Ericksonian Psychotherapy

Volume II: Clinical Applications

Editorial Review Board

Ericksonian Psychotherapy

Volume II: Clinical Applications

edited by

Jeffrey K. Zeig, Ph.D.

BRUNNER/MAZEL, *Publishers* • New York

All royalties from this book are the property of The Milton H. Erickson Foundation, Inc., 3606 N. 24th Street, Phoenix, Arizona 85016. Royalties will be used to foster educational and scientific efforts that pertain to Ericksonian psychotherapy and hypnosis.

Library of Congress Cataloging in Publication Data
Main entry under title:

Ericksonian psychotherapy.

   Proceedings of the Second International Congress on Ericksonian Approaches to Hypnosis and Psychotherapy, held in Dec. 1983, in Phoenix, Ariz.
   Contents: v. 1. Structures—v. 2. Clinical applications.
   1. Erickson, Milton H.—Congresses. 2. Hypnotism—Therapeutic use—Congresses. 3. Psychotherapy—Congresses. I. Zeig, Jeffrey K., 1947-   .
II. International Congress on Ericksonian Approaches to Hypnosis and Psychotherapy (2nd; 1983; Phoenix, Ariz,)

[DNLM: 1. Erickson, Milton H. 2. Hypnosis—congresses. 3. Psychotherapy—congresses. WM 415 E6854 1983]
RC490.5.E75E76 1985   616.89'162   84-24331
ISBN 0-87630-380-7 (v. 1)
ISBN 0-87630-381-5 (v. 2)

Published by
BRUNNER/MAZEL, INC.
19 Union Square
New York, New York 10003

MANUFACTURED IN THE UNITED STATES OF AMERICA

To Sherron S. Peters and Nicole Rachel Zeig

"Don't you think the Congresses should have their rewards?"

" Each person is a unique individual. Hence, psychotherapy should be formulated to meet the uniqueness of the individual's needs, rather than tailoring the person to fit the Procrustean bed of a hypothetical theory of human behavior. **"**

Milton H. Erickson, M.D.

Contents

Introduction

The two volumes entitled *Ericksonian Psychotherapy* present the proceedings of the Second International Congress on Ericksonian Psychotherapy held in Phoenix, Arizona, December 1983. Volume I on *Structures* includes theoretical issues and descriptions of technique. Volume II on *Clinical Application* presents case materials and information relevant to immediate application.

The First International Congress on Ericksonian Approaches to Hypnosis and Psychotherapy was held December 4-8, 1980, also in Phoenix. Erickson was a member of the organizing committee of that Congress and one of the purposes of the meeting was to give him the opportunity to see the impact of his work. Unfortunately, he died eight and a half months prior to the Congress. The proceedings of the first Congress were published in *Ericksonian Approaches to Hypnosis and Psychotherapy* (Brunner/Mazel, 1982).

Whereas the first Congress was organized to honor Erickson, the second Congress was intended to broaden and advance Ericksonian methodology, and it had a different tone.

CONGRESS FORMAT

The program was academic, experiential, and interactive. The academic program consisted of keynote addresses, invited presentations, accepted papers, and panels. In total, 100 speeches were made. The faculty was composed of 125 members (including moderators and co-presenters).

It is the academic portion of the Congress that is reported in these proceedings. Most of the 100 presentations were submitted for publication. Of those papers, 76 are included in the present text. A discussion by Haley and Weakland that was part of the Congress media program is also included.

The experiential component of the Congress consisted of three-hour workshops that were held each day. In total, 75 workshops were offered. A unique feature added to the workshop was small group practicums.

Each three-hour practicum consisted of no more than 12 students and was led by a faculty member. Topics included utilization of hypnotic phenomena, pain control, confusion technique, habit problems, metaphor, and family therapy.

On the third day of the Congress, the format changed to allow for interactive events; no workshops were conducted and no papers were presented. Rather, that day consisted of demonstrations, conversation hours, group inductions, discussions of videotapes of Milton Erickson, and special topical panels. Also presented was a special keynote address on Erickson's child-rearing techniques, featuring a panel composed of six of Erickson's eight children.

The evening programs of the Congress included an authors' hour, media events, a hospitality reception, and a banquet.

The Second International Congress was even larger than the 1980 Congress, probably making it the largest professional meeting held on the topic of hypnosis. More than 2,000 attendees came from 19 countries, a striking indication of the continuing influence and growth of the therapeutic legacy of Milton H. Erickson.

ACKNOWLEDGMENTS

The assistance of a great many individuals was instrumental in the success of the meeting. I would like to take this opportunity to thank them.

The following professionals reviewed abstracts of papers submitted for presentation at the Congress: Joseph Barber, Ph.D., Stephen Gilligan, Ph.D., Melvin Hector, M.D., and Bill O'Hanlon, M.S.

The Editorial Review Board is listed in the front of the book. The editors made an important contribution in reviewing papers for publication in these volumes. Each paper was read by a minimum of two editors and a maximum of seven.

On behalf of the Board of Directors of the Erickson Foundation, I want to take this additional opportunity to thank the distinguished Faculty of the meeting. It was their theoretical and clinical contributions that made the Congress a successful training event.

The staff of the Erickson Foundation worked endless hours in handling the registrations, meeting arrangements, and administrative tasks. The following people had the temerity to work on both the first and second Congresses: Sherron Peters, the Administrative Director of the Foundation, Mildred Pardee, Bookkeeper, and Barbara Bellamy, Administrative Assistant. Barbara deserves special recognition for the excellent job she did compiling the Congress syllabus. Other Foundation staff who were instrumental included Lori Weiers, Secretary and Coordinator of Volunteers, Curtis Stone, Tracy McVey, and Ranee Tran.

A number of volunteers helped both prior to and at the Congress, including Charles and Jean Achtenberg, Hazel Arnett, Alfred Cox, Ed Hancock, Philip McAvoy, Will Weiers, Martin Zeig, Ruth Zeig, and Edythe Zeig. In addition, there were 79 student volunteers who served as monitors, and photographers, and who staffed the registration and continuing education desks.

Deserving special recognition are Mrs. Elizabeth Erickson and Kristina Erickson, M.D., who gave generously of their time and energy to make many executive decisions about the Congress. They have worked tirelessly on behalf of the Erickson Foundation.

Jeffrey K. Zeig, Ph.D.
Director
The Milton H. Erickson Foundation

The Milton H. Erickson Foundation, Inc.

The Milton H. Erickson Foundation, Inc., is a federal nonprofit corporation. It was formed to promote and advance the contributions made to the health sciences by the late Milton H. Erickson, M.D., during his long and distinguished career. The Foundation is dedicated to training health and mental health professionals. Strict eligibility requirements are maintained for attendance at our training events or to receive our educational materials. The Milton H. Erickson Foundation, Inc., does not discriminate on the basis of race, color, national, or ethnic origin. Directors of the Milton H. Erickson Foundation, Inc., are: Jeffrey K. Zeig, Ph.D., Sherron S. Peters, Elizabeth M. Erickson, and Kristina K. Erickson, M.D.

ERICKSON ARCHIVES

In December 1980, the Foundation began collecting audiotapes, videotapes, and historical material on Dr. Erickson for the Erickson Archives. Our goal is to have a central repository of historical material on Erickson. More than 300 hours of videotape and audiotape have already been donated to the Foundation.

The Erickson Archives are available to interested and qualified professionals who wish to come to Phoenix to independently study the audiotapes and videotapes that are housed at the Foundation. There is a nominal charge for use of the Archives. Please write if you are interested in details.

PUBLICATIONS OF THE ERICKSON FOUNDATION

Books

The following books, in addition to the present volumes, are published by Brunner/Mazel, Publishers:

A Teaching Seminar with Milton Erickson (J. Zeig, Ed. & Commentary) is a transcript, with commentary, of a one-week teaching seminar held for professionals by Dr. Erickson in his home in August, 1979.

Ericksonian Approaches to Hypnosis and Psychotherapy (J. Zeig, Ed.) contains the edited proceedings of the First International Erickson Congress.

Newsletter

The Milton H. Erickson Foundation publishes a newsletter for professionals three times a year to inform its readers of the activities of the Foundation. Articles and notices that relate to Ericksonian approaches to hypnosis and psychotherapy are included.

The Ericksonian Monographs

The Foundation has initiated the publication of *The Ericksonian Monographs,* which will appear on an irregular basis, up to three issues per year. Edited by Stephen Lankton, M.S.W., the *Monographs* will publish only the highest quality articles on Ericksonian hypnosis and psychotherapy, including technique, theory, and research. Manuscripts should be sent to Stephen Lankton, P.O. Box 958, Gulf Breeze, Florida 32561. For subscription information, contact Brunner/Mazel, Publishers.

Audio and Video Training Tapes

The Milton H. Erickson Foundation has available for purchase professionally recorded audiotapes from its meetings. Professionally produced video cassettes of one-hour clinical demonstrations by members of the faculty of the 1981, 1982, and 1984 Erickson Foundation Seminars and the 1983 Erickson Congress can also be purchased from the Foundation.

Audiotapes of Milton H. Erickson

The Erickson Foundation distributes tapes of lectures by Milton Erickson in the 1950s and 1960s when his voice was strong. Releases in our audiotape series are announced in the *Newsletter.*

Training Videotapes Featuring Hypnotic Inductions Conducted by Milton H. Erickson

The Process of Hypnotic Induction: A Training Videotape Featuring Inductions Conducted by Milton H. Erickson in 1964. Jeffrey K. Zeig, Ph.D., discusses the process of hypnotic induction and describes the micro-dynamics of technique that Erickson used in this 1964 induction. Length: 2 hours.

Symbolic Hypnotherapy. Jeffrey K. Zeig, Ph.D., presents information on using symbols in psychotherapy and hypnosis. Segments of hypno-therapy conducted by Milton Erickson with the same subject on two consecutive days in 1978 are shown. Zeig discusses the microdynamics of Erickson's symbolic technique.
Length: 2 hours, 40 minutes.

Videotapes are available in all U.S. formats, as well as in the European standard.

TRAINING OPPORTUNITIES

The Erickson Foundation organizes the International Congress on Ericksonian Approaches to Hypnosis and Psychotherapy. These meet-ings are held triennially; the first two meetings were held in 1980 and 1983. Each was attended by over 2,000 professionals. The next Inter-national Congress is scheduled for December 3-7, 1986, in Phoenix, Arizona.

In the intervening years, the Foundation organizes national seminars. The seminars are limited to approximately 450 attendees and they em-phasize skill development in hypnotherapy. The 1981, 1982 and 1984 seminars were held in San Francisco, Dallas and Los Angeles respec-tively.

Regional workshops are held regularly in various locations.

Programs held at the Foundation include beginning and advanced ongoing training in hypnotherapy and strategic family therapy.

All training programs are announced in the Foundation's *Newsletter.*

ELIGIBILITY

Training programs, the newsletter, audiotapes, and videotapes are available to professionals in health-related fields, including physicians, doctoral level psychologists, and dentists who are qualified for mem-bership in or are members of their respective professional organizations (AMA, APA, ADA). They are also available to professionals with grad-uate degrees in areas related to mental health (M.S.W., M.S.N., M.A., or M.S.) from accredited institutions. Full-time graduate students in accredited programs in the above fields must supply a letter from their department certifying their student status if they wish to attend training events, subscribe to the newsletter, or purchase tapes.

Faculty of the 1983 International Congress on Ericksonian Approaches to Hypnosis and Psychotherapy

FACULTY

Leo Alexander, M.D.
  West Newton, MA
Nachman Alon, M.A.
  Yaffo, Israel
*Lonnie Barbach, Ph.D.
  Mill Valley, CA
*Joseph Barber, Ph.D.
  Los Angeles, CA
*John O. Beahrs, M.D.
  Portland, OR
*Patrick J. Brady
  Quincy, MA
*David L. Calof
  Seattle, WA
Chong Tong Mun, M.D.
  Singapore, Singapore
*James C. Coyne, Ph.D.
  Berkeley, CA
*O. Spurgeon English, M.D.
  Narberth, PA
Allan Erickson, M.S.
  Columbia, MD
Elizabeth M. Erickson, B.A.
  Phoenix, AZ

Kristina K. Erickson, M.D.
  Columbia, MO
Lance Erickson, Ph.D.
  Ann Arbor, MI
Robert Erickson, M.A.
  Phoenix, AZ
Betty Alice Erickson Elliott, B.A.
  Dallas, TX
John H. Frykman, M.Div.
  San Francisco, CA
Anthony Gaito, A.C.S.W.
  Syosset, NY
Stephen G. Gilligan, Ph.D.
  Newton Highlands, MA
*David Gordon, M.A.
  Lancaster, CA
*Harold Greenwald, Ph.D.
  San Diego, CA
Jay Haley, M.A.
  Rockville, MD
F. William Hanley, M.D.
  Vancouver, BC, Canada
*Norman W. Katz, Ph.D.
  Albuquerque, NM

---

*Indicates faculty who also presented invited workshops.

xxi

Roxanna Erickson Klein, M.S.
  Dallas, TX
Moris Kleinhauz, M.D.
  Ramat-Chen, Israel
*Alfred Lange, Ph.D.
  Amsterdam, Netherlands
*Carol H. Lankton, M.A.
  Gulf Breeze, FL
*Stephen R. Lankton, A.C.S.W.
  Gulf Breeze, FL
*Jean Lassner, M.D.
  Paris, France
*Marc Lehrer, Ph.D.
  Santa Cruz, CA
Alan F. Leveton, M.D.
  San Francisco, CA
Camillo Loriedo, M.D.
  Rome, Italy
*Herbert S. Lustig, M.D.
  Ardmore, PA
*Cloé Madanes
  Rockville, MD
Judith Mazza, Ph.D.
  Takoma Park, MD
Jesse S. Miller, Ph.D.
  Berkeley, CA
*Bill O'Hanlon, M.S.
  Blair, NE
*Robert E. Pearson, M.D.
  Houston, TX
*Martin Reiser, Ed.D.
  Los Angeles, CA

Madeleine Richeport, Ph.D.
  Santurce, Puerto Rico
*Michele Ritterman, Ph.D.
  Oakland, CA
*Sidney Rosen, M.D.
  New York, NY
*Deborah Ross, Ph.D.
  Santa Cruz, CA
*Ernest L. Rossi, Ph.D.
  Los Angeles, CA
Hans-Ulrich Schachtner,
  Dipl Psych
  Munich, West Germany
*Irving I. Secter, D.D.S., M.A.
  Lauderdale Lakes, FL
*Lynn Segal, L.C.S.W.
  Palo Alto, CA
*Margaret T. Singer, Ph.D.
  Berkeley, CA
*Charles R. Stern, Ph.D.
  Detroit, MI
Sandra M. Sylvester, Ph.D.
  Tucson, AZ
*Kay F. Thompson, D.D.S.
  Carnegie, PA
*Richard Van Dyck, M.D.
  Oegstgeest, Netherlands
*Paul Watzlawick, Ph.D.
  Palo Alto, CA
*Jeffrey K. Zeig, Ph.D.
  Phoenix, AZ

FACULTY PRESENTING WORKSHOPS ONLY

Norma Barretta, Ph.D.
  San Pedro, CA
Philip Barretta, M.A.
  San Pedro, CA

Richard Fisch, M.D.
  Palo Alto, CA
Edward Goodman, Ph.D.
  Dallas, TX

---

*Indicates faculty who also presented invited workshops.

Alan Griffin, Ph.D.
  Richardson, TX
Marion R. Moore, M.D.
  Memphis, TN

Lars-Eric Unestahl, Ph.D.
  Orebro, Sweden
John H. Weakland
  Palo Alto, CA

FACULTY SERVING ON PANELS ONLY

Carrell Dammann, Ph.D.
  Atlanta, GA

Carl Hammerschlag, M.D.
  Phoenix, AZ

ACCEPTED PAPERS

James R. Allen, M.D.
  Tulsa, OK
Brian M. Alman, Ph.D.
  San Diego, CA
Daniel L. Araoz, Ed.D.
  Mineola, NY
Christopher J. Beletsis, M.A.
  La Jolla, CA
Ronald R. Brown, Ph.D.
  Knoxville, TN
John D. Buksbazen, M.A. cand.
  Los Angeles, CA
Robert A. Burnham, Ph.D. cand.
  Cambridge, MA
Lisa Chiara, M.A.
  La Jolla, CA
Henry T. Close, Th.M.
  Coral Gables, FL
Klaus G. Deissler, Dipl Psych
  Marburg, West Germany
Richard E. Dimond, Ph.D.
  Springfield, IL
Yvonne M. Dolan, M.A.
  Denver, CO
John Edgette, M.S.
  Philadelphia, PA
Jeffrey B. Feldman, Ph.D.
  New York, NY
Steven H. Feldman, M.A.
  Seattle, WA

Julian D. Ford, Ph.D.
  Burbank, CA
Michael E. Forgy, A.C.S.W.
  Le Claire, IA
William B. Freeman, Jr.
  Burlington, VT
Wilhelm Gerl, Dipl Psych
  Munich, West Germany
Peter W. Gester, Dipl Psych
  Marburg, West Germany
Lawrence R. Gindhart, M.A.
  Indianapolis, IN
Eric Greenleaf, Ph.D.
  Berkeley, CA
D. Corydon Hammond, Ph.D.
  Salt Lake City, UT
Ronald A. Havens, Ph.D.
  Springfield, IL
C.A.L. Hoogduin, M.D.
  Delft, Netherlands
Lynn D. Johnson, Ph.D.
  Salt Lake City, UT
Marc Z. Kessler, Ph.D.
  Burlington, VT
Sung C. Kim, Ph.D.
  San Francisco, CA
Dee Krauss, Ph.D.
  Seal Beach, CA
Dennis Leri, M.A.
  San Francisco, CA

John D. Lovern, Ph.D.
  Marina del Rey, CA
Don W. Malon, Ph.D.
  Clayton, MO
Dan C. Overlade, Ph.D.
  Pensacola, FL
Burkhard Peter, Dipl Psych
  Munich, West Germany
Noelle M. Poncelet, M.S.W.
  Menlo Park, CA
Mark Reese, M.A.
  San Diego, CA
Helmut Relinger, Ph.D.
  Berkeley, CA
David Rigler, Ph.D.
  Santa Cruz, CA
George A. Sargent, Ph.D.
  Vista, CA
Gunther Schmidt, M.D.
  Heidelberg, West Germany
John C. Simpson, Ph.D.
  Charlotte, NC
Donna M. Spencer, Ph.D.
  St. Louis, MO

Harry E. Stanton, Ph.D.
  Hobart, Tasmania
George Stone, M.S.W.
  Morrill, NE
Bruce L.M. Tanenbaum, M.D.
  Reno, NV
Bernhard Trenkle, Dipl Psych
  Heidelberg, West Germany
James E. Waun, M.D.
  Ludington, MI
Dawn M. White, Ph.D.
  Whiteriver, AZ
James W. Whiteside, Ph.D. cand.
  Charlotte, NC
James Wilk, M.A. (Oxon.), M.Sc.
  Milwaukee, WI
J. Adrian Williams, Ph.D.
  Charleston, IL
R. Reid Wilson, Ph.D.
  Cambridge, MA
Michael D. Yapko, Ph.D.
  San Diego, CA
Hillel Zeitlin, M.S.W.
  Berkeley, CA

MODERATORS

James R. Allen, M.D.
  Tulsa, OK
Neil Di Capua, D.D.S.
  Woodland Hills, CA
Michael J. Diamond, Ph.D.
  Los Angeles, CA
Richard E. Dimond, Ph.D.
  Springfield, IL
Bengt Essler, D.D.S.
  Stockholm, Sweden
Jeffrey B. Feldman, Ph.D.
  New York, NY
Lawrence R. Gindhart, M.A.
  Indianapolis, IN

David Henderson, Ed.D.
  Mequon, WI
C.A.L. Hoogduin, M.D.
  Delft, Netherlands
Lynn D. Johnson, Ph.D.
  Salt Lake City, UT
David Northway, M.A.
  Eugene, OR
Jane A. Parsons, C.S.W.
  New York, NY
Helmut Relinger, Ph.D.
  Berkeley, CA
Donna M. Spencer, Ph.D.
  St. Louis, MO

Eric C. Steese, Ph.D.
  Olympia, WA
Michael D. Yapko, Ph.D.
  San Diego, CA

Lenora M. Yuen, Ph.D.
  Palo Alto, CA

Ericksonian Psychotherapy

Volume II: Clinical Applications

PART I

Keynote Addresses

Jay Haley and Cloé Madanes direct the Family Therapy Institute of Washington, D.C. As teachers and writers, their impact on the field of psychotherapy has been enormous. Haley has authored, edited and coedited eleven books and Madanes has authored two books. They are two of the most important figures in the field of psychotherapy.

More than any single person, Haley is responsible for popularizing Erickson's work. Throughout his career, Erickson was well-known in hypnosis circles. However, it was the publication of Haley's Uncommon Therapy *(Norton, 1973) that integrated Erickson's techniques into the mainstream of clinical practice.*

Haley has continued to be influenced by Erickson's ideas. His latest volume, Ordeal Therapy *(Jossey-Bass, 1983), describes how he has used and advanced a particular technique he saw Erickson using extensively in the 1950s and 1960s. Haley's keynote address is one of the chapters from* Ordeal Therapy.

Madanes has had a number of academic appointments and is an adjunct associate professor in the Department of Psychiatry at the University of Maryland. Her keynote address is a chapter from her recent book, Behind the One-Way Mirror *(Jossey-Bass, 1984).*

The keynote addresses by Haley and Madanes were two of the most highly rated presentations at the Congress. They demonstrate the depth and freshness of the authors' perspectives.

In his chapter, Haley describes types of ordeals, stages of ordeal therapy, and ordeals as a theory of change. Madanes discusses the strategic use of humor. She credits Erickson for being the first person to introduce humor as a legitimate aspect of therapy.

3

Chapter 1

A Review of Ordeal Therapy

Jay Haley

One day a man, an attorney, came to me for help because he could not sleep at night. His insomnia was beginning to cost him his career because he was falling asleep in the courtroom. Even with heavy medication he was sleeping less than an hour or two each night. I had just begun private practice, and the man was sent to me to be hypnotized to solve his sleep problem. He was not a good hypnotic subject. In fact, he responded to suggestions for hypnosis just as he did when trying to sleep: He would suddenly rouse up wide awake and alert as if frightened by some thought he could not describe. After several tries, I decided hypnosis would not be the way to influence this man's sleeping problem. Yet I felt I had to do something. He'd been through traditional therapy, and nothing had helped him with his problem, which was getting progressively worse to the point that he feared he would become unable to function.

The attorney insisted that nothing was wrong with him or his life; he was happy with his work and with his wife and children. His only problem was that he couldn't sleep. As he put it, "When I start to go to sleep, something pulls me awake, and then I lie there for hours."

Finally, I tried an experiment. I suggested that at bedtime he create a pleasant situation, with his wife bringing him warm milk, as she had before. Then when he lay down to sleep, he must deliberately think of all the most horrible things he might think about or might do or see himself doing. I asked him to practice, in the interview with me, thinking of those awful things, and he couldn't think of any. When I had him think of all the horrible things a hypothetical person, "Mr. Smith," might

Reprinted with permission from *Ordeal Therapy*, by Jay Haley. Jossey-Bass, San Francisco, 1983.

have on his mind, however, he thought of murder, homosexual acts, and other exciting things like that. I told him that he was to lie down to go to sleep that night, but instead of trying to go to sleep, he should deliberately think of all the horrible things he could bring to mind. As he was leaving the office, he said, "You mean things like putting my wife in a whorehouse?" I said, "That's a good one."

The man went home and followed the instructions. He fell asleep immediately and slept the night through. From that point on, he used that procedure, and he lost his insomnia.

At that time, during the 1950s, there was no therapeutic theory to explain the creation of such an intervention or its success. The only theory was the psychodynamic theory of repression, which would have assumed that telling the man to think awful things would keep the man awake rather than put him to sleep, since it would mean bringing repressed material near consciousness.

At that time there was also no explanation of a rapid therapeutic change because there was no theory of brief therapy. It was assumed that if one did brief therapy, one merely did less than was done in long-term therapy. Therefore, my directive had no rationale. As I puzzled over why that case and similar ones were successful, I decided I should go and consult Milton H. Erickson.

I had learned hypnosis from Dr. Erickson, and I had talked with him about hypnosis as part of a research investigation. Finally I had begun teaching classes in hypnosis myself to local physicians and psychologists. When I went into practice as a therapist, I realized at once that hypnosis in research and teaching was not relevant to hypnosis used clinically. I knew how to give people hypnotic experiences, how to provide deep trance phenomena, and how to talk with them in metaphors about their problems. But I really didn't know how to use hypnosis to change anyone.

At that time Milton Erickson was the only consultant available to me who knew something about the use of hypnosis in brief therapy. I was also aware that he had a variety of brief therapy techniques not using hypnosis. These had come up incidentally in conversations about other matters. Actually, he was the only person I knew who was offering anything new in therapeutic technique or theory.

When I consulted with Dr. Erickson, I discovered that he had routine procedures using special ordeals to cause a change and that they were similar to the one I had devised for the attorney. I also found explanations and ways of thinking about other cases that puzzled me. For example, I had been curing a woman's severe headaches by encouraging her to have the headaches as a way to get control of them. As I talked with Erickson, I realized that his therapeutic techniques included paradoxical interventions of just that kind.

Let me present in Dr. Erickson's own words an ordeal procedure for an insomnia case he described to me:

> I had a sixty-five-year-old man come to me who had suffered a little insomnia fifteen years previously, and his physician gave him sodium amytal. Three months previously his wife had died, leaving him alone living with his umarried son. The man had been regularly taking fifteen capsules, three grains each—a dosage of forty-five grains of sodium amytal. He went to bed at eight o'clock, rolled and tossed until midnight, and then he would take his fifteen capsules, forty-five grains, a couple of glasses of water, lie down, and get about an hour and a half to two hours' sleep. Then he would rouse up and roll and toss until getting-up time. The fifteen capsules no longer worked since his wife died. He had gone to the family physician and asked for a prescription for eighteen capsules. The family physician got frightened and apologized for ever allowing him to become a barbiturate addict. He sent him to me.
>
> I asked the old man if he really wanted to get over his insomnia—if he really wanted to get over his drug addiction. He said he did, and he was very honest and very sincere. I told him he could do it easily. In taking his history I had learned that he lived in a large house with hardwood floors. He did most of the cooking and the dishwashing, while the son did the housework—especially the waxing of the floors, which the old man hated. He hated the smell of floor wax, and the son did not mind. So I explained to the old man that I could cure him, that it would cost him at the most eight hours' sleep, and that's all—which would be a small price to pay. Would he willingly give up eight hours' sleep to recover from his insomnia? The old man promised me he would. I told him that it would mean work, and he agreed that he could do the work.
>
> I explained to him that instead of going to bed that night at eight o'clock he was to get out the can of floor wax and some rags. "It will only cost you one hour and a half of sleep, or two hours at the most, and you start polishing those floors. You'll hate it, you'll hate me; you won't think well of me as the hours drag along. But you polish those hardwood floors all night long, and go to your job the next morning at eight o'clock. Stop polishing the floor at seven o'clock, which will give you a whole hour for rising. The next night at eight o'clock, get up and wax the floor. You'll really polish those floors all over again, and you won't like it. But you'll

lose at most two hours of sleep. The third night, do the same, and the fourth night, do the same." He polished those floors the first night, the second night, and the third night. The fourth night he said, "I'm so weary following that crazy psychiatrist's orders, but I suppose I might as well." He'd lost six hours of sleep; he had two more to lose before I cured him, really. He said to himself, "I think I'll lie down in bed and rest my eyes for half an hour." He woke up at seven o'clock the next morning. That night he was confronted with a dilemma. Should he go to bed when he still owed me two hours of sleep? He reached a compromise. He'd get ready for bed and get out the floor wax and the polishing rags at eight o'clock. If he could read 8:15 on the clock, he would get up and polish the floors all night.

A year later he told me he had been sleeping every night. In fact, he said, "You know, I don't dare suffer from insomnia. I look at that clock and I say, 'If I'm awake in fifteen minutes, I've got to polish the floors all night, and I mean it, too!' " You know, the old man would do anything to get out of polishing the floors—even sleep.

When Dr. Erickson described that case to me, I realized at once that the procedure I had developed for the attorney was formally the same. I had arranged that the attorney go through an ordeal that he'd rather avoid by sleeping. Dr. Erickson had given his client a task that he'd rather sleep than carry out. Here was a procedure based on a rather simple premise: If one makes it more difficult for a person to have a symptom than to give it up, the person will give up the symptom. Over the years I have made use of this type of intervention in a variety of ways, and in this chapter I will describe the range of variations.

The ordeal process is different from some of the other therapeutic techniques originated by Milton Erickson. His use of metaphor, for example, when he would change "A" by emphasizing "B" in an analogous way, is not an ordeal procedure. In some uses of the metaphoric approach little is directly asked of the client except to listen. Similarly, Erickson's cumulation of change procedures is quite different from providing an ordeal. A person who is asked to give up pain for a second, and then to increase that to two seconds, and then to four, is going through a geometrical progression toward improvement in which no ordeal seems to be involved.

If we examine Dr. Erickson's innovations in the use of paradox, we can note that he had a person experience a distressing symptom deliberately, and that is not an ordeal procedure. Or is it? Doesn't it fall into the category of giving up a symptom to avoid an ordeal? It appears possible that ordeal therapy is not merely a technique but a theory of change that applies to a variety of supposedly different therapeutic techniques. Before proceeding further with this notion, it might be best to describe the variety of ordeal procedures and their stages.

THE ORDEAL TECHNIQUE

With the ordeal technique, the therapist's task is easily defined: It is to impose an ordeal appropriate to the problem of the person who wants to change, an ordeal more severe than the problem. The main requirement of an ordeal is that it cause distress equal to or greater than that caused by the symptom, just as a punishment should fit the crime. Usually, if an ordeal isn't severe enough to extinguish the symptom, it can be increased in magnitude until it is. It is also best if the ordeal is good for the person. Doing what's good for you is hard for anyone and seems particularly difficult for people who seek therapy. Examples of what's good for people are exercise, improving the mind, eating a healthy diet, and other self-improvement activities. Such ordeals may also include making a sacrifice for others.

The ordeal must have another characteristic: It must be something the person *can* do and something the person cannot legitimately object to. That is, it must be of such a nature that the therapist can easily say, "This won't violate any of your moral standards and is something you *can* do." There is one final characteristic of a therapeutic ordeal: It should not harm the person or anyone else.

Given these characteristics, the ordeal offered might be crude, like a blunt instrument, or ingenious and subtle. It may also be a standard one that can be applied to many problems. Or it may be carefully designed for a particular person or family and not be appropriate for any other. An example of a standard ordeal is to exercise in the middle of the night whenever the symptom has occurred that day. An example of an ordeal designed for a particular person would require too lengthy a description here; readers will find individually tailored examples throughout this chapter.

One final aspect of the ordeal: Sometimes the person must go through it repeatedly to recover from the symptom. At other times the mere threat of an ordeal brings recovery. That is, when the therapist lays out the ordeal as a procedure and the person agrees to experience it, he or she often abandons the symptom before the ordeal even goes into effect.

Types of Ordeals

A few of the different types of ordeals can be listed with examples.

Straightforward task

When the ordeal is a straightforward task, the therapist clarifies the problem and requires that, each time it occurs, the person go through a specific ordeal. During the interview, the therapist finds out, often without making it clear what the purpose is, what the client should do more of that would be good for him or her. A typical response is that the person should do more exercising. The therapist therefore directs the person to go through a set number of exercises each time the symptom occurs. It is often best to have these exercises occur in the middle of the night. That is, the person is asked to go to sleep with the alarm set for three o'clock in the morning and then to get up at three and do the exercising. After that, the person goes back to sleep, so the procedure is like a dream or nightmare. The exercise should be sufficient so it can be felt in the muscles the next day.

As an example, with a man who became anxious when he spoke in public as his job required, I had him exercise each night when he had been more anxious than he thought he should be. The exercise needed to be severe enough so that he could feel it in his muscles at a meeting the next day. He was soon surprisingly calm when he stood up to speak. I learned this from Dr. Erickson who described the procedure in the same type of case with an emphasis on using energy. His patient

> had a ritualistic, phobic, panicky reaction to his television broadcast—forced panting, breathing, and for fifteen minutes he would stand gasping, and gasping, and choking, and his heart would pound. Then they would say, "You're on," and he would broadcast over TV with the greatest of ease. But each day he became increasingly more miserable. At first it started with a minute or two; by the time he came to see me it was built up to fifteen minutes. He was looking forward to twenty minutes, thirty minutes, an hour; and it was beginning to interfere with his other work at the station. A day after I found out what his sleeping habits were, I gave him that concept of so much energy. As you would expect, his sleeping habits were rather ritualistic. Always in bed at a certain hour. Always up at a certain hour. After I got the concept of energy

pounded into his head, I pointed out to him, why not use up that energy that he spent that way? [Demonstrating panting] How many deep squats would it take each day? I told him I didn't know how much energy it would take, but that I thought he ought to start out with twenty-five (in the morning before he went to work), even though I thought at least a hundred would be requisite. But he could start out with twenty-five. . . . No one wants to do that. . . . His lame, sore legs all day long convinced him that he had used up plenty of energy. He had none left over for that [demonstrating panting]. He liked that use of his energy. He built up his knee squats, deep squats, as a health matter to reduce his obesity. Then he began going down to the gym to exercise, and he began to enjoy that daily ritual of going to the gym.

He came back to me and said, "My trouble is recurring . . . I noticed the other day I took three or four deep breaths, and the next program I increased the number, so it is starting to build up. Now what are you going to do? Because doing the exercises won't work. I've got a lot more energy." I said, "It's a profound psychological reaction you're showing." He said, "Yes." I said, "Well, suppose we work on it at the psychological level. Now, I know your sleeping habits. You sign off at ten o'clock. You go right home. You just summarize the day to your wife, and then you go right to bed. You sleep eight hours. You're a sound sleeper. You enjoy your sleep, you're a regular sleeper. After four hours' sleep, get up and do a hundred squats." He said, "That I would really hate." I said, "Yes, you can really use up a lot of psychological energy hating that idea. How do you think you'll feel psychologically every night when you set your alarm, as you always do, realizing that you can take up a lot of psychological energy panting in front of the microphone and the television camera? You can take out an awful lot of psychological energy in two ways: . . . setting your alarm for the regular time and psychologically considering with a great deal of intensity of feeling how you don't want to get up in four hours' time to do deep squats."

That analogy worked—for a while. He came back. . . . I said, "So you have got an excess of energy." He said, "That's right." I said, "Now tell me, what has been your lifelong ambition?" He said, "To own my own home for my wife and my child." I said, "It will really make you sweat, won't it, to buy a home and mow the lawn?" He said, "My wife has been after me for years, and I

flatly refused to budge, but we're buying one this month." He's
had no recurrence. He's got a home. He's got a yard. He's using
up all excess energy.

This is not only typical of Dr. Erickson's ordeal therapy but typical of
the way he created a therapeutic procedure and then arranged that it
be built into the person's natural environment so the influence would
continue without therapy.

When a straightforward task is chosen, it can be whatever individual
clients say is something they should do more of to improve themselves.
A classic approach of Dr. Erickson's with insomnia, for example, was
to have the person stay up all night reading those books he or she should
have read but had put off reading. Since clients might fall asleep if they
sat in a chair to read, Dr. Erickson would require them to stand up at
the mantle and read all night long. With such an arrangement, clients
either sleep, which is good for them, or read the books they should
read, which is good for them. Erickson reports that a person will say,
"I'm ready if I ever have the problem again. I've bought a whole set of
Dickens." The solution gives clients confidence that they can deal with
the problem if it occurs again.

Paradoxical ordeals

The ordeal can be the symptomatic behavior itself and so be paradoxical—defined as encouraging the person to have the problem he or
she came to the therapist to recover from. For example, a person wishing
to recover from depression can be asked to schedule the depression at
a certain time each day. Preferably it should be a time when the person
would rather be doing something else. For example, the therapist may
schedule someone to concentrate on being depressed at a time when
free of other obligations, such as just after putting the children to bed
during the time when one might relax and watch television.

It is a question whether a paradoxical intervention can be anything
but an ordeal insofar as individuals are asked to go through what they'd
rather recover from. An example is the flooding technique in behavior
therapy: A person afraid of bugs and wanting to recover from that fear
is asked to experience the fear of imagining bugs crawling all over him.
This type of paradoxical intervention is obviously an ordeal. Similarly,
requiring a quarreling couple to quarrel, or asking a couple to go through
a distressing sequence that they wish to stop, is not only paradoxical
but an ordeal.

To put this matter another way, insofar as a therapeutic paradox is defined as the person's rebelling against the therapist by not doing the problem behavior, there must be an ordeal involved for the person to resist doing it.

One other relevant aspect of the paradoxical intervention is the way it involves making an involuntary act, which is the definition of a symptom, voluntary. The person must deliberately do that which he or she says can't be helped, such as eat impulsively, or avoid eating, or have aches and pains, or be anxious. When done deliberately, it is, by definition, no longer a symptom. With an ordeal arrangement, one can ask that the person repeat the symptom deliberately each time it occurs involuntarily, thus making the symptom an ordeal for having experienced the symptom. If a person has two symptoms, one can be required each time the other occurs, thereby introducing a paradoxical ordeal that is effective with two symptoms at once. For example, a person who has a particular compulsion and also suffers from extreme shyness can be required to socialize as an ordeal whenever the compulsion occurs.

The therapist as an ordeal

There are several classes of ordeals that are effective because of the effect on the relationship with the therapist. All ordeals are in relation to the therapist and effective because of that, but some are specifically set up to be therapist-oriented.

For example, when a therapist "reframes" an act, the message becomes the ordeal. Any act that is defined in one way by the client can be redefined in a less acceptable way by the therapist so that it is something the person doesn't like. For example, something the client describes as vengeful can be redefined as protective and encouraged by the therapist. Or an act that the client defines as independent of the therapist can be redefined as done for the therapist, thereby reframing it in such a way that the person would rather not continue it.

Another class of ordeals is the confronting techniques used by some therapists. When a therapist forces the client to face what the client would rather not face, and the client has sought out this painful experience, it can be classed as an ordeal procedure. Similarly, insight interpretations that the client doesn't like are an ordeal to experience. In such cases the therapy itself, rather than a specific act by the therapist, becomes an ordeal for a person, and the ordeal must continue as long as the person has the problem.

The fee, or any other benefit to the therapist, can be used as an ordeal by increasing it when the symptom continues or is worse, a type of ordeal some therapists like to impose.

Ordeals involving two or more persons

An ordeal can be designed for one person or for a unit of any size. Milton Erickson had a series of ordeals for children's therapy in which the task was an ordeal for both parent and child. In a typical procedure, for example, a bedwetting child was required, each time his bed was wet in the morning, to practice his handwriting and improve it. His mother was to wake him at dawn each morning, and if his bed was wet, she'd get him up and help him practice his handwriting. If his bed was dry, he didn't have to—but his mother still had to get up at dawn each morning. The procedure became an ordeal for mother and child that resulted in their pride in his giving up bedwetting and improving his handwriting.

With a family, ordeals are possible that can include a couple's burying a past romantic affair by going through a ritual ordeal together that is ostensibly to make the offender suffer but is actually an ordeal for both of them. Or a whole family can be put through an ordeal when a member misbehaves.

These examples indicate a wide range of possibilities; the therapist need only provide something the person would rather give up the symptomatic behavior than do. However, a sharp distinction needs to be made between therapeutic, benevolent ordeals and those ordeals that cause a person to suffer either for the advantage of a therapist or for social control reasons. Simply to lock someone in jail when he or she steals does not fall into the category of ordeal therapy but is a method of social control. All therapists should be on guard against persecution of the public under the guise of therapy. To make it quite clear, the ordeal should be voluntary by the person and good for the person experiencing it but not necessarily for the person imposing it except insofar as there's satisfaction in successfully helping someone to change when he or she wishes to.

One must always keep clearly in mind the context of any therapeutic intervention. For example, Milton Erickson once devised a procedure in which a boy out of control was sat on by his mother as a way of helping him become less self-destructive. Later this procedure was adopted by inpatient institutions as a way the staff could force children to behave. There is a sharp distinction between a loving mother reforming a child for his benefit under a therapist's guidance and a staff getting revenge on a problem child under the guise of help.

Ordeals, whether in life as a happenstance or in therapy on purpose, do not in themselves have positive effects. Only when ordeals are used with skill are the effects positive, and skill is required in the use of this technique, as in all effective therapy. To use a knife correctly in surgery is rather different from accidentally slashing here and there with a knife while stumbling through an operating room. Similarly, to inadvertently cause a person to suffer is one thing; to arrange it deliberately is quite another.

Stages of Ordeal Therapy

As with any planned therapy, the use of an ordeal should be a step-by-step process with each stage carefully done.

1) The problem must be defined clearly

Since the person has a consequence, an ordeal, whenever the problem occurs, it is best to define the problem clearly. As an example, the person can be asked whether he can tell the difference between normal anxiety and the special anxiety he is coming to therapy to recover from. Everyone is anxious at times in some situations. The distinction must be clear because the ordeal will follow on the presence of abnormal anxiety only. Sometimes that distinction becomes clearer after the ordeal procedure has been suffered and the person is more serious about it. One can also use ordeals for a general feeling of boredom or lack of well-being as a way of driving the person into a more interesting life, but that procedure needs to be carried out with more caution than the more simple ordeal following on a clearly symptomatic act.

2) The person must be committed to getting over the problem

If a person is to go through an ordeal, he or she must really want to get over the problem presented. The motivation to get over it does not always exist at the time of entering therapy. The therapist must help motivate the person to take this kind of drastic step. Offering a benevolent concern, the therapist must bring out of the client a determination to get over the problem. The procedures are similar to getting a person to follow any therapeutic directive, with the additional fact that this type of directive will be unpleasant to follow. Typically the therapist must emphasize the gravity of the problem, outline the failed attempts to get over it, make it a challenge that the client is up to facing, and emphasize that the ordeal is a standard and usually successful procedure.

An important motivation of many clients in this situation is to be willing to go through the ordeal to prove the therapist wrong. Such people have usually tried many things to get over their problem; and if the therapist takes a firm position that this procedure will solve it, the client finds that hard to believe. Yet the only way the client can disprove it is by going through the procedure. Doing that has its therapeutic effect.

One way to motivate a client is to say that there is a cure that is guaranteed, but the client will not be told what it is until he or she agrees in advance to do it. Sometimes clients are asked to come back next week only if they're willing to do whatever is asked. Intrigued at the idea that something can be done to get over the problem, and not believing that, they are placed in a situation where they must agree to do something to find out what that something is. In that way they are committed to do the task.

One should keep in mind that in most cases the ordeal is effective *in relation to* the therapist. It is done to prove the therapist wrong, or else recovery is fast because of the therapist. Typically, for example, if the therapist is asking the person to stay up all night and lose sleep, or get up at night and clean house for an hour, it should be emphasized that the *therapist* is not going through that ordeal. The therapist can say, "I know how hard it is to get up in the middle of the night like that, because I myself so enjoy sleeping soundly all night through." Consequently, when the person is up in the night, he or she is thinking of the therapist enjoying a night's sleep.

3) An ordeal must be selected

The selection of an ordeal is done by the therapist, preferably with the client's collaboration. The ordeal must be severe enough to overcome the symptom, it must be good for the person so that he benefits by doing it, it must be something he can do and will accept in terms of its propriety, and the action must be clear and not ambiguous. It should have a beginning and an end clearly established.

The ordeal procedure is most likely to be followed if the client is involved in selecting the ordeal. Once it is explained to clients that they need to do something voluntarily and then the involuntary reaction of the symptom will cease—or some similar explanation—then they will think of tasks to be done. The therapist must require that the task be good for them so they don't set off punishing themselves in unfortunate ways. If they've designed a positive task themselves, they tend to carry it out with more enthusiasm, and if it's necessary to increase the severity of the task, they respond well.

4) The directive must be given with a rationale

The therapist needs to give the directive clearly and precisely so there is no ambiguity. He or she must make clear that the task is to occur only with symptomatic behavior and that there is a set time for it. Exactly what is to be done must be described. If appropriate, the task must be given with a rationale that makes it seem reasonable. Generally it should be a variation on the theme that if the client does something harder on herself than the symptom, the symptom will disappear. For some people, it is best to not explain but simply to tell them to do it. This more magical approach is best for the intellectuals among the clientele who can undo or explain away any rationale and find the whole thing not necessary.

If the ordeal is at all complex, or if there is a question about its nature, writing it down is helpful to both client and therapist.

5) The ordeal continues until the problem is resolved

The ordeal must be done precisely each time it should be done and must continue until the symptomatic behavior disappears. Typically the contract should be lifelong.

6) The ordeal is in a social context

The ordeal is a procedure that forces a change, and there are consequences to that. The therapist needs to be aware that symptoms are a reflection of a confusion in a social organization, usually a family. The existence of a symptom indicates that the hierarchy of an organization is incorrect. Therefore, when a therapist resolves a symptom in this way, he or she is forcing a change in a complex organization that was previously stabilized by the symptom. If, for example, a wife has a symptom that helps maintain her husband in a superior position as the one taking care of her, that changes rapidly when an ordeal requires the wife to abandon the symptom. She and her husband must negotiate a new relationship contract that does not include symptomatic behavior. Similarly, a man who stops drinking excessively must require his family organization to change because it is no longer adaptive to that symptom. It is best for a therapist to understand the function of a symptom in the social organization of the client. If not able to understand it, the therapist must resolve the symptom warily while watching for repercussions and changes.

It is the social changes that often lead the client to a reaction as the behavioral change occurs. Expectably, the client becomes upset, and that upset is a psychological change related to social consequences. When used correctly, an ordeal does not simply change minor behavior, the person restraining himself rather than go through the ordeal. This therapeutic approach can produce basic character changes as part of the disturbing changes that occur in the person's social organization. One sign of a basic change sometimes occurs when the client reports the experience of going out of his mind at the moment of change. Sometimes, just as the ordeal is proving effective, the client will telephone the therapist and say that something strange is happening. The therapist must reassure him that what is occurring is part of the expected change and help him through the reorganization of his life.

To summarize, symptoms have a function in an organization, and it is best if the designed ordeal takes into account the hierarchical situation of the client and his or her family. If, for example, a grandmother is siding with a child against his mother, it might be appropriate to have an ordeal procedure set up between child and grandmother to encourage more distance between them. Or if a father is abdicating his responsibilities in the family, he can become part of the ordeal procedure that would improve his child. Symptoms are adaptive to organizational structures, and with the change in a symptom the organizational structure will change.

Let me give an example that illustrates the procedures in designing an ordeal as well as the need to take the family organization into account when introducing a change. A sixteen-year-old youth recently out of a mental hospital had the distressing symptom of putting a variety of things up his behind. He would do this in the bathroom, inserting into his anus various vegetables, paper, Kleenex, and so on. He would then leave the bathroom a mess with all this material. His stepmother would have to clean it up, which she did furtively so the other children wouldn't know about his problem.

What ordeal might be appropriate for this unpleasant behavior? Not only should it be something more severe than the problem so he would abandon that behavior, but it should be good for him in some way. More than that, it should involve a change in the structure of his family organization.

What became apparent in a family interview by Margaret Clark, the therapist, was the way the stepmother was burdened by the problem, and the problems of all the children, while the father went about his business. She implied that when he had had several children to take care of after a divorce, he had married her and simply handed the children and their problems over to her. Clearly there was resentment on her part and a strain on the new marriage. The boy's problem became so severe that the parents did not have to deal with the marital issues between them; this appeared to be part of the function of the symptom.

The question was whether to arrange an ordeal with just the boy or to involve his family. It was decided to involve the family, partly because the boy did not seem motivated to get over the problem and partly to make a structural change possible so the symptom would be unnecessary. How to involve the family was the next step. It seemed logical to put the responsibility for an ordeal procedure in the hands of the father, since he should take more responsibility for solving the problem and burden his new wife less. Father and son could experience an ordeal together each time the symptom occurred. The next step was selection of an ordeal appropriate to the symptom.

The procedure decided on was as follows: Each time the boy put material up his behind and messed up the bathroom, the father would be told about it when he came home from work. The father would take the youth out into the backyard and have the young man dig a hole three feet deep and three feet wide. The boy would bury in the hole all the material that he had been messing up the bathroom with and then cover it up. The next time the symptom occurred, the behavior would be repeated, and this would continue forever.

The father methodically followed the procedure with his son, and in a few weeks the symptom stopped. It was not merely that the boy did not do it; he lost enthusiasm for it, as is typical with the use of the correct ordeal. The father, pleased with his success with the boy, began to associate more with him. The wife, pleased with her husband for solving this awful problem, became closer to him, so that the boy's misbehavior to help them became less necessary. There were other problems with this boy and his situation, so that therapy continued, but the particular symptom was promptly ended and remained gone.

This ordeal had the preferred characteristics: It involved and changed the structure of organization in the family by getting an irresponsible father involved. It was more severe than the symptom, since digging a deep hole in hard ground in the fall in the cold is not a simple task. The father had to stand in the cold with the boy until the task was done, so that his attitude toward a repetition of the symptom became more negative. The boy got exercise, which he wanted, in digging the hole. Digging the hole could be considered metaphoric, as well as paradoxical, to the symptom: He had been putting things in a hole, and he was required by the therapist to put things in a hole. So the procedure involved not only an ordeal but a metaphor, a paradox, and a family organizational change. As with most therapeutic procedures, the more an ordeal deals with various aspects of a situation, the better.

THE ORDEAL AS A THEORY OF CHANGE

Up to this point the ordeal procedure has been discussed as a therapeutic technique that can be considered one of many possible types of intervention to bring about change. If we examine the ordeal in a broader context, it appears to be more than a technique—it is actually a theory of change that encompasses many therapy techniques. Is it possible to say that all types of therapy are effective because an ordeal is explicitly or implicitly involved?

Examining other theories of change, one finds there are really not many contenders on the market. There is the insight theory in its different variations. This is based on the view that men and women are rational, and if they understand themselves, they will change. The schools of therapy based on this premise range from those that probe into unconscious processes through those that offer a rational consideration of alternatives to education of parents in dealing with problem children. Included in this school are the "emotional expression" theories, also based on the theory of repression, the central idea of this theory. Just as insight into repressed unconscious ideas is said to bring about change, so is the expression of repressed dynamic emotions, whether through insight or through primal screaming. The resistances must be "worked through" by discovering ideas and expressing buried emotions.

A second theory of change derives from learning theory and proposes that people change when the reinforcements that determine their behavior are changed. The procedures range from increasing positive reinforcements to replacing anxiety with relaxation to forcing people to change with "aversive" techniques.

A third, increasingly popular theory of change is the idea that people are participants in a homeostatic system and the governors of that system must be reset to bring about change. When reset, either by amplifying a small change or by disorganizing the system and forcing a new system, the problem behaviors of the participants will change. Most of the marital and family therapies flourish within the idea of the systems theory of change.

Theories of change of this kind have several characteristics. First of all, they can explain almost any outcome in any kind of therapy, even those of opposing theories. Enthusiastic advocates will say that the "real" cause of change is based on their theory. So an insight theorist will argue that people experiencing behavior modification procedures changed because they "really" discovered things about themselves during the experience. Similarly, the learning theorist argues that the insight schools of therapy actually change their clients' reinforcement schedules, and that is what "really" produces the change. In the same way, systems theory is broad enough so that its adherents can argue that any method of therapy "really" alters the sequences in a social system and so changes the people involved. Even the entrance of a therapist into a social system must change the sequences.

Another characteristic of theories of change is that they must be conceptualized in such a way that they cannot be disproved. It is the theory no one can disprove, like the theory of the existence of God, that has a fair chance of living forever, if there is money in it.

Can the ordeal as a theory of change meet the challenge of the other theories? Certainly it fits the criterion that it cannot be disproved. One can always argue that all people in therapy go through an ordeal. Even the most ingenious experimentalist could not set up a way of disproving the notion that any therapy is an ordeal. The mere fact that one must ask for help in order to begin therapy is an ordeal. It means that one has failed to solve one's problems and must concede that one needs help. Those who do not ask for help, but enter therapy involuntarily, demonstrate the point even more; it is an ordeal to be forced to go through therapy (and even to have to pay for what one does not want).

Once in therapy, the experience is hardly a rose garden. In the insight therapies one has the unpleasant experience of having all the unfortunate thoughts and deficiencies that one doesn't like to mention examined and dwelt on. If the person objects, the therapist is likely to argue that resistance, and working through that resistance, is expected. One must suffer the exploration of what one would rather not think about. Interpretations are always about what one is reluctant to admit. At a more elementary level, Freud (who knew an ordeal when he saw one) suggested that the fee should be a sacrifice to benefit the analysis, which is an unconscious recognition of the ordeal as the basis of analysis. Whether we examine psychodynamic orthodoxy or one of the spin-off confrontation groups where people face their innermost awfulness, the insight school clearly is based on the premise that an ordeal is basic to change.

Behavior modifiers don't force people to think about their more unpleasant thoughts; they emphasize the more positive side of reinforcements. However, the therapy experience itself often includes the tedium of being lectured on learning theory as well as having someone behave in a programmed way in response to one's intimate distress. The inhuman response to a human dilemma can be an ordeal. Of course, behavior modification also revels in aversive techniques involving explicit ordeals, such as shocking people by word or electricity when they manifest symptoms. Even apparently benign techniques that don't seem aversive, such as Joseph Wolpe's reciprocal inhibition procedure, in which clients imagine their phobic situations, are not cheerful moments. It is unpleasant and can be tedious to go through imagined scene after imagined scene of situations one fears and would rather not think about, and to pay money to do that.

Family therapy also offers ordeals, both intentional and inadvertent. To have to come together with one's family in the presence of an expert and concede that one is a failure as a parent or a child or a spouse is an ordeal. Exploring how one participated in producing a defective member, or even acknowledging that one did so, is ordealful. Therapists using acceptance techniques are likely to advise the family to continue in their misery, as is characteristic of the Milan group. Other therapists use experiential and confronting techniques, offering unpleasant insightful interpretations to the family, thereby causing a family to hint they would rather be elsewhere. Therapists who like to have families weep together and express emotions must focus on bringing out their misery.

Obviously, a sound argument can be made for the ordeal as the "real" cause of change in all contemporary therapy, whatever theories the therapists think they are following. Should we confine ourselves to therapy schools? What about other aspects of human life? One thinks of religion at once. Is not the ordeal the basic rock on which is built the Christian church? Change, or conversion, in Christianity was obviously not based on the idea that the soul is saved through wine and good cheer; rather, salvation comes through misery and suffering. It is when the Christian gives up the pleasures of sex and the grape and accepts the hair shirt that conversion has taken place. The benefits of distress are part of the basic, and curious, concept of salvation through suffering. Everywhere one turns in Christian edifices, one sees the sufferer going through his ordeal on the cross. Turning to specific procedures, in the oldest tradition of the oldest Christian church is confession—an ordeal in which one must, for the good of one's Soul, reveal to another that which one would rather not. Equally old in tradition is penance, a consequence of confession. Obviously, penance is a ritualized ordeal. Like therapy ordeals, penance takes two forms—penance as a standardized task and penance designed for the peculiar sins of a particular sinner.

In passing, it might be mentioned that not only Christianity and the Western world have found their way to the ordeal. If we glance at the Eastern philosophies and religions, we see that misfortune is part of enlightenment. Not only are there Eastern religions that emphasize accepting suffering as beneficial, but Zen Buddhism, with its 700-year-old procedures for changing people, includes specific ordeals. The Zen master is likely to bring about enlightenment by striking students with sticks and requiring them to respond to impossible koans. Enlightenment, like salvation and therapeutic change, has painful steps on the way to bliss.

The other area of human life besides religion where change takes place is in the political arena. Here we also find the ordeal. The great revolutionary movements, such as the Communist and Socialist movements, set out to change the masses of the world. To achieve this change, participants in the movement are expected to make sacrifices and go through disciplined ordeals. Every mass movement requires sacrifices and giving up the world of pleasure for the cause. It seems evident that if an individual, or a whole society, is asked to change, the ordeal is central to the process of transformation.

Whether we examine the ordeal as a technique or as a universal theory of change, its merits demand further examination and exploration. As a subject of research and training for many years to come, it has one aspect that needs great emphasis. Like any powerful means of changing people, the ordeal is a procedure that can cause harm in the hands of the ignorant and irresponsible who rush off to make people suffer. More than any other technique, it can be misused by the naive and incompetent. We should all keep in mind that society grants permission to therapists to impose their help on people to relieve suffering, not to create it.

Chapter 2

Finding a Humorous Alternative

Cloé Madanes

It was probably Milton Erickson who first introduced the idea of humor as a legitimate aspect of therapy. In his 1954 paper, "Indirect Hypnotic Therapy of an Enuretic Couple," Erickson described a young couple who consulted him because, shortly after their wedding, they discovered that they were both lifelong bed wetters. Erickson instructed them to wet the bed, deliberately and simultaneously, and then to sleep on it every night for two weeks. After the two-week period, as a result of this directive, the involuntary bed-wetting disappeared. It is doubtful that this instruction appeared humorous to the couple at the time that it was given, but Erickson wrote that they were amused when they came back to report the results.

Humorous interventions often do not appear humorous to family members and clients. It is only in retrospect, after the problem has been solved and people have a more optimistic view of life, that the humor becomes apparent. The uniquely human characteristic of being able to laugh at one's own predicament seems to disappear when people are involved in serious conflicts and is recovered only as these conflicts are resolved.

Humor, like all human efforts to make sense of the world, involves the issue of classification. That is, an event can be classified as sad or amusing, boring or exciting, trivial or important, depending on the context that defines it. In therapy, this context develops from the interaction between therapist and client. Therapists can create a humorous context to lessen their own power or authority, or to help a client feel at ease, or as part of the strategy to solve the presenting problem. A situation

This paper is a chapter in *Behind the One-Way Mirror*, by Cloé Madanes. Reprinted with permission from Jossey-Bass, San Francisco, 1984.

can be defined in various ways, just as the same story can be told as a comedy, a drama, a satire, a romance or a mystery. Therapy can often be seen as an effort to change the genre: from drama to comedy of errors, from tragic romance to adventure story, and so on.

Probably humor was being used by therapists for decades, but it was Erickson who brought it out of the closet in professional publications. Today there are numerous publications that deal with the subject, and it is accepted in a variety of modalities of therapy.

A therapist can follow either of two broad approaches in using humor to change the context of a person or the drama of a family. One is based primarily on the use of *language* to redefine situations. The other relies on organizing *actions* that change a course of events and modify sequences of interaction. Some therapists prefer one or the other approach, but some, like Milton Erickson, are masters of both. I will first discuss the approach based on the use of language to change people.

TALK

Strategic therapy often involves changing the genre and can begin with a redefinition of the problem that involves the use of humor. For example, a 30-year-old alcoholic refused to hold a job and lived with his retired and ill parents who were preoccupied with the young man and spent their time bickering about him. They described him as a bum, without either a goal in life or a career. The therapist said that the young man was not a bum and that he did have a career, but that his career was not recognized or socially acceptable in our culture. His career was to entertain his parents, to keep them busy and focused on him rather than bickering with each other. Was he on an alcoholic binge? Had he gotten in trouble with the law? Had he found a job and then lost it? All these concerns kept the parents entertained and kept him involved with them. He was like the recreation director on a cruise ship, keeping the old people amused, and he should really even be making a salary at this job instead of receiving only criticism. Perhaps if he were appreciated instead of only criticized, he would develop more interesting ways of entertaining his parents than getting drunk and raising hell. Maybe he would take them to a movie, a picnic, or even to a museum, to provide a wider variety of recreation for them.

The therapist, who was close in age to the son, said that he, in fact, respected and admired the young man for having chosen a career that is against the cultural values of our time and that does not lead to a good income or to a contribution in some area of endeavor, and is not conducive to marriage and children, the things that most men want to have. The therapist added that he himself had chosen a career as a therapist (against his father's wish that he be a banker) and he was not nearly as devoted to his own parents as the young man was to his, since he saw them only occasionally. This was because he, the therapist, had other interests, but, he remarked, "We are all different from one another and who is to say that my way is better than yours?" Although the therapist's view was taken by the family as more sarcastic than humorous, the young man improved and the parents went away on vacation for the first time in five years. They said that if their son would not leave them, they would move to another state and leave *him*.

Language can be manipulated in infinite ways that can be humorous and therapeutic. (In the example above, and the others I am presenting, the therapist was a trainee at the Family Therapy Institute of Washington, D.C., and I was the supervisor behind the one-way mirror. Our trainees are professional therapists learning a strategic approach.)

A middle-aged alcoholic was in therapy with an eager young man who was determined to cure him. This alcoholic was an expert at asking for help and then refusing to be helped. He constantly complained about his problems while refusing to do anything to change his situation. He appeared to enjoy frustrating the young therapist who responded to every rebuke with increased interest. The therapist was instructed to begin every statement he made during a session with the words, "I am not going to tell you," so that he would be negating what he would immediately say. The therapist said, for example, "I am not going to tell you that a man should not beat his wife," "I am not going to tell you that a man in your situation should be looking for a job," "I am not going to tell you that you should take care of your children." As the session progressed the man became more and more irritated with the therapist, until finally the irritation turned to laughter and he began to ask, "What else are you not going to tell me?" By disqualifying his own statements in this way, the therapist was able to disengage from his intense involvement with the alcoholic and was more effective in influencing him.

Often the wisdom of popular humor lies in the fact that it forces us to realize that the unit is the system. A favorite story about drivers is the one about the woman stalled in the middle of traffic. As she starts her car 20 times in a row only to have the engine fail before she can move, a man behind her keeps blaring his horn, even though he can see her predicament. Finally the woman gets out of her car, goes to the driver behind her and says, "I'm awfully sorry, but I don't seem to be able to start my car. If you'll go up there and start it for me, I'll stay here and lean on your horn." The humor in this story is similar to that in an intervention where the therapist says to a wife that he promises to criticize the husband himself if the wife is nice to the husband. Since it is necessary for someone to always be critical of the man, the therapist will be pleased to take on the job and free the wife for a more pleasant interaction. In this case, as well as in the story about the drivers, the unit is a dyadic pair that is working together to maintain the status quo. Many techniques of therapy are similar to the punch line of a joke, and the punch line in a joke is so often the truth about interpersonal relationships. Wife and therapist can change positions, just as the two drivers can change positions, leading to humor. Changing positions is similar to taking turns, a form of cooperation highly valued in our culture.

A young man described his position as the "life ruiner" in the family in that he ruined the family's life. He had been arrested several times for drunken driving, breaking and entering, and possession of drugs. He had a 26-year-old brother and a 23-year-old sister, and all three children lived at home and did not contribute financially to the household. The young man insisted that his siblings were good and that he was the only source of conflicts; he ruined the life of the family. The therapist proposed that the three siblings should take turns at ruining the family's life, that it was not fair that only one, the youngest, should have that position. If they took turns at causing trouble every week, then the young man would have two weeks out of three to devote to his own life and perhaps might get ahead on matters other than causing the family grief. There was much discussion and the older brother volunteered to replace his sibling and ruin the family's life for one week. The younger brother reluctantly agreed and during that week obeyed the law and found a job. The therapist stuck to the same strategy for three weeks with the result that the young man said he was interested in other matters and had given up on life-ruining as a way of life.

To share an unfortunate position by taking turns at causing distress is both humorous and therapeutic. Just as bringing the unconscious into consciousness can be the punch line of a joke, so the recognition of a tacit collusion in the family where one person is chosen to cause distress can be amusing. As the family discussed taking turns to be the life ruiner, the absurdity of their way of solving their problems became apparent.

Another approach that involves changing positions has to do with changing the perspective of a person in a family. A young couple consulted for divorce counseling when their divorce was about to become final. The young man was 22 years old and had an unstable job history. The wife was 26 and had married him when she accidentally became pregnant. At the time, her father had recently died and she was living with her mother, who was trying to overcome her depression. The two women had decided that it would be nice to have a baby. When the daughter got pregnant, the new grandmother went to work to support her daughter and grandchild. Both women excluded the young man who alternated between brave attempts to become a responsible bread-winner and aimless wanderings across the country. The wife sued for divorce, which was about to become final, when the baby was two years old. They came for divorce counseling to negotiate visitation and to improve communication to better deal with the child. The husband had the secret agenda of getting back together with his wife. In the second session the husband's wishes were made explicit and the wife made it very clear that she would not go back with him. Before the third session, the divorce became final. The husband unexpectedly appeared at his ex-wife's house and demanded to be driven somewhere. The ex-wife re-fused and he took a knife and slit his arms longitudinally, shouting, "This will give you pleasure!" Then he grabbed the baby and ran down the street. The wife caught up with him and took him to the emergency room where he got some stitches.

After this crisis, all available family members were invited to the next session. The young man, the ex-wife, the baby, an uncle of the young man, and the young man's father, who came from out of state, were present. The grandmother did not arrive until the session was over. The young man appeared depressed and humiliated. The therapist asked each one how they thought that this kind of dangerous act by the young man could be prevented in the future. The ex-wife and the young man said that surely he must be mentally ill. The father and the uncle said that the mistake had been for the young couple to continue to see each other when they were separated, that there should have been a cooling-off period with more distance between them. It sounded to me, the supervisor, like the two older men were right and the therapeutic error had been not to arrange for this distance. A strategy was planned to correct the mistake.

The young ex-wife was asked to leave the room with the baby because the therapist wanted to speak to the men alone. She said to the father and uncle that what the young husband needed was an attractive, strong young woman on *his* side to counteract the power of the ex-wife and her mother. He needed a woman with whom he could enjoy having sex and who would be jealous and possessive of him. It was the duty of the father and uncle to help him find such a woman, since he obviously was not willing to do it by himself; otherwise, a young man as handsome as *he* would be involved with one already. In fact he was probably occupied in fighting them off. Therefore, the father and uncle, right after the session that evening, had to take the young man out on the town to pick up a girl, or at least to meet women. The three men laughed and the atmosphere of the session turned to something similar to a bachelor party. The young man said that he did not need help and could pick up a girl by himself quite well. The therapist would not hear of it. The father and uncle said that they both were married and their wives would not look favorably on this idea. The therapist said that she understood that this was a sacrifice she was asking of them, and of their wives, and they would have to explain to their spouses that this had been a therapeutic recommendation. In fact, the therapist would be happy to write a letter to the wives explaining the situation. Father and uncle said, stroking their moustaches, that they would just have to sacrifice themselves and go out looking for girls. There was a great deal of joking and laughter as they planned where they would go. The young man forgot his depression and participated actively in the discussion, suggesting which would be the better places. The therapist said that that night would just be the beginning. From then on, father and uncle had to collaborate in finding the young man women until he was involved in a sexual relationship with a strong, beautiful woman who would protect him from his ex-wife and her mother. There was more laughter and the uncle suggested that attractive women could be found in places other than night spots, for example, in church. The idea was accepted and further plans were made. The session ended with the three men taking off for a night on the town.

From then on the sessions involved only the three men and had the same focus, for the father and uncle to advise the young man and help him find women. The father was put in charge of all decisions with regard to his son's life and it was decided that there would be no visits to the ex-wife until he was involved with another woman. To arrange for this involvement was not an easy task. There were ups and downs and it took more than two months for the young man to begin to have sexual relations with other women. Other issues were dealt with in various ways, and the ex-wife and grandmother were seen separately. The mood, however, remained changed. The humorous directive of asking the father and uncle to sacrifice themselves by helping the young man find women changed the focus of the therapy. Instead of dealing with mental illness, depression, loss and separation, the theme of the therapy was fun and sex.

The humor in a story often consists of some kind of reframing or relabelling of a situation. There is a story about how in the midst of a heated argument, a wife began beating her diminutive husband. In terror he ran into the bedroom and crawled under the bed. "Come out!" she cried. "No," he shouted back from under the bed, "I'll show you who's boss in this house!" In therapy it is often useful to relabel the weak as powerful and the powerful as weak, and the truth is always a matter of interpretation. A young, beautiful wife was always cutting down and rejecting her husband while complaining that he was inhibited, did not express himself, or communicate his feelings as she expected. The husband kept excusing himself but defending his need to spend long hours at his office involved with his promising career. The therapist said to the wife that in fact her criticism and rejection of the husband were extremely kindly to him, since he probably could not tolerate having a loving wife. He had not received enough love and caring from his father during his childhood (the husband had talked about this in therapy) and therefore he was not prepared to receive the love, of which he had been so badly deprived, from anyone, particularly not from a beautiful wife whom he loved. If she were *not* critical and rejecting, if she were loving and devoted to him, he would be overwhelmed, might not be able to tolerate her affection and might even leave her. Her rejection was really a manifestation of love that the husband should appreciate because it was a way of staying close to him in a fashion that he could tolerate. The therapist said that she would work to improve the couple's relationship, but that the wife had to make sure to always maintain a certain level of rejection so that the husband would not get upset, particularly since the therapist did not want to improve the relationship to the point where the husband would leave the wife. For several weeks the couple discussed in therapy what they could do to have more fun with each other and to have a better marriage, but always the therapist reminded the wife to be rejecting, and every session began with the therapist asking the couple whether the wife had been sufficiently rejecting since the last session. As a result the wife became considerably less rejecting, and the husband much more tolerant of having a loving wife.

A young man who was struggling to become an opera singer came to therapy referred by his voice teacher who thought he could not reach certain notes because of emotional difficulties. The young man was in his mid-twenties, lived with his parents, held a menial job even though he had a college degree and struggled to improve his singing. He spent a great deal of time keeping his mother company and was distant from his father, an engineer who was not sympathetic to the son's artistic vocation. The young man's difficulty in singing was solved in two sessions by asking him to make two mistakes deliberately: one that his teacher would notice and one that she would have trouble perceiving. As the young man struggled to make these mistakes, his skill improved and he reached the notes that had presented difficulties. He said to the therapist, however, that his main reasons for coming to therapy were that he wanted to improve his relationship with his father and that he wanted his father to appreciate him. The therapist, a young, attractive, exotic-looking woman, said that she found his concern about his relationship with his father extremely interesting because it was so unusual. The young man asked why it was unusual, and the therapist answered that most young men in therapy these days are concerned with other things, so she had not had the chance to work with one who was mainly concerned about his father. She found this very moving and, although she did not know whether she could help him, she was certainly interested in the therapy because it would be a new learning experience for her. The young man asked what things other young men were concerned about, and the therapist answered: "Oh, mainly having more sex and making more money. That is mainly what they want, and it is not half as interesting as your problem of improving your relationship with your father and getting him to appreciate you." The young man said that he, too, wanted to have more sex and make more money; in fact, he would like to spend some time talking about that. The therapist said she knew that that was not so and that he was mainly concerned about his father; what was so fascinating to her was that this was such an old-fashioned problem. Young men many years ago had brought that problem to therapy quite frequently but nobody at the Institute had heard of a young man having that problem in recent years. The problem was so old-fashioned that it could not have even been the subject of an Italian opera, only of a German opera because they were more boring. In fact, what the young man should do was write a German opera about a young man who wants to be appreciated by his father. There was a discussion of how such a story could go, the vicissitudes of such a young man, and how he would finally be appreciated by his father after a long life of suffering. The young man agreed to write the German opera and actually wrote it and read it to the therapist. As he was working on it, his interest in his father diminished and his interest in sex and money increased.

In relation to these new interests, it became apparent that there were no women in his life at all. He talked about his difficulty in finding a girl he liked and in approaching her. The therapist said that that was not his difficulty at all. His difficulty had to do with tolerating rejection. Because it was so difficult for him to tolerate rejection, he could not approach women for fear of being rejected. Therefore, what he had to do was to practice feeling rejected. For this purpose, he had to stand at a certain corner in front of a certain boutique and spend several hours during two weekends inviting women to have a cup of coffee with him. They would refuse, and he would have the experience of being rejected and tolerating it. Surprisingly, so many women accepted the invitation that the young man did not really have the chance to experience rejection.

As he began to feel more comfortable with women, the young man explained that one of his fears had always been that he would be taken for a homosexual. Because of his work in the theater, he thought that he had certain mannerisms that could be thought of as being effeminate. The therapist told him that that presented a wonderful opportunity and that he should practice leading a woman to believe that he was gay and then unexpectedly seduce her. The young man said that, in fact, he had already had that experience. Once he and a friend, after unsuccessfully trying to find girls at a beach resort, had pretended to be homosexual and had been very successful at convincing two girls to go out with them. The therapist said that she had not realized that he had such a range and that it would be difficult to arrange for experiences of rejection for him.

The therapy ended when the young man became involved with a girl who was very interested in sex. He then had to find a better job so he could move out of his parent's house and have some privacy with her. By this time, he had lost interest in whether his father really appreciated him. His concern about his father, his difficulties with women, and his fear of homosexuality had all been reframed in humorous ways that led to change.

The presentation of authority as fallible is a typical humorous device. Jokes abound about God, the pope, the president, and so on. Some difficult problems of young people involve rebellious acts against a parent who is seen by the young person (accurately or inaccurately) as being extremely powerful. The positions in the family appear rigidly established: the parent attempts to take charge of the young person and fails, the young person refuses to obey the parent, and the war escalates with each confrontation. Reversing the hierarchy, describing the parent as having a problem of unhappiness, and making the focus of the therapy a discussion with the children of what advice they could give the parent so that he or she could become a happier person, is a way of introducing humor, optimism, and the possibility of negotiation. Children, for example, can advise a parent to be more irresponsible, to have more fun and to engage in more adult activities instead of being so involved with the children. A variation of this approach that involves more action than talk is to actually put the children in charge of the parents' happiness, so that the children plan what the parents will do to be happier and the parents follow the children's instructions. In a session where such issues are discussed, the mood becomes considerably lighter because it strikes the parents as funny but true that the children are in charge of their happiness. It is also a moving experience for parents to see how concerned the children are about them and how wisely they can advise them.

Not only in therapeutic interventions but also in interviewing technique, there is a parallel between popular humor and therapy. Take the story of the young man who is going on his first blind date and is nervous about not having anything to say. His brother advises him with a formula that never fails: to talk about family, food and philosophy. Any of those topics is guaranteed to get a girl talking. So the young man goes to meet the girl who is pretty and shy. Eager to make a good impression, he follows his brother's advice and begins to talk about family. "Tell me, do you have a brother?" he says. "No," she answers. So he moves to the topic of food. "Do you like noodles?" "No," she says again. So the young man remembers his brother's advice. He'll talk philosophy. "Tell me," he says, "if you had a brother, would he like noodles?"

As in this story, in therapy, it is often necessary to ask questions about apparently unrelated subjects in order to obtain information on which to base a hypothesis for change. When these questions are combined with a request to one family member to comment on the relationship of two others, the effect is often humorous, as in the circular questioning of the Milan Group. "If your mother and your wife were to talk about your job, would they agree that you should strive for a better position?" "If your husband and your son were to talk about you, what would they say?" "If your daughter were worried about you, what would she be worried about?" "Would your wife be worried about the same thing as your daughter, or would she worry about something else?" The more guarded and reserved the family, the more humorous and off-the-wall the questions appear. However, as soon as an important issue is addressed, the questions no longer seem absurd or humorous.

ACTION

I will now discuss the approach that relies on organizing actions that change a course of events.

Slapstick is a form of humor that involves actions often mocking violence. It is sometimes used in therapy as a way of redefining a situation through actions rather than through verbal statements. A couple in their 60s consulted because of marital unhappiness. One of the problems was that the wife complained about the husband's irritation at what she considered to be her idiosyncracies that should be accepted benevolently. She had the habit of doing things quickly and walking fast so that he could not catch up with her. For example, she would hand him a cup of coffee and drop it on the floor before he could grab it. They would get out of the car to go to a movie, and she would rush ahead of him in a way that he considered rude. She was asked to show how she walked fast in the session, and she jumped out of her chair and sprinted toward the door. She was asked to do this once more, and this time the husband was to run after her, grab her, and give her a big Rudolf Valentino-style kiss. The couple did this with much laughter. They were asked to practice this scene during the next week. The wife was to purposefully run away from the husband, and the husband would grab her and kiss her dramatically whether they were with friends, in the middle of the street, in a restaurant or whatever. The slapstick routine counteracted the irritation and resentment of the couple's interaction and the humor freed them to try new ways of relating.

It is not uncommon when humor is used in therapy that a family member attempts to establish a secret coalition with the therapist. This is usually conveyed by nonverbal means, through a certain look out of the corner of the eye and a certain smile, twisted to one side, that implies that the therapist and that person are together in pulling the leg of another family member. In the previous example, when the husband was asked to act like Rudolf Valentino, he said with a wink and a smile that he did not know who Rudolf Valentino was and had never seen that type of a kiss, implying that he was too young to know. The implication was that the therapist and he would humorously coax the wife out of her bad habit, while in fact the therapist's plan was to change both their behaviors.

It has been said that in all humor there is an element of defiance, be it of authority, socially accepted norms or rules. Defiance can be used in ways that are not only humorous but therapeutic as antagonism is changed into playful challenge. Peggy Penn (1982) describes a technique to be used with young couples who may present marital, sexual or communication difficulties and where the situation can be understood as resulting from the difficulty of the couple in establishing a boundary around their relationship and protecting it from intrusions and overinvolvement with in-laws. The couple is asked to visit both sets of in-laws and during these visits the wife is to be overtly and exaggeratedly affectionate to the husband, holding his hand, whispering in his ear, kissing him, giggling, sitting on his lap. The husband is to respond showing that he is pleased but shy and not rejecting. The couple is then to go home and make notes of the behavior they observed in the older couples as they performed their parts. Usually the in-laws send the couple home early, since it becomes clear that they have something going on between them from which they are excluded. The young couple can separate more easily from their parents through playful defiance rather than unfortunate confrontations. The same approach can be used when one of the spouses is involved in conflictual ways with siblings, friends, or other relatives.

Not only defiance, but also violence, can be turned to a humorous encounter in a variety of ways. One young couple consulted because of the fighting and violence in their marriage. They described a sequence in which the wife would criticize the husband, he would withdraw, she would pursue him and eventually, in frustration at his silence, would start hitting him, and to her shock he would hit her back, sometimes quite painfully. They were both attractive, intelligent and successful, but they could not change this interaction which made them unhappy, horrified them, and prevented them from deciding to have children. The therapist conducted a long session exploring the consequences that a happy relationship would have for both their extended families and asked them to think further about those issues. Then he suggested that in the next two weeks, every time that the wife provoked the husband's anger, and particularly when she hit him, the husband, instead of hitting her back, would put his hand up her skirt or under her blouse. Some of their fights had been in public, so this behavior would also take place even if it had to be in public. The couple laughed and agreed to do this. The directive was repeated for six weeks and the violence and fighting disappeared. The husband said, however, that although they had not had the opportunity to follow the directive because there had been no fights or provocations, he had had opportunity to fondle the wife in different circumstances. When therapy was terminated in two months, the couple had decided to have a baby.

Often a story is humorous because there is an incongruity between a situation and the framework in which it takes place. Woody Allen, for example, a masterful humorist, depends in many of his characterizations on the incongruity between two factors: his alleged prowess as a lover and his mousy physical appearance. As a writer, he also works on the humorous aspects of incongruities. In "The Stolen Gem," a satire on detective fiction, a character says, "The sapphire was originally owned by a sultan who died under mysterious circumstances when a hand reached out of a bowl of soup he was eating and strangled him" (Allen, 1981).

The element of incongruity is common both to humor and to paradoxical directives. A couple consulted about their 12-year-old son who had been setting dangerous fires for seven years. This activity endangered the father's job because he worked for the government in situations where he and his family repeatedly needed to obtain security clearance, which was in jeopardy because of the child's firesetting. In fact, at an army party, the boy had set fire to explosives, an act which had driven the father to distraction. The mother could not leave the child alone in the house for five minutes for fear that he would burn it down. The father worked long hours and had little contact with the son. In the first session the therapist had the boy demonstrate how he set a fire to see if he could do it properly. For this purpose a coffee can, papers, matches and water to put out the fire were brought into the room. When the boy set the fire and put it out, the therapist criticized him severely, saying that he did not know the first thing about fires. He had not closed the match box; he had set the fire too close to the edge of the can so that a paper could have floated out and burned him; after pouring water in the can he had put one hand inside too soon while touching the hot can with his other hand, so either hand could have been burned. All this, said the therapist, proved that the boy was completely incompetent about fires and the irony was that he claimed to be an expert, judging by all the fires he had set. When the therapist left the room for a moment to empty the coffee can, the boy, who had listened incredulously to the therapist's harangue, said to his parents: "This guy is crazy." The therapist came back and asked the father to demonstrate for the son how to set and put out a fire correctly. Then he was told that he needed to spend more time with his son in a fatherly way, and what better way than to spend the time teaching the boy about fires like he had done in the session. He was directed to supervise the boy in this endeavor setting a variety of fires with different materials in different places and putting them out. They were to do this six times a day, every day. The mother was to keep notes on their activities. The parents complied and carried out the task for several weeks. Sometimes the father, because of his long working hours and difficult schedule, had to wake up the son in the middle of the night to set a fire. On several occasions the indignant child said that the therapist was crazy and on occasion the parents seemed to think the same. The spontaneous firesetting, however, stopped immediately and soon the boy asked whether he and his father could spend the time in more constructive ways than setting fires. Eventually, the therapist consented to this suggestion and father and son discovered common interests and enjoyed each other. The directive to set fires was incongruous in the context of a therapy designed to end the firesetting. The father was asked to encourage the son to set supervised fires rather than not to set fires at all. The ordeal of setting fires, first in the session and then several times a day to the point of having to get out of bed to set a fire in the middle of the night; the therapist's criticism of the boy as an inadequate firesetter; and the child's indignation at the therapist were humorous. In fact, the child was so provoked that he set out to demonstrate to the therapist that he was competent in all areas and his grades in school improved. There was a quality of the absurd in the therapist's directives. This element of ridicule is common to humor and to paradoxical directives.

An element of incongruity often is also useful in training therapists. Haley tells about his approach to a very shy student who was terrified of his supervision behind the one-way mirror (personal communication, 1983). He instructed her to go into the therapy room to interview a family and to be sure to make three mistakes. Two of these mistakes would be obvious and one mistake would be one that would not be evident to Haley. The student conducted the interview and after a while came out of the room to discuss the problem with Haley. He asked, "Did you make the three mistakes correctly?" She answered, "Screw you!" and was no longer overconcerned about his opinion. It is incongruous to ask a therapist to properly make mistakes in the context of teaching how to do therapy properly.

A therapist under supervision was a professor of behavior modification and was very concerned with telling people just what they should be doing. He had a difficult case of a little girl referred by her school for a variety of problems. She had been adopted by her grandparents after being abandoned by her mother. The therapist was instructed to deal with all problems by only saying to the grandparents, "I am curious to see how you will resolve that." This made sense in terms of increasing the grandparents' confidence as parents, but it was not the kind of directive approach the therapist was expecting to learn. However, he struggled to follow the supervisor's instructions, and problems of lying, failing in school, and thumb sucking were dealt with only by saying, "I am curious to see how you will resolve that." The grandparents benevolently resolved all problems in a couple of months, and school and therapist were impressed. To ask a student to make mistakes deliberately or to refrain from giving any directives is incongruent in the context of a directive therapy where the student is precisely interested in learning how to give directives properly. However, just as with clients, it is usually only later that the student sees the humor in the situation.

An understatement of a problem can lead to humorous directives. A compulsive vomiter came to therapy after 17 years of bulimarexia which had resulted in the loss of all her teeth, various somatic problems and years of unsuccessful therapy. She and her family were told that what she was doing was simply throwing away food by mushing it up in her stomach first and then throwing it into the toilet. Why not mush up the food with her hands instead and place it in the toilet directly? This would be less harmful to her body than having the stomach do the work. The family was to provide the food and supervise the process. To say that 17 years of compulsive vomiting was simply throwing away food by passing it through her stomach first, was an understatement of a severe self-destructive compulsion. The instructions were followed, however, and the vomiting disappeared after this and other paradoxical interventions.

A common element in popular humor and in strategic therapy is an ordeal designed to solve a problem, as in the cases of the firesetter and the compulsive vomiter. Take the story of the man who complains to the doctor about his uncontrollable cough. The doctor gives him a bottle of castor oil and tells him to go home, drink the whole bottle and come back the next day. When he comes back, the doctor asks, "Did you drink the castor oil?" "Yes," says the man. "Do you still cough?" "Yes." The doctor gives him a second bottle of castor oil and tells him to drink it and come back the next day. The man follows the instructions and reports the next day that he is still coughing regularly. The doctor gives him yet another bottle and repeats the instructions. When the patient returns, the doctor asks, "Do you cough now?" The patient answers quiveringly: "I don't cough any more. I'm afraid to."

This story is reminiscent of the ordeals often prescribed by Erickson to his patients. Haley presented in his address (Chapter 1) the case of the old man who complained of insomnia, and who hated waxing his floors. Erickson promised to cure him if he gave up eight hours of sleep.

The man agreed and Erickson instructed him to get ready for bed that night but instead of going to bed, to wax the floors all night. At seven in the morning he was to go to work as usual. He was to repeat this procedure for four consecutive nights. Since he only slept two hours a night, this meant giving up only eight hours of sleep. The man polished the floors for three nights but on the fourth night he decided to lie down for a few minutes and he slept until morning. A year later he was still sleeping soundly every night. Erickson said: "The old man would do anything to get out of polishing the floors, even sleep."

I used a similar approach in the supervision of the therapy of a woman who was a compulsive cleaner. The symptom developed when she married her second husband and quit her job. She cleaned the house and everything in it constantly and compulsively. It took her hours to clean the kitchen after each meal, and, to avoid the cleaning, her cooking was simple and uninteresting. Often her husband would bring home ready-made food to prevent her from having to wash and clean the kitchen for hours after cooking a meal. Frequently she had to get up in the middle of the night because she thought that somebody might have used a towel in the bathroom and she immediately had to put it in the washing machine. This aspect of her habit was particularly annoying to the husband because the noise of the washing machine prevented him from sleeping. The woman did not have this problem when she visited her mother's house, which was regularly, or at other people's houses, nor did she have this problem in hotel rooms when the couple went on vacation. At home, however, the husband would sit every evening by himself and read the newspaper or watch television, then he would go to bed and continue watching television by himself, and he would eventually fall asleep alone while the wife was still busy cleaning. He was 20 years older than the wife and, although he said that he cared about his wife and wanted to help her, he was very disagreeable and obnoxious to the therapist, insisting that he did not want to participate, that this was her individual problem to solve. He was somewhat annoyed at having paid for five years of psychoanalysis and for behavior modification and several experiences of the encounter and growth variety without results. The husband also objected to the fact that the couple had to drive two hours to come to the sessions. It was apparent that the therapy would have to be extremely brief if it was to involve the husband. A humorous ordeal is particularly appropriate to brief therapy and might succeed where other approaches had failed. Given the information provided in the first interview, it was postulated that the wife spent her time cleaning compulsively to avoid being with her husband. If this were so, it would follow logically that if the consequence for exaggerated cleaning would be for her to have to be closer to her husband, the situation would be reversed and she would clean less in order to avoid him. Based on this hypothesis, two directives were given to the couple. One was a short-term intervention designed to introduce an element of playfulness in the relationship and the other was a long-term recommendation that could continue to be effective without a continuing therapeutic involvement.

The first intervention was to tell the couple that in the following two weeks, every day the wife would leave something in the house purposefully uncleaned. When the husband came home in the evening he would search the house and try to discover what it was that she had not cleaned that day. If he discovered it, he had won and she would make dinner for him as usual. If he lost, he would take her out to dinner. However, it was important to ensure the wife's truthfulness and for this purpose, before the husband came home, she would have written what it was that she had not cleaned on a little slip of paper and stuck the paper in her bra. The husband had to find out whether he had won or lost by finding the slip of paper and reading it. In this way, the problem of compulsive cleaning was leading to the husband getting closer to his wife. Even though the couple might not follow the suggestion, the mere fact of giving the directive had introduced playfulness into the situation. During those two weeks the wife was also to make a detailed description of her cleaning and a log of the time she spent at it to use as a baseline for the next intervention.

In the next interview, the husband said that he understood that the therapist wanted him to take a more firm position in relation to his wife and he was planning to do just that. He had searched the house, failed to discover what she had not cleaned, and found the slip of paper a few times, not every day, but they had frequently gone out to dinner. The therapist reviewed the time log that the wife had brought to the session and proposed the following to the couple: A housekeeper works eight hours a day, the wife was working now as a housewife and housekeeper since she had quit her job; therefore it would be normal for her to clean eight hours a day, but no more than that, like any hired housekeeper would. The husband said that only five hours a day of cleaning could possibly be necessary, but agreed on eight hours of cleaning during the week and two hours on weekends and holidays as normal for a housekeeper. The wife said that would be normal for another woman but not for herself. Then the therapist said that she had a cure and if the couple followed her instructions the problem of compulsive cleaning would be solved, but they had to promise to follow her directive before she would tell them what it was. The couple refused to promise so the therapist gave them the directive anyway. Every day the wife was to stop cleaning at five o'clock (she had reported that she never started before nine). She then would shower and dress to look nice for her husband. When he came home, there would be no more cleaning; the wife instead could read, do needlepoint, or whatever she liked. She was only allowed half an hour to do the dishes after dinner. If she spent any time cleaning beyond that, the husband would force her to get in bed with him to watch television (which was what he enjoyed doing in the evening), and she would have to stay in bed with him until they fell asleep. If the husband preferred, instead of watching television together in bed, the punishment that he could enforce would be that the two would go out together either that evening or the next. The wife said that this would not work, and the husband said, "Excellent, I understand, excellent!" He commented that he had known all along that he should have taken a firmer position with her.

With this the couple terminated the therapy. They were followed up with phone calls every three months for the next nine months, and they reported that the wife was cleaning only from nine to five and for only two hours on weekends. Some days she preferred to go out and did not clean at all. However, the wife emphasized, the improvement had nothing to do with the therapy.

In the case of the insomniac, Erickson knew that the man thought that he should wax the floors but did not want to do it. In the case of the compulsive cleaner, it was suspected that the woman thought she should spend more time with her husband but did not want to do it. The case of the insomniac is most similar to the story of the man with the cough in that in both cases a worse alternative to the symptom is offered (castor oil and waxing floors). In the case of the compulsive cleaner a worse alternative is also offered (to get into bed with the husband or to go out with him), but this alternative is precisely the one behind the symptom, the one that in the therapist's view the woman had construed the symptom in order to avoid. She could not be with her husband because she had to clean. The therapist turned cause and effect around and proposed that if she cleaned she had to be with her husband. The purpose of the symptom was defeated.

Passing the ball is a well-known theory of mental health. If anything upsets you, you should immediately tell your story to others until you find someone who is willing to be more upset about it than you are. At that moment you will feel good once again and be able to go about your business. Often a therapeutic intervention consists of arranging to pass the ball, as in taking turns. Sometimes, however, the same goal can be accomplished with a contract. For instance, when a single woman and her son agree that every time the son brings home an A the mother will go out on a date, the problem has been passed to the mother. The problem has become the mother's loneliness rather than the son's academic difficulties. When an anorectic with an alcoholic father agrees that if the father does not drink she will eat, but if the father drinks she will starve herself, the ball has been passed to the father, and his alcoholism becomes the issue. The father who came in to solve the daughter's eating problem finds that he has to stop drinking. Similarly, the mother who brought her son in for a school problem finds that she has to start dating.

The humorous effect of these approaches is related to passing the ball, but the therapeutic effect consists of solving the original problem that was expressed through the symptomatic behavior which was itself a misguided attempt at a solution (in the case of the student, the child's concern about the mother's loneliness; in the case of the anorectic, the anorectic's concern about her father's alcoholism).

Humorous interventions in therapy include an element of surprise, of the unexpected. A humorous redefinition, explanation or directive takes the family by surprise in a way that gives strength, drama, and impact to the intervention. Humor often allows the therapist's creativity to match the creativity of the symptom. To have impact, a therapist must have the ability to tolerate ridicule, to appear absurd, to risk loss of face, since sometimes the laughs turn on the therapist in unexpected ways. Humor should not be confused with sarcasm, however. It is therapeutic to laugh with the client, not at the client. It is better for a therapist to ridicule himself or herself than to ridicule a patient or a family.

What makes change possible is the therapist's ability to be optimistic and to see what is funny or appealing in a grim situation. Humor involves the ability to think at multiple levels and in this way is similar to metaphorical communication. When a therapist talks about a meal or a game of tennis in ways that are metaphorical of a sexual relationship, the humorous aspect of the communication becomes apparent as soon as the connection is made between the two levels. To think at multiple levels also involves the ability to be inconsistent, to be illogical and to communicate in nonsequiturs, jumping from one subject to another, associating what seems to be unrelated in ways that appear humorous and are therapeutic. In order to use humor in therapy, it is the therapist who must have a sense of humor, whether or not the client does.

REFERENCES

Allen, S. (1981). *Funny people*. New York: Stein & Day.

Erickson, M. (1954). Indirect hypnotic therapy of an enuretic couple. *Journal of Clinical and Experimental Hypnosis, 2*, 171–174.

Haley, J. (1963). *Strategies of psychotherapy*. New York: Grune & Stratton.

Penn, P. (1982). Multigenerational issues in strategic therapy of sexual problems. *Journal of Strategic & Systemic Therapies, 1*, 1–13.

PART II

Family Therapy

Milton Erickson was not a family therapist in the sense that the term "family therapy" is commonly used (i.e., he did not often see entire families in a joint interview). However, Erickson was one of the first practitioners to see patients and their families.

Aspects of Erickson's approach have been integrated into family therapy. Erickson's strategic methods have been utilized and developed by practitioners such as Haley, Madanes, and the MRI group. More recently, Erickson's formal hypnotic methods have been integrated into family therapy.

In this section, authors describe the use of both strategic and formal hypnotic methods to promote change in family systems.

Michele Ritterman, Ph.D., earned her degree in clinical psychology from Temple University. She is engaged in private practice and consultation in Oakland, California and travels widely to conduct workshops. Ritterman's book, Using Hypnosis in Family Therapy (Jossey-Bass, 1983), is the first volume that describes how hypnotherapy and family therapy can be used in unison. In it, she also presents some pioneering work in using hypnotic family therapy with hemophiliacs.

Ritterman describes how intrapsychic and interpersonal approaches can be joined. Systems can induce symptoms in individuals. Ericksonian methods can be used to understand the effectiveness of these negative inductions and they can be used to formulate counterinductions.

David L. Calof is in private practice at the Seattle Family Institute which he cofounded. He specializes in the treatment of psychophysiological and dissociative disorders.

Calof is earning a Master's degree in psychology from Antioch University in Seattle. He conducts a private practice and is actively involved in teaching and consultation.

Erickson's impact on interpersonal approaches is discussed and the literature on hypnosis and couples therapy is reviewed. Innovative techniques utilizing hypnosis within marital counseling are presented and described. Where Ritterman emphasizes the structural approach of Salvador Minuchin and the strategic approach of Haley and Madanes, Calof emphasizes the transgenerational approach of Murray Bowen.

Alfred Lange, Ph.D., is on the faculty of Group Psychology at the Psychological Laboratory of the University of Amsterdam. He coauthored a volume with Onno van der Hart, Ph.D., entitled Directive Family Therapy *(Brunner/Mazel, 1983).*

Lange and his colleagues have been influential in the training of psychotherapists in the Netherlands. Their work is strongly influenced by strategic approaches. They authored two volumes in Dutch entitled Directive Psychotherapy, *and they established the* Journal of Directive Therapy and Hypnosis *in conjunction with the Netherlands Society of Clinical Hypnosis. Lange is a coeditor of the journal.*

To be effective, interventions need to be tailored to individuals. Motivation techniques can be used to increase the probability that clients will respond. A framework for motivation techniques is presented.

George Stone earned his M.S.W. at the University of Maryland at Baltimore and conducts a practice in brief psychotherapy in Morrill, Nebraska. When he lived in Phoenix, between 1975 and 1977, he received training from Milton Erickson.

Following Haley's strategic approach, family structure can be used metaphorically to induce change in individual family members. Ray Birdwhistell's linguistic methods can be used to describe the microdynamics of interactions and interventions in family systems.

George A. Sargent, Ph.D., earned his degree from the United States International University in San Diego, California. He is director of a group practice in psychology and family therapy in Vista, California, and is a core faculty member at National University in San Diego. He is a California licensed marriage, family, and child counselor, and served as president of the Mental Health Association in San Diego. Sargent has published on the topic of Logotherapy and served on the Board of Advisors of the First World Congress of Logotherapy.

Sargent describes the strategic use of rituals in family therapy. He compares the approach of a character from a popular series of children's books, Mrs. Piggle-Wiggle, *to the approach of Milton Erickson. Both use rituals involving ordeals to promote change.*

Gunther Schmidt, M.D., is one of the chief clinicians at the Family Therapy Institute in Heidelberg, West Germany, that was established by Professor Helm Stierlin. Bernhard Trenkle, Dipl Psych, is a psychologist who also practices in Heidelberg.

Schmidt and Trenkle have been two of the leading exponents of Ericksonian techniques in West Germany. They have sponsored numerous workshops and have been presenting and developing their own methods of applying Ericksonian techniques in family therapy.

Schmidt and Trenkle describe their eclectic conceptual model. Theoretical approaches of family therapy can be combined with pragmatic Ericksonian methods. Special emphasis is placed on the integration of the Milan model and Ericksonian psychotherapy.

Camillo Loriedo, M.D., earned his degree and specialization in psychiatry from the University of Rome where he currently serves on the Family Therapy Service. He conducts a private practice and training of family therapy at the Centro Studi di Richerche per la Psicoterapia della Coppia e della Famiglia, which is one of the major family therapy training centers in Rome.

Loriedo has authored a book on Relationship Therapy *published in Italian. He is the leading practitioner of Ericksonian techniques in Italy.*

Ongoing behavior can be used to promote change in families. Ideas for tailoring interventions are presented.

Chapter 3

Family Context, Symptom Induction, and Therapeutic Counterinduction: Breaking the Spell of a Dysfunctional Rapport

Michele Ritterman

The true logics of behavior . . . are in a social, cultural, or symbolic space which is no less real than physical space and is, moreover, supported by it. For meaning lies latent not only in language, in political and religious institutions, but in modes of kinship, in machines, in the landscape, in production, and, in general, in all the modes of human commerce. (Merleau-Ponty, 1963, p. 56)

In 1979, having studied structural and strategic family therapy and Ericksonian hypnotherapy, I began routinely using hypnotic principles and trance induction techniques in my work with families. Nevertheless, there seemed to be an either/or philosophy about the two approaches, and this concerned me. If one regarded the symptom as representing a unit of one, (i.e., the symptom-bearer), one logically might seek entry into the individual's mental set or context-of-mind (Ritterman, 1983).* Therefore, one ideally might use hypnotherapy to help the person mobilize private resources. On the other hand, if one

---

*This term is used to represent a structured, and in part hierarchically organized set of thoughts, feelings, ideas, etc. within each individual. Although a person may impact upon that context, he or she is also subject to it.

focused on the unit of symptom-bearer-in-context, appreciating the symptom as a functional representation of the logics of that structure, one might not attend to inner phenomenal realities of the symptom-bearer, assuming that when personal social arrangement changes its configuration, interior furniture will spontaneously rearrange itself. Many therapists arrived at this confusing historic juncture with a hypnotic map saying "turn in here" and a family map saying "no, this way, the problem's really out there." Erickson indicated that the most useful attitude for a clinician is that of curiosity and hopefulness. It behooves us to clear up our unnecessary confusions.

I began considering *symptoms as a moment in which the suggestive influences of an individual's belief system and broader relational systems converge.* In thinking about the role of families in the activation of symptoms one might consider that a certain context-of-mind and a certain family-context interface in such a way that individuals end up producing mixed-up messages about how to behave—a hybrid that we call a symptom.

One case in particular demonstrated this point: a young man was brought to a child-guidance clinic by his parents because he was having trouble thinking from one thought to the next. He had chest pains he experienced as a heart attack, and problems breathing. A basic rule in his belief system was that his mother was the only reliable barometer of his inner states. In his family structure, he was prevented from moving to his next developmental stage by relational rules which placed him as a buffer between his parents.

The informative session was one I viewed later on videotape, in which the young man was one week from college registration and the family had convened to help him register. Instead, the interview opened with mother telling the therapist how sick her husband was with Parkinson's disease. Father then described his condition, physically and psychologically. The whole family, despite the intention to convene about an event which might be a source of pride and happiness in another member, locked into *an intense grievous rapport.*

With admirable if unintended indirection, father then suggested to his son that he "need not feel guilty" for his father's condition. Now, in an intense and grievous rapport, the young man's attention was directed away from immediate relational concerns, and directed inward toward a specific category of private associations.

Mother then, paradoxically, if inadvertently, suggested that the young man be specific about guilty feelings, memories, and associations, by compelling his attention toward past scholastic failures. She then began a "confusion technique" based on interruptions of logical communicational flow between father and son, and by shifting subjects, each of which carried different implications about how her son ought to feel and behave. She drew on shared memories and private family cue words to do so, and thereby unwittingly, locked the therapist out of the most private aspects of family rapport. Just as the son began to recognize what his mother was doing, she would change subject and affective tone (from blaming to assuaging) or would speak to someone other than son.

Even as the young man protested his parents' unhelpful procedures, it was as if he had been told: "Now go ahead and try to stop thoughts of guilt, and find out that you can't." The automatic components of his symptoms—including inability to think from one thought to the next, chest pains, and breathing troubles—all were activated "spontaneously." Using the young man's mental set and the structures of the family to influence it, the family awakened a particular ambience and exclusive rapport in developing a suggestive sequence which culminated in the production of components of his symptoms. These symptomatic expressions were used by parents and son to confirm that there was something wrong inside the young man, and to confirm that family structure and family ambience were not the problem.

I realized that trained hypnotists are not the only people who may gain entry into otherwise automatically regulated psychophysiological phenomena, or induce special states which culminate in seemingly automatic behaviors in others. There can be multiple hypnotists. And perhaps most importantly, *contexts, once functioning on automatic pilot, may hold special suggestive powers which are effective because they operate below our threshold of ordinary awareness.* The suggestive aspects of family life began to take on increasing importance in my clinical work.

MIND, CONTEXT AND SUGGESTION

Let me clarify briefly the way I use the word "context." I regard the symptom as often identifying a moment at which there is a confluence of three suggestive contexts: the individual's context of mind, family context, and broader social arrangement (Ritterman, 1983). In this chapter aspects of both self-instruction and social suggestion are temporarily placed in the background. The focus is on breaking down significant elements of family rapport and family suggestive techniques into some observable units.

Within each of the three contexts mentioned, symptom-bearers have the potential to play a dual role. On one hand, they are an organizer of each context they inhabit. In this capacity, the scanning self or "homunculus" (Crick, 1979) selects from the various selves-in-context (such as the self at work, at home, at church or synogogue, or in a professional society) and uses aspects of self somewhat strategically in creating an orientation to survival and productivity. On the other hand, symptom-bearers are subject to each context inhabited, including the rule-bound atmosphere of their own mind. In this capacity to be structured by existing contexts, symptom-bearers ignore certain aspects of those contexts and behave on automatic pilot within established (if unspoken) and now out-of-ordinary awareness rules and roles of those contexts. Although capable of organizing contexts, at the point of entry into therapy, symptom-bearers often behave as if they were prisoner to this side of the human dialectic, as if they had lost their margin of personal freedom from any one context inhabited.

The capacity to behave automatically or spontaneously without conscious intention within various social contexts shares some commonalities with the human capacity to be hypnotized. *However, the trance state, particularly as elucidated by Erickson, does not only tap into a person's ability to behave "automatically," but rather embodies the dialectic relationship between automatic behaving and drawing on one's creative and context-making resources.* Symptom-bearers may be in a destructive abuse of the trance state in which creative coping capacities are in use, but in a misguided or perverted manner within the confines of certain contextual requisites.

SPELLS OF POWER AND SPELLS OF RAPPORT IN FAMILIES

Structural and strategic therapies have made major contributions to our understandings of power and responsibility aspects of family context and symptoms (Haley, 1976; Minuchin, 1974). In hypnotic family therapy, we use our knowledge of the symptom-bearer's position in family hierarchies and cross-generational alliances to understand how it might suggest certain behavior, given his or her mental set.

For example, the young man who cannot think from one thought to the next, when his mother interrupts his speech with father, his father disappears into the periphery, and mother picks a fight with him, often seems to be structurally "cued" into becoming mother's "little husband." It is here (between him and mother) that the intense rapport, however negative it may seem, does exist.

However, hierarchies and power relations are not sufficient for appreciating the powers of family contextual suggestions. Consider that the subject of family suggestions need not be in a lower position within a family hierarchy, nor *under* the spell of certain more powerful family mesmerizers. *Once subjects believe in and uphold certain family structures and certain family mythology, they may become susceptible to those structures.* Their own position of power in one family hierarchy can render them suggestive to certain structural influences. Likewise, conflicting positions in different units of family life may effect a family confusion technique as symptom-bearers reel from changes in altitude from being "family failure" in one subunit and "family rescuer" in another. Also, once within the intense rapport of family life, any number of family members, close or distant, weak or strong, and any number of memories *may carry the weight of family inductive power to the symptom-bearer.*

Any element of the family ambience which bears its feeling tone of guilt, blame, denial, violent rage, pity, terror, etc. to the symptom-bearer may likewise suffice to "cue" him or her into a certain mental set in a manner which culminates in seemingly automatic production of certain behaviors. As mentioned earlier, these behaviors may then reverberate outward as proof of unimportance of contextual structure or rapport features which may in fact be essential elements to the change process.

SEARCHING FOR THE FAMILY SYMPTOM-INDUCTIVE MOMENT

Research has shown that family interactions may somehow violate the natural rhythms of human psychophysiology, leading, for example, to life-threatening rises in levels of free fatty acids in the bloodstream of a superlabile diabetic child (Minuchin, Rosman, & Baker 1978). In the case of a child like this, it has been shown that conflict between a child's parents may cue the child into a state in which levels of free fatty acids—a type of stress-marker—rise. As this stress-marker increases, which in the child's case is dangerously associated with the disease of diabetes, the same stress-marker decreases in the parents. They tend to stop fighting and focus instead on what is going on inside the child. The ebbs and tides in family bloodstream contents begin to carry its own psychophysiological undertow, which is particularly threatening to the symptom-bearer. If we think of this and related phenomena from the symptom-bearer's standpoint, we consider that external contexts may penetrate him or her somehow, creating neurohormonal, cardiovascular or other psychophysiological events.

As we look at a symptom-bearer's lack of self-possession, and preoccupation with family conflict from a hypnotic model, we consider automatic behavioral and physiological products as indicators, if not of a trance state, then of the reception of suggestions by the unconscious mind or by the autonomic nervous system. We also consider aspects of the symptomatic state and its component behaviors—including subjective experiences of time, space and personal identity—as a form of trance state. This symptomatic state occupies periods of psychological time which might otherwise provide for rest or renewal. In other words, we consider the symptomatic state as *partly* a destructive or constricting use of trance capacities in which the symptom-bearer is carrying out some reconciliation of seemingly irreconcilable suggestions from his or her social context, meta-cues from the family context, and/or his or her own context of mind. We recognize that symptoms are also functional and derive in part from active coping and defensive attempts. Symptoms are thus mysteriously multipurposed.

In hypnotic work with families, therapists work to observe moments within which specific family rituals, which correspond with recognized hypnotic induction rituals, seem to activate symptomatic behaviors. We do not use the eyeroll or arm-levitation tests as ratifiers of family trances. Instead, *we pay special attention to the culmination of observable family sequences in the seemingly spontaneous expression of observable components of symptomatic behavior.* We are particularly interested in the microcomponents of the symptom, such as those microcomponents associated with the classical ratifiers of the trance state. These include changes in rate of respiration, facial tone, reflexive response, and subjective experiences, such as amnesia, positive or negative hallucination and dissociation.

Although we appreciate that the family has a special *generalized* power of emotional and suggestive continuity, clinically we are best informed when we can actually catch an *inductive event.* We may then pattern both the microdynamics and the macrodynamics of our therapeutic counter-inductions on related techniques, using family suggestive channels to carry new tonality, mood and other "bits" of directive about how to behave, and helping family members mobilize new internal processes which can then be projected outward into transforming actions and new relational arrangements.

When an inductive moment occurs, the undertow of family emotional life suddenly opens up, pulling the symptom-bearer with it, regardless of his or her conscious intention. The event just as often closes up quickly, leaving no observable tracks, except a symptom-bearer wondering, "What's wrong with me? Am I making all this up?" The symptom-bearer is left holding the bag of elusive family variables with a feeling tone of guilt, and a disheartening scan through personal memories for times he or she disappointed people, with no idea how the bag got there in the first place. As one young "schizophrenic" man expressed it to me: "When my mother looks me in the eyes like that and talks in that voice, she hypnotizes me. I lose 30 seconds in your time, but to me, I lose eternity. A hole opens up. Then, I can't remember where I was or what I was doing." Inductive moments are slippery—that may be part of their power—but we look for them, and try to catch a glimpse of them when possible.

Two main problems are posed for those of us who would be Induction Catchers:

1) The family is the most *private* human institution. All institutions have a private aspect and a public aspect, an "us" and a "them." Many of us have discovered this phenomenon in leaving an institution which had "felt like family." No sooner are we out the door, than we become "them." And "them" are treated differently. Being "us," particularly in a family, has a lot of meanings, many of which are secret or cloistered privately within the family, contained exclusively within the intense rapport of family we-ness. Non-kin, even members of extended family, are locked out of certain of these most private features. One of the problems the us-them dichotomy of family life poses for the therapist is that often we are not let in to see a private enough slice-of-life to grasp how family context and the symptom-bearer's belief system weave in and out of one another in the long ticker tape of family development. If we want to observe a family inductive moment, this becomes a problem because these powerful events disappear as rapidly as they opened up, and are often hard for therapists to find especially if they are locked out of the "spell" of family rapport.

2) The family has a *unique power of suggestive-continuity.* Family therapists often hope to grasp the essence of family contextual "cueing" by observing sequences of interaction that occur within a therapy session. This hope comes in part from the idea that patterns within the same structure tend to replicate themselves, such that sequences about eating will reveal ways sexual problems are handled, or how money is dealt with as well. However, certain sequences of family life are longer than we can catch in our session. Certain messages can be on a variable inductive reinforcement schedule, they can be transmitted by a certain innuendo-resonant tone of voice, by multiple family members, across great gulfs of time, well disguised or hard to decode. Therefore, the most powerful inductive moment may be the fish that gets away in our interview. The climate or ambience we create within the clinical setting

is important for getting clues about suggestive-continuity. The more powerful and intense our therapeutic rapport, the more likely it can help "break the spell" of dysfunctional features of family rapport.

UNIQUE FAMILY INDUCTIVE CAPACITIES AND TECHNIQUES

In hypnotic family therapy, we are particularly interested in meta-cues about how to behave that families convey in part by their ambience and feeling tone (blame, hope, despair, rage). Some of the variables we attend to exist below the threshold of perception of family members. Unless we are aware of ways they typically manifest themselves, we too may be induced to "not see" them.

Basically, we consider the family to be an institution which has certain powers of suggestion which derive from the family as a context. The power of the family to make effectively received suggestions comes from: 1) economic and life-stage developmental-biological dependencies; 2) the power and responsibility structures and hierarchies of the family; and 3) the unique rapport which permits the transmission of unconscious (or out of ordinary awareness) messages from one family member to the unconscious mind of another family member. Both family structural alignments and family mythology belie certain unconscious categories upheld by the family as a unit, and converge in the production of meta-cues about how to behave. *Structural and rapport-inductive forms may be similar, even inseparable, but they are not identical.* Neither one alone explains the algebra of family context in symptoms. Both together begin to capture the role of the family in activating automatic behaviors in a susceptible or ready-to-respond family member. To paraphrase a Goethe poem: "All forms are similar, and none is like the others. So that their chorus points the way to a hidden law."

One of the capacities of families which makes catching an inductive moment difficult, is family "we-ness." This feature of rapport is an always available trigger of an individual member's readiness for focusing attention inward. This capacity can manifest itself in many different ways. Consider that the power of majority consensus is an aspect of family we-ness. As such the family may exert pressure of conformity over individual members. If you are like us, you are "in," and have access to all our "goodies" from love to money; if you are not like us, you are "out," and we take our "toys" away. Likewise, the family can produce positive and negative hallucinations, for example, by not seeing what the rebellious child does when the rebellious child is not being rebellious, and only noting the rebellious behaviors. They may arbitrarily start and stop sequential analyses of daily events in such a manner that the end point of blame is consistently one parent, spouse or child. In this way, families may use family we-ness to shape the machinery of the self and its feeling tone.

Likewise, family we-ness is founded upon shared family history. Just as when a parent disciplines a child, the parent may be skillful at eliciting feelings of responsibility, shame, guilt or regret; the family in trouble may inadvertently use shared family memories in a manner which brings an individual member back to the kinds of thoughts and feelings that make it hard to step forward with confidence. In the context of family we-ness, family members can draw on physical resemblances, even to long-dead family members, which may also exert a special power of suggestion for a symptom-bearer. For example, "Joan looks exactly like Aunt Milly" (who was a prostitute), or "Jim reminds *me* of Uncle Bill" (who never amounted to anything, was a drunk, but was superficially good-looking). Likeness inductions may draw on certain temperamental features. Real, if thin, threads of commonality are in some way woven into the fabric of family alliance patterns and then radiate with tremendous suggestive color. Once symptom-bearers lock into a certain piece of shared family history, their brains may be activated to continue to search unconsciously through their memory system, even after the family analogy has been consciously dismissed as ridiculous. This unconscious search on an autonomous level is the essence of indirect suggestion which enters "invisibly" and starts a search outside the respondent's ordinary frame of reference.

Most critical in terms of powers of family context to transmit effective meta-suggestions to members is the concept of the *cue word*. *Entire relational structures and ambience can be summarized, even by a single word*. Just as a sequence of interactions (father talks to son, mother interrupts, mother and son fight intensely) summarizes and epitomizes family structural rules, so a single word can summarize chains of family interaction and rules of relating. This word then becomes an economical signal, a form of shorthand, and the original inductive sequences need not be repeated. The cue word itself carries the hidden power of family structure. Claude Levi-Strauss (anthropologist) refers to this capacity, in which a piece of a culture conveys a representation of the whole institution, as "metonymy." He contrasts it with "metaphor." (Leach, 1974). The capacity of the human mind to use key representations of a whole context to cue a member about a meta-message of that context seems to have a basis in the material conditions of the human mind.

Crick (1979) wrote that we have easily demonstrable blind spots in each eye. Our brain fills in the holes with visual information borrowed from the immediate neighborhood of the spot. (This capacity to "fill in" may lie behind Erickson's making a class of suggestions and letting the person fill in the blind spots himself, drawing from his own mental set, or telling a therapeutic tale in which the led-up-to but withheld information contains the directive.) It seems that cue words function in a similar manner. They evoke elements of the context we are part of, and we "fill in" the rest of the data based on our "idea" of the context we are part of. Once a person operates within a certain contextual rapport, any number of elements within that rapport can signal it. Erickson used a special trance name as a cue word to a person to return to that previous hypnotic rapport, that same inner state inhabited before (Erickson, 1976). In a family, once a certain power structure and rapport is established, many elements can cue individuals to draw selectively in some precise ways from their surroundings and come up with a contextually "suitable" or logical behavior.

For example, if a family member wants to bring a spouse, child or parent "back" to a past memory or line of association (inner *or* outer) he or she has cue words that can be used including nicknames for the person at that time, or for important places or pets. Because dysfunctional families tend to dwell on the past, they may easily and unnoticeably mobilize the symptom-bearer's past failings as a kind of unconscious undertow which sucks him or her back into the family—especially when the family member is trying to disengage.

In the family of the young man who cannot think from one thought to the next, the name of an expensive parochial school he attended served this function, directing the young man's attention to what he had already cost his family and to what avail, when he is trying to make plans for the expensive endeavor of going to college (expensive both financially, and in terms of shaking up the family structure).

Consider also that a parent may have many different names for a child, each of which is "automatically" used in conjunction with a certain feeling state, a certain task at hand, often without the parent's awareness of which name is used for what. In an immigrant Jewish family, the formal American name may be used in disciplining, the American nickname in routine usage, the Hebrew name (associated with the modern state of Israel) in times of intense pride, the old country Yiddish name in times of deepest personal affection. *Not only does the name-calling convey the parental feeling tone, it may just as automatically evoke a certain feeling tone or inner state within the child.* In fact, as in many cultures, there is an implicit recognition in Jewish culture of the power of naming as a cue word. After a serious illness, a child may be renamed a name that will not ever again evoke the "self which became ill," only the new "healthy self." The child may be renamed "Godlike One" or "Blessed One" to serve this healing-cueing function.

In a family inductive moment that we will examine, the very word "loneliness" so epitomizes the family ambience that it makes the index patient tighten up with fear and cues her into a lifetime of personal meanings about her failures, inadequacies, the badness, and sickness of her own body. Affecting the impact of a cue word may alter family mood and even the nature of relational valences between family members. The therapist often must affect the use of associated meaning of the word(s) that serves as summary for cues of central family troubles.

To summarize thus far then, the hypnotic family therapist appreciates both family power relationships and unique suggestive rapport as potentially symptom-relevant features of family context. Each of these features derives its suggestive power from the underlying grammar of the family kinship system within our society. This system of kin has material and economic power as well as the powers of privacy and we-ness which humans, as social beings, tend to find forceful and formative. As a hypnotist, one recognizes a scanning self, an attention-directing aspect of the individual which selects from messages and meta-cues of the multiple contexts of which he or she is part. Nevertheless, the symbolic meanings and material powers of family life can sometimes override the individual's margin of personal freedom, cluttering inner realities with excessive family conflicts, and interfering with self-possession. We use our understandings of family structure to help recognize that this family is a "waltz" and that family is a "calypso." Our analysis of the nature of family rapport tells us whether the music of family life is played in a "lively" or "mournful" tone, and tells us other fine points about nuance, ambience and innuendo.

FAMILY UTILIZATION OF THE ERICKSONIAN INTERSPERSAL TECHNIQUE

Let us now look closely at an inductive moment in a family interview. This interview has been called to help a family decide what to do about their 20-year-old daughter's symptoms, which include 1) suicide attempts (by wrist-slashing); 2) conceptual rationales for these attempts; and 3) the carrying of a stuffed animal in public. The young woman, Gretchen, has been in and out of therapies and psychiatric hospitals since she was five and is a "famous" client in her locale. To date, she has not been interviewed within her entire family context. This interview is conducted by an out-of-town consultant informed about the young woman's history by the ongoing therapist.

The young woman is a member of a German immigrant working class family, which draws on the Fundamentalist religion to determine rules and roles of family life. However, economic hardship necessitated mother's working, transgressing the family belief that a woman's place is in the home, and intensifying gender-related conflicts between mother and father. These conflicts in turn exacerbated the parents' difficulties helping their two older children, both female, to leave home.

At college, the young woman was troubled about whether to stay in college, get a job, or just look for a husband-caretaker. She had trouble concentrating on schoolwork and fitting in with peers. The night before the interview, she quit school unexpectedly and moved home with her parents and two brothers.

At this point in the interview, the consultant has some cues about power-structure contributions to the suicidal young woman's symptoms. In one hierarchy of family life the young woman is in a female vs. male gender alliance with mother against father about women's rights and economic realities. In another hierarchy she is in a transgenerational alliance with dad against mother's excessive demands for intimacy and affection. However, these same alliances might exist without providing the young woman with a rationale for being symptomatic. What is it that characterizes the rapport within this context which prevents the young woman's movement home from being seen as a normal, atavistic regression, a refueling in preparation for separation, rather than a sign of present failing and a prognosticator of failures to come? The interviewer sets the stage to observe the nuances of family we-ness, the techniques whereby the family contributes to the young woman's feeling-tone of hopelessness. Elsewhere I have described the steps involved in creating a "hypnotic atmosphere," an intense, multiperson-focused rapport in which the likelihood of catching a family symptom-induction is increased (Ritterman, 1983).

At this point in the interview the consultant has already been allowed into the power and responsibility aspects of the family, and now seeks to further strengthen her position as "head" of the therapeutic context by entering more deeply into the contextual rapport or ambience of the family. Her goal is to activate family members to relate as they do around the symptom in *private*. In this way, she hopes to catch a glimpse of how family members may help shepherd processes in a symptom-bearer in a manner that mobilizes symptomatic behavior. The study of the family induction will then lead to the construction of the scaffolding for a therapeutic counterinduction.

In this case, the induction follows Erickson's interspersal technique. Erickson used that technique to help a florist deal with cancer pain. Ostensibly, in his induction Erickson sang only one "song," that of growing tomato plants, to a man intimately familiar with growing plants. Erickson "grew" the plant from seed through ground swell, stalk, branch, bud leaf, to sun-ripened, rain-washed tomato plant. However, sprinkled throughout the tomato story was a fine rain of progressive hypnotic suggestions (a second sequential line of conversation, in a different voice) about comfort, curiosity, things that work well, listening without seeing or hearing, feeling more and more comfortable each day, desiring to have food in one's stomach, and taking it one day at a time. It was the *embedded* or *interspersed* message Erickson most hoped would get through to the man's unconscious mind (Erickson, 1966).

Erickson's approach depends upon the human capacity to absorb simultaneously different levels of cultural category, such as conscious and unconscious information, much as one might apprehend both harmony and melody at the same time. This phenomenon is in keeping with the algebra of the brain, which, it is believed, can process information on millions of channels in parallel (Crick, 1979). As we mentioned earlier, the unique features of family rapport provide a suggestive continuum in which an induction initiated by one family member can—despite interruptions—be picked up at a later time when that family member speaks again, as if nothing relevant to that issue had occurred between speeches. Also, as in the therapeutic moment under examination, multiple family members can pick up an induction process. When several lines of speech or other communication converge, even across persons, one may conceal the other, in effect constructing an interspersal technique, from the vantage point of the listener. In this technique, *at least two levels of communication* occur at once, weaving in and out of one another, like harmony and melody. As in some scores, one or more of the melody lines is hidden, deriving its power from being in the background, less detected by the listener, unless that background suddenly becomes the primary theme, compelling then a different form of attention.

In Gretchen's case, we will see that messages from mother and father together have the effect of a single hypnotic interspersal technique. Here the family is directed to talk about Gretchen's homecoming, why she has to come home. While consciously the parents intend to give Gretchen the support she needs, interspersed throughout their speeches is a message about loneliness, how unbearable life is, and even thoughts of taking one's life. Following is a synthesis of mother's and father's speeches across 20 minutes in a session. The embedded lines of unintentionally interspersed *suggestion* to Gretchen are in italics.

Father: Umm—I am a little bit leery. I think Gretchen has a *hard time functioning* on her own (voice lowers and speech becomes slower while looking at Gretchen). . . .

Mother: She found it *lonely* here *where we live.* . . .

Father: Yah. You see, for a while there she was staying with that elderly lady and for a while she was *alone* up here. We didn't know what time the college started up here and she came up a week earlier. And, *she was alone in the house* and I don't think it is best for her. . . . I didn't want her to come back, but then she would be better off at home. . . .

Mother: I *worry* about her, especially like—even when she is at home—when she cut her wrist, she *did it at home* and I am scared of what she would do if *she will do it*—maybe not like, I think suicides are usually accidents. They try to prove something (nervous laugh). They do a good job, and I am *afraid*—like, I cannot imagine going and *finding her really hurt or dead*, like that bothers me. She says she won't do it anymore. . . .

Father: No—but I think that Gretchen has a *hard time* if she lives alone. I guess everybody gets *lonely*, but she has a *harder time* to function on her own, I guess. . . . I think the story with me—I *try to ignore* the fact that she wants to take her life because *I cannot understand it*. Personally, I am an optimist and *I cannot understand* why anybody would want to take their lives. You know what I mean?

Mother: I know *it's serious*. I can understand, in a way. When I was 14, *life* at home was *unbearable*. . . . (to Gretchen, leaning forward, gazing intensely into her eyes) And, I tried to—*I took* a whole bunch of *aspirins*. I took too many and so *all I did was get sick*. I just threw up. And, every time *I take an aspirin now*, my stomach goes yecch because I remember the taste of throwing up 22 aspirins. *And, life is so unbearable* and I can understand that feeling of *anything is better than living*, in me, but I *cannot understand* it in you because I am good (looks into Gretchen's eyes) to you and dad's good to you and we love you and we don't fight and I don't go out with men and I don't drink and dad doesn't beat me up. And that is why *life was unbearable* at home. Because my mother called me a whore and I was a virgin. Just because—I don't know why. And so, I don't understand it—like I don't understand—*I can understand life being unbearable* but I don't understand why it would be for you. Because, the circumstances aren't the same. And yet, if you believe that *life is unbearable,* why, why is *life unbearable,* and how can I help you to make it bearable? That's why I said to you, if you come home, one of the conditions is that we have to continue to see the therapist until you're better, because *I cannot handle it* on my own. Because *I don't know how.* You are a Christian and we are Christians. And you know that *the only reason to live is to go to heaven afterwards,* and if you *take your own life,* there is no—it makes it *hard for me to understand.* Because, that is *not right* as a Christian to feel that way. If I was a Christian then, I wouldn't have done it when I was a kid.

Father: Well . . . *even to carry those thoughts in your mind is not right* (shaken, biting lip).

Mother: And, I have to help you or else your being home would be *too hard on me* if *I can't help you* and you help me. And, I don't know why. Why do you *feel* so *angry?* Do you *feel angry* because you *don't feel well* (crying)? Why *don't* you *feel well? Like—physically, emotionally? You know that we are a lot alike, you and I.* We have a lot of feelings the same and what makes me different from you—like, how did I cope and *you don't.*

Father: Well, I can understand that a person *gets depressed* once in a while. This is understandable. (to Gretchen) I do understand that you *do get depressed* sometimes, but why so *depressed* that you want to *take your life?* That's one thing I don't understand. So, things don't always go the way we want them to go and then we have a *hard time* dealing with problems here and there. It is no reason to *think about taking your life,* though. That is something I just *cannot understand* (bites lip, folds arms, holds back tears). (Ritterman, 1983, pp. 115-117)

When shortly after this induction the consultant begins to work to activate the young woman against her parents' unintentional message, she obtains verbal confirmation of the behavioral observation of the parents' effect on the young woman. When the consultant asks, "What happens to you when your parents are talking to you like this?" the young woman answers, "I get scared . . . I kind of feel guilty, in a way."

The point for this moment is that while mother and father intend to save their daughter from hurting them and herself, their tone and approach, their two voices converging, carry an interspersed message, which, in a family failing financially, feeling depressed and inadequate, carries an inadvertent suggestive message that life is unbearable. In short, they unintentionally activate that emotional state in the young woman which easily spawns the rationale for suicide.

At this point, then, the consultant wishes to create an in-kind counterinduction, which can impact upon the dysfunctional features of family rapport, and in doing so paves the way for related structural alignment changes. The therapeutic counterinduction employs its own interspersal techniques to intervene, first to counter the contextual tone, then the contextual structure. Is this waltz to be a dance of life, or a dance of death?

CREATING AN IN-KIND THERAPEUTIC COUNTERINDUCTION

The consultant has "caught" a moment in which the family has revealed spontaneously and in its own unique symbolic "language" how it contributes to the activation of potentially self-destructive feelings in Gretchen. This family induction has culminated in mother looking angry, with tears in her eyes, father biting his lip to hold back his sea of tears, and Gretchen having proceeded from monosyllabic conversation to staring vacantly and looking sad and guilty. She has become a passive subject to some confusing prescriptions: "Suffer all you want. Life is unbearable, but pretend it is not because knowing it or acting on the fact that it is is against our religion. Perhaps you are a little bit of a latent un-Christian, from your mother's side."

The consultant sees Gretchen's present state as not only a consequence of sequences of enactment of family grief; Gretchen and her interior realities are also a starting point, an initiating moment in family interaction. The consultant wants to enter into such a moment in Gretchen's inner processes in order to introduce to it suggestions that may awaken a different mood. The goal of this counterinduction is *not* to rescue Gretchen from her parents, but rather to block family members from being "homeostatic discouragers" of Gretchen's self-help efforts; to invite family members to *effectively* catalyze Gretchen's self-help attempts; and to help Gretchen transcend the confusing logic by which she is confined in order to *asymptomatically* rescue herself.

As is typical in this approach, the consultant has already set up specific "cues" with each family member, such that she can carry out *ostensibly* an indirect hypnotic induction with the young woman in her family's presence, while she is *actually* making related indirect suggestions to all family members. By selecting content which is symbolic of critical life-cycle phenomena, she can address specific developmental requisites of this phase for *each* member, *while* talking to Gretchen about her *own* idiosyncratic and personal developmental requisites for living out the reign of the symptom. Just as Gretchen's parents had engaged in developmental doubting procedures by looking to the future through a mood and tone of despair, so the consultant intersperses through her hypnotic communication with Gretchen an indirect communication to parents and brothers: messages of developmental hopefulness. The seeding for "joy" and "curiosity" is paired then with "growing-up" and with "moving on" to one's coming life stage.

The therapist uses an indirect hypnotic induction procedure to help Gretchen direct her attention inward, within the new context of her private rapport with the consultant, and to defocus from other aspects of her immediate surroundings. Note that "cues" established are such that when the consultant talks about Gretchen's body, and Gretchen says that she has a bad body, the other members of the family consider that she is referring metaphorically to other parts of the "body-familial" as well.

In the induction, the consultant has the young woman focus on her hands. Gretchen says, "They are part of this body." The consultant says that Gretchen keeps it (this body) all wrapped up as if it's something terrible—something to be ashamed of. Gretchen goes on to say, "It's not a very good body . . . it doesn't work very well," and, "It's sick," and this is because "it is sad all of the time," especially, "the sadness is in the heart." The consultant has just redefined Gretchen's original complaint of a dysfunctional or evil body, saying, "It's a sad body." Gretchen has acceded, "Yeah, it feels sad." As the counterinduction begins, the consultant assumes that each family member is feeling some of that sadness and badness about bodies, reproduction, development, and is seeking help for these concerns *through* Gretchen.

Consultant: When was the first time you remember feeling really, really sad?

Gretchen: I don't remember not feeling sad . . . it's in the body . . . it is always there . . . it was there when the body was born.

Consultant: (each looking into the other's eyes using private rapport to help detach Gretchen from family context) Well, when a child comes into the world and gets a first smack on the butt and screams, that's a cry of *shock*, but not of sadness. It seems like all babies start out with some degree of *shock* and *curiosity* at just what hit them. And, early on in your life you *do discover* your hands. When you were a tiny baby in your crib. (Consultant wiggles her fingers *playfully* as if waving, while talking seriously.) That took a lot of *learning, discovering* those hands. (Gretchen starts to cry.) And that was a *joyful* experience for you. You are going to have to *find* those tiny, *happy times.* Look back on those *happy* times. Your problem in concentrating isn't in terms of learning schoolwork—it is in terms of *memorizing the joy,* even if it only lasted 30 seconds. You need that *joy* for yourself and for your parents. (Gretchen is sobbing.) And even the saddest of bodies has a right to feel some *joy.* You have a right to feel sadness—it's your own sadness. It's not mine. To feel your mother's sadness or your father's sadness—it's useless, isn't it? And you know that your father and mother suffered a great deal. When was the first time you smelled a *flower?*

Gretchen: Uh-huh (slowly wiping tears). I must have smelled flowers before . . . I must have been that small.

Consultant: You were just a toddler.

Gretchen: Yeah (head keeps nodding).

Consultant: Do you remember the kind it was, or just the smell of them?

Gretchen: (sniffing) Daisies.

Consultant: Daisies?

Gretchen: Daisies. Couple of daisies. I think so (sniffing).

Consultant: The smell of the daisies is *special* for you.

Gretchen: Yeah. They are pretty.

Consultant: (as if in there with her) They *do smell good.*

Gretchen: Yes . . . they do (wiping tears, rubbing under her chin).

Consultant: When you cried just now, you cried for yourself. And you cried for some of the things you've lost. You're only 20 years old and you've lost a great deal. And you know it.

Gretchen: Yes (very faintly).

Consultant: And you paid a heavy price, heavier than you knew at the time. And what other *positive* memories do you have besides *smelling the daisies* at three?

Gretchen: I remember riding on my dad's shoulders and we were delivering toothpaste and we were going down the hill (laugh). It was cold, it was freezing cold that day, and we were delivering toothpaste to people's houses (laughing). And I remember it was fun, it was fun riding on his shoulders.

Consultant: It was freezing cold but *you and dad were comfortable.*

Gretchen: Yeah. Then I got to ride on the sleigh, too. He pulled me on the sleigh. And I was small and I was comfortable. And it felt good. There was fresh air. It was wintertime.

At this point in the counterinduction process, the entire family is in a trance state. As Gretchen has thought of her father her head has moved slowly toward her father, as if she is seeing only him. She looks intensely and happily at him, as if she were a wide-eyed little girl. In her memory she is three. Following her lead, and given the ongoing family trance, the consultant can readily invite parents to participate in a basic hypnotic family therapy technique, the *shared family reverie*, in which the family is allowed selective participation in a shared recollection of a therapeutically desirable event, in this case a memory of a time of hope and joy. The critical therapeutic issue is to activate developmentally and clinically useful memories, and to draw a boundary between Gretchen and her parents if they begin to induce her associations away from comfort and pleasure. The consultant now carefully invites father to join in the remembered day.

Consultant: Do you remember that day?
Father: That's how it was (perseverative nodding).
Gretchen: I remember we were giving out toothpaste.
Father: I didn't remember that part of it.
Mother: You must have mixed up two things. Dad wasn't selling toothpaste yet. I came home from the hospital with baby John that day.
Consultant: Yeah. Seventeen years ago, that makes you really think about that memory. You were little, you could *see it as if it's happening now.*
Gretchen: (her memory not impeded by family participation) I remember that. Yeah. I just remembered that about a year ago. I started thinking about that and I remembered it.
Consultant: About a year ago?
Gretchen: Yeah. It just popped into my mind for a day and I started thinking about that happening.
Consultant: And that was something *very special*, to be on dad's shoulders. And *warm*, even though it was cold.
Gretchen: Yeah. That was fun, yeah. I remember that.
Consultant: So the little girl in the little body had some *good times* after all. (It is the growing up, the developing body that is hinted at as the family trouble.)
Gretchen: I think she did, yeah.
Consultant: I had *good times* when I was little. Getting older I had to give up the toys of my childhood. (Gretchen has her stuffed animal, mother has Gretchen.) It's a sad thing when we give them up. It's been a lonely thing to give up those toys of being a little girl. It's been a frightening thing to give up those toys of being a little girl. I felt safe on my daddy's shoulders and I knew he wouldn't let anything harm me. We all have to learn how to *grow up, grow up* or die. And death might not *look attractive* after all.
Gretchen: Why do people want to die?

Consultant: They'd rather die than give up the toys of their childhood.
Gretchen: (wistfully) Yeah.
Consultant: The *daisy* should be your *special flower* to remind you of the
  talk we have had and of your *hope* for the *possibility* that you can *go
  beyond* where your mother's gone. And you might *be something really
  special.*
Gretchen: Uhmmm. I think so.
Consultant: Do you think she'd forgive you if you even *did her one better?*
Gretchen: Yes. I think she would.
Consultant: And would your dad? How *well* would he put up with it?
  A more *grown-up* you.
Gretchen: I think he would. Yeah, I think so.

Even in this brief segment of the therapeutic interview we can see the
impact of the interspersal of developmentally related features of joy and
comfort upon Gretchen and her family. These interventions go practically unnoticed by the family, because they flow so naturally from the
communication patterns typical to them. They strike deep, because they
are interventions based on patterns which are central to symptom induction in Gretchen. The joy and development interspersal technique
helps to resurrect hope in multiple family members, so that each of them
can draw on and develop resources of refuge within themselves (such
as daisies for daughter, giving birth for mother, being a good provider-
carrier for father); and improve their attempts to be useful resources to
each other. Ultimately, the interview ends with the production of a new
affective tone, which awakens a sense of hopeful reunion, while blocking
family members from imposing new unrealistic expectations on one
another. Ultimately, this and related procedures lay the way for a young
woman to come home for help briefly, without having to be disguised
as a baby for her mother, or so desperately in need of help as to be
suicidal, to convince father of the gravity of her need.

SUMMARY

The entire field of family therapy, and even of psychoanalysis, is a
testimony to the powers of the family over individual members. The
family, in hypnotic terms, is characterized by a unique rapport. This
rapport—whether positive or negative—contains the family within a
private reality. Once inside of this private context, the contents of family
life and family communication may be charged by certain organizational
arrangements or structures, and a certain mood or feeling tone or family

ambience. Often—but by no means always—a symptomatic individual is somehow sustained in a symptom in part by his or her family. Often, we can get a glimpse of activations of a person's symptom in our therapeutic interview of the family. In this setting, if we are let in on an intimate enough slice-of-life, we can study the roles of both family structure and family ambience in inducing seemingly automatic symptom-behaviors. And we may then produce therapeutic counterinductions which can activate new family structures as well as new family inductions.

Most importantly, we have emphasized that there is an interdependence of social arrangement and emotional logic in families. These two aspects of family context interweave with one another. If we fail to develop strategies for affecting aspects of family abilities to "spellbind" one another other than via power and responsibility units, we may miss a key therapeutic opening. It is the unique rapport of family life and its powers of suggestive continuity which permit a family to transmit a message over great gulfs of time, across multiple voices (as in the interspersal technique), on telephone wires—to pick up, as if nothing had happened in between, a line of association left off years before. The very sound of a parent's voice, its feeling tone, may so deeply reverberate within even a grown child that after 30 seconds on the phone, the person may sob with the abandoned sobs of children and reamers or radiate an extraordinary sense of pride and joy.

In hypnotic family therapy we look to an individual's context of mind, family context, and immediate social context to identify a symptom-inductive pattern. We try to confirm our hypothesis through observation of individuals in their context. We attempt to provide the individual and responsive members of the family with means to alter their inductive effects, while sticking as closely as possible to the inductive patterns they are already employing.

When I first came to see Erickson (in 1975) and study with him, I told him I had come to learn his philosophy of life, and what he thought therapy was. In his manner then, he said, "And what is *your* definition of psychotherapy?" I said something about planning strategies to change families. He leaned forward and looked me intensely in the eyes. "In psychotherapy you change no one. People change themselves. You create the circumstances under which an individual can respond spontaneously and change. And that's all you do. The rest is up to them." It is this philosophy which underlies the idea of the therapeutic counterinduction: to create a climate of enabling.

REFERENCES

Crick, F. H. C. (1979, September). Thinking about the brain. *Scientific American, 219–232.*
Erickson, M. H. (1966). The interspersal hypnotic technique for symptom correction and pain control. *American Journal of Clinical Hypnosis, 3,* 198–209.
Erickson, M. H., Rossi, E. L., & Rossi, S. I. (1976). *Hypnotic realities.* New York: Irvington.
Haley, J. (1976). *Problem solving therapy: New strategy for effective family therapy.* San Francisco: Jossey-Bass.
Leach, E. (1974). *Claude Levi-Strauss.* New York: Penguin.
Merleau-Ponty, M. (1963). *In praise of philosophy.* Chicago: Northwestern University Press.
Minuchin, S. (1974). *Families and family therapy.* Cambridge, MA: Harvard University Press.
Minuchin, S., Rosman, B., & Baker, L. (1978). *Psychosomatic families.* Cambridge, MA: Harvard University Press.
Ritterman, M. (1983). *Using hypnosis in family therapy.* San Francisco: Jossey-Bass.

Chapter 4

Hypnosis in Marital Therapy: Toward a Transgenerational Approach

David L. Calof

INTRODUCTION

It is the thesis of this chapter that techniques of "conjoint hypnosis"* can enhance a transgenerational family systems approach to marital therapy and that such techniques are particularly helpful in resolving points of therapeutic impasse in marital therapy by expanding the "working context"** of the therapy to include more of the intrapsychic lives of the spouses within the interpersonal contexts (the therapy triangle) and in their respective transgenerational families (living and dead). The working medium of conjoint marital hypnotherapy al-

The author gratefully acknowledges the research and editorial assistance of Linda Nolting, M.A., of Seattle, Washington. Sue Foss of Seattle is gratefully acknowledged as well for contribution to the research and the preparation of the manuscript.

*By conjoint hypnotherapy, I mean the induction and therapeutic utilization of trance in individual(s), in or out of their conscious awareness, in the presence of others who might also be being induced, either in or out of their awareness and either in or out of rapport with other hypnotized individuals. Conjoint hypnotherapy of couples corresponds to Ritterman's (1983) notion of "convergent trances," Araoz's (1978) classification of mutual and couple hypnosis, and Morris' (1979) definition of "concurrent mutual hypnosis."

**The medium of marital therapy is a complex intersection of many different possible "working contexts" (or mediums) in which the therapy may occur. The following are representative examples of possible working contexts of marital therapy in three broad categories: 1) *Interpersonal (systemic)*—marital couple, therapy triangle (or group), nuclear family, household, network, family of origin; 2) *Intrapsychic*—psychodynamics, individual personality, conscious mind, unconscious mind, internalizations, introjects, dreams, psyche, soma; 3) *Temporal*—present, past, future, distorted time.

lows that therapist to work with the unconscious of both spouses in the contexts of the transgenerational families of each.

One of the basic problems in traditional marital therapy has been whether to focus on the intrapsychic or the interpsychic lives of the couple and whether to work in the present or to pull in past history. Because of the time-distorting properties and possibilities of hypnotherapy, the marital hypnotherapist may work with the past (internalizations, introjects), the present (projections in the therapy triangle or in the family), and even with the future (hypnotically distorted time).

Milton Erickson's interpersonal/interpsychic view of hypnotherapy, as well as his vast clinical and field experimentation with conjoint technologies of trance induction and utilization, has now given transgenerational family workers a therapeutic tool that recognizes both psyche and system as subsets of one another.

After presenting a discussion of Erickson's contribution to conjoint hypnotherapy and a literature search, I will then develop a perspective of the hypnotic unconscious in the context of the transgenerational family. I will conclude by offering a summary of the intervention varieties according to specific proposed therapeutic objectives, along with a representative case vignette.

MILTON H. ERICKSON'S CONTRIBUTION TO CONJOINT HYPNOTHERAPY

Perhaps as a result of his atheoretical stance, Milton Erickson seemed perfectly at ease operating clinically in either an intrapsychic or an interpersonal model of psychotherapy. Thus, he became the first noted hypnotic practitioner to work in an expanded context of inquiry, which was not the custom in traditional, individual hypnotherapy. Erickson pioneered a view of the relational, interpersonal dimension of hypnotherapy and developed several conjoint forms. Because of his new perspective of "atheoretical flexibility," current schools of family therapy *and* individual therapy have roots in Erickson's garden.

Erickson was the first noted hypnotic clinician to utilize the interpersonal dynamics of networks, families, and couples to systematically influence the behavior of the so-called identified patient. The film of Erickson working hypnotherapeutically with "Nick and Monde" (Lustig, 1975) is an excellent demonstration of Erickson's utilization of an interpersonal field (in this case, a triangle) to obtain satisfactory trances in each demonstration patient. Erickson's classic "My Friend John" technique of hypnotic induction (Rossi, 1980) is another example of utilizing a triangle (albeit imaginary) to potentiate a patient's trance experience.

Erickson also demonstrated that the hypnotic behavior of the subject could be utilized to influence interpersonal dynamics. For example, in his later years, Erickson often recounted the story of how he hypnotized a trained somnambulistic subject in the presence of a difficult target subject and instructed the hypnotized subject to induce a trance in the difficult target subject once Erickson had left the room. After recounting this story, Erickson would smile broadly and ask his students, "Who can resist a hypnotized hypnotist?" (M.H. Erickson, personal communication, 1979). The author once remarked to Erickson that it didn't appear as though he (Erickson) did much conjoint family work and asked why he often elected to work hypnotically and, seemingly, individually with a symptomatic child. Erickson remarked, "Some people think you need to change the family so that the child will change. I say, why not change that child and let the family learn to live with him differently?" (M.H. Erickson, personal communication, 1979).

Erickson published a number of anecdotal clinical reports of the conjoint use of formal hypnosis and naturalistic techniques with married couples in which he hypnotized either one or both spouses in the presence of the other (Erickson & Rossi, 1979; Haley, 1973; Rossi, 1980). Perhaps the best known of these (due to its wide dissemination on audio tape) is the case of the elderly couple that Erickson hypnotized simultaneously for the conjoint therapy of the husband's phantom limb pain and the wife's chronic tinnitus (Erickson & Rossi, 1979). Erickson used an informal, conversational approach, interspersing suggestions about their relational dynamics while ostensibly providing hypnotherapeutic treatment for their individual symptomatology.

Traditional hypnotherapy mainly focused on the subjects' behaviors and then, to some extent, on the dyadic relationship between the subject and the operator. It has consequently not developed a model or language for describing the dynamics of systems. For example, traditional hypnotherapy does not consider therapeutic triangles. The family therapy movement's quantum leap "from psyche to system" over the last two decades, coupled with the popularization of Erickson's notion that hypnosis is an interpersonal as well as an intrapsychic phenomenon (Rossi, 1980; Haley, 1963), adds an interpersonal dimension to the study of the individual unconscious in the context of the transgenerational family.

As a consequence, we must view such qualities formerly designated as intrinsic—e.g., "hypnotizability" and "suggestibility"—as contextually dependent. Why not think of the so-called unhypnotizable as simply responding to a posthypnotic block, ordered up by the transgenerational context and put in place by the parent/hypnotist(s)? For example, in his keynote address at the First International Congress on Ericksonian Approaches to Hypnosis and Psychotherapy, Carl Whitaker alluded to the hypnotic-like quality of transgenerational, hierarchical family relationships. Several times, he referred to the concept of "mother hypnosis" directed towards her children. He cited his own 35-year history of falling asleep in therapy sessions as his "hypnotic life pattern." And with reference to the hypnotic-like quality of his therapy, he noted, "The posthypnotic residuals of such right brain fun often echo through the living room, dining room and into the backyard" (1982, p. 501).*

LITERATURE SEARCH: HYPNOSIS IN COUPLES THERAPY

In preparing this chapter, the literature pertaining to the use of hypnosis in couples was carefully surveyed. Apart from Erickson's anecdotal reports (along with the few specific references to his use of hypnosis with couples), little exists directly pertaining to the use of hypnosis with couples per se. No specific references were found prior to Araoz's 1978 article, "Clinical Hypnosis in Couple Therapy."

A decade ago, a listing of 70 publications that had published one or more articles on marital therapy (Gurman, 1973) did not include even a single journal that regularly published articles on hypnosis or hypnotherapy. Clinical reports of the use of hypnosis in marital therapy since 1978 exist, but tend to be anecdotal. However, a few investigators (notably Araoz, 1978, 1979a; Braun, 1979; and Ritterman, 1980, 1983) reported systematic inquiries into the use of hypnosis in couples and family therapy. Lankton and Lankton (1983) also advocated the expansion of traditional applications of hypnotherapy to include systemic or relationship alterations (in addition to the traditional, intrapsychic applications).

The most common current use of hypnosis in couples therapy seems to be for sexual dysfunction. Clinical reports tend to be anecdotal and stereotypic. For example, hypnotherapy is done with a symptomatic spouse (e.g., an impotent husband or preorgasmic wife), not in the presence of the asymptomatic spouse and usually from within a psychodynamic or behavioral orientation. Examples of such clinical reports include: Alexander (1974), Beigel (1971), Caprio (1973), Crasilneck and Hall (1975), de Shazer (1978), Fuchs, Hoch, Paldi, Abramovici, Brandes,

---

*Although several of the authors cited in this paper report primarily on family (as opposed to marital) therapy, it is my position that marital therapy is a special case of family therapy.

and Timor-Tritsch (1973), Leckie (1964), Nuland (1978), Richardson (1963, 1968), and Wassilk (1966).

The use of hypnotic-like techniques (such as metaphor, symptom utilization, paradoxical intention, surprise and confusion, binds, suggestion, play, provocation, humor, reframing and reconnoting, guided imagery, role play, homophonics, clang associations, puns and other means by which logical, critical censorship may be blocked or circumvented) is becoming quite widespread with couples in the clinical practice of marital therapy due to the work of investigators such as Alger (1976), Anderson (1980), Bandler and Grinder (1981), Bergner (1979), Bockus (1980), Braun (1979, in press), Brink (1981), Cameron-Bandler (1978), Dammann (personal communication, June 24, 1983), de Shazer (1980), Erickson (1980, in Rosen, 1982), Erickson and Rossi (1976), Gordon (1978), Haley (1963, 1973, 1976), Lankton and Lankton (1983), Madanes (1981), Mazza (personal communication, July 1983), Morrison (1981), Papp (1976, 1982), Ritterman (1980, 1983, personal communication, July 1983), Starr (1977), Stricherz (1982), Watzlawick (1978), and Watzlawick, Weakland, and Fisch (1974).

A TRANSGENERATIONAL PERSPECTIVE OF MARRIAGE: THE HYPNOTIC UNCONSCIOUS IN THE CONTEXT OF THE TRANSGENERATIONAL FAMILY

The Transgenerational Marriage

The family therapy movement contributed a variety of viewpoints on how marital problems of one generation may be thought of as consequences, reenactments, or symbols of difficulties, distortions, incompletions, and/or perceptions of previous generations. Paul wrote that

> the marital couple is quite different from other couple relationships. When couples marry and become parents, they become conduits between the generations with implications far beyond their awareness. As conduits, parents transmit . . . the biological genetic code, relational patterns, behavior patterns, and cultural patterns from their forebears to their children. (Bockus, 1980, p. ix)

Of the multigenerational model of family therapy, Guerin and Guerin (1976) observed,

> As the marriage is worked on, and the marital fusion unfolds, the process inevitably involves a tie into the extended family. The

interlocking character of the three generations comes into view. . . .
A focus will develop on each spouse's primary parental triangle.
Marriages of grandparents and siblings will be compared. (p. 93)

A common theme in each of the various schemes or models of transgenerational transmission is that the couples' symptoms (or the symptomatology of the identified patient spouse) are seen as having meaning
in some larger, multigenerational, context rather than some circumscribed context which the couple may present (e.g., "functional and/or
dysfunctional spouses," or as an ongoing argument about how to properly squeeze toothpaste tubes, or seeking how to deal with a symptomatic "problem child").

Kerr (1981), commenting on Bowen's theories (1978), pointed out that
a multigenerational concept expands the context of our perception of
the **nuclear family** as an emotional unit to the perception of the **multigenerational family** as an emotional unit. In this expanded working
context of the therapy, the couple can circumvent the therapeutic im-
passes that arise in marital therapy, particularly when the couple presents a narrowly defined individual symptom or a circumspect relationship
problem.

The Hypnotic Unconscious

The major transgenerational marital therapy models can be put into
two broad categories: interpersonal and intrapsychic. The purely interpersonal approaches do not posit the existence of an unconscious. They
chiefly are concerned with relational factors and, as such, do not consider
intrapsychic factors relevant to problem maintenance. This theoretical
point of view is presented in the transgenerational work of Bowen (1976),
Williamson (1981-1982), and others.

The intrapsychic/interpersonal approaches emphasize a living interplay between the intrapsychic and interpersonal vectors in the transgenerational matrix (characterized by the work of Bockus, 1980;
Boszormenyi-Nagy & Spark, 1973; Framo, 1965, 1981, 1982; Whitaker,
in Neill & Kniskern, 1982; and Morrison, 1981, and others). Simply put,
in both interpersonal and intrapsychic/interpersonal schemes, the prov-
erbial "sins of the fathers" are visited upon the sons who are the fathers
of the men (and indeed, the mothers on the daughters who are the
mothers of the women, etc.).

Whether these complex multigenerational processes are described as
the "family projection process," "intergenerational power structures,"
or "patterns of covert loyalties," each, in some way, is a description of

a complex process of interplay between interpersonal and intrapsychic factors. For example, Boszormenyi-Nagy and Spark (1973) stated, "There is a conscious and unconscious interlocking between systems—individual, marital, parental, and the extended family" (p. 254). Furthermore, they specified,

> The key issue for a theory of relationships is: how does the process of internalization interlock and remain connected with an active arrangement with relational partners; therefore, in what way is the internalized object also an "active agent" and representative of the "objects" of my needs? (p. 171)

A basic problem in marital psychotherapy has been whether to focus on the intrapsychic or the interpersonal life of the patient(s). Family therapy workers have demonstrated convincingly, that it is **unwise** to acknowledge the importance of the patient's individual history and introjected, internalized, reconstructed family, while systematically ignoring the patient's mother sitting and breathing in the waiting room week after week. However, it is **just as unwise** to deny that the character of a patient is being influenced by internalized reality, or that that patient's internal (unconscious) processes may be the royal route to the transgenerational family dynamics.

Gurman (1981) proposed an integrative marital therapy (including psychodynamic, behavioral, and structural/strategic approaches) **emphasizing** the interrelationships between intrapsychic and interpersonal dimensions. Commenting on the therapeutic technology of an integrative model, he observed, "There are few techniques in the practice of marital therapy that have derived directly from an appreciation of the **psychodynamics of intimate relationships**" (Gurman, 1981, p. 431).

The typical practice of the nonhypnotic, transgenerational family worker (as opposed to the individual therapist) has been to avoid using "the past hidden in the unconscious of the individual," and rather to "use the disruptive, regressive, negative behaviors expressed in the relationship in vivo to create change" (Boszormenyi-Nagy & Spark, 1973, p. 226). Consequently, the clinical strategy of much psychodynamic (object-relations) systems-based marital therapy has been to first work with the marital (family) projections in the live context of conjoint therapy and then (perhaps) attend to the introjects and distorted internalizations of the individual spouses (possibly in individual therapy). It would seem that such practice has grown partly as a consequence of a lack of technology for working with the living interplay of intrapsychic and interpersonal spheres.

Expanding the Therapeutic Context

A fortunate merging of systems thinkers and Ericksonian hypno-therapists is beginning to produce new and interesting developments. One bright example is Ritterman's recent work (1983) synthesizing hyp-notic techniques with a structural/strategic approach to family therapy. Ritterman describes family transactions in hypnotic terms and employs techniques of hypnosis to create new relational boundaries.

Conjoint transgenerational marital hypnotherapy provides a new set of techniques enabling the parties, with the aid of the therapist in the marital therapy triangle, to gain greater access to the intrapsychic di-mensions within the interpersonal context of both the marital and family relationships.

The transgenerational marital hypnotherapist works with the intro-jects (past) and projections (present) simultaneously (and mainly, con-jointly) in the couple. The working context of the therapy (and thus of the "marital problem" impasse as well) thereby is expanded to include (and perhaps even to manifest in living color in the room or inside the eyelids of the couple!) the couple's introjected and internalized families of origin and miscellaneous split-off fragments of self in a medium of hypnotic time that can be distorted so that the living, dead, present, past (and even future) can be brought together in the hypnotic moment.

As the Zen saying goes, "If you can't keep your cows in the corral, build a bigger corral." Through the use of techniques of marital hyp-notherapy, the therapist assists the couple to peer back and forth over the time and space of their (and their families') lives to have the expe-rience of being actors and actresses on the much larger, multigenera-tional stage. In this way, the couple has a working medium in which to express and come to terms with disappointments, hostilities, and unfinished family business in a field outside of or greater than each other, themselves, or the therapist (the building of a bigger corral). The couple graduates from "having a marriage problem" or a symptom, to being conscious of their roles as vectors in a larger field over time and space, of which they are but part(s) and in each of whom is contained the whole. (Minuchin and Fishman, 1981, discuss concepts of "part" and "whole" in families.)*

---

*Minuchin and Fishman (1981) address the problem of not having an adequate language for describing units of more than one. They quote Arthur Koestler addressing this con-ceptual difficulty, ". . . to get away from the traditional misuse of the words 'whole' and 'part,' one is compelled to operate with such awkward terms as 'sub-whole' or 'part-whole.' " Koestler coined a new term, "holon," from the Greek holos (whole) with the suffix on (as in proton or neutron), which suggests a particle or part. Minuchin and

In practice, many nonhypnotic transgenerational marital and family workers make use of hypnotic-like technique by employing certain procedures or principles that seem to create intersections between the intrapsychic context and the interpersonal context in the therapy. Also, the membership in the therapy is strictly regulated and manipulated to provide access of the intrapsychic in the interpersonal context as well as to generate and manage (therapeutic) affective intensity and to engender the belief that marital (family) problems are determined extrapersonally.

For example, consider Whitaker's special emphasis on the "absurd" and on "play therapy" and his rather dogged insistence on getting (at least) three generation systems together in therapy; Whitaker used words such as "homogenizing" to describe the process that then ensued (in Neill & Kniskern, 1982). It is clear that such a reference is not to any linear, reality-oriented, conscious-based, secondary-process strategies. In fact, when Scheflen (1973) studied therapy films of Whitaker (working along with Malone), he documented instances of "dissociation" in their patients.

Williamson (1981-1982) described the use of "playful intervention" utilizing such (hypnotic-like) procedures as play, humor, paradox, the absurd, and "going slowly." Williamson believes that such techniques are a particularly effective type of intervention in intergenerational work considering the intense emotionality of such work.

VARIETIES OF TRANSGENERATIONAL MARITAL HYPNOTHERAPY INTERVENTION

Neither the summary of intervention types below nor the specific examples of each are intended to be an exhaustive listing. Rather, they are offered as representative examples to give the reader an operational

---

Fishman, writing about the holons of family therapy state, ". . . the unit of intervention is always a holon. Every holon—the individual, the nuclear family, the extended family, and the community—is both a whole and a part, not more one than the other, not one rejecting or conflicting with the other. A holon exerts competitive energy for autonomy and self-preservation as a whole. It also carries integrative energy as a part. The nuclear family is a holon of the extended family, the extended family of the community, and so on. Each whole contains the part, and each part also contains the 'program' that the whole imposes. Part and whole contain each other in a continuing current and ongoing process of communication and interrelationship. . . . The individual holon incorporates the concept of self-in-context. It includes the personal and historical determinants of self. But it goes beyond them to include the current input of the social context. . . . It is easy to view the family as a unit and to see the individual as a holon of that unit. But the individual includes other aspects that are not contained in the individual as a holon of the family . . ."

sense of practice within the transgenerational marital hypnotherapy model and to stimulate clinical research and reporting. The categories are broad and are not intended to be mutually exclusive.*

Generating and Managing Therapeutic Intensity

The task of moving a married couple past an impasse to a higher level of inquiry (or to an expanded working context) often necessitates the generation of a greater measure of therapeutic (affective) intensity. To generate intensity, prior to employing techniques of hypnosis with marital therapy couples, I used to rely mainly on family of origin visits by the spouses as well as on conjoint therapy sessions with members of the spouse's family of origin. The addition of conjoint techniques of hypnosis has provided a greater degree of control over the generation and management of therapeutic intensity in transgenerational work (particularly related to material that is repressed or suppressed). The conjoint session with the family of origin, or the family of origin visit itself can be valuable in accessing the internalizations of marital therapy patients in the family context, but they are temporally bound to the present for the most part (barring spontaneous hypnotic regression of the patient in the presence of the family).

Examples of clinical procedure:

1) At the peak of an argument of inappropriate intensity (or one which seems unrelated to the alleged issues), one partner may be hypnotized and regressed to a time in the past (perhaps to childhood in the family of origin) where the feelings belonging to the fight seem to fit. The hypnotized partner is then helped to work through the past experience in the presence of the other partner, after which the couple is led in a discussion of the experience and encouraged to continue the discussion outside the office.

2) In trance, one of the spouses, in the presence of the other, is regressed to reexperience some troublesome sequence(s) of cognition,

---

*Each of the interventions described in this section is a description of just the hypnotic technique of a hypothetical marital hypnotherapy session. They do not give any information about the context in which these procedures are used, which is always a matter of the individual case. For example, each of these techniques may be delivered within a paradoxical imperative; or the hypnotherapist may wish to fail at hypnosis with the couple initially (as the distraction phase of the hypnotic therapy) and then to impotently deliver "marital therapy," but while utilizing indirect hypnotic technique. As with all techniques, the possibilities are endless.

affect, or behavior in the marriage and then is directed **to determine for whom in their family of origin they are behaving in that way.**

3) With one or both members in trance, the "spirits" of the family(s) of origin may be evoked (in fantasy or hallucination) to comment on the marriage or the therapy process and/or to answer questions.

4) Using hypnotic dissociation procedures, each spouse can be dissociated into "parts" (or ego states) that correspond to the compartmentalized elements of self that often come into play in the marital battle: e.g., "the little boy or girl" (dependent, depressed, passive); "the angry side" (rageful, immature, symmetrical); the incorporated mother or father (distorted internalizations of parents or other significant objects); a "core" or "center" and others. These circumscribed fragments or elements of both partners are then directed to interact in various ways to foster interpersonal (and intrapsychic) integration.

Transferring Loyalties (From the Family of Origin to the Family of Procreation)

Because of its ability to juxtapose and manipulate both the interlocking intrapsychic and interpersonal systems to bring the past into the present (the hypnotic moment) in the presence of the spouse, couples hypnotherapy may be a valuable clinical tool for transferring a spouse's primary loyalties from the family of origin to the family of procreation. Through the time-distorting capabilities of hypnosis, **partners may be caused to meet at any point in their individual "histories"** to tackle the problems of divided loyalties in the contexts in which they occur.

Examples of clinical procedure:

1) A nonhypnotized spouse can be introduced (put into rapport) with the hypnotized, regressed partner and instructed to develop a relationship of trust and support **(at a point in time before the couple actually met).**

2) A hypnotized partner, in the presence of the observing spouse (and either in or out of rapport with that spouse), can be asked to experience or reexperience the death (or abandonment) of both parents and the consequent grief related to the end of the family home. At this point, the partner can be encouraged to provide support for the grieving spouse, which then can be combined with future shared imagery of the family of procreation in which supportive, communal aspects are emphasized.

3) In trance, the partners may be asked to see the others as they appear to them at troublesome times and then to see the "masks" of the parent(s) or other significant other being peeled away to reveal the "true" face of the partner. With posthypnotic suggestion, such an intervention can be generalized to nontherapy, nontrance contexts.

Creating Desirable Expectational Sets

Conjoint marital hypnotherapy indirectly can create desirable expectational sets in the working couple such as, "We'll finally get to the bottom of this once and for all," or, "Neither one of us will be able to resist telling the truth." Because the approach is conjoint and works to expand the working notion of the place of the "marital problems" to the transgenerational family, there is no implication that one person is the identified or pathological patient. Also, the interplay between conscious and unconscious, past and present, as well as interpersonal and intrapsychic factors, is implied by the form and nature of this approach.

Examples of clinical procedures:

1) Early in the therapy, the couple can be mutually hypnotized and then given general suggestions for ego-strengthening, tension relief, or teaming, and for some variety of self-improvement, such as habit control or improved "concentration" (as an individual motivational measure). Suggestions also can be given for incidental symptomatic relief (as a couple's motivating factor), particularly if the symptom is in some way the focus (or an unwitting result) of a marital battle, such as a performance-based sexual problem or—the Great American universal—"a failure to communicate."

2) In mutual trance, the couple can be directed to create imagery of the successful conclusion to their therapy and, further, to imagine how they might be able to deal effectively with whatever setbacks or "therapeutic crises" they might encounter.

3) In mutual deep trance, the couple can be oriented to a pseudo-future—one in which they have completed their therapy successfully. It is further explained to them that they will find themselves sitting in the therapist's office in order to give the therapist a "follow-up" report. The couple are interviewed in this **as-if** state concerning how they **now** view their progress ("looking back . . ."), how they had managed setbacks or tangents, and what they remembered from their therapy that was especially helpful or unhelpful. Such confabulations can become the outline for an entire marital therapy.

Altering Interpersonal Dynamics

Conjoint marital hypnotherapy can be used to alter the relational patterns or "control dynamics" in couples through the use of interventions such as "symptom-cueing" (Ritterman, 1983) in which intrapsychic or interpersonal signals that previously cued symptomatic behaviors or patterns are blocked or redirected to "turn on" newly suggested sequences of counter-symptomatic behavior. The indirect use of hypnosis in couples therapy such as the "My Friend John" form of intervention can be invaluable in circumventing the conscious resistance of a recalcitrant partner.

Examples of clinical procedure:

1) To circumvent the conscious resistance of a recalcitrant partner, a spouse can be hypnotized in the presence of the recalcitrant one, and then directed to interpret a dream of the other (previously given) in a way to positively connote the other's apparently resistant behavior as a form of protection for the spouse and for the couple.

2) An external or internal cue which may have previously signaled an undesirable sequence can be reordered hypnotically to produce a different, more adaptive outcome (cf. Ritterman's symptom-cueing above).

3) Interventions in the relational dynamics may be delivered through the symptom, as in Erickson's case of the phantom limb pain husband and tinnitis wife; and Zeig's smoking cessation couple (Zeig, 1982).

4) Araoz (1978) wrote on the value of using mutual hypnosis (in which each spouse is taught to hypnotize the other while entering self-hypnosis) as a means of "balancing the dynamics of authority" in couples.

Fostering Intimacy

Conjoint applications of hypnotherapy can foster greater intimacy in the couple. Through the use of conjoint intervention types, trance, and symbolic reenactments, the conscious perceptions (projections) of the partners may be circumvented and each partner is thereby better able to understand the unreasonable demands of the other (particularly through the use of regressive techniques). Unconscious to unconscious communication also is potentiated and the experience of intimacy can be immediate rather than mediated by intellect or by other linear, conscious processes. Suggestion also can be used to foster a freer expression of repressed, suppressed, or denied feelings between partners. Transference operations are increased and the therapist is more likely to enter the marital (family) system as a symbolic parent rather than as a rival lover.

Examples of clinical procedure:

1) The couple can be mutually regressed (in rapport with one another) to some happy, successful preproblem time and then directed in this "**as-if**" state to look into the actual (problematic) future as though it were only a "probable possibility" (perhaps by pretending) and plan corrections or actions to ensure a desirable outcome. Techniques of age progression can be used in tandem with this procedure to enhance the development of the ideal images and to secure commitment and build motivation for desired courses of action.

2) Through the use of shared trance techniques, the couple can use mutual fantasy or hypnotically induced dreams* to image progress in therapy, mutual goal attainment, changes in relational patterns, etc.

3) The couple, both in deep trance, can be asked to assume each other's identity (deep trance identification) and renegotiate marital issues. As a means of expanding the working context of the therapy with the use of this technique, the couple also can be directed to visit the spouse's family home (in hallucination or fantasy) to gain understanding of the spouse's childhood experience.

The Use of Self-Hypnosis

Couples may be taught self-hypnosis or mutually induced hypnosis. The spouses may apply techniques of self-hypnosis to obtain personal goals that may foster marital accord (such as weight loss, smoking cessation, assertiveness, tension reduction, and anger management). Practicing the techniques of mutual hypnosis (in which the couple is taught to go into self-hypnosis while hypnotizing the other) can lead to an emerging culture in the marriage in which more of the intrapsychic lives of the spouses are shared.

As an example, Morris (1979) describes a self-help technique for couples in which one partner hypnotizes the other after the other has iden-

---

*Because conjoint marital hypnotherapy adds a greatly expanded working context for working with dreams, I often utilize them. Consider that in the hypnotic medium, dreams may be created, edited, and interpreted (both consciously and in trance) by each spouse and that each may reexperience and interpret the other's dreams and the dreams of other family members as well.

tified an adverse reaction arising from some recent interpersonal situation. The partner/hypnotist then uses suggestion to intensify the hypnotized partner's feelings and uses these to form a bridge back to some key event from childhood which the subject reexperiences, redecides from an adult perspective and then re-creates the childhood scene in some new way incorporating the insights.

Facilitating Adaptation to Developmental Events

Marital hypnotherapy can be used to facilitate adaptation to various developmental events, such as the birth of a child, death of a parent, marriage of a child, retirement, or death of a spouse.

Examples of clinical procedure:

1) Techniques of mental rehearsal can be used in advance of major developmental events such as imminent death of a terminally ill parent or spouse to promote coping strategies and appropriate affective responses.

2) A retrospective approach to couples' poorly handled events of the past is the use of regressive and redecision techniques to provide an opportunity for the couple to integrate the past event through the medium of hypnotic imagery.

CLINICAL VIGNETTE

A 62-year-old man requested hypnotherapy to arrest active alcoholism. He explained that his wife had recently left due to his drinking and that he was depressed, having suicidal ideations. He was informed that the author would be unwilling to see him without his wife, a condition to which he consented.

In a conjoint session it was determined that the wife was 60 years old and had been married to this man for two years. Each had been married before and had raised families. The man's previous wife had died a few years earlier and the woman had divorced her husband within the same time period. Within the two-year marriage, the wife had moved out of the couple's home to her mother's residence four times; her chief complaints concerned the man's behavior when he drank. She complained that the husband was heavy-handed, sexually assaultive, highly manipulative, and "two-faced."

She went on to explain that in recent years she had tried to put some distance between herself and her mother, who refused to take her daily insulin whenever the daughter moved toward differentiation. The wife felt doubly trapped, since each time she moved to escape the mother's manipulations, the husband castigated her and threatened suicide. Many times, when she went to visit her mother, however, the husband became highly volatile and accused the wife of infidelity.

The wife's stance in the session was patronizing toward the husband while she attempted to form an alliance with the therapist. She insisted that the husband was the source of all their marital problems and that her demands were all perfectly reasonable since the husband was insensitive, evil, or both. Any attempt to point to the wife's responsibility was met with indignation and the husband's meek agreement that the wife was right in her assessment of him and the situation. Any attempt to bring the husband to point out any aspect of the wife's behavior which he resented or objected to just met with pitiful and depressed responses and his praise for his wife for tolerating him.

I reasoned that neither the husband nor the wife would be willing, for the most part, to treat the husband as more than a second-class citizen in the therapy until he stopped drinking. So I told the couple I was unwilling to use hypnosis with the husband unless they recognized three things: 1) they would need couples therapy (starting right then) to examine their mutual roles in the impasse; 2) they should expect that I could be helpful (the man appeared to be an excellent hypnotic subject); and 3) I "agreed" with the wife that the husband would need some help **if he was to become a working member of the therapy** and not waste my time **or hers**.

The husband was seen for a series of weekly individual hypnotic appointments over the next three months, during which time he did not drink at all. Finally, after three months, the husband remarked how much better he was feeling and stated how much he now realized he wasn't the only one who needed to change (a reference to his wife). I told him that it was time to commence the conjoint therapy. In the next session, both husband and wife were present. But while the husband had obviously improved and the couple reported having dated a few times successfully, the wife was still insistent about the husband's low character and carried on to the therapist about the husband in much the same way she had in the initial session.

In this session, the husband was hypnotized into a somnambulistic trance in the wife's presence and was told to regress to a time that had some bearing on the "matters at hand" concerning his wife. He regressed to age 10 and reported that his mother had just died in a house fire. He explained that she had been badly burned by the fire and that he was the only one home at the time and their house was many miles away from the town. He had helplessly watched as his mother died before him. As he told the story, he had the affect and beliefs appropriate for a 10-year-old enduring such an ordeal. He felt that his mother's death had been his fault and **he regretted that he wasn't dead instead of her.** As the wife heard this last remark, her jaw dropped visibly and her eyes began to water. (Later, she explained that at that moment she realized that the husband's suicidal behaviors were not directed toward her and she knew she didn't have to take them personally.) **She had felt a wave of caring and compassion for the little boy who she realized was her husband.** (Subsequent to this, the wife divulged that her son from her previous marriage had killed himself just before she met her present husband.)

I helped the regressed 10-year-old begin to come to terms with the awful calamity as being a terrible, random act and assisted him to discharge his feelings about the loss. When he had gained some of his composure, he was asked **what advice he would give to people who still had their mothers.** Without hesitation, he blurted out, *"Never leave them!"*

At this remark, the wife finally could no longer contain herself. She burst out crying, ran to the other side of the room (where her husband was sitting), and began to kiss and hug him and dry his eyes. The man, still in deep trance, sat apparently oblivious of her ministrations. I pointed this out to the wife and the man was awakened with his wife sitting beside him. Instructions were given to recall the trance experiences slowly. As he did, both the husband and wife cried together.

In the next session, the couple reported significant improvements in the relationship though the wife was still adamant that she didn't trust the husband not to become physically abusive with her again if she were to move back with him. In a fashion similar to the previous time, the husband was hypnotized and told to go back to a time that would again have something to do with "those matters at hand" concerning his wife. The husband regressed to a time just a few months after the death of his mother at which time the family (the man, his older brother, and their father) had moved to town. The regressed little boy described how his older brother beat him regularly and how his father, at best, was neglectful. He described how the other kids at school regularly teased him because of his worn, "country bumpkin clothes" and his small size.

He lamented that **"nobody ever listened to me,"** as he broke down in tears. (Again, the wife's eyes grew moist as they remained fixed in a glassy gaze on the husband.)

I then asked the little boy, **"What do you do when someone doesn't listen to you?"** Making fists and sticking his chin out, he exclaimed, **"I hit them!"** Once again the wife's jaw fell. After awakening the husband in similar fashion to the previous session, the husband and wife embraced and cried together.

Discussion

Certainly, these two interventions do not constitute the total marital therapy in this case. The clinical vignette is included because it is a cogent example of how the use of hypnosis may assist couples to dissolve longstanding, rigid conflicts out of their marital relationship into a much larger, transgenerational context in which they may hopefully be better tolerated and perhaps completed and integrated.

SUMMARY AND CONCLUSIONS

Conjoint marital hypnotherapy used within a transgenerational model of marital problems is an elegant and direct way of accessing the marital impasse. Particularly at points of therapeutic impasse, hypnosis can expand the working context of marital therapy to include the intrapsychic, within the interpersonal context of the therapy triangle and the multigenerational families of origin. Also, because the context of time becomes elastic, the marital hypnotherapist is able to juxtapose the past, present, and future in the hypnotic moment.

Hypnotic techniques in marital therapy can be used to generate and manage therapeutic intensity; to increase intimacy and cooperation in the couple; to help transfer primary loyalty from the family of origin to the family of procreation: to create certain desirable expectational sets in the couple; to alter control and relational dynamics; to facilitate adaptation to various developmental events; and to teach the couple self-hypnosis, which may be used to obtain personal goals that may facilitate marital accord.

The current dialectic between systems theorists, Ericksonian hypnotherapists and psychodynamic-oriented object-relations thinkers is developing and promises to produce more clinical experimentation of many kinds with marital couples utilizing various forms of unconscious communication such as hypnosis and various "hypnotic-like" and "as if" procedures.

For example, Araoz (1982) has led work for the integration of hypnosis with sex therapy and the synthesis of a systemic model of couple work originating from an object-relations orientation. Morrison (1981) has explored pathways into couples' and family's internalized constructs through the use of imagery techniques from within a transgenerational perspective. Ritterman (1983) has formulated a pioneering model of family therapy in which she conceptualizes hypnotic technique as a means of "creating new relational boundaries," synthesizing an Ericksonian hypnotic approach within a structural family therapy paradigm.

There is a significant need for continuing clinical research and documentation of the use of hypnosis in marital therapy and the beginning of a body of knowledge of the use of hypnosis within a transgenerational model of marital therapy.

REFERENCES

Alexander, L. (1974). Treatment of impotency and anorgasmia by psychotherapy aided by hypnosis. *American Journal of Clinical Hypnosis, 17*, 33–43.

Alger, I. (1976). Multiple couple therapy. In P. J. Guerin (Ed.), *Family therapy*. New York: Gardner.

Anderson, A. (1980). *New approaches to family pastoral care*. Philadelphia: Fortress.

Araoz, D. L. (1978). Clinical hypnosis in couple therapy. *Journal of the American Society of Psychosomatic Dentistry and Medicine, 25*(2), 58–67.

Araoz, D. L. (1979a). *Hypnosis in couples group counseling.* Paper presented at the 87th Annual Convention of the American Psychological Association, New York.

Araoz, D. L. (1979b). Hypnosis in group therapy. *International Journal of Clinical and Experimental Hypnosis, 27*(1), 1–13.

Araoz, D. L. (1982). *Hypnosis and sex therapy*. New York: Brunner/Mazel.

Bandler, R., & Grinder, J. (1981). *Reframing*. Moab, UT: Real People Press.

Beigel, H. (1971). Therapeutic approaches of impotence in the male. II. The hypnotherapeutic approach to male impotence. *Journal of Sex Research, 7*, 168–176.

Bergner, R. M. (1979). The use of systems-oriented illustrative stories in marital psychotherapy. *Family Therapy, 6*(2), 109–118.

Bockus, F. (1980). *Couple therapy*. New York: Jason Aronson.

Boszormenyi-Nagy, I., & Spark, M. (1973). *Invisible loyalties*. New York: Harper.

Bowen, M. (1976). Theory in the practice of psychotherapy. In P. J. Guerin (Ed.), *Family therapy*. New York: Gardner.

Bowen, M. (1978). *Family therapy in clinical practice*. New York: Jason Aronson.

Braun, B. G. (1979). Hypnosis in groups and group hypnotherapy. In G. Burrows & L. Dennerstein (Eds.), *Handbook of hypnosis and psychosomatic medicine*. New York: Elsevier-North Holland/Biomedical Press.

Braun, B. G. (in press). Hypnosis in family therapy. In A. H. Smith & W. C. Wester (Eds.), *Comprehensive clinical hypnosis*. Philadelphia: Lippincott.

Brink, E. (1981). *Imagery in family therapy.* Paper presented at the 1981 Conference of the American Association for the Study of Mental Imagery, New Haven.

Cameron-Bandler, L. (1978). *They lived happily ever after.* Cupertino, CA: Meta Publications.

Caprio, S. F. (1973). Hypnosis in the treatment of sexual problems. *Hypnosis Quarterly, 17,* 10–14.

Crasilneck, B., & Hall, A. (1975). *Clinical hypnosis: Principles and applications.* New York: Grune & Stratton.

de Shazer, S. (1978). Brief hypnotherapy of the sexual dysfunctions: The crystal ball technique. *American Journal of Clinical Hypnosis, 20,* 203–208.

de Shazer, S. (1980). Investigation of indirect symbolic suggestion. *American Journal of Clinical Hypnosis, 23*(1), 10–15.

Erickson, M. H., & Rossi, E. (1976). Two level communication and the microdynamics of trance. *American Journal of Clinical Hypnosis, 18,* 153–171.

Erickson, M. H., & Rossi, E. L. (1979). *Hypnotherapy: An exploratory casebook.* New York: Halsted.

Erickson, M. H., Rossi, E. L., & Rossi, S. I. (1976). *Hypnotic realities.* New York: Irvington.

Framo, J. L. (1965). Systematic research on family dynamics. In I. Boszormenyi-Nagy & J. L. Framo (Eds.), *Intensive family therapy.* New York: Harper.

Framo, J. L. (1981). Integration of marital therapy with sessions with family of origin. In A. S. Gurman & D. P. Kniskern (Eds.), *Handbook of family therapy.* New York: Brunner/Mazel.

Framo, J. L. (1982). *Explorations in marital and family therapy.* New York: Springer.

Fuchs, K., Hoch, Z., Paldi, E., Abramovici, H., Brandes, J. M., & Timor-Tritsch, I. (1973). Hypnodesensitization therapy of vaginismus. *International Journal of Clinical Hypnosis, 21*(3), 144–156.

Gordon, D. (1978). *Therapeutic metaphors.* Cupertino, CA: Meta Publications.

Guerin, P. J., & Guerin, K. B. (1976). Theoretical aspects and clinical relevance of the multigenerational model of family therapy. In P. J. Guerin (Ed.), *Family therapy.* New York: Gardner.

Gurman, A. S. (1973). Marital therapy. *Family Process, 12,* 145–170.

Gurman, A. S. (1981). Integrative marital therapy: Towards a development of an inter-personal approach. In S. H. Budman (Ed.), *Forms of brief therapy.* New York: Guilford.

Haley, J. (1963). *Strategies of psychotherapy.* New York: Grune & Stratton.

Haley, J. (1973). *Uncommon therapy.* New York: Norton.

Haley, J. (1976). *Problem solving therapy.* San Francisco: Jossey-Bass.

Kerr, M. E. (1981). Family systems theory and therapy. In A. S. Gurman & D. P. Kniskern (Eds.), *Handbook of family therapy.* New York: Brunner/Mazel.

Lankton, S., & Lankton, C. H. (1983). *The answer within.* New York: Brunner/Mazel.

Leckie, F. H. (1964). Hypnotherapy in gynecological disorders. *International Journal of Clinical and Experimental Hypnosis, 12,* 121–146.

Levit, H. (1971-72). Marital crisis intervention: Hypnosis of impotence/frigidity cases. *American Journal of Clinical Hypnosis, 14,* 56–60.

Lustig, H. S. (1975). *The artistry of Milton H. Erickson, M.D.* (Parts 1 and 2). [Videotape]. Haverford: Herbert S. Lustig, M.D., Ltd.

Madanes, C. (1981). *Strategic family therapy.* San Francisco: Jossey-Bass.

Minuchin, S., & Fishman, H. C. (1981). *Family therapy techniques.* Cambridge: Harvard University Press.

Morris, F. (1979). *Hypnosis with friends and lovers.* New York: Harper & Row.

Morrison, J. K. (1981). The use of imagery techniques in family therapy. *American Journal of Family Therapy, 9*(2), 52–56.

Neill, J., & Kniskern, D. P. (Eds.). (1982). *From psyche to system: Evolving therapy of Carl Whitaker.* New York: Guilford.

Nuland, W. (1978). The use of hypnosis in the treatment of impotence. In F. Frankel & H. S. Zamansky (Eds.), *Hypnosis at its bicentennial.* New York: Plenum.

Papp, P. (1976). Brief therapy with couples groups. In P. J. Guerin (Ed.), *Family therapy.* New York: Gardner.

Papp, P. (1982). Staging reciprocal metaphors in a couples group. *Family Process, 21*(4), 453–468.

Richardson, T. A. (1963). Hypnotherapy and frigidity. *American Journal of Clinical Hypnosis, 5*, 194–199.

Richardson, T. A. (1968). Hypnotherapy in frigidity and para-frigidity problems. *Journal of the American Society for Psychosomatic Dentistry and Medicine, 15*, 88–96.

Ritterman, M. (1980). Hypno-structural family therapy. In L. Wolberg & M. Aronson (Eds.), *Group and family therapy*. New York: Brunner/Mazel.

Ritterman, M. (1983). *Using hypnosis in family therapy*. San Francisco: Jossey-Bass.

Rosen, S. (Ed.). (1982). *My voice will go with you*. New York: Norton.

Rossi, E. (1980). (Ed.). *The collected papers of Milton H. Erickson on hypnosis* (Vols. 1–4). New York: Irvington.

Scheflen, A. (1973). *Communicational structure*. Bloomington: Indiana University Press.

Starr, A. (1977). *Rehearsal for living: Psychodrama*. Chicago: Nelson-Hall.

Stricherz, M. (1982). Social influences, Ericksonian strategies and hypnotic phenomena in the treatment of sexual dysfunction. *American Journal of Clinical Hypnosis, 24*(3), 211–218.

Wassilk, J. (1966). Vaginismus responses to hypnotical treatment. *Journal of the American Institute of Hypnosis, 7*, 31–37.

Watzlawick, P. (1978). *The language of change*. New York: Basic Books.

Watzlawick, P., Weakland, J., & Fisch, R. (1974). *Change*. New York: Norton.

Whitaker, C.A. (1982). Hypnosis and family depth therapy. In J.K. Zeig (Ed.), *Ericksonian approaches to hypnosis and psychotherapy* (pp. 491-504). New York: Brunner/Mazel.

Williamson, D. S. (1981–1982). Personal authority via termination of the intergenerational hierarchical boundary: A "new" stage in family life cycle. *Journal of Marital and Family Therapy*, Part 1, *7*(4), 441–451; 1982, Part 2, *8*(2), 23–37; Part 3, *8*(3), 309–322.

Zeig, J. K. (1982). Erickson approaches to promote abstinence from cigarette smoking. In J.K. Zeig (Ed.), *Ericksonian approaches to hypnosis and psychotherapy* (pp. 225-269). New York: Brunner/Mazel.

Chapter 5

Motivating Clients in Directive Family Therapy

Alfred Lange

INTRODUCTION

Many descriptions of psychotherapy place emphasis on the nature of interventions and their effect on clients. One seldom reads about what the therapist has to do to ensure that intended interventions have a chance of success; not much has been written about how clients are motivated to make them amenable to both the therapist's suggestions and enduring change. This is unfortunate, as one particular characteristic of the practice of directive therapy is that a great deal of attention is given to motivating clients. A set repertoire of routine interventions or techniques is not used, and the way in which clients are motivated and the "timing" of interventions should be carefully adapted to the individual client (cf. Haley, 1976; Lange, 1980; van der Velden & van Dijck, 1977; van Dijck, 1980a).

This chapter categorizes some of the strategies and techniques used to motivate clients, a number of which are mentioned in the above literature. The categories are not exhaustive or mutually exclusive. They are merely an aid to sum up the great variety of implicit and explicit motivation tactics. The final section of this chapter deals with how reluctant clients can be persuaded to participate in family sessions.

CATEGORIZATION ON THE BASIS OF TWO DIMENSIONS

Two dimensions can be used to categorize motivation techniques and strategies. The first dimension is *general-specific*. Some motivation techniques, tactics, and strategies are fairly general and aim to motivate clients for the therapy as a whole, i.e., give them confidence in the therapist and enable them to work on the proposed treatment. There are also techniques and tactics which are designed to magnify the effect of specific interventions, for example, to ensure that clients accept the therapist's feedback or to increase the chance of their carrying out homework assignments.

The second dimension relates to the nature of the approach, which may lie on the continuum from strictly *congruent* to *judo-like*.* Congruent motivation occurs when a therapist explains directly what is expected of the client and why a particular thing is important. Other congruent motivation techniques include explaining exactly what is to take place in therapy and giving clients hope that there is a fair chance of success provided they work in a certain way. Judo-like motivation techniques may be called for when a client tends to oppose everything the therapist or the other family members say. In such cases the therapist should be wary of presenting an over-optimistic view of the problems and solutions. It is also advisable not to be "too persuasive" with such clients. Table 1 presents the various motivation techniques which can be applied.

General Congruent Motivation Techniques

Rabkin (1977) considers the principle of *giving the patient hope* an essential basis for motivation. The therapist imparts the idea that a gloomy outlook and feelings of hopelessness are not entirely justified and that it is possible to do something about the situation.

Positive labeling can engender hope at the outset of therapy. For example, in an assessment session, John, age 45, stated that he was "completely stuck." He worked half days in a warehouse and received supplementary welfare. After a childless marriage and a period of living

Table 1
Categories of motivation techniques

	General	Specific
Congruent	1	3
Judo	2	4

---

* In their categorization of interventions, van Dijck et al. (1980) use the *"congruent-paradoxical"* dimension. As this article is not concerned with typically paradoxical interventions but with a broader approach which may seem paradoxical but is not really so in all cases, I shall use the term "judo-like" here (cf. Lange, 1977).

with a girlfriend, he again was living alone. During the session he talked about his loneliness and his attempts to build satisfactory relationships with friends and girlfriends. At one point he said, "Basically I'm lazy, I suppose. I always let people down after a while, and then I try to forget about the whole thing. . . ." The therapist did not react at once. He looked thoughtful for a moment and then said, "You know, I don't believe you're lazy at all. You probably find it strange that I can be so sure after talking to you for only half an hour. I'm not usually like that, but what you've told me, has given me a completely different impression. From what you've said you're a perfectionist and in all your previous relationships you've tried to be honest and talk things out." The therapist pointed out several examples to support his view and then continued, "I can imagine that it's this perfectionism that has got you into trouble in the past and that it is difficult for other people to deal with, and perhaps you could reduce it eventually, but I don't think you're lazy." The therapist ended by supportively pointing out another of John's positive characteristics—his very obvious sense of humor, which even in his unfortunate circumstances made it possible for him to see his situation in perspective.

John was quiet for a while, and then the assessment session continued. At the end, the question of a preliminary treatment contract arose. The therapist did not have a place for him in his schedule, but because he considered immediate treatment necessary, he suggested referral to a colleague. John did not even want to discuss it. Crying, he said, "You're the first person in years who's said anything good about me. I need that too from time to time." It was decided that John would wait until the therapist had time to take him in therapy.

The above example shows how positive labeling can lead to hope for a fresh start, the beginning of a new self-image and faith in the therapist and the therapy, all of which increase general motivation at the beginning of treatment. Hope can also be created in the early stages of therapy by *asking about a client's positive qualities,* instead of concentrating on failures and difficulties as has been the fashion in most psychotherapeutic orientations. With John, who had hinted at being interested in art, the therapist asked him how he manifested his interest. Similarly, it is often useful to ask clients how they have tried to deal with their problems in the past, thereby eliciting new possibilities for treatment which fit in with solutions the client independently may have considered.

By displaying self-assurance, confidence in his or her own ability, and a certain air of authority, the therapist may also increase the patient's hope and confidence in a successful conclusion of therapy. Vulgar displays of status or boasting are uncalled for. For example, Rabkin (1977) mentions the case of a physician who had a photograph of himself with President Kennedy in his consulting room. Just as transparent and equally unnecessary are some of Goldstein's (1975) recommendations. He described an experiment which is supposed to prove that therapy in which the therapist introduces himself as "doctor" was more successful than when the therapist simply used his own name. Fortunately subsequent research refuted his findings.

Self-assurance can be demonstrated more modestly, as for example by a calm attitude and by probing in a competent manner when one is not satisfied with vague complaints. Stimulating clients to be specific is a motivating factor because they then realize that it causes them to talk about their complaints in a different way and that it gives them insight.

Hope and positive expectations are engendered particularly when clients notice at the outset that *their situation is changing.* This may mean that in an individual discussion the client experiences problems becoming clearer or his self-image changing or that he realizes that there are previously unconsidered ways of dealing with problems. What might emerge in a first family session is that clients immediately experience that they are talking to each other differently than they do at home. For example:

1) Everyone is being more specific;
2) Certain members of the family who do not normally discuss problems are now talking about them directly;
3) There are ways of reaching a compromise in conflicts.

A second general principle of congruent motivation techniques is "*joining*," a term introduced by Minuchin (1974). This implies the following:

1) That the complaints the clients bring up be taken seriously; and
2) That therapists show interest in their clients by inquiring about matters not directly related to therapy, such as hobbies, jobs, children's schools, etc.

A good example of the second point is provided by what took place in a first family session. It initially was difficult to persuade the father to come. The problem was the son, and the father felt it had nothing to do with him. He eventually came, after his wife was advised over the telephone how to get him to agree at least to the first session. He walked in sullen, ill-tempered and openly protesting. Due to lack of suitable space, the therapist's racing bike was in the therapy room. As coincidence would have it, the client was a keen cyclist too and seeing the bicycle changed his mood completely. After discussing racing for five minutes they were on such good terms that the man was perfectly willing to talk about the problems in the family.

Another example of joining is provided by Yvonne, 14 years old. Her mother told the therapist over the telephone that she was unmanageable and that she wanted to talk to him with her husband, but without Yvonne. The therapist asked her to come with the whole family. She said that she did not think Yvonne would be prepared to come. The therapist instructed her how to put it to her daughter. Several days later, the woman telephoned to make a definite appointment. Yvonne agreed to come but announced that she did not intend to say a word. At the beginning of the session, the therapist asked Yvonne which schools she had been to. One of them was where he was about to send his own daughter. An animated discussion ensued regarding what the school was like and the various teachers. Subsequently, Yvonne participated in the rest of the session in a lively and positive manner.

Admittedly these are not everyday examples, but showing interest in clients and their work and hobbies, and wherever possible showing some knowledge on subjects which interest them, increases the degree of contact with clients and consequently, their motivation for therapy.

Giving a clear picture of what they can expect from therapy is also motivating. This means that the therapist should not be afraid to reveal his or her working methods at the outset, and should propose a *preliminary treatment contract* (cf. Lange & van der Hart, 1983, chapter 6) at the end of the first session, providing information about possible working methods. The therapist should naturally exercise judgment; too much theoretical information is demotivating. Therefore, it is important that the presented information correlate with what the clients have "experienced" during the first session. For instance, the principle of homework assignments may be explained during the first session by describing an assignment which may be used at a later date when dealing with that particular problem. Patients might be told that at a later date they might be asked to register how often a certain problematic situation arose. This technique is more motivating than providing written information before therapy starts, as recommended by Goldstein (1975).

An effective procedure which both provides information and is motivating is showing film or video sequences of potentially similar therapy with clients who have related problems.

Providing information at the outset on a possible treatment approach also has the advantage of providing the clients the opportunity of having some say in the therapy right from the start. Therefore, clients may "amend" the therapist's suggestions and express their own preferences. This procedure alone is motivating, increases involvement in therapy and promotes a sense of responsibility for carrying out the therapy program.

General Interventions of a Judo-Like Nature

The above general congruent motivation techniques probably are characteristic of good therapists of all disciplines. This notion correlates with the research cited by Frank (1976) that therapy results are much the same regardless of the therapist's discipline. What is of significance, though, is the degree to which therapists use the nonspecific variables mentioned above, especially "confidence in one's own ability" and "being capable of inspiring hope in clients."

It is perhaps characteristic of directive family therapy that congruent approaches are not the only ones used. There is an awareness that for certain clients a positive congruent approach does not have a beneficial effect.

In general there are three kinds of clients who are not served by optimistic prospects, explanations and conclusions.

1) Clients who are accustomed to having chronic complaints and who draw a large degree of secondary gain from them (in the form of attention or convenience);
2) Clients for whom symptoms may be regarded as an adaptation strategy (cf. van Dijck, 1980b) used to protect themselves or others in a system. For example, a child who tries to keep its family together by exhibiting symptoms of depression or psychosis (cf. Selvini Palazzoli et al., 1978);
3) Clients who genuinely want to change, but at the same time are unwilling to accept the therapist's authority and tend to get involved in a struggle for power.

According to Haley (1963), the last category is the largest; almost every therapeutic relationship contains a struggle for power. Even if one cannot entirely accept Haley's claim, it must be agreed that a large number of clients fit into this category, and a congruent approach would not at all be helpful with them.

While some congruent approaches can be used, it certainly would be wrong to give these clients hope, to draw attention to genuinely positive matters and to emphasize positive aspects of their characters.

Therefore, therapists can provide general interventions of a judo-like nature. What is a "judo intervention"? It is an approach in which the therapist provides explanations and pinpoints the complaints, but avoids giving hope or drawing positive conclusions. Rather, the complaints are taken excessively seriously and the therapist acts pessimistic about his ability to help the client (cf. Lange & van der Hart, 1983). Criticism of the therapist and other forms of resistance are given positive labels, e.g., "being critical at least shows that you do not mindlessly accept what other people tell you," which neatly turns resistance into a form of cooperation.

The therapist's dilemma is to decide if judo-like or congruent motivation techniques are more appropriate. It is not easy to decide, but there are several types of disqualifying behavior which may serve as an indication.

1) Constant correction of the therapist by the client;
2) Regularly pointing out that the therapist's point of view perhaps applies to other clients, but not to this particular (and special) case;
3) Continually stating that nothing will change because "that's the way I am."

When confronted with attitudes and behavior such as these, it is useful to apply the judo technique for a while. Critical remarks can be preempted by telling the client, "I could give you my opinion, but I don't think I really know enough about the situation, so it wouldn't be right." Curiosity aroused, the client will not be able to resist pressing the therapist into revealing more.

After repeated objections, the therapist "reluctantly" gives in. This technique is indicated when clients demonstratively try to create the impression that they have no faith in therapy, and that although they come to sessions, they do not expect to be helped.

It is not wise to try and persuade such clients that they can reasonably derive benefit from therapy. It is better to "go along" by saying:

1) "Things definitely don't look good";

2) "There is indeed only a very remote chance of success";
3) "It might be better not to embark on therapy at all."

Only at the client's insistence should the therapist agree to several sessions, simply to "give it a chance." The advantage of this approach is that the therapist ensures that clients cannot seduce the therapist into "pulling" at them. Instead, clients have to "draw it out" of the therapist, thereby increasing motivation. For example David, a concentration camp survivor, was referred for symptoms of apathy and depression. During the first session he did not pass up an opportunity to tell the therapist that he neither wanted therapy nor had any faith in the outcome. He had so many negative experiences with therapy that he had no reason to believe that this time would be any different. However, the more the therapist outdid him in gloominess, the more David started looking for positive points in himself.

The judo approach is also indicated when there are psychosomatic complaints which the client regards as purely somatic. It is usually best to go along with the client's position, but preferably in an inconvenient way, such as making the client undergo yet another physical examination, or by imposing a "burden," such as extensive registration of symptoms or by prescribing "rest" (cf. Hoogduin & van der Velden, 1978). One then waits until the client tries to get out of the bind by suggesting that there are perhaps "minor" areas to work on in the psychological field.

A similar attitude may be adopted when clients strongly emphasize intrapsychic factors, when problems of interaction clearly exist. Here again, the therapist should not try to convince the client directly. The therapist may, "as a matter of routine" ask about interactional problems, "but only to complete the picture—not because there is anything wrong in that direction."

So much for the judo motivation technique for "obstreperous" clients. Let us now return to more specific congruent motivation techniques.

Specific Congruent Motivation Techniques

This category may be divided in two: motivation can relate to interventions during a session or to homework assignments. Examples of motivation techniques during a session are reinterpretation and reframing, which cause clients to view themselves and their problems in a different light. If the therapist attempts to place problems in a favorable light, the client must be motivated to trust the therapist's interpretation.

For example, a woman admitted to a psychiatric hospital for depression was receiving a fair amount of medication. After six weeks, the team decided to involve her husband in the treatment, since the woman gave the impression that fear of him and his lack of understanding were important factors in her condition. At first he refused to come. After some persuasion he agreed, but arrived shouting and swearing, "It's a scandal. You bunch of jerks are giving my wife so many pills. She's coming home now and then everything will be O.K. again. Talking isn't going to help her." The therapist waited until he was quite finished, and then asked if he had any more complaints about the clinic staff. After about a quarter of an hour of criticism there was a silence and the therapist asked, "Would you like to hear what I have to say now?" The man grudgingly muttered his consent.

The therapist was silent for a moment, then looked straight at the man and said, "I'm sure you'll think it's strange, but I'm very pleased about everything you just said. Most spouses simply want to see more medication given. It makes life easier for them. I can see that you are deeply involved in what's happening to your wife here and that you're prepared to fight for her recovery. I'll support you, but you must help me too. We can only decrease the dosage once we've started working on the preparations for going home—for example, by the three of us talking together. Would you be ready to cooperate?"

This is not the point at which to discuss the way in which the therapist formulated what he had to say or its content and effect; it is merely an illustration of how a therapist can effect this type of intervention. What is essential is that the therapist allowed the husband to get everything off his chest and then had him say he did want a reaction from the therapist. The "motivating impact" was heightened by lengthy pauses, talking slowly and a dramatic tone of voice.

When a therapist is trying to provide a client with insight it is important that he *adapts his use of language to that of the client*. Van der Velden & van Dijck (1977) provide a clear example of this technique with a retarded client who had hyperventilation problems. To explain what was wrong with the client's breathing, the therapist compared the process of hyperventilation with the results of an incorrect mixture of air and gas in the patient's motorcycle.

The above example concerns accepting feedback and interpretations during a session. It is often necessary to persuade clients to carry out homework and other assignments. Naturally, careful explanation using the client's own phrases and clearly recognizable symbols are of utmost importance. The effect can be heightened by diction, i.e., consciously regulating the speed of speech, the tone, and emphasis.

A common mistake in giving an assignment is trying to "sell" it by making it sound easy. This is demotivating, as the client has the feeling that anyone could do it. It is, therefore, usually better to introduce an assignment by saying something such as, "I'm about to ask you to do something which is difficult, and I'm wondering if it isn't perhaps too difficult. Take your time to think about whether or not you want to do it." An explanation follows and then the client has a period of time in which to consider a reaction. If he says "yes," it means that he is undertaking something which will increase his self-respect. Van der Velden & van Dijck (1977) express this principle succinctly: "Doing something any fool could do is not very motivating, but doing something which the therapist has made seem a challenge is more attractive."

In conclusion: presenting a task as difficult, and specifically asking for cooperation, is a useful and legitimate way of motivating people to take on and carry out a homework assignment. Apart from this, clients may also make amendments in the therapist's suggestions so that the assignment becomes a task they have set themselves thereby further increasing their motivation.

Specific Judo-Like Means of Motivation

As with general judo-like interventions, these techniques often apply to clients who not only are inclined to take on a fight with the therapist but would also like to win. If these clients are to be persuaded to carry out their homework assignments, specific motivation techniques are necessary. A particularly elegant technique, appropriate for this type of client, is based on the "illusion of alternatives" principle (cf. Erickson & Rossi, 1975). The client is offered a choice of home assignments. The therapist does not say, "This week I suggest you do . . .," but, "There are two possible approaches and I'd like you to think about which would be more suitable." There are few clients who at that moment realize that there is a third and far more effective means of getting the better of the therapist, namely not choosing either.

The alternatives offered may differ widely. For example, the client may be given the choice of a relatively slow step-by-step approach, or a faster method, possibly with paradoxical intention. This may not always be part of a judo-like motivation, rather it may be a genuine effort on the part of the therapist to find out how the client would like to work. It is then more the application of the principle of negotiation which has a congruent character. However, if the therapist presents two explanations for an assignment based on exactly the same principles and has the sole purpose of giving the client the feeling that he himself is in charge, we may speak of a specific judo-like intervention.

The element of choice may be a matter of the time in which the patient is to do the assignment. The therapist may say, "Decide for yourself when you are ready for it. Definitely not now, but think about when you would like to do it." If the client comes back next session with the announcement that he or she is perfectly ready or has already done it, then it is the client's decision and not that of the therapist.

With clients who seem to call for judo-like means of motivation, giving detailed explanations and pointing out the importance of every step is not usually advisable. It may be best to refer to an intervention only indirectly and in passing (cf. van Dijck et al., 1980), e.g., "I had a relative with that problem and you know what he did . . .? but I don't think that would be right for you." The therapist is silent for a moment and then pursues another matter. There is a strong chance that the client will bring up the subject again. "That relative of yours, how did it end? Don't you think I should give it a try?" Depending on the client/therapist relationship, it may be necessary to hold back for a while and eventually "give in," allowing the client to set himself the assignment.

Some clients are not inclined to expend a great deal of energy on combatting their problems, for example, if they derive secondary gain from them in the form of attention from others and the therapist. For this reason they will deflate every form of support and positive labeling. With these people often it is helpful for the therapist to paint a very gloomy picture of the situation (cf. van Dijck et al., 1978). Before we saw an example of the use of negativity by the therapist where a client's general attitude was concerned, but it may also be necessary when introducing a specific intervention. Hoogduin & Druijf (1980) describe a number of examples of how the therapist can precede certain assignments with a speech on how badly things will end up if the clients do not make a concerted effort to carry out assignments and apply themselves to therapy. Another example is provided by Erickson (cf. Haley, 1973), who was treating a small boy with a "malicious streak." He gave the mother a curious assignment. She was to sit on her son for one whole day. Beforehand he described in some detail how the child would run wild and could even wind up in prison. Admittedly this is an extreme example, not suitable for everyday practice, but it does give an impression of the possibilities provided by *extrapolating into the future* (thanks are due to Kees van der Velden for suggesting this term). Telling clients how grim their prospects are without therapeutic intervention often motivates them to exert themselves for assignments or other aspects of therapy.

MOTIVATING FOR FAMILY THERAPY

So far only motivation techniques for directive therapy in general have been considered and categorized. This section deals with specific motivation techniques for directive *family* therapy. The central issue is how to motivate a family to participate in treatment when only one of its members has been referred. Often, the therapist has to consider whether to have one or more sessions with the patient alone and then decide if the rest of the family should participate, or whether to insist on having the whole family at the first session. I agree with Haley (1976) and Selvini Palazzoli et al. (1978) that it is particularly important to invite and motivate the whole family for the first session. This makes it possible from the outset to assess the following points in the family situation:

1) The degree to which the complaint of the referred patient has a function within the family;
2) The effect of the complaint on the rest of the family;
3) The sources of aid which exist within the family.

If family sessions are instituted at a later date, they are often problematic because a relationship has already been established between the therapist and the referred patient. The previous relationship plays a part in talks with the rest of the family. Furthermore, certain subjects have already been dealt with in detail and cannot easily be covered again. The reaction of the rest of the family has not been observed and this makes such talks awkward and unproductive. It is, therefore, of the utmost importance to have the largest possible relevant unit present at the first session.

How does one persuade a reluctant client to bring the rest of the family? Naturally, there are clients who are only too pleased when the person doing the intake over the telephone says, "I don't want to go into your problems too deeply now. I would rather talk first with your partner and children there too." The client may agree readily, expecting to be less isolated in this scenario. With this category of clients, motivation techniques are not extremely necessary. In most cases, however, one does come up against some resistance. In certain cases the client wants to bring the partner but not the children, and in others, neither. How does one motivate such families for a family session?

A number of techniques are available:

1) It is important to give clients an *explanation*. It should be emphasized that the rest of the family is being asked to come only to provide as much information as possible and not because they are regarded as the cause of the problems. A person with problems undoubtedly influences and is influenced by the other members of the family. As the therapist wants to work as cautiously as possible, it is necessary to know about this influence before therapy starts. This kind of explanation is often sufficient to get a client to ask the rest of his family to come to the assessment session.

2) The patient can be told that the initial contact involves *only one session*, after which there may be no need for further full family sessions. Therapy may be continued alone or with any subsystem of the family. Thus, being present at the first session does not imply further commitment. This fact alone removes a barrier. Motivation for future family sessions which may be necessary then takes place during the first session. If the clients find the first session beneficial it will not be difficult to get them back. If not, their reluctance is probably justified. In psychotherapy as elsewhere, quality is the best sales talk.

3) Sometimes clients will say that they are prepared to ask their families to come, but that they are certain one or more family members will refuse. In such cases it is advisable to discuss all the possible objections beforehand and to do a sort of *role playing* to model how to ask the rest of the family to come at least once. The emphasis will often be that they are coming to one session simply to be of assistance and as a special favor to the therapist. Very few people can resist this sort of appeal. Sometimes a client asks the members of his family to come and then telephones to say that one or the other has refused. If on closer inquiry it is apparent that the client has indeed done his or her best, the therapist can speak directly to the person in question. Frequently the objections are not all that serious, and the referred client has simply accepted a mildly negative response. Occasionally the client has not even really asked.

4) Perhaps the most fundamental requirement for motivation for family sessions is the therapist's conviction that the request is justifiable. "O.K., come alone if that's what you want" should not be said too quickly. If the therapist shows conviction, clients are more likely to cooperate than if they notice in the therapist's hesitations and tone of

voice the possibility of making him change his mind and agreeing to an individual session. Here again, confidence is vital for a positive outcome. We may speak of a "self-fulfilling prophecy;" therapists who expect their clients to follow their lead will seldom experience otherwise, while those who have doubt will often be faced with situations in which they cannot convince the referred client of the need to bring in the rest of the family.

DISCUSSION

From the above, one could conclude that motivating clients is simply a matter of applying the correct technique. It may be superfluous, but I should like to caution the reader explicitly: The techniques and principles presented are no more than aids which are effective only when a number of therapist variables are present. Some of these factors are: interest in the client, courtesy and respect, knowledge and an attitude of being prepared to stand behind the necessary therapeutic strategies. This is, of course, an arbitrary list which is neither objective nor exhaustive and serves only to place the above motivation techniques in the proper perspective.

Similarly, the categories presented are more a framework and an aid in considering motivation techniques than a system of mutually exclusive categories. The border line is not always sharply defined. Allowing a client to make minor amendments to a proposed home assignment may be depending on the existing therapeutic relationship, either congruent (have the character of negotiation) or judo-like. The same applies to how the importance of a certain assignment is stressed, and as shown before, the way in which a choice is offered. In directive therapy and directive family therapy there is no question of a set repertoire of motivation techniques to be used on all clients in all circumstances. I hope that this chapter has made clear that there are a variety of techniques available—sometimes quite contradictory—and that the decision of which to use depends on the situation, the type of complaints, the relationship between client and therapist and the stage therapy has reached.

REFERENCES

Dijck, R. van (1980a). Timing en motivering. In K. van der Velden (Ed.), *Directieve therapie 2.* Deventer: Van Loghum Slaterus.
Dijck, R. van (1980b). Modellen in psychotherapie. In K. van der Velden (Ed.), *Directieve therapie 2.* Deventer: Van Loghum Slaterus.

Dijck, R. van, van der Hart, O., Scharree, C., van der Velden, K. (1978). Negatief etiket-teren. *Tijdschrift voor directieve therapie, 5*, (4/5), 47-53.
Dijck, R. van, van der Velden, K., van der Hart, O. (1980). Een indeling van directieve interventies. In K. van der Velden (Ed.), *Directieve therapie 2*. Deventer: Van Loghum Slaterus.
Erickson, M.H., & Rossi, E.L. (1975). Varieties of the double bind. *American Journal of Clinical Hypnosis, 17*, 143-157.
Frank, J.D. (1976). Psychotherapy and the sense of mastery. In Spitzer & Klein (Eds.), *Evaluation of psychological therapies*. Baltimore: Johns Hopkins University Press.
Goldstein, A.P. (1975). Relationship-enhancement methods. In F.H. Kanfer & A.P. Goldstein (Eds.). *Helping people change*. New York: Pergamon Press.
Haley, J. (1963). *Strategies of psychotherapy*. New York: Grune & Stratton.
Haley, J. (1973). *Uncommon therapy*. New York: Norton.
Haley, J. (1976). *Problem-solving therapy*. San Francisco: Jossey-Bass.
Hoogduin, K., & Druijf, T. (1980). Directieve interventies bij de ambulente behandeling van psychosen. In K. van der Velden (Ed.), *Directive therapie 2*. Deventer: Van Loghum Slaterus.
Hoogduin, K., & van der Velden, K. (1978). De welwillende beproeving. *Tijdschrift voor directieve therapie, 4*, (4/5), 54-64.
Lange, A. (1977). Judo, oftewel het niet trekken aan cliënten. In K. van der Velden (Ed.), *Directieve therapie 1*. Deventer: Van Loghum Slaterus.
Lange, A. (1980). Timing. In K. van der Velden (Ed.), *Directieve therapie 2*. Deventer: Van Loghum Slaterus.
Lange, A. & van der Hart, O. (1983). *Directive family therapy*. New York: Brunner/Mazel.
Minuchin, S. (1974). *Families and family therapy*. Cambridge: Harvard University Press.
Rabkin, R. (1977). *Strategic psychotherapy*. New York: Basic Books.
Selvini Palazzoli, M., Boscolo, L., Cecchin, G., & Prata, G. (1978). *Paradox and counter-paradox*. New York: Jason Aronson.
Velden, K. van der, & van Dijck, R. (1977). Motiveringstechnieken. In K. van der Velden (Ed.), *Directieve therapie 1*. Deventer: Van Loghum Slaterus.

Chapter 6

Family Structure as Metaphor

George Stone

Milton Erickson was a master at indirectly inducing people to change through the use of metaphor. He was also interested in the social situation of his clients. In this chapter I discuss one aspect of his legacy: using the family structure in metaphoric ways to indirectly produce change in the behavior of family members.

Haley, a leader in the use of this technique, defines family structure as "the repeating acts among people" (1977, p. 105). Metaphor is a form of comparison between two things. For example, what one parent says of a child can be understood as a metaphor about the other parent as well as a statement about the child. A therapist can respond to the family in metaphor as well as listen to the metaphors they produce about themselves. This particular form of analogy can be called "structural metaphor" because it focuses upon implicit comparisons between family members.

Structural metaphor is a special form of a broad class of analogical communication. Haley (1981) credits Erickson with introducing new ways to use this class of communication to produce change (p. 169). Rather than make interpretations to his clients, Erickson spoke to the person in analogy. There are two requirements for therapy done in this way: First, A is discussed as an analogy to what one wishes to change in B. Second, in the discussion one must take a position on how A should be in order to change B. In Erickson's view the analogy is not as effective if the patient becomes aware of it.

When a parent says that a child cannot be "trusted," the therapist should be alerted to the possibility of "mistrust" as an issue between the parents as well as between the parent and child. The therapist would then talk to the parents about how they could solve this problem in their child. As the parents start to behave differently toward the child they will behave differently toward each other. The goal of this procedure is to indirectly influence the parents through focusing upon the child's presenting problems.

In this approach it is assumed that when a child displays a problem, especially a social problem, it is usually due to the way the parents are behaving towards each other. In this sense the parents are the target of the therapeutic procedures, although it is emphasized here that the focus of therapy is kept upon the child's presenting problems at all times.

STRUCTURAL METAPHOR AND THE SOCIAL SITUATION

To understand the social situation of individuals it is best to observe them with their intimates. This is a complex process, in which each message by each participant usually has multiple referents. When a family interacts together, there are certain classes of behavior which are helpful in guiding a therapist to an understanding of how that family uses analogies. Using these guides does not require the legendary powers of observation demonstrated by Erickson himself. For example, much can be gleaned by attending to pronouns used by family members. The ambiguous quality of a pronoun lends itself well to metaphoric expression. For example, "he" can stand for a particular male in the family, but it can also refer to all of the men in the family as well. The source of metaphoric comparison is the relationship between family members, and the use of open pronouns invites implicit comparisons.

Body movements found in association with pronouns are useful as well. Birdwhistell (1963) calls this class of movements "kinesic pronominal markers." He states that this class of movement is easily recognizable because the movements "are normally associated with or may be, in certain environments, *substituted for*, pronominals" (emphasis added) (1963, pp. 154-159).

In address or reference the proximal or distal movement of the head, eyes, hand, or finger is recognized by Birdwhistell as a kinesic pronominal marker. Movements of the leg or foot should be included in this class as well—at least for therapeutic purposes.

Proximal movements are found in association (or substitute for) the verbalizations, "I," "me," "us," "we," "this," "here," and "now." Distal movements of the same body parts are associated with (or substitute for) "he," "she," "it," "those," "they," "that," "than," "there," "any," and "some."

Some English sentences do not require accompanying kinesic pronominal movement. For instance, "The dog is barking" requires no markers. The utterance, "He's barking," requires a distal movement over the word "he." The English sentence, "I gave you the book" requires kinesic pronominal movement which would look like this: A proximal movement (toward myself) of the appropriate body part should occur over the "I" as it is uttered, and a distal movement (toward the location of you in space) should occur as the word "you" is spoken. That is, kinesic pronominal movement is patterned in association with certain English sentences.

The variations on this common pattern can be of therapeutic interest. One variation can be illustrated by repeating the sentence, "I gave you the book," while changing the kinesic pronominal movement slightly. One can make the expected proximal movement as the word "I" is spoken. However, more than one distal movement could be made as the word "you" is uttered. In other words, there can be many referents for the "you" involved. One can be offered by the verbal pronominal "you," and the second "you" can be offered by *pointing* toward the location of a different "you" than the one I am addressing verbally.

It is this incongruent use of kinesic pronominal that marks a metaphoric context. A therapist who observes this incongruent kinesic pronominal should consider it to be a context marker which has the meaning, "I am using metaphoric comparison now, in this situation." At a more direct level, such usage of the kinesic pronominal should be understood to mean, "I am inviting you, the therapist, to compare *implicitly* the two referents in my statement."

The notion of structural metaphor at the linguistic level alone is sufficient for therapists to identify the relationships to be compared, and for therapists to respond in therapeutic analogies as well. Kinesic pronominal data observed in addition to linguistic data simply provide a cross-referencing, which in turn provides increased confidence that metaphor is, indeed, being employed by family members at that moment.

Therapists can consciously use their own kinesic pronominal behavior to help influence family members out of their awareness. For example, when a mother talks about her son, a therapist can *assume* that she is talking about her husband as well. When she casually points toward her husband while talking about her son, a therapist can have more confidence that she is *really* using a structural metaphor to refer to both her son and her husband. Likewise, when a therapist answers her by talking about her son, he or she can point casually toward the husband over certain words to indicate to the woman that he or she hears and understands the mother's metaphors. The mother is likely to apply what the therapist says of her son to her husband as well. The metaphoric comparison is implicit, and therefore unconsciously performed. Only the therapist need be consciously aware of the process.

Structural metaphor with kinesic pronominal data can be compared to the artistic metaphor. Artists often present their audience with an explicitly described image, in the hope that their image will be compared with some (often unstated) object. The linguistic utterance should be considered the image half of the structural metaphor, while the kinesic pronominal should be considered the object half. This can be illustrated by an example drawn from a videotaped therapy session.

STRUCTURAL METAPHOR WITH KINESIC PRONOMINALS

A father made the following statement about his two teenage sons: "I expect them to do what they are told, when they are told, without any back-talk. And that's not what we get!" Over the word "that" he made a distal gesture with his left hand toward his wife. The movement is incongruent in at least two ways: 1) Over "that" it should indicate the location of the sons, not the wife; and 2) there is no accompanying proximal movement over "we" to indicate "my wife and I." Such a variation of kinesic pronominal patterning can be understood as an invitation to compare his relationship with his sons to his relationship with his wife. His explicit statements "about" his sons can be understood as the image half of a metaphor, while the kinesic pronominal toward his wife can be understood to mark her as the unstated object half of the metaphor. One issue between the couple could be that the wife does not do what the husband asks of her, and that she "back-talks" him in a way similar to his sons. I do not know this to be a fact, but I am alerted to the possibility that this is an issue for the father.

Almost at once the mother comments about her elder son, "He has a very bad attitude. Every time I ask him to do something he snaps at me." She marks both occurrences of the word "he" with kinesic pronominals indicating the location of her *husband* rather than her son. In this way she marks a metaphoric context, and invites me to compare her relationship with her son to that of her husband along the dimension of "attitude." From her point of view both her son and her husband have bad attitudes.

RESPONDING IN STRUCTURAL METAPHOR WITH KINESIC
PRONOMINALS

There are two levels of response that therapists can make to a family member in structural metaphor. At a general level therapists should just let the family members know that they hear and understand their metaphors (Haley, 1977, p. 32). This is done to encourage further metaphoric expression by the family members. In the case example given above a therapist could respond very generally to the mother by saying, "What do you do with a *fellow* who has an attitude like that?" The use of the ambiguous noun "fellow," rather than the more specific noun "son" or "John," should alert the mother that the therapist hears her communication and wishes to converse further in her language. When this is done properly, the mother is more likely to continue to describe her situation in metaphor.

Encouraging the use of metaphor in this way can provide a therapist with a very rapid assessment of the family situation. When the issues in that particular family are clear to the therapist (but not necessarily to the family) structural metaphor can be used in more specific ways. For example, in the situation described above I actually responded to the mother's statement about her elder son by saying, "A boy learns a lot from his mother. He needs to learn how to show affection, but he also needs to learn how to show respect." Her immediate response was, "That's what bothers me. He doesn't [show respect]."

Through my use of an ambiguous pronoun "he" I presented her with an implicit definition of the situation which could be applied to her husband as well as to her son. Note also that I took the position in relation to the metaphor, "He also needs to learn to show respect." The explicit position I took in relation to what the boy should do could be applied to the father as well. The statement, "A boy learns a lot from his mother," implies that the mother should teach her son to show respect, and therefore a comparison of husband with son implies that mother should teach her husband as well to be more respectful. The position taken in my metaphor is a metaphoric directive to the mother.

Just as the mother made it easier for me to grasp her metaphors by using kinesic pronominals, I attempted to make my usage easier for her (but not for her conscious awareness) to grasp by using kinesic pronominals incongruently. When I said the word "boy" I marked her son properly with a congruent kinesic pronominal. However, with both occurrences of the word "he" I shifted my kinesic pronominals to indicate the location of her husband. The movements marking this shift were done casually.

By listening and watching I formed a hypothesis about one aspect of this family's situation. My intervention, based on the notion of structural metaphor, aimed at 1) defining the problem situation indirectly, and 2) making an indirect suggestion to the mother to "do" something about it. This procedure was applied to the father as well as the mother, and the focus of therapy was kept upon the boys' problems at all times. At one point both parents stated that they felt like they had "failed" as parents. I declined this invitation to shift from the children to explore the parental relationship by saying, "I don't think you have failed." And then I listed the boys' positive attributes, and said that their sons' problems were the result of a stage the boys' were going through in growing up. The parents accepted this and stopped talking as if they were failures. I continued to discuss their relationship to each other through structural metaphors derived from their relationships to their children.

Using structural metaphor to create indirect change in the parents is important because it protects the parents from unnecessary criticism while at the same time moving them toward new behaviors. In the case reported above, the problems presented by the parents around the teenage boys disappeared, while at the same time the parental relationship improved. A four-year follow-up contact indicates that these positive changes have been stable.

THE ABSURD TASK AS METAPHORIC CONTEXT MARKER

Like a kinesic pronominal, a special task assignment or directive can mark a metaphoric context. Madanes (personal communication, 1978) maintains that when a person in therapy produces a non sequitur, a therapist should understand this to mean, "What we are talking about now is not 'really' what we are talking about." In other words, a non sequitur should alert a therapist to the possibility that metaphor is being employed by the speaker. As noted above, it is also helpful for therapists to alert the family members when *they* employ metaphor as well. Absurdities in an assigned task can accomplish this goal.

Watzlawick, Weakland, and Fisch (1974, pp. 142-146) developed what they call "benevolent sabotage" which they prescribe to the parents of problem children. Parents are instructed to put crackers in the child's bed, or starch the child's laundry, and then are told to pretend that the event was accidental. Such a solution to a serious problem is absurd, and yet it is being offered by a professional person, in a serious way, as the solution to the problem. It seems that the absurdity of this kind of task makes a statement about the context in which it occurs: It invites the parents to search the request (and others in the context) for new or comparative meanings. The absurdity forces the parents to begin to think (or continue to think) in metaphoric ways.

In addition to marking metaphoric contexts, a well-placed absurd task also functions at a direct level: It should alter the sequence of events, the parental solutions which have maintained the problem behavior in the situation, or other sequences such as parental disagreement.

I used ideas from "benevolent sabotage" to treat the case described above. That is, I asked this mother to put crackers in her sons' beds whenever they were disrespectful to her. She did not like this idea and said, "I'm not that kind of person, I don't like revenge." I insisted that she do this task for at least one week, and then I assumed a stance advocated by Madanes (personal communication, 1978): "I want you to do this because I think everybody needs a harmless way to get back at someone." In effect, this stance can be seen as a position in my metaphor, "You should get back at *both* your son and your husband in the harmless way of putting crackers in their beds."

The mother was still unhappy with this task and turned to her husband for his help. The videotape indicates that the couple had their first reasonable discussion of the therapy at the moment this task was assigned; that is, they talked together in a positive way, and this altered their habitual sequence of events. The father concluded the discussion by saying, "I know you don't like this! They aren't supposed to like it either! But if it will work it's worth it! [long pause, and then spoken almost as an aside] Just so you don't put crackers *in my shoes* when I leave them out!" This almost humorous aside shows how clearly the father realized the consequences for *him* if the mother really did the task. Yet, his joking manner indicated that this knowledge was more or less out of his awareness.

The parents went home and talked this over further on their own. In spite of having promised me that they would do this task, they reached agreement on something else that proved effective in disciplining their sons. They reported to me two weeks later that they thought my idea was stupid, and "how can we teach our kids to be adult-types if we act so childish?" The presenting problems were resolved and the couple's relationship strengthened. This was done outside of the parents' awareness, and thus they did what was needed, while at the same time they were protected from undue criticism.

CLEARING THE TABLE: STRUCTURAL METAPHOR WITHOUT KINESIC
PRONOMINALS

The final section of this chapter will illustrate the use of structural metaphor by itself. Kinesic pronominal data are not relevant in this case because only one member of the family, the mother, was seen after the first interview. Proximal and distal movements such as I have described here are not easily applicable to individuals in session.

The mother of this family of four presented her 13-year-old son as a glue sniffer and discipline problem. He went places he was not supposed to go with boys he was not supposed to be with. He also made a mess around the house, and he refused to do his clean-up chores unless he was very closely supervised by the mother. His 11-year-old sister also contributed to the mess, but she was not presented as a problem. Based on this information provided by the mother I assumed that the problems with her son were "like" her problems with her husband. That is, the husband probably went to places of which she did not approve, with people of whom she did not approve, and he probably messed up the house much like his son. These two notions were verified later in therapy. But the idea that the boy's glue-sniffing problem paralleled a similar problem in the father was not substantiated.

In addition to problems that the mother felt were "in" the boy, the mother reported that the father had switched the boy "until he was black and blue" after the last episode of glue sniffing. The father also smashed the boy's new guitar, and confiscated his TV, stereo, and tape recorder. The father refused to join the mother in therapy because, as she put it, "He just can't admit that he can't handle a 13-year-old boy!" I took this statement "as if" it meant that neither father nor mother would like to admit to anyone that they have trouble handling their marital relationship.

Therefore, I formed a plan to see the mother alone and to use structural metaphor to induce change in both parents indirectly, through her. If this initial approach failed to achieve results in one month I planned to contact the father personally and invite him into the therapy to help his son over this serious problem. In the first session the mother gave the following account of the events leading up to the beating:

My husband was gone to work; he holds three jobs. My daughter was visiting a friend. My son wanted to go with her, but I kept him at home with me because I was afraid that he would get into trouble if I let him go. It was Saturday afternoon, and I was just lying there leafing through a magazine in my bedroom. My son came in and just turned around and left. He came back into my room in about 10-15 minutes and just reeked of glue. I knew it had to be in his room because he hadn't left the apartment. So, I jumped up and dragged him in there to look for it. I watched him as I looked for the glue, and when he got fidgety I knew I was getting warm. When I found the glue I called his father. His father rushed right home from work and cut a switch. I said, "Don't do that!" He told me he would handle it his way, and if I didn't like it he would go back to work and I could take care of everything myself. It was after he switched the boy so terrible that I came in here.

This is an unusually clear description of a sequence of events by a participant in the sequence. The sequence can be described by a series of commands like a computer program:

1) Father is absent or distant, go to line 2.
2) Boy remains at home close to his mother because of problem, go to line 3.
3) Mother communicates sadness or depression to son, go to line 4.
4) Son sniffs glue in a way that he will be discovered, go to line 5.
5) Crisis activates mother to signal father for help, go to line 6.
6) Father returns to help, go to line 7.
7) Mother criticizes way father deals with son, go to line 8.
8) Boy behaves, go to line 9.
9) If mother and father agreed, go to line 10, if not, go back to line 1.
10) Go on with life.

This family is caught up in a repeating cycle of events, and it will take someone from "outside" the system to alter the sequence. In computer program language this kind of repetitive cycle is called an "infinite loop" of the "repeat until" variety. In this kind of a program the loop repeats infinitely *until* some new condition obtains, or until it is broken up by an "interrupt function." The job of the therapist is to push the parents together, and thereby create the condition necessary for them to escape the loop. Metaphoric comparison and directive help move people together without labeling them defective for being apart in the first place.

In this case the mother was told in the initial session that there is a "sure cure for his problem," and she would be told what it was next week provided she promised to do exactly as she was told *before* she knew what she would be told. Meanwhile, she was asked to "take over *his* discipline yourself." She was asked not to call her husband in for help.

In setting up this intervention, I was careful to protect the father, even though he was not present. To do this I used a variation of a procedure taught by Madanes (personal communication, 1978; 1984, p. 20) for uses in abuse/neglect situations. To protect the father, blame for the abuse was placed upon the child in a benign way. I said, "Your husband was probably half-mad with worry over this glue-sniffing business." In this way the husband's abusive acts were reframed as coming from his desperate concern for the son's welfare, rather than the father's pathology, or a hatred of the mother at that moment. The mother and I agreed to stop this boy's problems without resort to further violence. When violent solutions are blocked in a positive way, it becomes easier to find more productive behaviors to replace them.

I gave the mother the idea that there was a cure for "his" problem; at the same time I asked her to take over "his" discipline. Since this was said of the son, my hope was that the mother would make an implicit comparison between her son and her husband, and that she would take over "disciplining" both of these fellows. This task assignment also operates as an "interrupt function" and alters the sequence of acts 1 through 9 at number 5. If the wife takes over the full discipline of her son and does not call in her husband for help, the sequence will be altered. If the husband does not come in to help, he is not likely to beat the boy again. Therefore, the boy is "safer" in this situation than before the task was assigned.

Therapy is successful when it helps resolve or significantly improve the presenting problem. As such changes are occurring, there are various cues to guide the therapist en route. In the second session of this case, one week later, the two most serious problems of glue sniffing and abuse had not recurred. However, the boy had been a discipline problem and had not done his clean-up. The improvement in the presenting problems was considered evidence that the therapy was on the right track and that the plan should be continued.

I urged the mother to continue to "discipline *him* yourself." And then I presented her with the benevolent sabotage of Watzlawick et al. (1974) as the "sure cure" for the problems at hand. Whenever the boy sniffed glue or whenever he misbehaved, the mother was instructed to "put crackers in his bed, and starch his underwear stiff." She reluctantly agreed to keep her word and do these things, and the remainder of the session was spent on such practical matters as, "Do you have crackers and starch on hand at home?"

In the third session the mother gave the following account:

Mother: I'm really surprised, but I'm very pleased. Miracle of miracles! I don't know what is happening in my house but I like it! I went straight out last week and got my crackers and starch; haven't had to use them one time. I can't believe it!

All the presenting problems except the clean-up problem cleared up, and clean-up improved significantly. Change accelerated after the assignment of the benevolent (absurd) sabotage. The mother emphasized that she "didn't know what was happening" in her house.

I remained skeptical:

Therapist: I'm sorry that that's happened. I wish you would have had a chance to use this procedure.
Mother: Well, they'll slide. I mean it *can't* go on. After all these years it can't go on. Even my husband is participating (pause) in cleaning up.

Her statement, "even my husband is participating," ratifies a goal set for the therapy two weeks earlier, namely, to involve indirectly a distant father in the change process through metaphoric focus on a child's presenting problem. Moreover, the father is "participating" in "cleaning up," which is a first hint he might mess up as well.

The mother continued to talk about her son briefly, then abruptly shifted to her husband:

Mother: He told me—he's smart as he can be—he said, "Mom I can see what Dad's doing. As I progress and show him that he can trust me, I think he'll eventually give my stuff back." So he got his TV set back last night. And my husband rekeys locks, so naturally the dining room table is covered with locks and cylinders and all that stuff. Well, my husband says, "I'll pick this up when you give me a place to put it."

This statement is important in at least two ways. First, this seems to be an interesting variation of structural metaphor used by the mother. There is a need to let me know what the issues are from the father's point of view, yet the father is not present. I think the mother contrives to give her husband's view by reporting what *her son* says to her. Her report of the boy's statement, ". . . show him that he can trust me," indicates that trust is an issue between father and son. If this is so, trust may be an issue between father and mother as well. It was no surprise, therefore, to learn later that the mother often threatened to leave the father. She did this indirectly, and usually qualified it by saying that she would only "move into my daughter's room." The father probably did not trust her to stay with him, or was uncertain about it in some way.

The mother made several indirect threats to leave her husband in the third session. No comment was made on these threats, and no effort was made to explore this issue or change it at that time.

Second, it is learned that the husband rekeys locks and "naturally" renders the dining room table unusable as a result. This ratifies the original assumption about the metaphoric nature of the presenting problem: the boy messes up the house, and so does his father. The crucial question is what has the mother done about this problem since therapy began? The mother's next statement continues the topic of the locked up table:

Mother: So I cleaned my desk out and said, "There! Take it! Just get that stuff off the table!" And he says, "Well, I'll come home tomorrow evening and I'll really clean it up. I'll put some in my closet." I said, "You can't get anything else in there!" So he says, "Well, tomorrow I'll take some things over to the shop." He didn't disagree or anything. I'm really surprised! We had a long serious talk the other day. . . .

The mother makes it clear that the father has begun to clean up because she pushed him on this issue. This is a ratification of the original therapeutic structural metaphor in which she was asked to "take over *his* discipline." She has done with her husband what I asked her to do with her son—and subsequently the presenting problems are gone or improved. The couple has begun to talk directly with each other, rather than talk through the children.

The husband had cleaned the dining room table that week, as he had promised. I asked the mother what she was going to do with her "new table." After a short, thoughtful pause she replied, "Well, we could eat off of it." In this way I learned that this family of four ate in their small kitchen in shifts, since the kitchen table was small and had only two chairs. The next week the mother began to serve meals in the dining room, and the family began to take their evening meal together for the first time in more than a year. Within several weeks the parents began to eat out several times a week, both with and without their children. The father dropped one of his three jobs, and began spending a great deal more time with the family, especially with his son. He also stopped spending so much time playing his musical instrument with friends.

The mother's disciplining of the father opened up new sequences for the couple and their children. Although none of the presenting problems recurred after the third session, the mother presented a special challenge at that time: She based her "discipline" on the premise that she would leave if her husband did not do what she asked. This is not a suitable foundation for lasting change, even if it is acceptable to get changes started. These threats by the mother were dealt with indirectly in the fourth session.

Perhaps needing a metaphor for expressing her situation to me, the mother brought up a problem in her extended family. She related that her sister-in-law had frequently run away from her husband's brother. During one of these flights she had taken their son (who was the same age as the boy in treatment with me) with her. Unfortunately, the car she was driving crashed; she was killed and her son seriously injured. He recovered from his injuries, but he was "never the same again." I took this story as the image half of a structural metaphor which invited me to compare this mother's situation with that of her sister-in-law. As her sister-in-law left her husband, so did this mother threaten to leave her own husband.

I responded to this story by taking a position on what the sister-in-law had done to solve her problems; that is, I took a stance that clearly put the sister-in-law's behavior in an undesirable light. I told the mother, "While I don't want to disparage the memory of your dead relative, wearing out a suitcase packing and unpacking it is *the worst possible way* to solve that kind of problem." I spent about 15 minutes disparaging this suitcase solution to my client. The mother promptly dropped her threats to leave her husband, and the couple continued to improve their relationship. I saw the mother for two more sessions to make sure that the change was stable, and then terminated the therapy.

Therapy comprised six sessions over two months. The presenting problems were all resolved, and the parental relationship substantially improved. I knew of improvements on both these levels because I continued to keep the focus upon the son during the therapy. Yet, in each session she would also talk about her husband, and I would always listen with interest. I did not provide any kind of direct help during these discussions. I thought of her references to her husband as tangential, like the kind reported by Erickson to Haley (1973, pp. 249-256). In this therapy we were "really" talking about her son, so it was safe for her to make a tangential remark about her *husband*. When I intervened indirectly, as with the table, I was not doing so in relation to helping her with her husband, but rather with her son.

A one-year follow-up indicated that these changes were stable, and that the presenting problems had not recurred. I left the drug treatment center about one year after this case. A two-year follow-up contact indicated that the mother had returned to the center for therapy with her husband. At that time she felt that she was *potentially* abusive. Both of these problems were resolved by another therapist at that agency.

A recent five-year follow-up contact with the mother indicates that the changes gained through both therapies have been stable. She and her husband have remained together in a good relationship. The son graduated from high school, and has been employed full-time over the last two years. There have been no further problems with him.

It is most intriguing to me that during this follow-up discussion the mother thanked me several times for "teaching us the importance of communicating together." In fact this had never been done directly, but her perspective five years later was that it had been done successfully, and she talked openly and consciously about it. I did not share my theory that all I had done was arrange the situation so that the mother could use her native ability to communicate, and that I had taught her nothing about "how to do it." I played down my part and emphasized how her hard work had paid off.

The positive results of the initial therapeutic effort can be summarized as follows:

1) The presenting problems were eliminated and did not recur over a five-year period.
2) The marriage improved greatly over the one-and-a-half-year period following therapy. And when the mother returned to therapy the father came in with her.
3) Although the *question* of abuse came up again in relation to the mother, this was resolved without the occurrence of actual abuse.
4) The positive changes within the family have lasted at least five years.

The initial handling of the case probably influenced the father to become involved in the later therapy, the success of which may have been related to his presence.

CONCLUSION

This chapter discussed the use of structural metaphor in therapy. Structural metaphor is a special class of analogy which makes implicit comparisons between two or more members of the family group. The idea of structural metaphor did not originate with this author. However, several contributions to the theory are made here. First, an application of kinesic pronominal markers has been demonstrated for therapy. The use of kinesic pronominals with structural metaphor in this way is an original contribution. The value of kinesic pronominal data is that it is easy to learn to use, and very helpful in listening to metaphors and in marking therapeutic metaphors.

Second, while Haley (1973, 1977, 1981) has emphasized the importance of taking a position in therapeutic metaphor, the importance of position in *structural* metaphor has not received extensive treatment. This chapter reviews the general notion of position, describes how to take a position in structural metaphor, and provides guidelines for assessing client response to therapeutic metaphor. For example, by taking a position on how a mother should treat her son, a therapist also can give the mother an implicit directive on how she should treat her husband. If the therapist told her directly what he wanted her to do in relation to her husband, she might simply refuse.

Third, the introduction of benevolent sabotage into a context in which structural metaphor is being used seems particularly potent, perhaps because of the absurdity of the task. When parents are directed to do something absurd to their child (and, indirectly, to their mate), they often end up doing something more reasonable—and of *their* own choice.

Finally, two cases were presented to illustrate these ideas. Each case presented a different problem, yet structural metaphor and benevolent sabotage were used in each with positive results, which were shown to have endured over time.

REFERENCES

Birdwhistell, R. (1963). Movement with speech. In B. Jones (Ed.), *Kinesics and context* (pp. 110-128). Philadelphia: University of Pennsylvania Press.
Haley, J. (1973). *Uncommon therapy: The psychiatric techniques of Milton H. Erickson, M.D.* New York: Norton.
Haley, J. (1977). *Problem-solving therapy*. San Francisco: Jossey-Bass.
Haley, J. (1981). The contributions to therapy of Milton H. Erickson. In J. Haley (Ed.), *Reflection on therapy and other essays* (pp. 151-173). Chevy Chase, MD: Family Therapy Institute of Washington, D.C.
Madanes, C. (1984). *Behind the one-way mirror: Advances in the practice of strategic therapy*. San Francisco: Jossey-Bass.
Watzlawick, P., Weakland, J., & Fisch, R. (1974). *Change: Principles of problem formation and problem resolution*. New York: Norton.

Chapter 7

Prescribing Rituals in Family Therapy: Mrs. Piggle-Wiggle Meets Milton Erickson

George A. Sargent

By incorporating the language, behavior, and symbolism of ritual into family therapy, an entire cultural history of curative experience can be summoned into the present (Seltzer & Seltzer, 1983; Selvini Palazzoli et al., 1974, 1977; van der Hart, 1983). Rituals can change interactions and provide linkages with old "hypnotic" structures. They can rearrange unconscious patterns and lend power from the collective past to the therapist working on current problems.

Tracing the anthropological roots of ritual to different times, contexts and cultures, van der Hart (1983) shows that ritual prescription in therapeutic situations can be a potent change-producing device and elucidates guiding principles for designing and prescribing rituals in psychotherapy. In regard to traditional rituals, he distinguishes between rituals of transition (often tied to marking changes in the life cycle, such as leaving home) and rituals of continuity (activities that perpetuate social groupings, or ongoing cultural practices like holiday celebrations, birthdays, and anniversaries). Rituals are "prescribed symbolic acts, or a series of acts, which must be performed in a certain order, and may or may not be accompanied by verbal formulas" (van der Hart, 1983, p. 5). Rituals must be performed with emotional involvement by the participants, or else they become meaningless and empty (Plaut, 1975).

When traditional rituals are not available, or when they have been performed without useful effect, then a prescribed, uniquely designed therapeutic ritual can be useful (van der Hart, 1981). Examples of such ritual prescriptions from the work of Mrs. Piggle-Wiggle and Milton Erickson will be used to highlight principles and properties.

MRS. PIGGLE-WIGGLE

Unlike Milton Erickson, Mrs. Piggle-Wiggle, the fictional and eccentric parent helper of author Betty MacDonald (1947), lived in a topsy-turvy house (Bodin & Bodin, 1976). As a child lying in bed staring at the ceiling, she often had wondered what it would be like to live in an upside-down house. As an adult she built a house where everything structural (with certain convenient exceptions like the stairs) was inverted. The neighborhood children would use the chandelier in the dining room as a campfire, sitting around it and telling ghost stories. (Mrs. Piggle-Wiggle was pleased that her chandelier was the only one in town that was put to good use.) The sloped ceilings, which were on the floor, of course, made excellent sliding boards, and so on (MacDonald, 1947).

Cookies were always baking, and children were very much in evidence around Mrs. Piggle-Wiggle's house. They adored her. She understood the ways of children and never lost her appreciation of what it was like to be a child. Small wonder that parents called her when their children had problems they as parents didn't understand, especially since she seemed to have all the solutions. In the second of the four books (MacDonald, 1949) about Mrs. Piggle-Wiggle, she actually had witchlike magical powers; in all the others she only seemed to have magical power because her family problem-solving was so effective.

MILTON ERICKSON

Milton Erickson didn't live in an upside-down house, but he liked creating structures upside down and backwards, and he enjoyed observing the different perspectives such changed contexts provided. As a child bedridden with polio he made a habit of listening to and watching the most subtle behaviors of those around him. As a result of this and a lifetime of study, he understood people and the intricacies of human nature. Small wonder many people called him when they encountered problems they didn't understand and couldn't solve, especially since he seemed to have the "magic" to make things change. Many people thought of Milton Erickson, the professional therapist, as a kind of modern-day wizard.

As far as we know, Dr. Erickson and Mrs. Piggle-Wiggle never knew each other (J. Haley, personal communication, February 19, 1983; Erickson, Elizabeth, personal communications, June 25 and June 27, 1983). Lenthall (1975) brought them together in an article on the similarities between Mrs. Piggle-Wiggle's nonprofessional approaches and the nontraditional practices and ideas of Milton Erickson and Gregory Bateson. However, the use of ritual prescription in therapy was not specifically described by Lenthall; apparently, Mrs. Piggle-Wiggle's work in training family therapy professionals is not yet complete.

THE SLOW-EATER-TINY-BITE-TAKER-CURE

One day Allen, a boy who in all other ways seemed quite normal, virtually stopped eating. Despite his mother's concerned prompting, he refused to eat more than a few grains of cereal in the morning, or do much more than float crackers on his favorite soup at lunch. At the evening meal Allen cut his meat into the smallest bits imaginable. When his father offered to bring him a magnifying glass, Allen simply smiled and said, "I guess I'm just a slow eater. I choke if I take larger bites" (MacDonald, 1947, p. 93).

The next day Allen's mother called some of her friends to see if they had any problems with their children like those she was having with Allen. Mrs. Crankminor couldn't get her daughter to *stop* eating. Mrs. Wingsproggle had trouble getting her Pergola to chew everything one hundred times. Patsy's mother simply suggested she call Mrs. Piggle-Wiggle, which Allen's mother did immediately. Allen had not eaten a tablespoon of food in the last two days.

"So Allen has become a Slow-Eater-Tiny-Bite-Taker, has he?" said Mrs. Piggle-Wiggle. "I'll send over the Slow-Eater-Tiny-Bite-Taker dishes. He'll be all right in a day or two, although he may get a little pale" (pp. 95-96). Mrs. Piggle-Wiggle gave Allen's mother explicit instructions on the order in which she was to serve Allen his meals on the dishes. She was to use the largest dish and cup for dinner that night, the medium-sized set for the next day and the small set for the following day. By the fourth day he would be using the tiny set, with a plate the size of a penny, a cup that would hold only a drop, a fork like a needle and a spoon like a pin. At first Allen was delighted. His eating pattern became even more deliberate and focused on cutting and picking. He went from pale white to pale green and by the fourth day he was so weak that he had to crawl into breakfast on his hands and knees, with only a sick smile for his mother.

The telephone rang. It was Mrs. Piggle-Wiggle reminding Allen it was his turn to exercise the spotted pony. Although he was delighted, Allen was too exhausted to walk there on his own, so his mother pulled him in his red wagon and two of his friends laid him across Spotty's back like a sack of cornmeal. By lunchtime Allen had headed the pony for home and rolled off the pony onto the grass and lay crying. As he and his mother discussed the problem—including the fact that he wouldn't have the chance to ride Spotty again for a long time—his mother told him it was all due to his becoming a Slow-Eater-Tiny-Bite-Taker. If he would eat, he could gain enough strength to ride Spotty that afternoon. Allen was carried limply into the breakfast nook. Soon his mother handed him the smallest cup and instructed him to drink it in one gulp. The two cracker crumbs on the penny plate he was to put into his mouth all at once. He did. She handed him the next larger set of dishes (with the doll cup and plate) with a little soup and cottage cheese. "Drink the soup right down," she said, "and here is a large fork and I want that cottage cheese eaten in two bites!" Before he was finished Allen had gone through all four sets of plates and cups and was sitting up and asking his mother for more food; she made it for him. As he rode off that afternoon on Spotty, his mother had him drop the basket of Slow-Eater-Tiny-Bite-Taker dishes off at Mrs. Piggle-Wiggle's.

SYMBOLISM AND METAPHOR IN RITUAL BEHAVIOR

"Metaphors provide organizing images which ritual action puts into effect," writes Fernandez (1977, p. 101). "This ritualization of metaphor enables the persons participating in ritual to undergo apt integrations and transformations in their experience." While it is true that strategic-systemic therapists have typically eschewed interpreting insight to clients in their approach to change, they have not ignored the meaning of the symptom when constructing their interventions. One of the more compelling aspects of rituals, in this regard, is that they address so many levels of experience simultaneously.

Fasting is often a part of transition rituals. Food, as a symbol, is often shared, sanctified, or set aside, as a metaphor of nourishment or worldliness incorporated or temporarily abandoned (van der Hart, 1981). Timing of eating, or the order in which food should be eaten, even the portion size, are often carefully circumscribed symbols in traditional rituals.

"I guess I'm just a slow eater," said Allen, "I choke if I take bigger bites." Perhaps Allen's self-selected metaphor can be seen as suggesting that he has trouble swallowing the potential nutrition available in his household. He would rather "starve" than choke on a bigger bite. A problem that all children cope with, of course, is how much to "eat" of mother's or father's "food." The anorectic, for example, is often seen as making her stand on the issue of food simply because it is the last bastion of "self" possible. She may have to swallow everything *but* food. Certainly a trace of such a metaphor lies in Allen's unexplained (or at least unexplored) refusal. He may not yet be anorectic—few, if any, of the childrens' symptoms in Mrs. Piggle-Wiggle are described as pathological—but he *is* weakened, pale, and failing.

If the reader can allow such an understanding of Allen's metaphor, then the ritual required by his mother when he decides he *wants* to eat also can be understood metaphorically. "You can eat now" (I allow you again to take in our nourishment) "but I suggest you take small bites to begin with" (don't bite off more than you can chew). Gradually she resumes parental control by telling him how to eat, and even by finally helping him to break out of her ritual by eating beyond the special plates. The ritual pattern is broken and, for both, no longer required. Allen has demonstrated his ability to discriminate, chew, change speed of assimilation, and survive. His mother has demonstrated the benevolence of her authority as well as her willingness to accept his metaphor of growth and independence. By working through the mother, Mrs. Piggle-Wiggle has minimized the period of her intervention as well as limited the dependence created by it. The family system is successfully functioning again without her help. They can return the dishes (a task delegated to Allen and one he graciously accepts).

DISCUSSION

In the Slow-Eater-Tiny-Bite-Taker cure, we have an excellent example of the work of Mrs. Piggle-Wiggle. It is typical that her help is sought, in desperation, by the parent (mother) or parents (Lenthall, 1975), and typically she knows the child involved, pleasantly frames her relationship to that child when speaking to the parents, and responds in such a way that conveys that the cure will be rather simple though anxiety-provoking for some days. By responding "Oh, so Allen has become Slow-Eater-Tiny-Bite-Taker, has he," she lays claim to her reputation as having had great experience. Clearly she has dealt with such problems before, because she will send over the Slow-Eater-Tiny-Bite-Taker dishes. By suggesting that he may become a little pale before he is "cured," she is reassuring the parents, predicting a worsening of symptoms, and getting ready to prescribe the curative ritual by gaining their commitment to "the guaranteed cure." But the genius and core of the change effort lies in her knowledge that by rearranging the sequences of Allen's already ritualized eating, the parents can make the ritual their own, and Allen will have to give up the symptom or become enslaved by it. True, the giving of the progressively smaller dishes and portions of food to Allen can also be seen as "prescribing the symptom" (Haley, 1963), and having him use the progressively smaller plates in reverse sequence as a "deviation-counteracting process" (Hoffman, 1971), but the concept of ritual integrates these pattern-focused ideas with greater elegance.

Mrs. Piggle-Wiggle also makes a second significant intervention beyond the prescription of a ritual. When she called on the fourth day to offer Allen the opportunity to ride the pony for the day, she was establishing the turning point for his symptom. Although she did not do this type of second intervention in all of her cases, she was typically ready to do so (Lenthall, 1975, p. 380). Just as Milton Erickson was ready to follow up his first intervention with a second, third or fourth until he found a cure (Haley, 1982), so is she.

Both Erickson and Mrs. Piggle-Wiggle developed a gift for knowing (or predicting) whether follow-up intervention would be needed. From a ritual perspective, one could suggest that their gift was related to their understanding human nature and the natural history of family life. Erickson's habit of diagnosing problems as stuck transitions from one life cycle stage to another enhanced his appreciation of the need for rituals and, perhaps, helped him predict when a second intervention would be required.

Ordinarily, the consequences of prescribing the symptom and having the parents stop trying "more of the same treatment" are enough of an ordeal that the children themselves voluntarily give up their problematic behavior. In "The Radish Cure," Patsy—who seems to be avoiding a purification ritual—finally *begs* for a bath when she sees little radish leaves sprouting from her dirty arms and forehead. Mrs. Piggle-Wiggle had instructed her parents to plant radish seeds in the dirt that would naturally accumulate on her because of her refusal to bathe. In "The Selfishness Cure," Dick Thompson pleads with his mother not to continue making signs that say "Dick's sandwiches—Don't touch," or "Dick's apple—Don't touch," or "Dick's lunchbox—Don't touch." Even though at first he was pleased to have his possessions labeled with "Don't touch" signs and to have his toys locked up, the natural consequences of having the school children make fun of him were so unpleasant he eventually gave up his selfishness. When his father saw him finally sharing his toys with friends and his dessert with the dog, he packed up Mrs. Piggle-Wiggle's Selfishness Kit, with all the padlocks, keys, name labels, and stickers, and had Dick return it the next day (MacDonald, 1947).

In her Foreword to van der Hart (1983), Peggy Papp discusses possible reasons why such rituals have a beneficial effect:

> Since rituals make use of the stuff that dreams are made of—symbolism, fantasy, myths, and metaphors, they address themselves to the most primitive and profound level of experience. This is also the level where resistance to change lies, where emotional impasses from the past block new resolutions to problems. This level is difficult to reach as it is beyond awareness and usually remains immune to logical explanations or interpretations. It is this primitive level of experience that is reached by the therapeutic rituals, and it is on this level that change takes place. . . .One can only wonder why the mental health profession has only recently begun to tap the power of this immense and natural source of healing. (p. vii)

RITUALS IN STRATEGIC THERAPY

As Haley (1973) noted, "When one examines the ways Erickson deals with the problem of weaning parents and children from each other, it would appear that he sees therapy at this stage as an 'initiation ceremony.' Most cultures have such ceremonies, and they function not only to allow the young person to shift to the status of an adult, but also to require his parents to deal with him as an adult. . . .If a culture lacks such a ceremony, then an intervention by a therapist becomes the ritual that disengages child from parent" (p. 254).

Haley described the traditional ritual in India designed to help both sons and mothers successfully disengage from each other at the critical life stage. It begins when the son is about five years old. Each year the mother, supervised by the home guru, sacrifices "little fruits of which she is very fond" (p. 255). She is to increase the size and preciousness of the sacrifice each year until the natural fruit sacrifices are made from metals: iron, then copper, then bronze, and finally gold. The last and most extreme stage of the sacrifice is a total fast and a ceremony attended by the guru, the relatives, and the household servants, where the mother finally gives her son to the world, although she would like to keep him forever.

If a ritual of transition for an event such as leaving home is not available in a culture, then a uniquely designed ritual may need to be performed. I remember one such ritual that my mother performed on my twenty-first birthday. With great ceremony she presented me with an elegantly wrapped gift about the size of a tie box. I unwrapped it, opened the box and stared curiously at the two pieces of flowered material about 14 inches long. I looked up questioningly at her. "My apron strings," she said with a big smile, kissed me and walked away.

It is necessary to consider the parents (and siblings) as well as the adolescent in the construction of a complete ritual so that all parties can reorient their lives without feeling such a vacuum that they rush back together to fill it. An example from Erickson highlights this point as he worked with a 70-year-old mother and her 50-year-old schizophrenic son. They were constantly together, and yet the mother complained she wanted the son to grow up. Erickson instructed the mother, in her son's presence, to drive out into the desert and take him and a good book. At a deserted point she was to let him out, drive three miles down the road, sit out in the sunshine and, reading the book, wait for him to walk to her. He said, "Now listen, your son is going to fall down, he's going to crawl on his hands and knees, he's going to wait out there helplessly to stir up your sympathies. But on that road there will be no passersby, and the only way he can reach you is by walking. He might try to punish you by making you sit there and wait for five hours. But remember, you have a good book, and he's out on that ground for a period of time. He'll get hungry" (Haley, 1973, pp. 253-254).

Of course the son eventually straggled up and the mother told him how she had enjoyed reading in the out-of-doors. At Erickson's suggestion, the mother decided to relent somewhat the next time. If her son voluntarily asked to go walking, she would only drive a mile down the road. He began walking more briskly and on his own initiative. Eventually he found other exercises which he chose on his own, furthering the process of individualism begun with a ritual.

Certainly this intervention by Erickson falls within the category of ritual prescription. The behavior had to be performed in a particular fashion, i.e. in a certain location, with the distance to be walked rigidly prescribed, and the behavior of the mother clearly limited, denoted, and sequenced. While this ritual did not celebrate the total differentiation of mother from son, it did connote some degree of individuation for each.

One might consider this Erickson example as a mini-ritual, a preview or a part of the preparation phase of a fuller, more complete rite of passage. The Piggle-Wiggle cures almost always fall in this category of mini-rituals, probably because they deal with younger children and are more appropriate to puberty than to leaving home.

The most striking use of therapeutic ritual prescription is usually connected with either a *major* transition (moving from one life stage to another) or performing a leave-taking ritual which involves saying goodbye to a lost relationship (Sargent, 1981, p. 60). Selvini Palazzoli and her colleagues (1974, 1977) have written about several powerful ritual prescriptions which involve such major life transitions.

In reality, Mrs. Piggle-Wiggle and Milton Erickson cannot be fairly compared. He was a paid professional; she was a volunteer homespun advisor. She had no credentials; he was a trained medical doctor. Mrs. Piggle-Wiggle's fictional cures were the products of Betty MacDonald's imagination; Milton Erickson's cures were imaginative solutions to real problems. The popularity of both these talented individuals, however, is undeniable. Tens of thousands of children and adults have enjoyed the exploits of Mrs. Piggle-Wiggle, and tens of thousands of people in the helping professions have enjoyed the stories and cases of Dr. Erickson, probably for many of the same reasons. The wizard and the witch both understood people, with a humorous and wise appreciation for their similarities and differences. They both knew how to use magic. Part of that magic lay in their understanding that people are creatures of habit, that habits are patterns, and that rituals are the patterns that connect and disconnect families, cultures and life stages.

REFERENCES

Bodin, A. M., & Bodin, L. J. (1976). The topsy-turviness of Mrs. Piggle-Wiggle: Its symbolic significance. *Family Process, 15*(1), 117.

Fernandez, J. W. (1977). The performance of ritual metaphors. In J. D. Sapir & J. C. Crocker (Eds.), *The social use of metaphor: Essays on the anthropology of rhetoric*. Philadelphia: University of Pennsylvania Press.

Haley, J. (1963). *Strategies of psychotherapy*. New York: Grune & Stratton.

Haley, J. (1973). *Uncommon therapy: The psychiatric techniques of Milton H. Erickson, M.D.* New York: Norton.

Haley, J. (1982). The contribution to therapy of Milton H. Erickson, M.D. In J. Zeig (Ed.), *Ericksonian approaches to hypnosis and psychotherapy*. New York: Brunner/Mazel.

Hoffman, L. (1971). Deviation-amplifying processes in natural groups. In J. Haley (Ed.), *Changing families*. New York: Grune & Stratton.

Lenthall, G. (1975). A tribute to two masters. *Family Process, 14*(3), 379-388.

MacDonald, B. (1947). *Mrs. Piggle-Wiggle*. New York: J.P. Lippincott.

MacDonald, B. (1949). *Mrs. Piggle-Wiggle's magic*. New York: J.P. Lippincott.

Plaut, A. (1975). Where have all the rituals gone? Observations on the transforming function of rituals and the proliferation of psychotherapies. *Journal of Analytic Psychology,* 20, 3-17.

Sargent, G. (1981). Een begrafenis aan zee (A burial at sea). In O. van der Hart (Ed.), *Afscheidsrituelen in psychotherapie.* Baarn, The Netherlands: Ambo.

Seltzer, W. J., & Seltzer, M. R. (1983). Material, myth, & magic: A cultural approach to family therapy. *Family Process,* 22(1), 3-14.

Selvini Palazzoli, M., Boscolo, L., Cecchin, G. F., & Prata, G. (1974). The treatment of children through brief treatment of their parents. *Family Process,* 13(4), 429-442.

Selvini Palazzoli, M., Boscolo, L., Cecchin, G. F., & Prata, G. (1977). Family rituals: A powerful tool in family therapy. *Family Process,* 16(4), 445-454.

van der Hart, O. (Ed.). (1981). *Afscheidsrituelen in psychotherapie.* Baarn, The Netherlands: Ambo.

van der Hart, O. (1983). *Rituals in psychotherapy.* New York: Irvington.

Chapter 8

An Integration of Ericksonian Techniques with Concepts of Family Therapy

Gunther Schmidt and Bernhard Trenkle

Our approach to family therapy is based on a unique conceptual model. In order to understand our approach, it is necessary to look at its roots. In the 1970s concepts from family therapy aroused interest in Germany. Stierlin, Boszormenyi-Nagy, Wynne and Singer, Bateson, Lidz, Minuchin, Norman Paul, and Selvini Palazzoli provided additional understandings about observing patients, problems and symptoms. We agree with Stierlin et al. (1980) that "family therapy is a new paradigm—a frame of reference that reveals and reorganizes so that significant new meanings emerge and new perspectives open up" (p. 6). Further, "the unit of treatment is no longer the person, even if only a single person is interviewed; it is the set of relationships in which the person is embedded" (Haley & Hoffmann, 1967, p. V).

With the publication of Haley's *Uncommon Therapy* (1973) an additional dimension was revealed. Erickson's ideas and methods inspired us to experiment with such techniques as storytelling, the use of metaphor, encouraging both relapse of symptoms and resistance, and utilizing resources. The more we used Ericksonian ideas, the more it became clear that, just as systems thinking is a new paradigm for theory, the treatment strategies and techniques of Erickson are a breakthrough for practice.

For a long time, family therapy and Ericksonian therapy were unconnected worlds. For example, when we heard or read about a concept of

The authors wish to thank Megan Lawler for her editorial assistance.

family therapy for the first time, it often brought a sudden insight, a surprising new possibility for therapeutic intervention. In studying a case or videotape of Erickson's work, the experience was different. As with seeing a Picasso, or hearing a piece of modern classical music, it was necessary to review the experience more than once, and thereby move from spontaneous fascination to a deeper understanding of human responsiveness.

We became aware of variations in the emphasis of training workshops and seminars. In the family therapy seminars of therapists such as Stierlin, Boszormenyi-Nagy and Norman Paul, the dynamics of the family were discussed in detail and one was trained to think about complex multigenerational theory; not much emphasis was placed on therapeutic interventions. Although we often saw skillful therapy, the behavior of the therapist was not the central issue, rather it was defined in general terms such as "empathy," "cognitive stability," or "multidirectional partiality" (Stierlin et al., 1980).

In training workshops in Ericksonian methods, the emphasis was on effective communication. The focus was on the interaction between the client and the therapist. The psychodynamics or family dynamics of the clients were secondary; emphasis was placed on the multiplicity of communication possibilities and the adaptation of therapeutic strategies to the unique personalities of the clients.*

This can be further illustrated by examining Erickson's case transcripts (Erickson & Rossi, 1979). One sees a great difference in the amount of space used to describe the client and his/her problem in comparison to the amount of space devoted to considerations of responsiveness to Erickson's therapeutic communication. Another example can be seen in Erickson's (1944) article about the induction of an experimental neurosis where he wrote several lines of "explanatory remarks" to discuss the significance of just a single word in the therapy.

To summarize, we value a focus on family dynamics and a focus on the interactional process between client and therapist. In our own work we are attempting a synthesis of the two. Our efforts are described in the following two sections. The first section presents an attempt to combine the conceptualizations of family therapy with Ericksonian principles and techniques. The second section describes some ways of integrating Ericksonian techniques with the systemic family therapy approach of the Milan team (Selvini Palazzoli, Boscolo, Cecchin, and Prata).

---

*A thank you to Jeff Zeig, Stephen and Carol Lankton, and Paul Carter.

I. ERICKSONIAN AND FAMILY THERAPY: AN ATTEMPTED SYNTHESIS OF THE TWO

To organize our thinking about the therapeutic process, we can use the mathematical equation, FD × X = G, where "FD" represents a description of a family, "X" is a set of therapeutic interventions, and "G" represents the therapeutic goals. To put it in another way, "FD" (family dynamics) is a description of the family before therapy, "G" denotes the state of affairs after successful intervention, and "X" is the series of interventions and communications which lead to the desired state, "G."

The FD Operator: Diagnosis and Family Dynamics

The FD operator consists of observations about a family, as condensed and accurate as possible, expressed in the terms of everyday language as well as in the terminology of family therapy. In the process of gathering information there are five important epistemological presuppositions. After listing these, we will present aspects of the mathematical formula that we view as specially relevant to devising effective treatment:

1) The therapist's theoretical orientation shapes and limits his/her perceptions. Moreover, the therapist's observation of the family enhances his/her knowledge of theoretical concepts.

2) Conceptualizations are like "settings of a telescope, [whereby] each perspective reveals different, though often overlapping aspects of human reality" (Stierlin et al., 1980).

3) "The map is not the territory" (Korzybski, 1933). As applied to family therapy, this concept translates into "the words and conceptualizations are not the family." This is not to say that the patient's words should be minimized—these communications provide useful data. Rather we are in agreement with Erickson and Rossi who state,

> When you are doing psychotherapy, you listen to what the patients say, you use their words, and you can understand those words. You can place your own meaning on those words, but the real question is, what is the meaning that a patient places on those words. You cannot know, because you do not know the patient's frame of reference. (1981, p. 255)

4) One of Erickson's basic principles is that each person is a unique individual. It is important to gain a picture of the uniqueness of each family and each family member.

5) This last presupposition emphasizes another Ericksonian principle,

namely, identifying and strengthening personal resources. Erickson was brilliant in his ability to turn what seemed to be overwhelming handicaps into resources which changed the lives of his clients.

The First Interview

In the first interview with the family, we especially attend to five diagnostic levels. There are many other factors that can be considered. The following five are most beneficial in establishing therapeutic formats that family therapists can easily utilize.

Planes of FD operator

1) The five perspectives of Stierlin et al. (1980): related individuation; transactional modes of binding and expelling; delegation; multigenerational legacy and merit; state of mutuality
2) The Circumplex Model of Olson et al. (1979): cohesion; adaptability
3) Stage of family life cycle
4) Resources, potentials
5) Symptoms, problems

The above list consists of levels which we use to describe a family. It mainly contains the actual inventory of effective strengths.

The G operator: The goals

G contains the therapeutic goals. Goals are defined by family members, as well as by the therapist. Goals are partially derived from diagnostic conceptualizations and depend on the perceived resources of the family.

Planes of G operator

There are six levels of goals that we emphasize in our model:

1) Goals stated by family members
2) Goals derived out of the five perspectives of Stierlin et al.
3) Goals derived out of the Circumplex Model
4) Goals directed to moving to the next stage of the family life cycle
5) Goals related to the presence of a resource
6) Goals involving problem solutions or symptom change

The X operator: Communication, interventions, techniques

Equipped with FD and G, the task remains to find the operations which make it possible to move from FD to G. Remaining in the mathematical metaphor, when the operator and the result are stated, the multiplier which will equalize the equation must be found. It is in this level of therapeutic interaction that Erickson's influence is of tremendous importance. Ericksonian intervention strategies include storytelling, metaphor, paradox, symptom prescriptions, indirect suggestions, the use of hypnotic phenomena as resources, tasks, the use of symbols, multiple-level communications, and reframing.

Planes of X operator

Techniques of family therapy:

• initiation of dialogue
• active restructuring
• insight and reconciliation
• initiating blocked mourning
• family sculpting
• paradoxical prescription, rituals
• tasks
• circular questioning

Techniques of Ericksonian therapy:

• storytelling, metaphor, anecdote, symbols, multiple-embedded metaphor
• paradox, binds, symptom prescription
• reframing
• indirect suggestions, interspersal technique, analogical marking
• depotentiating habitual framework, humor, shock, surprise, confusion
• using hypnotic phenomena: age regression, dissociation, etc.
• yes-set
• tasks
• ordeals
• retrieving and building resources

Techniques in family therapy are often vague. Experienced family therapists often use Ericksonian techniques without making them explicit.

However, it was not Erickson's ingenious interventions that constituted the core of his genius; rather, his brilliance was his special style of uniquely meeting the needs of each individual. Therapists would do well to emphasize tailoring treatment to the individual rather than striving to use particular techniques.

In discussing diagnostic parameters, Zeig (1980) describes four important factors: absorption, responsiveness, attentiveness, and control. He states:

> For example, the hypnotic and psychotherapeutic techniques that one applies to a one-down, externally oriented person, who is highly responsive to direct suggestion should be different from the therapeutic techniques one applies to a one-up, internally absorbed person who is more responsive to indirect suggestion. (Zeig, 1980, p. 17)

We try to use similar diagnostic categories* to tailor our communication and interventions to meet the needs of the individual families we see.

Returning to our mathematical equation metaphor, we find it useful not to include these diagnostic aspects in our framework. Rather, we use them as an "elegant operation" similar to using shortcuts in calculating fractions. For example, one can save considerable time and effort in calculating fractions by using prime numbers and calculation tables of simple and compound multiplications; the actual effort is thereby condensed. Before giving you a table of "Ericksonian prime numbers," we would like to give an example of the use of the whole equation in the context of the Circumplex Model.

The Equation in Context of the Circumplex Model

We can create hypothetical examples using "Cohesion" (Table 1) as one of the dimensions of Olson's Circumplex Model (Olson et al., 1979). With an enmeshed family, the goal would be to work towards a connected family. For present purposes we will direct our analysis only to the sublevels of "space" and "time."

Using our formula the equation would be:

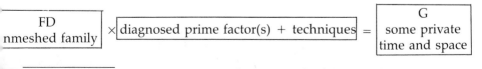

$$\frac{FD}{\text{nmeshed family}} \times \boxed{\text{diagnosed prime factor(s)} + \text{techniques}} = \boxed{\begin{array}{c} G \\ \text{some private} \\ \text{time and space} \end{array}}$$

*Zeig's diagnostic criteria, workshop handout Fuschl/Austria, May 1983.

Table 1

Family Cohesion Dimension: Interrelated Concepts

	DISENGAGED (Very Low)	SEPARATED (Low to Moderate)	CONNECTED (Moderate to High)	ENMESHED (Very High)
Independence	High independence of family members	Moderate independence of family members	Moderate dependence of family members	High dependence of family members
Family Boundaries	Open external boundaries; closed internal boundaries; rigid generational boundaries	Semi-open external and internal boundaries; clear generational boundaries	Semi-open external boundaries; open internal boundaries; clear generational boundaries	Closed external boundaries; blurred internal boundaries; blurred generational boundaries
Coalitions	Weak coalitions; usually a family scapegoat	Marital coalition clear	Marital coalition strong	Parent-child coalitions
Time	Time apart from family maximized (physically and/or emotionally)	Time alone and together is important	Time together is important; time alone permitted for approved reasons	Time together maximized; little time alone permitted
Space	Separate space both physically and emotionally is maximized	Private space maintained; some family space	Family space maximized; private space minimized	Little or no private space at home
Friends	Mainly individual friends seen alone; few family friends	Some individual friends; some family friends	Some individual friends; scheduled activities with couple and family friends	Limited individual friends; mainly couple or family friends seen together
Decision-Making	Primarily individual decisions	Most decisions are individually based; able to make joint decisions on family issues	Individual decisions are shared; most decisions made with family in mind	All decisions, both personal and relationship must be made by family
Interests and Recreation	Primarily individual activities done without family; family not involved	Some spontaneous family activities; individual activities supported	Some scheduled family activities; family involved in individual interests	Most or all activities and interests must be shared with family

Next, we consider what unique attributes (prime factors) enmeshed families have and tailor our strategies to meet these needs. Attempting to open up "space" for an individual family member may depend on the family's definition of "space." Depending on the *representational system* the family employs (cf. Bandler & Grinder, 1976), it may mean, "No one can hear me," or "No one can see me." Some people need merely close the door for privacy, while others need a distance of 2000 miles to obtain it.

Families also differ in *tempo*. Some prefer quick, dramatic change; others prefer a slow, careful process. Some families are of the opinion that they need a great deal of time with the therapist before they can be understood. Others, demand a diagnosis and solution after 20 minutes.

Enmeshed families can be either *compliant* or *defiant*. With compliant families we work with direct suggestions and assignments. Defiant families may benefit from paradoxical techniques (cf. Papp, 1980) or indirect methods.

The Circumplex Model differentiates levels of adaptability between "chaotic" and "rigid" families. In the latter case, we often use confusion techniques to overload rigid sets, and then intersperse the idea of developing private space. In a chaotic family we attempt to fixate attention and then speak precisely and repeatedly about developing space.

Some families are good in *thinking* or analyzing; others have excellent access to their *feelings*; others are good in *doing* or approaching things practically. We can use these strengths as resources to develop a less-developed aspect in regard to personal space. But we can also prescribe an overdeveloped aspect and prohibit an underdeveloped one. So we may prescribe *thinking* about family dynamics and strictly forbid any action. In other cases we may prescribe a more or less senseless ritual and forbid thinking about it.

For a mother whose attentional style is *external*, it might be more acceptable to say that her child needs space to develop sensory awareness. A father who is *internal* would more easily accept the idea that his child needs private space to daydream and develop his own fantasies.

Families differ in relation to *giving and taking*. For example, there are families where parents feel guilty, thinking they have not done enough for their children. Therefore, they hold on to the children so they can keep giving. Defining a private room as an immense sacrifice can give a rationale for providing space that the parents can accept.

The therapist can use the family's *philosophy of life* or *religion*. With a family interested in Eastern esoteric religions and meditation, one can suggest meditating about marriage:

Marriage
Sing and dance together and be joyous,
but let each one of you be alone,
even as the strings of a lute are alone,
though they quire with the same music,
and stand together yet not too near together. . . . (Gibran, 1968)

People differ as to one-up or one-down behavior. With one-up people we prefer to use more indirect techniques; with one-down people we are more direct.

In summary, adapting Zeig's diagnostic categories we consider the following "prime factors" as especially important in tailoring treatment approaches:

- compliant/defiant
- representational systems
- handling of time
- chaotic/rigid
- thinking/feeling/doing
- external/internal
- giving/taking
- philosophies of life
- one-up/one-down

In discussing the "prime factors," we have used aspects of Ericksonian therapy described in other places as "meeting the clients at their model of the world" (Lankton & Lankton, 1983, p. 18), "pacing and leading" (Bandler & Grinder, 1975) and "utilization" (Rossi, 1980, Vol. 4, p. 147).

The following case illustrates additional aspects of our approach. A 33-year-old man came to therapy accompanied by his parents because of his severe stuttering. The relationship between mother and son was one of high cohesion and a low level of related individuation. The son was delegated responsibility for the family's restaurant. In the family's multigenerational legacy it was not permissible for the son to go his own way as the mother was still obedient to her parents. The son never had an intimate relationship with a woman. He spent his time working in the restaurant and with his mother and grandparents.

After the first few sessions it became obvious how difficult it was for the mother to let the son speak for himself. Whenever the son started to comment, she stopped looking at him, went "internal" for a moment, and seemingly did not hear him. Then she would jump to other topics (cf. Singer, 1978; Wynne & Singer, 1966). At these times the son looked bewildered.

The therapist's goal was to attain more structured communication and a higher level of related individuation and lower cohesion. We ended one session with a story and related assignment.

> I (B.T.) recently saw a man in his thirties for therapy. He was good-looking and successful. However, he wanted to commit suicide because he lost his voice after surgery for a brain tumor.
>
> At the time I saw him, he had learned to speak without using his voice. The speech therapist understood every word. I only understood the first four or five words and then I lost track. It was hard work to find out why. Finally I recognized that I had to learn to hear in a new way. I recognized that when I was very engaged or liked someone very much I was in danger of thinking too much about possible ways to help; thinking about what to say. . . .

I discussed at length how to concurrently hear and think; how such processes are automatic and unconscious. I repeatedly interspersed "learn hearing in a new way."

> . . . I have had to learn in the past to hear and think concurrently but not see and think concurrently. So I said to myself, "You have to learn to hear others in a new way." *And I say this to you*, because I know you are also very involved with your son and you love him very much. Because of this, my guess is that you also are very quick to go inside, to try to help him but then you miss what he is saying.
>
> So I give you the assignment to find out and report at the next session how many words he says that you can remember. Count before you start thinking how to help him, and do this because you love him so much.

Mother came to the next session obviously shocked and reported that most of the time she was not able to recall a single word her son had said. This was an important step. We then reiterated how important her help was, because for the stutterer it is important that others really hear during their speaking.

Among the various Ericksonian techniques used were:

- Storytelling and metaphor
- Interspersal technique to seed and suggest new behavior
- Communicating to the conscious and unconscious mind
- Reframing intrusive behavior as love and care, and using this resource
- Interrupting an unconscious behavior pattern through a task
- Changing a behavior sequence ending in an internal state of awareness and attention to a sequence ending in an external state of attention

Having indicated our basic model and how it can be used to tailor treatment, we next describe how Ericksonian and Milan models intersect.

II. ERICKSONIAN AND SYSTEMIC FAMILY THERAPY

Among the different concepts of family therapy in the last 10 years, the approach of the so-called Milan team (Selvini Palazzoli, Boscolo, Cecchin, & Prata, 1978) has gained a strong influence. Known as the "systemic approach," it is based on the theories of Gregory Bateson and on General Systems Theory. These theories are widely accepted as epistemological foundations of family therapy. Besides the publications of the Milan group itself (e.g., Selvini Palazzoli et al., 1978, 1980), there are some important contributions by Peggy Penn (1982) and by Lynn Hoffman (1982), which elaborate different aspects of the approach. One important therapeutic tool of the Milan group that has received special attention in the literature is circular questioning.

In circular questioning, the therapist asks questions about differences in the relationships between family members and changes in relationships over time. Usually one family member is asked about the relationship between two or more of the other members who are almost always present. (There is also the possibility of asking strategic questions about persons not present in the interview, but we will not discuss these aspects here.) This process is continued with every member.

The information so gained is then used to carefully design an intervention which is presented at the end of the session (Selvini Palazzoli et al., 1980). Such an intervention usually contains the positive intent of behaviors of family members. Sometimes rituals are prescribed and sometimes "paradoxical" reframings are presented.

We have been working successfully with this approach for several years. In the beginning (just like the Milan team) we held the assumption that the main purpose of the interview is to increase the therapist's knowledge about the system. Although Lynn Hoffman takes a softer position at another point, she comments that the Milan team and she herself assume that this process of circular questioning gives no instructions, answers, or interpretations, consisting as it does only of questions (Hoffman, 1982).

As we worked with the Milan approach, we began to see that these assumptions are too pat. We realized that the process of circular questioning itself can be an extremely useful therapeutic tool—in many aspects even more effective than prescriptions and positive connotations at the end of the sessions. From our point of view, the therapeutic potential is limited in an unnecessary way by the assumption that the interview is a process of only increasing the therapist's knowledge. We gave up this assumption two years ago. We see the main task of the interview as *giving* relevant information to the family; as evoking patterns of associations, potentials of behavior, and attitudes which can be used by the family members for the solution of their problems. Of course, we do not mean to imply that getting information is not important. Every bit of information which clarifies the picture of the organizational patterns of the system is of great help for the therapist in proving hypotheses and in modifying strategies for more therapeutic effect. But we see getting and giving information as a synchronous event, and in many cases the giving seems to have much more impact than the getting. In summary, *we use questions mainly as a vehicle for the feedback of information and the intensive seeding of new ideas.*

We now conceptualize the whole interview as a frame for indirect hypnotherapeutic strategies. We find that Milton Erickson's understanding of the therapeutic process and his masterful techniques can be combined quite well with the advantages of the systemic approach and circular questioning, so that each session becomes an indirect hypnotherapy, without hypnosis ever being mentioned.

For the following explanations, let us remember a rough scheme of Ericksonian trance induction:

- Getting and keeping the attention of the subject
- Focusing attention towards some relevant internal realities (feelings, abilities, memories, etc.)
- Depotentiating the habitual patterns of thinking and experience (by means of distraction, confusion, doubts, etc.)
- Activating unconscious processes by evocation of personal associations, thought sequences, search processes, etc.

• Eliciting responses as a result of these evoked patterns of experience (The subject experiences them as appearing autonomously.) (Erickson & Rossi, 1979)

Our opinion is that the original Milan approach already contains indirect hypnotherapeutic elements, although this is not the goal of the concept. (In several personal discussions with L. Boscolo and G. Cecchin, they have confirmed that they had not aimed in this direction.) Moreover, this aspect is mentioned nowhere in the literature.

We will now discuss some examples of typical elements of indirect hypnotherapy as they appear in the Milan approach.

1) The therapists actively structure the course of the session. The family is brought into a *complementary position* (Haley, 1963) by means of continuous circular questioning. This process takes place without being commented on verbally. The therapists are in charge of the process in the session (at least they *usually* are). Their behavior *presupposes* this structuring; no discussion of the structure is needed or intended. It is presupposed by behavior.

2) The continuous flow of questions results in a strong *fixation of attention*; this is also an effect of the fact that nobody in the family can ever be sure about when and how questions will be directed towards them. There is no need for overtly suggesting a fixation of attention. The situation in itself contains mild uncertainty which helps make the therapist's questions important for the family members.

3) *Cue words* of the family are picked up. They are understood as important hints of the "family paradigm" and become embedded into the context of the whole family through questions about differences. This picking up and redefining is an effective *utilization strategy* with pacing (picking up the cue words) and leading (transferring them into the family context). In this way an increase in rapport is created while new ideas are being elicited.

4) Almost all questions are asked in a circular fashion. (Hoffman, 1982; Penn, 1982; Selvini Palazzoli et al., 1980). The structure of the questions is isomorphic with feedback loops in the family. Each of these questions is basically an *indirect suggestion, a presupposition* which suggests that there are circular relational patterns to be found in the interactions between people and that they obviously play an important role in the family.

Most families who come to therapy use a linear epistemology in organizing their perception and their explanation of the world. One can usually assume that this linear world view stabilizes the family problem (Watzlawick et al., 1967, 1974). Through circular questioning the family receives continuous indirect suggestions to see relations in a circular way. This takes place without any open attack against the linear epistemology. Experience shows that the family members can smoothly take over the new point of view and incorporate it into their autopoietic organization (Maturana & Varela, 1980). Thereby, they often create new and more functional solutions for their problems in an autonomous way without having the specific problem *content* as a focus of the therapeutic session.

This process demonstrates communication on multiple levels. The complicated questions promote new perspectives and intensely absorb conscious attention. At the same time, the implicit message to see the interactions in a circular way can easily bypass the conscious mind and drop into the unconscious.

5) The questions are often surprising and complex. They generally lead rather quickly to *conscious mind overload*. As a result of the active structuring of the therapists, there is already an effective pattern disruption of the redundant problem stabilizing behavior sequences in the family. Overload reinforces this process, and thereby people lose track of their usual conscious patterns (e.g., as a result of a question such as: "What do you think that your mother is thinking when your father is behaving in such and such a way in relation to your sister?"). This evolves into an intuitively conducted *confusion technique* (Rossi, 1980).

It is not surprising at all that a variety of trance phenomena develop as a result of overload. These moments of common, everyday trance are good times to bring in useful problem-solving suggestions which would be rejected in the waking state. Unfortunately, because these communication processes are not acknowledged, they often remain unused in circular interviews.

6) In the Milan approach, "resistance" is handled much as it was by Erickson. Reframing the positive intent of *all* behavior, especially problem behavior, is, as mentioned, a basic procedure. The premise is that all observed behaviors are directed for the purpose of keeping the cohesion and unity of the family group (Selvini Palazzoli et al., 1978).

7) The way one deals with family secrets in the Milan approach can be seen as a *utilization strategy*. The therapist starts from the premise that the content of the secret is not nearly as important as the relational structure around the secret. So the therapist asks that the secret be kept, while continuing to ask such questions as, "Who knows something about it? Who does not? Who would like to know? Who wouldn't? How

do the people who do not know feel?" With this approach, in most cases the function of the secret dissolves without it ever being necessary to urge people to talk about the secret itself. This procedure also is a strong context marker (Wilk, 1982), interrupting behavior which had occurred spontaneously in the past.

The Milan approach includes a variety of other interesting indirect hypnotherapeutic communications such as prescriptions and rituals, questions which induce new ideas, provocation by means of questions which challenge the value system of the family, and hypothetical questions.

All these hypnotherapeutic processes lead, even without any prescriptions or tasks, to the evocation of patterns of association, perceptions, behaviors, and experiences which contain constructive and relevant problem solutions. But this often happens rather intuitively and unsystematically. Therefore, processes already evoked are often disturbed again by unwitting interventions leading in the opposite direction. For example, hypothetical questions often "spontaneously" have the effect of an interspersed suggestion (e.g., when the therapist says, "Let's assume X would get active again and would make satisfying contacts"). A therapist who does not realize the effect of presuppositions might inadvertently phrase questions which are countertherapeutic. In the example above, an unaware therapist might phrase the question to suggest *inactivity* rather than activity. We often see such processes in supervision of therapists working with the Milan approach.

In our own work with an Ericksonian orientation, we assume that a formal trance is not necessary to effectively convey suggestions. Erickson pointed out that "response attentiveness" or "common everyday trance" is sufficient. We rely on the suggestion of Erickson and Rossi that Braid evoked hypnotic phenomena in people who seemed to be awake by asking specific questions (Erickson, Rossi, & Rossi, 1976). We also build on Sternberg's findings. He described that when questions are asked, the human brain, even after having found a seemingly satisfying answer on a conscious level, searches through the whole memory system on an unconscious level. On the basis of this understanding, we systematically apply questions in the different phases of the therapy process.

Building Rapport and Defining the Context

A primary goal is to build rapport with the whole family and to orient them to the therapeutic context. Frequently, we work as a team with a one-way mirror and video. The explanation of this setting offers many possibilities for indirect suggestions. For example, "Before we decide which problems and what possible solutions there are in the family, we want to explain about the equipment in the room," or "Before we begin an open exchange about the relevant issues, we want to explain. . . ."

The intervals between the sessions in our work are usually about four weeks. We explain this structure like this: "In these sessions many important issues for the family are discussed, consciously or unconsciously. New knowledge is gained which consciously or unconsciously can trigger new perspectives and possibilities for solutions." Here we add a longer explanation of the terms conscious and unconscious. These explanations are, of course, laced with numerous indirect suggestions. Their content depends on the goals we want to achieve.

Co-therapy Possibilities

To work in co-therapy offers a broad variety of possibilities for indirect utilization. For example, the therapist who is asking the questions can pace on different levels (body posture, etc.) of the person being questioned, while the co-therapist sequentially paces remaining members of the family. In our experience this increases unconscious rapport.

In some cases we find open disagreement on the part of the therapists useful, either during the session or in the commentary/prescription at the end. This allows us to handle ambivalences in an isomorphic way, and is useful in families with strong splitting tendencies, e.g., schizopresent families (Stierlin, 1983).

One therapist holds the position of one part of the family epistemology, the other one the other part. If one therapist also takes the "ugly" part (the unpopular and disliked position), he or she usually absorbs all rejections with his or her statements and it is usually much easier for the other therapist to induce important directives.

We also use this method at the end of the session when we give a task or an interpretation. The "bad" therapist suggests the worse alternative, the "good" one suggests the alternative which we actually want to be accepted. In other words, if a behavior of a family member is seen as a sign of illness by some members and as laziness by others, the "bad" therapist uses the definition of "illness," the "good one" uses the definition of "laziness."

We also use disagreement in the phase in which we clarify the reasons for family therapy. One therapist can hold the doubtful position, while the other one shows neutrality or empathy for the motivated side. In this way we pace both poles of the family. With such a procedure we get much important information about the meaning of family therapy for the family. Recommending therapy will often be experienced as establishing a coalition with one side of the family, so that the therapist loses neutrality and "resistance" may emerge. In most cases the procedure described above evokes motivation for therapy.

The Use of Anchoring, Interspersal, and Metaphor

The use of anchoring and interspersal is proving to be among the most effective therapeutic elements in our work. One use of this tool is to establish a "yes" anchor (perhaps turning to the right and using a soft voice tone) and a "no" anchor (perhaps turning to the left with some other voice tone) as we begin work with a family.

Circular questioning provides a wonderful opportunity for interspersal. We ask hypothetical questions as in the original Milan approach but formulate them in the indicative instead of the subjunctive mood.

If we want to suggest that X behave in such and such a way, we say, "Let's assume X *will behave in such and such a way.* How will father react?" connecting the suggestion with the anchor for "yes."

We usually do not limit ourselves to this simple and unspecific form, but integrate as many communicational elements as possible. This means that we include whatever kind of signal we perceive in the particular situation, and any specific accessing cues. Using Zeig's diagnostic formulation,* for a person with an internal, diffuse, mosaic structure with strong visual accessing, we would say something like this: "Let's assume that X will be sitting somewhere sometime in the days or weeks to come, and just when that will be even he himself does not consciously know, and he will sit in a _____ (use his actual seating position at the moment for the description) and he will just drift along with his thoughts, all those different thoughts in his head, and slowly he will see again something which will remind him of his ability to solve this problem constructively, in his own way, and he also may see that it's time to do Y (the desired behavior) or something else even more suitable for him. How will he feel then? And how will his father see the situation then? What will he feel? And will he even realize it in the first place? What will be the signals which will show a change for him? And what will he do then? Will it be acceptable for him? What will he need to accept it?"

---

*Zeig's diagnostic criteria, workshop handout Fuschl/Austria, May 1983.

The questions are not directed explicitly to the person for whom the suggestions are meant, but to other members of the family. Usually we get common everyday trance phenomena at once with this procedure, and not only with the indicated person but with the whole family. This technique functions as an indirect guided imagery process. We formulate questions to either suggest new solutions or access resources already used in the past.

Michele Ritterman has pointed out how the identified patient (IP) can be led hypnotically to a symptomatic behavior by the other family members (Ritterman, 1980). We want to add that this is a circular process in which the IP also influences the other family members in a hypnotic way. Therefore, with our questions we try to model patterns of experience in which family members could behave in a functional way. We then formulate these questions in such a way that triggers, which have previously served in a dysfunctional way, can be rewired for functional behavior. Then, the old context markers lose their effect and can either be replaced by new ones or acquire more functional meaning themselves.

Whenever it is possible we introduce or pick up metaphors to illustrate the ongoing homeostasis. The use and effectiveness of metaphors are discussed so widely in the Ericksonian field (Gordon, 1978; Lankton & Lankton, 1983; Rossi, 1980; Zeig, 1980), that we will not elaborate on this topic extensively. For now we just want to point out that we use metaphors to bring all the family members to the same level of value analogically. Metaphor design demonstrates the equal participation and responsibility of all elements of the system, which functions as a strong context marker that is incorporated into old steps of the pathological sequence. The meaning cannot stay the same.

It is interesting that sometimes the family will respond metaphorically at first before realizing the new solution. We want to illustrate some of these aspects with a case example.

The family consisted of father, age 50, mother, age 46, daughter, age 24, and son, age 17. The identified patient was the son. The daughter was married to a 25-year-old man who also participated in this session. The IP was the second son in the family, the first son having died of pneumonia at the age of 10 months. The parents still expressed intensive guilt feelings over this. They told us that they had been refugees from East Germany. At the time of the death of the first son, they had been in a bad financial situation, and so they believed that the baby had not gotten optimal nutrition. The IP himself at the age of one year almost choked in bed accidentally. Since that time both the parents interacted with him in a very overprotective manner, treating him like a nine- or

10-year-old boy almost all the time. He himself often behaved like a young boy.

The family came to therapy because the IP had stolen things such as horns and reflectors from cars. He also was described by the parents as shy and depressed, having no friends of his age. His only lasting contact outside the house was with a 13-year-old boy. We diagnosed the family as extremely centripetal and enmeshed. The diagnosis was confirmed by the fact that the daughter lived with her husband in a rented flat next door and had practically no household of her own.

In the third session we addressed some questions to the IP. He hesitated for a short time, and the mother at once stepped in and gave the answers for him. The sister and father did the same. Everyone in the family obviously perceived the son as weak. We understood this as a typical redundant sequence, showing an important rule structure in the family. We followed up on that in this way:

Therapist A (to Therapist B, who just asked questions concerning a totally different problem area): Did you see that? That's fantastic. I'm really very impressed. I really wouldn't have expected him to be so skillful (pointing to the IP). I think I will use him as a model for myself for some situations.

(Therapist A does not indicate what he is talking about and is talking in a rather dramatic way. The family members look surprised, curious and confused. The fixation of attention is intense. Then Therapist A asks father, mother, sister and her husband the same questions that he asked Therapist B, still not mentioning what he's talking about. They get more uncertain and look rather helpless.)

Therapist A (to all of the family): You really didn't realize how successful he is in getting other people in the family to step in and do the work for him? (Then Therapist A gives a short hint about the particular interaction sequence.) He's competing really well with the labor exchange office. He's a fantastic provider of work for helpful press commentators. (to the daughter's husband) How does he manage that so well? Who in the family does he usually get to accept this job as a commentator first?

Daughter's husband (after some thinking): Mother.

Therapist A: Then who?

Husband: His sister.

Therapist A: Who next?

Husband: Father.

(In this sequence the other members show signs of common everyday trance.)

Therapist A (to husband): How does he get mother to do it? How does he telegraph his message, his labor offer?

Husband: Well . . . (looks helpless).

(Then Therapist A asks the sister the same question.)

Sister: Well, he looks kind of helpless or looks at mother insecurely.

Therapist A: Aha, that's his way of sending out labor offers. He really has a successful labor exchange office for commentators and for social workers. He's competing very well in this field.

Then we expanded this metaphor in other directions, asking what the workers get paid, whether they send bills or not, and if not, why not. What would happen if nobody took the job? What can the mother do to refuse to take the job? What will she do instead. How will the others react if she doesn't take the job? Will there be somebody else to step in first? Is there a competition for the labor, or not? Who will be the next not to take the job after the mother? How will they do that?

To go into double description (Penn, 1982) we asked how it would be if the IP decided to close his labor office, when would he do that, what would bring him to the decision, how the others would handle their being unemployed, how he would keep up his decision and resist possible demands for labor, what could possibly bring him to change his decision, etc. When we added general indirect suggestions such as, "Sometimes people begin to change old habits after having talked about it in a certain way," and "One can do something the old way [using the "no" anchor] or create new and interesting ways of being ["yes" anchor]."

As in cases where resistance could emerge if the interventions are remembered consciously, we induced a *structured amnesia* (Zeig, 1985, Vol. 1: *Structures*). In this case, that was done when therapist B, without any transition, picked up the topic he was on before the interruption by therapist A, behaving as if nothing had happened and no interruption had taken place.

In addition, we usually give some general indirect suggestions for amnesia. Our experience with this procedure is that in many cases amnesia occurs and the desired behavior appears. That was the case with this family.

In the next session (four weeks later) the mother reported that she had persuaded the father to go to the seashore for a weekend without the children for the first time since the birth of the children. The son appeared much more self-confident and had made some ongoing contacts with his peers. The daughter introduced the idea of moving to another part of the city, which was done eight weeks later.

Subsequently, we again picked up the metaphor and asked the son to open his labor exchange office in times of such intense change. He adamantly refused such a silly idea, as did his parents.

Other Possibilities for Integration

We see ourselves just beginning an exploratory journey into a land with many rewarding treasures still to be found. Here are some possibilities we have glimpsed:

- "Group trance inductions" for the family by asking questions leading their attention and fantasy to important unresolved problem areas or to needed resources, ordering them not to answer those questions (a form of guided imagery).
- The use of "scramble" techniques (Lankton & Lankton, 1983), letting the family describe the steps of a pathological circle and then asking hypothetical questions about different orders of the steps in the sequence until confusion about the "real" sequence is sufficient to interrupt the old pattern.
- The design of symbolic symptom prescriptions including all relevant members. For instance, in a family with a depressive member, giving the task of carrying a bag of coal, with the whole family taking turns so that first the IP carries it for a week, then the husband, etc. (Zeig, personal communication, 1982)
- The systematic tailoring of interventions and commentaries at the end of the session in the form of a trance induction.
- The systematic induction and use of trance phenomena (amnesia, dissociation, etc.) for problem resolution.
- The use of provocation and *reductio ad absurdum*, either in the session or in homework assignments.

SUMMARY

In conclusion, even when a therapist is not working primarily in the systemic therapy style, he or she can use circular questioning for gaining and giving information or for focusing attention. Even if the question cannot be answered, a complicated question has some of the above described effects: overloading the conscious mind, fixating the attention, etc. An Ericksonian family therapist can use this technique in different ways: for example, as a starting point for a therapeutic metaphor or as a deepening technique.

In working primarily in the systemic style, therapists will use their knowledge about family dynamics to hypothesize and to determine the content of questions. While giving information with circular questions or through interventions at the end of a session (paradoxical prescriptions, rituals, tasks, etc.), therapists have goals in mind. Tailoring interventions to the individual family makes them even more effective; using what we call "prime factors" can be a powerful tool.

REFERENCES

Bandler, R., & Grinder, J. (1975). *Patterns of hypnotic techniques of Milton H. Erickson, M.D.* (Vol. 1). Cupertino, CA: Meta Publications.

Bandler, R., & Grinder, J. (1976). *The structure of magic* (Vol. 2). Palo Alto, CA: Science & Behavior Books.

Erickson, M.H. (1944). The method employed to formulate a complex story for the induction of an experimental neurosis in an hypnotic subject. *Journal of General Psychology, 31,* 67-84,

Erickson, M.H., & Rossi, E.L. (1979). *Hypnotherapy: An exploratory casebook.* New York: Irvington.

Erickson, M.H., & Rossi, E.L. (1981). *Experiencing hypnosis: Therapeutic approaches to altered states.* New York: Irvington.

Erickson, M.H., Rossi, E.L., & Rossi, S.I. (1976). *Hypnotic realities.* New York: Irvington.

Gibran, K. (1968). *The prophet.* New York: Knopf.

Gordon, D. (1978). *Therapeutic metaphors.* Cupertino, CA: Meta Publications.

Haley, J. (1963). *Strategies of psychotherapy.* New York: Grune & Stratton.

Haley, J. (1973). *Uncommon therapy: The psychiatric techniques of Milton H. Erickson.* New York: Norton.

Haley, J., & Hoffman, L. (1967). *Techniques of family therapy.* New York: Basic Books.

Hoffman, L. (1982). A coevolutionary framework for systemic family therapy. *Australian Journal of Family Therapy, 4,* 9-21.

Korzybski, A. (1933). *Science and sanity: An introduction to non-Aristotelian systems and general semantics.* Lancaster, PA: The Science Press Printing Co.

Lankton, S., & Lankton, C. (1983). *The answer within.* New York: Brunner/Mazel.

Maturana, H., & Varela, F. (1980). *Autopoiesis and cognition.* Boston: Reidel.

Olson, D., Sprenkle, D., & Russell, E. (1979). Circumplex model of marital and family systems. I: Cohesion and adaptability dimensions. *Family Process, 18,* 3-28.

Papp, P. (1980). The Greek chorus and other techniques of paradoxical therapy. *Family Process, 19,* 45-57.

Penn, P. (1982). Circular questioning. *Family Process, 21,* 267-280.

Ritterman, M. (1980). Hypno-structural family therapy. In L. Wolberg & M. Aronson (Eds.), *Group and family therapy: An overview.* New York: Brunner/Mazel.

Rossi, E.L. (Ed.). (1980). *The collected papers of Milton H. Erickson on hypnosis. New York:* Irvington.

Selvini Palazzoli, M., Boscolo, L., Cecchin, G., & Prata, G. (1978). *Paradox and counterparadox.* New York: Jason Aronson.

Selvini Palazzoli, M., Boscolo, L., Cecchin, G., & Prata, G. (1980). Hypothesizing —circularity—neutrality: Three guidelines for the conductor of family interviews. *Family Process, 19*, 3-12.

Singer, M. (1978). Attentional processes in verbal behavior. In L. Wynne, R. Cromwell, & S. Matthysse (Eds.), *The nature of schizophrenia.* New York: John Wiley.

Stierlin, H. (1983). Reflections on the family therapy of schizo-present families. In H. Stierlin, M. Wirsching, & L. Wynne (Eds.), *Psychosocial intervention in schizophrenia.* Berlin: Springer.

Stierlin, H., Ruecker-Embden, I., Wetzel, N., & Wirsching, M. (1980). *The first interview with the family.* New York: Brunner/Mazel.

Watzlawick, P., Beavin, J., & Jackson, D. (1967). *Pragmatics of human communication.* New York: Norton.

Watzlawick, P., Weakland, J., & Fisch, R. (1974). *Change: Principles of problem formation and problem resolution.* New York: Norton.

Wilk, J. (1982). Context and know-how: A model of Ericksonian psychotherapy. *Journal of Strategic and Systemic Therapies, 1*, 2-20.

Wynne, L., & Singer, M. (1966). *Schizophrenic impairment in sharing foci of attention.* New Haven, CT: Yale University Press.

Zeig, J. (1980). Symptom prescription techniques: Clinical applications using elements of communication. *Journal of Clinical Hypnosis, 23*, 23-33.

Zeig, J. (1985). *Ericksonian psychotherapy. Vol. 1: Structures.* New York: Brunner/Mazel.

Chapter 9

Tailoring Suggestions
in Family Therapy

Camillo Loriedo

Linear causality is too elementary as a model to understand the complexity of events that take place in the family system. The Ericksonian model, more than any other, demonstrates how it is possible to avoid linear interpretations not only on a theoretical level but also on a clinical one.

In Ericksonian psychotherapy, the patient's behavior is rarely interpreted. Rather, the behavior itself is used to guide the therapeutic process. Erickson was able to recognize and utilize tendencies toward change even in rigid symptomatic patterns and use them in his therapy. The possibility of using rigid patterns of symptomatic behavior to tailor therapeutic interventions makes available a tool of great value in working with the family system.

Due to the complexity of the family organism and its internal mechanisms which tend to preserve the steady state of the system, radical restructuring of the family is often rejected. However, a therapy that has the flexibility to shape itself to the family system and its pattern of symptomatic behavior may obtain a desired outcome in a short period of time.

Tailoring suggestions in this manner is based on two premises: 1) respect for the patterns which already exist in the family, and 2) recognition that the potential for change exists in even the most regressed behavior. Instead of using one particular form of treatment to which every family is forced to comply, the Ericksonian therapist designs strategies to conform to each individual family. A therapeutic model which conforms to the features and needs, not only of each family, but also

155

of each family member, provides a structure for individuation and models one of the primary goals in family therapy.

To tailor individual therapeutic strategies, it is necessary to select among the cues which the family offers. Many cues have been considered in relation to their use in hypnotherapy (for example, the diagnostic categories taught by Zeig in his workshops). Here we will focus only on some of the more relevant cues in the family, particularly the cues found in family structure, family themes, family language, and the presenting problem. Each of these will be examined in turn.

FAMILY STRUCTURE

In order to choose an appropriate suggestion for each family, we must know the structure of the family. Matching the family's style can be effective in pacing and establishing rapport. For example, vague statements may be ineffective for a family with a rigid obsessive-compulsive pattern. Instead, one should use a meticulous ritual with well-detailed instructions. On the contrary, for a family with a chaotic structure a confusion technique would be more effective than a highly organized plan of rules and procedures.

FAMILY THEMES

Every family has recurring issues which the family spends most of its time discussing. These themes indicate areas that have special meaning for the particular family. The family members talk about education, food, money, etc. The therapist could think of these areas as tangential to the therapy. Actually, they reflect an attitude of the family which is critical to the family, either directly or metaphorically. Sometimes families may say more in speaking about the weather than when they speak about their specific conflicts. Likewise, a therapist might accomplish more speaking metaphorically about the weather than by directly confronting specific conflicts.

FAMILY LANGUAGE

Every family has its own language. To promote understanding, the therapist needs to fashion interventions in the family's language. A classic example of misunderstanding occurs when a therapist uses sophisticated language with a family that uses simple language.

Some families are more sensitive to nonverbal communication, whereas other families prefer a therapy in which there is a lot of talking. When a family uses a language in which fantasy has a prominent role, the use of metaphors, anecdotes, and fables may be indicated as the best treatment language.

THE PRESENTING PROBLEM

The problem the family presents to the therapist derives from a long process of selection that has taken place inside the family. It is a special problem which contains many other problems within it. The problem or symptom that the family presents is the only behavior that is perfectly coherent with the family's logic, although this logic may appear to be distorted and inadequate. The coherence between the symptomatic behavior, the family's logic and repetitive behavior patterns can be used as a lever to obtain change in the entire family system.

The quantity and the quality of information that the presenting problem (or symptom) contains are the key to therapeutic change. According to the Ericksonian model, the presenting problem becomes the guide for the therapeutic process. The therapist's task is to identify the cues that activate and modify the problem, and then to tailor suggestions using these cues as much as possible. In this perspective, the well-known position of Watzlawick, Weakland, and Fish (1974) that the solution itself is the problem may be reversed into the more paradoxical one that "the problem itself is the solution."

Now let us consider some cues in the presenting problem on which it is possible to mold therapeutic interventions. These cues are: a) the *formulation*; b) the *request*; c) the *evolution* and d) the *content*.

The Formulation of the Problem

The family may present the problem or symptom as a suffering they want to end, as a desire to change, as an intolerable situation, and/or as a need for help. The therapist may use the specific formulation proposed by the family to motivate change by tailoring suggestions which underline the importance of ending the suffering, of satisfying the desire to change, of resolving an intolerable situation, or of receiving help. When the family formulates the problem as the symptom of only one member, the problem is often more severe. In these cases, tighter tailoring of the suggestions to the cue of a one-person problem is needed.

If the therapist tries to focus on other aspects of the family life, the symptom may be exaggerated in order to correct the "digression" made by the therapist.

The Request

The family presenting a problem will propose different types of requests to the therapist. These should be considered carefully. They are looking for an explanation when they ask, "Why does he behave like this?" To tailor a suggestion to this request, the therapist should not give a prescription, but rather an explanation of the identified patient's behavior. This is usually accomplished best with a positive connotation such as, "He is withdrawn because he wants to take his time to think about the decisions he will be making in the future."

When the family asks, "What can we do when he behaves like this?" they are no longer asking for an explanation but for guidance in how to handle the situation. In this instance, the therapist should give a prescription, if possible a symptom prescription such as, "Leave him alone so that he may think about his future decisions without any hurry."

Finally, the family may want the therapist to predict the future by asking, "What will happen if he goes on behaving like this?" In this case, a paradoxical prediction is indicated. An example of this type of prediction is, "He will continue to be withdrawn because he needs to think until he is sure enough of his decisions."

Use of a powerful therapeutic tool like the paradox should be restricted to applying a specific form (positive connotation, paradoxical prescription, and paradoxical prediction), according to the requests made by the family.

The Evolution of the Presenting Problem

The presenting problem usually manifests a high level of stability and redundancy. Yet, the problem changes continuously. Sometimes the changes are small, at other times large. The capacity to identify changes is one of the therapist's most important skills. Whenever the therapist notices a change in the presenting problem, he or she must modify suggestions to tailor them to the new conditions. Moreover, each small change can be built on. If therapists do not possess these capacities and exercise their skill, they may mistakenly persist in the attempt to obtain changes when changes have already taken place.

The Content of the Problem

The content of the symptom is a basic cue on which to tailor the therapeutic strategy. An interesting way to do this is to use the content of the problem to cure itself. In order to give a clearer explanation of how this is done, and how to tailor different suggestions and different cues, some clinical examples of this approach are presented.

CASE ONE

A physician referred a family with a five-year-old daughter who had serious congenital language and motor handicaps. The first session was attended by the mother, father, daughter, and maternal grandmother. It was clear from that session that though the presenting problem was the daughter's handicaps, the true problem was the delusional belief of the father that the daughter's handicaps were not congenital but due to an incident which occurred when the daughter was a baby. The man was convinced that his own sister had placed pressure upon a small angioma on the baby's forehead. The father felt that this resulted in her handicaps. He kept saying that the doctors were not telling the truth about his daughter, and that he doubted their competence. He maintained his strong doubts concerning the diagnosis of congenital brain damage even though others tried to convince him otherwise. During the session, while the father was expressing these doubts, the mother and grandmother looked at him and shook their heads. They tried to make sure that the therapists understood how impossible their life was with this man.

Even though the therapists were aware of the little girl's learning and social difficulties, they decided to cue in on the immense and persistent doubts presented by the father. To use the symptom as a lever and to tailor the therapy on it, the therapists stated that they *were skeptical about the father's doubts*. The man was surprised by this statement. For a moment he stopped his stubborn complaints concerning his sister's supposed crime and the incompetence of the doctors. He asked the therapists to explain their reasons as to why they were skeptical about his doubts. One of the therapists answered that if he really had these doubts he should have done more to seek the truth and to verify his suspicions. The man tried to justify his beliefs by saying that he had already consulted two different doctors. The therapist replied that to be reassured by only two doctors was not enough. They both could have been wrong or they could have been accomplices of his sister who were trying to trick him into believing that she was not responsible.

Although the man had been convinced that the sister was responsible for his daughter's illness, the doubt introduced by the therapist was too much.

"I don't believe that," he said nearly stuttering, "my sister is not capable of doing things like that."

The therapist responded, "How can you be sure of this? Have you really ever examined what your sister is capable of doing?" Gradually the father began to doubt his own misgivings. "Perhaps I was wrong, my daughter's illness was already present when my sister touched her."

During subsequent sessions when the man would again bring up the subject of his sister, the therapist suggested more accurate investigation. Then, he would drop the issue and return to the problems the daughter had in school and in establishing relationships with her peers. In the end, with the cooperation of the father, it was possible to help the family and improve the daughter's adjustments in school.

CASE TWO

A family requested that the therapist help bring about at least "a very small change."

Within this family the identified patient was the father who was diagnosed as depressive. According to the family, "he never said a word." Everybody agreed that they would be happy if he would only speak a few words.

The therapist structured a minimal change. He suggested that the father should say one word each day—no more—for an entire week. At the end of the week, with the seven words that the father had pronounced, the family was able to reconstruct a complete meaningful phrase: "When I speak nobody listens to me." Cueing in the request for a "small change" brought out new possibilities for listening and led to a radical change in the family's interactions.

CASE THREE

In this case, the suggestions were tailored not only to the presenting problem, but also to the obsessive-compulsive structure of the family.

The index patient was an 11-year-old boy with an obsessive-compulsive ritual. He engaged in a series of silent prayers for several hours before both lunch and dinner. The symptom had completely altered the family's life. The father was forced to return earlier from the office. The mother was forced to remain at the table, beside her son, whereas previously she had been so busy preparing the meal that she had no time even to sit at the table. The parents had tried to stop this behavior in many ways by threatening him, imploring him, but to no avail. Finally, they accepted the suggestion of the school psychologist and began family therapy.

The parents asked the family therapist what they should do about the presented symptom. They were told to refrain from attempting to stop the boy's prayers. Instead, their task was to methodically control a task assigned to the boy.

The task given was the following: That same evening, as soon as they sat down to dinner, the mother was to give a signal and the boy was to begin an entirely new prayer. This prayer would be silent like the other one; however, its content would be completely different. This would be "a prayer to stop the prayers." The mother was to begin the new prayer and at the same time she would start a stopwatch. She would pass the stopwatch to the father who, after exactly 57 minutes, would give a signal for the boy to stop.

After finishing "the prayer to stop the prayers," the boy could take all the time he wanted for his habitual silent prayer, without being blocked by the parents. The father was to return the stopwatch to the mother so that she could register the length of the symptomatic prayer. Every day "the prayer to stop the prayers" should be three minutes longer and the parents were asked to carefully control this amount of time.

From the first day the boy realized that "the prayer to stop the prayers" was difficult to perform. He started to silently implore his parents, but they still did not allow him to stop before the agreed time. The first day the symptomatic prayer lasted exactly three minutes. After that, it became shorter and shorter until it finally disappeared. Nevertheless, the parents wanted the boy to continue "the prayer to stop the prayers" even if in more abbreviated form. After a few months they were satisfied with having the boy say the therapeutic prayer only once a week, but in a very precise way.

Understanding reality in terms of circular causality and tailoring suggestions to family needs can be an effective way of introducing change. Quite often this orientation is in conflict with the original training of the therapist, and it typically requires a therapist who is sophisticated in professional development. An Ericksonian approach to family therapy provides techniques for individual treatments and avoids the linear model pitfall of single-set hypotheses or predetermined interventions.

REFERENCE

Watzlawick, P., Weakland, J.H., & Fisch, R. (1974). *Change: Principles of problem formation and problem resolution.* New York: Norton.

PART III

Naturalistic Approaches

Naturalistic approaches entail using hypnotic technique without using formal induction. Basically, these techniques involve using multiple-level communication when patients are in responsive "common everyday trances."

R. Reid Wilson, Ph.D., earned his degree in clinical psychology at the Fielding Institute. Currently, he is director of hypnosis training at the Southeast Institute in Chapel Hill, North Carolina. Wilson is active in the North Carolina Society of Clinical Hypnosis and edits their newsletter. He has a number of publications on human sexuality and pain control.

Practitioners of brief psychotherapy can naturalistically guide patients into common everyday trances and help them develop hypnotic phenomena. These phenomena can be used as powerful resources. A case transcript demonstrates the efficacy of interspersing hypnotic phenomena within ongoing treatment.

J. Adrian Williams, Ph.D., earned his degree in counseling psychology from the University of Illinois, Urbana-Champaign. He is in private practice in Charleston, Illinois. Williams has published and presented at a number of professional meetings on the topic of Ericksonian techniques.

Communication does not merely consist of the actual words that are used. Therapists need to be aware of the effect of the implications of their communication. The ambiguous nature of communication can be used to mobilize patients toward self-induced change.

John H. Frykman has a Master of Divinity degree from Philadelphia Lutheran Theological Seminary and he is a California licensed marriage, family, and child counselor.

Frykman is founder and president of the Cypress Institute which provides training in psychotherapy and communication. He is also pastor of the First Lutheran Church in San Francisco. As an internationally renowned teacher of brief strategic therapy, he regularly conducts workshops throughout the United States and Europe.

Indirect suggestions can be presented through anecdotes and through manipulating contexts. Strategic task assignments are effective methods to promote change in individuals and families.

Donna M. Spencer, M.S.W., Ph.D., earned her degrees in social work and education from St. Louis University. She has served as an assistant professor of social work at St. Louis University. Currently, she is in private practice at the Marriage and Family Institute in Clayton, Missouri.

Spencer describes some of her experiences with Milton Erickson. She emphasizes a specific form of multiple-level communication and presents personal and clinical experiences to illustrate her concepts.

James Wilk, M.A. (Oxon.), M.Sc., earned his degree from the University of Oxford in London. He was active in promoting Ericksonian approaches in England until he recently moved to Wisconsin to take a position at the Brief Family Therapy Center in Milwaukee. Wilk has coauthored with Bill O'Hanlon a book entitled Shifting Contexts: Clinical Epistemology and the Generation of Effective Psychotherapy *(Guilford, in press).*

Gregory Bateson's theoretical formulations can be applied strategically in clinical practice. By modifying contexts, therapists can help patients reclaim their power to change.

Chapter 10

Interspersal of Hypnotic Phenomena Within Ongoing Treatment

R. Reid Wilson

Within hypnotherapy, the development of hypnotic phenomena is often a primary procedure. Dissociation, age regression, hypermnesia and pseudo-orientation in time are deliberately used to assist in diagnosing, ratifying trance, retrieving information and resources, and providing new learnings. In other forms of psychotherapy, though, the presence of trance phenomena may be one of the most frequent and yet least consciously utilized occurrences. When identified and skillfully used, these experiences can have a profound impact on the success or failure of therapeutic interventions.

This chapter describes the frequent presence of trance phenomena in psychotherapy and outlines their therapeutic benefits. Specific methods of eliciting and enhancing such phenomena are illustrated.

To take charge of the trance as a therapeutic endeavor, the therapist must maintain a constant vigil over trance phenomena. "Spontaneous" trance does not imply a haphazard event. It is an unintentional outward manifestation of an internal, unconscious process which can directly affect the outcome of the treatment session. Whether trance phenomena are consciously or unconsciously elicited during treatment, their power lies in their ability to permit unconscious processes to mediate client responses. The therapist's task is to ensure those unconscious processes will be directed toward helpful change.

PURPOSE OF TRANCE PHENOMENA

Trance phenomena develop during moments of concentrated attention such as when attention is fixed on a narrow range of matters which
have great meaning or interest. At any moment during a treatment
session, the client is engaged in a "generalized reality orientation" (Shor,
1959) or is in some stage of developing trance phenomena. Generalized
reality orientation is a maintaining of the *status quo*. The client's limited
conscious frame of reference is engaged in interpreting events on the
social, psychological and biological levels. Only at the point of dissociation from that state does therapeutic change have the greatest potential
to take place.

Erickson, Rossi, and Rossi (1976) defined hypnotic phenomena as the
dissociation of any behavior from its usual context. Since the client does
not continue to hold the habitual notion of restrictive choices, hypnotic
phenomena can provide the opportunity for the client to experience the
possibility of change: to create vivid sensory experiences when not asleep
(positive hallucination), to feel pride in success before a project is complete (pseudo-orientation in time), to relive a past event as though it
were today (age regression), to recall a forgotten memory (hypermnesia),
to lose an unwanted sensation (anesthesia). When conscious attention
is fixed and role-taking behavior is unconsciously directed in this way,
the therapist has the opportunity to influence change through the association of phrases or images (indirect suggestions). At the same time,
the client has increased attention to his own newly formed associations
which can then surface to awareness.

The objective of psychotherapy is not to elicit superficial other-re-
sponsive behavior but to provide the context within which the client can
reorganize his or her inner reality sufficiently to better meet the requirements of external life. Trance phenomena are the tools which enhance
and utilize internal experience toward the meeting of therapeutic goals.

HYPNOTIC PHENOMENA OUTSIDE THE HYPNOTIC CONTEXT

Mott (1982) defined the hypnotic context as any time when, with prior
agreement of the subject, a hypnotic induction is performed. In the
formal induction process of traditional hypnosis, the therapist suggests
experiences which are to be consciously accepted by the client. Erickson
(1959) introduced techniques of utilization, which essentially reversed
roles in the relationship: The client presents behaviors which the therapist accepts and employs. In this manner, Erickson proved highly suc-

cessful in eliciting trance phenomena in clients who were otherwise unresponsive to hypnotic suggestion (Erickson, 1964b; Erickson, 1965, p. 58; Haley, 1973, p. 115).

The utilization approach can enhance treatment sessions outside the hypnotic context. What Erickson and Rossi (1976) called the "common everyday trance" takes place frequently within psychotherapy. When the normal frame of reference is suspended, the person can unconsciously search for an understanding which will return him or her back to the equilibrium of the general reality orientation. Outward signs of this search phenomenon (Lankton & Lankton, 1983, p. 66) are those of light trance: pupil dilation, flattened cheeks, increased skin pallor, some catalepsy, suppression of blink and swallow reflexes, reduced rate of respiration, and detachment from the surroundings.

Erickson believed that psychotherapy involved extending this phenomenon and using it for the client's betterment. During demonstrations, he would seek out those in the audience who were *already* manifesting these traits and invite them to serve as subjects (Erickson, Rossi, & Rossi, 1976, p. 303). In treatment, he supported spontaneous development of hypnotic phenomena as the most valid indicators of trance, since when they occur the client performs a natural relinquishing of ego control. Thus, alterations are no longer guided by conscious sets (Erickson, Rossi, & Rossi, 1976, p. 307). Although they appear spontaneously, these alterations are an external indication of an active process of unconscious dissociation and reorganization.

Each time the client lapses into a hypnotic state, he or she offers the potential for a special class of interventions to encourage unconscious reorganization. The following example illustrates how a brief moment of search behavior can be capitalized upon in treatment. The client has been reporting anecdotes regarding her increased independence from her mother:

Th: If you continued in this same direction to get the changes that you need in this relationship, what will you need to do in the coming months?

Cl: I can't quote unquote break down my defenses. Break down my defenses, in other words, "Oh, well, maybe if I give into her this time, I can continue at a later date." I can't do that. I've got to stay consistent with the way I'm feeling now.

Th: So the defenses you have up now keep you strong.

Cl: Right. I've got to keep up those defenses. I can't let them lag, or I'll be right back where I started twenty years ago. (pauses, mouth turns downward, eyes become moist) But I feel like I have such a big wall around me. It's uh . . . (remains motionless and absorbed)

Th: (speech slows, voice quiets, looks away and defocuses eyes) You sense a need for some kind of separation though. What kind of . . . if you were to build something literally to represent that separation, (pause) . . . it wouldn't be an eight-inch-thick wall . . . I wonder what choice there is. . . .

Cl: (turns head downward, stares at floor) Hmmm (pause) . . . a picket fence. (eyes remain fixed on floor)

Th: Lovely. Uh-huh. (pause) And what does that represent, that picket fence?

Cl: (pauses, then looks up at therapist, smiling) There's just enough space between each picket to allow us to keep the lines of communication open. But don't go beyond the picket, or you're going to get hurt . . . on her side.

The client was conversing within the general reality orientation until an internal conflict arose. She was expressing pride at separating from her mother, then suddenly recognized and felt her emotional loss. At this point she entered a light trance. The author altered his presentation to gain rapport with the client's trance and to encourage a positive hallucination. It can be presumed that the client developed an image of the picket fence, then envisioned a time in the future where that fence successfully provided both individuation and relationship (pseudo-orientation in time). Subsequently, she returned to a generalized reality orientation to proudly report her new resource.

ELICITING AND ENHANCING TRANCE PHENOMENA

Certain principles can guide a therapist in the effective use of trance phenomena in psychotherapy. These principles should not be perceived as delimiting the field; in fact, they are presented to encourage further expansion and elaboration.

1) Therapist Skill Acquisition

Three skills are essential as the foundation for an interspersal approach of hypnosis in therapy. *Competence in delivering indirect suggestions* can provide great benefit within the treatment session. It would be redundant to review the essentials of indirection here since a comprehensive presentation is given in Erickson and Rossi (1980) and Erickson (1966).

A second important skill is the *presentation of therapeutic metaphors*. Facilitating the arrival of trance phenomena is a subtle craft. The client's conscious attention to psychological change should be present only when it supports and stabilizes such alteration. Embedding indirect suggestions within a metaphorical framework further enhances alterations on an unconscious level while maintaining a conscious rapport (Lankton & Lankton, 1983).

To recognize the client's shift into trance is also essential. The skills of observation are well-developed in the competent therapist. To utilize trance phenomena in a directed fashion requires a renewed study of verbal and nonverbal communication. The cues for such phenomena as unconscious search, dissociation, amnesia, age regression, time distortion, and positive and negative hallucination are plentiful. Analysis of a single hour of communication will reveal dozens of such alterations in consciousness, whether the context is a therapeutic session or a dinner table discussion.

2) Development of Trance Readiness

"Trance readiness" within a client represents an ability to become absorbed in an active unconscious experience without a conscious need to maintain social rapport with the therapist. In this way, trance phenomena such as catalepsy, eye fixation and dissociation become acceptable modes of operation within the therapeutic setting.

Obtaining rapport and a relationship with the client is usually the first task of the competent therapist. One also wants to model the ease, acceptability and comfort of *breaking* conscious rapport. Through this process, the therapist gives the patient permission to ignore conscious indications of rapport in order to engage at a deeper level of experience. Returning to the traditional social indicators of rapport a few moments later reinforces the natural interrelationship of conscious and unconscious processes. The previous transcript indicates how easily the client can move between internal and external focus of attention.

Six methods are commonly used to promote trance readiness:

1) The therapist can set the stage for trance readiness through indirect suggestions, metaphors and interspersal. The following is an example of Erickson's Interspersal Technique (1966), in which the client's conscious attention is directed toward a particular subject matter, while suggestions are interspersed that invite unconscious responses. Here I am describing to the client my experience of writing this paper:

. . . I had struggled at my desk all afternoon to place that line of reasoning into words, and didn't get very far. That night, while out to dinner with friends, I found myself (voice quiets) *sitting there frozen* in thought (pause). . . . It seems like out of nowhere comes an idea of how to verbalize that concept. And fortunately I was able to *hold fast onto that idea* until I jotted it down. . . . I don't know if you've ever had that kind of experience, like *letting your mind drift* just before sleep and stumbling onto some creative solution to an old problem. . . .

2) Erickson would often introduce the concept of "wonder" to invite exploration on an unconscious level (Erickson & Rossi, 1976). When uncertainty is aroused, the unconscious searches experience to resolve doubt. Words such as "surprise," "imagine," "understand," and "explore" serve the same function. For example, "Now, as that tear rolls down your cheek, you may *wonder* what emotion it really reflects."

3) Adding a negative adjective or adverb increases internal search by adding confusion: "I'm not sure whether or not you've experienced that in a completely satisfying way before." Or, "You may not want to just sit with that thought for a moment."

4) Communication can be phrased so that the client is invited to produce a response internally but not present that response to the therapist. "And that change could affect certain people more than you expected, couldn't it?" It is as though the therapist is asking a rhetorical question on which the client is free to just ponder for a few moments.

5) In addition, the therapist can model trance behavior within the session. While delivering a metaphor, the therapist can begin with conscious attention focused on the client, then slowly shift the eyes away in a gaze, turning the head or body slightly away from him or her.

6) The therapist can develop overt trance phenomena by requesting information which requires an unconscious search. For example, the therapist might ask, "That part of you that's like your father . . . I wonder, does it have a way of presenting itself in public?"

Trance readiness is an overt or covert acceptance by clients, verified by their behavior, that conscious and unconscious processes have equal roles within the therapeutic relationship. Through experience, they appreciate that a passive, receptive stance consciously permits an active, creative unconscious process which has an equal contribution to problem-resolution. As Erickson said, "If you are sufficiently tired physically, you can fall asleep as your head hits the pillow. If you are sufficiently prepared psychologically, you can develop a trance just as easily" (Erickson, 1964a, p. 297).

3) Set the Therapeutic Intention

This principle is basic to all psychotherapy: The therapist is responsible for setting his or her intentions with regard to the abrogation of the client's distress. The use of trance phenomena is placed within this context. In initial sessions the intention might be to develop trance readiness. Thereafter, trance phenomena should be elicited or enhanced by the therapist only when he or she senses their potential contribution to the therapeutic objectives.

Focus on the client's resources is a cornerstone of the Ericksonian approach. Therapist intentions should not only include what changes are needed for the client but which client resources will be utilized to produce that change. This is not to imply that intentions are rigidly set and pursued. Therapist control is reflected in the flexibility to constantly modify intentions based on the therapeutic interaction. Even when interventions are unconsciously directed, conscious hindsight should be able to identify the objective.

By allowing trance phenomena to develop outside of his or her awareness, the therapist runs the risk of having these same powerful tools work against the therapeutic endeavor. Schafer (1981) spoke of clients who enter altered states as an ego defense, such as protecting themselves through amnesia from a present trauma. Erickson and Rossi (1979) stated:

> We could even conceptualize that the typical states of depression and uncertainty with which most people enter therapy are actually spontaneous manifestations of the second and third stages [*depotentiating habitual conscious sets*] and [*unconscious search*] of our general paradigm of trance induction and suggestion. (p. 77)

Such phenomena as dissociation, age regression, pseudo-orientation in time, amnesia and hypermnesia are likely to occur whenever one is exploring areas of a client's life which might stimulate negative emotions or cognitions. If not accounted for, they may sabotage the therapeutic intentions. However, if the therapist expects, even anticipates, their arrival, he or she can intervene at a profound level.

4) *Engage the Unconscious in the Problem-Solving Process*

When the therapeutic intention is set and when hypnotic phenomena are judged as potential tools, two avenues are open. The therapist may elicit the experience through his or her conscious intention or may await a spontaneous trance experience.

The skills of eliciting trance phenomena are similar to those used within the formal hypnotic context. To focus attention internally, the therapist can direct the client to various aspects of the presenting problem. Questions or instructions can be formulated to encourage a particular phenomenon. "Tell me what you experienced when you first became anxious," supports a conscious report of the initial circumstances. This instruction can be altered to assist in the development of several phenomena: "How clear is your image of those first days of anxiety? . . . Take a moment to get a sense of that experience. . . . When you can, just give me a few words to describe your feelings. Better yet, just sit with them a minute until you really know them." The therapist's attitude is one of utmost confidence regarding the client's ability to recreate that experience. While the therapist sets the stage for the experience and tends to direct the client's conscious mind, he or she takes direction from the client at the same time. It is the *client* who always chooses the experience.

In the above example, a variety of phenomena are possible. As a simple illustration, we can consider only the verbal responses of the client: "That time was so frightening. I don't even want to remember it." Here is an invitation to develop the resources of amnesia or of negative hallucination. Through metaphor and indirect suggestion, the desire to forget can be enhanced. Amnesia could allow the client to face similar stressful situations in the future with only a sense of his or her coping strategies, instead of retrieving the fears of the past. Negative hallucination could encourage focus on other experiences during that period of time while the anxious moments are left in the background.

"Boy, I can see myself standing there, ringing my parents' doorbell, shaking in my boots." The client is experiencing an age regression from a dissociated position. The therapist can continue to develop dissociation as a resource ("Now, while we're still sitting here comfortably, keep watching what happens. . . .") or can aid in the detailed remembering of hypermnesia. ("When the door opens, watch for the very first expression on your father's face.")

"I'm sweating . . . my stomach's tense . . . I'm really feeling like I could jump out of my skin." The client's use of the present tense and report of physical alteration indicates an age regression without dissociation. The therapist now shifts in tone, posture, vocabulary, sentence structure and tense to join the client in the past as though it is the present. "That's right, you're feeling tense and jumpy . . . and you can be there now. . . . What do you see around you?" (positive hallucination)

Spontaneously occurring trance is far more frequent in the treatment hour than trances generated by the conscious direction of the therapist. Erickson and Rossi (1979) state that therapists "can ignore and actually ruin these moments when the other is engaged in inner search and unconscious processes by talking too much and thereby distracting the person" (p. 16). One choice, instead, is to remain quiet and carefully observe. What the therapist has to offer at these times is often less beneficial than allowing the client to have an inner moment to formulate a response.

If a client defocuses his or her eyes and begins to cry, it can be unnecessarily disruptive to state, "I see that you are crying. . . ." or to ask questions which encourage intellectual curiosity. These interventions tend to lift the client back to a conscious interaction. To state, "You can continue to follow that feeling quietly" establishes rapport during the client's shift away from conscious focus, maintains the client's self-esteem and invites a continuation of the process. Indirect suggestions such as, "Emotions can express our past and can guide our future," can add meaning to the current experience. Thereby, the client can be drawn toward more profound trance phenomena.

When the therapist intervenes, it is with these objectives:

1) To create a permissive atmosphere which allows a break in conscious social rapport;
2) To presuppose that a shift in consciousness has taken place;
3) To establish rapport with that altered consciousness;
4) To aid in the continuation of that experience, even if only for a few moments;
5) To use the unconscious and to invite a reassociation of resources toward a resolution of the client's discomfort and fulfillment of the therapeutic contract.

CASE EXAMPLE

The following example, excerpted from the fifth session with a 33-year-old man, illustrates several of the principles of this paper.

Cl: That's more what I want to work on today . . . really trusting unconscious process because there's still . . . now I more experience it as blocks. I feel . . . there's nothing . . . there's no response coming out and the way I see it now is that I'm keeping something from coming out. So that's what I want to work on today, one of the things. The other is that . . . ah . . . kind of as a consequence of what I originally came to you for . . . I don't seem to have the ability to confront a lot of unpleasant things directly and especially in confrontations with people where I would like to have that choice but don't seem to be able to. And it's not that I can't get what I want from people. It's that . . . because I've certainly developed other ways of doing it to avoid having to confront at times. But it's . . . it's . . . I don't feel that I have that choice. I can't do that. When I should do it or want to do it I don't feel I can.

Th: When you get the urge that comes up inside you, perhaps, to do it or you have the sense that you ought to be doing it, you can't follow through from either the urge or the sense.

Cl: Right. (eyes gaze upward)

Th: You seem to get an image, a picture of that as we talk. Do you have a sense of an experience?

[Here the therapist identifies search behavior and suggests that the client consciously attend to it.]

Cl: (pause) Hmm. I don't know. (eyes focus on therapist) A lot of the searching I do is visual, anyway. I'm not conscious of having an image.

Th: Could you get one?

[Again the therapist encourages a return to the search behavior.]

Cl: Aaa . . . (pause . . . gazes in distance over therapist's head) Hmmm . . . yeah, I could. Huh. (smiles)

Th: (quietly) And stay with that as you talk to me. Just stay with the image and not me. And I'll be here.

[The therapist implies that rapport can be maintained while the client shifts to an internal focus of attention.]

Cl: OK

Th: Whatever you need to do to enhance the image, feel free to do that, whether your eyes are opened or closed, to keep focus.

Cl: Yeah . . . Umm. Yeah, the image is real old. Umm. I can't remember how old I was at the time, but it was, ah . . . took place in a park in New Jersey. Ah, I was being chased by someone, someone who I didn't remember, I didn't know. I don't think I saw him before or really ever saw him afterward. [The client is experiencing age regression with dissociation.] But he was chasing me with a water balloon. And I let him chase me. And, as I see it now, with my experience of being adult, I allowed myself to be intimidated by him instead of standing up to him. And several weeks ago it hit me that I had done that and that for some reason it seemed like a very important experience, a turning point that was . . . umm . . . something that if I had treated that incident differently, my life would have been different. I don't know why I feel that way. It's just that, looking back, it's something that . . . umm . . . I feel was important.

[The client's field has narrowed to a few specific thoughts. If he can sense that helpful change pivots on a small but significant area of his reality, and if that area itself can be altered then he has a greater chance of promoting a creative reorganization of his mental set.]

Th: And do you feel yourself as an observer watching the scene or do you feel yourself as that boy?

Cl: No, an observer. I see both boys.

Th: Can you describe (quietly) *your emotion* there as you look down? [The therapist intersperses the suggestion to no longer remain dissociated from the experience.] Can you describe his emotion?

Cl: His emotion.

Th: Mmm . . . and perhaps even his thoughts?

Cl: Yeah. A sense of outrage at being chased for no particular reason by someone who I didn't know.

Th: Outrage.

Cl: Outrage.

Th: Where do you feel the outrage?

Cl: It's . . . in my chest. Kind of a burning.

Th: Follow the outrage and see where the outrage takes you. . . . Whether it remains in that scene, changes scenes . . . let it guide you . . . anywhere it goes. Just trust it. . . . Perhaps it will change, increase or stay the same.

Cl: (pause) It changes only insofar as somebody wants to impose on me something that I don't choose.

Th: Keep following it.

Cl: Well, (hard, slow swallow) he basically wants to make me soaking wet. I have no desire to be wet. I'm outraged, especially because he just won't go away. I have to do something about it to maintain something that is my right: to be the way I want to be.

Th: Go ahead . . . do something about it.

Cl: (talking slowly, still gazing) He chased me. I ran into trees next to the park. And I was ahead of him and could have strategically ducked behind a tree so that, though he was chasing me, surprise would have been mine. I could have, for his troubles, gotten him wet instead of me.

Th: And watch yourself do it.

Cl: I am. (brief, pleasing grin)

Th: Find out what happens to the outrage, to the warmth in the chest. Stay with it. . . . That's it. (closes eyes for first time) That's it. (grins broadly) Just enjoy that.

Cl: (chuckles) . . . Just be funny . . .

Th: Feel the sensations in the body. You might even be surprised to find they're not static, those sensations. And when you like, report to me what you're experiencing, what you're seeing.

Cl: Kind of delight. Being able to do something. To defend myself. To . . . not just to thwart his purpose, but to turn it back on him.

Th: Can you enjoy that delight, for any length of time?

Cl: No. I have enjoyed it.

Th: See if you can enjoy it for a little length right now. Notice what happens. See whether or not you can. And if you find you can, you can give me a little nod.

Cl: (pauses, then nods slightly)

Th: Enjoy that delight again, for as long as it lasts, and no longer.

[For the next few minutes the therapist guided the client in pseudo-orientation in time to create scenes in the future which would culminate in that same sense of "delight." He developed images of both work and social situations where a direct confrontation was required.]

Th: (as the client opens his eyes) Is there any way that you can put that review into words so that we can talk about it? (pause) Don't feel like you have to lift too far out of trance to do that.

Cl: (talking slowly) What strikes me most about it was a lack of recognition that something would have to be done, done quickly. That I had a feeling that by the time I recognized where I was and what I was doing, I'd missed my first, perhaps best, opportunity to take control of the situation.

Th: And do you know what cue might have been used to let you take control more immediately? Do you have any sense of . . .

Cl: Not consciously, no. 'Cause I wondered about that.

Th: Yes, you're wondering. . . . What do you think of the idea of looking back again at those scenes . . . discovering what you used then?

Cl: Yes, but before I do . . .

[Here the client describes certain sensory experiences from the trance he had while his eyes were closed, with comments such as ". . . almost entirely swept away conscious thought processes. . . ," ". . . a reassuring force that carried me away . . . ," "like one side of my head drifting out and the other side crashing into trance. . . ." The therapist supports the client's conscious discussion of these "side effects" of trance. The client thus learns to expect and accept these responses during periods of intense internal involvement.]

Cl: (deep breath) I'm ready to look for cues . . . (closes eyes)

CONCLUSION

Several benefits can be highlighted when considering the interspersal of hypnotic phenomena within ongoing treatment:

1) Clients are more receptive to presented ideas.
2) As clients increase their control over physical and psychological responses, they increase the responsibility for their own experiences.
3) As clients come to understand and trust the trance experiences, they will be capable of allowing the unconscious to operate more freely in the treatment sessions.
4) Clients can learn to accept and expect brief periods of time distortion, psychosomatic responses, visual fantasies, etc., as potentially creative moments.
5) The therapeutic relationship can then be used to explore with greater frequency experiences which are outside of the client's usual frame of reference.
6) As trance experience increasingly becomes a part of the treatment session, profound phenomena such as age regression, hypermnesia and pseudo-orientation in time can be accessed.
7) At certain moments there can be a blending of conscious understandings and expectations with unconscious participation. New unconscious insights and learnings can be immediately gratifying to conscious needs. As described in Bandura's (1977) self-efficacy theory, the client can acquire a sense of confidence that he or she will have adequate resources to cope with the problematic situation.
8) Simply acknowledging change at the moment it takes place can be beneficial in reinforcing the therapeutic process and undoing negative beliefs or attitudes. After all, "consciousness does not always recognize its own altered states" (Erickson & Rossi, 1979, p. 10).
9) Since hypnotic phenomena are accessible, they can serve as tools to enhance a variety of nonhypnotic treatment interventions. For instance, in behavior therapy, pseudo-orientation in time can

strengthen the visualizing and fantasizing needed for behavioral rehearsal.

10) Owing to the fact that a trance state can be elicited within a brief period, the client can be restricted to limited patterns of response indicative of the hypnotic phenomena. This interrupts the usual development of resistance and renders the client vulnerable to therapeutic suggestion.

11) Successful utilization of brief trance establishes a permissive environment for formal hypnotherapy. When an extended trance experience is needed to increase the therapeutic leverage, the client is more likely to perceive its potential.

REFERENCES

Bandura, A. (1977). Self-efficacy: Toward a unifying theory of behavior change. *Psychological Review, 84*, 191-215.

Erickson, M. (1954). Pseudo-orientation in time as a hypnotherapeutic procedure. *Journal of Clinical and Experimental Hypnosis, 2*, 261-283.

Erickson, M. (1959). Further clinical techniques of hypnosis: Utilization techniques. *American Journal of Clinical Hypnosis, 2*, 3–21.

Erickson, M. (1964a). The "surprise" and "my-friend-John" techniques of hypnosis: Minimal cues and natural field experimentation. *American Journal of Clinical Hypnosis, 6*, 293–307.

Erickson, M. (1964b). An hypnotic technique for resistant patients: The patient, the technique and its rationale and field experiments. *American Journal of Clinical Hypnosis, 7*, 8–32.

Erickson, M. (1965). The use of symptoms as an integral part of therapy. *American Journal of Clinical Hypnosis, 8*, 57–65.

Erickson, M. (1966). The interspersal hypnotic technique for symptom correction and pain control. *American Journal of Clinical Hypnosis, 3*, 198–209.

Erickson, M., & Rossi, E. (1976). Two-level communication and the microdynamics of trance and suggestion. *American Journal of Clinical Hypnosis, 18*, 153–171.

Erickson, M., & Rossi, E. (1979). *Hypnotherapy: An exploratory casebook*. New York: Irvington.

Erickson, M., & Rossi, E. (1980). The indirect forms of suggestion. In E. Rossi (Ed.), *The collected papers of Milton H. Erickson* (Vol. 1, pp. 452–477). New York: Irvington.

Erickson, M., Rossi, E., & Rossi, S. (1976). *Hypnotic realities*. New York: Irvington.

Gruenewald, D. (1982). Some thoughts on the hypnotic condition. *American Journal of Clinical Hypnosis, 25*(1), 46–51.

Haley, J. (1973). *Uncommon therapy: The psychiatric techniques of Milton H. Erickson, M.D.* New York: Norton.

Lankton, S., & Lankton, C. (1983). *The answer within: A clinical framework of Ericksonian hypnotherapy*. New York: Brunner/Mazel.

Mott, T. (1982). The role of hypnosis in psychotherapy. *American Journal of Hypnosis, 24*, 241–248.

Schafer, D. (1981). The recognition and hypnotherapy of patients with unrecognized altered states. *American Journal of Clinical Hypnosis, 23*(3), 176–183.

Schor, R. (1959). Hypnosis and the concept of generalized reality-orientation. *American Journal of Psychotherapy, 13*, 582–602.

Chapter 11

Erickson's Use of Psychological Implication

J. Adrian Williams

The sophisticated use of language and interpersonal behavior was a trademark of Erickson's approach to psychotherapy. Successful therapeutic outcomes were secured as a result of Erickson's ability to communicate in ways that made psychological sense to the patient, and that simultaneously facilitated a development of new options for utilizing existing, though perhaps consciously unrecognized, resources. One of the methods that Erickson employed with casual elegance was the procedure of communicating through implication; he gave directions, suggestions, and instructions in such a manner that patients often ended up "spontaneously" developing the idea for themselves. This chapter will examine some of the ways in which Erickson made use of psychological implication (multilevel communication) to effect therapy.

Erickson often pointed out that many times it was what one *didn't* say that was important (personal communication, September 27, 1978). He believed that the learnings that occurred *inside* were the ones that the patient was most able to use, and that learning at unconscious levels could occur more easily, and even more effectively when patients or students did not really know just what they were learning. Thus, in therapy Erickson often made use of simple, ambiguous words that allowed patients to assign personal meaning to the communication.

Through psychological implication understandings can be communicated so casually that people generally accept what they are hearing without really thinking about what they have accepted. For example, I worked with a male patient who had a strong need to exert conscious control through recollection of every word spoken while he was in trance. This need to scrutinize consciously all of his hypnotic work could

179

have posed a serious obstacle to his progress in psychotherapy. A comprehensive amnesia for trance experience was effected simply by allowing him to experience a profound visual, auditory, and kinesthetic hallucination, emphatically pointing out that he was to recall every detail of *that* experience in utter clarity. I elaborated that upon awakening he would recall that experience absolutely completely in each and every detail, and that he would be able to describe it fully to me, to his wife, and to certain friends. As these suggestions were in accord with his own needs, he responded fully and was satisfied, apparently dismissing the rest of his therapeutic work in that session as being of such secondary importance that it was not worth bothering to pay any attention to, let alone remember. The amnesia was effected by implication! He did remember *that* experience (the hallucination) in great detail, but in his acceptance of the suggestion he also accepted the implication, i.e., that he would *not* have to recall *any other* trance experiences. Direct suggestion of a comprehensive amnesia for the therapeutic work would have only encountered resistance from this patient, and probably resulted in a total rejection of the amnesic suggestions. The use of psychological implication allowed the patient both to meet his needs to remember *and* to progress by handling certain parts of his therapy outside of his conscious awareness or recollection.

Another form of implication is the communication of meanings through presupposition. This form of psychological implication makes use of the tendency people evidence to accept as fact, without conscious scrutiny, those things presented to them in a presuppositional format. For example, one may point out to hypnotic subjects during an induction that they can go even deeper into trance today than they have ever gone before. The implication is, of course, that they will go into a trance again today. A second implication is that they have gone deeply before, which serves to ratify previous work, thus providing a base for more extensive therapeutic work. The only question subjects tend to have is whether or not they have gone "even deeper" than any previous experience. They obviously have to go into a trance to answer such a question. Though such a use of presupposition is rather straightforward, and actually contains little subtlety, it can be quite effective.

More complex therapy, however, may require greater sophistication. I may point out to patients in the trance state that they can deal with problems in the trance state that they wouldn't dare to consider in the waking state, and that they can do so with no more discomfort than they are comfortably willing to experience. Through this format of the apposition of opposites (Erickson, Rossi, & Rossi, 1976) I am able to structure my suggestion in such a manner that any resistance tends to be depotentiated into confusion and a concern with just how much discomfort can be experienced without discomfort. The question of whether or not patients will deal with the issues causing the problems in the first place is bypassed. I have frequently observed patients deepen their trance in response to the suggestion described above, apparently with a desire to ensure that they will deal with the problem material more comfortably. Thus, careful construction of verbalizations to patients can result in suggestions with multiple psychological implications that can greatly increase the potency and therapeutic effectiveness of communications.

Erickson was always concerned with his language usage and, as noted above, typically utilized simple, ambiguous words that allowed patients to assign personal meaning to the communication. A classic example of this is Erickson's assignment to a young woman to "go home and draw a picture of yourself in the nude" (personal communication, September 29, 1978). Such a communication has at least two immediate meanings, depending on how the patient interprets the directions. One interpretation would be that the patient should go home and construct a picture in which she appears without clothing, while the other interpretation is that she should go home, remove her clothing, and then draw a picture of herself, in which she might appear either with or without clothing. One of the interesting effects of this type of communication is that patients tend to only make one interpretation of the communication. They do not seem to question that there might be alternative interpretations of the communication. It has also been my experience that patients will tend to interpret such a communication in terms of their own individual personality needs.

The tendency to interpret ambiguous wordings in terms of one's own personality needs allows for indirect therapy to be performed. I once had a patient who had a number of sexual problems which caused her intense emotional upset. Yet, she was unable to discuss these problems with a male therapist. In early hypnotic sessions I was able to praise her as being "a very sophisticated subject, who had no recognition of her sophistication." I was able to elaborate on this statement by commenting on the fact that hypnosis was new to her, and that undoubtedly as she progressed in her hypnotic training she would come more and more to recognize and be comfortable with her own sophistication. Therapy progressed rapidly; two weeks later she hesitantly reported that she ought to tell me that she had withheld information about her problems from me. She had experienced sexual problems for a number of years, but for some reason she no longer was having difficulties with her sexual adjustment, and she was increasingly comfortable in dealing with sexual matters. She never recognized that I had anything to do with her progress in that area. Her sexual therapy, however, was based on the initial use of the concept of "sophistication." She consciously accepted that term in relation to her abilities as a hypnotic subject, yet the psychological implications of being a sophisticated *woman* did not escape her unconscious mind, which was then free to respond outside her awareness to other meanings of my therapeutic communications to her.

This form of multilevel communication was frequently employed by Erickson. It involves a tactic of casually, even perhaps obscurely, referring to areas of personality function hypothesized as being clinically relevant for the patient. Erickson noted that people tend to respond to things that hold personal meaning to them, even if that meaning was outside their conscious awareness. Erickson's style of handling threatening or simply unconscious material was so casual that patients often found themselves responding to the psychological implications of his comments without really realizing how the topics came to their minds. This approach can be used both diagnostically and for purposes of treatment. In general, use is made of the tendency for the mention of different mental mechanisms to in fact evoke those mechanisms (Erickson, 1944; Erickson & Rossi, 1979; Erickson, Rossi, & Rossi, 1976). For example, casual mention of the mechanism of forgetting serves to activate those processes in the patient. Once activated, these processes can be systematically utilized in order to effect an amnesia.

Erickson used this type of implication in a teaching seminar. He mentioned a mechanism, apparently didactically, and then demonstrated the multilevel responsiveness of a subject. Erickson's comments were as follows:

> Now in your use of hypnosis, you secure the sub, uh, the patient's *attention*. You talk to them. Express ideas. It isn't necessary to tell them *relax*, or *feel sleepy*. Close their eyes *slowly*. Lift their hand *higher* and *higher* and *higher*. You merely speak in such a way that you command their attention *more* and *more*. And when they give you *full* attention, they *become immobile, unresponsive* to a lot of *unimportant* stimuli. . . . (personal communication, September 25, 1978)

As Erickson made these remarks to those present, the person sitting next to him blinked his eyes, began to lift his left hand, and then closed his eyes. The body movements gradually ceased completely, and the person remained immobile for some period of time. The mention of the specific behaviors underlined above served, in the responsive subject, to effect a casual, yet elegant induction of hypnosis.

Thus far I have focused on the verbal means by which Erickson utilized multilevel communication. He also made use of nonverbal communications. Despite his physical limitations, Erickson was a master at the skillful manipulation of body postures, gestures, and voice qualities such as tone, rhythm, inflection, and pitch in dealing with his patients and students. This was illustrated in a teaching seminar at his home in Phoenix.

A rather abrasive female student had been annoying both Erickson and everyone else present. A female companion of hers commented that she was beginning to recognize some of her own rigidity, and asked Erickson to please help her deal with that. He responded in characteristic fashion, and told a rather long case report of a female patient who was frigid. All the while he stared at the Navaho rug on the floor in front of him. As he finished the story, the first woman interrupted, saying rather obnoxiously,

> Dr. Erickson, you just didn't understand. She said that she was *rigid*, not that she was frigid!" Erickson listened to this outburst, still staring at the floor. Finally, with great deliberation, he looked up, gave the woman his famous fixed stare, and replied, "I know that *she's* not frigid." He then returned his gaze to the floor, and soon began telling another story. The woman sat stunned, and created no further problems during the seminar. (personal communication, July 11, 1979)

The use of psychological implication was an extremely important part of Erickson's approach to psychotherapy. It is, by definition, a situation in which multiple level communication is taking place, allowing one to communicate far more than what one is merely saying at a content level. By his subtle use of psychological implication, Erickson structured situations in such a manner that his patients and students developed ideas, plans, and behaviors which they experienced as originating from within themselves. As a result, changes implemented by Erickson's therapy and teaching proceeded from the inside out, rather than vice versa.

Erickson eschewed theoretical models, and never really provided a formal categorization of all the various methods by which he utilized the process of psychological implication. This attitude was a result of the individualized nature of his approach to therapy, and of his genius in using whatever was available to facilitate therapy under whatever circumstance he saw his patients. Thus, it should be understood that psychological implication is not a system to be applied *to* a particular patient. Rather, interaction with the patient provides a stimulus for whatever implications can be introduced with therapeutic intent. This point is critical in understanding Erickson's work. He did not develop a theory or technique which was then blindly applied to every patient. Erickson developed a vast repertory of approaches that he could then implement in an experimental fashion when provided the stimulus of a unique individual with a unique problem constellation.

REFERENCES

Erickson, M. H. (1944). The method employed to formulate a complex story for the induction of an experimental neurosis in a hypnotic subject. *Journal of General Psychology, 31,* 67-84.
Erickson, M. H., & Rossi, E. (1979). *Hypnotherapy: An exploratory casebook.* New York: Irvington.
Erickson, M. H., Rossi, E., & Rossi, S. (1976). *Hypnotic realities.* New York: Irvington.

Chapter 12

Use of Indirect Suggestion in Brief Therapy

John H. Frykman

Once I asked Milton Erickson if he thought his Norwegian heritage contributed to his skills as a therapist. He surprised me by telling a story about another part of his genetic makeup: his American-Indian ancestry.

"Do you know about the ways white people and Indians hunt? White hunters gather on one edge of the forest, stationing only one or two hunters on the other border. The troop then charges loudly through the forest, banging the trees, flushing out the prey toward the guns of the waiting hunters. Alternatively, white hunters will make a great production of tracking, using dogs, binoculars, four-wheel vehicles, a vast array of technology.

"The Indian hunter goes alone into the heart of the forest, sits on a rock with his face toward the wind, and quietly watches and waits for the animal to come to him. Now, that's how I do therapy" (personal communication, December 5, 1979).

Milton Erickson is the only therapist I have observed who seemed to *know* what he was doing. Some of us pretend to others that we know, or even talk ourselves into believing it, but Erickson always rang true to me. I may not have caught on to the point of his every observation or suggestion, but I did not doubt his sureness—that he was secure on a rock, right in the heart of the forest.

People's conscious minds are so easily distracted, their unconscious minds never. During one of my first visits with Erickson, I found it difficult to understand his partially paralyzed speech. He said, "John, close your eyes for a moment, and see how much more easily you can hear, when your conscious mind is not distracted by the way I look. Allow yourself to hear the words." He also told me that when I returned home and listened to my tape recordings, I would have less difficulty understanding, for the same reason. Picking up his suggestion, I tried looking at his eyebrows rather than directly into his eyes when he spoke, and my listening and understanding improved immediately. In this way I could bypass my conscious distractions and allow myself to hear.

Indirect suggestions allow people to close their eyes in order to hear what is being said without being distracted by the problem, the solution, what's right, and so forth. A therapist can use the language and the imagery of a person or family to tailor suggestions that will draw out their own resources. Throughout a therapy session, there are countless opportunities to make verbal and nonverbal indirect suggestions—for example, by manipulating the environment or telling stories, and in efforts to engender rapport and change thinking.

ENGENDERING RAPPORT

A therapist can unwittingly obstruct rapport and trust by dressing in a way that hides the person; both a uniform stereotype and an outlandish style of dress can make clients uncomfortable, uncertain who the person is. In my first meeting with clients, I nearly always wear a jacket and tie. Later, it may be quite natural to relax and loosen up, but to go the other way, to impose formality, is to risk the trust that has been gained.

Clients can be just as easily reassured and intrigued by a genuine expression of the therapist's uniqueness. Erickson's use of purple (he often wore purple clothes) is a case in point. My own irrepressible sloppiness seems to disarm people—although I don't claim that this is by design.

Recently a probation officer referred a Japanese immigrant family with the information that the identified patient was a teenage boy "into rock music." Borrowing a "Police" (rock band) button from my son, I wore it in my lapel at the first meeting. When I noticed the boy eyeing the button, I nodded affirmatively in his direction; thereafter, whenever he looked at me with interest, I nodded again. Soon his body was relaxed and he began to enter into the discussion.

To the parents I said, "It must be very hard for you, as people who take pride in the way you manage your own lives, to have an outsider like me looking in on your privacy." They relaxed immediately.

When clients first enter a therapist's office, they can be set at ease by noticing evidence of the therapist's "real life," such as personal objects, pictures, plants, books, decorative touches, etc.

As therapists develop security in the heart of the forest, they learn a multitude of behaviors for engendering rapport: posture; gestures; position taken in the room (avoid having a "therapist's chair"); management of time; style of note-taking; choosing strategically what order family members are addressed; using "trigger" words that engender cooperative responses (may be slang or life-style related, i.e., "straight," "bad," "hip," "cool," etc.); sympathetic breathing, sighing, movements, expressions—in fact, taking seriously everything one does and what effect it can have in the therapy situation.

STORYTELLING

Stories provide the vehicle for many of my indirect suggestions. The individual or family can relax and "not do anything" while the story is told, which helps them to open their minds to suggestions for change.

I told a story to a family that was having difficulty talking about the real issues that were troubling them. In this case the husband and wife had become almost totally disengaged from each other while becoming overly engaged with their two teen-aged sons (sports, Boy Scouts, school, etc.) and one of the boys emerged as the "deviant."

"You make me think of the times when I was a young boy and used to play hide-and-seek. What a feeling it was to be in a really good hiding place, to feel my heart start to race as 'It' drew near, knowing full well that I wouldn't be found, yet still fearful that I would. Or, being so crafty that I would begin to follow 'It' as she moved about looking for me and the others. I always tried to keep the way 'home' clear. Or, when 'It' myself, seeing someone, I would wait for just the right moment when it was most advantageous to reveal my discovery, in such a way that others would be caught as well."

On another occasion a 19-year-old "schizophrenic" woman talked of the powers that were controlling her from another state. A man there had a stone. When he touched the stone he had direct communication with her, "as if there is a radio in one of my teeth. . . ."

"As you're talking, Ginny, I can't help but begin to feel frightened myself (at which point she comforted me and reassured me). I think of the time I was stranded behind enemy lines in Korea, living in a cave for almost three weeks. The soldiers would come very near the cave, but I couldn't understand what they were saying, whether they had seen the cave, whether they were friendly or hostile. I knew no Korean. I would start to sing songs without uttering a sound. I'd begin to fight with hand-to-hand combat without moving a muscle. It was all so real, so . . ."

There are so many ways in which storytelling can allow us to reach that which otherwise has been unreachable, and suggest that which has been unacceptable in ways that can be received.

ENVIRONMENTAL MANIPULATIONS

Staging conversations in waiting rooms that can be overheard; spilling a cup of coffee all over one's self; prescribed journeys or expeditions; arranging the positions where people sit; strategically planned interruptions (phone calls, persons coming to the door); changing appointment times, varying appointment times; hanging certain pictures or posters; having a wide range of usable items in one's office (books, timers, clickers, puzzles, games, cups, spectacles, counters, rosaries, worry beads, Tarot cards, Biorhythm gadgets, egg timers, pedometers, etc.); controlling temperature, light, noise; use of video and audio recording equipment; the one-way mirror—the hidden authority; colleague consultation; supervisorial intervention; and, most important, being continuously aware of how much influence environmental factors have in the family's situation—these are but a few examples of the utilization of environmental factors.

To illustrate the last point, I offer two striking examples:

A couple presented what seemed to be rather ordinary sexual problems. The man suffered from occasional impotence and episodic ejaculatory incapability. The woman was "turned off to sex," and didn't know why. This was after seven years of marriage without any significant sexual problems. A modified Masters and Johnson approach was initiated with the couple—touching exercises, "I" message training, sensate focus, etc. It was to no avail. After four sessions it was decided that the author would visit the couple's home. On the wall over their bed hung a picture of their three-month-old, dead baby, in a white casket, surrounded by flowers. Imagine, if you will, the impact of that picture (approximately 11" × 16") on their bed-entering activities.

The couple was instructed to take a long weekend trip. Before departing, they were to hang a draw curtain in front of the baby's picture so that they would be able to show their respect and concern for the child in a new way. When they returned from their "adventure" and to their own bed, they would draw the covers over themselves and then "draw the covers over their baby," to allow her to sleep peacefully as well.

To point out the influence of the picture would have been to invoke a new form of guilt. They were able to discover that they slept well and had no more serious sexual problems.

In another case, parents came to me concerned about a 14-year-old daughter who was wetting the bed. She shared a room with an 11-year-old sister who did not wet the bed. A great deal of the meal time conversation centered around Rachel's problem. In gathering information I learned that the parent's bedroom was four steps up from the girls' in a split-level house. Every morning the girls were awakened by the father shouting down the stairs, "Time to get up, girls. Are you awake?" Rachel was on the high school swim team and afraid to go on overnight meets because of her problem.

I instructed the father to have a talk with Rachel and say: "You are really quite grown-up now. I shouldn't really have to be calling down and waking you up in the morning. If I get you your own alarm clock, would you be willing to get yourself and your sister up in the morning?" She readily agreed.

I instructed the mother, who often went to observe Rachel's swimming, to call her aside as she came out of the water and say: "I don't know what it is about you lately, but you sure seem different. Your body seems to be changing, you're walking straighter, you seem so much more like a young woman."

The bed-wetting stopped in less than one week.

In terms of some of the other items on my list: Have you ever tried not to listen to someone who was whispering in a waiting room? How does a person react when the picture on the wall is a metaphor of their own situation (a poster with three little tiger kittens tangled in balls of twine comes to mind)? Or, people who are having trouble letting go of an ended relationship taking a cruise on the "Red and White" fleet in San Francisco, taking with them an artifact that represents the ended relationship (picture, special gift, etc.), and casting it into the sea as the boat goes out under the Golden Gate Bridge. They are asked to sit down, close their eyes and listen to what their unconscious mind is trying to teach them. When they do, they hear the noises, voices, laughter, and the recorded narrative telling them all the wonderful things about San Francisco. Hard to stay a captive of grief in those circumstances.

Or, the magical power of an egg timer measuring three minutes of anger, three minutes of eating, three minutes of sorrow, three minutes until my next cigarette (drink), three minutes to make believe that I am beautiful/handsome—and much more (Madanes, 1981).

There is so much happening all around us that can be used to strengthen and enhance the work we do. So often therapy is crippled by being confined to what we say and what our patients/clients say.

From "benevolent sabotage" (Watzlawick, Weakland, & Fisch, 1974) to "squirting water between your front teeth" (Haley, 1973) to an "addict eating three oranges a day" (Frykman, 1972)—environmental manipulation can provide rich resources from which to offer indirect suggestions to our clients.

INTRODUCING NEW, CHANGING OLD IDEAS

Certainly, there are many ways to approach dealing with a "bridge" phobia. But what happens to a person when they *learn* that they have been on a bridge for almost 10 minutes, and haven't been frightened at all?

A 33-year-old man came to me because he could not drive from Oakland to San Francisco to visit the theater, restaurants, museums, because of the bridge. Upon entering the bridge in his car, he would begin to sweat, have heart palpitations, and eventually have to stop the car, trembling, and wait until a tow truck came to rescue him. He came to me for therapy via BART (the train in the tube under the Bay) and bus, a journey that would take him about an hour and a half. I arranged for him to visit one of my friends who worked in an office building which had a bridge to an adjoining building, 10 floors above the street. I instructed him to learn what he could. My friend was instructed to take him on a walking tour of his office, ending in the middle of the bridge. He was, after a certain period of time, to take the client to the window to show him something on the street below. Imagine the surprise. The client learned at that moment that it was safe to be on a bridge, even one that was 10 stories above the ground. New ideas like this one are learned far more easily when they are *discovered* than when they are pointed out.

Parents will often become victims of their children's power (Haley, 1976). Helpless, unable to act or to exercise the normal prerogatives of parenthood, they can be helped in a variety of ways to regain their authority with indirect suggestions. They can be instructed to "go home and learn how really bad your children are. Both of you keep a notebook and write down all the things that they do that show you how bad they are. Don't try to correct them this week, merely learn how bad it really is so that we will be able to know where to go from here."

Parents in that situation unwittingly communicate a quiet confidence and authority which begins improvement in the children. Therapy becomes a task of simply "going from here."

Recently, in a session where parents were sabotaged by the children (wandering off to other parts of the room, talking about things totally unrelated to the session, bickering with each other, etc.), I said to the children, "I'm going to ask you to leave for a while so that I can speak with your parents alone. There are things that I have to say to them that you may not hear. I'll bring you back in a few minutes for the conclusion of our session."

Even if no specific suggestions are given to the parents, their authority and position in the family have been enhanced by the intervention. An old idea, "I can get away with anything I want," has begun to be changed.

Other examples of such indirect suggestions include: instructing clients to write letters to family and friends in a precisely prescribed way; making a series of phone calls to learn about a crucial issue; sending patients out to buy a special gift for a special person; learning a prepared and practiced response to invoke in common situations that precipitate crises—whenever you feel you are being criticized say, "I'm not so sure I understand you, could you tell me that again?" or other variations on "counting-to-ten," etc.

One final illustration: About five years ago while doing a workshop at a mental health center, I was asked to do a demonstration interview with one of their "chronically ill" patients. Samson was brought into the room from the inpatient ward next door. I had no knowledge of his history.

I learned subsequently that he had been diagnosed paranoid schizophrenic and that the evening before our interview he had thrown a bed out through the window of the board and care home where he resided under the conservatorship of the state. He was a very tall, muscular, young man and had a history of violence. He had started many brawls in bars and at one time had holed up in a mountain cabin with several guns and other weapons "because the *Losers* (a motorcycle gang) were out to get me." He also had a "Social Worker" who followed him around to take care of him. She was presently in England and unable to help him.

As the story unfolded, it was learned that he had broken the window to go out and rescue "a boy who was being whipped by some men, and was yelping like a dog in pain." He had a seven-year history with the mental health center.

The interview was conducted with about 60 therapists gathered in a small classroom. As Samson and I talked at the front, one of the group sat with a hand-held video camera in the front row.

Time and space prohibit going into detail about this case. Let it suffice to say that I was concerned that he *learn* that he was not out of control and that he could direct his behavior in successful endeavors. After all, he had spent many years as a lumberjack and everyone knows how difficult and complex that is.

I told him how sometimes I yearned to be in a position like his, to have someone to care for me, feed me, see to it that I was washed—without the worry of working 50-60 hours a week to support myself. Then I gave him this instruction: "There are many things in your situation that puzzle me. It doesn't seem to fit together, to make sense. What you have told me that the doctors have said, though it *may* be true, does not add up. Would you be willing to do something that sounds a bit crazy to find out?" (Full affirmative response.) "As soon as you are allowed to leave the hospital, would you go to your favorite bar, buy one drink, and *try* to pick a fight. And while you are *trying*, I would like you to pay very close attention to what is going on around you and in you so that you can report it to me."

About a week later he followed through on the assignment. He was unable to pick a fight. He learned a great deal through that experience. Within two months he had taken the legal steps to become independent from the state. When I last heard of him, he was serving admirably as a detective in a large urban department store. Psychotherapy had been his Delilah.

Indirect suggestions in brief therapy provide powerful tools for the therapist to intervene in the whole range of human problems. Each situation is unique; each family is unique; each person is unique. In a real sense the craft of therapy is getting someone to accept a suggestion that they have not been able to accept before. The more indirect the suggestion, the more powerful the discoveries and changes will be.

REFERENCES

Frykman, J. (1972). *A new connection*. San Francisco: Scrimshaw Press.
Haley, J. (1973). *Uncommon therapy*. New York: Norton.
Haley, J. (1976). *Problem-solving therapy*. San Francisco: Jossey-Bass.
Madanes, C. (1981). *Strategic family therapy*. San Francisco: Jossey-Bass.
Watzlawick, P., Weakland, J., & Fisch, R. (1974). *Change: Principles of problem formation and problem resolution*. New York: Norton.

Chapter 13

The Playful Use of Words in Therapy (The Case of the PUNishING Therapist and the SUPERFISHal Client)

Donna M. Spencer

Poetry is often considered the language of the soul—the means by which humans give expression to concepts difficult to express. One could argue that the language of therapy is often akin to poetic expression. Words in therapy, like those in poetry, can take on multiple meanings and the words themselves can stimulate behavior change at an unconscious level. The utilization of this language process in therapy outside conscious awareness is the topic of this chapter.

I will trace the development of my awareness of the phenomenon of unconscious language utilization. Chronologically, the phenomenon presented itself in a sequence of interactions over a three-year period and emerged through distinct stages: 1) Erickson's teasing with words; 2) my spontaneous playing with words; 3) my utilization of language forms outside conscious awareness; 4) Erickson's and my communicating with words at a conscious and unconscious level; and 5) my experience of clients' utilization of language outside conscious awareness.

In a qualitative research sense, I attempt to step into the situation by describing the interactions as they were personally experienced. Such a method enables one to go beyond a linear understanding of the phenomenon and creates the beginnings of a more in-depth understanding of what actually occurred.

THE UTILIZATION OF LANGUAGE
OUTSIDE CONSCIOUS AWARENESS

Milton Erickson was intrigued with words. Much has been written about his masterful use of embedded messages, metaphors and paradoxical injunctions. Erickson loved ethnic jokes, accents and any form of plays on words. He related to me early on in our relationship that he was fascinated with the power of poetry in expressing thoughts. One evening he had me climb high onto a chair in his family room to reach a particular book of poetry. He then asked me to open to one selection after another and read certain poems aloud to him. This went on for some two hours. He asked me, "What have I had you read all *these* poems for?" He then added, "These poems got me through my first bout with polio and then through medical school." He next asked me to look at the inscription on the front cover. It was inscribed, "To Milton from Your Nurse." Shortly thereafter, he asked if I had ever read *Archy and Mehitabel*. He then asked me to read all three volumes that evening and to return to let him know how I liked them. They were delightful reading and I recall Archy lamenting:

boss i am disappointed in
some of your readers they
are always asking how does
archy work the shift so as to get a
new line or how does archy do
this or do that they are
always interested in technical
details when the main question is
whether the stuff is
literature or not

I decided to go with the flow; Erickson never would directly explain the reason behind all this reading—I decided to just relax and enjoy whatever my mind consciously or unconsciously would do with the material. I had by this time spent many formal training hours with Erickson in which he had used me as a hypnotic subject. Hypnosis was such a common phenomenon by this time that it was difficult to differentiate clearly when I was in or out of the trance state. As the trance state became less discernible, so did its need. Eventually, unconscious processing, primary logic, holistic perception, time distortion and catalepsy were all occurring quite easily and without ritualistic trance induction.

I also knew something was occurring in reference to my perception of words. Words became fascinating without conscious effort on my part. Milton and I began to banter in a double entendre vaudevillian style of humor. As a friend presented him with a gift of home-canned beans, he glanced at me and said, "Melba's bean here" and I answered to his delight—"Well, she's just stringing you on."

One evening after finishing some rigorous videotaping with Ernest Rossi, we decided to have a dinner party for Milton and his wife Betty. I was quite tired and homesick. Frankly, I did not feel like socializing. Reluctantly, I went to the dinner and even performed a little skit for Erickson's entertainment. Immediately on finishing the skit, I decided to leave. Sandra Sylvester of Tucson saw me getting ready and said, "That's all the entertainment, right, Donna?"—to which I replied slowly, and in a spontaneous trance, "Yes."

When I arrived at the motel room I experienced cramps in my stomach, diarrhea, and a rush of early childhood memories. I began relating these early memories and feelings on the phone to my friend, Donald Malon. As I would relax with one set of images I would cramp again, have diarrhea and then experience another amazingly clear, dreamlike series of associations from my childhood and early adult years. This went on for three or four hours. I felt quite exhausted and relieved. The next morning I was to be a subject for Erickson as he demonstrated hypnosis to a group. I went in the kitchen to see him before the group assembled in his office. He greeted me with a smile and the comment—"You had diarrhea last night, didn't you?" I said yes, and asked if he had given me some kind of posthypnotic suggestion! He smiled more broadly and said, "No, I did nothing—you figure out when your unconscious decided it had more work to do."

As the day went on I tried to figure out what had happened. Finally, on the way to the movies that evening I recalled the events of the night before. I heard consciously what I had heard unconsciously the night before. I experienced delight and humor as I could hear Sylvester unwittingly say to me, *"That's all the entertainment"* and I realized that my mind had translated this outside of conscious awareness as "that's all—end retainment!" My conscious mind had been tired and weary of all the hypnotic work, yet, unknown to me, my unconscious had given my conscious mind information to process all night long.

This was the first instance I experienced that my unconscious could process information outside conscious awareness. Previously I could not quite believe that my mind could function without conscious thinking being in control. It was truly unbelievable and quite unsettling. I realized how deeply set is the bias that conscious control of inner processes is necessary. At first I experienced an insecure feeling, a feeling of being out of control. It is no small matter that Erickson spends so much time assuring clients that they can trust their unconscious processes and allows them to experience the positive functioning of these unconscious processes.

After this experience, I continued to work with Erickson and with clients. I began to experience a spontaneous poetry coming to me often in the middle of the night. One poem I wrote and did not find until three weeks later. The poem is as follows:

Mad MAD MADelaine
    mad made maiden came
mean dream   So unseemly
    S/he intolerably tame

Where there's hair there's joy
    or nought   there ought

to be for living—now giving—getting
    even Stephen paul—and all
especially Mother   so bear   no hair
        emptinest
    so full of shit
Split   and let be both

This poem was about a client who was a dual personality. She had experienced a great deal of trauma growing up with a repressive mother in wartime England who punished her daughter for disobedience by lighting a match to her vagina. The client married, moved to the United States, had six children and lived with her mother and family. Shortly after the death of her mother, she discovered that her husband, a very straitlaced fellow, had an affair. The client experienced a psychotic breakdown and was hospitalized. She began then showing two distinct personalities—the good mother and wife, and the bitch. She was unaware of the dual personalities. With treatment, the "bitch" was kept in control; she was allowed to be angry and to hate men, was instructed to stay out of the couple's bed. I worked long hours trying to help the client integrate the personalities. It seemed impossible for the two personalities to function compatibly for very long. However, I did not consciously realize the impossibility of integrating the two personalities until three weeks after my unconscious had composed the poem with the accurate diagnosis and prognosis:

Split   and let be both.

During this same period I was calling long distance to Erickson. He always wanted to hear about clients. When I related instances such as the one above, he would comment, "Your unconscious mind is much smarter than you think." I had the habit of prefacing questions to him with the phrase "I was thinking. . . ." He would always quickly stop me mid-sentence and interject: "That's probably the problem—you are *thinking*."

In an October 1978 visit with Erickson, he asked my opinion of a person who had been participating in the group earlier that day. I immediately wrote on a piece of paper, without consciously thinking about it:

in   no   sense

Erickson laughed and agreed that the person appeared open, but yet in his words, "He has no sense; opportunity will knock at his door and he'll waste his time sweeping the floor." It wasn't until a year later that I could see the behavior that confirmed Erickson's hunch and my unconscious diagnosis. This person had every opportunity to grow personally having worked with Erickson over several months time, yet he resisted any interpersonal growth in spite of the fact that he was an excellent hypnotic subject, experienced deep trance, and could demonstrate any number of hypnotic phenomena.

It should be noted that in his earlier years Erickson would spend up to 200 hours working with a particular client in order to induce a hypnotic trance. In his last years of clinical practice he relied less on the traditional hypnotic trance and seemed to have confidence that transitory trance states were adequate for therapeutic purposes. Most participants in his training groups conducted at his office in Phoenix report that they slipped in and out of trancelike states. Few were used as hypnotic subjects in the traditional sense of a ritualized trance induction, yet many or most experiencing the transitory trance state reported experiencing changes in their behavior after these encounters.

Regarding another patient, a poem spontaneously flowed:

in
no sense
Manger's load of childhood
7 up-side down
WOW

I did not understand this poem at first, until I saw the last word WOW upside down as MOM. The critical issue with this patient was that she had been raped at age seven and was still angry at her mother for coldly taking her to a doctor for a physical exam and refusing to allow the child to let go of any emotion about the rape. The mother was perfectly rational and expected the daughter to stay in complete control of her feelings. Ever since that time this woman has been perfectly proper, especially with her mother, and has experienced much ambivalence about herself as a woman, emotionally and sexually.

In 1979, Erickson and the organizing committee invited me to present a paper at the First International Congress on Ericksonian Hypnotherapy to be held in Phoenix for his 79th birthday in December of 1980; however, Erickson died in March 1980.

In preparing for my paper, I decided to review some audio tapes recorded during a two-week seminar with Erickson in August 1978. I was reluctant to listen to the tapes since I was still grieving his death. I was not sure what memories and feelings the tapes would release. As I listened to the tapes, I was astonished at what I heard that I had not heard consciously while the tapes were being recorded.

It sounded as though two conversations were simultaneously taking place between Erickson and me. One conversation was digital, logical and conscious, and could be easily verified by anyone listening to the tapes. The second level conversation was also digital and logical but was occurring outside conscious awareness. The meaning of this conversation is subjectively deduced from my understanding, in retrospect, of myself at that point in time.

I had no conscious awareness of sending or receiving these messages. On the one hand I had no conscious understanding at the time of the taping that these were problem areas for me. On the other hand, I was conscious of being in the presence of other professionals and colleagues in the group and I was aware that I did not want to be "opened up," in a therapeutic sense, by Erickson. Yet in retrospect I know two facts: 1) each of the personal concerns discussed outside of conscious awareness proved to be issues which not only logically fit into my life history but which became concerns that I worked through in the two years following the taping; and 2) certain concrete behaviors can be documented which indicate a problem resolution in these same areas. It is these behaviors experienced at a conscious level that validate to some extent that some communication was occurring outside any conscious awareness.

I will attempt to explain the process by which I became consciously aware of changed behaviors. It should be noted that these "pieces" of awareness occurred periodically over a two-year period. They occurred prior to studying the tapes of my interaction with Erickson and prior to my discovery of the pattern of communication occurring outside conscious awareness. As I look back on the experiences, they each followed

a certain pattern with discernible characteristics. The pattern of awareness followed a sequence:

1) I would spontaneously perform a new behavior or behavior set.
2) I would experience an odd trancelike pause and then become aware
   of viewing myself as subject and object simultaneously.
3) I would experience a rush of feelings at both a subjective and objective
   level.
4) The experience at both levels was perceived as humorous, positive,
   fulfilling and significant.

Usually I would write the experience down in detail and share it with
Milton. His response was always delight and laughter and a teasing
taunt to me to stay open to what else my unconscious had to tell me.
We began to refer to these experiences as "AHA'S." They were similar
to the spontaneous "aha" one experiences when catching a joke. One
is caught at one level in the logic of the story and simultaneously one
is aware of another logic within the punch line which opens up a new
meaning. Our immediate response to such leaps in awareness is laughter. It is a childlike delight not very different from that open response
we see in a baby who sees three images reflected in the three-way mirror.
(I will discuss the theoretical descriptions of this type of awareness at
the end of the chapter.)

As illustration, I will detail one such "aha" experience. To preface the
experience I should explain that I was 36 years old at the time. I had
spent eight years as a Sister of Mercy. After leaving the convent, I lived
a normal life including enjoyable relationships with men. Four years
later I married and subsequently had two sons. I considered myself well-
adjusted and felt positively about my femininity and sexuality. This
"aha" experience happened shortly after leaving Phoenix while I was
working out at a St. Louis health spa. As usual, after the workout I took
a steambath and shower. I stepped out from the shower into the dressing
room which had one mirrored wall opposite the shower. I had been
stepping from this same shower into this same room for over a year.
This day as I stepped from the shower I *saw* a beautiful black woman
standing nude in front of me, her back to the mirror, her front facing
me. I could also *see* myself nude in the mirror. This stepping out could
only have lasted two or three seconds, before this woman passed me
into the shower, and I had myself wrapped in the towel. However, the
experience seemed to last for hours. I was totally delighted, as though
I had personally discovered a whole new universe that no one else had

knowledge of. I experienced joy and an intense desire to share the experience. I saw each part of her body and thought it magnificent. I saw my own body and thought it too was beautiful. This was not a judgment of the merits of either body on a 1 to 10 scale. It was an aesthetic appreciation of a beautiful piece of art. There definitely was a sensory awareness along with the intellectual awareness, but it was not erotic. It was more of the nature of discovery. On a subjective level, I experienced immense pleasure at knowing something new—at seeing something I had never seen before.

At the same time, I could see myself viewing myself and objectively thinking about what I was experiencing subjectively. I was aware that I was having a "first" experience. In all my years of living with my mother, sister, friends, and even with 40 women in a convent, this was the first time I had seen a woman's body. How, I asked myself, could I have not *seen* these bodies?

Then I became aware of an even more ridiculous situation. I had enjoyed sex, had given birth to two sons, had been living in my body for 36 years. How could I have not seen my own body? These questions along with the awareness of now seeing and appreciating the sight of these bodies created an ecstatic feeling of humor and joy.

In the two years between the first meeting with Dr. Erickson and my preparation for the paper in Phoenix approximately ten such experiences were recorded. Each experience followed the same pattern and each included a behavior which would fit logically into the problem areas discussed between Erickson and me in words utilized outside of conscious awareness. Analyzing the original tapes, several parallels were found between Erickson's choice of words and the words used by me in interacting with him. It is as though two conversations were simultaneously taking place between us. The conversations were embedded in the same sentences, yet the words chosen had meanings at two different levels.

To illustrate the process without detailing all the personal information on the tapes I will select some of the many examples of this type of communication.

At the beginning of the sessions Erickson got the lay of the land and began exploring the openness of the individual group members to trance work. One person, who had been with Erickson at a previous workshop, easily slipped into a deep trance. Erickson complimented her on the depth of the trance and asked:

E: Do you know where you are?

Cl: (The client elaborates a number of specific visual experiences which she and Erickson enjoy together in the trance.)

The other group members, many of whom had never experienced hypnosis, were utterly amazed that this person was in such a deep trance and communicating with Erickson. He then pointedly asked:

E: Where are you?
Cl: Nowhere um and it's nice. I'd rather be there with you than anyplace else.
E: How do you feel about nowhereness? (no awareness)
Cl: Just really good. It's OK.
E: Why do you say nowhereness is OK?
Cl: I like being here. It's comfortable.

Erickson said nothing, the client continued the trance. As Erickson moved his body, a microphone dropped and made quite a clatter. Erickson laughingly commented, looking at no one in particular:

E: Somebody dropped something?
I immediately responded: But what?!

It was at this point that Milton H. Erickson and I first met. He commented on the seat I had chosen in the group, indicating that I wanted to be "vulnerable" and then he guided me through my first traditional hypnotic trance.

This first encounter was replete with double-level communication. The first subject (Cl) explained that no awareness was quite comfortable for her. Erickson appeared to accept her unconscious communication and moved on to find another subject. My first words to his invitation "drop something?" were "But, what?" The next two hours of taping find me uttering the word "but" an endless number of times.

"But, what?!"
"Yes, but. . . ."
"No, but. . . ."
"I agree but. . . ."
"The butt of the problem. . . ."
". . . a kick in the butt. . . ."

In an unusual display of directness, Erickson later on in the first day shared with me his awareness of my overuse of the word "but." He stated, "You can't keep your mind off your butt." He continued, "It's not just your butt—it's all of you." Later in a far less direct manner he told the story of Herbert, a former client. Erickson used the following sentences which can be heard at a conscious and unconscious level.

E: Herbert became my patient. . . .
   (Her butt became my patient. . . .)
E: I really listened to Herbert's story. . . .
   (I really listened to Her butt's story. . . .)
E: Herbert knew he had been fed the wrong thing.
   (Her butt knew she had been fed the wrong thing.)

   Bandler and Grinder (1975) had written several books detailing Erickson's ability to pace a client's representational system. Here we see this ability to pace the client refined to include utilizing the same exact word the client uses unconsciously in order to communicate to the client outside of conscious awareness.

   In the session the following day, I stated to Erickson: "I need a good belly laugh." He responded: "Would you like to wake up with a good belly laugh? Go ahead and enjoy it." I continued: "My mother's life is full of belly laughs."

   I seem to be saying that I need a good belly in order to fulfill my life as a mother. Erickson is telling me to go ahead and trust my uge to have a baby. At a conscious level, I had intellectually decided that two children were enough and that I wanted only to pursue my doctoral degree. I had become quite serious about life. Unconsciously, I seem to be saying something different. I needed another child, and I needed to laugh. Behaviorally, I did later become pregnant and was overjoyed. I definitely did want another child at some unconscious level.

   Erickson seemed to encourage this thought as he used certain words in his description of when he lay acutely ill with polio for the first time at the age of 17.

E: As I lay in bed that night I overheard the three doctors tell my parents in the other room that their boy would be dead in the morning. *I felt intense anger* that anyone should tell a mother *her* boy *would be dead by morning* (mourning). *My mother then came in with as serene a face as can be.* I asked her to *move the dresser up against* the side of *the bed* at an angle. *She did not understand why, she thought I was delirious.* My speech was difficult. But at that angle *by virtue* of the mirror on the dresser *I could see* through the doorway, through the west window of the other room. I was damned if I would die. *I was going to see one more sun* (son) *set* (yet).

He later began to tell a story about a patient whom he treated by getting her to grow African violets. He explained that he had the patient do her own therapy. I immediately interjected, supposedly talking about his patient.

"Which she is already doing." Erickson agreed with me.

As Erickson went through this patient's story, he repeated again and again that at the end of his treatment with her there were:

> . . . African violet(s)　(I can violate) in the kitchen.
> . . . African violet(s)　in the dining room.
> . . . African violet(s)　in the bedroom, etc. . . .

Listing all the rooms of the house, he finally said there were so many violets in her house there was no room for depression. Interestingly, Erickson repeated this story to me so many times over the months that I became quite bored with it. One evening he started telling me the story during the night, and I remember thinking that perhaps he was getting senile. I said to him, "Milton, you've told that story several times. I think I know it by heart." He ignored me and continued rambling on with it. Several weeks later he laughed as I described an "aha" in which I was enjoying making love with my husband and realized that this was the first time we were not in our bedroom!

Beyond experiencing new awareness within myself, I began to *hear* more messages coming from my clients. Denzin (1978) points out that in qualitative research the ability to document the same phenomena occurring in other situations is a sound method of validation. Therefore, I will conclude this section of the chapter with some examples of this type of communication which transpired between my clients and me in my clinical practice.

One particular client had a gruesome personal history of having a schizophrenic mother and spending a good deal of her childhood in foster homes and institutions. She had had polio as a child and walked with a slight limp. She married at age 16 and gave birth shortly thereafter to a daughter. The marriage was a disaster and involved some wife beating. She divorced, completed her schooling and functioned well as a single parent. She eventually remarried, held a responsible job, and presented herself as a mature and competent woman. However, she brought her daughter to innumerable therapists because she feared the child inherited the schizophrenia potential from her mother. Some therapists found problems in the little girl; most diagnosed her normal. When this woman came to me, her preoccupation with the fear that she produced a potential schizophrenic was destroying not only her relationship with her daughter through smothering, but was causing her otherwise fine marriage to deteriorate. I diagnosed the daughter as normal and the mother as functioning at a creative level. This woman had linked herself to significant role models who enabled her to develop far beyond what would have been expected of a crippled girl of a schizophrenic mother. She was intelligent and she related to me that her daughter Gina was okay. However, she could not seem to accept that message when people told her. "No matter how many people say that she's well I still worry." This woman was really unable to feel relief at an emotional level. It was as if the words did not register. I found myself interspersing into my interviews with her the words "Gina grows"—"Gina is fine." I would tell her in the midst of the interview:

> *Gee, nothing grows* in my garden.   *Gee nothing is fine all the time.*
> (Gina grows)   (Gina is fine, all the time.)

In a short period of time (three interviews), the client told me that she didn't understand why, but she felt better about her daughter. Her words were, "I don't know why, but I feel like I really know down deep that Gina is fine." She described her knowledge as "intuitive" not rational. Following up with her the next year, it was apparent that she had no manifestation of the earlier anxiety. It seemed as though her unconscious was able to bypass her conscious bias and allow her to know without understanding exactly what she knew.

Another client defied all methods of traditional treatment to deal with her guilt and anxiety about a marriage outside the Church. This woman was frigid sexually and extremely anxious to the point of severe depression. After several methods of treatment were unsuccessful, she commented. "I guess nobody can help me but myself and I certainly don't know what to do." I decided to let her help herself and simply suggested that she stay open to whatever method her unconscious would use to solve the problem. Within a few days she called me frantically saying that she had a dream that must mean bad luck. She said all she could remember was a series of numbers that added up to "13"—an unlucky number. I asked her to come in for an appointment. She began telling me the dream. She had a wonderful glow on her face as she recounted the dream but she insisted the numbers added to "13" and must mean something unlucky. I asked her if the number 13 appeared in the dream. She said it did not. I then explained that the 13 and feeling of bad luck was conscious. I asked her what numbers had occurred unconsciously in the dream. She exclaimed with a smile on her face:

$$6 \quad 4 \quad 2 \quad 1$$

They were exactly in that order. I said, "Well—no wonder you're smiling—God's given you your Christmas present." She was baffled. I explained.

$$6 \quad 4 \quad 2 \quad 1$$
Sex for two, won!

She then cried with joy. She felt that that was the message. She went home to plan a second honeymoon with her husband. When they returned from Hawaii her husband called to ask what kind of sex therapy I had used on her. He said she was terrific.

Over and over again I have experienced clients sending and receiving messages about their problems outside of conscious awareness. When I simply pay attention to this level of communication, therapy becomes simple. However, I have also tried this method on numerous clients who have no propensity for playing with words. They lack humor, often are rigid in their thinking and use generalized verb forms. These people do not usually send messages at an unconscious level and they do not seem to respond to them no matter how creatively they are presented in therapy.

CONCLUSION

This chapter has been an attempt to describe the process by which words are utilized outside conscious awareness in the therapeutic setting. This utilization of words can be seen as a more specific association at the unconscious level of Rossi's stages three, unconscious search, and four, unconscious processes (Rossi, 1980).

The two-level communication which occurs can be described more explicitly as 1) The conscious process fixates attention on the ordinary meaning of the word. The meaning is translated from the context of the sentence and the subject's conscious frame of reference. The individual and literal associations are excluded by consciousness in its effort to grasp the general meaning; and 2) The unconscious process can activate the suppressed associations and heighten the ability to recognize literal meanings and new associative patterns.

Jenkins (1974) summarized research in the area of verbal association, event recognition, information integration and memory that places a similar emphasis on the significance of context to understand conscious and unconscious communication. In normal conversation it is usually the general context that establishes meaning rather than the structural units or the idiosyncratic interpretation. The obvious exception is the use of puns, allusions and verbal jokes.

In the same way, Erickson's two-level communication utilizes a general context to fixate the attention of consciousness while the individual associations of the meanings of words are registered at the unconscious level. The end result is that the conscious mind is surprised at its new awareness.

It was the activating and utilizing of these natural attentive processes that delighted Erickson. He believed people had not only the resources within themselves to change but that the change process could be an enjoyable learning experience. His utilization theory of hypnosis emphasized the need to capture each patient's unique resources in terms of mental processes outside of conscious awareness.

It is hoped that the examples presented here will validate, in a limited sense, the fact that utilizing particular words sent and received by clients outside conscious awareness can result in changed behavior in therapy.

The major conclusion of the chapter is the fact that some people do send and receive messages at an unconscious level. These communications can become efficient means of effecting change in therapy.

Language, which is generally perceived as logical, digital and conscious, can become a resource of unconscious processing. The language clients use to describe the problem can be utilized to solve the problem. Language can be processed in therapy with much the same primary logic as found in dreams and in some schizophrenic communication (Watzlawick, 1978).

Implicit in this utilization of language outside conscious awareness is the idea that we can accept what clients tell us in therapy. Clients know unconsciously (better than the therapist) exactly what the problem is and what alternatives are available for resolution. Clients can do their own therapy. Therapists control and manipulate the conscious biases of clients in order to free them to utilize their inner resources for problem resolution. It is the therapists' responsibility to be flexible enough to fit their clients' frames of reference and devise methods of treatment that are not necessarily wedded to a school of thought but which allow for change.

Integral to this change process is a pacing of the clients' language system, particularly language utilized outside conscious awareness. To pace and/or lead clients in this unconscious processing demands an intense encounter. Implied in this emphasis on two-level communication is the necessity for congruence on the therapist's part. A client functioning at conscious and unconscious levels is acutely in touch with the therapist's functioning on both levels. In order to utilize these resources in clients, therapists must relate consciously and unconsciously with the client. In effect the therapist's congruence models for the client the need for compatibility of conscious and unconscious processes within the client.

Therapists, being persons first, should learn to trust their own unconscious processing in treating clients. As Ralph Waldo Emerson once said, "The greatest virtue of the scholar is self-trust." This is not meant to encourage a mindless enthusiasm for some intuitive or psychic power. It is the self-trust that emerges from being open to phenomena subjectively and being disciplined enough to organize the new data into patterns that can be understood and critically evaluated by others.

Finally, Ericksonian hypnotherapy, by its essential insistence on the utilization of unconscious inner resources, presents us with an attitude toward knowledge and knowledge acquisition that rejects the notion of blind allegiance to any one theory of human behavior and encourages constant exploration, organization and evaluation of data. The attitude is one of the pilgrim rather than of the disciple. As Erickson once succinctly stated to me, "You must expand your limits"—i.e., one should open one's arms (limbs) wide enough to embrace new ideas which extend the limits of thinking.

In gratitude to Milton for all the wonderful learnings he shared with me—most of which I am still unaware of knowing—I conclude with a poem of e. e. cummings. The poem expresses for me most beautifully the characteristics of Milton which made him *the* therapist of therapists.

one winter afternoon*

(at the magical hour
when is becomes if)

a bespangled clown
standing on eighth street
handed me a flower.

Nobody, its safe
to say, observed him but

myself; and why? because

without any doubt he was
whatever (first and last)

Mostpeople fear most:
a mystery for which I've
no word except alive

— that is, completely alert
and miraculously whole;

with not merely a mind and a heart
but unquestionably a soul—
by no means funerally hilarious

(or otherwise democratic)
but essentially poetic
or etherally serious:

a fine not a course clown
(no mob, but a person)

and while never saying a word

---

who was anything but dumb;
since the silence of him

self sang like a bird.

Mostpeople have been heard
screaming for international

measures that render hell rational
— i thank heaven somebody's crazy

enough to give me a daisy

REFERENCES

Bandler, R., & Grinder, J. (1975). *Patterns of the hypnotic techniques of Milton H. Erickson, M.D.* (Vol. 1). Cupertino, CA: Meta Publications.
Denzin, N. K. (1978). *The research act* (rev. ed.). New York: McGraw-Hill.
Jenkins, J. (1974). Remember that old theory of memory? Well, forget it! *American Psychologist, 29,* 785–95.
Marquis, D. (1982). *Archy & Mehitabel.* New York: Doubleday.
Rossi, E. L. (Ed.). (1980). *The collected papers of Milton H. Erickson. Vol. II: Hypnotic alteration of sensory, perceptual and psychophysical processes.* New York: Irvington.
Watzlawick, P. (1978). *The language of change.* New York: Basic Books.

Chapter 14

Ericksonian Therapeutic Patterns: A Pattern Which Connects

James Wilk

The psychotherapy of Milton H. Erickson was basically simple. It is simple to understand and its principles can be simply stated in simple terms. It is simple to learn.

Now, "simple" does not mean "not difficult." A lot of hard work is involved—at least at the beginning, or at each beginning. As the fruits of that hard work begin to ripen, and each hard-won learning becomes automatic and falls into its place in the coherence of one's smooth, autonomous, unconscious functioning as a therapist, the hard work gets progressively easier. I say "each" beginning because there are always further pieces to learn and master, following the same sure course of hard work, practice, and gradual mastery.

"Simple" also does *not* mean "not complex"—it *does* mean "not complicated." The pieces are simple and the arrangement of those pieces is itself simple but the resulting picture is complex, many-layered. We must, without being pedantic, distinguish between "complicated" and "complex."* In swimming, the breaststroke is complex but not complicated. The individual movements are simple, the arrangement and sequencing of those movements are simple, and the resulting pattern is

---

The writer wishes to acknowledge Bill O'Hanlon, M.S., for his editorial assistance in the earlier stages, and Penelope Birch-Campian for her generous help in the preparation of the final manuscript.

*"Complex" derives from the past participle of the Latin *complecti*—"to entwine around, embrace, comprise"—and has the sense of being compound or composite, i.e., comprising many constituent parts. "Complicated" derives from the Latin *complicare*—"to fold together"—and has the sense of consisting of many parts which are not easily separable.

quite complex. The better a swimmer you are and the more you *master* the breaststroke, the *less complicated* it becomes. It gets smoother, more refined, more elegant, more economical—*simpler* in its stark and uncluttered complexity.

Erickson's work was elegant and economical. Like a Japanese sumié ink painter, he could conjure up a powerful and emotive landscape with a couple of brushstrokes. This is complexity *and* simplicity. But never anything complicated.

There is mastery of skills and of the coordination of those skills (which is itself a skill) and then there is *opportunity*. And the greater one's mastery, the more frequently one finds the opportunity to exercise many skills at once. To the "uninitiated" it may *appear* complicated afterwards, but to the practitioner in the heat of the moment it seems obvious and unavoidable. A star Welsh rugby player, as humble off the field as he was dazzlingly brilliant on the pitch, was interviewed after making a spectacular run through seemingly endless obstacles. Asked how he'd managed the feat, he shrugged his shoulders and replied honestly, "What *else* could I do?"

Erickson's work was simple in this sense. At the practice level its complexity consisted of a simple, skillful arrangement of many skills each of which was simple in itself and simple to learn. (Once again, not *easy* but *simple*.) Equally, at the level of theory and therapeutic principles guiding the choice of intervention, Erickson insisted, "My work isn't really all that complicated, elaborate, or unfathomable. There's nothing mystical. It's really quite simple: all of what I do boils down to simple commonsense psychology" (Beahrs, 1982, p. 64).

My aim here will be to make some of Erickson's therapeutic interventions comprehensible, even "obvious" with hindsight. Along the way I will trace a number of threads in Ericksonian psychotherapy and indicate a pattern or two connecting Erickson's diverse therapeutic patterns, in order to enable practitioners to "hit upon" such interventions themselves. More than that, I hope to make clear how Ericksonian therapists can make use of this pattern-of-patterns to open up a number of different avenues of intervention at any point in therapy.

WHAT'S THE PROBLEM?

And so when a patient comes to me, I have all the doubts. I doubt in the right direction. The patient doubts in the wrong direction.—Erickson (Zeig, 1980, p. 46)

Now when patients come to you they come to you because they don't know why exactly they come. They have problems . . . if they knew what they *really* were they wouldn't have to come, and since they don't know what their problems really are they can't tell you. They can only tell you a rather confused account of what they think, and you listen with your background and you don't know what they're saying but you better know that you don't know. (Erickson, in Gordon & Meyers-Anderson, 1981, pp. 122-23)

So you listen to your patients' words and you don't know what those words mean and you cannot put your own interpretations on those words, nor can you simply take your patients at their word either. You can bet that your patients seek therapy because there is something they *do* in life that they do not want to do, or something they do *not* do in life that they would like to do, or something they do one way that they would like to do differently. But that's all you can count on.

Now your patients come to you and tell you their problems. But do they tell you their problems or do they tell you what they *think* are problems? And are they problems only because they *think* that the things are problems? (Erickson, in Zeig, 1980, p. 79)

Your patients will speak with great *certainty* about why they cannot do something different or differently; they will tell you what they *know*. So the Ericksonian therapist's attitude is one of benevolent skepticism, for life is fundamentally simple but people keep insisting on making it so damn complicated. Erickson was fond of quoting Josh Billings: "It ain't what we don't know that gives us trouble; it's what we know that *ain't so* that gives us trouble."

People have the kinds of problems for which they end up going to psychotherapists because they *assume* things—i.e., tell themselves things—that are terribly limiting: about their lives, about life, about their minds, their children, their families, their past, their present, the things they want to do and the things they don't want to do. And to top it off, they tell themselves they need to get themselves fixed.

The fact is, they need to *do* something different or differently, and the *only* way for them to do that is for them to do something different or differently. That's it. People can behave differently and often act as if they cannot. They do not always exercise the choices they have. They have all the learnings, the *know-how* they need to solve their problems, but they do not use that know-how. They know and they don't know that they know. So they go on without using their know-how, in the same habitual patterns over and over again, and see their options as limited. And so they are.

People behave in rigidly patterned ways, and much of Erickson's teaching and therapeutic work emphasized that we do not realize how rigidly patterned our behavior and thinking really are. But it is important not to miss the point that rigid patterning is both necessary and desirable. In psychotherapy we would seek to intervene in a rigid pattern only if the pattern did not contain the behavioral option or options necessary to solve the problem. Far from there being anything wrong with rigid patterning per se, Erickson and Gregory Bateson alike maintained that not only does much of our functioning go on unconsciously and autonomously, following rigidly recurring patterns, but, indeed, it could not be any other way.* Bateson writes, "The conscious organism does not require to know *how* it perceives—only to know *what* it perceives," and goes on to draw attention to the fact of *skill* "as indicating the presence of large unconscious components in the performance" (1967, pp. 108-110).

Compare Erickson's remarks: "Now, the unconscious mind is a vast storehouse of your memories, your learnings. It has to be a storehouse because you cannot keep consciously in mind all the things you know. Considering all the learnings you have acquired in a lifetime, you use the vast majority of them automatically in order to function" (Zeig, 1980, p. 175).

While it is therefore necessary that the majority of our behaviors follow, more or less rigidly, *some* sort of a pattern, the *particular* rigid pattern that obtains is to a great extent optional. Even more important, the rigid patterning of human behavior and experience is a feature of *organization*, not of *control*. However rigid the pattern, at every point in it, individuals are free to do something different, if they so choose. The pattern may not *contain* certain options, but neither does it *constrain* the individual from exercising those options. Although some systems thinkers sometimes write or talk as if the interactional patterns control individual behavior, this is nonsense. The fact that interaction displays rigidly recurring patterns does not in any way constrain the individuals concerned

---

*Bateson considers "the impossibility of constructing a television set which would report upon its screen *all* the workings of its component parts, including especially those parts concerned in this reporting" (1967, p. 109), and argues that "consciousness, for obvious mechanical reasons, must always be limited to a rather small fraction of mental process. If useful at all, it must therefore be husbanded. The unconsciousness associated with habit is an economy both of thought and of consciousness; and the same is true of the inaccessibility of the processes of perception" (1967).

from acting outside those patterns (Wilk, 1982; Wilk & O'Hanlon, in press).

PATTERNS OF INTERVENTION

Psychotherapists can intervene in two possible directions: either abolishing the pattern/system and throwing individuals back on their own devices (resources/know-how) *or* enabling individuals to exercise the necessary know-how and thereby abolish the pattern/system. *Either way, the ultimate aim of therapy is to allow a new, equally rigid, automatic pattern to be established, but one which does not contain the undesired behavior or experience and which is otherwise satisfactory* (Wilk, 1982; Wilk & O'Hanlon, in press).

TRANSFORMING CONTEXTS

Now how do you go about abolishing the pattern or system? "Simple commonsense psychology!" For human beings, reality is necessarily contextual: The context of something is part of what that something *is*. The significance of anything for humans depends on the context in which we find "it." In another context, an experience or communication or piece of interaction would have a completely different significance and therefore would *be* something completely different.

A toddler who was screaming to annoy his mother would have the contextual rug pulled out from under him if his mother urged him to scream louder, because his screaming would no longer be what it was, no longer a member of the class of "things that bother Mother." Therefore, we can alter the "fundamental nature" of any behavior or experience or communication by introducing some communication altering the context. Parents, for example, learn this through common sense and bitter experience when dealing with their two-year-old who topples over. When the child looks up to scan their faces to find out whether any great calamity has just occurred, only to see a big smile and hear, "Whoops—that was silly!" it becomes possible for the child to giggle and get on with it instead of bawling.

So, to change the pattern or system, all that is required is to transform the context. One option would be simply to abolish the present context and (as it were) leave the choice of new context up for grabs; to this option I will assign the overlong and unnecessarily ugly term "*de*contextualization." The other option would be to transform the old context into a new one specifically preselected by us—with the new context (if we wish to be fanciful about it) rising like a phoenix from the ashes of the old. To this latter option I will give a term no shorter and no less ugly, "*re*contextualization" (Wilk, 1982).

All this is easier than it sounds, and far easier done than said. For context is a product of human communication. The communication which gives rise to context and maintains specific contexts includes not only the ongoing stream of verbal and nonverbal communication and relatively durable features of the environment but equally, laws, rules, traditions, institutions, and even Weltanschauungen. The aspects of communication (in this wider sense) which serve to signal, to classify, to differentiate contexts, I call, following Bateson, "context markers." Bateson (1978, pp. 250-279) gives these examples from among "the diverse set of events (falling) within the category of context markers":

(a) The Pope's throne from which he makes announcements *ex cathedra* which are thereby endowed with a special order of validity;
(b) The placebo, by which the doctor sets the stage for a change in the patient's subjective experience;
(c) The shining object used by some hypnotists in "inducing trance";
(d) The air raid siren and the "all clear";
(e) The handshake of boxers before the fight;
(f) The observances of etiquette.

Of course, context markers are artificial abstractions imposed on the data by the observer, so we cannot count them or decide how many can dance on the head of a pin, but we *can* consider the sources of information heralding the news that this is one sort of context rather than another.

Contexts need to be maintained, either by a continuing stream of context markers or by context markers with some durability through time (such as police uniforms or stop signs or chessboards or houses of parliament). If not continually maintained, contexts tend to fade or generally evanesce in the special way contexts have of evanescing—they become ambiguous. Once ambiguous, the very context is at the mercy of the first unambiguous context marker to happen along and exploit the situation by claiming the context for its own (Wilk, 1982).

Contexts can be transformed or abolished by manipulating context markers. And Erickson was second to none in his mastery of the art of transforming and abolishing contexts.

RECONTEXTUALIZATION

Reemploying Existing Context Markers

Recontextualization, transforming one context into another quite specific one, is accomplished through (in effect) introducing new context markers. This introduction of new context markers can be achieved either by actually introducing new objects or behaviors (through behavioral prescription) to serve as new context markers or, alternatively, by giving a new sense to signs (including behaviors) currently serving as markers of one context, in order to reemploy them as markers of a new context altogether ("recycled" context markers). Let us consider an example of the latter.

Case one

An alcoholic came to Erickson for help with his drinking problem. He would go into a bar and set up two boilermakers, drinking one whiskey and washing it down with a beer and then drinking the other whiskey and washing it down with a beer; then he would be off on his drinking binge. He had been a flying ace in the First World War and, though now a lush full of self-pity, he was still proud of his past achievements. He brought in his scrapbook for Erickson to see—full of newspaper clippings, photographs of himself, the full record of his times of glory. Erickson perused the album and threw it in the trash, saying, "This has nothing to do with you." Then he told the man what he was to do. He was to go to the bar and set up two boilermakers as usual. As he finished off the first one he was to say to himself, "Here's to that bastard Milton Erickson, may he choke on his own spit." And as he finished off the second one he was to say, "Here's to that bastard Milton Erickson, may he rot in hell." Then Erickson dismissed him (Bateson, 1975; O'Hanlon, personal communication, October 1982).

That was the end of his drinking problem.

This time, and forevermore, it was Erickson who set up those boilermakers; he set them up as context markers of another context altogether. This context we may characterize as one in which the man's indignant, self-righteous anger confronted Erickson's glib dismissal, an anger full of his inner insistence that these achievements (the man he had been, full of self-confidence, self-discipline, and stoic courage) did *so* have *everything* to do with him. And this (in place of the old context of self-pity, self-indulgence, and compulsion) was now the context those boilermakers unambiguously marked.

Note that this recontextualization is accomplished irrespective of any-thing the patient may think of Erickson's prescription. Even if he rejects it out of hand and vows not to give it another thought, the problem context is now irrevocably altered. As Stewart Brand said of this patient (in an interview with Bateson who told the story), "He's been colonized" (Bateson, 1975).

Case two

A woman had a recurring, highly disturbing dream featuring one of her colleagues at work. Every time she saw him he reminded her of the dream and so "gave her the creeps." She would start acting strangely and then so would he, thus confirming her creepy feelings. She became increasingly unable to stand being in his presence, started avoiding him, and was badly disrupting her work relationships. When she told me she had been trying not to think of the dream when she saw him, I told her that was like trying not to think of a pink elephant. I asked her to recall the dream in her mind's eye and challenged her to see the scene in the dream *without* seeing a baby pink elephant frolicking about on the fur-niture. She laughed at finding she couldn't get rid of the elephant. I told her that her only remaining problem was how not to offend her colleague if he thought she was laughing at *him*, because she would think of the dream when she saw him and would not be able to keep that mischie-vous elephant off the furniture. Later that morning she reported all was well at work, and the dream never recurred.

Case three

A man who sought therapy for depression was in a rigid pattern of brooding for hours on end over the impossible situation with his married girlfriend. After extensive questioning, he explained how this problem got in the way of his life. He would get this powerful sinking feeling in his chest whenever thoughts of his relationship crossed his mind. If he was with his mother and grandfather at the time, he would start snap-ping at them and being nasty. If he was studying, he would abandon his work and go out on a binge of drinking or spending. As a result, he was failing in his studies, getting into terrible rows with his mother and grandfather, and spending most of his time either broke or loaded or, in his words, "crawling on the floor."

I told him that for the next month, as soon as he got that sinking feeling in his chest, he was to write down the time in a little notebook and give himself exactly five minutes from that time to reach a decision:

If he was studying he was to decide whether to go on studying in spite of the feeling in his chest, or to go out drinking or spending; if with his relatives, he was to decide whether to be nasty or civil. In other situations, he was to decide whether to "crawl on the floor" or to accomplish something useful. He was to write down the decision he reached at this "choice point."

A month later he reported that he only had to write the decision down once, completing four solid hours of studying after this choice point. He said he stopped snapping at his folks, got on with his studies, stopped binging, and was "finding choice points all over the place" and not letting his feelings run his life. His depression has not recurred.

Case four

Here is one last example of recontextualizing by recycling existing context markers to mark out a new context. In a case in which the referrer recommended family therapy because of frequent rows in the family of a phobic teenager, the teenager was seen individually. I noticed the girl's rigid pattern of clenching her left fist in a stereotyped way whenever she became angry and argumentative. Trance was induced conversationally, and clenching the left fist in this manner was selected and utilized as a cue for the reinduction of trance and, subsequently, as a cue for inducing self-hypnosis (which, incidentally, she used in overcoming her anxiety hysteria). Subsequent reports revealed that peace was mysteriously reigning in the family, and the teenager spontaneously reported that she was having difficulty picking a fight at home because her left fist would clench automatically and this would immediately calm her down.

Introducing New Context Markers

Case five

New context markers can be introduced rather than reemploying existing ones. Parents who sought assistance because of the "non-stop" violent rows between their teenage sons could not get the boys to the first session because they "wouldn't go to see any shrink." I told the parents to tell the boys that since I could not hear their arguments in person, I needed the parents to bring me some good data. I instructed the parents to follow them around with a tape recorder and catch the rows on tape. The boys cockily assured the parents, "You'll never catch *us* arguing; you're gonna go back to that shrink empty-handed!" The boys were proved right. Thus utilizing their reluctance to have anything to do with any shrink and their desire to show up their parents, I sent their parents home with a shrinking context marker.

Case six

In a case of Bill O'Hanlon's (personal communication, June 1982), a woman sought therapy for binging on food. She felt awful about herself whenever she was binging, but had no clear idea what triggered it; she would just suddenly find herself raiding the refrigerator. She was asked whether she had a favorite pair of shoes, a pair she wore when she felt really good about herself and that felt good whenever she wore them. She said she had. She was instructed to keep the shoes on top of the refrigerator and to put them on before she binged. She agreed and only had to do the assignment a couple of times before she stopped binging altogether. She was then instructed to throw the shoes away. More than a year later this long-standing symptom had not recurred (O'Hanlon, personal communication, April 1983).

Case seven

A child of 12 who was acutely afraid of the dark and of being on her own, was given the opportunity in the session to practice making silly faces, putting her thumbs in her ears and waggling the fingers, and so on. She was instructed to make these faces whenever she was alone or in the dark and felt afraid, and to do so (simultaneously hopping up and down on one foot in extreme instances) until the fear subsided. The task was to be repeated as often as necessary. This context marker made it difficult if not impossible for the fear context to be maintained. In the next session, three weeks later, the child reported having had to do the exercise only two or three times, thereafter having no opportunity, "because I just don't get scared anymore."

Case eight

The odd-numbered and even-numbered days of the month are frequently introduced by the author as context markers. For example, a 25-year-old woman had a lifelong history of being unable to get up in the morning before midday, a severely disabling pattern which had resisted all previous attempts at treatment. She was told that every morning when the alarm rang she was to take note of the overwhelming feeling of wanting to go back to sleep. Then, on odd-numbered days she was to give in to this feeling and go back to sleep; on even-numbered days she was to get out of bed and start the day. Within a week she had altered the directions herself and was getting up on time *every* day, a pattern she has continued to maintain.

DECONTEXTUALIZATION

In decontextualization—simply abolishing the old context through the introduction of ambiguity—the therapist obscures or obliterates existing context markers. Again, this is more easily done than explained. In Bateson's famous definition, information is a difference which makes a difference (1978, p. 286). In other words, information is a perceptible difference (perceptible by the receiver) that *makes a difference* to the receiver. Context markers are information about context—differences which make a difference as to the context. Thus, context markers can be obscured/obliterated in one of two ways: by obscuring the perceptible difference itself (i.e., so that it is no longer perceptible *as* a difference), or by obscuring the difference it *makes* to the receiver.

When we speak of "the signaler" and "the receiver," it may well be, in a given instance, that the signaler and the receiver are the same person. The considerations apply equally to this limiting case, for it is in the self-reflexive nature of human beings that we can both behave and be the observers/interpreters of our own behavior. For heuristic purposes and purposes of presentation, however, it is sometimes simpler to deal with cases in which the signaler and the receiver are stationed in different bodies—though this is by no means a necessary requirement.

Obliterating the Difference (Signal) Itself

To obliterate the perceptible difference itself is to prevent reception of the signal in the first place by means of communication in effect introducing other signs indistinguishable from the signs used in the signaling, so that the signal can no longer be differentiated *as* a signal (e.g., the story of the boy who cried wolf). The sign (in this case, the cry) which otherwise would have signaled a wolf context cannot any longer be received as a context marker of a wolf context because of all the preceding false alarms.

In radio communications one speaks of "jamming"—preventing the reception of certain signals by sending out other signals of approximately the same frequency. Noise or "static" has thus been introduced. In the story of "Ali Baba and the Forty Thieves," when Ali Baba's house is singled out for some sort of attack by a red mark placed on it, his wife puts an identical mark on all the other houses (James Warner, personal communication, July 1983).

In psychotherapy, there are two general strategies of introducing "noisy" communication to prevent reception of the putative context marker as a signal in the first place by camouflaging the context marker altogether: (a) by arranging for additional signs indistinguishable from those used in the signaling *actually to be introduced*; (b) by simply *requesting* the introduction of such additional signs, doing so in front of both the "signaler" and the "receiver." In the latter case (b), even if the signaler disregards the request, noise will have been introduced for the receiver. I will provide examples of the latter case first.

Case nine (merely requesting the introduction of camouflage)

In a case of Haley's (1963) a man referred for ejaculatio praecox had been striving for years to give his wife an orgasm. In the husband's presence the wife was told that one day she might experience some sexual pleasure and "when she did she was to tell her husband that she did not enjoy it. If her husband insisted on her saying whether she really had not enjoyed it or was just following this directive, she should say she had really not enjoyed it" (p. 143). Robbed of any source of information as to his wife's enjoyment, the husband found that his potency was soon restored and with it, no doubt, his wife's pleasure in sex. In this case, the wife needed to do nothing in response to the intervention—the uttering of the directive itself was sufficient to obliterate existing context markers, abolish the old context and throw the husband back quite literally on his own devices.

Case ten (merely requesting the introduction of camouflage)

A boy of 14 had been stealing from home for many years and recently had begun to steal from the family's shop and from elsewhere. I saw the boy on his own and told him all he needed was to learn how to resist temptation, and that I had a surefire way to teach him to resist temptation—but that he wouldn't like it one little bit. I had already secured his desperate parents' agreement to carry out anything I asked of them, and I told him so. I explained I could either give his parents the surefire cure right now or I could give him two months to see if he could teach *himself* to resist temptation. However, if he failed, his parents would teach him with the surefire method I would give them. I gave my somewhat reluctant, skeptical consent in response to his pleading to be given a two-month period to try on his own, and I called his parents in.

I explained the deal and in front of the boy I secured their cooperation in helping him teach himself to resist temptation by providing as much temptation for him as possible. I instructed them to leave money around for him to find, to accidentally-on-purpose leave doors or drawers or cash registers unlocked, and so on. They were to conspire with other family members, friends, neighbors, school, and local shopkeepers to provide this temptation for him in ways so indirect and subtle that sometimes the boy would be unable to imagine any possible way the parents could have had anything to do with planting the temptation. At every opportunity they were to deny planting any temptation for him and indeed to deny they were following this assignment at all. They were to keep careful records of how well he was succeeding in teaching himself to resist temptation, and to bring me the results in two months.

Note that the success of this intervention did not depend on the parents actually *doing* anything at all, as the decontextualization was accomplished merely through the "noise" introduced in the delivery of the directive. Note also that this intervention can to some extent also be viewed as a *re*contextualization employing existing markers.

Case eleven (arranging for camouflage actually to be introduced)

As noted earlier, context markers can be obscured as signals by arranging to introduce *actual* additional signs indistinguishable from those used in the signaling. A young teenage girl with numerous phobias since early childhood could not be left on her own for even five minutes without working herself up into an acute state of panic which would often escalate into a full-blown panic attack with all the physiological concomitants. I found her to have a pattern of obsessively telling herself frightening things about any situation she was in. For example, if she was walking home she might tell herself she might forget the way home, or she would find the house had burned down, or her parents would not know her, or that man across the street was really following her, or she might be pulled into the bushes and raped, and so on.

After playing a game in which we took turns naming all the scary things that might happen if she were left alone in my office, she was left alone in the consulting room at first for five minutes, then ten, then for half an hour, with instructions to "silently tell yourself all the scary things you can think of about what might happen, and write down each thing you tell yourself." No degree of panic occurred, and she was able to repeat this exercise at home and elsewhere for increasing lengths of time. No panic attacks have occurred since.

Case twelve (arranging for camouflage actually to be introduced)

Here is another example of arranging for camouflaging signs actually to be introduced. The writer saw the parents of a six-year-old boy whose behavior at home and at school was so extreme and uncontrollable that he had been labeled variously as psychotic or mentally subnormal. He seemed oblivious to standards set by adults. The parents, it turned out on questioning, gave in to his every whim. A daily occurrence, for example, was his "making" his parents take a game down off the shelf for him, rejecting it after five minutes, making them take down another game, and so on until all the games were down. Then he would make them put them all back up and repeat the procedure. (Not surprisingly, the school found he had a nonexistent attention span!) Psychologists, school counselors, teachers, neighbors, friends, grandparents, and even the minister of the church (where they were active churchgoers) failed to convince the parents to "be firm" and "not give in." No one could shake them from their rigid belief that what their child needed was more patience and more attention.

The parents, who were fond of playing games, agreed to play a "diagnostic game." The boy was to play for five-pence coins, and at the end of every week he could keep half his winnings to spend as he liked and half would go in the collection plate at church. He was told in front of his parents that there were four rules in this game; that he would love the sound of the first three and his parents would hate the sound of them; but that his parents would *love* the last rule.

I spent a long time going over the first three. The first rule was that the boy would win five pence for every game he got his parents to take down off the shelf for him, five pence for every time they had to tell him to do something or not do something, and five pence for every time he asked for something after having been told "no." The second rule was that his parents could not fine him money for being naughty and could not threaten to end the game before the month was over. Rule three was that they could not spank him or slap him as punishment during the next month.

The parents responded with relief and mischievous delight when the significance of Rule Four dawned on them—that "There are no other rules." "You mean I can ignore him?" Mom hoped. "Yes." "You mean I can say 'no TV tonight if I have to ask you again'?" Dad asked, brightening up. "Yes." The young lad did his level best to win his shilling pieces, but he had not reckoned on having such firm parents as he turned out to have. Parents and school reported that he was "a completely different child." This was confirmed by my own observations. Improvements were sustained as of follow-up 18 months later.

Note that even if the boy had played no part in the game the intervention would have worked in the manner of the interventions discussed above in which the decontextualization is accomplished merely through the therapist's *request* for the introduction of "noisy" communication.

Case thirteen

This is what in fact happened with a similar intervention, in which a family with two girls was to play the following "therapeutic game": Each started out with a bag of 20 shilling-pieces, and the deal was that they could ask something of anyone else in the family up to *twice* for free, but from the third time onwards they had to pay them five pence each time they asked. For two months they each tried conscientiously to play the game but despite their efforts only five pence changed hands, and that on the first day. Mother stopped nagging, father stopped indulging, the girls stopped disobeying and making excuses and learned to accept "no" for an answer. The younger girl (the identified patient) went from being a depressed, isolated child with a nervous tic to a well-adjusted, cheerful 12-year-old. But the game, alas, never got off the ground.

Case fourteen

Here is a final example of a decontextualization that could have worked either way. In a case I supervised, there were violent rows over trivial matters between the teenage patient and her stepmother, made worse by father's "inability" to stay out of the middle. The therapist gave the family an assignment to help father learn how to stay out of these fights. Stepmother and stepdaughter were to give him plenty of practice by deliberately picking fights with each other over the most trivial things and trying to draw him in; and his job was to stay out. Everyone was to deny ever picking such a fight deliberately.

If they had managed to fight, the intervention would have worked through camouflaging the context markers father depended on. Equally, the girl and her stepmother might never have managed to fight at all because the context markers of the start of a fight had been obscured for both of them.

Obscuring the Difference that the Difference (Signal) Makes

As noted earlier, since information is a difference which makes a difference, context markers (being differences which make a difference as to the context) can be obscured *not only* by obscuring the difference (the signal itself) so that it can no longer be distinguished *as* a signal but additionally, by obscuring the difference that that difference (signal) *makes*.

When some American cities introduced the right-turn-on-red, red could still be perceived as a detectable difference (perceptibly distinct from green), but for the driver wanting to turn right, at least once he had briefly stopped and looked both ways, red no longer *made a difference* distinct from the difference green made. Thus such decontextualization can be accomplished simply by attribution. The signal can still be received but it no longer makes a difference to the receiver—the response required in its presence is no different from the response required in its absence (Wilk, 1982).

In terms of the pragmatics of the communicational situation, the net effect of this attributional communication is the same as that brought about by jamming the signal altogether (in one of the two ways already described). An example of obscuring the difference itself would again be the story of the boy who cried wolf—his false alarms obscured the genuine S.O.S. Another example of obscuring the difference itself would have been if the story had been rewritten as follows: "A young shepherd-boy-in-training who needed further practice at raising the wolf alarm was instructed, in front of the entire assembled village, to pretend to raise the alarm of "wolf" at least once in the coming week. The next day a real wolf came and the frightened shepherd boy raised the alarm but no one came to his rescue."

An example of *obscuring the difference that the difference makes* would be if the story had been rewritten as follows:

A young shepherd boy had never raised any false alarms about wolves, but one day all the villagers heard on the radio that a disease was going around among shepherds that gave them vivid hallucinations of wolves. The next day a real wolf came and the frightened shepherd boy cried out but no one came to his rescue.

The therapist can decontextualize a situation through obscuring the difference that the difference makes by attributing (in the presence of the receiver but usually preferably in the absence of the sender) a further significance, Y, to the signs currently marking the context as X and "informing" the receiver that those signs do sometimes classify the context as X but may equally sometimes classify the context as Y. Y is chosen such that X (the old significance) and Y are mutually exclusive and, preferably, require opposite courses of action from the receiver, thus making the pragmatic situation thoroughly ambiguous.

Case fifteen

A mother felt that her son, Melvin, was always being "picked on" by her husband, the boy's stepfather. The stepfather would scold the boy about some small bit of misbehavior or bad manners, and the boy would dig in his heels and persist all the more. Then the stepfather would get increasingly annoyed and become more insistent in his demands, the cycle punctuated frequently by mother's demands that stepfather "stop picking on Melvin." The results of this escalation could be pretty unpleasant.

In the second session with the mother and Melvin alone, the mother sought my help in getting the stepfather to stop picking on the boy. After getting a description from the mother of the specific situations she was referring to, I told her this tallied well with the interaction I had witnessed in my office in the initial family session and that I wasn't sure if the stepfather *was* picking on Melvin. From what I had seen and what she described he *may* have been picking on him and she may be right in thinking that he disliked and resented Melvin. However, it seemed it *might* be that he loved Melvin very much and was trying to bring him up as well as if he were his own son, but getting very frustrated in the process. If so, the best thing was to help the stepfather; but *if not* she should defend Melvin from being picked on. In the next session the mother reported that she had stayed out of these battles and sometimes told Melvin to behave himself. She found that not only was her husband going easier on the boy but she could see that most of the time he was right.

Case sixteen

A stepmother sought my help because in the 18 months since her 14-year-old stepdaughter had started her periods there had been many battles over the girl's habit of hoarding and hiding used sanitary napkins. The stepmother would "have to" make daily searches of drawers, closets, mattresses, bookshelves, and so on. For a year and a half she had begged, pleaded, cajoled, bribed, punished, nagged, shouted, wept, and had one-way heart-to-heart talks in an effort to get the girl to inform her when her period started and to dispose of the sanitary napkins properly. She could not get an answer to why the girl was "doing this to me" but was convinced it must be an attempt to provoke her. When I asked whether her stepdaughter didn't mind her friends seeing these used napkins all over her bedroom, I learned the children had not been allowed to have friends over for the past two years because the stepmother was so ashamed of the state of the house. The father had knocked down walls, torn up floorboards, and pulled out pipes two years before in a burst of renovating enthusiasm, but had bitten off more than he could chew; two years later the house was still like a bombsite and she was forever urging her husband to put it right.

I said she was probably right that her stepdaughter was just trying to provoke her, but that I could not be sure she was not just joining her stepmother in a silent protest about the state of the house and the fact that no one will ever *see* her room anyway. The stepmother thought about this but left still convinced the girl was getting at her. As for the problem, it just disappeared. The next month the girl announced, "Mom, I've come on—what shall I do?" and all went as well as the stepmother could have wished. The problem never recurred. Note that this intervention altered the context without changing what the stepmother thought about the situation.

KNOW-HOW

. . . And it's what we know and don't know that we know that gives us even more trouble.—Milton H. Erickson (Zeig, 1980)

The discussion of decontextualization and recontextualization has been concerned with ways of transforming or abolishing the context in order to abolish the pattern or system and throw individuals back on their own devices, resources or know-how. But as was said at the outset of this discussion, it is equally possible to intervene in the opposite direction—i.e., by enabling individuals to exercise the necessary know-how and thereby abolish the pattern/system. The essence of intervening in this latter direction is this: The therapist enables individuals to transfer across contexts the know-how they already have (and perhaps do not know they have) by helping them to see the context where they *already* apply the know-how and the context where they *need* to apply the know-how as two versions of the same thing.

Intervening in this direction involves altering the individual's "frame"—the psychological (or at least the *intraorganismic*) counterpart of context. Such "reframing" interventions differ significantly from context interventions in that a therapeutic reframing can achieve its effect of enabling the transfer of know-how to the problem context only if clients come to accept the reframing at a conscious level (though they need not be conscious of having done so). Context interventions, on the other hand, achieve their effect irrespective of how clients choose to view the relevant context.

Case seventeen

Parents were beside themselves with despair over the soiling and smearing of their nine-year-old boy. They could not cope with his smearing feces all over the bathroom towels and walls. They did, however, know how to cope with his being messy at the dinner table. They had made him responsible for keeping the tablecloth clean and set penalties for any untidiness. The parents were told that whether he was smearing in the dining room or in the bathroom he could be made responsible for his cleanliness; whatever the cause of his soiling there was no excuse for untidiness. The mother carefully showed him how to clean himself and keep the bathroom clean, and the parents laid down strict penalties for any lapses. They also made him responsible for making sure to use the toilet and they set penalties for the results of any lapses. The smearing stopped immediately and the soiling stopped within a week. The parents knew nothing about encopresis but they knew how to deal with untidiness.

Case eighteen

In a case of Erickson's, an enuretic girl of 11 whose sphincter had been stretched through cystoscopy for a bladder infection years before, wet her pants whenever she laughed. Erickson asked her, "If you were sitting in the bathroom, urinating, and a strange man poked his head in the doorway, what would you do?" She replied, "I'd freeze!" Erickson said, "That's right. You'd freeze—and stop urinating. Now, you know what you already knew, but didn't know that you already knew it. Namely, that you can stop urinating at any time for any stimulus you choose. You really don't need a strange man poking his head in the bathroom. Just the *idea* of it is enough. You'll stop. You'll freeze. And when he goes away you will start urinating" (Rosen, 1982, pp. 113-117).

Where the therapist cannot readily find a context in which the client already applies the relevant know-how or has done so at some time in the past, the therapist must, as a preliminary step, provide the client with a context in which the know-how can be acquired. Such a context may be provided either in the therapy room or in the outside world by means of a behavioral prescription, so long as the context arranged is related at most tangentially to the problem context. Above all, it must be a context in which acquiring this know-how is the *natural* response that this individual would have to being in this context (given what we know about his patterns of responsiveness). Often we need only rely on the fact that our client is a human being and on what we know about the natural patterns of responsiveness universal among human beings.

Erickson's work is replete with examples of providing in the therapist's office a natural context for acquiring the relevant know-how. And, of course, many opportunities are afforded by trance.

Case nineteen

A boy of nine who was afraid to go to the toilet by himself or to be alone in his bedroom was told by the author that his problem was one of not being able to get rid of certain unwanted feelings, namely scary ones. Through the use of trance he was quickly taught (in less than an hour) how to change bad feelings into good feelings, anxious feelings into relaxed feelings. He was told to practice this at home. Of his own accord, he started applying this skill to the problem situations themselves, rapidly freeing himself of his unwanted fears and limitations.

Case twenty

In a case where trance was not used, another nine-year-old boy was continually provoked into fights at school when the other kids baited him by calling him names. He felt he "couldn't help it" because he just got so angry. In my office he quickly acquired the know-how he needed through the simple expedient of my calling him every name in the book—he supplied the names and I called him those. In my office he *had to* control himself, and he soon "couldn't help" giggling uncontrollably. At school he was no longer provoked by name-calling, and so the other kids, of course, gave it up.

Case twenty-one

The client often can be sent out on an assignment to get the know-how required. In one of Erickson's cases, a father who was being rather overprotective of his six-year-old son was sent with his son up Squaw Peak. The father found he could hardly keep up with the boy, and learned how to let him look after himself—know-how he was afterwards able to apply in other contexts.

Case twenty-two

A prim and proper young woman who was told by the author that she needed to learn how to feel good about learning from her "own stupid mistakes" was given the assignment to go out and make five stupid mistakes in public in the next two weeks and to be curious about what she might learn. She completed the assignment as perfectly as she had always done everything. For example, she stood in a major street asking passersby directions to that street; she "accidentally" went swimming without changing out of her clothes; and she asked at a London Underground ticket-counter for a ticket to a nonexistent station. She insisted the ticket seller was mistaken and had an argument with the Station Master, still insisting on her station. She reported she had felt freer and happier than at any time in her life and had learned she was "happier not trying to be so perfect all the time." She was soon feeling free to make and learn from mistakes in many areas of her life and so began to overcome her neurotic limitations.

Unhooking

Sometimes the simplest route to enabling the transfer of know-how across contexts through getting the client to view the problem context and a nonproblem context as two versions of the same thing is to *unhook* the client from limiting beliefs by appealing to universal life experiences or learnings.

A mother who felt she *had* to shout and scream whenever her teenage children were being disobedient was asked whether she would still shout and scream if a baby were sleeping in the next room. When she said no, I advised her to keep a baby sleeping next door in her imagination. Clients hooked on the idea that they *had* to do such-and-such (e.g., have a cigarette) whenever they *desperately felt* they had to do it would be reminded that they (indeed most people) feel desperately like going back to sleep when they shut the alarm off in the morning, and, still feeling that way, get themselves out of bed. Parents hooked on the idea that they had to *agree* would be told there's no law that says they have to agree. They would be reminded that children have to learn to adapt to different individuals with different standards, rules, and tolerances, and so why deprive the kids of one of the benefits of having two parents? Depressed patients who fail to take necessary action because they mistakenly take the depth of their gloom as *proof* of the hopelessness of their situation may never have had the experience of coming out of a deep depression yet will undoubtedly have known times when "after the rain comes the sunshine." Hokey sounding or not, such a typically down-home Ericksonian reminder may enable the patient to reapply his or her know-how of maintaining hope and planning for a breakthrough at times when all seems gloomiest, and thereby see his or her way to *doing* something.

SUMMARY

What is most fundamental in Ericksonian psychotherapy is the conviction that individuals already have the learnings, the know-how they need to solve their problems. The psychotherapist needs only to provide a context in which they can utilize that know-how. No one needs to change or to get themselves repaired; one needs only to do something different or differently, and the only way to do that is to do something different or differently. That's it.

If this sounds too simple, that is because what clients bring to therapists are illusory complications, the things they tell themselves that are so terribly limiting. The therapist's job is to enable clients to see their way to using their know-how to do something different and thereby get different results, more satisfactory outcomes in their lives, instead of staying locked in the illusory prisons of their rigid patterns of thinking and behaving.

In accomplishing this job, therapists have limitless possibilities for intervention, falling into a number of broad areas: 1) They can appeal to universal life experiences and learnings as challenges to *unhook* clients from rigid beliefs that have kept them from applying their know-how in the problem context, thus assimilating the problem context to a nonproblem context. 2) They can employ metaphor or anecdotes or presupposition or implication or simple redefinition or other forms of verbal communication (often with multiple levels) to *reframe* the problem context and a nonproblem context (in which the client already applies or has applied the relevant know-how) as two versions of the same thing. In doing so, as a first step, therapists sometimes need to provide a context, either 3) in the therapy room or 4) in the outside world in which the client's natural response would be to develop the know-how which can then be transferred across via a suitable reframing.

Alternatively, therapists can choose to extricate the individual from rigid personal or interactional patterns by abolishing or transforming the context. One way would be to abolish the context through a decontextualization, obliterating or obscuring a context marker or markers in one of two ways: 5) using attribution to obscure the difference the signal makes, so that it cannot continue to signal a particular context; or obscuring the signal itself by introducing noise. The latter can be done by either 6) introducing additional signs indistinguishable from those used to signal the old context or 7) simply requesting (in the receiver's presence) the introduction of such signs. In any of these variations, the resulting introduction of ambiguity leaves the context up for grabs and throws individuals back on their own devices.

Another possible avenue of intervention would be to unambiguously transform the old context into a new one, specially preselected by the therapist. Such recontextualization would be accomplished by either 8) irresistibly conferring a new significance on existing signs and thus reemploying them to mark out the new context or 9) introducing new context markers altogether, often through a behavioral prescription.

In all of this it is absolutely essential for therapists to shrug off any and all hypotheses or interpretations about meanings or causes, and instead to concentrate efforts on obtaining the precise *facts*, the specific details of the pattern. What is needed is a "video description" unembellished by interpretations—i.e., stripped of all the things clients tell themselves about the significance of the raw data. Once equipped with these details at the level of the client's *sensory* experience, therapists can selectively introduce bits of communication to irreversibly transform the *significance* of that sensory experience.

Then, the client's situation is no longer what it was. And so the client can do something different—which she could have done in the first place. For, really, there is no such thing as the client's situation—apart from what the client takes her situation to be. And, in the end, nothing will alter for the client until the client does something different—which means nothing more than carrying on with the business of living and learning. "Live and learn."

There is no other way to do something different but to do something different. That's it. A client of mine, following successful one-session psychotherapy, reflected on over 20 years of failed psychiatric and psychotherapeutic treatment and how his life had changed dramatically as a result of this single session. He quoted a line from Confucius: "The way out is *through the door*; why is it that no one will use this method?"

REFERENCES

Bateson, G. (1975, Fall). Caring and clarity. *Co-Evolution Quarterly, 7*, 32-47.
Bateson, G. (1978). *Steps to an ecology of mind* (pp. 101-125). London: Paladin Books. Originally published 1967.
Beahrs, J.O. (1982). Understanding Erickson's approach. In J.K. Zeig (Ed.), *Ericksonian approaches to hypnosis and psychotherapy*. New York: Brunner/Mazel.
Gordon, D., & Meyers-Anderson, M. (1981). *Phoenix: Therapeutic patterns of Milton H. Erickson*. Cupertino, CA: Meta Publications.
Haley, J. (1963). *Strategies of psychotherapy*. New York: Grune & Stratton.
Rosen, S. (1982). *My voice will go with you*. New York: Norton.
Wilk, J. (1982, Winter). Context and know-how: A model for Ericksonian psychotherapy. *Journal of Strategic and Systemic Therapies, 1*(4), 2-20.
Wilk, J., & O'Hanlon, B. (in press). *Shifting contexts: Clinical epistemology and the generation of effective psychotherapy*. New York: Guilford Press.
Zeig, J.K. (1980). *A teaching seminar with Milton H. Erickson, M.D.* New York: Brunner/Mazel.

PART IV

Paradox

Paradoxical technique or prescribing the symptom entails telling the patient to do exactly what he or she is already doing. This technique binds the patient. If the patient complies, he or she takes conscious control and thereby modification has taken place. If the patient rebels against the directive, there can be a "flight into health." Any change can be used as a stepping stone to effect additional change.

Harold Greenwald, Ph.D., earned his degree in social psychology from Columbia University and is a California licensed psychologist. He has authored and edited a number of books on psychoanalysis, human sexuality, and psychotherapy, including Active Psychotherapy *(Jason Aronson, 1967) and* Direct Decision Therapy *(Educational and Industrial Testing Service, 1974). He has held numerous academic appointments; currently, he is president of the Professional School for Humanistic Studies in San Diego, California.*

Greenwald is a Fellow of both the American Society of Clinical Hypnosis and the American Group Psychotherapy Association. He is former president of The Association for Applied Psychoanalysis, The National Psychological Association for Psychoanalysis, and the Academy of Psychologists in Family and Sex Therapy.

Greenwald indicates how paradoxical technique can therapeutically elicit humor. Case examples elucidate his approach.

Herbert S. Lustig, M.D., is a psychiatrist who earned his degree at Albert Einstein College of Medicine. Lustig practices in Ardmore,

Pennsylvania, and travels extensively to teach Ericksonian techniques. He is producer of the two videotapes, "The Artistry of Milton H. Erickson, M.D.," and "A Primer of Ericksonian Psychotherapy."

Lustig illustrates how paradox can be used with individual symptoms and in family problems. Unexpected therapuetic tasks and ordeals also can be used to promote rapid change.

Chapter 15

Beyond the Paradox

Harold Greenwald

It was quite a surprise when I found that the use of the paradox was a "technique." Members of my family had always communicated in this manner. So I was happy to find out that it was a technique and I was "allowed" to speak with patients in the way I usually spoke at home without having to cloak myself in the fictional sincerity of the therapist.

The trouble is, when you learn psychotherapy, the one thing they don't tell you is what to do when you see a patient. You learn the theory, but what do you do? I found out by going to the movies. In the movies I discovered that the way you do therapy is to be a dedicated co-sufferer. The patient comes in and he suffers and you sit there and suffer with him. No matter how much he suffers, you suffer along, and that led me to one particular utilization which I describe below.

I did not get permission to use paradox from reading Erickson but rather from studying psychoanalysis. From the psychoanalytic point of view, probably the first and most important practitioner of what we now call paradoxical therapy was the Hungarian psychoanalyst, Ferenczi, who made a tremendous contribution to the technique of psychoanalytic treatment. One of his major innovations was something he called "joining the resistance." That was where I started. For example, when somebody comes late and they say they're sorry they're late, you say it's alright to be late. If they don't want to talk, you say it's OK not to talk. The technique is similar to prescribing the symptom but it was called joining the resistance. This meant that you did not have to trace the resistance through to its infantile derivatives as one would in classical psychoanalysis.

In minority cultures paradoxes are constantly utilized. Ferenczi gave an example, taken from animal psychology, of a contest of coachmen to see who could control the horses best. Powerful men pulled back on the reins with very little result; the horses ran away with the coaches. Finally, one coachman got up and said, "Go ahead." He gave them the reins and they slowed down.

When I was able to use that principle, it made a tremendous difference in my whole feeling about being a therapist. Up until that time, I thought you had to be grim all the time and that was a terrible strain on me. I would be so tired from hearing so many funny things without being allowed to comment on them; I certainly wasn't allowed to laugh. Joining made a big difference for me. Here are some simple examples of this approach.

CASE ONE

A woman whom I had seen many times and who was very depressed was able to transform every triumph into a disaster. As a nursery school teacher, she had to take and pass a certain number of courses, because she didn't have a degree. She kept complaining in session after session about a particular teacher and the course he was giving, how she would never pass and it would mean the end of her career. She would have to go on relief. There was constant complaining.

Then one day she called me late at night at home and said, "You know what that son of a bitch did? He gave me an A plus." So, I was prepared for what would happen. The next day she came in her depressed clothes. She had a special costume. Ordinarily she dressed well, but this time she came in a dark, shapeless dress.

I sat in the corner and appeared very depressed. She started to talk to me and as she talked, I started to sigh. This went on and on. I was beginning to enjoy it because I'm hardly ever depressed and here I was letting myself be depressed. Finally, she stopped and said, "You know, Dr. Greenwald, when my last analyst didn't feel well, she would cancel the session."

I said, with my voice quivering, "Yes, I suppose I could have done it, but what good would it have done? You're only going to die, anyway" (which is what she would always say).

We went on a little bit more in this manner. She didn't like my depression and she kept working on it, trying to get me angry. Finally, she stopped and said, "I know what you're doing, you son of a bitch. You're showing me how miserable I am. How do you put up with me?" Thereafter, the session went much better.

CASE TWO

I used a similar technique on another occasion with a similar kind of person. Whatever I said she would say, "Gee, I'm sorry, I'm blocking, what did you say?" Then I would repeat it. Finally she said something to me and I said, "I beg your pardon?" She told me again and I replied, "I don't know what was the matter with me, I'm blocking."

This was in a group and the rest of the group got mad at me and demanded, "Why are you treating poor Anna this way? You're making fun of her."

She said, "Shut up, he knows what he's doing."

CASE THREE

One of the most striking successes I had was in Norway where I was conducting grand rounds at a mental hospital. They brought in one of their prize patients. She looked like a typical back-ward schizophrenic. She had straggly hair, wore a shapeless bathrobe and carpet slippers, and screamed constantly. She was known to every therapist in town and when they told me whom I was going to see, everybody said, "Oh, boy, you're in for it now."

So I talked to her and she started to scream at me. I said, "Hey, what the hell are you yelling about? You can talk straight like everybody else."

She said, "How did you know?"

I answered, "It takes one to know one." After that we were in good shape. Some years later she came to a seminar I was conducting and I asked her, "Would you tell these people what I did that helped you get better?"

She said, "Oh, that was very simple."

I asked, "Well, what was it?"

She replied, "I finally met a doctor who was crazier than me."

CASE FOUR

One time I had a woman who had seen many different therapists. The problem was that she had great difficulty in speaking during therapy as soon as it was so labeled. So I asked her to try to trace it back. (This was analysis.)

T: Did you ever speak?
P: No, not really.

T: Didn't you ever speak to your family?
P: Only at dinner time.
T: OK, instead of meeting in the office, we'll meet at dinner. We'll have dinner out and talk.
P: It wasn't like that. We had this big dinner table and I would get under the table and then while I was under the table, I could talk to them.
T: Why don't we get under my desk and talk?
P: What do you think I am—crazy?

So, I got under the desk, and we had a very good session. She spoke very nicely. The next session she came in and lay down on the couch again. She was not talking so I started to get up and get under the desk. She said, "I'll talk, I'll talk. Just don't get under that damn desk again."

That technique backfired because a week later her husband called and said that his wife was beginning to hallucinate. He said, "You know what she told me happened in your office?"

CASE FIVE

On another occasion, a woman wouldn't talk because she "couldn't stand my face." So, I turned away from her. She said, "No, it's no good, you're still in the room."

Here was a real challenge. But at that time, I had a little closet in my office in which I kept the chairs for group therapy. So, I went into the closet and sat down and left the door slightly ajar. We had a very good session. We went on this way and I think it was three weeks before I came out of the closet.

In all of these cases, you might call what I am demonstrating paradoxical; another way of looking at it is as play. I once wrote a paper called "Play therapy for children over 21." I think a lot of what we get out of paradox is that it's a playful approach to life.

Why do I call this approach "beyond the paradox?" When I first started some of these techniques, I looked upon some of these things as a ploy. For example, if somebody didn't talk, I would say, "You don't have to talk." Well, I was trying to get them to talk. Sometimes it worked and sometimes it didn't. But then, I came to the conclusion that *people have a right to make the choices that they make as long as they understand what they're doing.* If they make them in awareness, they have a right to that choice. I do not believe that people make irrational choices; I think, from their point of view, their choices are rational. The trick is to put yourself in their place, to understand their language, to speak in their language, until it makes sense. If their choices don't make sense, you don't understand them.

Now, if I say to somebody, "You don't have to talk," I mean it. They don't have to talk. Why should they?

CASE SIX

I had one man come to see me and for the first two weeks he didn't talk. As an analyst I tried to wait him out. After two weeks, I hesitantly said, "Would you like some help in speaking?" (I wasn't going to report this to my supervisor because I was supposed to wait.)

He said, "Oh, am I supposed to speak here?"

I said, "Well, that's what most people do."

So he spoke. At the end of some months he was much improved and I said to him, "How do you explain the improvement?"

He answered, "Well, you said some very wise things and I began to understand. However, the best times were those first two weeks when I didn't say anything but faced myself."

So, they don't have to talk. I really believe that. And going "beyond" is when you understand that what seems paradoxical, what seems like a ploy, what seems like manipulation, is really dealing with the literal truth.

CASE SEVEN

A woman had been brought to the hospital the previous day and they didn't have a chance to knock her out with medication. She had not reached a state of tranquilization so I had a chance to talk with her. She started to talk in clang associations and so on. I said, "Well, a woman like you."

She said, "Wo-man, man-wo, male, female, are you male?"

And I answered in double-talk, "Well, that depends if the cojun is on the stranum part or on the other side."

She said, "Cojun, what's that?"

I said, "I don't know. I just made it up."

She said, "Oh, you speak a private language."

CASE EIGHT

A woman who had been diagnosed as schizophrenic had been in therapy for many years. She had serious handicaps, her mother was a counselor and her father was a psychiatrist. She had two younger siblings who seemed comparatively normal. I think there was some kind of arrested development neurologically. It couldn't be determined what it was, but I felt certain there was something else going on. They put her in a home with a bunch of old people and there was no attention really paid to her. The only therapy that happened was when she came to see me once a week.

The first thing I insisted upon was seeing the whole family. When I saw the whole family, the second sister was quite normal, reasonably so, and the brother was OK, too. The patient was the odd one in the family. When she first came, there was no conversation. She just talked to herself without talking to me, going on in schizophrenese: "I was here . . . the man came out . . . that was my husband . . . there was five children . . . and on the way here. . . ." Her voice was low with little expression.

The first problem was to get communication going. That was achieved finally by speaking like her. I could do that, too. So, I spoke like her and she laughed delightedly when I spoke like that. I have found very often that it worked very well.

I was able to finally make contact and after a while there would be maybe 15 or 20 minutes during the session when we could converse. One day she came alone. Her family was away on a trip and they didn't want to have her around. I said to her, "You're a remarkable person. You are really a fantastic person."

She looked up at me and said, "What do you mean?"

I said, "What you have sacrificed to keep your father and mother together. You know, they don't have much going for them."

The mother was the nag of all time. When this poor girl would come in, dressed a little bit all right, Mother would say, "Look at your hair. With hair like that, how do you even expect to get married?"

When the second daughter decided to become a social worker, the mother said, "A social worker—what kind of men would you meet becoming a social worker? You will work with bums, tramps." So the daughter found a toothless itinerant worker with whom she lived to get even with mother. Mother's attitude was wearing everyone down. The father was off someplace, doing his own thing.

When I had the daughter alone, I said, "It's marvelous. They don't pay much attention to each other. The only thing that keeps your father and your mother together is you. You've sacrificed your entire life to keep them together and it's working. Not only that, you knew that your mother didn't know much about being a good mother. You've been training her to be a mother so she will be a better mother for your sister and brother than she was for you. That's why they've turned out so much better."

She looked at me and said, "That's amazing."

I said, "Why?"

She answered, "It's amazing that you knew."

That was the most remarkable thing of all. At the next session the parents came with her and I repeated the same thing. Static broke out. The mother started to nag irrationally about everything. The father started to discuss some experiments he was making. He had had a dream in which he was told how to cure herpes and he was spending tens of thousands of dollars on the experiments based on this dream. Mother was criticizing him for all the money he was spending. It was pure static, there was no rational talk between them. The only one who was rational and trying to keep the thing together was the identified patient who was now saying, "Why don't you listen," and things like that. At the end of the session, the mother said, "You know, did you notice she didn't say one crazy thing during the whole session."

We had switched the whole process. What had seemed to me to be a far-out ploy was seen by the patient as the literal truth. Again and again I have found that what we call paradox is the way people see the world. If it's the correct intervention, it mirrors the way they see things and, therefore, it has remarkable effect and power.

CONCLUSION

The goal of therapy is not just to do therapy; it is to help the people you are working with. I remember having a debate with a more orthodox psychoanalyst. I was doing something called active psychoanalysis and I said that it helped people. He replied loftily, "My goal is not to help people, it is to conduct analysis in the correct way." I think that very often we are too busy conducting our therapy in the correct way rather than helping people.

Now I train many of my students in how to speak to their supervisors, because there are certain things you don't report to supervisors. You know, they'll think you're crazy. Often students ask, "What do I do when the supervisor tells me something stupid."

I answer, "Look them straight in the eye and say, 'I never would have thought of that.' " Because of course you never would.

Chapter 16

The Enigma of Erickson's Therapeutic Paradoxes

Herbert S. Lustig

If you were given six sticks of equal length, and asked to make four equilateral triangles with them, so that only the ends of the sticks touched each other, how would you do it?*

To patients, some psychotherapeutic interventions seem as enigmatic as this puzzle. Patients often do not understand our interventions, because we examine the problematic situation from a perspective that is different from theirs. What seems enigmatic to the patient is matter-of-fact to us, because the patient usually continues thinking about the problem—even in our office—with the same logical system that produced the symptom in the first place, and which cannot produce any beneficial change. Effective therapists use some other system of logic to appreciate the world that the client lives in, and then use that new system of logic to introduce the client to a new way of solving the previously insoluble problem.

How does a therapist develop this skill? By finding out what it is in each of us that allows us to be most creative, and that allows us to develop a different and constructive way of perceiving familiar situations.

When I began my child psychiatry training at the Philadelphia Child Guidance Clinic, I discovered that I was most comfortable working with families who shared my ethnic origins. However, the clinic was in an area of the city where few of my patients did. Consequently, I had to learn about theirs.

Since the Philadelphia Child Guidance Clinic under Salvador Minu-

---

* The answer to the six-stick puzzle is a tetrahedron.

chin's directorship fostered creative psychotherapy, I was allowed to experiment with ethical therapeutic interventions that seemed unorthodox, so long as they had some clinical merit. One time, I treated a patient whose family was sporadic in keeping appointments. They were missing appointments not because they intended to, but because time was not an important concept in their lives. The only fair thing to do, I decided, was to share our "homes." I suggested, and they agreed, that we would take turns in hosting the appointments. One week I'd come to their house, and the next week they would come to my "house," the clinic.

Their house was about four blocks from the clinic. When I went there for the inauguration of this "home and home series" of therapy sessions, everyone was punctual and present. The family was very proud that the doctor was coming to visit them, and the head of the household offered to provide me with some refreshment. The identified patient was dispatched to the corner grocery store with instructions to buy me the soda of my choice. The soda was brought back to the house and ceremoniously poured into a sparklingly clean one-pint jar. I thanked them very much, and drank its contents.

For the next appointment, it was my turn to be host. They were coming to the clinic. But how could I offer them coffee in styrofoam cups when they had, with solemn dignity, given me soda in a one-pint jar? Therefore, I got some one-pint jars. At the session, they took the coffee with great ceremony, and we all drank from the jars with great pleasure. The therapy session, that day, went very well.

From then on, there was never a problem about promptness or therapeutic progress. The family would come to my home and I would go to theirs. The clinic became my patient's second home. Even the receptionist came to befriend my patient, because the patient would drop in at unscheduled times to say hello to people. The patient's psychotherapy and that of the family were successful.

After the therapy was over, one of my supervisors asked me, "How did you know to offer them coffee out of one-pint jars?"

I answered, "I learned about this in two ways when I was a kid. I once had a babysitter whom I liked very much, and who one day proudly took me to her house on the other side of the tracks. It was one-quarter the size of the two-story home in which I was living. She took me to the kitchen and showed me what her mother was cooking. Her mother was cooking lima beans for dinner! To me, lima beans were the yukkiest food in the whole world. I figured that they must be really poor if they *had* to eat lima beans, and if they had *only* lima beans for dinner. I couldn't get that experience out of my head for months.

"The second way was that when I was growing up we often had other uses for things—empty cans made excellent containers for storing important items. I already had some appreciation of the fact that people could lead their lives and use ordinary objects in different ways. It didn't seem to matter how well off the people were, or how they used the objects, just as long as they lived and functioned with integrity. So the one-pint jars didn't surprise me."

What was curious about the whole process, though, was that I had to stop thinking about things in my habitual way. Otherwise, what was happening with my patients made no sense whatsoever. I had to think about things their way, and then somehow find some new way of appreciating what was happening. It's that way with all paradox.

Many times, when a client presents a personal difficulty for treatment, we do not have a way of understanding it. Often, we attempt to understand it from our own frame of reference. In the process of doing so, we often have no conception of what is going on. It is much more helpful to understand it from the client's framework, and then, since it is still a real problem for the client, to find some way of demonstrating an understanding that makes sense to the client *and* creates a solution.

THE FUNCTIONS OF PARADOX

Controlling the Symptom

Paradox has several functions in psychotherapy. The first is that paradox controls the symptom. For instance, anytime that a symptom prescription is used as a therapeutic intervention, the patient's seemingly involuntary behavior is brought under voluntary control. Consider the following scenario:

"Oh, I couldn't do that. I can't. That's why I'm here."

"Well, do me a favor, will you? The headache that really bothers you, it would be most helpful to me if I could see you having it here in this office, so that I'd know what would be the best treatment for you. Could you please get it a little bit—not a lot—just a little bit, so that I can find out exactly what it's like?" And they usually get the headache.

I carefully observe them and question them about the symptom, and finish with, "Thank you very much. You can get rid of it now." And they get rid of it.

They are then told, "I understand that you got this just a little bit, and then were able to get rid of it. Could you practice doing it some more? Could you get the headache again, just a little bit, and then get rid of it again? You've already done it once." And they usually can.

Why does paradox work in this situation? Because the patients are placed in a situation where their original way of thinking about their symptom are no longer valid. That is, they demonstrate to themselves that they *can* do something that they did not think was possible, i.e., control their own symptom. This method works for habits, it works for many physiological symptoms, and it works for a lot of emotional states where people are confused, anxious or out of control.

The principle is the same. The patients are presented with a new model, a new way of thinking about their symptom. Then they experience it which allows them to regain control over themselves.

Providing a New Logical Framework

Comments and therapeutic tasks provide patients with new perspectives and new logical frameworks for their clinical problems. It was the old perspective, the old framework, and the old logic that helped produce the symptom in the first place. If a new perspective is created for patients, one they can accept and understand, then inherent in that new perspective is a potential solution to their problem.

That's why, if you are still trying to figure out how to construct four equilateral triangles with six sticks, so that only the sticks' ends touch, you are discovering that some of your old frameworks don't apply too well.

Reducing Resistance to Change

The third function that paradox has clinically is to reduce greatly a client's resistance to change. This occurs because paradox brings confusion into the situation. When a client is confused about the purpose or meaning of a therapeutic intervention or strategy, but agrees to accept it because the therapist is trusted, any reluctance that the client might have had about personally changing is diminished. In the process of thinking about the therapist's comment or in performing the therapeutic task, the client is also involved in the process of changing. It is the client's faith and belief and trust in the therapist that allow the confusion of paradox to be tolerated, and clinical change to occur.

CASE ONE

Since I am both a child psychiatrist and an adult psychiatrist, people often come to my office with questions and concerns about their children. Occasionally, they complain that their children are "misbehaving at home and always getting into fights."

Therapist: What do you mean by "fights?"
Parent: Well, they're always hitting each other.
Therapist: I have a sure-fire way of having your children not hit each other, but first I need to know whether that's what you really want.
Parent: Absolutely. That's what we want, no more hitting.
Therapist: Fine, here's what to do. Tell your children the following: The next time I hear or see any child in this family hitting another child in the family, *both* children will be sent to their rooms immediately.
Parent: How can that be? You can't do that! It's not fair, doctor!
Therapist: Wait a minute. I asked you whether you wanted to stop the hitting.
Parent: Yes, we do want to stop the hitting, but your way is cruel.
Therapist: Well, this is a very fair way to do it. So far, though, the method makes little sense to you, because it seems that the put-upon child will always be taken advantage of, right? The bully of the family will be able to smack the little guy whenever he wants, and then the poor victim will have to spend time in his bedroom nursing his wounds, right?
Parent: Exactly! Why should the child who gets hit be sent to his room?
Therapist: I'll tell you why. Let's say that the little guy is getting pounded daily by the big guy, and both are being sent to their rooms. The little guy has no revenge, right?
Parent: Right.
Therapist: But let's say that the big guy has an important date coming up. He has borrowed the family car, rented a tuxedo, bought a corsage. He is going to the big formal dance of the year. And just as the big guy is walking out of the house, saying goodbye to Mom and Dad, the little guy walks up and wallops the big guy right in front of Mom and Dad. Both have to be sent to their rooms—immediately.
Parent: Oh yes. That'll work just fine!

It usually does—within a week. As soon as it's explained that both children are equally vulnerable and that both children are equally powerful, it makes perfectly good sense. The little guy understands immediately, and the big guy is worried silly. And, there is no more hitting.

CASE TWO

When my son was about eight years old, he manifested a chronic case of napkin agnosia; he didn't remember to use his napkin after eating a snack or meal. Back then, it was easy to tell what Jason had just consumed: You could ask him directly, you could look on the table around his plate, or you could look at his face after the meal was over. At Thanksgiving dinner that year, since his mother had made an especially delicious feast for the three of us, Jason's face was particularly artistic.

After the meal, having now decided that reminding the boy was not being effective, I called him over to my chair. He was accustomed to my doing that, because I frequently hugged and kissed him after he had been excused from the table. So he came over to me, and I bent down to him. And I licked his face! Then I gently said to him, "There's some food that you didn't wipe off."

Well, he was horrified! But that was the last time Jason didn't remember to use his napkin. And he still remembers the incident—not so much for having been taught to use his napkin, but for how grossed-out he was by his dad's behavior.

How can we use paradoxes and unexpected tasks therapeutically? First, we must accept at face value the patient's statement about the problem and the patient's logic about the problem. We really have to find out exactly how the patient conceptualizes the problem, what is the logical system being used, what are the sequences and circumstances in which the symptom occurs, and what are the logical exceptions to that system. By examining the patient's system from a different perspective, exceptions will appear as obvious irregularities.

After we have discovered the *patient's* logical system for the symptom, then we can apply *our* new logical system, derived from our clinical perspective, and create a different cognitive framework for the symptom. This allows us to devise a solution to the patient's problem based on logical extensions of the new cognitive system, and it provides the patient with at least one logical method for symptom abatement.

CASE THREE

A young girl was brought to me by her parents because she was fearful in her bedroom at night. She slept alone in a moderately sized room that had some windows through which moonlight and streetlight entered. Her bed was about 12 inches above the floor, and she feared that monsters were continually skulking beneath her while she slept. Keeping lights on didn't help diminish her fear. Consequently, she slept as little as possible at night and took long naps during the day. Unfortunately, the naps occurred while she was at her desk in school.

After finding out from her that the monsters appeared only when the sun was not shining and that they were ugly and tall and thin (six inches thick), I asked her whether there were any other frightening creatures anywhere else in her room. We discussed her entire bedroom and closet, talked about every drawer, corner and cranny, and even considered the hallway outside her door.

"No," she said, "the monsters hide only under my bed."

I told her that I had a way of getting rid of the monsters permanently, but that I first needed to be sure they were only under her bed. I asked her to go home and, for the next week, whenever she was awake at night, to look in every conceivable place in her room for the hiding monsters. I assured her parents that her health would not be adversely affected and that she could make up her schoolwork on the weekend if she was too tired to stay awake in school.

The next week, she reported to me that the monsters had been under her bed every night, and that they had not been hiding anywhere else. She agreed when I asked if it was all right if no more monsters lived in her bedroom—since the cellar and attic already housed a sufficient number.

I then turned to her father and asked about the cost of his daughter's bed. He replied that it wasn't worth too much.

"Would you be willing to do some carpentry on your daughter's bed, so that she won't be frightened by the monsters under it?"

"Yes," he replied. The girl volunteered that it would be fine with her, too.

I told the father, "Cut off the legs of your daughter's bed, so that it sits directly on the floor. The monsters won't be able to live there, then."

He did as I suggested, and the little girl was no longer bothered by monsters at night. Her schoolwork and disposition improved rapidly.

CREATIVE THINKING

Erickson's therapeutic paradoxes and riddles were creative solutions to his patients' clinical problems. Creative thinking and problem solving were skills that he constantly taught in his seminars, although often his students did not appreciate exactly what they were learning.

People who went to Erickson's house for seminars were regularly challenged with a variety of mental puzzles. He would ask all the ways that the number 710 could be read. The responses would usually produce numerical answers. Then Erickson would turn the number upside down, and show them the word OIL. To discover OIL, it was necessary to look at 710 from a different perspective, with a different frame of reference for the written characters.

Likewise, Erickson often asked people, "What are all the ways that you can go from this office to the adjoining room?" Students usually answered with a variety of methods for ambulation and with ingenious methods for exiting his office and entering the adjacent parlor. When they had exhausted their solutions, Erickson would then delight in telling them additional ways that they could have solved the problem. *After* they had exited his office but *before* they had entered the adjoining room, they could have gone anywhere in the world, or done a colossal number of intermediate activities, and then returned to enter the room through its doors or windows. It *was* necessary to accept the architectural limitations of Milton's house and the physical limitations of the human locomotor apparatus to answer the riddle, but it was *not* necessary to accept the limitation of brief elapsed time that most people assumed. By showing that a different frame of time reference was also valid, Milton provided his students with an infinite number of new solutions to the problem he posed.

The stories and riddles that Erickson enjoyed telling his patients and students had, as one of their functions, the purpose of teaching people to examine their life situations from different frames of reference. That, too, is our task as therapists—to assist our clients to change their worlds and create more comfortable and meaningful lives for themselves.

PART V

Ericksonian Approaches with Specific Populations

Ericksonian techniques can be applied across clinical categories and with all patient groups. The chapters in this section demonstrate the wide applicability of Ericksonian methods.

Yvonne M. Dolan, M.A., earned her degree in psychology from West Georgia College in Carrollton, Georgia. She now practices in Denver, Colorado. Dolan recently completed a book on the utilization of Ericksonian techniques with chronic patients which will be published by Brunner/Mazel.

Dolan describes some Ericksonian methods that can be used with severely disturbed patients. Formal techniques of hypnosis are not used; rather, the emphasis is on naturalistic methods.

Noelle M. Poncelet, M.S.W., earned her degree at the University of Pittsburgh. While pursuing a Ph.D. in clinical psychology at the Fielding Institute, Poncelet conducts a private practice in the San Francisco Bay area. Also, she is actively involved in training professionals to use Ericksonian hypnotherapy.

Poncelet describes an integrated treatment program for using Ericksonian methods to facilitate the process of childbirth. A novel part of the procedure is to work with both members of the couple.

John H. Edgette earned his Master's degree in community psychology at University of Bridgeport, Connecticut. He is working on a Psy.D. in clinical psychology from Hahnemann Medical College and Hospital. Edgette describes how Ericksonian techniques can be integrated with behavioral methods to treat agoraphobics.

C.A.L. Hoogduin, M.D., is a psychiatrist who practices in Delft, Holland. He is the president of the Netherlands Society of Clinical Hypnosis. Hoogduin is a member of the Dutch directive therapy group and is one of the coauthors of Directive Therapy, Volumes I and II, *published in Dutch.*

Hoogduin describes his treatment strategy for cigarette smoking which consists of three parts: classical trance induction, a paradoxical approach which includes ordeals and symptom prescription, and an Ericksonian approach which involves indirect technique.

David Rigler, Ph.D., is a clinical psychologist practicing in Santa Cruz, California. Formerly, he was a clinical professor at the Medical School of the University of Southern California and chief psychologist at the Children's Hospital in Los Angeles.

Rigler discusses the use of hypnosis with adolescents. Developmental issues must be considered. Hypnotherapists who work with adolescents were queried about their approach and Rigler reports the results of his survey.

Nachman Alon has a Master's degree in clinical psychology from the Hebrew University of Jerusalem. He is codirector with Moris Kleinhauz, M.D., of the Clinic for Multidimensional Therapy in Tel Aviv. Alon is in the Israeli Military Reserve where he serves as a Lieutenant-Colonel and Commander of an Infantry Unit.

Alon describes his approach to patients with posttraumatic stress disorder. The personality characteristics of these patients are delineated and strategies for treatment are presented.

Ronald R. Brown, Ph.D., earned his degree in clinical psychology from the University of Michigan. He is a staff psychologist at the Counseling Center at the University of Tennessee in Knoxville and an adjunct assistant professor in the Clinical Psychology Department. He has conducted training seminars on hypnosis for professional organizations.

Dr. Brown describes how Ericksonian methods can be used to treat rape victims. Comparison between an Ericksonian orientation and traditional approach is offered.

Donald W. Malon, M.S.W., Ph.D., earned his degrees in social work and sociology at St. Louis University. He is an associate professor at the School of Social Services at St. Louis University, and codirector of the Marriage and Family Institute of Saint Louis.

Malon describes the use of Ericksonian-based techniques with "super-rational" clients. Personality aspects of these patients are presented. Malon describes five approaches for dealing with super-rational clients and illustrates how techniques can be used to bypass resistance.

O. Spurgeon English, M.D., is a professor in the Department of Psychiatry, Temple University Medical Center. He received his M.D. from Jefferson Medical College. Dr. English is well known as a lecturer and a writer and has coauthored five volumes on various aspects of psychiatry and mental health. He is a Fellow of the American Psychoanalytic Association, the American Psychiatric Association, and the American College of Physicians.

Similar to Malon, Dr. English discusses a particular type of patient, namely, the kind of patient who responds to confrontation, especially the kind of indirect confrontation which Erickson often used. Three case examples illustrate his approach.

Chapter 17

Ericksonian Utilization and Intervention Techniques with Chronically Mentally Ill Clients

Yvonne M. Dolan

This chapter describes case examples of interventions selected from a group of 23 chronically mentally ill clients successfully treated with Ericksonian techniques in a small-town psychiatric day hospital between 1979 and 1981. I will provide illustrations of some practical ways to apply Ericksonian methods to the treatment of the chronically mentally ill, the world's most experienced and possibly most challenging clients. To date (1983), none of the above clients have required further inpatient psychiatric hospitalization.

For the purposes of this chapter, "chronic" refers to individuals hospitalized two or more times yearly in psychiatric inpatient settings for three or more years in succession without achieving significant symptomatic relief.

In the demanding context of working with chronic clients, the Ericksonian approach offers a perspective of pragmatism coupled with integrity. In many cases, utilization strategies enable a client to bridge the gap between acceptable behavior that is tolerated in the community and bizarre symptomatic behavior that results in being sent to psychiatric inpatient facilities or jails.

UTILIZATION

Ericksonian utilization is both a way of looking at the client and a way of interacting with the client. It is a perspective of optimism and confidence in the client's ability to respond to psychotherapy (Erickson & Zeig, 1980). A crucial condition for success with chronic clients is the therapist's expectation that the client will respond to treatment (Erickson, 1980b). The concept of utilization implies that all aspects of the client's behavior, personality, relationships and situation are potentially valuable and useful in enabling the client to achieve more rewarding behavioral choices (Erickson, 1980d).

The concept of utilization is essentially a nonjudgmental way of looking at human behavior (Erickson, 1980b). Stephen Gilligan (personal communication, 1982) tells an anecdote in which Milton Erickson says, "You cannot rigidly assign values to human behavior; they're always changing." Therapists must maintain a nonjudgmental attitude if they are to enable the chronic client to become unstuck from rigid symptomatic patterns of behaving and perceiving. Direct or implied criticism of the chronic client's behavior and perceptions—of the client's model of the world—will merely strengthen symptomatic patterns. If directly challenging a psychotic client's belief system would lead to successful intervention, it would have worked long before the client became chronic with a long clinical history of unsuccessful treatment. Erickson, with Zeig (1980), writes:

> . . . No two people necessarily have the same ideas whether they are psychotically based or culturally based. When you understand how Man really defends his intellectual ideas and how emotional he gets about it, you should realize that the first thing in psychotherapy is not to try to compel him to change his ideation; rather you should go along with it, and change it in a gradual fashion and create situations wherein he himself willingly changes his thinking. (p. 336)

Before symptomatic behavior can be therapeutically incorporated into the change process, the therapist must be willing to accept and appreciate the problematic behavior as a potentially valuable therapeutic resource (Erickson, 1980a). It is essential that this acceptance be real and not merely the therapist's attempt to trick the client into giving up the problem behavior. The experienced client, involved with the mental health system long enough to be considered chronic, will quickly sense dishonesty on the part of the therapist. The therapist's attempt to utilize symptomatic behavior will then result in distrust and further loss of rapport.

By joining the chronic client in his or her model of the world, the therapist enables the client to feel safe enough to make contact (Erickson, 1980b). The client's symptomatic behavior or perceptions then can serve as initial stepping stones to voluntary choice of less constricting, more socially acceptable behavioral options.

THE CASE OF PETER

With some chronic clients, the therapist's first task is to get the client to show up for regular treatment long enough for an intervention to be accomplished. Such was the case with Peter, a 34-year-old male who suffered from panic attacks and chronic depression, and had made repeated suicide attempts. He had been seen by virtually every inpatient and outpatient mental health professional in his community. However, he never stayed in treatment long enough for rapport to be established. Several local therapists refused to see him. The day hospital staff's initial task was to identify Peter's treatment attendance pattern so that pattern could be utilized to lead to more regular attendance. Peter stated that while he wanted relief from the anxiety and depression that led to recurrent suicide attempts, he felt ambivalent about treatment and experienced difficulty motivating himself to continue once treatment was started. When his suicide attempts led to inpatient hospitalization, he characteristically checked himself out of the unit within 48 hours, only to make another suicide attempt within two weeks.

In the day hospital setting, Peter's characteristic attendance pattern was identified as attending two consecutive days of treatment, then missing a week or more. To utilize his problematic attendance pattern, the day treatment staff gave Peter the following directive which was later written into a contract which he signed:

> We realize you are not sure that coming here is good for you. It is our experience that people have difficulties when they don't do what is truly good for them. Therefore, we believe that it is most important that you learn to do what you feel is truly good for you. After giving this long and hard thought, we have come up with the following rules to insure that you only do what you feel is truly good for you:
>
> 1) You are only to come to the day treatment program if you feel it is truly beneficial to you.
>
> 2) To discourage you from coming unless it is really helping you

feel better, once you start you will be allowed to continue to come only if you have attended the previous treatment day.

3) If you stay home on a scheduled treatment day, in order to return to the program you must be able to demonstrate verbally that you spent that day or days doing something good for yourself that you enjoyed.

4) If you fail to do something good for yourself that you enjoyed while gone from the program, you will be required, as a penalty, to stay away from the program for one week following the absence.

Peter reacted with a look of surprise and then said softly, "You really DO want me to do what makes me feel better." The following week he predictably attended two days and then missed a week. The following week Peter returned and was warmly greeted by the day treatment staff who enthusiastically welcomed him back, casually remarking that he was in compliance with his agreement of missing one week following an unexcused absence. The following week Peter missed one day and returned the following day. He said that he had been miserable at home the previous day and had not bothered to do even one thing that he enjoyed or was good for himself. He was told, therefore, that he would be penalized by having to stay away from the program for at least one day. If he spent that day doing something he enjoyed that was beneficial to him, he could return on the following day. If not, he would be suspended for a minimum of a week.

Peter was first incredulous and then indignant. He angrily protested his right to attend treatment regularly. At this point, the therapist assumed a posture of humorously exaggerated amazement. Peter than began to laugh and quietly left the therapist's office. He spent the rest of the day enjoying himself fishing and then attended to several long-neglected chores which gave him a sense of accomplishment. Peter subsequently participated regularly in the day treatment program long enough for other interventions to be accomplished.

"Shock" Therapy

Sometimes the most effective intervention depends on the therapist's ability to not interfere with the process of a naturalistic intervention. The intervention that led to a change in Peter's chronic suicidal behavior was accomplished by other clients in the day hospital setting. During a large group therapy session, Peter announced to the therapist and his peers that he planned to go home that night and kill himself with a drug overdose. Before the therapist could respond, the other 15 clients actively voiced their concern and objections, stating versions of, "You can't do that!" Peter protested that he could do it. To his great discomfort, the other clients unanimously agreed among themselves that they would go home with him that night and remain with him indefinitely in his tiny apartment until the danger of suicide was over! He began to protest loudly and angrily but was overruled by his peers who voiced deep concern in tones even more hysterical, loud and demanding than his. For several hours, Peter and his peers argued about whether he could safely go home alone.

Despite the crisis nature of the incident, the therapist resisted the temptation to intervene. Finally, Peter succeeded in convincing his peers, the therapist and himself that there was no need for him to attempt suicide again. The reality of 15 deeply caring, allegedly "crazy" people threatening to come to live with him indefinitely was enough of a shock to enable Peter to successfully interrupt and permanently change his chronic suicidal behaviors. In the three years since, there have been no further suicide attempts.

UTILIZING A PSYCHOTIC EXPERIENCE: THE CASE OF BRIAN

The author does not employ direct hypnotic techniques with psychotic or semipsychotic clients. Instead, it is assumed that these clients are already in a state of altered awareness, and that the therapeutic task is to assist the client in reorienting to a more lucid, comfortable, and functional state. Psychotic clients tend to be in a highly suggestible state (Zeig, 1974). The therapist's nonverbal expressions of comfort and security often are helpful in eliciting comfort and security in the client.

Brian was a 24-year-old male seen to evaluate the necessity of immediate inpatient psychiatric hospitalization. He was in a semipsychotic state and had not slept, bathed, or eaten for several days. It had been learned previously that the client had grown up on a farm, liked cars, and liked to go to parties.

The client reported that he had spent the past week obsessively worrying and compulsively arguing with family and friends about an apparently hallucinated experience. Brian's hallucinated vision was an experience of traveling down a long road and encountering a fortune-telling machine which told him, "Your future is in your past." He said, "I now realize I've been traveling backwards for a long time. Maybe this means my life is over. I'm thinking about killing myself." He felt that the fortune-telling message was the "key" to his long-term difficulties.

Numerous people, including Brian's family, friends and previous therapists had unsuccessfully attempted to convince him that his experience was hallucinated, not real, and should be forgotten so he could go on with his daily life. This had the effect of heightening his conviction of the importance of his hallucination, and produced mild paranoia.

I listened to Brian's obsessively detailed hour-long account of the fortune-telling machine and waited until he became silent and began to look expectant and comfortable. I then told him a long and detailed account of a farm girl who, in order to comply with her father's request not to put more than ten miles on the car, drove backwards down a country road to a party where she enjoyed herself listening to music. Later, she drove forward home without exceeding her allotted mileage. She had enough mileage left to go to the movies. Suggestions for experiencing comfort, security and an externally focused (lucid) state of awareness were interspersed in the story, which concluded with the observation that "she found out that you can also use a backward route to get directly to the places you need to go forward to." Brian reoriented to a lucid state, went home that night and slept for nearly 24 hours. The next day he reached a decision to seek treatment for a long-standing substance abuse problem. To date (three years later), there have been no further psychotic episodes or apparent mention of the fortune-telling obsession. A recent inquiry indicated that the client has maintained his sobriety.

THE CASE OF ALICE

One of the primary difficulties facing the therapist who works with a chronically aggressive, belligerent or threatening client is that success is often in proportion to the therapist's willingness to become closely involved with the client. This is difficult because the chronic client's aggressive behavior serves as a well-practiced and powerful means of keeping others at arm's length. Such was the case with the following client:

Alice was a 25-year-old female client with a four-year history of violent acting-out behavior resulting in repeated arrests, suicide attempts, and cyclical hospitalizations. Typically, Alice formed romantic liaisons with rough, alcoholic men who cheated on her. She characteristically attempted to surprise her boyfriend and the woman he was cheating with at one of the local bars and then attempted to beat them up. Although

Alice was petite, she was a skilled street fighter and usually delivered several respectable blows before the police came to take her away.

Alice was referred to the psychiatric day hospital program through a court order. For the first three months, she spoke rarely, sulking angrily around the unit, snarling that she was technically in compliance with the court order. My direct attempts to make contact with Alice served only to elicit anger and threatening behavior. For two months, I said little to Alice but progressively moved in closer and closer physical proximity, beginning from across the room and eventually achieving a conversational distance of a few feet without eliciting anger or threats. However, any direct expression of support or interest brought an angry or suspicious response.

The staff arranged to make "random" positive observations about Alice's improved appearance, behavior with peers, skills at crafts, etc., deliberately intended to be overheard by the client. Any marginally positive behavior was framed in a positive light. After six months of overheard comments, Alice began to seek out the staff. She refused to speak directly about her difficulties, but talked only about her craft and needlework projects. The staff responded by repeatedly telling her, "This is good . . . and you really can find a way to use your abilities in a way that lets you win." Her characteristic reaction to this comment was, "You're nuts!" However, she began to smile and her behavior continued to become more gentle and sociable. Suggestions for self-esteem and security also were interspersed in comments to other clients, made with meaningful looks at Alice. The staff wondered, however, if these messages were actually reaching her.

After six months of treatment Alice was in desperate need of a job, was sleeping in her car, and had little to eat. No one would hire her. One day she came late to the program and announced triumphantly, "I found a way to use my abilities!" She had gotten a job as a bouncer in one of the rough local bars. Her previous reputation for erratic and violent behavior served her well. When she asked customers to leave, they left quietly despite her diminutive stature. Within a year, Alice progressed from bouncer to barmaid and began to dress appropriately and attractively.

No further violent outbursts or suicide attempts occurred. Three years later, the client still maintains contact with me. Alice reports that she currently is completing a college degree in psychology, has enjoyed a rewarding and stable relationship with a man for over a year, and is employed as a secretary. In repeatedly suggesting that she could find rewarding ways to use all her abilities, the staff could not have predicted how Alice would find a way to productively use her violent street fighting behavior. However, even the most problematic behavior can be utilized as a therapeutic resource.

THE CASE OF CARL

Carl was a 35-year-old man who was repeatedly hospitalized because of episodes in which for days he refused to eat, drink, bathe or speak. When pushed by family to care for himself, he struck out physically. This behavior often led to intervention by the police. Attempts at family and individual therapy were unsuccessful because Carl refused to speak. He gave no evidence of being delusional and appeared intelligent. Previous to the onset of his withdrawn behavior, he had earned a college degree.

The author asked Carl what he thought would make him feel better about his life. After a fifteen minute pause in which the author waited expectantly, Carl sighed heavily and began to speak. He stated emphatically, "I want to be left alone!" Rapport was achieved by offering to assist him in his stated goal of getting his family and service providers to leave him alone. Since Carl had been repeatedly hospitalized over the past three years, he was receiving services from virtually every agency in town.

Carl was asked how each service provider and family member specifically bothered him and what he thought it would take to get them to leave him alone. Carl was uncertain. He reluctantly agreed to attend one of his own treatment staffings to get a more accurate idea of what, specifically, it would take to get all those people to leave him alone.

Carl's previous treatment decisions had been made either in his absence or with him present as a passive, withdrawn observer. In this treatment staffing, he reluctantly became the active, central participant. With the therapist's support, Carl gradually found out from his parents and each of his service providers what change in behavior he could use to "manipulate" them into leaving him alone. The parents and service providers' descriptions of behaviors that would allow them to leave him alone were listed on a piece of paper. I then assisted Carl in negotiating some of the stated details with his parents and the other service providers. This agreement was written up as a contract and signed by Carl, his family and service providers, all of whom agreed to meet for a treatment staffing once a month to assess how the arrangement was working out and to negotiate changes in the contract.

Initially, Carl agreed to bathe, eat, and attend the day hospital program provided that his parents would not nag him and the various social service and mental health workers would leave him alone. Later, the agreement evolved into Carl's living independently in his own apartment and getting job training while no longer needing to attend the day hospital program. He became more expressive and outgoing with his peers and requested individual therapy which he utilized well.

The treatment staffings were held every six to eight weeks and eventually comprised Carl's only continuing form of psychotherapy while he continued to function independently in the community. After two and one-half years, only two service providers continued to be involved in Carl's case. When one of them abruptly stopped attending the meetings, Carl almost immediately regressed to his former withdrawn symptomatic behavior. However, he did not regress to the point of requiring inpatient hospitalization. Instead, he voluntarily returned briefly to the day hospital program and continued to live in the community.

I believe that follow-up is useful in avoiding the risk that the former chronic client might feel abandoned by the therapist who is seen less frequently as the client no longer exhibits symptomatic behavior. Some chronic clients like Carl may regress as a way to maintain contact and continue to get needed support from the therapeutic community. The follow-up can take the form of continued involvement with the treatment system through a support group, follow-up appointments, or occasional phone calls or letters. Erickson frequently made personal follow-up inquiries at casual social gatherings.

The above case histories suggest that Ericksonian utilization and intervention techniques can be powerful tools for enabling chronic clients to move beyond symptomatic limitations to more rewarding behaviors and perceptions. In order to utilize symptomatic behavior to lead to therapeutic change with chronic clients, a highly personalized and flexible approach is likely to be required from the therapist. The therapist must be willing to view the client's symptomatic behavior in a nonjudgmental manner and successfully communicate this to the client as evidenced by deep rapport.

Once rapport has been achieved with the chronic client, the therapist must identify an aspect of the client's ongoing behavior or current perceptions that can be incorporated into the therapeutic change process in such a way as to enable the client to willingly move closer to a desirable therapeutic outcome. In the context of the Ericksonian approach, all of the chronic client's symptoms can be viewed as potential therapeutic resources.

REFERENCES

Erickson, M. H. (1980a). Naturalistic techniques of hypnosis. In E. Rossi (Ed.), *The collected papers of Milton H. Erickson* (Vol. 1, p. 168). New York: Irvington.

Erickson, M. H. (1980b). An hypnotic technique for resistant patients: The patient, the technique, and its rationale and field experiments. In E. Rossi (Ed.), *The collected papers of Milton H. Erickson* (Vol. 1, p. 299). New York: Irvington.

Erickson, M. H. (1980c). The use of symptoms as an integral part of hypnotherapy. In E. Rossi (Ed.), *The collected papers of Milton H. Erickson* (Vol. 4, pp. 213-215). New York: Irvington.

Erickson, M. H. (1980d). Psychotherapy achieved by a reversal of the neurotic processes in a case of Ejaculatio Praecox. In E. Rossi (Ed.), *The collected papers of Milton H. Erickson* (Vol. 4, p. 348). New York: Irvington.

Erickson, M. H., & Zeig, J. K. (1980). Symptom prescription for expanding the psychotic's world view. In E. Rossi (Ed.), *The collected papers of Milton H. Erickson* (Vol. 4, p. 336). New York: Irvington.

Kramer, E., & Brennan, E. P. (1964). Hypnotic susceptibility of schizophrenic patients. *Journal of Abnormal Psychology, 64*, 657-659.

Zeig, J. K. (1974). Hypnotherapy techniques with psychotic inpatients. *American Journal of Clinical Hypnosis, 1*, 56-59.

Chapter 18

An Ericksonian Approach to Childbirth

Noelle M. Poncelet

In the last 20 years, there has been much effort in the health field to bring "normalcy" back into the childbirth experience, e.g., by using a home environment; by focusing on the emotional and interpersonal experience; and by using nonpharmacological pain control methods. Concurrently advances in obstetrics offer the pregnant woman and her child the most sophisticated medical and nursing care in a hospital setting. Yet technological advances are too often at the cost of emotional comfort for the mother, the father, and their newborn (Palmer, 1983).

Elements of Ericksonian principles and techniques are ideally suited to enhance the process of childbirth. The model described herein emphasizes intrapersonal and interpersonal factors that foster a heightened awareness of the totality of oneself in the processes of childbirth.

This approach to childbirth training was developed for patients receiving traditional obstetrical care. It evolved as an effort to: 1) pay attention to the nonmedical factors involved in childbirth, such as the psychological aspects of the pain experience and the stress on the marital relationship; and 2) prepare the couple for a normal childbirth experience, despite the limitations inherent in the medical setting. These limitations, such as time pressure, multiple demands, and hospital care based on symptomatology and emergency readiness, can encroach upon the medical and nursing staff's capacity to be sensitive to the woman and to the couple. The current approach is also a response to postpartum reactions in both men and women including the male reaction to role

The author gratefully acknowledges the editorial assistance of Alan Leveton, M.D., in the preparation of this manuscript.

changes; the male's emotional and physical isolation from his wife and child; and female sexual dysfunction.

CHILDBIRTH AND ERICKSONIAN PRINCIPLES

Erickson stressed the need to understand human behavior in context—as a communication between individuals and the environment (Haley, 1973). To understand behavior during childbirth, I looked at the interaction between the pregnant woman, her husband and the medical staff in the hospital setting. If the hospital's focus is solely on the safety of the woman and her child, if the husband colludes with this focus, and if there is little else for the woman to do but respond to the hospital's concern, there exists a powerful, although admittedly unintended, environmental (hypnotic) suggestion for her to concentrate on the physical sensations of her contractions, translate those into the performance criterion of centimeters of dilation, be cheered and prodded along by her husband, and worry (while hooked onto the monitor) about her safety and her child's safety. To this stew, add a dash of family myths about pregnancy and childbirth and a few tall tales from well-meaning friends, let an overworked staff stir this stew in the sterile environment of a hospital where sick people go to get well or die, and it is no wonder that anxiety and pain are the prevalent "main dish of the day." Indeed, I suspect that only couples who are naturally good at dissociation and reframing make it comfortably through childbirth.

Erickson demonstrated the usefulness of thinking in terms of patterns and polarities in understanding human behavior and in planning behavior change. The polar side of psychosomatics is that, if the body can somatize in the form of muscular tension and pain, feelings of fear, anger, and boredom, this same body can express physical well-being, feelings of anticipation, joy and love. In other words, where there exists a capacity for pain, there coexists a capacity for pleasure. This is analogous to Erickson's approach to amputees: "Now if you have phantom pain in a limb, you may also have phantom good feelings. And they are delightful" (Erickson & Rossi, 1979, p. 107).

Erickson delighted in teasing out the capacity of students and patients to enjoy life at multiple levels, to have the deeply satisfying experience of self-appreciation, of sensory awareness, of interpersonal connection, of intellectual curiosity and discovery, of personal growth and evolution (Erickson & Rossi, 1979; Erickson, Rossi, & Rossi, 1976). So much of this enjoyment has only been tapped haphazardly during childbirth.

Erickson also taught a deep respect for life cycles—for the process from birth to death that occurs in the interpersonal context of the nuclear and extended family. He looked at the transitions created by life events as rich opportunities for transformations, and for cognitive and emotional reorganization of issues such as sexuality, work/play, pain/pleasure (Haley, 1973). The physical body can be involved during those rites of passage which evolve entry and/or separation. Certainly the pregnant woman experiences, in the passage from internal connection to external bonding with her baby, a separation and an entry. Similarly, her husband moves from physical isolation to connection and bonding with his child. The couple experiences a shift from being a pair to becoming a triad, sometimes at great expense. Such transformations need not be translated into physical pain.

Erickson considered anxiety a transformative element, a positive energy that can be harnessed and utilized. Negative anxiety occurs when the frame of reference for understanding events and behaviors is too narrow, when intrapersonal and interpersonal needs are not acknowledged and utilized, and/or when the circularity of such needs and processes between individuals and the environment is not recognized (Erickson & Rossi, 1979). Erickson approached anxiety by pacing, i.e., by overtly accepting its specific manifestation in an individual and/or in the couple. He acknowledged its positive function, and respected attempted solutions.

When the nature of the anxiety found in every couple facing childbirth is explored carefully and gently, one finds fear of dying for the woman, and fear of loss of baby and wife for the man. It is easy to identify and explain the potential dangers inherent in the childbirth process (for which hospitals are so well prepared). Yet there may exist a deeper explanation. Milton Erickson repeatedly said, "Your body knows, . . . your unconscious is your best friend." As I witnessed a close friend die, I marveled at the similarities between the contractions that give life and those that surrender it. When I have shared with couples my observation of the similarities between these contractions, in some instances, and the possibility of links being established between the two experiences of life and death by their unconscious, the result has been paradoxical: By reframing their anxiety in a context broader than potential medical emergencies, I have found a relieved willingness in couples to acknowledge this anxiety with new respect, to use it, and then let go of it.

Milton Erickson trusted his own belief system and used it to give structure to his therapy with his patients (Haley, 1973). Couples preparing for childbirth can be approached with total conviction that childbirth can be a pleasurable experience, the natural outcome of their love relationship. Two people created a baby through an act that is pleasurable. Nine months later, the events of procreation and childbirth are linked and involve for the woman the same genital organs and the same mechanisms of tension/release. Erickson and Moore knew of the potential orgasmic pleasure, "the joyful shaking" brought forth by the pressure of the baby's head as it rotates through the cervix and down the vagina and by the rhythmic contractions of second stage labor (Erickson & Rossi, 1979, p. 311). How can childbirth *not* be potentially a totally satisfying experience? In my experience women immediately recognized the link; men have been intrigued by it.

Having repeatedly witnessed in my office the envy and yearning experienced by men as they recalled their wives' birth and nursing experiences, I searched for patterns, for common trends underlying the male and female experience that could be used as a bridge.

I observed that fortunate men have vivid dreams of giving birth, at night or in trance. Those dreams can be so realistic that women, upon hearing their descriptions, have validated their accuracy. Thus I took literally the statement that Milton Erickson told Monde (Lustig, 1975): "You can pretend anything you want and master it!" I began to utilize the power of imagination and invited the husband to participate in his wife's experience as fully as he wished to because he was capable of experiencing it all.

Seen in this context, there exists during childbirth a possibility for a rich and profound intrapersonal experience. The primary context is the love relationship between man and woman, and not the health care system, no matter how nurturing it is. Childbirth is a unique opportunity to deepen the marital relationship.

To facilitate the shift in focus described above, hypnosis is an ideal tool. Ericksonian hypnotherapy is particularly suited for this purpose, as it recognizes individual strengths, and utilizes problem-solving styles. Anchoring can be used to establish new ways for the couple to fulfill needs mutually.

Anchoring, a neurolinguistic term and technique developed by Bandler and Grinder (1979) is based on Erickson's hypnotherapy. It consists in pairing a behavior, thought or emotion with a sensory stimulus in such a way that the sensory stimulus can elicit these phenomena in the future (see Erickson working with Monde, Lustig, 1975).

Ericksonian hypnotherapy uses naturalistic inductions and the reframing of meaning, and replaces with positive and playful metaphors, previously frightening images of isolation, danger or pain. Furthermore, Ericksonian hypnotherapy recognizes the need to establish a link between conscious and unconscious processes so that the childbirth experience in the trance state can be recalled at the conscious level (Erickson, Hershman, & Secter, 1961; Erickson & Rossi, 1979). It can be an adjunct to natural childbirth (Dick-Read, 1973) and Lamaze training (1970), which are well-established methods relying on relaxation, breathing, visualization and education regarding the birth process. For pain control, Milton Erickson particularly enjoyed creating dissociation and body catalepsy from the neck down, which he referred to as a hypnotic "sacral block" (Zeig, 1980).

THE PROTOCOL

The Setting

The couple is seen in the third trimester of pregnancy when labor and delivery are immediate concerns. An audiotaped two-hour session usually suffices. I make clear I need not be present during labor and delivery. I am available for "booster" sessions or by phone if necessary. I request follow-up contact after the baby is born.

I send the woman's physician a letter that explains the nature of hypnosis and helps him or her recognize trance behavior. I make suggestions for ways the obstetrician can reinforce the trance, including a hand on the woman's shoulder, and/or simple sentences such as: "You are doing fine, (first name)." I recommend lower trials of analgesic medication, if that is necessary, to avoid oversedation. I indicate that hypnotic training includes suggestions for appropriate responsiveness to interactions with the medical and nursing staff.

The Information-Gathering Interview

The information-gathering interview consists of two phases: 1) the identification of needs and "anchoring" of need fulfillment; and 2) fostering an understanding of hypnosis.

Anchoring

In order to tailor the hypnotic training to the unique characteristics of the couple, I proceed by first asking detailed information regarding: 1) their assumptions about the childbirth experience or their expectations if this is not their first pregnancy, and 2) their needs.

Questions about assumptions and expectations allow me to hear facts and myths transmitted by significant others and the health staff, and determine if they are accepted to any extent by the couple. (Poncelet, 1983). Particular attention is paid to metaphorical "organ" language. I question each spouse sequentially and treat them equally. Similarly, I question what their needs will be before, during and after labor and delivery.

Most often the woman is quick to identify general needs, e.g., love and support from her mate, and relief from pain. There is usually a pause when I ask her, "*How* will you recognize his love and support? What form do you wish his love and support to take?" I help her to identify whether she wants him to look at her, talk to her, touch her. What exactly does she want to hear? Where does she want to be touched? When? How much pressure? As I encourage her to create a totally satisfying sensory experience, I frequently am amazed at how specific many women can be, especially when invited to exclude some disagreeable behaviors.

It is delightful to observe the appreciative look of her husband as he sighs deeply, and acknowledges the relief of knowing specifically how to be helpful. Many suggestions are elicited and the husband is then asked to state sincerely which behaviors he is willing to offer and which he would rather not. I will express disbelief at "blanket" acquiescence and will state that any need met out of obligation is poison to the relationship while those met out of desire are fertilizers. Helpful behaviors he agrees to are immediately rehearsed and anchored.

The process is then reversed and the husband is asked what his needs will be and how he would like his wife to best meet them. Stupefaction is a common response. Men have told me they do not need anything; this is not their time; all they want is to help their wife and make sure she is all right. I respectfully disagree and wonder aloud about their personal concerns and their isolation from the physical experience between their wife and child during the pregnancy. Tentatively first-time fathers begin to tune inward. Men who already have a child have less difficulty stating their inner experience. Needs can now be formulated, agreement elicited from the woman, and their needs can be anchored. Encouraging husbands to voice their concerns provides two crucial points of relief for the woman: It is a validation and explanation of a worried look on her husband's face or perceived concern in his voice.

She is less likely to interpret these behaviors as rejection or criticism. Moreover, it prompts her to get away from her preoccupation with herself, and attend to his needs. Two cases illustrate this process:

Kevin, the father of a young child, remembered feeling cut-off, helpless, unimportant and concerned about the safety of his baby, as his wife, Cathy, fought for two hours against the need to push because of the pain accompanying each contraction. Unable to meet his perceived standard of excellence, she had walled herself off. Everything he said was wrong and, worse, prompted the opposite response. What did he need for next time? "Let me into your world. Share your sensations, observations, concerns, not just the pain. Be with me." Cathy checked her memory, and was delighted to remember that there were comfortable parts in her body and pleasant experiences. She readily agreed to oblige, although she reserved the right to be silent during contractions. From him, she needed language that validated her experience and the intensity of her pain, rather than suggestions which she interpreted as criticisms. She wanted to hear, if needed: "You are in a lot of discomfort and it is very hard for you to push in such circumstances."

Rachel, a Hassidic Jew who could not be touched by her husband during menstruation, labor and delivery, feared the birth of her third child. Her previous childbirths had been experiences of anxiety and pain. Each time, she had cut herself off from her husband. Profoundly religious herself, she now asked that he sing hymns and psalms and look at her. He requested that she share some of her experience and remain in contact with him. Suddenly aware of how calming touch and massage would be, she decided with her husband to invite her closest female friend to be with her, since the Hassidic rule against touching does not apply to women.

Mutual anchoring of needs can occur at the visual, auditory, and kinesthetic levels in a way that is unique to each couple's needs. Anchoring is rehearsed in the office. It is a natural posthypnotic suggestion for a satisfying interaction and for personal comfort and relaxation during labor and delivery. Furthermore, clarifying and negotiating needs clear the way for privacy to be respected by each, since such withdrawal no longer is interpreted as rejection and abandonment.

Knowledge about hypnotic experience

The last part of the information-gathering interview focuses on the couple's knowledge of, and previous experience with, hypnosis. Successes, failures, myths and fears are carefully identified, again in behavioral terms. Experience with Lamaze and natural childbirth training, meditation, prayer and relaxation are acknowledged as useful and overlapping with the hypnotic state. Needs to be in control of the experience and complete responsiveness to the medical and nursing staff are stressed as being compatible (and in fact enhanced) in the hypnotic experience.

Such attention to the hypnotic experience is in itself the beginning of a naturalistic induction and, most often, signs of light trance behavior become evident at this point.

Hypnosis Training

The couple is invited to enjoy the trance together, to make themselves even more comfortable than they already are. They are encouraged to readjust their body positions any time they wish to increase their comfort and relaxation. This is especially important because the pregnant woman may need to move if only in response to her baby shifting position. In fact, some pregnant women exhibit active trance behavior similar to that seen in hypnotized children; the main clue that a trance state has been experienced is the reorientation behavior seen as the trance is terminated (Poncelet, 1982).

Eye fixation

Both are invited to focus on a "spot" on the ceiling in anticipation of the many ceiling fixtures they will see at home and in the hospital. Thus an orientation to the future is suggested. Experienced subjects are invited to recall their most satisfying trance, meditation or relaxation training experience while untrained subjects are specifically led toward an eye closure. Other trance inductions may be used to meet the specific needs of either partner.

Dissociation

Dissociation is suggested to a "favorite place filled with happy memories, where you have felt so relaxed, so comfortable, so safe. You can be by yourself or with each other, it does not matter." The couple is encouraged to use the power of their imagination and to step into this place. Ideomotor finger signaling ratifies that this step has been accomplished and that trance is deepening.

Relaxation

Relaxation is suggested in a variety of ways. Always added is an invitation to "focus on the most comfortable part of your body . . . and with each breath in, increase and spread the feeling of relaxation, with each breath out, let go of unnecessary tensions and concerns. They can be put on hold and dealt with later, just like dirty dishes in the sink sometimes need to wait for an appropriate time to be washed." Thus, anxiety is not discounted but postponed.

Trance deepening

Deepening is achieved by the use of learning sets, suggestions about conscious and unconscious processes, truisms, and double binds. Many observations on the couple's trance behavior and appreciation of their accomplishments are also given.

Partial amnesia for previous childbirth experience

At this point, suggestions are given to multipara couples for retrieving the positive aspects of, and the lessons learned from, their previous childbirth experience and for forgetting what was "uniquely negative about those events."

Pseudoorientation in time

The couple is invited to "think of the time soon in the future, the appropriate time only, when the baby will be ready to be born." It is important in orientation to the future to stress that the rehearsal is for the future only and not an invitation to go into labor now. Perhaps she will recognize a contraction, the rupture of her membrane. These will be signals for her to feel very joyful, excited, curious, relieved that the time has come . . . and to go into a very soothing and comfortable trance. Therapeutic suggestions can be added: "Your body knew how to learn to walk; how can childbirth not be the most satisfying, pleasurable experience when it is linked to your love for one another now and several months ago?"

As her husband learns from his wife that labor has started, he is invited to use her message to go deeply into an active trance which will enable him to help himself, his wife, and the obstetrical team. He is invited to tap within himself the ancient genetic primary knowledge that he has about the childbirth experience. He is reminded that he is the product of one sperm and one egg, that he started as a female embryo before differentiating as a man. Moreover, he will be pleased to know that men have vivid accurate dreams of giving birth. Both are reminded of ways to meet the needs they have agreed upon and that are now available to them so that each can be maximally comfortable, confident and present to the other.

Analgesia

Contractions are described as "the long abdominal muscles contracting while the cervix opens and the vaginal walls stretch. Your body knows what to do; your body leads, your mind observes and enjoys the experience." To maximize comfort, the metaphor of a switchbox in the mother's inner mind is offered. She is invited to identify the wires that connect every organ and muscles involved in childbirth and to connect each one with a switch of specific color. She is alerted to the light above the switch which goes on at the start of a contraction. This signal gives her the pleasure to recognize how well her body is working. She then can turn the switch off or lower it so that all she needs to feel is a dull pressure, a numbing cramping sensation, massaging her baby.

Amnesia

She is encouraged to appreciate the work of each contraction and to recognize it as _completed_ and therefore ready to be forgotten as she immediately becomes absorbed in other activities: preparing herself to go to the hospital, enjoying leisure, conversation, rest, dreaming, sleep.

Posthypnotic suggestions

The woman is encouraged to remain active during the first stage of labor, to follow her physician's advice on the proper time to go to the hospital, and to use the breathing and focusing techniques learned during childbirth training. She is invited to notice her trance and relaxation deepen with each contraction (or, as she gets in the car; at each traffic light; as she approaches the hospital, talks to the insurance clerk, as she is greeted by the medical and nursing staff, as she sees uniforms; or when her physician and assigned nurse examine her, etc.). She is alerted to fluctuations of trance level as a normal phenomenon, especially in the lighter trance level necessary for verbal communication.

Reframing pain

Both partners are invited to recognize that if contractions are one minute long, for example, in one hour there will be 12 minutes of work for 48 minutes of comfort. Therefore, boredom and fatigue are identified as unnecessary enemies and the couple is encouraged to play, move, listen to favorite music, dissociate to favorite places and rest.

Reframing anxiety

Anxious feelings are welcomed because "if you can say hello to them, you obviously will be able to bid them. . . ." I encourage the couple to observe their anxiety, to recognize its appropriateness, e.g., the contraction/release mechanisms of the body, fear of the unknown, concerns about the baby, doubt about parenting abilities. I suggest they seek information if it is needed. "An 'A+' for your childbirth performance is not necessary; all that matters is to enjoy and fully experience a special shared moment. If you feel you need medication, trust yourself, and take some; you can be pleased to know you need less because you are using hypnosis." Another metaphor is offered: "Anxiety is like driving down the highway and coming to a railroad crossing. The light is flashing red and so naturally, you stop, and listen. Before long you see the train coming from one side as you feel the ground tremble beneath you. You watch it crossing the highway and disappear out of your awareness as you proceed safely and cheerfully on your journey."

Reframing hospital language

In the hypnotic state, any sentence is a potential positive or negative suggestion. At this point, with humor in my voice, I direct the couple's attention toward the peculiar way some people have of expressing themselves. For example, if a nurse comes in and says: "Are you in much pain, honey?" or "You don't look uncomfortable yet!" or "How bad are your contractions?" or "You are only six centimeters dilated," I tell the couple to immediately adjust such a potentially negative suggestion with tolerance and delight to: "How comfortable am I?" or "I am already six centimeters dilated with four more to go." Similarly, in response to the well-meaning physician saying, "This is your last chance to receive medication before your baby is born," the woman is invited to think, "I have a choice: do I want medication?"

Time distortion

"Welcome to the second stage of labor (or transition, if such terminology is used): your baby is near! Your contractions are stronger and
more powerful (rather than more painful); they are closer to one another.
Trust your body; it will know how to breath and flow with the pressure,
if you let it use all it knows and has practiced." Suggestions are given
for time distortions so that in between contractions, time is experienced
as relaxing and resting: "Take a few moments . . . , all the time your
unconscious needs to feel rested, regenerated with energy and refreshed." Dissociation is particularly encouraged at this time.

Reframing the straining

The straining, the panting, the buildup of tension are linked gently
to preorgasmic experience (when one can look and sound in pain and
not experience it as such). Low vocalizing is a natural vehicle that can
help push the baby down. She can use her energy as a powerful drive
(Peterson calls it aggressive [1981]) that will massage the baby down the
stretched and flexible passage without any harm to her or the baby (see
Peterson, regarding the woman's fear that she will be ripped open and
her baby's head be crushed). I prepare the woman for the possibility of
experiencing the orgasmic-like pleasure, the "rush" and "joyful shaking" at the moment her baby rotates its head through her cervix and
down her vagina. I reinforce that it will be a private and enormously
satisfying experience.

Her husband is encouraged, if she so desires, to fondle her breasts
during contractions (Gaskin, 1978), to massage her back and apply counterpressure, to squeeze her shoulders, her ankles with an intensity that
parallels the contraction, using his own intuition and responding to her
direction.

It follows naturally to talk about the joy of actively bringing her baby
into the world as the couple focuses next on the pleasure of seeing the
baby's head, hearing its sounds, feeling him/her in one's arms, on one's
belly, close to one's breast.

Reframing the nursing experience

I describe the baby licking the nipple before suckling, the familiar
sexual pleasure that facilitates vaginal contractions. I talk in general
about the pleasure for their baby to enjoy both the feeding breast, full

of milk, and the empty breast, the one that pacifies. I explain the delight for the baby to experience two different sensations. Here I offer the possibility for the man to consider comfortably giving in to his natural yearning for the nursing experience, if he so desires as some men do, and if social mores have not inhibited his capacity to recognize this need and to act upon it.

Bleeding control

As the couple is absorbed in the trance state imagining the pleasure of discovering their newborn, it is easy to slip in some rather direct suggestions for prompt expulsion of the placenta, bleeding control, comfortable stitching of the episiotomy if necessary, quick and effective contracting to prepregnancy shape, and speedy and smooth healing and recovery.

Posthypnotic suggestions

Husband and wife are asked to share their unconscious experience of childbirth with their conscious mind upon awakening from the trance in the hospital.

Both are encouraged to appreciate what they have accomplished in this office and to take time to practice going into a trance with or without the audiotape of this hypnotic training session, with heightened confidence that they will pleasurably experience the birth of their baby.

Termination of trance

Suggestions for reorientation to the office are given. Comments, questions and clarifications are welcomed at the end of the session. Joyful anticipation is shared and my availability for "booster" sessions, if necessary, is made clear.

CLINICAL CASES

Debbie

Debbie was one of my earliest patients and the only one who requested I went to the labor suite since she was unhappy with the way her pain was controlling her. In those days I had not developed the mutual anchoring technique, and her husband was busy focusing on her breathing pattern and timing contractions. To counteract her external locus of control and her rigidity, I gave her a lot of suggestions for flexibility and stretching. After I left, she started stretching her body during contractions, evolving this movement into a dance that lasted the rest of her labor's first stage, leaving the staff bewildered by her metamorphosis.

In her case, the hypnotic suggestion for an internal process was thus spontaneously acted out in a way that facilitated comfortable contractions in a continued trance state.

Although retrospectively pleased with the experience, Debbie came back to my office complaining that something was missing. In a hypnotic revivification of labor and delivery, she acknowledged the comfort given by her husband looking at her and touching her and the delight of her "dancing" trance. She identified her physician *not* talking to her at the time of delivery as the missing element. She was then invited to correct that moment to her satisfaction through fantasy.

Debbie's description highlighted to me the importance of giving suggestions for stretching and elasticity, and the link between satisfaction and complete sensory experience. This prompted me to teach couples to identify the sensory modes of communication that each needed and to ask for them from each other and from the staff.

Lisa and Jim

Lisa and Jim were a couple in their twenties expecting their first child. Lisa was experienced in hypnosis, Jim was not. In the information-gathering part of the interview, Lisa requested that Jim hold her hand and talk to her during childbirth; in turn, he asked for time to leave the room if he needed to "sort things out at the bad moments" and not to have his behavior interpreted as rejection.

They were both led into a trance using the previously described protocol. Jim experienced a deep trance with amnesia, Lisa a moderate level trance from which she emerged stating: "I believe I have a job to do, and if I do it well, I can relax and enjoy it in between [contractions]." Both felt prepared.

Lisa went into a trance as she felt the first contractions. She prepared herself and the house, and went for a walk with Jim. She called her physician when her contractions became harder. The ride to the hospital intensified her trance. Upon her arrival she was six centimeters dilated and was allowed in the birthing room because she was doing so well as a primipara. She recalled: "There was only one time when Jim did not hold my hand during a contraction and I felt like I was off the table during that time. The pain at other times was far more bearable, I would not even call it pain . . . but a cramping sensation. Jim would talk to me about places we had gone on vacation, and I would even ask questions during a contraction. I felt like my head and my eyes and my mind were in one place, and my body was on the bed doing its job. My breathing with the Lamaze technique went well as long as I held Jim's hand."

Lisa also noticed how obnoxious some nurses were: "When I started to hear things that were either negative or rubbed me the wrong way, I did not want to get anxious over it, so I would just tune them out. At times when I realized that there was something I needed to hear, I would just say: 'Would you tell me that again?' "

Lisa spontaneously discovered that by pinching her thumb and forefinger which were holding a lollipop, she was able to shift the focal point of her discomfort. She took Demerol after being told by her physician that this was the last opportunity and it would "take the edge off." "I actually wish I had never taken it because it made me more lightheaded and dizzy. I just did not like that feeling of being out-of-control especially during this process where I felt I had so much to do." The medication wore off during transition. She used a combination of Lamaze and hypnosis and developed a consistent rhythm which she maintained both during and in between contractions. Initially afraid to be ripped open by the action of pushing, she found the pain no different and allowed herself to push with intensity.

"The birth itself was tremendous. It was such a release and such a relief. . . . The baby was very calm."

The stitching process did not hurt. Lisa's physician was impressed at the ease with which Lisa delivered using hypnosis. He observed the process without interfering.

Having delivered her baby in such a deeply dissociated trance, Lisa found herself during the next two days waking up in the conscious state, briefly afraid that her baby had not yet been born. She soon integrated her childbirth experience at the conscious level. This alerted me to the fact that it is important to link both conscious and unconscious processes so that integration can occur as one comes out of trance.

Because the birth experience was so positive, Lisa found it easy to bond with her daughter. One month later, she stated: "I feel sad the whole thing is over and I look forward to having more children really quickly."

Jim felt as if he had given birth to his daughter, having had an opportunity to concentrate on childbirth, to think about it beforehand, and to work so closely with Lisa during labor and delivery. As Lisa became adept at using the Lamaze breathing, he felt free to invite her to dissociate to meaningful and pleasant shared memories. At the birth of his child, he experienced "a tremendous rush to the head of blood and of energy. I felt good that Lisa was safe and that my daughter was born a healthy and beautiful baby. It was an experience of ecstasy. . . . We had a very full and meaningful experience and we did it together, and I felt part of it and a great oneness from that experience, and the three of us are very much one kind of entity as a family.

CLINICAL FINDINGS

The findings summarized here are based on information gathered from more than 20 couples. Although each couple experienced childbirth uniquely and used hypnotic phenomena selectively, several general trends emerged:

1) Each woman used the anchoring of need fulfillment which acted as a deepening cue for the trance experience. All felt free to adjust the original agreement to better adapt to actual labor and delivery.
2) The women wanted to feel the contractions, and did. They were able to achieve partial or complete well-being during contractions by focusing on comfortable parts of the body rather than on the pain, or by applying counterpressure. While awareness of discomfort remained, the affective and evaluative components of pain were positively altered.
3) The majority did not want and did not use medications. Some who requested or accepted analgesic medication regretted their decision because pain relief was accompanied by somnolence, dizziness and decreased awareness of the birth experience. A few went to the hospital fully intending to use medication and found they did not need to. Several thought they did not need an epidural or a local infiltration for episiotomy. A few wanted to relax even more fully and to control the pain even better.
4) Fatigue, while present, was not an issue, and exhaustion was absent. Many women mentioned forgetting the contractions; several were delighted at the speed with which time passed. Ann, a primipara with no hypnotic training prior to the session, wrote: "Five hours

collapsed into one. I could not believe it was time to push." They successfully used dissociation for rest and sleep; all mentioned being active and relaxed during the first and second stages.

5) Women found it humorous to hear some linguistic mishaps on the part of the staff and were quick to tune them out or to reframe them. They similarly were unbothered by the moans and screams of other women, by the uninspiring hospital setting. They were all the more appreciative of the help and sensitivity they experienced from their physician and nursing staff.

6) Many babies were described as being born calm. No one voiced any difficulty enjoying either the baby or the nursing experience.

7) Recovery was prompt. There was no problem with healing.

8) No husband turned down the invitation to learn hypnosis with his wife or chose not to use the training received. Many men called personally to say they were elated with the experience. They had felt prepared and had become fully involved. They were delighted by the ways they had used hypnosis with their wives, sometimes using my "soothing" voice, many times improvising upon the suggestions they had heard, amplifying their wife's dissociation by describing common memories, deepening their wife's trance, etc. Unanimously, men and women felt the childbirth experience had brought them closer.

9) Multipara women had a better experience; they found hypnosis more versatile than the Lamaze method, especially during the second and third stages of labor. They no longer worried about concentrating on specific breathing which previously had been so difficult for them. Trusting their body, breathing became again a natural experience rather than a chore. They remained active longer and deliberately focused on enjoyment. These women particularly noticed a change in their relationship with their husbands: "He was so much there for me." Guesses were eliminated and clear communication substituted: "We were working as a team of experts." There is evidence that this change in the relationship carried beyond childbirth.

10) Even in cases where childbirth was not problem free, participating couples expressed satisfaction with the use of anchoring and the selective use of hypnosis. A few women had prolonged back labor and posterior presentation of the baby. One woman delivered a stillborn child.

11) The response of physicians to their patients has been positive, even

though they were not familiar with medical hypnosis. They have either supported fully the effort of the couple and liked the results, or they have left the couple alone and proceeded as usual.

CONCLUSION

From the information provided by these women and their husbands, hypnosis in combination with Lamaze and other natural childbirth methods has been found effective. Hypnosis is particularly helpful in providing amnesia for contractions and discomfort, time distortion for lengthening of the restful period between contractions during the second stage of labor, and dissociation to facilitate rest. The immediate result is normal fatigue rather than exhaustion, energy left to enjoy husband, baby and childbirth, moderate use of drugs and quick recovery, findings similar to those mentioned by Erickson, Hershman, and Secter (1961). This approach offers an opportunity to enhance sexuality, to deepen the marital relationship by opening communication at multiple levels, and to facilitate bonding with the baby.

Several applications of Ericksonian hypnotherapy were particularly effective: 1) mutual anchoring which stirs the interaction between the spouses away from assumptions and judgments into a satisfying connection; 2) verbal pacing by the husband of his wife's experience which allows her to feel validated and therefore more accepting of his help; 3) mutual hypnosis, to heighten the intimacy between husband and wife, and posthypnotic suggestions which make the presence of the hypnotherapist unnecessary; 4) reframing of the hospital environment: the setting, the moans, the ill-phrased language that needs to be translated or tuned out; and 5) accessing unconscious processes to establish links between separate experiences (in our culture) such as sexuality and childbirth, male and female experience.

Links facilitate for the woman the uninhibited understanding and use of her body, breathing and voice. At a deeper level, the use of unconscious processes to retrieve primal knowledge of childbirth enables the woman to trust her body's capacity to deliver safely, and enables her husband to heighten the quality of his participation and of his sensitivity to his wife. Together they can as fully as they wish, share the physical, emotional and spiritual processes involved in giving birth to their child.

REFERENCES

Bandler, R., & Grinder, J. (1979). *Frogs into princes.* Moab, UT: Real People Press.
Dick-Read, G. (1973). *Childbirth without fear: The principles and practices of natural childbirth.* New York: Harper & Row.
Erickson, M. H. (1980). In E. L. Rossi (Ed.), *The collected papers of Milton H. Erickson.* (Vols. 1-4). New York: Irvington.
Erickson, M. H., Hershman, S., & Secter, I. (1961). *The practical application of medical and dental hypnosis.* New York: The Julian Press.
Erickson, M. H., & Rossi, E. (1979). *Hypnotherapy: An exploratory casebook.* New York: Irvington.
Erickson, M. H., Rossi, E. L., & Rossi, S. (1976). *Hypnotic realities.* New York: Irvington.
Gaskin, I. M. (1978). *Spiritual midwifery.* Summertown, TN: The Book Publishing Company.
Haley, J. (1973). *Uncommon therapy: The psychiatric techniques of Milton H. Erickson, M.D.* New York: Norton.
Lamaze, F. (1970). *Painless childbirth: Psychoprophylactic method.* Chicago: Henry Regnery and Co.
Lustig, H. S. (1975). *The artistry of Milton H. Erickson, M.D., Part I* [Videotape]. Haverford, PA: Herbert S. Lustig, Ltd.
Palmer, H. (1983). Can we view labor as normal? In S. Humenick (Ed.), *Expanding horizons in childbirth education* (pp. 3-12). Washington, D.C.: Aspo-Lamaze.
Peterson, G. F. (1981). *Birthing normally: A personal growth approach to childbirth.* Berkeley: Mindbody Press.
Poncelet, N. M. (1982). *The training of a couple in hypnosis for childbirth: A clinical session* [Videotape]. Western Psychiatric Institute and Clinic Library, 3811 O'Hara Street, Pittsburgh, PA 15213.
Poncelet, N. M. (1983). A family systems view of emotional disturbances during pregnancy. *Clinical Social Work Journal, 11,* p. 1.
Zeig, J. K. (1980). *A teaching seminar with M. H. Erickson.* New York: Brunner/Mazel.

Chapter 19

The Utilization of Ericksonian Principles of Hypnotherapy with Agoraphobics

John H. Edgette

Agoraphobia can be described as a marked fear of being alone, or without available help. Sufferers are incapacitated in a public place such as in crowds, tunnels, bridges, and restaurants. Ventures to the feared places are frequently accompanied by anxiety, or even panic attacks, often resulting in an increased constriction of normal activities as the fear or avoidance behavior comes to dominate the person's life (American Psychiatric Association, 1980).

In recent years behavior therapy has been used for treating agoraphobia. Most notably, desensitization techniques and graduated in-vivo exposure have been used successfully, to the point of currently being considered the treatments of choice (Mathews, Gelder, & Johnson, 1981).

Hypnosis also has been seen as valuable in the treatment of phobias in general, including agoraphobia. Moll (1891), saw agoraphobia as due to autosuggestion and accordingly listed hypnosis as particularly suitable for its treatment. Schilder (1956) recommended light hypnosis for mild phobias, leaving the more severe cases for psychoanalysis. Wolberg (1977) recommended that hypnosis be used to speed age regression, and hence illuminate the dynamic origins of phobic symptomatology.

The results of the one study that experimentally pitted desensitization against hypnosis in the treatment of agoraphobia favored the desensitization approach (Marks, Gelder, & Edwards, 1968). However, the authors stated that the findings were difficult to interpret due to the confounding use of medication. It also can be argued that the study's sole reliance on direct "authoritarian" suggestion limited the impact of the hypnotic work. An approach based on direct suggestion lacks flexibility and tends to be effective only with highly suggestible clients (Barber, 1980).

In the last few decades Erickson and others have expanded the techniques of hypnosis far beyond the use of direct suggestion (Zeig, 1982). Indeed, techniques derived from hypnosis have been used in psychotherapeutic work outside the realm of the formal trance. Some of this naturalistic use of hypnotherapy, including cases Erickson himself described, concerned the treatment of various phobias (Haley, 1973).

This chapter proposes the integration of Ericksonian principles of hypnotherapy with behavioral methods. The two treatment approaches are compatible, and the therapeutic power of behavioral methods can be enhanced by incorporating ideas derived from Erickson. From a practical viewpoint there is no need to see the two approaches as mutually exclusive, as has sometimes been the case in the literature.

THE PATIENT POPULATION

The therapeutic work was done with a group of 12 white, blue-collar class women ranging in age from 26 to 48. While all were agoraphobic, some were diagnosed neurotic while others were considered suffering from character disorders. Diagnosis was established by the cotherapists after an intake interview and was later confirmed independently by a psychiatrist.

PARAMETERS OF THE THERAPY

The treatment site was an outpatient clinic in a major city. While the work described here was done in a group setting, most of the clients were also in individual therapy with one of the cotherapists. The group met once a week for 90 minutes.

At the time of my departure from the group, one and a half years after its inception, all but three dropouts had evidenced highly significant improvement. Therapeutic gains were measured by subjective reports, therapist evaluations, and pre-post comparisons of the daily charts kept by the patients. These charts recorded the distance traveled and the time spent outside during assigned daily practice.

THE USE OF FORMAL HYPNOSIS

Formal hypnosis played a large part in the therapy group. Following Erickson, inductions utilized the patient's preferred sensory modality to bring about trance (Zeig, 1983). Since agoraphobia is marked by an inability to move in physical space and since anxiety attacks largely are experienced somatically (i.e., dizziness, sweating, heart palpitations, limb weakness, general autonomic arousal), kinesthetic cues were used to facilitate induction. Hence a variation of Jacobson's (1983) muscle relaxation procedure was used to begin the inductions. Also used was imagery, including the staircase method. Trance induction constituted a starting point of relaxation from which ventures could be taken during the in vivo exposure portion of treatment.

Once trance was established, but before outside exposure, metaphorical stories often were told by the therapist. These usually centered around gradual patterns of successful separation from mother and family during normal development. This theme was chosen because overcoming agoraphobia entails being able to tolerate being alone and away from the security of home. Indeed, ego psychologists such as Mahler (1968) and Rhead (1969) have cited difficulties in the separation-individuation phase of development as instrumental in the later development of agoraphobia. In this phase, the child of one to three years of age uses locomotion to progressively master the anxiety of being physically separate from the mother. Individuation is achieved by means of the child maintaining a stable and unified internal representation of the loving mother.

Members of the agoraphobia group seemed to be stuck endlessly recapitulating this stage. For example, being home entailed a blissful, "all good" sense of maternal security and warmth which ultimately was unsatisfactory because it became engulfing and smothering. Going out, on the other hand, involved moving into territory deemed "all bad," with concomitant feelings of being apart, separate and cut off—without a sense of object constancy. The metaphors used in the group sessions focused on the successful resolution of this conflict between dependancy and autonomy.

One metaphor told during group trance was developed over a number of weeks. It was about a young girl learning to ride a bike. First she was on a tricycle, moving to and from her mother, bringing back interesting things that she found. Next the young girl rode a two-wheeler with training wheels. Finally, she progressively was helped (with the guiding aid of her mother's hand on the back of the seat) to balance on her own and ride off. This separation-individuation story was relevant because it related a kinesthetic experience of mobility where the protagonist coped with the loss of balance and control.

There was an additional element to the last portion of the story. The mother suddenly released her grip and the child rode on without help, only to eventually look back, see no one, get scared, lose her balance, fall and scrape herself. Following Zeig (personal communication, 1982) the use of such mildly anxiety-provoking elements in otherwise comforting stories, with subsequent return to the relaxed state, allows for a naturalistic desensitization to occur. Since the story was told while the group was in trance, it was easy to help members regain calm feelings.

While the provoked anxiety resembles abandonment fears often felt by agoraphobics, it is overridden both by eventual successes developed in the story and by the realization, common to all children, that parental "dirty tricks" can turn out to be in the child's best interests. Turning the bike "loose" allows children to learn they can ride alone. This story can reframe developmental and life traumas of the agoraphobic as being precursors to eventual success. The scrapes and bruises of childhood, while painful at the time, eventually are remembered as bittersweet, if not forgotten.

Interestingly, after weeks of work with the biking metaphor, a number of group members went out and purchased bikes. One even learned to ride for the first time. This subgroup further added to their improvement by buying shirts paradoxically imprinted, "The Agoraphobic Bike Club"!

ERICKSONIAN METHODS DURING GRADUATED EXPOSURE

While the foregoing describes the blending of imaginal desensitization with formal Ericksonian trance work, the use of in-vivo exposure entailed a greater reliance on Ericksonian principles of therapy. In traditional behavior therapy, graduated exposure takes place with consideration only of spatial and temporal factors, for example, distance from home and time spent outside the home (Mathews, Gelder, & Johnson, 1981). An Ericksonian approach, in addition to utilizing in-vivo desensitization, can address dimensions such as the intrapsychic, developmental, symbolic and cognitive at no expense to the "time spent outside."

One example of this multidimensional effect occurred when the therapy group went outside. Developmental themes of separation and individuation again were employed. The male and female cotherapists, reminiscent of mother and father, sat on the clinic stoop while individuals ventured into the neighborhood. Like the separating child, they returned to "touch base" and regain security, bringing back tales of adventure and various items found or purchased.

There are numerous other ways to integrate Ericksonian techniques with behavior therapy for agoraphobia. For example, Erickson placed great importance on the patient gaining control over symptoms. This often involved purposefully making symptoms worse—a form of symptom prescription.

During graduated exposure, this principle was used by having clients teach a therapist how to look as if he were having a panic attack on the street. Also, some patients volunteered to try to mimic or actually evoke anxiety in themselves. This not only helped patients gain control but also enhanced risk-taking abilities, encouraged counterphobic reactions, and discharged the agoraphobics' commonly held fear of being a public spectacle.

The gaining control principle also was employed by occasionally prescribing "relapses." Patients were told to either return to their original pretreatment state of agoraphobia or to go beyond even that—to confine themselves to different rooms of their house on successive days. Similarly, some were instructed to "develop inner space" by reading six hours a day. Subsequently, the therapist passed out bookmarks with a picture of a boat and the quote, "There is no frigate like a book to take us miles away." It became easier to give up the symptom than to follow the assignments.

Erickson often made use of elements of a symptom to defeat the symptom. He would utilize and side with important parts of a complex problem in the service of fracturing the gestalt of a maladaptive pattern. In our therapy group, the therapist asked women volunteers to do their homework of going out into the world by becoming "bag ladies." In their shopping bags they carried all the essentials for the day and it was suggested that they were "carrying their homes" with them. Another example of symptom fracturing occurred when one woman, while declining to buy a mobile home, did return to work after years of unemployment by selling hot dogs from her new truck. She never left it when around town. In these examples, patients were allowed to keep the problem of "having to stay home" while the real life limitations this imposed were progressively overridden.

Erickson was fond of creating tasks that would prove therapeutic no matter what the outcome. One example of this occurred when a therapist spotted an extremely decrepit vagabond who was living on the street. Before the group saw him, the therapist gave a long discourse on how the group was about to witness the public reaction to a sight far more disturbing than any agoraphobic in panic could ever produce. The group turned around to watch this man for 15 minutes while virtually none of the passersby gave him even a glance. Should someone have stopped, the therapist was prepared to frame the interaction as demonstrating public concern for even the lowest members of society. In any event, the agoraphobic's fear of being a ridiculed public spectacle while having a panic attack was reduced. Making an asset out of a problem is an important technique of hypnotherapy. In the agoraphobic group this was illustrated when one shy woman was encouraged to utilize her anxiety in public as an excuse to ask attractive men for support. Long after her recovery she reported continuing to use this "line" to meet men.

SUMMARY

Many Ericksonian techniques of psychotherapy can be integrated with currently popular behavioral methods. Practically and theoretically this union detracts nothing from either approach. For the behavior therapist using in-vivo exposure, the gain will be in increased depth and power at previously unaddressed levels, and increased options for dealing with resistance. For the hypnotherapist, the benefit is in the prospect of quicker therapeutic success through a simple behavioral method that has received much experimental support.

REFERENCES

American Psychiatric Association. (1980). *Diagnostic and statistical manual of mental disorders* (3rd ed.). Washington, DC: American Psychiatric Association.

Barber, J. (1980). Hypnosis and the unhypnotizable. *American Journal of Clinical Hypnosis, 23,* 4-9.

Haley, J. (1973). *Uncommon therapy.* New York: Norton.

Jacobson, E. (1983). *Progressive relaxation.* Chicago: University of Chicago Press.

Mahler, M. (1968). *On human symbiosis and the vicissitudes of individuation.* New York: International Universities Press.

Marks, I. M., Gelder, M. G., & Edwards, G. (1968). Hypnosis and desensitization for phobias: A controlled prospective trial. *British Journal of Psychiatry, 114,* 1263-1274.

Mathews, A., Gelder, M., & Johnson, D. (1981). *Agoraphobia, nature and treatment.* New York: Guilford Press.

Moll, A. (1891). *Hypnotism.* London: Walter Scott.

Rhead, C. (1969). The role of pregenital fixations in agoraphobia. *Journal of the American Psychoanalytic Association, 17,* 848-861.

Schilder, P. (1956). *The nature of hypnosis.* New York: International Universities Press.

Wolberg, L. R. (1977). *The techniques of psychotherapy.* New York: Grune & Stratton.

Zeig, J. K. (Ed.). (1982). *Ericksonian approaches to hypnosis and psychotherapy.* New York: Brunner/Mazel.

Zeig, J. K. (1982, March). *Ericksonian psychotherapy.* Workshop conducted at the Philadelphia Child Guidance Clinic, Philadelphia, PA.

Zeig, J. K. (1983, February). *Ericksonian hypnotherapy.* Workshop conducted at the Philadelphia Child Guidance Clinic, Philadelphia, PA.

Chapter 20

Classical Trance Induction in Ericksonian Psychotherapy: Smoking Control

C.A.L. Hoogduin

INTRODUCTION

People seek expert help, not only because they have problems, but primarily because they are desperate; they have problems which they can no longer solve alone.

When articles appear in the press about the possibility of using hypnosis to solve problems, people see it as *the* solution to their own specific problems and apply for treatment by hypnosis. A wide variety of problems is presented with the request, "Hypnotherapy please!"

Hypnotherapists, however, usually are trained in other forms of therapy, and it may well be that the therapist does not consider hypnosis to be the most suitable form of therapy for a particular case. A bed-wetter, for example, probably can be better treated by the "bell and pad" method.

Patients who ask for hypnotherapy may be dissatisfied, however, when another kind of therapy is suggested, even if the therapist has good reason for the recommendation. They want hypnotherapy and reject any other suggestion. Lazarus's (1973) investigation elucidates this point. During a course of systematic desensitization some patients were treated by means of relaxation, others by so-called hypnotic relaxation. Actually, the addition of the word "hypnotic" was the only difference in procedure. No difference in effect between the two forms of treatment was observed in people who had not asked specifically for hypnosis.

However, the people who asked for help by means of hypnosis responded better to the treatment which used the word "hypnotic."

Frank (1978) quite plausibly has noted that patients' expectations about the kind of treatment they receive has a considerable effect on the end result; when treatment meets with patients' expectations of it, there is a greater chance of success.

This chapter describes a treatment strategy in which emphasis is placed on patients' expectations of treatment. The treatment of undesirable habits, in particular that of cigarette smoking, is used here by way of example.

THE TREATMENT STRATEGY

The treatment presented here is made up of three major parts: classical trance induction, paradoxical approach, and the Ericksonian approach.

Classical Trance Induction

Patients who present themselves for treatment for a specific undesirable habit, e.g., cigarette smoking, often have attempted on numerous occasions to break themselves of the habit. They no longer have faith in their ability to stop, and they believe that if they are treated by hypnosis they themselves will not have to stop smoking—that, however incredible this may be, cure will happen automatically. Thus, hope for a solution is manifest, and this is precisely what is needed in order to solve the problem. In such cases the patient has to receive a form of treatment which he recognizes as hypnosis, notably, classical trance induction, usually by means of eye fixation.

Paradoxical Approach

In this approach the three therapeutic paradoxes as formulated by Haley (1963) are applied:

1) *Prescribing the symptom: Do what you were doing, but do it on my conditions.* You do not have to give up smoking; you will develop a gradual resistance and aversion to smoking, so that the habit will, as it were, wear off itself; until that happens, enjoy yourself, take pleasure in every cigarette that you smoke.

The therapist advises the patient *not* to cut down on smoking! For example, the patient is not told to smoke only one half or two thirds of the usual number of cigarettes. Rather, the symptom is implicitly prescribed through a registration assignment: "Carry on with what you were doing—you were already doing it as little as possible anyway—but register it, write down each time you smoke."

2) *The benevolent ordeal: Do what you were doing, but it will be less pleasurable and more bothersome.* The patient can still smoke as much as he or she likes, but smoking is made more difficult. The patient has to smoke a different brand of cigarettes. He or she can smoke only in particular places, preferably outside the study or living room. Before or after smoking a cigarette, the patient has to *do* something, e.g., engage in physical exercise "for the good of his or her health."

These elements may be compared to the self-control procedures used in behavior therapy, in which clients receive programs that make it possible for them to establish the desired behavior changes by themselves. The programs are constructed from measures which can be taken before the problem behavior gets the chance to show itself (stimulus control, stimulus response intervention), and after the behavior has taken place (response consequences, especially self-reward and self-punishment).

Stimulus control (organizing the environment) refers to the client arranging the environment in such a way as to decrease the chance of the undesired behaviors being performed. For example, a tin of cookies standing on the table can tempt someone with eating bouts to start eating. By placing the cookie tin out of sight, the chance of an eating binge is diminished.

Stimulus response intervention (interrupting the response chain) refers to the client intervening in the chain of thoughts and behaviors that ultimately lead to the performance of undesired behavior. For example, in the behavior analysis of a client with binge eating, these binges appear to be preceded by a feeling of tension. As soon as this feeling is experienced, the client will bike for an hour or take a long walk. The chance that the undesired behavior is thwarted increases, as the intervention in the response chain occurs in an early stage.

Response consequences (behavior programming) refer to the client linking the consequences to the occurrence of a certain behavior (cf. Thoreson & Mahoney, 1974). In positive self-rewards, clients reward themselves after they have done something difficult, e.g., buying something nice after losing some weight. In negative self-reward, clients reward themselves after a desired behavior has been displayed, e.g., the poster of a fat pig can be removed after losing some weight.

In positive self-punishment, the client withholds something pleasant when the undesired behavior has taken place. In negative self-punishment, the client inflicts a punishment after displaying undesired behavior, e.g., physical exertion after breaking the diet rules.

3) *The metacomplimentary relationship: Follow my directions and you are on the way to improvement.* The patient is always "the ideal patient," who is already on the way to improvement. To a patient who smokes a lot, the therapist can say, "You're a real smoker and that's the sort of person this treatment is intended for"; or to someone who smokes little, "You're well on your way to giving up."

The therapist can motivate the patient, who often sees him/herself as a weakling—a person so lacking in willpower that a therapist is needed—by saying, "You are just the sort of person who wants to stop smoking, otherwise you wouldn't have come to a therapist; you are the sort of person who takes no pleasure in the undesirable habit, unlike other people who want to stop but don't do anything about it."

The images of the patient as someone who has sought treatment—someone who is no longer prepared to put up with smoking—are given here as illustrations of the above characterizations of the patient as a fighter.

The Ericksonian Approach

The patient has requested treatment by hypnosis. During the session it is discussed and understood that hypnosis will take place at the end of the session. The first part of the session is used for discussing and drawing up the self-control program. The chance that there will be resistance to these arrangements is minimized because of the patient's belief that treatment will really begin at the moment hypnosis begins.

Therefore, the patient is susceptible to suggestions such as the following: "There are patients who, once having begun treatment by means of hypnotherapy, notice that they become very sensitive to the hot, burning feeling in the throat caused by smoking," or, "Some patients notice that they sense a kind of distaste when they think of cigarettes and get a satisfied, pleasant feeling when they haven't smoked one for a while. Or they immediately notice a sense of irritation when they light a cigarette and this makes them decide to stub it out." The therapist also can express surprise at the effect that hypnotherapy sometimes has, namely, that even confirmed smokers suddenly decide to give it up. This effect is then ascribed to the strong, unconscious distaste for their habit, which already exists within them.

When the trance induction finally begins, the treatment has already been provided. A registration assignment has been given, the "benevolent ordeals" have been arranged and the indirect suggestions made.

The trance induction then takes place in a way that is in accord with the patient's expectations. The method used is usually eye fixation. The induction is carried out in such a way as to avoid failure. When introducing the trance it can be mentioned that some people do not enter into a deep trance the first time, that sometimes they achieve only a slightly relaxed state, but that that in itself is enough. Also, it is advisable to give the patient some information about the feeling of "being aware" during hypnosis, because many people imagine that hypnosis induces a kind of sleep from which they will awake a nonsmoker.

As far as possible permissive techniques are used to induce the trance. Preparation for this method is made during the preinduction talk: "It may be that, on fixation, your eyes will start to blink, feel heavy and then close; it may also be that you will feel a strong desire to close your eyes. Other patients simply do not blink at all. In that case, I will, at a given moment, ask you to close your eyes slowly." When the patient has entered into a trance, the various therapeutic arrangements are reiterated.

The patient receives an audiorecording of the hypnosis session that is taken home to be practiced with on a daily basis.

During the subsequent sessions the various ordeals gradually can be made more difficult. For instance, at the beginning of the treatment the ordeal consists of a 20-minute walk after 15 cigarettes have been smoked. A next step could be a 30-minute walk after 10 cigarettes, a 40-minute walk after eight cigarettes, and so on. Finally, tasks could be given contingent on any cigarette smoking, like doing physical exercise for 10 minutes.

DISCUSSION

The treatment consists of the following parts:

1) *Anamnesis:* Collection of information about such things as the antecedent and subsequent factors, frequency, etc.

2) *Benevolent ordeals:* Negotiating arrangements that will make continuance of the symptom behavior more difficult.
3) *Indirect suggestions:* Using the "explanation of procedures" in an Ericksonian way in order to have an effect upon the complaint.
4) *Applying classical trance induction:* The various arrangements are reiterated while the patient is in a trance.
5) *Taped practice:* The patient receives a cassette tape recording of this classical trance induction to take home so that he or she can perform autohypnosis on a daily basis.

With patients who apply for treatment by hypnosis, there is a positive expectation that the treatment will be successful, and the therapist can use this to advantage. In the strategy described here, an indirect Ericksonian method is applied before the treatment (i.e., hypnosis) begins. The patient does not realize that treatment already has begun and therefore remains open to the therapist's suggestions. The chance of resistance during this phase of the session is small; the application of indirect suggestion improves the chance of successful treatment (cf. Zeig, 1982).

What is true of probably all psychotherapeutic programs is also true when setting up this kind of treatment plan: The general outline can be constructed in advance but almost always the therapist has to take into account the peculiarities of the problem behavior of the particular patient.

Making the various arrangements requires a good knowledge of the patient's situation. Herein also lies one of the major objections to the kind of fixed time planning (21 days) that, for example, von Dedenroth (1964a, b; 1968) employed. This method affords the therapist no chance of continuing to help a patient who still smokes a little on the 21st day. It is better to let patients fix a time limit for themselves. The therapist can then express doubt as to whether this is long enough. Then, if the patient does not succeed within the proposed time limit, the treatment can be extended a few weeks without much difficulty.

The chances of successful treatment increase when the spouse or another member of the family is given information about the treatment and participates in it. Preferably, the spouse at least should be present at the evaluation session. The significance of the effect of the symptom on the relationship and the family can then be assessed. Also, the chances of treatment being negatively affected by the partner are diminished. Moreover, the partner can fulfill the role of social reinforcer. For example, patients can be advised at the communal session to hang the graphic reproduction of their progress over their bed and to discuss it with their partner every evening.

The abrupt termination of treatment when the symptom disappears is inadvisable. Relational problems can sometimes arise after the successful treatment of a mild complaint. Even families or couples who function "normally" can go through a difficult period as a result of one member's becoming more secure and fit after successful treatment. Even in the treatment of a "harmless" bad habit, some attention should be devoted to systemic issues in the follow-up.

REFERENCES

Frank, J. D. (1978). Expectation and therapeutic outcome—The placebo effect and the role induction interview. In J. D. Frank, R. Hoehn-Saric, S. D. Imber, B. L. Liberman, & A. R. Stone, *Effective ingredients of successful psychotherapy*. New York: Brunner/Mazel.

Haley, J. (1963). *Strategies of psychotherapy*. New York: Grune & Stratton.

Lazarus, A. A. (1973). Hypnosis as a facilitator in behavior therapy. *International Journal of Clinical & Experimental Hypnosis, XXI* (1), 25–31.

Thoreson, C. E., & Mahoney, M. J. (1974). *Behavioral self-control*. New York: Holt, Rinehart & Winston.

von Dedenroth, T. E. A. (1964a). The use of hypnosis with tobaccomaniacs. *American Journal of Clinical Hypnosis, 6* (4), 326–331.

von Dedenroth, T. E. A. (1964b). Further help for the tobaccomaniacs. *American Journal of Clinical Hypnosis, 6* (4), 332–336.

von Dedenroth, T. E. A. (1968). The use of hypnosis in a thousand cases of tobaccomaniacs. *American Journal of Clinical Hypnosis, 10* (3), 194–197.

Zeig, J. K. (1982). Ericksonian approaches to promote abstinence from cigarette smoking. In J. K. Zeig (Ed.), *Ericksonian approaches to hypnosis and psychotherapy*. New York: Brunner/Mazel.

Chapter 21

Adolescence and Hypnotherapy

David Rigler

Adolescence is sometimes taken as synonymous with puberty, that is, as a biological bridge that lies between leaving childhood and becoming an adult. Although all societies seem to acknowledge a transitional period between child- and adulthood, adolescence as a concept appears to have emerged comparatively recently in Western culture, perhaps somewhere in the late 18th to mid-19th centuries.

In contemporary society, adolescence has emerged as a significant developmental period from many vantage points, ranging from its impact on the marketing of clothing, music and motion pictures to the emergence of a medical subspecialty. "Adolescent medicine" boasts its own professional societies, training programs, and literature. It was from the comparatively recent perspective of association with a division of adolescent medicine in a pediatric hospital that I became especially interested in the application of hypnosis and hypnotherapy to this group of patients.

I began to wonder to what degree what was going on with my patients might be related not merely to what I was doing, but more specifically to distinctive qualities associated with being adolescent. What I was encountering, on the one hand, was success with some of my clients. With others I was able to establish good rapport but the proposal to employ hypnosis was too often a cue that signaled an early break in the therapy relationship.

Let me start by giving an example. I present this with what I hope is some humility, aware that other therapists might have responded differently, even more wisely.

Thirteen-year-old Patrice was referred at the end of her second hospitalization in a pediatric unit. Most mornings, Patrice spiked temperatures in the range of 104-105° F. The fevers plus severe pains and weakness in one leg made it impossible for her to attend school regularly. Despite laboratory tests and other studies, no cause had been found.

Patrice was an attractive, bright and exceptionally well-read youngster who had excelled in her studies until the onset of her ailment. She had been socially popular prior to the illness, and she still had many friends, but she was now out of the mainstream at school. I found Patrice sincere in her wish for help. She was intelligent, she seemed to be nondefensive and she had a striking capacity for playfulness and fantasy that made relating to her a satisfying experience.

Because of a number of suggestive factors in her history, I began to suspect that the fevers were either factitious or fictitious; the school and family history as well as Patrice's own development suggested that Patrice was motivated to be sick. The question still remained whether this fever was conscious or unconscious, whether the fevers were a fiction, or whether the fevers did exist, being brought about by some as yet unfathomed process.

The pediatrician could not enlighten me. He adopted a conservative stance, that is, until there was solid evidence to the contrary, he had to conclude that the fevers were real even though the cause was unknown. The weakness and pain in the leg were better understood by him, and were clearly of organic origin.

I found myself wanting to believe that Patrice's fevers were real. But I think I wanted them also to be psychogenic, perhaps so that I could cure her, rather than catch her in a lie. I was required to record a DSM-III diagnosis and I settled on conversion hysteria, but I did not have data persuasive enough to show that Patrice was not in fact suffering from some mysterious infection or some oddity in metabolic functioning.

Patrice and I worked together for several weeks, both in family therapy and individually, initially with some symptomatic improvement. During this period I introduced Patrice to thermal biofeedback, to help her to learn how to control her body temperature. The early improvement, unfortunately, was of short duration. The school year was coming near its close, and Patrice had been absent virtually the entire year. It seemed certain that she would have to repeat the school year, something that she found devastating. Still lacking convincing data, my suspicion was growing stronger that this charming young lady was not hysteric and did not have an infection but had been faking her fevers.

If so, it was apparent that Patrice was confronted with a situation which had grown beyond her control. Whatever function her illness had initially served, it was now exacting too heavy a price. Notwithstanding, she could not recover unless there was a good explanation. If indeed she was faking, Patrice had created new but serious problems. Her mystified parents believed and trusted her, as did her friends, and so did the many members of her church who were praying for Patrice's recovery. In fact, her mother was correspondent for a national church network, and I learned that there were people all over the United States who were praying for her. If this fever was a lie, Patrice could not admit it without humiliating not merely herself but all of her family. How could she ever return to school and face the other kids? Most of all, how could she face herself? On the other hand, the cost of continuing to feign illness was extreme, given all her other wants.

Still uncertain about the source of her symptoms, I proposed at this point to teach Patrice self-hypnosis. Whether or not her symptoms were "real," I wanted to provide a graceful way out. My thought was that Patrice could learn to hypnotize herself, ostensibly or actually acquiring in the process the skill of controlling her body temperature. With this new skill, she could emerge with a public rationale for bringing her illness to an end. Of course, if she was faking, she would still have to live with that knowledge, but others need not know. On the other hand, if this was a conversion reaction, it might still prove effective. And if it was neither, little harm would be done.

Patrice's response to this gently presented proposal was to refuse resolutely to continue further in treatment. Hitherto a conforming child, she now told her parents, who tried to persuade her otherwise, that she would not ever return to see me. Her stated reason, astonishingly enough, was that I was not a Christian, and therefore could not help her. If her parents insisted, she would still refuse, but she would pretend to be well. She would have no more of me. Nor would she agree to see anyone else.

Patrice did, in fact, return to school within the week. Her teachers thought it was not possible, with but one month left in the school year, to pass her schoolwork, but Patrice made up for the missed year and passed all her classes, mostly with B's.

End of case report. Patrice was better, or at least she so pretended and although I was left with a lot of uncertainty, the pediatrician counted it as a success and began to refer more cases.

One year later, I received a tearful call from Patrice. She announced that she wished to see me again. We made an appointment and she started back into treatment, remaining until my departure from that clinic a few weeks later. Patrice confessed to her bewildered but forgiving parents that she had faked her fevers to avoid problems at school. She had fled from me and from psychotherapy, not because I was not a

Christian, but because she sensed that I was on to her. Despite my careful efforts to assure her that she would always remain in control of what she revealed, despite her awareness that therapy was privileged, and despite what I thought was a nonjudgmental response, Patrice expected and feared exposure. This serious and spiritual youngster feared not so much disgrace as a fall from grace. A high level of motivation to escape from her self-wrought trap was not sufficient to permit Patrice to trust herself. And even self-hypnosis, in which she would reveal no information to me, was too fearful to contemplate.

While many elements in the Patrice story may not be uniquely age-related, others reflect the special problems associated with being a teenager in psychotherapy. Dr. Richard MacKenzie, the director of the Teenage Health Center, is fond of saying that it is not so much that teenagers have problems, as that they have solutions. It is the solutions that so characteristically get them into trouble. Patrice's first solution was to exaggerate her temperature. Her next was to escape from treatment. With such tactics, teenagers may not be unlike many adults who present themselves for psychotherapy, except that lacking adult experience, even small setbacks may be experienced as irreversible disasters.

Another difference between teens and adults is that many of the developmental tasks that confront teenagers bring them into conflict with the demands of the psychotherapeutic process in general and the circumstances of hypnotherapy in particular. Children are habituated to conformity. If not in the company of a parent, a young child is in the custody of someone who assumes a parental role, be it babysitter, teacher or older sibling. A young child's world is bounded by adult-imposed borders which generally are not seriously challenged. But an adolescent seeks to define activities, whereabouts, social relationships, belief systems and a host of other defining parameters. Young children may not like the idea of being taken to the doctor, but adolescents are much more likely to indicate, with legitimacy, that they should have some control, some input into the process of decision. How many of you recall yourselves as teens calling out to your parents about some decision, "Well, it's my life, I should decide."

Teens who enter into a psychotherapy relationship often do so with at least a subtle measure of coercion. Something in their life is not working right. As a result, a parent, a teacher, a judge, a physician, or one or more other adults urge them to seek help. By accepting that counsel, teenagers yield a bit of the autonomy that they are striving to attain. Indeed, in too many instances the very thing that is not working right for the teenager is the effectiveness of this striving for autonomy.

It should be clear that I am not referring solely to adolescents who are in open rebellion. As Josselson has noted, adolescents may not even differ observably from their parents with respect to values and attitudes for individuation to be taking place. "Opposition is only important," she writes, "in that negativism makes clear—to the self and to others—that one is autonomous and not surrendering" (1980, p. 192). In the psychotherapy situation, adolescents are confronted by an adult who functions as and who takes on the quasiparental role of expert, counselor, and authority. The therapist becomes further invested with magical power associated with the popular image of hypnosis. I am not saying that one cannot do hypnotherapy successfully with adolescents, rather that it does present a special challenge. Therapy with young teens may not differ greatly from that which is employed with children; with older, highly motivated teens who are seeking help on their own initiative, therapy will not differ from that which is accomplished with adults.

In an effort to go beyond this kind of speculation, I sought to learn about the experience of others. I do not pretend to have exhausted the literature, but two findings stand out. Books that deal with adolescents make little or no reference to hypnotherapy; and books concerned with hypnotherapy make little mention of adolescence.

Since I could not find it in books, I sought help from my colleagues. With limited time and with limited facilities, I designed a preliminary survey of hypnotherapists who treat adolescents. To save time, I conducted this survey over the telephone among a small, select and decidedly nonrandom group of psychologists and pediatricians, about a dozen in all. Each of the persons who were questioned treated adolescents as well as patients who were younger, older or both. I included no rating scales and invoked no statistical measures in analyzing my data. Standard questions, however, were read to each individual.

Respondents were asked about similarities and differences they encountered between teenagers treated by them, and adults and children, with respect to nine patient variables. These variables were: motivation, trust, fear of loss of control, expectations, hypnotizability, overall resistance, depth of trance, physical activity, and incidence of imagery. Respondents were encouraged to note not only differences between teens, and adults and children, but also systematic differences observed among adolescents, for example, between teenagers under and over the age of 16, and between boys and girls.

Two other areas were explored. Therapists were asked about the kinds of induction procedures they utilized with teens, and whether these differed systematically from those used with patients older and younger.

They were asked about differences with respect to directive versus permissive methods, and they were also presented with a list of commonly used techniques. Finally, therapists were asked about the relative effectiveness of treatment for each of a list of problems or symptoms.

Some of the variables concerning differences in what teens bring to hypnotherapy were cited by several respondents as being unimportant to them in their work. This is particularly true for *hypnotizability* and *depth of trance*. These variables, they found, are not associated with effectiveness in treatment. *Trust* and *fear of loss of control* are seen as more relevant, and are linked to each other, with the achievement of *trust* being seen as prerequisite to overcoming *fear of loss of control*. With respect to *motivation*, perceived differences relate more to the kind of problem presented and the context of treatment than to the age of the patient. All of the therapists who work with young children agree that high levels of *physical activity* are typically present among young children, but are rarely observed in the teens.

Observers disagree regarding differences in the imagery presented by teens, especially in comparison with that manifested by children. Imagery of children is seen by some respondents as more vivid, but also as more primary and less complex than that reported by either teens or adults. Substance of the imagery is noted as reflecting age-related interests, so that boys more often utilize imagery of active sports. But differences in the *capacity* for imagery is seen as reflecting life experience rather than developmental level. Individuals who had been read to as young children, it was suggested, and who had been encouraged to engage in make-believe fantasy, found it easier to invoke imagery in hypnosis. I do not know of any systematic data supporting this interesting suggestion.

With respect to methods of induction there is wide variability. All of the respondents favor permissive over directive methods. Some therapists deny ever using directive methods with teens, but at least one pediatrician, used to working in acute emergency situations, acknowledged that directive methods are sometimes unavoidable. Within this small sample, ideomotor techniques are rarely used with adolescents, and the use of storytelling is limited to children. Perhaps more important than which techniques are favored or disfavored, are the reasons offered. Confusion techniques, for example, are disavowed by several respondents, to avoid conveying the impression of manipulation.

When these therapists were asked about the kinds of problems for which they had found hypnotherapy useful with teens, some of the disagreement on earlier questions was clarified. Therapists were asked about eight symptom or problem areas: anxiety, pain (including head-ache), nausea and vomiting, eating disorders, enuresis and sphincter control, other psychosomatic disorders, substance abuse, and work or study effectiveness. The question was intended to learn for which disorders each therapist finds hypnotherapy useful in the treatment of adolescents. What the question revealed instead is the area of specialization of the practitioner, and hence the kinds of patients he or she is accustomed to treating. In retrospect, that appears obvious. But knowing what kinds of patients are being treated is the key to understanding what each therapist concludes about the qualities shown by teenagers. For example, the practice of one of the responding pediatricians is family-oriented primary care. Many of the adolescents he treats have known him as their primary physician since they were infants. Trust, on the part of this pediatrician's patients is rarely an issue. One of the psychologists, in contrast, is accustomed to working with teens with behavior disorders. His patients come with suspicion, fear and hostility. For him, the first and often the largest task is overcoming distrust. Another pediatrician works with adolescents with serious, chronic and life-threatening disease. Adolescents treated by this physician are often arrested in their physical development by debilitating illness. Chronic illness has locked up equally the growth of their psychological development. Illness has forced a dependency from which many fear to outgrow. It should be no surprise that these teenage children respond more like youngsters than like adolescents of like age developing under optimal circumstances. In short, what I learned from my survey is that what adolescents bring to hypnotherapy is by no means uniform, and varies not only with their age, but with the kind of problem for which help is being sought.

This brought me back to my own situation. There was much variability in my own case load. For example, I was being called upon to help teens who were suffering from traumatic injury, from severe physical discomfort, and from phobic responses to medical treatment. With such patients, I found hypnosis frequently to be immediately and even dramatically effective. Other patients, however, had been referred because they had attempted suicide, or been traumatized sexually, or were engaged in socially unacceptable behavior. The initial response of these patients was often guarded or even hostile. It is often possible to establish good rapport with these teens and to engage and hold them in treatment. That is not the same thing as engaging them in hypnotherapy. What I found, as with Patrice, is that it frequently leads to early termination of the treatment relationship.

Why is this so? I mentioned earlier that adolescents are faced with developmental tasks. Erik Erikson called one of these the achievement of autonomy, and that is as good a name for this process as can be found. Hypnosis raises for the adolescent, as it may for an adult, the prospect of yielding control to another. Never mind the sincerity of the therapist whose very goal is to enhance the adolescent's search, because it remains a paradox. To get help, the adolescent must accept a dependent role, must yield a measure of control to the therapist. The teenager does not necessarily think through what is happening, he or she just reacts. But the reaction is one perhaps best seen as a "transference" reaction. The response is not so much to what the therapist is doing or saying, it is to what the patient is feeling, that here is another parent seeking to impose control. And if it can be a negative transference, equally it can be a positive one which distorts reality no less, in which the patient's eagerness, gratitude and compliance reflect dependency and helplessness that carries with it equal risk for the patient and therapist alike.

REFERENCE

Josselson, R. (1980). Ego development in adolescence. In J. Adelson (Ed.), *Handbook of adolescent psychology*. New York: Wiley.

Chapter 22

An Ericksonian Approach to the Treatment of Chronic Posttraumatic Stress Disorder Patients

Nachman Alon

Posttraumatic Stress Disorder (PTSD) is a comparatively new term (DSM-III, 1980) for old clinical entities which have been treated by psychiatry for about a century. Effective treatment of the acute phase was mainly established during the First World War (Salmon, 1919). Its basic principles are still valid today and offer a rather high rate of success. The chronic phase, although well-known, proves to be less amenable to treatment due to patients' resistances, hostilities and poor motivation.

In recent years, mainly due to the sequelae of the Vietnam War, a new interest in the syndrome has been aroused, and there is a growing literature concerning its treatment (e.g., Aleson, 1983; Caknipe, 1983; Figley, 1978). However, little has been said about *specific* strategies for dealing with the basic problems of treatment: overcoming resistance and motivating the patient. This chapter summarizes a treatment approach which was used with 58 patients with a promising rate of success. The approach is based upon the therapeutic principles espoused by Milton H. Erickson, which seem to overcome some of the limitations occurring in other approaches that attempt to tackle therapeutic problems in a direct manner.

Haim Omer and Dr. Noga Rubinstein were very helpful in the conceptualization and writing of this paper. Amalia Urbach effectively treated some of the patients described in this work and contributed greatly to the treatment of the PTSD family.

The PTSD syndrome consists of contradictory psychological tendencies:

1) Reexperiencing of the trauma, as evidenced by recurrent and intrusive recollections of the event, recurrent dreams of the event, and sudden acting or feeling as if the traumatic event was recurring because of an association with an environmental or ideational stimulus.
2) Numbing of responsiveness to, or reduced involvement with, the external world, beginning some time after the trauma. It is shown by a marked decrease in one or more significant interests, feeling of detachment or estrangement from others, and constricted affect.
3) Various symptoms such as hyperalertness, sleep disturbances, survivor's guilt, problems in memory and concentration, avoidance of activities that arouse recollection of the traumatic event, depression and anxiety, unpredictable explosions of aggressive behavior, etc. (DSM-III, 1980, pp. 236-239).

PREMORBID FACTORS

Kelman (1945) analyzed the character of the PTSD patient and the difficulties in therapy which are posed by it. The characteristics of the premorbid personality are:

1) A compulsive need to attain and maintain an idealized image of oneself, along with self-absorption in attaining the overexacting set of standards included in this image; hence, total intolerance of failure.
2) A great need for self-control and control of the environment. "Loss of control has violent repercussions, and is regarded as a loss of face, a failure, a depletion and an extreme humiliation. Occurrence of the unexpected feels particularly defeating and humiliating" (p. 139). The need to control anger often leads to avoidance of conflict situations.
3) A strong need to be unique and self-sufficient. As a result, there is an aversion to any form of cooperation, discipline, help and dependency, all of which are perceived to be humiliating.

The basic experience in a traumatic event is unexpected utter helplessness and loss of control (Seligman, 1983). For the person described above, this sort of experience may be shattering. He may react to this experience in several ways:

1) Depression, guilt, preoccupation with trauma, self-hate, sense of

helplessness, hopelessness, doom, depression and guilt. Such reactions were defined above as the reexperiencing reaction. Patients of this group can be readily treated by direct approaches.

2) Withdrawal and blaming, that are aimed to ". . . preserve whatever illusions are left and to insure themselves against another exposure and defeat . . ." (Kelman, 1945, p. 141). "Because they cannot tolerate blame, they must project the cause for their failure onto others or make others shoulder the burden. They are constantly building a case for themselves as the abused ones and as the ones who have been unfairly treated" (p. 140). The trauma turns into a face-saving device to account for the personal failure. This blaming and externalizing attitude, which is accompanied by emotional numbness, has been noted by various workers in the field and constitutes one of the most difficult problems of therapy (Brock, 1960; Caknipe, 1983; Titchener & Ross, 1974). Patients of this group do not respond well to direct approaches, and it is with them that an indirect approach is indicated.

The Process of Chronicity

Sometime after the occurrence of the traumatic event, the typical patient starts to exhibit symptomatic, withdrawn angry behavior. Family members, employers, friends, therapists and the patient himself try to "do something to solve the problems," but these attempted solutions only make things worse. They set in motion vicious cycles in the manner described by Watzlawick, Weakland, and Fisch (1974).

For example, upon discovering that the husband has somehow changed, the wife may attempt to help him by temporarily taking responsibilities off his shoulders. As we shall see later, for the PTSD patient, being weak or perceiving that he is thought to be weak arouses anxiety and depression, which results in even less effective functioning. This, in turn, forces the spouse to assume even more responsibilities and so the cycle repeats itself. Eventually the wife starts getting frustrated and angry, since her hopes of aiding her husband to recover are not met; the more she helps, the worse he gets, which is totally incomprehensible to them both.

This cycle also affects the children: As father withdraws, his position in the hierarchy gets more marginal. The children, trying to regain their father's attention, become demanding, withdrawn or symptomatic, sometimes resulting in open rejection by the father. The atmosphere at home, with a withdrawn father and a frustrated mother who holds the sole responsibility for running the house, becomes tense and angry.

Things get worse if the father bursts into anger, as is often the case.

These family processes exemplify the vicious cycles which lead to chronicity, sometimes with surprising speed. There develops an interconnected net of other vicious cycles, which adds fuel to the process. For example, temporary decreases in responsibilities at work for benevolent reasons on the part of the employers and colleagues tend to leave the patient in a one-down position, thus deepening depression. The same vicious cycle may be seen even in the bodily sphere. For example, insomnia, which is frequent at the acute stage, increases fatigue, tension and irritability by day, which in turn increases obsessive preoccupation with one's situation, which in turn increases difficulties in falling asleep.

PROBLEMS IN THERAPY

The above analysis clarifies some of the difficulties which are often encountered in the treatment of chronic PTSD patients, especially of the second, "numb" type. When I first started to work with these patients, I found that work towards rehabilitation or towards "working through the trauma" tended to mobilize "therapeutic vicious cycles" which aggravated rather than alleviated the problems.

Every attempt by any potential helper to bring the patient to rehabilitation reactivates the conflict described above (Kelman, 1945). The patient reacts with anxiety, resistance and antagonism. The helper assumes a "pushing role," conveying the message, "You are able if you want to." The patient, feeling misunderstood and victimized, reacts with further proofs of incapability. Thus, each rehabilitation attempt aggravates the problem and becomes a further link in a cycle *away* from rehabilitation. The problem gets even more severe when secondary gains are present.

Moreover, ceaseless preoccupation with being the victim of a trauma brought about by others is an important part of the process of establishing chronicity. Patient and therapist alike may get entangled in a progressive mystification of the trauma. The therapist often assumes that cognitive and affective processing of the trauma will lead to the resolution of present problems. That is often true with acute patients and sometimes with the "reexperiencing patients." However, with "numb" patients this actually *reinforces* the trauma's neurotic value. Every further attempt in this direction justifies the patient in his self-conception as a helpless victim of his past, for which others are to be blamed. In this light, it becomes clearer why these patients are often considered to be noncooperative, unmotivated, aggressive, antagonistic and resistant to therapeutic intervention. Therapy openly threatens them with assuming responsibility for their problem and for rehabilitation.

STRATEGY AND TACTICS

The strategic aim in the treatment of PTSD is to gradually provide the patient with a series of active coping experiences, thus counteracting his vicious cycles *without directly pushing him to abandon his self-image as being an incapacitated victim of abuse and neglect.* The assumption is that as coping improves and the sense of failure lessens, self-image will change itself. The overall strategy is accomplished by several tactics which are described and exemplified by case vignettes below.

Establishing and Maintaining Therapeutic Alliance

Utilization (Erickson, 1980) is the single most important means for establishing therapeutic alliance with the PTSD patient. Erickson describes it thus:

> The patient's behavior is a part of the problem brought to the office; it constitutes the personal environment in which the therapy must take effect, it may constitute the dominant force in the total patient-doctor relationship . . . sometimes . . . therapy can be established on a sound basis only by the utilization of silly, absurd, irrational and contradictory manifestations. (p. 212)

This principle may appear in many forms, both on the tactical and strategic levels.

CASE ONE

An example of the utilization of pathology is a family, consisting of husband, wife and three children who were referred to therapy because of a family PTSD reaction after the loss of a son in a military accident four years prior to therapy. The family was of low education and low income level. The mother was especially depressed and withdrawn, and her functioning as a housewife and a mother deteriorated to the point that not even meals were served at home. Family therapy helped to some extent, but nothing could get us beyond the impasse of the wife's depression. Medication was recommended but was rejected by her. I started to suspect that she considered therapy a threat rather than an aid: her mourning was endangered by it. When this became clear, she was told that her general condition severely impaired her ability to mourn. For example, her problems in concentration made her distractible; the impairment of memory caused her recollections of her son to be blurred; her constant crying brought her to emotional and physical exhaustion, which made further crying impossible; her lack of appetite made her overtired and drowsy. If she wanted, *really* wanted, to revive her ability to mourn to the full extent, she had to overcome these obstacles—and therapy, especially medication, could alleviate them. This reasoning was readily accepted and antidepressants were taken. She reported within six hours that her mind had become crystal clear and that she could now mourn much better. When her depression lessened, she started to take an active role in a project of commemoration of her son through the synagogue, and this paved the way to further, less sad, activities.

Most PTSD patients exhibit ambivalent and conflicting attitudes concerning therapy: they want a brief and efficient therapy for problems which they consider insurmountable, they want the therapist to be omnipotent enough to overcome these problems, and yet they want to maintain complete control over whatever happens in therapy. This ambivalent attitude has to be indirectly dealt with by assuming a one-down position (Haley, 1963) and by using multilevel messages.

The position of an omnipotent, self-assured authoritarian therapist is necessary in treating the acute PTSD. However, the therapist who assumes this position with the chronic patient is likely to lose his patient. The following attitude is taken as a standard step in the first session of most treatments: The therapist takes a "one-down" position. He speaks of the enormity and duration of the complex problems; of the lack of sufficient therapeutic tools necessary for a thorough change; of previous eminent therapists who did not seem to help much, most of whom are as experienced as himself and maybe more so; and of his personal feelings that he is not capable of helping much, except, perhaps, for some marginal and insignificant matters. When the patient objects to these reservations and cites the recommendation made about the therapist, his objections are dismissed as merely pointing to the fact that the recommending agent is not familiar enough with the therapist's shortcomings, which will surely become obvious as therapy progresses. Again, these messages are stated in a manner which is also indicative of the confident and secure standing of the therapist.

Sometimes, the therapist simultaneously gives *overt* messages which conform to the patient's point of view and a contradictory *covert* message. Whereas the overt message is verbal and is therefore within the patient's awareness, the covert message judiciously uses *implications* (Erickson & Rossi, 1979, pp. 38-40) and nonverbal language and is usually out of the patient's awareness.

CASE TWO

An intelligent and talented patient, whose paranoidal criticism made him quit previous therapy, was treated by me for several months with no change taking place. His ambivalence towards therapy was apparent, as were his needs to see me both as an omnipotent and an impotent therapist. One day he criticized me severely for poor planning of therapy, for lack of insight and understanding, and for being just like any other standard psychologist who works by the book, etc. He then stated that my useless strategy was absolutely clear to him, and that he could see through all my maneuvers which were meant only to degrade and humiliate him. Triumphantly, using military metaphors and tactical analysis, and with much insight, he explicated the indirect therapeutic approach as an enormous deception plot and distraction campaign. Astonished, I sank back in my armchair, lowered my head mournfully, and said in a firm tone and with a very, very slight smile: "I am shocked! No patient has ever succeeded in grasping these manipulations before, and very few therapists did, even after attending workshops I have given. I am totally disarmed now. I have no more tricks to play, no maneuvers to perform. The victory is all yours; I can't see any more tricks by which I can hold you in therapy (although I am very willing to). Nothing more can be done here, except for useless chattering and gossiping. I will not be surprised if you will leave right now, as my real face has been unmasked."

It was now the patient's turn to get off-balance. He was obviously struggling between a wish to exhibit even more aggressive behavior and a wish to respond in a friendly manner. A long pause took place before he said half-smilingly: "OK, OK. Can you imagine that I would travel the 90 miles back home before the session is over and before I get my money's worth? You won't get rid of me that easily. What's on our agenda next?" And the crisis was over. The neutralization of the patient's aggression and its turning into a sportslike interaction were achieved by the double message I gave: verbally expressing a one-down acceptance of all accusations and simulating loss of face, while nonverbally express-

ing confidence and lighthearted warmth. The overt statement satisfied
the patient's need to be stronger than the therapist, while the covert
one-up message conducted him to unwittingly adopt a complementary
one-down position, which was needed for further therapeutic work.

An important maneuver in attaining rapport, combatting resistance
and creating a new context for change is *relabeling* or redefining (Watzlawick, Weakland, & Fisch, 1974). One example of useful relabeling with
PTSD patients involves defining the situation as "a crisis" (implying it
is transient) rather than "a state." The PTSD is explained as a natural
response to the encounter with death, rather than a breakdown, stress-
response anxiety or depression. "You were pretty sure that you were
going to die, were you not? After such an encounter, who can enjoy life
anymore?" (This nonblaming formulation is the only one which never
aroused any resistance among any of my patients.) Therapy is often
defined as retraining, as "brushing up on rusty vocational and social
skills." Homework assignments devised to covertly bring about change
are defined as means of behavioral data-collecting, etc.

Another relabeling maneuver which is closely related to redefinition
is *positive connotation* (Selvini Palazzoli, Boscolo, Cecchin, & Prata, 1978):
Whatever the patient does or experiences is defined as positive. For
example, when the patient reports some good feelings during the past
week, he is praised for his efforts in bringing about this good feeling.
If he reports bad feelings, he is praised for overcoming them quickly.
If he still does not feel well, the therapist is happy at the chance to deal
with the real problems *in vivo*. And if the report is of "no change," the
patient is praised for his success in stabilizing the process of deterioration.

CASE THREE

A PTSD patient got severely depressed and apathetic; he complained
bitterly of his inability to get out of his apathy and said he was sure
nobody could help him. I readily agreed to this and said that what I
could do was to at least help him *enjoy* his apathy. He was hypnotized,
deeply relaxed, and got acquainted with the freedom of not having to
choose between any of the many imaginable things and possibilities his
life could offer him. He was taught to enjoy being "apathetic" at the
beach, after having orgasm or after jogging. He also started physical

fitness exercises in order "to enjoy more deeply the apathy that followed." These exercises served as the starting point for further changes.

Closely related to positive thinking is the dissociation between good intention and debatable behavior. This patient's anger toward his parents was defined as immunizing them against possible depression on his leaving home in the future—a feat we were discussing at the time.

This form of therapy *avoids insight*. As explained before, the whole psychological makeup of these patients is geared towards warding off introspection and insight. Trying to achieve these goals would be working against the point of highest resistance, an approach which hardly can bring about change. Moreover, some patients are engaged in obsessive ruminations which *seem* to be introspective but are actually futile. For them, further introspection serves only to aggravate the obsessive process.

CASE FOUR

D. is the "model patient," the dream of every therapist. A veteran of years of former therapies and an intelligent man, D. was able to grasp totally and fully the meaning of all aspects of his problems, conscious, preconscious and unconscious, and to elaborate perceptively. The only problem was that he did not change a bit and his main complaint—pain in his chest—never got better. We spent 18 months in futile attempts at therapy.

One day, upon taking his seat he contemplatively commented: "I wonder why I *always* take the same seat. . . ." Suddenly it dawned on me that D. was stuck in therapy not *in spite* of his introspective ability but *because* of it. He was wasting most of his energy on the most insignificant matters as if they were the key to his problems. I asked him to come to the window and to look into the garden intently for two minutes. It was May and the garden was blooming. D. stood there, gazing out in a manner which indicated that he was really busy with inner thoughts rather than observing. He was then seated and I asked how many different flowers he had seen. He said, bewildered, that he saw one, but maybe there were one or two more. He was deeply surprised to find out about the other six types that he just had not seen because he was preoccupied with worries and inner dialogue. From then on therapy was geared to *decrease*, rather than to increase, self-involvement, and to turn attention to the external world. This change of focus brought about a marked decrease in his physical complaints and paved the road to excellent therapeutic progress.

The following table summarizes the multilevel messages that have to be simultaneously given by the therapist in order to maintain a balance between conflicting attitudes:

Overt Message (Verbal)	Covert Message (Nonverbal; By Implication)
1. Therapist is impotent.	1. Therapist is competent and knows what he is doing.
2. Problems are insurmountable.	2. *Some* problems are surmountable.
3. Patient is incapable of coping.	3. Patient *and* therapist can cope together.
4. The cause for problems is external and objective.	4. Change is possible irrespective of cause.
5. The patient is not responsible for change.	5. The patient may be interested in learning slight changes.
6. Changes is an all-or-none matter.	6. There is a spectrum of changes.
7. Rehabilitation seems impossible, and will not serve as a goal.	7. Learning to cope is possible.
8. The patient's perception of the world is correct.	8. The patient's perception of the world may be correct, but other perceptions might be as valid.

Motivating the Patient for Activity

The tactics reviewed so far are aimed to engage patients in therapy in spite of initial reluctance, and to give them the feeling they are at last understood and not condemned. Once this is achieved, the task is to start engaging the patient in activities that will counteract vicious cycles, and initiate "beneficial cycles" instead. Erickson was a master of devising and mobilizing these processes, often out of the patient's awareness. A classic example of this kind of therapy is his treatment of Harold, "the feeble-minded moron" (Haley, 1973, pp. 120-148).

This case served as my model of therapy with PTSD, and the principles underlying it are applied accordingly.

Choice of first interventions. The first task of the therapist, once rapport is established is to judiciously choose the first assignment for the patient. This assignment has to be nonthreatening (on the route of least resistance), yet powerful enough to mobilize some beneficial cycles which will counteract the various vicious cycles that have evolved. Once the task has been successfully performed, and a minor change occurs, the therapist gradually can initiate tasks that will tackle more central issues in a more direct manner, *but without letting the patient notice the long-range goals.* The patient is left with the impression that he performs discrete tasks from one week to another. A good rationale has to be given to the patient to make the demands put on him plausible.

In the treatment of PTSD patients, the beginning target for therapeutic intervention is usually the problem of insomnia or some other problem in the somatic field. Insomnia is a highly distressing symptom, and yet it seems minor as compared to other problems. Therefore, overcoming it does not imply the "threat" of further rehabilitation. With a paradoxical intervention, insomnia is generally controlled within a few sessions. The patient, somewhat surprised and confused, is motivated to continue with further assignments.

Choice of further assignments. Sometimes the patient is taught relaxation by self-hypnosis. At other times, a process begins in which therapist and patient conduct a negotiation on the next goal the patient wishes to attain. In this process the therapist consistently *rejects* goals that are too ambitious or too complex to be attained within a few weeks, or that constitute the patient's central complaints. Acceptable targets may be: qualifying for a driver's license; pleasing one's children without getting involved in too much direct contact with them; being able to enjoy one's apathy, and so on. Examples of targets which are unacceptable are: overcoming stuttering; improvement of family relationships; vocational rehabilitation.

Whenever the patient proposes unacceptable targets, the therapist presses for a restriction. In this manner, the "pusher" and "pushed" relationship is inverted, and the patient is the one who presses for progress. This negotiation is sometimes followed by an analysis of the steps needed to attain the chosen goal. Once the general analysis has been made, the therapist focuses on one step at a time and refuses to deal with the next steps or even to discuss them. From now on, every step is dealt with separately, but in the general context of the long-range goals. This process covertly serves for the patient as a model for realistic appraisal of goals and for lowering overexacting self-demands, thus serving as an indirect therapeutic move which aims at a basic pattern of the patient.

PTSD patients are often reluctant to perform "therapeutic" homework assignments. However, they will perform many activities—ranging from quarreling with their spouse to studying art therapy, as long as they see them as either activities aimed at a better diagnosis or as training for the attainment of a goal which is important to them. I found, for example, that *all* the patients started to do physical exercises when it was put to them as a "means to combat the physiological aspects of stress through redistribution of adrenalin and other biochemical components." Many PTSD patients went to a movie or a party or took a vacation for the first time in years in order "to monitor their anxiety, restlessness, moments of self-abandonment, physical discomfort," etc. Paradoxical techniques are useful, e.g., combatting insomnia by "writing down all interfering thoughts that come to mind," and by insisting on conscious monitoring "even when one gets extremely sleepy, eyelids heavy, falling asleep . . . because we will be able to analyze what it is in your head that prevents you from falling asleep."

CASE FIVE

A soldier patient wanted to obtain a driver's license. He was asked to gather information concerning whether his commanders would agree to send him to a driving course, what recommendations they would give, what schedules of courses were available, etc. He asked for an interview with his commander, who was surprised that this chronically passive complainer did, after all, want to do something positive. This led to a relatively open and comfortable interview in which the soldier allowed himself to explain things thoroughly, which in turn further enhanced rapport with his commander.

CASE SIX

Another example is a patient who was reluctant to perform any sort of homework assignment. He was asked to resume an old habit he had not practiced for the two years following his injury "in order to see what bodily sensations would occur while shopping." He was to buy one kilogram of toffee candy in the military canteen and bring it home on Friday night. *That much* he could do. The following week he complained about the misbehavior of his kids at a football game. When asked how come they had all gone to the game—which they had not done for years—he said that his kids were happy to receive the candy "just like in old times" and behaved accordingly. This, in turn, led to the common leisure activity.

Another important agent in enhancing the patient's motivation is the therapeutic *metaphor* which exemplifies the problem and the possibilities of solution. For example, when asked in the initial stage of therapy what are the chances of change, I abruptly open my drawer, pull out a big rusty screw stuck in a nut, and ask the patient how to free the screw from the nut. We run a long technical discussion about oil, tools, rust and corrosion, until a solution is reached. I then ask what is the most difficult part in the freeing process. We both agree that the first motion is the hardest, but once motion starts, things get easier. This serves as a metaphor for the process of freeing the patient's rusted skills. Many patients remember the metaphor of the screw better than they remember any other item in therapy.

Moving to more central issues. Once the initial tasks have been success-fully accomplished, a gradual shift can be made towards more central issues. Often trust develops to a degree which enables the therapist to speak more directly and to be less cautious.

CASE SEVEN

M. is a senior teacher who lost his job due to PTSD. During therapy he was working in a minor job under a woman manager. She did not like him there, but had to obey *her* boss who did want M. The course of problems tackled in the treatment was:

1) Combatting hyperventilation by self-hypnosis.
2) Combatting hyperhydrosis by self-hypnosis.
3) Dealing with his boss with humor rather than with aggression: He was to thank his superior for relieving him of his responsibilities (which originally infuriated him tremendously). "Being without a great deal to do enabled him to take it easy, to earn a living without having to work too hard, to contemplate the realities of bureaucracy, etc."
4) Dealing with his boss with candor: He was to invite her to lunch and

tell her that he thought their situation was absurd; that each of them was a pain-in-the-neck for the other, yet they had to work together; that they could either keep fighting each other or attempt peaceful coexistence; and that he personally preferred the second alternative although deep in his heart he wished her every possible misfortune.
5) Dealing with conflict in work through assertiveness: He was to warn his superiors that he would complain to the Administration unless they took some action to solve some organizational problems.
6) Dealing similarly with a deep marital conflict.

CASE EIGHT

Another example is H., who had quit his studies in geography six months before completion. (This kind of self-destructive impulsive act is not uncommon among PTSD patients.) He had 20 three-page reports to submit and felt he could not possibly complete them; besides, nobody would find him a job in this field anyway. He refused to write any more reports, but agreed to show me how a report looked. He agreed to *copy* one report, so as to be able to diagnose his inhibition about writing. The following week he was asked to rewrite it from memory, so as to train himself in remembering. Next he was to write a false report. After three months of working in that manner, one task a week and never mentioning completion of his studies, he had his 20 reports, went back to school and completed his studies.

An important issue is the way the therapist is to relate to what the patient does. During this process the therapist should *avoid giving direct positive reinforcements*. These are perceived by the patient as patronizing, a proof that he is looked upon as a child. Reinforcement should apply to *traits*, not to *specific behaviors*. For example, when a patient successfully completes a task, he may be praised for his *courage* in following the therapist's strange directives or for his persistence, but not for the perfect manner in which he performed the directives. Praise for the latter can easily lead to undoing of that behavior. The same indirectness has to be practiced in *assessing change*. PTSD patients seldom volunteer information concerning change, let alone improvement. On the contrary, their complaining is incessant even when change is obvious. The therapist must, to a large extent, ignore verbal reports and seek indirect evidence for change, mainly by looking for what the patient's report *implies*.

Multidimensionality of treatment. The multidimensional nature of PTSD problems necessitates a multidimensional therapeutic approach. The therapist has to employ flexible interventions taken from various schools of therapy, e.g., psychodynamic, behavioral, gestalt, hypnotherapy, cognitive behavior-therapy, family therapy, sex therapy, etc.

CASE NINE

The case of the S. family (Alon, 1980) is relevant here. The S. family lived in a house which was assaulted by terrorists in 1979. During the attack the father was captured by the terrorists and had a narrow escape. The family was separated, each member staying on his or her own, believing the others were dead. Stress reactions appeared a few days later. A marathon crisis-intervention session proved insufficient in overcoming the severe PTSD manifestations in all family members: depression, isolation, severe fears, especially during the night, watching for terrorists at the windows for hours, refusal on the children's part to sleep anywhere except in the parents' bedroom, etc.

The therapeutic strategy was to engage the parents as cotherapists in the treatment of their daughters, as it was assumed that vicarious learning would thus take place. A host of interventions were used:

1) Indirect suggestions and therapeutic double binds using apparently casual remarks like: "Of course it's absolutely *impossible* for you to leave your parents' bedroom—at the moment. It will take a *very* long time before you'll be able to do so—maybe even a whole month!"
2) Grading of rooms by level of fearfulness.
3) Putting up signs in the girls' room, reading "The Room of Terrible Fear."
4) Directives to write in a "Fear Diary" whenever fear is felt at night.
5) Training in "springing out of bed in panic" to noises made by the therapist.
6) Detailed drawing of frightening fantasies with emphasis on small inappropriate details such as putting a wristwatch on a monster.
7) Singing the therapeutic poem "Song of Fear" in moments of light fear: "I'm terribly afraid/I'm terribly trembling/woe is me/my suffering is fathomless," etc.
8) Using the Fear Diary for self-analysis of physical and psychological anxiety reactions.
9) Mothering of "frightened dolls" at fearful moments.
10) After the girls had returned to their own room: "fearful" escape to parents' bedroom on a preplanned night.

11) Defining fear as legitimate and essential to self-preservation.
12) Under light hypnotic trance: dissociating helpful self-preserving fear from superfluous fear; the latter is then "permitted" to leave.
13) *In vivo* desensitization, through play, to the traumatic shelter at which the terrorists were met.

The net result was that the girls' phobias disappeared altogether after four two-hour sessions. Marked decreases in the parents' fears was also achieved.

In order to work multidimensionally, the therapist needs to flexibly assume different roles, among which are the roles of coordinator, coach, instructor, etc.

CASE TEN

Y., a former high-ranking officer, had lost many soldiers of his battalion in battle ten years previously. He had tremendous guilt feelings (objectively unjustified). In therapy, his guilt was tackled directly in an extreme implosion-like technique (Ramsey, 1980); as a consequence it subsided considerably. However, in his work as a factory manager he often suffered temper tantrums in the face of minor incidents. For nearly a year therapy consisted almost entirely of coaching in problems such as how to allocate authority; how to persuade the owners to accept more modern views of management; how to initiate intrigues; how to counteract intrigues; how to gain the support of peers; how to use outside consultants to bring about change; how to use authority and when to avoid authority. No *overt* psychotherapy was done and the sessions looked like amateur managerial counseling. I often had to press Y. not to quit his job prematurely, because of his low tolerance of frustration. The joint endeavor enabled him to overcome his urge to quit. Comprehensive changes took place in the plant and it became economically and organizationally successful. Y. is still there and does not intend to quit.

An important aspect of multidimensional therapeutic work is teamwork with support-systems agencies. One has to work in close collaboration with several systems, including the family and various governmental agencies in veterans' affairs, job placement, vocational education, medical care, etc. Sometimes the therapist has to assume the role of coordinator between various systems in order to lessen hostility and suspicion among the agencies toward the patient and to build hope and optimism, while at other times, after careful planning, he has to detach himself from such agencies.

Stages of Therapy

Most treatments follow some general plan and stages, but the order and relative importance of each stage vary markedly with different patients. Seldom is there a clear-cut distinction between stages. The tendency of the patient to switch from one problem to another forces the therapist to adhere firmly to a central issue and to insist on the need to follow the stages he delineates. The general plan of treatment consists usually of the following stages:

(a) Evaluation and establishing the therapeutic alliance.
(b) Initiating beneficial cycles.
(c) Stabilizing work, an essential factor for further improvement since therapy often fails if the patient does not start working.
(d) *Family:* Although various family interventions may take place from the beginning of therapy, I have found that a more comprehensive approach can be taken only after some self-esteem has been restored. Hypnosis is used in a family setting or with children, frequently serving as an indirect tool to treat one family member while ostensibly treating another.
(e) A multidimensional approach to dealing with symptoms; techniques can be taken from all schools—psychodynamic, behavioral, family therapy, hypnotherapy, etc.
(f) Dealing with the various aspects of the trauma: Only now, when the trauma is no longer needed as a face-saving device can it be handled and relieved. Hypnosis serves as a means to achieve cognitive and emotional restructuring or abreaction.

Emotional Aspects

Therapy has to deal with basic emotions, especially with anger, guilt, fear and sadness. The tendency for emotional numbness makes dealing with emotions a complex task. Anger is especially difficult, since many patients have difficulty in its direct expression and resort to passive-aggressive patterns. The therapist can encourage direct expression of anger by utilizing occurrences of anger against the therapist. He lets the patient be angry at him, thus serving as a model through whom the patient learns to endure conflict and survive it. Anger in the patient's daily life is dealt with either by self-control or by assertiveness. Techniques like self-relaxation, desensitization, emotional detachment, or symbolic expression of anger all serve to enhance self-control, whereas cognitive rehearsal, guided imagery, etc. serve to enhance assertiveness.

Guilt, and especially survivor's guilt, is not easily amenable to therapy. Guilt underlies much of the patient's behavior, and may be seen as a major source of self-destructive behaviors. The therapeutic paradigm I often utilize is the behavioral exposure approach (Ramsey, 1980). The patient, usually under hypnosis, is flooded with self-reproaching ideas and images, in which his "disgraceful" deeds are reexperienced through the therapist's verbalization. It takes 60 to 90 minutes before the patient is totally exhausted and is desensitized to his feelings. The procedure is repeated for as many as 10 sessions, usually twice a week. Even long-standing problems of guilt are much relieved by this radical intervention. For example, the senior officer with guilt (Case Ten above) who felt he was responsible for the death of more than 30 soldiers was relieved of 10 years of guilt to the degree that he could get out of his "anniversary depression" within a few days whereas in the past it would have taken weeks or even months. The only therapy still needed is periodic 6-month "booster shots" of the same procedure around the anniversary period. That approach seems to work because it is an ordeal which serves also as a *self-inflicted intrinsic punishment*, which some of these patients seek.

CONCLUSION

The principles underlying the therapeutic approach described here are by now well documented in the literature by Erickson himself and by his followers and colleagues (Fisch, Weakland, & Segal, 1982). Among these principles one can find the following: the utilization approach; using two-level communication; using one-down position; reframing in its various forms; utilization of homework assignments as change producers; avoidance of insight; mobilizing positive "beneficial cycles" and counteracting vicious cycles; avoidance of too ambitious goals; avoidance of positive reinforcement; utilizing therapeutic metaphors; dealing with social support systems; assuming several therapeutic roles; making parts of therapy an "ordeal therapy"; working multidimensionally, with techniques taken from several approaches and frameworks.

What distinguishes the therapy described here from other therapies based on Ericksonian approaches is not the mere utilization of certain therapeutic principles; it is their systematic application to a special population, presenting all the complexities of chronic states, in the framework of long-term therapy with an ever-present resistance. As I have shown, this difficult syndrome is multidimensional, and it takes a multidimensional therapy to counteract it. Treatment cannot be brief, and therapy may become a long-term constant combat to maintain the therapeutic alliance in spite of continuous resistance.

Traditionally, the above-mentioned principles are thought to work best with well-focused problems in a context of brief therapy of the nature of problem solving. Most of the case reports are of this sort, and only a much smaller proportion is devoted to the presentation of long-term therapies with schizophrenics or other chronic patients. My experience in treating PTSD proves that Erickson's principles are not only applicable to extremely complex situations, but that this application is necessary in dealing with such problems, which are considered to be nonresponsive to other therapies.

The utilization of Ericksonian principles in this context does *not* preclude the application of other principles and techniques; on the contrary, one cannot do much with PTSD without a good psychodynamic understanding of the problem, without a good understanding and skill in behavioral processes and techniques, and without a good systemic reasoning; moreover, one also has to have a good ecological, societal, and organizational outlook. But the Ericksonian approach serves as a meta-approach, a unifying overall set of principles, without which the best techniques prove not to be strong enough to bring about change. Successful outcome with 26 patients and partial success with another 17 patients, with only six drop-outs and eight failures among the 58 treated in this manner, seems to back this conclusion.

REFERENCES

Alon, N. (1980, July). *Treatment of a family with phobic reactions following terrorist assault.* Paper presented at the First World Congress on Behavior Therapy, Jerusalem, Israel.

Aleson, E. (1983). *A comprehensive treatment program for post-traumatic stress disorders (PTSD) among combat veterans.* Paper presented at the Third International Conference on Psychological Stress and Adjustment in Time of War and Peace, Tel Aviv, Israel.

Bandler, R., & Grinder, J. (1979). *Frogs into princes.* Moab, UT: Real People Press.

Brock, S. (1960). The neuroses following head (brain) injury. In S. Brock (Ed.), *Injuries of the brain and spinal cord.* New York: Springer.

Caknipe, I. (1983). *Beyond post-traumatic stress reactions—Etiology and aftermath.* Paper presented at the Third International Conference on Psychological Stress and Adjustment in Time of War and Peace, Tel Aviv, Israel.

Diagnostic and statistical manual-III. (1980). Washington, D.C.: American Psychiatric Association.

Erickson, M. H. (1980). Utilization approaches to hypnotherapy. In E. L. Rossi (Ed.), *Collected papers of Milton H. Erickson on hypnosis* (Vol. 4, pp. 147–234). New York: Irvington.

Erickson, M. H., & Rossi, E. L. (1979). *Hypnotherapy: An exploratory casebook.* New York: Irvington.

Figley, C. R. (1978). *Stress disorders among Vietnam veterans.* New York: Brunner/Mazel.

Fisch, R., Weakland, J., & Segal, L. (1982). *The tactics of change: Doing therapy briefly.* San Francisco: Jossey-Bass.

Haley, J. (1963). *Strategies of psychotherapy.* New York: Grune & Stratton.

Haley, J. (1973). *Uncommon therapy: The psychiatric techniques of Milton H. Erickson, M.D.* New York: Norton.

Kelman, H. (1945). Character and the traumatic syndrome. *Journal of Nervous and Mental Diseases, 102,* 121–153.

Parker, N. (1977). Accident litigants with neurotic symptoms. *Medical Journal of Australia,* 2(10), 318–322.

Ramsey, R. W. (1980, July). *Bereavement—A behavioral treatment of pathological grief.* Paper presented at the First World Congress on Behavior Therapy, Jerusalem, Israel.

Salmon, T. W. (1919). The war neuroses and their lesson. *New York Journal of Medicine, 109,* 993.

Seligman, M. E. P. (1983). *Helplessness, depressive attributional styles and vulnerability to severe stress.* Paper presented at the Third International Conference on Psychological Stress and Adjustment in Time of War and Peace, Tel Aviv, Israel.

Selvini Palazzoli, M., Boscolo, L., Cecchin, C., & Prata, G. (1978). *Paradox and counterparadox.* New York: Jason Aronson.

Titchener, J. L., & Ross, W. D. (1974). Acute or chronic stress as determinants of behavior, character and neurosis. In S. Arieti (Ed.), *American handbook of psychiatry,* (2nd ed.). New York: Basic Books.

Watzlawick, P., Weakland, J., & Fisch, R. (1974). *Change.* New York: Norton.

Chapter 23

The Treatment of Two Cases
of Rape Using
Ericksonian Hypnosis

Ronald R. Brown

You have lived through this problem and you
can live through other types of problems.
You can pretend anything and master it.—(Lustig, 1975, Part I)

"Rape—the forceful act of sexual intercourse," say Renshaw
(1979), "is legally defined as 'carnal knowledge by fear, force or fraud.' "
Silver and Stonestreet (1978) indicate that a reported rape occurs approximately every ten minutes in the United States. They also observe
that 55,000 or more rapes are reported annually throughout the country.
Moreover, between 50 and 90 percent go unreported according to FBI
estimates.

The large percentage of unreported rapes may be attributed to the
widely held societal myth that the rape victim "wanted it to happen,"
or that, "she asked for it!" Kamara (1982) observes that the black victim
of sexual assault often has to contend with several additional myths
including:

1) Blacks are inherently more active sexually;
2) Black women are strong under stress and therefore are not affected
   by being raped;
3) Blacks are accustomed to violence in their daily lives, so rape is not
   considered too serious an offense by black women.

Heppner and Heppner (1977), Renshaw (1979), Whiston (1981), and

Kamara (1982) maintain that these myths and other societal mixed messages have added to the trauma of the attack and intensified the feelings of guilt and shame experienced by the rape victim. Consequently, she may feel unclean, dirty, confused, and unable to relate to members of the opposite sex.

The sequelae from rape often include symptoms such as inability to eat, to sleep, or resume normal social relationships. The combined factors of societal myths and psychological problems and symptoms often make it extremely difficult for the rape victim to seek out assistance —especially professional assistance (Heppner & Heppner, 1977).

Given this unfortunate situation, what kind of treatment might prove substantially beneficial to the rape victim? This question will be answered by providing the following:

1) A brief look at the traditional way of treating rape victims;
2) A brief examination of an Ericksonian orientation to the treatment of rape victims;
3) The presentation of two cases of rape utilizing an Ericksonian orientation.

TRADITIONAL TREATMENT OF RAPE VICTIMS

Silver and Stonestreet (1978) have urged that a supportive and understanding atmosphere be established before any major psychological intervention be undertaken. Once this has been achieved, Freiberg and Bridwell (1976) emphasize that one of the primary objectives of therapy for the rape victim is to assist her to verbalize and review the situation surrounding the rape and the rape experience itself. Other therapeutic objectives, according to Heppner and Heppner (1977) are to help the rape victim identify, clarify, and accept her feelings, reorient her perceptions, and begin reestablishing a normal life style.

These therapeutic objectives are indeed laudable and reasonable; however, the important issue is implementation. That is, even if therapists were to adopt these objectives, how would they proceed to implement them? Moreover, little is said about the rape victim's inability to engage in the therapeutic process because of such factors as: (a) the sex of the therapist (Silverman, 1977); (b) the race of the therapist (Kamara, 1982); and (c) the feeling that rape is being handled more like a legal or medical problem than a psychological one (Hilberman, 1976). Fortunately, the problem of implementation and related issues can be resolved with an Ericksonian approach.

An Ericksonian orientation to treatment using hypnosis, metaphors and indirect suggestions affords the clinician the opportunity to encourage the rape victim to do the following: 1) deal with the trauma of her rape experience in a gradual and dissociated manner; 2) safely experience herself sharing the rape and the circumstances surrounding it with significant others; 3) experience herself as a worthwhile person; 4) utilize her previous learning experiences and mental skills as a means of reviving a sense of mastery; and 5) become involved with groups or agencies, such as rape crisis centers, whose primary focus is helping rape victims. Thus, in the context of working with rape victims, an Ericksonian orientation to hypnosis encourages strengths and positive actions; clinicians can avoid the role of the traditional diagnostician making observations about "paranoid tendencies," resistances, or psychopathology.

TREATMENT OF TWO CASES OF RAPE

Case One

Ms. A., was a 20-year-old black coed, a sophomore majoring in art. Her presenting concerns were an inability to sleep, concentrate, or study for her classes and uncontrollable crying. She was brought to the author's attention by a supervisee, who was apprehensive about the client's behavior in therapy, offering the following description:

> I have this client who acts weird and unusual; she frequently attempts to scratch her face and bang her head against my office wall. In the course of behaving this way, she cries out, "I'm unclean! I'm unclean!" Then all of a sudden, she stops and stares off into space. As she does so, she mumbles some unintelligible sounds like a word-salad. I don't know what to do with her or for her. Would you care to see her, or should I refer her out for hospitalization?

I also was informed that the client had arrived at the university after most of the available on-campus housing had been assigned. The only possible housing left was a series of hotels designated as the university's overflow facilities. The client was assigned to one of these hotels on a temporary basis. During the first week there, she was raped. Her rapist was an older white male who gained entrance to the client's room while the client was sleeping by posing as a repairman.

Concurrently with her efforts to seek assistance at the university counseling center, she also sought help, under a different name, at the local Rape Crisis Center (RCC). This fact came to the surface when my supervisee was consulting with one of the workers at the Center. It appeared that the client had decided to deal with the rape episode at the RCC and deal with the symptoms of rape, the crying spells, and the inability to sleep and study at the university's counseling center. It wasn't until after my supervisee and the RCC counselor had compared notes that they discovered they were working with the same client and that rape was a primary issue.

The discovery prompted several decisions with respect to treatment: One, the client would be seen at the university center and not referred to a psychiatric facility. Two, I would work to replace a negative experience with a pleasant, more positive one, as Erickson had done with "Monde," a black woman, in the tape series, *The Artistry of Milton H. Erickson, M.D., Part One* (Lustig, 1975). His objective was to have "Monde" utilize some of her earlier learning of positive times, comfortable times, pleasant times, in an effort to provide a foundation for and expand her present and future endeavors. Three, the fact that the client was inclined to dissociate and go into trance states suggested that hypnosis would be a viable technique in this case.

Upon meeting the client for the first time, I perceived a grubby and unkempt young woman who, in the middle of the session, demanded hostilely, "What the fuck can you do for me, now?" To be sure, she was not the most cooperative, approachable, or trusting client one would want to meet; however, it was obvious from her previous attempts that she desperately wanted help. I assured her that I considered her concerns, whatever they were, to be important, and added:

> To coin a phrase, whatever the fuck I planned to do would be of some help to you. And now could you tell me about your most comfortable time of day, a pleasant place, your family and what you hoped to do with your life?

My remarks appeared to shock the client and precipitated a glazed look in her eyes. Then I inquired if she were familiar with any of the psychiatric hospitals in the area. She answered affirmatively in a subdued fashion. I knew I might be able to make use of her aversion to hospitals in a later session. At the close of the first session, I wondered if she had in her possession a makeup kit with perfume and a comb. I also asked about presentable clothing. She nodded, indicating that she had both. Then I asked if she might do a favor for me. Though surprised by the request, she consented. I asked if she could come to the next session having experimented with these items. Still surprised and somewhat confused, she nodded that she would.

The next session, the client's appearance was drastically improved. Her hair was combed and she wore makeup and an attractive outfit. I asked if she had seen herself in the mirror that morning? She responded that she only had taken a brief glimpse. She was encouraged to enjoy taking a deeper and fuller look when she returned to her room. This was done indirectly by asking her to check the length of the hem on the back of her skirt. Two other requests were made of her during the session. The first involved her ability to visualize. Thus, she was asked to see several pleasant memories of her early childhood. The second request dealt with the kind of childhood scratches and injuries she might have experienced growing up. Her recollections afforded me an opportunity to end this session with an anecdote of a childhood accident I had experienced which left a facial scar that was only visible upon very close inspection. This anecdote was meant to indirectly guide her associations in positive ways.

Subsequently, the client was seen for a period of five months, once a week, or on an as needed basis. Highlighting the therapy were three occurrences which proved helpful to her. The first was a moderately confrontative incident, which set the stage for doing trance work. In the course of a more in-depth discussion about the rape, the client reverted to her face scratching and head banging. She was restrained and was asked if she thought I could be of some help to her or did she think one of the local hospitals could do a better job? The client's response was to enter a mild dissociated state.

Further work around the rape episode was handled first by my prescribing the behavior. I stated, "You are about to scratch your face and bang your head." Then I hooked that statement to an eye/hand induction which included the ideas: "As you think about what I have said, while watching your hand come down slowly, you can wonder if you want to do something else like enjoying the comfort and peace of a familiar place, letting your eyelids comfortably close." After this procedure was adopted, the face scratching and head banging subsided.

The second occurrence was the client's increased interest in discussing the rape episode with her brother and sisters. This interest emerged after a trance in which she visualized and experienced the rape assault and imagined telling family members about that painful experience. Several sessions were required to assist her in working through and integrating that experience.

The third occurrence involved further trance work, where the client experienced herself working productively as a commercial artist, interacting with both men and women, and helping other women who had been through similar painful experiences. In the spring of the academic year the client terminated therapy, after indicating that she felt comfortable enough with herself to continue working on her degree.

Case Two

Mrs. C. was a 23-year-old black coed, a senior majoring in communications. She was short and stocky, and had a light complexion. In contrast to the client discussed in Case One, she was neatly attired for each session. She initially came into the counseling center during the spring quarter for vocational counseling. She was uncertain whether to remain in the area of communications. At that time, she was seen for two sessions to take vocational tests and discuss the results. The most striking aspect about these sessions was her lack of warmth and the distance she manifested.

She returned to see me again during the fall and continued through the winter quarter of the academic year. It was during this second set of visits that she revealed that she had been raped. Her revelation, however, first was preceded by a request for assistance with depression, anxiety, and inability to concentrate. In discussing these concerns, she stated that something terrible had happened to her, but that she was not able to say what it was that had taken place. Siding with the resistance, I encouraged her to reveal only what made her feel most comfortable and to take her time while doing so. She finally revealed that she had been raped on an intermittent basis by her stepfather since she was 12 years old.

The physical assaults by her stepfather took place when her mother was out of the house and continued through the end of high school. Upon her entrance into the university, her stepfather forbade her to date and frequently phoned to check up on her whereabouts. As a result of previous assaults and current harassment, she viewed herself, in her own words, as being "fucked up!" She seemed to feel that she was locked into a lifelong tragic drama over which she had little control. The "locked-in" aspect came from feeling that she could not tell anyone in her immediate family about the repeated assaults because she could not trust them. More importantly, the client could not tell her mother because her mother was indebted to the stepfather because he had assumed the responsibility for her three young children. The client's inability to discuss the assaults with anyone and the continued harassment by the stepfather served to maintain her feelings of shame and guilt. Somehow, *she* felt responsible for the terrible thing that had happened to her.

The client was encouraged to consider the possibility of using hypnosis to view the rape experience and deal with it at a pace she could control. After a few sessions of experiencing trance, the client was taught self-hypnosis and various hypnotic phenomena (e.g., arm levitation, and feelings of lightness and heaviness). During trance, it was suggested that she would enjoy learning new and different things, despite the unfortunate aspects of her life. The client was also asked, during trance, to respond through ideomotor signalling as to whether or not she could do some basic things for herself (e.g., get up in the morning, wash herself, clothe and feed herself). She was also assigned the task of visiting a local psychiatric hospital. Again, positive and negative associations could be stimulated indirectly and used to promote change.

Subsequently, trance was used to gradually have her see, feel, and hear the rape experience. She was directed to place the experience on a television screen and encouraged to change the channel, turn the volume down, or even turn it off if the scenes became too upsetting. There may have been times in the past when she was not in control of things happening to her, but *now* she could be more in control of her life! In this connection, it was suggested that her unconscious mind would help remember when she had experienced greater control in her life. Added to this suggestion were metaphors about large towering trees which had survived violent storms and lightning. It was further suggested that she let no man or woman "write her epitaph."

Prior to termination, I shared with the client some brief information about a serious injury I had experienced, an injury which could have left me crippled with a severe limp and unable to continue any athletic endeavor. I shared with the client my lingering despondency about these grim prospects. Subsequently, I was confronted by the attending physician who made the observation that healing can often be enhanced if the injured limb becomes very special to the patient. The patient has to care for, nourish, and love that injured limb. To reject it may cause partial and incomplete healing or prolong the healing process over an extended period of time. That's control! What was required of her now was to learn to care for, nourish, and love herself!

As a postscript to the work, the client returned several months later for a single session to discuss and explore how she might learn to relate to men better. She was more relaxed and congenial. I expressed my pleasure that she had been willing to trust me with her concerns. Her request was put into the context of the many ideas and understandings discussed during the earlier sessions. I stated that she would move gradually at her own pace in the direction of the things that had been discussed and the client terminated treatment.

REFERENCES

Carter, P. (1982). Rapport and integrity for Ericksonian practitioners. In J.K. Zeig (Ed.), *Ericksonian approaches to hypnosis and psychotherapy*. New York: Brunner/Mazel.

Erickson, M.H., Rossi, E.L., & Rossi, S.I. (1976). *Hypnotic realities*. New York: Halsted Press.

Freiberg, P., & Bridwell, M.V. (1976). An intervention model for rape and unwanted pregnancy. *The Counseling Psychologist, 6*, 50-53.

Heppner, P.P., & Heppner, H. (1977). Rape: Counseling the traumatized victim. *Personnel and Guidance Journal, 56*, 77-80.

Hilberman, E. (1976). *The rape victim*. New York: Basic Books.

Kamara, B.F. (1982). *Dealing with myths and bridging gaps: The black sexually assaulted victim*. Paper presented at the Tennessee Statewide Conference for Rape Prevention, Tennessee Department of Public Health, Nashville, TN.

Lustig, H.S. (1975). *The artistry of Milton H. Erickson, M.D., part one* [Videocassette] New York: Irvington.

Renshaw, D.C. (1979). Rape. *Journal of Sex Education and Therapy, 4*, 11-14.

Silver, S.M., & Stonestreet, S.D. (1978). Rape counseling: A model for sensitizing and training helpers. *Personnel and Guidance Journal*, 283-287.

Silverman, D. (1977). First do no more harm: Female rape victims and the male counselor. *American Journal of Orthopsychiatry, 47*, 91-96.

Whiston, S.K. (1981). Counseling assault victims: A loss model. *Personnel and Guidance Journal, 56*, 363-366.

Chapter 24

The Indirect Use of Directness with Super-rational Clients

Don W. Malon

Milton H. Erickson (1967a) defined "utilization" as adapting the therapeutic technique to the behavioral activities of the subject. It is clear from his work and writings that "behavioral activities" meant any expression of the person's attitudes, beliefs, thinking, feelings, and behavior, and even includes the overly rational, intellectualizing verbal style that often mitigates against successful therapy. Many therapists, especially beginners, have difficulty dealing effectively with such client behavior because their personal therapeutic style tends to be rational and direct.

Schactel (1947) employed the term "conventionalization" to describe the "siege conducted by society against human potentialities and inclinations" (p. 25). He observed that so-called civilized intelligent people tend to develop literacy and logic to an addictive degree. More recently Philip Slater (1978) applied the more cynical term "Ego Mafia" to the disproportionate authority of the ego that "seeks a world of simple mechanical processes." Slater (1978) provided a brief but accurate description of the super-rational traits belonging to the Ego Mafia:

> It loves to classify, to pigeonhole, to categorize, to analyze . . . it tends to be obsessed with avoiding mistakes. Instead of acting, and learning from the feedback it gets, it likes to plan, calculate, and predict before doing anything. (p. 18)

Virginia Satir (1972) described this type as a communication style and referred to people exhibiting this super-reasonable style as "computers." Such people are very correct and very reasonable and are preoccupied with choosing the right words so they do not make a mistake. "The sad part about this role," according to Satir, "is that it seems to represent an ideal goal for many people. Say the right words; show no feeling; don't react" (p. 68).

Erickson had the ability to avoid, deflect, and utilize the intellectualizing patterns of his patients and students. In his therapeutic discourse he was a man of few words—but those were well-chosen, descriptive, and sensory-based. This ability by the master of nonrational therapy was enough to leave a too-rational, laid back therapist like myself with a therapeutic inferiority complex!

On the one hand, "too-rational" therapists face a potential pitfall, namely that their rationality may serve to reinforce the client's defensive rationality. On the other hand, therapists who control their rationality can use it as a therapeutic resource. It took a while for me to discover that my direct, conversational style (which I had considered inappropriate for an Ericksonian therapist) could be employed to therapeutic advantage. I only happened on this discovery after some inadvertent successes with super-rational clients convinced me that I knew more than I thought I knew; I discovered that I really was not being as rational as I thought.

Rational clients were comfortable with me because I appeared to be like them. Therefore, it was easy for me to "pace" their behavior. Having established a strong rapport, I could employ various indirect means in the context of my rational-direct style to lead clients to access their latent capabilities for growth and change.

Before discussing these indirect means I will clarify why indirectness is a major orientation of Ericksonian therapy. In Ericksonian therapy, as Gilligan (1982b) points out, the unconscious is the agent of change. The therapist works to encourage unconscious processing and discourage analytical processing. Ways must be found to depotentiate conscious frames of reference, ways that cannot be resisted: direct ways tend to be resisted. As Erickson said:

> A healthy person is direct. . . . A patient himself is a person who is afraid to be direct. If you directly force patients, they are going to resist for the very same reasons that they resist directness in their life anyway. The indirectness can somehow circumvent the patient's resistance in many ways. (Beahrs, 1977, pp. 57-58)

Thus, the super-rational person only *appears* to be direct and straightforward; his personality traits are actually indirect expressions for achieving social importance and personal satisfaction. For example, the educationally privileged, pompous Major Winchester of the TV show M.A.S.H. elevates himself at the expense of those who are less educated, urbane, witty, and informed. His abilities are not the direct reflection of an integrated personality, but rather a means of avoiding intellectual honesty, sensory openness, and emotional vulnerability.

I have delineated five approaches for helping super-rational clients contend with their fear of directness. The approaches are neither exhaustive nor for use exclusively with super-rational clients. The five indirect means are: therapist "response-attentiveness," use of sensory-based language, utilization of visual representation, the seeding and utilization of dreams, and the "nonuse" of trance.

RESPONSE ATTENTIVENESS

Erickson coined the term "response-attentiveness" to refer to the ability of excellent trance subjects to become absorbed in what another person (the hypnotist) was communicating. He viewed this altered state as the common everyday trance (Erickson, Rossi, & Rossi, 1976, p. 303). It is evident, however, that Erickson viewed response-attentiveness as a desired state for both client and therapist:

> If I have any doubt about my capacity to see the important things I go into a trance. . . . It happens automatically because I start keeping close track of every movement, sign, or behavioral manifestation that could be important. (Erickson & Rossi, 1977, p. 42)

Gilligan (1982a, p. 93) referred to this state as an "externally oriented trance" in which the therapist suspends conscious processing in order to let the unconscious respond. Lest one equate this trance state with inactivity, consider Bandler and Grinder's (1979, p. 55) description of the state they call "uptime," which means to be completely in sensory experience, i.e., to be undisturbed by anything internal, such as voices, feelings, and pictures. One cannot keep sensory channels open and receptive, when attending to internal consciousness.

Response-attentiveness becomes the therapist's fundamental orientation for contacting and engaging the unconscious aspects of the client. Like the artist who requires a certain amount of objective technology in which to do creative work, a response-attentive orientation can be maintained in the context of a consciously directed interview. For example, one still can make direct use of Carkhuff's (1980) helping model or employ Bandler and Grinder's (1975a) Meta Model.

People usually experience one overriding reaction in the continued presence of super-rational individuals, namely boredom. A response-attentive attitude with all senses open permits one to inattend selectively to the boring words and behavior while responding with focused attention to the really interesting fragments of the client's presentation of self.

In other words, as I altered the way I perceived my super-rational clients, I began to notice behaviors that previously were masked by the rational defenses. Some very verbal people have wonderful voices; others have screechy voices but expressive eyes; and, so many are so physically uptight that I cannot wait to help them drop their shoulders and learn to slouch in the chair. For example, one client's ritual complaining would have been a boring irritant to me, but I liked the melodic, pouty sound of her voice. I noted her affect, independent of what she said. Her anger and sensuality were important self-expressions in spite of her obsessive self-justifications and blaming. I can be interested in such human expressions, and my interest permitted the client to tolerate my extinguishing of her intellectualizations, as it induced her to be responsive to me. Because I could maintain a positive attitude, I felt that she knew I was highly motivated to help her.

Ernest Rossi once commented to Erickson on how moved patients were by "the extremely attentive and expectant attitude" he showered on them, to which Erickson replied:

> It places the patient in a new frame of reference charged with an expectancy. . . . (Erickson & Rossi, 1981, p. 252)

USE OF SENSORY-BASED LANGUAGE

Super-rational people tend to ignore the sensory base which is the foundation of the use of language. It is as if their words are more than representations of experience; it is as if they *are* the experience. In actuality their language is poorly representative of sensory experience, since they avoid personal pronouns, use nouns without referential indices, and like to turn processes into things via nominalization (Grinder & Bandler, 1976, p. 53). For example, one of my clients, a 30-year-old language teacher named Susan described an experience on meeting a man in a bar. When she discovered he was married and on the make, it only affirmed the utter uselessness of asserting her need for male companionship. Knowing her penchant for hasty generalizing I engaged her in the following dialogue:

Therapist: What did you think of him?
Susan: His sexual pass made me mad.
Therapist: But what kind of a guy was he?
Susan: Oh, a nice guy.
Therapist: How did you feel there in that bar with him?
Susan: Okay. Better than sitting at home.
Therapist: How uncomfortable was it?
Susan: Actually, not bad; we laughed at lot.
Therapist: How much?
Susan: Most of the time.
Therapist: How long a time?
Susan: Four hours.
Therapist: Four hours! Was that like you to enjoy yourself four hours
   with a man who made you angry and disillusioned about men?
Susan: Well, actually, I can't remember when I've had such fun.

That simple interchange focused Susan's attention on the sensory
aspects of her experience in the bar and marked the turning point in
her therapy. My questions were very direct, but when therapists ask
sensory-based questions, the client does not know how important such
questions are. Susan only discovered later that week that something was
different about her. Words are a large part of our stock and trade as
therapists; but, they are also the main staple of the super-rational client.
Lankton pointed out a trade secret that should underlie therapeutic use
of language (1980):

> . . . words only have meaning insofar as they are associated to
> internal representations or sensory experience. (p. 50)

Lankton (1980, p. 58) pointed out that words can be thought of as a
series of "anchors" which stimulate or elicit various conscious and unconscious experiences in clients. Our task as therapists is to elicit the
kinds of responses that can be corrective of the client's situation. What
needs to be corrected in the typical super-rational client is the limited
connection between words and real life experience. It is not that sensory
words necessarily are absent, rather they are simply treated as abstractions. Therefore, I deliberately select from the verbalizations presented
the sensory-based, action words and phrases. I do so by slowing down
the verbal pace and changing the inflection in my voice. Then I ask a
number of sensory-based questions with the aim of indirectly putting

the client *in* that actual experience. If I judge the experience to be an important one, then I anchor it by emphasizing key words, or by a gesture or tonal shift. With Susan, for example, just the mention of the phrase "four hours in a bar" would elicit a laugh.

Of course, the use of anchoring is not limited to verbal representations. I use a common anchoring maneuver in order to "train" my rational clients to recognize the difference between thoughts and feelings. To signal and reinforce feelings, I motion with my hand and arm from the neck down, while lowering my voice tone. Conversely, I signal the presence of "headtripping" thoughts by raising my voice tone and motioning from the neck up. I agree with Lankton (1980, p. 57) that pairing of a visible gesture with a voice tone shift is often effective.

An important thing to keep in mind is Erickson's (Erickson & Rossi, 1981, p. 3) statement that, "One merely needs to know how to talk to a patient in order to secure therapeutic results." We should never lose sight of the multilevel nature of communication. What we say at one level (conscious-rational) can be understood at another (unconscious-experiential). As Erickson and Rossi (1981) have said:

> The presentation of ideas on an apparently intellectual level actually evokes psychodynamic processes that alter the listener's psychological state . . . talking about food can make us actually hungry. (p. 25)

Like my rational clients, I can "intellectualize" about things: dreams, physical sensations, memories, comfort, the mind's eye, the sound of ocean surf, making love, the glow of a fireplace, and so on. But when I talk about these things I try to access experiential responses.

UTILIZATION OF VISUAL REPRESENTATION

Many super-rational people are visual; they process information through visual imagery. However, they are so busy thinking about what they are saying that many are not consciously aware of the images playing across their mind's eye. Although in their mental processing they are accessing sensory experiences through internal visualization, they spoil the freshness of the sense experience by rationalizing and intellectualizing what they see.

Erickson (1967a, p. 9) placed special emphasis on the utilization of imagery because of its strong role as a trance phenomenon. As Bandler and Grinder (1975b) pointed out, "seeing a picture in the mind's eye is apparently a nondominant-hemisphere activity" (p. 186), therefore a means of accessing the nondominant hemisphere and bypassing the controlling activities of the dominant hemisphere.

By paying attention to "accessing cues" and predicates one can determine the presence of visual representation (Bandler & Grinder, 1979). I have been surprised at the regularity with which my rational clients see things by looking up to the left and right or by looking straight ahead with eyes defocused. If the client's predicates tend to be visual one can be more sure that his primary representational system is visual. For some, visualization is a primary means of representing experience; for others it is secondary and completely unconscious.

The most common way to utilize clients' visual representation is to make their visualizing explicit. One simply can ask in a direct manner what they are seeing as they are describing a situation. This kind of question will elicit a more concrete, sensory-based response than the more general question, "How do you see this situation?"

If someone can have a visual representation of a life experience, then they are in a position to have access to the other sensory aspects of that experience. And, with super-rational clients we are particularly interested in helping them get in touch with their feelings. This can be done by utilizing the visual mode to "overlap" to the kinesthetic (Bandler & Grinder, 1975b, p. 190).

For example, Denise, whose eyes moved up and to the left with great regularity, began to describe a visual memory of a time when she was three years old. On an airplane, she saw herself sitting next to her rather stern mother with her brother's small head resting in her lap. I asked her how she felt with her brother's head resting in her lap. She said warm and motherly. I asked her to look at her mother's face. She looked and was surprised to see a smile. I asked how she felt about her mother's smile. She had a warm, comfortable feeling of approval. By helping Denise retrieve the kinesthetic as well as the visual portion of this memory, she was able to correct a lifelong impression that she had never felt any approval from her mother.

Bandler and Grinder (1979, p. 85) claim that about 90% of what goes on in therapy involves changing the kinesthetic responses that people have to auditory and visual stimuli. Denise saw and also heard a lot of disapproving signals from her mother that left her feeling anxious and uncertain. In such cases, the therapist can overlap from visual to positive kinesthetic experience.

Not all super-rational clients conceal their feelings; some can have anxiety attacks or acute depression. Bob was a 44-year-old businessman with long-standing anxiety attacks. He had been under the care of a psychiatrist for ten years where the primary treatment was drug therapy. My co-therapist and I, working with Bob and his wife, succeeded in helping him gain control of the anxiety attacks, only to discover that his pent-up anger found expression behind the wheel of his car. He would become so outraged by speeders and tailgaiters that he would turn into an "expressway vigilante." He would chase a car until it would come to a stop, then confront the occupant with his 240-pound muscular frame and threaten to beat him up. Actually, Bob, who was a moral ex-marine, was not concerned about the dangers of his vigilantism, until one day he chased a speeding car which turned out to be carrying a prosecuting attorney and a sheriff.

That incident motivated Bob to use therapy to put an end to his vigilante behavior. Since he produced such rich imagery (as evidenced by his eye movements and his dreams), my co-therapist and I decided to utilize that visual lead system for an *in vivo* experiment. We helped Bob to become fully aware of the body sensations associated with feeling enraged. We then gave him the instruction to pull his car off the highway at his first awareness of those enraged sensations. Next, he was to look up in his mind's eye and note the images generated by those feelings. Sure enough, on his first try he got a picture of his deceased father stomping out of the house after a fight with Bob's mother, burning rubber as he pulled away in his car.

Bob needed one more experience of overlapping from kinesthetic to visual representation. As he felt the rage sensations a second time on the highway, he saw the image of a heavy metal gate being lowered in front of his car, preventing him from increasing his speed. He pulled over immediately to think about what he had just seen. He could not wait to see his therapists to find out if he was losing his mind. On hearing the story we congratulated him on the creativity of his unconscious mind and concluded it was not his mind he was losing but rather the need to be the expressway vigilante. It has been two years since he chased a car.

SEEDING AND UTILIZATION OF DREAMS

Because the unconscious is the agent of change, dreams should hold a special interest for Ericksonian therapists. Some super-rational clients rarely recall their dreams, while some have rich dreams that they recall readily even though they typically discount them. With the former I seed dreams, i.e., plant suggestions about remembering dreams. With the latter I engage their interest and curiosity in what their dreams might be trying to communicate, realizing that dream work can be a direct means of bypassing the client's conscious, resistive sets.

Seeding dreams is an elusive task because one cannot direct something to happen that must happen spontaneously. Actually seeding dreams is similar to seeding ideas, a process that Zeig (1980, p. 11) defines as, "building expectancy through small steps." There are at least three ways of building expectancy about recalling dreams: 1) by calling attention to visualization, 2) by using hypnosis, and, 3) by discussing dreams.

As Jones (1979, p. 12) observes, "dreaming is a form of thinking experienced as action." The dreamer is perceiving an active event, and visualization is the primary means of perception. If I have a client who does not recall dreams but who represents visually, then I call attention to the ability to visualize internally by having him or her experience that ability. Denise only began to report rich and meaningful dreams after she succeeded in picturing long-forgotten childhood memories. Mary, 27 years old, did not produce many memories during hypnosis, but she could see in her mind's eye one successful sexual experience that made her feel good about herself. Finally, she had a series of dreams that contained important content for helping her overcome her sexual inhibitions.

The experience of hypnosis can help to seed dreams. Hypnosis evokes non-dominant-hemisphere activity (Bandler & Grinder, 1975b). As Erickson pointed out, "trance is a time when you turn over your activities to your unconscious mind" (Note 1). The unconscious content of hypnosis might stimulate indirectly increased awareness of dream content. Furthermore, suggestions for dreaming are additional helpful stimuli if they are made while the client is in trance. Sacerdote (1967) noted that some of his patients became dreamers after one or more experiences with trance; he helped the process along by deliberately associating sleep with trance.

The third way of building expectancy about dreaming is by simply discussing the value of dreams. I discuss how dreams provide another kind of knowledge base about ourselves, and how uncluttered they are by the limitations of consciousness. I also point out how fascinating the symbolism is which serves to protect us from premature awareness. I discuss the historic importance of dreams in having generated creative and inventive ideas. I mention the amazing Temiars, a Senoi people from Malaysia, who purportedly have learned to control and change their dreams and use them as a source of learning (Garfield, 1975). Sometimes I just take the client off guard with a farewell of "Pleasant dreams," only to find later that they actually had pleasant dreams.

Working with dreams is a straightforward way to engage a client's unconscious resources. However, the traditional methods of analyzing and interpreting dreams based on Freud's work contain an inherent pitfall. Analyzing and interpreting are conscious, rational processes. Super-rational clients are too ready to analyze and interpret *ad infinitum.* In the Ericksonian tradition insight is not necessarily the aim of dream work. Sacerdote (1967) describes the more experiential outcomes which are possible:

> . . . the confabulation carried on by the patient during his dream sequence can often be a corrective intellectual and emotional experience capable of therapeutic results with a minimum of difficult-to-handle reactions, and with little need for conscious interpretations. (p. 138)

At the beginning of therapy Cindy dreamt that she was nursing her mother. In reality her mother had been a critical, possessive, and demanding parent, and no matter how hard Cindy tried she could not elicit approval for just being herself. A series of dreams over a period of months culminated in the following dream: Cindy saw her mother drowning. She reached her hand out to her mother who, although desperate to be saved, refused to take hold of it. Her mother drowned. Cindy shrugged her shoulders in mild dismay, and without guilt or remorse, thought to herself, "Oh well! I guess she didn't want to take my hand."

In keeping with an experiential view of dream work, there was no need to interpret Cindy's dream. The last dream represented an unconscious experience of separating from her mother, just as the first one indicated Cindy's inability to do so. In her last dream Cindy underwent a corrective experience. From that time on she actually enjoyed significantly greater independence from her mother.

In addition to an experiential utilization of natural dreams, I use the approaches to "redreaming" and "induced dreams" which Erickson (1967a) and Sacerdote (1967) developed. These approaches extend the dreaming process to the therapy sessions where the therapist can have more control of the process. By having the client dream the same dream or by suggesting new dreams under hypnosis the therapist helps the client feel more comfortable about dreaming as a means of self-communication and self-development. Once engaged, the super-rational client becomes intrigued by the free-associated, sensory-based content that arises spontaneously with little if any conscious, rational control.

A simple example is provided by John, a 45-year-old train yard technician who suffered from anxiety attacks which produced severe diarrhea. John had the following dream: he and a co-worker were pushing a train along a track when it suddenly began rolling downhill. However, someone inside the train applied the brake. Then, realizing that the train must be pulled from behind to get it back in the yard, John struggled to get the air-hose coupling connected so an engine could pull it. The bosses were watching, but John was not concerned about their watching. This is an interesting dream for a man who was afraid to "let loose," had diarrhea, and was afraid of what people thought of him. I saw the dream as evidencing significant growth. However, I wanted John to gain a deeper appreciation of its meaning, so I asked him to redream it.

He relaxed nicely as I reminded him of the essential content, and he described the dream, but with one additional detail: he found hamburger on the air-hose coupling which made it more difficult to connect up. Interpretively it is not difficult to understand the association between hamburger and diarrhea. However, I simply summed up for John what a productive dream it was, how strong and self-assured he felt in spite of the bosses' watching and in spite of the inexplicable interference of the hamburger. John replied with an impish grin, "Well, I think I can explain that. *I'm* the hamburger." Since then John quit being a hamburger.

THE NONUSE OF TRANCE

In his own words Erickson (1964) expressed the view that trance can be overused "for every little old thing." He was simply pointing out that when hypnosis is used indiscriminately it loses impact and the therapist loses credibility. Super-rational clients tend to be afraid of trance, yet if persuaded to try it, they can have unrealistically high expectations of its power. In other words, they will rationalize it as a technique that is supposed to produce an outcome in some way unknown to them and with no effort required from them. If the therapists cannot ease the fear or break the rationalizations, they lose credibility and therapeutic control.

The way to ease concerns about use of trance with such clients is by deciding not to use it. For an Ericksonian therapist, however, to not use trance, means to look for opportunities to use it indirectly. Trance is a naturally occurring phenomenon. As such, one can expect to find opportunities to use it by maintaining a positive relationship and staying response-attentive.

For example, after previous psychotherapy a 25-year-old physician thought she knew all she needed to know about her past which only confirmed for her how miserable it was. She was afraid of hypnosis and was not about to close her eyes much less go into a trance. Yet, at my request she did not hesitate to look up and allow her unconscious memory bank to select a childhood memory. She was surprised to remember laughing in the park with her father, dancing with her brother, and at age three taking and experimental bite out of a clump of grass. There was no need to tell her she was in a trance.

While there are many opportunities to use trance indirectly, there appear to be times when the amount of indirection needed requires a strategy of nonuse. In fact, Erickson (1980, pp. 440-441) provided a model for the nonuse of trance. In the case of the 40-year-old chronic respiratory patient for whom hypnosis had failed repeatedly, Erickson lists a number of things for this patient to do instead of being hypnotized. Here we have a masterful strategy for rationally and systematically pacing the needs of the super-rational mind through direct instructions, but with indirect suggestions for trance "logically" interspersed. Note that in four of the following instructions all the representational systems are engaged. Also, notice the simple but elegant one-two pattern in each instruction, which consists of, first, pacing the conscious resistances and, second, interspersing the indirect trance suggestions. In a slightly modified order and form the eight instructions are as follows:

1) Fixate visually upon something, any object in view—"to hold the eyes still."
2) Listen attentively to some sound, like the ticking of a clock—"to hold the ears still."
3) While paying attention to one continuous sound—it is all right to have auditory awareness of any other discernible sounds.
4) Be constantly aware of the physical self—"with attention fluctuating from one part of the body to another," from the feet to the hands or the thighs, to the cloth around the neck or shoulders, "to the hair on the head, and back again with any variation desired."
5) Random, orderly, and systematized thoughts are—to be "free to wander through the mind freely and spontaneously or even to linger."
6) At all times you should feel wide awake, alert, and attentive—"to the adequate performance of the tasks assigned."

7) Should you at any time notice any hint of hypnotic suggestion or attempt to induce a trance—you are to give full attention to the therapist and to disrupt the assigned tasks.

8) At all times you are to feel free to listen consciously to whatever the therapist is saying—although this is actually unnecessary, since the "unconscious mind will be within hearing distance of the therapist and can listen by itself, "while the conscious mind busies itself with the clock or with thoughts, or with various sounds, and whatever else of interest including the fluctuations in body awareness." (Erickson, 1980, pp. 440-441)

In effect this nontrance induction consists of a series of gracefully intricate benign double binds. I have used the instructions with variations, depending upon the person's need and my own preference at the time. One example occurred in my Family Therapy course where I spend 15 minutes each 3-hour class permitting the graduate students to experience the effects of a variety of trance and relaxation inductions. During one course 25-year-old Dan responded to every such induction with something like, "That didn't work either. I just can't relax." Knowing that Dan was a bright, analytical fellow, I suggested that he simply pay no attention to the successful trance and relaxation experiences of other students, that he had his own needs and would have to investigate his own body's responses to the inductions. Of course, like the others, he could fix his gaze on something in the room, eventually permit his eyes to close, sit motionless at his desk, listen to this week's version of an induction, and then use his rational curiosity to notice his body responses or lack of responses, and finally, he could be tolerant of his need to remain alert since it apparently held some importance for him.

In effect, I had used four of Erickson's eight directives. However, it was to no avail, until the sixth weekly induction which was a variant of Erickson's (Erickson, Rossi, & Rossi, 1976) early learning set. On opening his eyes after my delivery, Dan raised his hand, glared at me and said, "I certainly did not relax this time." To which I asked, "And what was different this time?" "When I heard the word 'child,' " he said, "I felt angry, and I am still angry. My childhood was unhappy and I never want to think of it again." I simply assured Dan that his response to this induction was immediate and real, because I could see that he was angry. His alertness had paid off; he had good reason not to relax.

Three weeks later Dan wrote the following in his course journal:

> In all the years I can remember I have probably dreamed six times per year. Now I dream every night in vivid color. For 16 years I

have hated children. Now I am bothered frequently by a desire to have a child. Perhaps these major changes occurred simultaneously and coincidentally with relaxation exercises and in reality are in no way causally related. However, I have no good explanation of why, all of a sudden, they have occurred. I am not ready to say hypnosis is responsible, but I would like your comments on this.

It is always amazing to me how a person can experience what Erickson (1980, p. 441) termed "the reorganization of unconscious thinking taking place without conscious awareness." That is exactly what happened to Dan. I told him that the culprit was his unconscious mind and not hypnosis. If I had tried to hypnotize Dan his analytical, super-alertness would have prevented him from doing any unconscious work. Not trying to hypnotize him prevented him from consciously interfering with his potential for unconscious reorganization.

CONCLUSIONS

In describing the five approaches for dealing with super-rational clients I suggested some indirect means of bypassing these clients' fears of being direct, and showed that the more rational-direct therapists can utilize their own and their clients' tendencies for directness in implementing these approaches. The five approaches—therapist response-attentiveness, use of sensory-based language, utilization of visual representation, the seeding and utilization of dreams, and the nonuse of trance—are not exhaustive. However, they provide the requisite variety (cf. Bandler & Grinder, 1979, p. 74) for dealing therapeutically with most super-rational clients.

The approaches may be employed singly or in combination. The first two are the most essential and provide the widest applicability, because they have the potential for shaping the entire context of therapy. The response-attentive and sensory-based orientations are not independent of each other nor of the other three approaches, but rather permeate and enhance the use of other approaches. They are what makes it possible to "get a fix" on the difficult-to-engage super-rational client and hold him in therapy. After establishing that fix other approaches and techniques can help direct the course of treatment.

REFERENCE NOTE

1. Seminar with Dr. Erickson, August, 1978.

REFERENCES

Bandler, R., & Grinder, J. (1975a). *The structure of magic I.* Palo Alto: Science & Behavior Books.

Bandler, R., & Grinder, J. (1975b). *Patterns of the hypnotic techniques of Milton H. Erickson, M.D.,* (Vol. 1). Cupertino, CA: Meta Publications.

Bandler, R., & Grinder, J. (1979). *Frogs into princes.* Moab, UT: Real People Press.

Beahrs, J.O. (1977). Integrating Erickson's approach. *American Journal of Clinical Hypnosis, 20,* 55-68.

Carkhuff, R.R. (1980). *The art of helping IV.* Amherst, MA: Human Resources Development Press.

Erickson, M.H. (1964). *General considerations in hypnosis* [Audiotape]. The Milton H. Erickson Classic Cassette Series, American Society of Clinical Hypnosis Meeting, San Francisco.

Erickson, M.H. (1967a). Deep hypnosis and its induction. In J. Haley (Ed.), *Advanced techniques of hypnosis and therapy.* New York: Grune & Stratton.

Erickson, M.H. (1967b). Further techniques of hypnosis—Utilization techniques. In J. Haley (Ed.), *Advanced techniques of hypnosis and therapy.* New York: Grune & Stratton.

Erickson, M.H. (1980). Innovative hypnotherapy. In E.L. Rossi (Ed.), *The collected papers of Milton H. Erickson,* (Vol. 4). New York: Irvington.

Erickson, M.H., & Rossi, E.L. (1977). Autohypnotic experiences of Milton H. Erickson. *American Journal of Clinical Hypnosis, 20,* 36-54.

Erickson, M.H., & Rossi, E.L. (1981). *Experiencing hypnosis.* New York: Irvington.

Erickson, M.H., Rossi, E.L., & Rossi, S.I. (1976). *Hypnotic realities.* New York: Irvington.

Garfield, P. *Creative dreaming.* (1975). New York: Simon and Schuster.

Gilligan, S.G. (1982a). Ericksonian approaches to clinical hypnosis. In J. Zeig (Ed.), *Ericksonian approaches to hypnosis and psychotherapy.* New York: Brunner/Mazel.

Gilligan, S. (1982b). *The unconscious as the major agent of change.* [*Audiotape*]. Seminar on Ericksonian Approaches to Hypnosis and Psychotherapy, Dallas.

Grinder, J., & Bandler, R. (1976). *The structure of magic II.* Palo Alto: Science & Behavior Books.

Jones, R. (1979). *The dream poet.* Boston: G.K. Hall.

Lankton, S. (1980). *Practical magic: A translation of basic neuro-linguistic programming into clinical psychotherapy.* Cupertino, CA: Meta Publications.

Sacerdote, P. (1967). *Induced dreams.* Brooklyn, NY: Theo. Gaus.

Satir, V. (1972). *Peoplemaking.* Palo Alto: Science & Behavior Books.

Schactel, E. (1947). On memory and childhood amnesia. *Psychiatry, 10,* 1-26.

Slater, P. (1978). The Ego-Mafia and American social character. *Social Policy, 9,* 15-20.

Zeig, J. (1980). *A teaching seminar with Milton H. Erickson.* New York: Brunner/Mazel.

Chapter 25

Confrontation in Psychotherapy

O. Spurgeon English

There are patients for whom empathy, emotional support, interpretation or confrontation are not sufficient in themselves to create involvement of patient and therapist toward a successful outcome. They also need a strong and *continuous confrontation*, often presented in the indirect manner at which Milton Erickson was so expert; otherwise, they do not relate to therapy in a way that will result in therapeutic movement of any kind, much less therapeutic success. The cooperation of spouse, family and sometimes others may be necessary to achieve results or prevent flight from treatment.

These patients include the anxious, the phobic, and especially the angry. Others are the passive, unmotivated characters, usually between the ages of 15 and 30. Also included are patients who are not reflective or curious people and who are insensitive to nuances of interpersonal relations. In fact, they may possess what amounts to an almost delusional fixation that they are not worth anything, are never going to get well, and are not liked by anyone. They consider life meaningless, if not downright malicious. Since resistance to change is one of the most crucial problems we encounter in therapy, we must pursue further knowledge of its presence and devise methods of reducing and eliminating it, so patients may be freed to proceed to the desirable goal of symptom removal.

Resistance is minimized when patients are susceptible or responsive to reward for more mature behavior. Reward and appreciation feel good to most people. Approval and praise promote growth and conformity and adaptation toward better behavior. But the puzzling and frustrating aspect of resistance is that patients engage in errant behavior which results in personal detriment as well as in the exasperation of, and sometimes punishment by, those around him. There has to be some reward in this behavior, but whence is coming the reward? It may be from within, or from some gratification they receive from the irritation of others.

The repetition of acts or even thoughts which coincide with the pleasure principle, as elucidated by Freud, seems easy to understand. The best educational principles as well as the principle involved in animal training, use reward to promote change, but exceptions to this rather simple principle tax the thinking as well as the patience of educators and therapists. Resistance to change is rarely, if ever, responsive to direct reason, logic, suggestion or command. The thinking processes of the patient must be reached more indirectly and hence, we must seek the help of the more indirect communication so prevalent in Ericksonian techniques.

All resistance is basically a reluctance or refusal to utilize the ego functions toward the widest and most varied utilization of self personally as well as in extension to the lives of others. To put it another way, people hold onto fears, hates, grudges, angers, various forms of helplessness and depression, phobic activities, somatic symptoms, and even delusions and hallucinations as the best way they know of dealing with a world they feel they cannot live in productively and happily.

An important question is why these forms of adaptation are used when friendliness, altruism and a variety of other adaptations receive so much more approval from the environment. The answer seems obvious. Whatever the symptom picture, or whatever form the personality takes, it is the best that patients were able to learn in the environment in which they grew and developed. When they become old enough to note a better adaptation being practiced around them, they discover they were so indoctrinated in the one they had previously learned, and were so impressed with their teachers, that they are convinced they are incapable of learning a better way of meeting life and the people in it. Moreover, the symptoms have served them so well to date that they would feel it foolhardy to change their behavior to a way that would seem strange and which might bring rebuff, ridicule, misunderstanding and perhaps exploitation. In short, they would like to change but they have no power within themselves to get the process underway.

THE DEPTH OR STRENGTH OF RESISTANCE

Patients vary in the power that resistance to change exerts. In some people, there is little resistance to change. They possess a willingness to adapt and learn new ways; they show this even as young children as they socialize well in school. They find rewards in new experience, adopt more mature attitudes as they develop, and seek new growth experiences daily. Others show much resistance to change and are sometimes labeled loners, misfits, obnoxious. They retain earlier learned patterns of behavior in preference to choosing to adopt the pattern of success seen around them—whether it be classroom success, social success, vocational success—which could bring about greater acceptance. They feel safe in restricted and limited expression of themselves and feel uncomfortable in trying new endeavors. Occasionally, if sufficiently uncomfortable, they may be helped by friends to expand themselves, especially if they request assistance. But if, in addition to experiencing anxiety, they are self-righteous in their isolation, the combination of anxiety and narcissistic pride hardens into a fixation of personality pattern which makes therapy difficult.

These people are rarely found in treatment during their early years. The school system, including college, rarely makes the demands for adaptability that are made by the work world or marriage. These two social systems, i.e., job and marriage, make many more demands for flexibility and adaptation, and the pressures of either one or both are what usually force individuals into our offices.

A form of resistance exists in those who live in a disorderly way and are unable to keep up in their work. They neglect their letters, their records, their checkbooks, their papers, and deplore their disordered desk and home. After they have been helped to recall memories of overindulgence at home or feelings of rebellion against overstrictness and censure in childhood, they still continue their delinquent pattern of behavior. They could talk indefinitely about their procrastination and anguish over it. A better way to live is to change thinking and behavior to gratify more facets of the ego, and, at the same time, bring more approval from the environment. This is what these patients cannot see at first, and they must be shown how change can occur.

Obviously, Erickson had a keen awareness of patients with strong resistance. Efforts to understand what we call Ericksonian technique take into account his enormous knowledge of human nature, his serious and confident manner, his reputation, his presence, his ability to give orders in a way that commanded attention and obedience, and his desire to help. It takes time and experience to acquire these traits and we can come one step closer to them with every case we treat.

Erickson did not hesitate to ask things of his patients in the course of helping them solve problems. In the beginning of my career, I did not ask much of patients. I was trained to ask them only to free associate, and with only a few exceptions, this was not asking very much. Considering the time expended, it did not accomplish very much. I soon began to change this attitude in spite of my indoctrination, but it took a long time to lose the conviction that resistance to change would dissolve with enough free association activity. As time went on, I became more of a teacher but I still remained too passive about whether patients made use of what I taught. I left patients too free to either choose the road to healthier functioning or to remain as they were. To do otherwise was being "too directive" or "too coercive" to be a good therapist. I allowed patients too much choice about the renunciation symptoms—almost like a surgeon who said the patient had a choice in leaving his diseased appendix untreated. I was following a democratic procedure which did not always work to the patients' benefit.

The first exponents of hypnotherapy were too peremptory and demanding for my personality, and I saw that they often failed and aroused more resistance. Erickson's permissive approach, e.g., "Would you like to go into a trance now or later," and, "Your unconscious is your friend and knows more than you and will help you with my assistance," made me interested to study and know more of his way.

CASE STUDIES

Case One

A 40-year-old divorced woman with three children developed lower back pain. She was in the midst of trying circumstances: her working conditions were uncongenial; her eldest child, a daughter, became incorrigible and disruptive and left home; and her live-in male friend was depressed and irrascible. She was given leave from work for a time. Her orthopedist assured her she had no disc protrusion.

When the time came to return to work, she was still feeling pain and did not wish to go back, even though she was adequately mobile for work at home. Her orthopedist reassured her that there was no organic pathology and offered the diagnosis that her discomfort and pain were of psychosomatic origin. She greatly resisted this possibility.

In a state of relaxation, she revealed two fears regarding a return to work. The first was that she had overheard the orthopedist say she might have "bulging discs" even though there was no pressure on her nerves. So she feared work might make these "bulging discs" into severe impingement on the spinal roots. The second fear was that her employer stated he wanted her to get treatment before she returned. She felt she had no evidence of having been treated; she thought she had only been examined and told she was psychosomatic. I gave her assurance that she need not fear further harm from work, for she had been susceptible to back pain all her adult life, but I agreed that she could avoid any possible damage with a support brace, and with this she would satisfy her employer by having had treatment. I wrote a letter to her orthopedist explaining her dilemma and asking his cooperation in obtaining back support. Subsequently, her resistance to returning to work was overcome.

A therapist must ascertain the problem and offer an acceptable solution. Erickson communicated to the patient the messages: "Do something new to show to yourself that you possess the ability to alter your traditional pattern of behavior," and, "Do something in a different way in order that you lose your pain and suffering or change the behavior that is giving you so much trouble for yourself and others around you." In this way, Erickson met resistance head on, and did not listen indefinitely to repetitious complaining without requiring some action.

Case Two

A 38-year-old woman with two teenage sons complained of her husband's several delinquencies. He drank, was unfaithful, had served time for theft and was unproductive in helping her to support the family. The family interaction deteriorated into mutual recriminations. She nagged, for which he condemned her, and she condemned him for his poor performance and disinterest in her. She had been ambivalent about taking him back after a separation in which he had been involved with another woman, but did so anyway and continued to reproach him for it. In their arguments, he would depict her as "the big angry cat" and himself as "a little mouse," defenseless against her destructiveness.

She was told that for 30 days she was to make no criticism and no reproach and wait to see what his response would be. If his response was positive, then she would know three things: 1) that she, being the stronger of the two, could change; 2) whether he was capable of response to her warmth and acceptance; and 3) if the marriage could be made a better one or whether she preferred to dissolve it and go alone.

After 30 days, she demonstrated her strength to be kind, and he responded with more help and consideration. They continued to improve in their marriage. It seemed clear that nothing would have occurred unless or until she was strongly confronted to make a change herself since she was the stronger and more contentious one of the pair.

Case Three

A single man of 32 was depressed and discouraged in his work, and never had any ability to enjoy the opposite sex. He dated girls at times and they liked him, but he could not become intellectually, emotionally or sexually intimate with them. He told them quite bluntly he did not care about them and advised them to seek a more lively and caring man. Two of them gave up after a year, but a third one, instead of quitting, scolded him for being so cold and conceited and stingy with himself.

It was decided her criticism could be of help. I told him that he must tell her he was seeing a psychiatrist in order to let her know he was trying to change but that he was afraid to reveal an important personal side of himself to her. I felt she could do something with this information that would be helpful to him. Much against his nature, he told her. She responded well, taking his admission to be a mark of sincerity rather than shallowness. From that time on, they became more genuine friends. I am hoping to see her with him in the near future and have her help in making him a more open and real person, able to see and feel the enjoyment of living with others.

SUMMARY

Erickson's methods and philosophy of treatment help me to confront the life-negating facets in the human personality in a more rapid, forceful way. Therapists in the past have listened too long and confronted too little. Once people develop symptoms which are faulty ways of meeting life and dealing with it, they seem to have a vested interest in retaining and maintaining the unsatisfactory pattern. Instead of listening and tacitly condoning, we should act as resourcefully as possible to eliminate resistance. The ego is, in most instances, more resourceful and durable than we have believed and supported.

PART VI

Alcoholism

Effecting change in alcoholics is a difficult problem for psychotherapists. The powerful communication techniques espoused by Milton Erickson may be especially valuable in this area where traditional psychotherapy often shows limited success.

Christopher J. Beletsis conducts a practice of psychotherapy in San Diego. He earned his Master's degree in psychology from International College and often conducts training programs through the Meta Institute in San Diego. Beletsis describes four general phases of an Ericksonian approach and indicates how they can be used with alcoholics.

John D. Lovern, Ph.D., earned his degree in clinical psychology at the University of Connecticut in Storrs. He is a clinical psychologist at the Chemical Dependency Recovery Complex at San Pedro Peninsula Hospital in California. Lovern served as an assistant professor of psychiatry at Loma Linda University School of Medicine. He has published and presented at professional meetings, especially on the topic of alcoholism.

Lovern discusses the approaches that a number of theorists have had to alcoholism and compares these ideas to Erickson's perspective on the process of change. Recovery from alcoholism can entail a "conversion experience" and Ericksonian techniques can be facilitative.

Chapter 26

An Ericksonian Approach in the Treatment of Alcoholism

Christopher J. Beletsis

Alcoholism is recognized as one of today's leading mental health problems affecting one in every eleven adults (Royce, 1981). It is the third leading cause of death in the U.S. behind cancer and heart disease. Alcoholism is a progressive problem, often leading to deterioration of many parts of an alcoholic's life, including health, personal relationships, career, and self-esteem. It is evident that there is a need for the development of more effective therapeutic treatment strategies.

Alcoholics share several characteristics which are central issues in the treatment of alcoholism, such as the need to control certain aspects of their experience, and progressive social and emotional difficulties. Denial is the major defense which allows the problem to continue. These issues are common to many individuals; however, alcoholics are uniquely different because of the exaggerated and extreme degree to which the issues progress.

Many medical and mental health professionals consider the alcoholic difficult and "resistant" to work with; most treatment modalities have a low success rate. Failure frequently has been blamed on the alcoholic for being unmotivated or hidden within the web of denial or unwilling to adapt to the particular mode of treatment being used.

The purpose of this chapter is to present a conceptual model for treatment of alcoholism based on Erickson's approach to hypnosis and psychotherapy. Four phases of treatment are identified and information presented on how the utilization technique, a distinguishing characteristic of the Ericksonian approach, can be used uniquely in each phase of treatment. Special clinical issues relevant to alcoholism are also discussed in this chapter, such as when not to use hypnosis, permissive vs. confrontive approaches, and handling relapses and crises.

I should mention at the outset that I confine my discussion to how the Ericksonian approach can be used with individuals. This is not to say that group therapy, family therapy and Alcoholics Anonymous are not valuable, but rather that the Ericksonian approach with individuals can complement and enhance these approaches.

PHASES OF TREATMENT

In one case, Erickson described his therapy with an alcoholic man where there was a history of alcoholism in both his family and his wife's family of origin. The alcoholic client worked on a newspaper where alcohol use was an occupational hazard. At one point in therapy, Erickson told the man:

> All right, you want me to do something about it—with that history. Now, the thing I'm going to suggest to you won't seem the right thing. You go out to The Botanical Gardens. You look at all the cacti there and marvel at cacti that can survive three years without water, without rain. And do a lot of thinking. (Rosen, 1982, p. 80)

In discussing his unique approach, Erickson said, ". . . you ought to look at your patient to figure out what kind of a man he is—or woman—then deal with the patient in a way that fits his or her problem, his or her unique problem" (Rosen, 1982, p. 81).

After reading case studies such as this one, I "do a lot of thinking" about why Erickson's therapeutic strategy was successful. My approach to treatment of alcoholics, based on his techniques, can be conceptualized in terms of four primary phases of treatment: 1) Setting the Context (e.g., rapport, trust, securing agreements and motivation); 2) Destabilizing the System (e.g., confusion, exaggeration and interruption); 3) Transforming the System (e.g., hypnotherapy, metaphor, reframing and developing resources); and 4) Consolidating the Changes (e.g., homework assignments, future pacing, self-hypnosis, and self-appreciation) (Carter & Gilligan, personal communication, 1978).

These phases of treatment do not always occur in this order. The steps frequently overlap, and it is more important that the therapist adapt the treatment to the ongoing needs of the client than follow the steps in the "right" order. However, generally it is important to complete steps one and two prior to moving on to steps three and four. Additionally, as far as techniques are concerned, strategies discussed in one phase of treatment may be just as useful in other phases of treatment.

SETTING THE CONTEXT

In this initial stage of treatment the therapist's primary goals with the alcoholic client are to develop rapport and trust, gather information, secure therapeutic agreements and develop the client's inner motivation to change. The intention of this treatment phase is to create an environment in which therapeutic change can most easily take place.

It is important for the therapist to be willing and able to adapt his communication and therapeutic strategies to meet the ongoing needs of the unique individual in treatment, rather than expecting the individual to fit into the treatment being offered. In this "utilization approach," the therapist accepts and utilizes the client's "own attitudes, thinking, feeling, and behavior, as well as . . . aspects of the reality situation" (Haley, 1967, p. 50).

This process is referred to as "pacing and leading" by Bandler and Grinder (1975), who emphasize pacing and leading the client's directly observable behaviors. Erickson clearly accepted and utilized the client's ongoing behavior to initiate rapport and therapy, and, in addition, he accepted and utilized complex psychological aspects of the client's non-observable experience.

Many aspects of the alcoholic's unique reality may be utilized by the therapist to formulate effective communication and therapeutic strategies. Therefore, it is useful for the therapist to gather information about the clients' drinking patterns (e.g., how long have they been drinking, how often, what, with whom?), other problems (e.g., familial, social, occupational, health, emotional), beliefs about their problems as well as what they have been told by others, resources (hobbies, interests or skills which will assist in the process of change), goals, and finally any experiences they want to avoid in the future. Information about personal history, including childhood and traumatic experiences, is also useful. Rather than disregarding or ignoring this information when it seems distorted or untrue, the therapist should accept this as valuable information about the client's own beliefs and perceptions. As denial decreases, the alcoholic's accuracy in self-perception increases.

Utilizing the client's drinking patterns and resources in alcohol treatment is well illustrated in a case study of Erickson's concerning a medically retired traffic officer who indicated that he wanted help because he drank too much, and his blood pressure was too high (Rosen, 1982, pp. 149-150). He had been a "good cop" for fifteen years who "always went by the book." He wanted to quit drinking and eat sensibly.

Erickson's therapeutic strategy was to have him walk a mile for each pack of cigarettes, a mile to the store to buy food for one meal, and a mile between each drink. Erickson accepted his need to eat, drink and smoke, making no attempts to restrict or control the man's substance abuse. Instead he gave him the opportunity to walk, to get in better shape, and to recognize that his behavior was voluntary.

In contrast to other treatment approaches, Erickson did not focus directly on whether the client was going to stop drinking; instead, he evoked and utilized the client's past discipline of being a good cop who always followed the book, and utilized it in his therapeutic strategy. Much of the therapy focused on developing and reassociating the client's own inner resources with his current goals. Recognizing the man's willingness to follow orders, Erickson offered a solution which accepted the client's desire to drink alcohol and smoke, but he altered the nature of how the client did them. Had the solution more directly threatened the alcoholic's drinking, it most likely would have been rejected.

Securing Agreements and Developing Motivation

One particularly important objective in treating the alcoholic is developing motivation to change. Motivation is such a pivotal aspect of the therapeutic process that it can make or break the success of therapy. It involves bringing clients to the point where they undeniably experience the desire to change and do something to make life work more effectively.

Clients must be internally motivated to change for their own welfare, rather than changing for some external force such as a family member, friend or the legal system. There are two kinds of motivation which may be developed and used in the therapeutic process.

Negative motivation occurs when an individual wants to avoid some experience and recognizes that the consequences of continued drinking are very high (e.g., dying, breakup of the family, loss of employment). Positive motivation occurs when an individual wants to move towards some experience (e.g., better health, a satisfying relationship, peace).

When simply given a solution to their problems without first being motivated to accept it, alcoholics will typically either reject it immediately and argue about it or accept the solution and agree with it but never act upon it. The individual must first deeply acknowledge personal need for change and agree to participate fully in the therapeutic process. The utilization approach, effective especially for working with resistant clients, consists of acknowledging and accepting the client's reality, then utilizing it to initiate a change.

Questions can be used to develop motivation in the following way. In a meaningful and intense fashion, I said to one alcoholic client,

> You've come here to get some help from me. You've been drinking for a long time and have had some fun, but it has also resulted in several problems. Your health is failing, sometimes you feel lonely, you may lose your job, and you enjoy a good drink. You've mentioned that you would like to develop some changes and resume dancing again. Things can be different. You may want to disagree with me on a number of points, but I believe you are here because you realize something has to change, aren't you? Yes or no? Your life isn't working for you, is it? Yes or no?

These were statements which the client was already in agreement with regarding existing positive motivation (e.g., you would like to develop some changes) and negative motivation (e.g., you may lose your job). I simply reflected the client's experience, focusing on important emotional topics and then asking pointed, direct questions which could bring the client to a decision. Any denial or disagreements the client might have were acknowledged by saying, "You may disagree with me on a number of points." Thus this technique supported all opposing aspects of the client's experience as valid, which reduced his defensiveness and need for denial and rationalization.

Challenges are another way to increase the alcoholic's involvement in the therapeutic process. To achieve this, the therapist brings up a topic or issue possibly important to therapy and then breaks it off by saying, "You probably wouldn't be interested in that," or "I'll bet you couldn't do that." Thus, first one builds up the client's interest in some topic, and then one changes the topic or distracts from it. This sparks the client's interest and then frustrates it. The client's resulting response potential assists him or her in being the driving force. For example, I developed one alcoholic's interest in learning how to go into trance by saying,

> Life has been difficult for you lately. In trance you really could develop changes that you've been avoiding for a long time, resolve old feelings, and learn effective ways to handle your problems. It's too bad you're not ready to do that yet.

Then I began talking about something else, which allowed the client's own interest and motivation to develop.

In discussing the motivation of a particular client Erickson commented that,

> Usually when he came to see me he would try to proudly tell me of his progress, but I would make disparaging remarks and accuse him of laziness and giving up too soon. . . . I continued to be unkind in all my remarks goading him into further effort. When he was in trance, I was very gentle. . . . (Rossi, 1980, p. 326)

In this example, Erickson challenged the conscious mind and then balanced his approach by supporting the unconscious mind. In these examples the client's own inner experience is accessed and utilized in order to develop motivation.

Behavioral tasks can be used to effectively confront the alcoholic with the reality of his situation. In the beginning of treatment, alcoholics often believe that they can control their drinking and that drinking is not the problem. Any attempt to convince them otherwise is usually unsuccessful. Demonstrating to clients from their own experience their inability to control drinking can be powerful and persuasive.

With one alcoholic client, I accepted and utilized his beliefs regarding his drinking and requested that he predict how many and what kind of drinks he would have each day for the next two weeks. Since he claimed he could control his drinking, I assumed there would be a few days during which he would not drink at all. He agreed to this task. After writing his predictions on a piece of paper, we set an appointment for the following week. He returned admitting both his inability to keep his agreement and the fact that he was alcoholic and needed help.

An alcoholic is usually unsuccessful at this assignment to control drinking and the result is undeniable. When the individual finally recognizes and accepts that he is alcoholic, then the therapist can secure an agreement that sobriety is a primary goal of treatment. Otherwise the alcoholic's struggle for control may vacillate for long periods of time without therapeutic progress.

One of Erickson's greatest contributions to the field of hypnosis is the use of indirect communication and metaphor. The greater the client's resistance and conscious interference to change, the more the hypnotherapist will find indirect communication and metaphor to be an effective therapeutic strategy. These techniques distract the conscious mind, access and utilize the unconscious mind and elicit the client's own associations and experiences (Gilligan, 1981).

The following guidelines are helpful in using metaphor to increase the client's motivation. The first part of the story must sufficiently acknowledge the alcoholic's problems yet be dissimilar enough so that the client is not sure the story is about him (e.g., stories about other clients with similar problems, characters in movies). In the second stage of the story, the therapist exaggerates and intensifies the client's experience of his problems, especially the emotional aspects, such as frustration, sadness, or hopelessness. As the client's discomfort increases he or she will eventually become motivated to reduce it. In the final stage of the story this motivation is utilized to access and develop the client's own possible resolutions to his problems.

In order to ensure sufficient motivation, the therapist may want to use several metaphors which access and intensify the alcoholic's problems and feelings but do not lead to any resolution (e.g., stories which have bad or tragic endings or simply lead to failure). By utilizing the client's own associations he recognizes that his life is not working and the problem must be dealt with. Once the alcoholic is motivated, additional stories may be offered which follow the above structure but focus increasingly on accessing and developing new choices, attitudes, and behaviors. Again the importance of utilizing the client's reality and ongoing processes cannot be overemphasized, therefore the content of the stories should be absorbing and interesting and incorporate the client's ongoing responses to the story.

The interpersonal relationship between the therapist and client is of utmost importance. The primary goal of accepting and utilizing the client's reality is to increase the therapist's sensitivity to the client's ongoing needs in order to facilitate change. In the framework of Ericksonian hypnotherapy, "resistance" signals a lack of utilization.

DESTABILIZING THE SYSTEM

Erickson often spoke about the value of destabilizing an individual's or family's system, believing that once existing patterns have been destabilized the system is prepared to accept and develop alternative patterns. Exaggeration and interruption techniques, particularly effective for destabilizing the alcoholic's system, are not used by many therapists because the techniques seem incongruent with therapeutic goals.

Erickson illustrates these techniques in the case of a couple who went to him for therapy (Haley, 1973, pp. 238-240). The wife was a severe alcoholic. She drank secretly, hid her bottle, and was always drunk by the time her husband returned home from work. Each evening they argued intensely as he searched the house for the bottle. The wife enjoyed gardening and found pleasure in drinking whiskey secretly. The husband enjoyed simply relaxing and reading all weekend. Much to the couple's surprise, Erickson utilized their reality by requesting that they continue to do exactly as they were doing. She was to keep hiding the bottle and he was to search for it. If he was unable to find it, then "she was entitled to empty it the next day." They had already been doing this for 12 years, but by encouraging their usual pattern Erickson changed it; he "robbed" her of the privilege of hiding the bottle secretly. Erickson's prescription exaggerated their patterns and destabilized and changed the system. Her behavior was no longer secret, resistant or pleasurable.

Erickson continued in this fashion, next destabilizing their typical weekend behavior which had become boring and was marked by avoidance of each other. He had them buy a camper and go fishing for the weekend, which they said they hated. However, they ended up loving camping. After encouraging and amplifying a small change in the system, Erickson then built on the small change to develop larger ones which then established new patterns.

Exaggerating the Patterns

To exaggerate the existing patterns the therapist simply has the client not only keep doing what he is doing but do it a little more. As illustrated in the above case, prescribing the symptom effectively makes maladaptive patterns obvious and redefines "resistant" behavior as cooperative. This is sometimes confusing or disorienting for the alcoholic because previously everyone has attempted to prevent or get rid of the behavior, and now it is not only being completely accepted, but also prescribed. The alcoholic has become proficient at defending or denying his behaviors and problems, but has not developed strategies for dealing with the exaggeration of his symptoms.

Interruption

To interrupt the alcoholic's existing patterns, the therapist causes a slight change or deviation in the pattern. In the above example, the couple was asked to keep doing what they were doing, but to do it a little differently than they were accustomed to and under new circumstances. An alternative is to have the client drink a different kind of alcohol, at different times, in different locations, or with different people.

Interruption and exaggeration techniques often disorient the client. However, they must be utilized so that the client feels trusting and supported in the process of changing; these techniques need to be balanced with a supportive approach. Thus, the therapist's integrity is crucial. When the therapist effectively creates instability in the system, a context is created which may be used to transform the system therapeutically.

TRANSFORMING THE SYSTEM

Alcoholics have a tendency to adhere rigidly to the existing rules and patterns of their system and to repeat solutions in order to maintain the system's homeostasis. Relatively few rules govern many aspects of behavior and communication. For alcoholics the attempted solution to problems is to drink alcohol. Once this system has been destabilized, a variety of hypnotherapeutic procedures, such as metaphor, age regression, pseudo-orientation in time, reframing, and homework assignments may be utilized to transform the existing rules and patterns of behavior in the system. Several points particularly relevant to alcoholism will be noted below.

Underlying this treatment approach is the recognition that drinking and abusing alcohol are functional behaviors within the unique context of the individual's life situation. The meaning and function of drinking are unique to each individual. Alcoholics often use alcohol to control their feelings (e.g., to repress anger, resentment, or physical or mental pain, or to access confidence, relaxation or rage) and to control family and friends. They experience themselves as being unable to have (or let go of) control without the use of alcohol. Because of alcohol's contextual functionalism, treatment must be multidimensional, assisting the alcoholic to remain sober while simultaneously developing other changes which will support a sober lifestyle, e.g., behavioral and attitudinal changes, increased self-esteem, better health, skill development, and appropriate emotional expression. Sobriety is a primary goal of treatment, but is not the end point or the only goal of therapy.

Speaking about transformation as a learning process, Erickson noted that, "The chronic alcoholic can be induced by direct suggestion to correct his habits temporarily, but not until he goes through the inner process of reassociating and reorganizing his experiential life can effective results occur" (Rossi, 1980, p. 39). This treatment program is characterized by the belief that individuals already have within themselves the necessary resources to transform their experience, and that these resources extend far beyond the limits clients impose upon themselves.

Case Example

A woman came to treatment reporting that she had been alcoholic for more than 30 years, since age 15. Ann had been to many therapists and doctors, followed everything they said, but always found a way to sabotage things. Confrontational approaches had been tried, but resulted in her feeling terrible. Supportive approaches, such as Alcoholics Anonymous, were also unsuccessful. She had an unpleasant childhood and had no memories of feeling happy or valuable. At the time of our meeting, her daily activities included nothing more than drinking, worrying about her children, and reading magazines. She lived an isolated life, was afraid of people, felt depressed, worthless, and lonely, and was overweight. She believed no one would want to talk to her.

Ann explained that she drank alcohol to relax, relieve boredom, cope with emotional problems, communicate in social situations, and block out her past. She believed alcohol had served her well for these purposes, and I wasn't about to give her an argument. Ann had a wealth of resources and interests from which she had become dissociated. She was friendly, creative and intelligent, had studied and enjoyed interior design, loved working with children, and enjoyed going to church, but had stopped these activities due to alcoholism.

I utilized her unique needs by developing a homework assignment which increased her ability to be more associated with herself and others. I had her go to see *Arthur*, a movie about a wealthy alcoholic, and to think deeply about the ways in which she was different from and similar to the title character. He was a character she could identify with and seeing the film was an insightful and emotional experience. This helped her to be more aware of herself and began to get her in the habit of doing new activities around people, while utilizing her need to remain in a safe situation.

Another goal was to apply her increasing self-awareness and communication skills to improving her social life. I had Ann begin to go to church again and pay close attention to the feelings that came up and the ways that she attempted to avoid going to church. At first she objected, saying that she no longer liked the pastor. Following the utilization approach, I told her that was absolutely fine, that she should exercise her right to the quality of experience she wanted and try different churches. After attending other churches, she realized that she liked her old church best and returned there, helping with the children at Sunday school. For this client, attendance at church and sobriety were deeply connected.

A third goal was to help her learn from and integrate past experiences which, up until that time, had been the source of a great deal of pain and depression. Metaphor and age regression were used extensively to assist Ann in exploring her early relationships with her mother and father from an adult perspective. After hating her parents for years, she was able to realize how unhappy they had been. She forgave her mother and recognized some of their similarities, such as loving animals and traveling. She also felt the love her father had given her and remembered some of the good times they had together. By resolving her relationship with her parents, she was able to let go of many old programs they had given her, e.g., "You're hopeless." "Who will want you anyway?" "You are never good enough." They could now be replaced with supportive and appreciative programs. During the latter part of treatment, she worked with problem teenagers in a halfway house, worked for an interior design business, and eventually co-led a group for adults with alcohol problems at her church.

These simplified examples illustrate how the changes and progress she made were built upon and utilized to develop further changes. Subsequent follow-up indicated that this client was still sober after one year, with no relapses during that time.

CONSOLIDATING AND INTEGRATING THE CHANGES

Many new behaviors and psychological changes take place throughout the therapeutic process and are evident in the therapeutic context. However, they do not always generalize to the client's daily life situations. The changes can be consolidated and integrated by the use of such methods as homework assignments, future pacing, self-hypnosis and self-appreciation (Gilligan, 1981).

Since alcoholics typically have a great deal of trouble liking themselves or feeling good about themselves, developing self-appreciation is a particularly valuable part of treatment.

Even after accomplishing something significant, alcoholics often will discount their accomplishment with remarks like, "I could have done it better," and "Anyone could do that." They are skilled at feeling terrible about themselves; thus, it is an essential part of consolidating and integrating changes that they learn to appreciate themselves deeply and congruently. I usually take a few minutes prior to the conclusion of each trance to develop the client's self-appreciation.

One method I use is to have clients remember an enjoyable experience in which they felt loved, nurtured or cared about by another person. I offer suggestions which assist in seeing, hearing and feeling how that person appreciated them, focusing finally on a general feeling of appreciation and how that feels in their body.

Another method, which can be used as therapy progresses, is to remind the client of changes and accomplishments already made. Because of the alcoholic's diminished capacity for self-appreciation, previous changes often go unrecognized. It comes as a pleasant surprise when they are pointed out. I acknowledge a nice difference that I observe in my client and communicate my genuine and honest appreciation. This can be followed by general self-appreciation suggestions.

Each of these methods follows the utilization approach. Rather than attempting to put something new into clients, I access experiences they have had and use them to further develop self-appreciation. Self-appreciation creates a context of support which makes the process of changing easier. Thus, it is fundamental to developing other potential changes.

SPECIAL CLINICAL ISSUES REGARDING ALCOHOLISM

When Not to Use Hypnosis

There are certain situations during which it is not advisable to utilize trance with the alcoholic client. Two are especially evident: 1) When alcoholics are drunk or on drugs, they are much less flexible, although they often perceive themselves as more flexible. It is important that the client's ability to go into trance and make therapeutic progress not be associated with alcohol or drug states. Trance is a special therapeutic process to be respected; 2) Hypnosis should not be employed prior to establishing rapport and trust with the client. Depending on the readiness of the individual client, the therapist may need to provide education about hypnosis, clear up misconceptions about hypnosis, utilize previous pleasant and unpleasant trance experiences, and alleviate any fears the client may have about exploring internal experience. Many alcoholics are afraid to go into trance because they may recall traumatic past experiences or intense emotions from which they have remained dissociated. In these cases, the therapist should be supportive of the alcoholic's reality and continue at a pace that respects the needs of the entire individual.

Permissive vs. Confrontational Approaches

Alcoholics tend to deny and therefore lie to themselves and to others. Therefore, it may be necessary to use confrontational communications and therapeutic strategies to enhance contact with the reality of the situation, increase self-awareness, and destabilize self-destructive patterns. Yet an entirely confrontational approach is incomplete and can result in loss of rapport and trust, extreme defensiveness and denial, and possible termination of therapy. Confrontations should be balanced with permissive and supportive approaches which serve to maintain rapport, provide support and caring, and distract the client from confrontational communications. The consequences of an overly permissive approach are that the alcoholic may continue down self-destructive pathways and perpetuate limiting ways of being. The alcoholic also may avoid meaningful issues in therapy and assume control of the relationship, believing that the therapist does not know what to do.

One way to balance permissive and confrontational approaches is to shift back and forth between the two. One may begin by listening to clients, accepting and supporting their experiences, and then pointedly confront a particular behavior or belief, followed by a return to support. This communicates to the alcoholic that life is not working effectively and that the therapist has a positive regard.

The therapist must be careful about the alcoholic's attempts to control the relationship. I accept and acknowledge my client's patterns, but always remember that the alcoholic's way of operating doesn't work, or he or she would not be in therapy. To the degree that the therapist gets hooked into the alcoholic's games, or remains within the existing patterns, therapy will fail.

Handling Relapses and Crises

Relapses and crises are a natural part of the therapeutic process. Alcoholic clients tend to think of relapses and emotional crises as failures and feel disappointed and guilty about their inability to change. Often, their response to a relapse is more harmful than the relapse itself. Relapses are an acceptable and often important aspect of deeply integrated change and it is necessary to utilize them accordingly.

After a client reports a relapse, I acknowledge the need and function of the relapse and link it to the development of further and more profound changes. By utilizing the symptom, one effectively changes the client's self-image and provides needed support at a time when family members are apt to blame and be unsupportive. Erickson frequently found it necessary not only to accept a client's relapse, but to prescribe a relapse. This is a paradoxical strategy. If the client relapses, he or she is following instructions and, therefore, not being resistant; if there is no relapse, therapeutic progress still continues.

In cases where the alcoholic is not making any therapeutic progress and still relapses, a more effective strategy is to go back to setting the context and secure the alcoholic's motivation and acknowledgment of the need to change.

CONCLUSION

Throughout the therapeutic process there is no tool more valuable and effective than respecting and utilizing the individual's entire personality and unique needs. All opposing aspects of a person, all parts of a person, can be developed, expressed and accepted as valuable (Carter, 1983). A therapist's integrity and effectiveness is directly related to the ability to see the existing wholeness and completeness of an individual and utilize it in order to assist in the process of change. This model of treatment provides an effective way of treating the alcoholic person.

REFERENCES

Bandler, R., & Grinder, J. (1975). *Patterns of the hypnotic techniques of Milton H. Erickson, M.D.* (Vol. I). Cupertino, CA: Meta Publications.

Carter, P.M. (1983). *The parts model.* Unpublished doctoral dissertation, International College, Santa Monica, CA.

Gilligan, S.G. (1981). *Hypnotherapeutic changes: An Ericksonian approach.* Unpublished manuscript.

Haley, J. (Ed.). (1967). *Advanced techniques of hypnosis and therapy.* New York: Grune & Stratton.

Haley, J. (1973). *Uncommon therapy.* New York: Norton.

Rosen, S. (Ed.). (1982). *My voice will go with you.* New York: Norton.

Rossi, E.L. (Ed.). (1980). *The collected papers of Milton H. Erickson on hypnosis* (Vol. 4). New York: Irvington.

Royce, J. (1981). *Alcohol problems and alcoholism.* New York: The Free Press.

Chapter 27

Unconscious Factors in Recovery from Alcoholism: The James-Jung-Erickson Connection

John D. Lovern

Most alcoholism treatment programs are based on the philosophy of Alcoholics Anonymous (AA). Central to this philosophy is the belief that recovery can occur only after the alcoholic experiences a profound unconscious change in which the individual surrenders conscious, willful control and assumes a completely altered set of thoughts, feelings, and behaviors; in short, a conversion experience. Currents of psychological thought which converged in AA to form this belief came primarily from William James and C. G. Jung. Refinements and elaborations were added by other theorists, such as Harry Tiebout, Gregory Bateson, and Vernon Johnson. A comparison of these ideas with Milton Erickson's views on therapeutic change reveals a remarkable congruence. In fact, an Ericksonian analysis greatly expands treatment possibilities because it suggests previously untried techniques for stimulating and enhancing the conversion process.

THE JUNG CONNECTION

A successful American businessman, Rowland H., traveled to Switzerland in the early 1930s to undergo treatment for his alcoholism with Dr. Carl Jung (Lois W., 1979). Approximately a year later, he completed the therapy with high hopes for recovery, yet he was drunk again within a short time. When Rowland returned to Switzerland and asked what had gone wrong, Jung stated his opinion that alcoholics of Rowland's type were utterly hopeless, that the only chance of recovery lay in what he called a "vital spiritual experience" (Anonymous, 1976)—a comprehensive "rearrangement" within a person of his or her ideas, emotions, attitudes, and basic motives. He suggested that Rowland return to the United States, involve himself in a religious group of his choice, and attempt to bring about such an experience.

Jung commonly encouraged his patients to join religious groups; in a 1935 lecture, he stated that several of his patients had gone to the Oxford Group movement "with my blessing!" (Jung, 1968, p. 182). He regarded religions as "psychotherapeutic systems" which had the goal of helping people detach from external objects, "persons, ideas, or circumstances," so that "the center of gravity is *in* the individual and no longer in an object on which he depends" (Jung, 1968, p. 182).

Rowland followed instructions carefully. He joined the Oxford Group movement, a nondenominational organization prevalent at that time, which aimed to revive the spirit of early Christianity by practicing self-examination, confession of character defects in group meetings, making restitution for past wrongs, and basing one's decisions on guidance received through prayer.

Rowland experienced what Jung described and became sober. He later shared this experience with another alcoholic, Ebby T., who also became sober. Ebby soon visited one of his old drinking buddies: a New York stockbroker named Bill W.

Bill was skeptical at first, yet he was unable to stop thinking about what Ebby told him about surrendering his will to a Higher Power. These ideas simmered in the back of Bill's mind through several more days of continued drinking and finally came to fruition during Bill's last treatment for alcoholism at a New York hospital. His physician there, William Silkworth, pronounced Bill's condition hopeless, a verdict that threw Bill into a state of turmoil. He remembered Ebby's suggestions and desperately sought guidance from "whatever God there *might* be." The response was instantaneous and dramatic (Anonymous, 1957):

> My depression deepened unbearably and finally it seemed to me as though I were at the very bottom of the pit. I still gagged badly on the notion of a Power greater than myself, but finally, just for the moment, the last vestige of my proud obstinacy was crushed. All at once I found myself crying out, "If there is a God, let Him show Himself! I am ready to do anything, anything!"
>
> Suddenly the room lit up with a great white light. I was caught up into an ecstasy which there are not words to describe. It seemed

to me, in the mind's eye, that I was on a mountain and that a wind not of air but of spirit was blowing. And then it burst upon me that I was a free man. Slowly the ecstasy subsided. I lay on the bed, but now for a time I was in another world, a new world of consciousness. (p. 63)

Following the experience, Bill remained sober and went on to become one of the cofounders of Alcoholics Anonymous. The other cofounder was Bob S., an Akron, Ohio surgeon and another Oxford group member, who became sober shortly after Bill visited him.

A vital spiritual—or conversion—experience was of central importance to Bill's and Bob's recoveries, and to the recoveries of countless subsequent AA members. The importance of the phenomenon led to its incorporation in the first three of AA's Twelve Steps of recovery (Anonymous, 1952):

Step One: "We admitted we were powerless over alcohol—that our lives had become unmanageable."

Step Two: "Came to believe that a Power greater than ourselves could restore us to sanity."

Step Three: "Made a decision to turn our will and our lives over to the care of God *as we understood Him.*" (p. 5)

THE JAMES CONNECTION

Shortly after Bill's conversion experience, Ebby gave him a copy of William James's, *The Varieties of Religious Experience*, a book based on James's 1901 lectures on the psychology of religion. Bill found in the book descriptions of many experiences remarkably similar to his own. Of particular interest were the sections dealing with the phenomena of conversion.

James defined conversion as an experience in which "the habitual center of [an individual's] personal energy" (p. 163) is shifted and rearranged. These rearrangements of mental systems often seem to occur suddenly or spontaneously. But, James saw them as actually following a period of "ripening" or unconscious undermining of the habitual system. Once the mental system is prepared,

a new perception, a sudden emotional shock, or an occasion which lays bare the organic alteration, will make the whole fabric fall together; and then the center of gravity sinks into an attitude more stable, for the new ideas that reach the center in the rearrangement seem now to be locked there, and the new structure remains permanent. (p. 163)

In short, James viewed conversion experiences as "subconsciously maturing processes eventuating in results of which we suddenly grow conscious" (p. 169).

James saw conversion as a naturally occurring, adaptive process, in which an individual strives for change at two levels, conscious and unconscious. The goals and efforts operating at the two levels differ and may come into conflict.

A man's conscious wit and will, so far as they strain towards the ideal, are aiming at something only dimly and inaccurately imagined. Yet all the while the forces of mere organic ripening within him are going on towards their own prefigured result . . .; and the rearrangement towards which all these deeper forces tend is pretty surely definite, and definitely different from what he consciously conceives and determines. It may consequently be interfered with . . . by his voluntary efforts slanting from the true direction. (pp. 171-172)

In other words, James believed that a person could block the unconscious healing process by trying to impose conscious, willful control over it. To do so, according to James, would be to rely on a less effective means of solving one's problems.

Where . . . the subconscious forces take the lead, it is probably the better self *in posse* which directs the operation. Instead of being clumsily and vaguely aimed at from without, it is then itself the organizing center. (p. 172)

For this unconscious "better self" to operate unimpeded, it is necessary for the "conscious self" to relax, yield, or surrender. In James's terms:

When the new center of personal energy has been subconsciously incubated so long as to be just ready to open into flower, "hands off" is the only word for us, it must burst forth unaided! (p. 172)

Bill and other early AA members took James's perspective on self-surrender and conversion seriously and made it a cornerstone of AA's philosophy of recovery. The contributions of other theorists were overlaid on this basic foundation.

TIEBOUT'S CONTRIBUTION

Harry Tiebout was a psychiatrist with close ties to early members of AA. After witnessing several AA-inspired recoveries among his alcoholic patients, he became intrigued with the conversion experience and wrote extensively about it. Tiebout agreed with James that surrender of self-will was necessary for an unconscious conversion to occur:

> With respect to the act of surrender, let me emphasize this point—it is an unconscious event, not willed by the patient even if he should desire to do so. It can occur only when an individual with certain traits in his unconscious mind becomes involved in a certain set of circumstances. (1949, p. 3)

Tiebout added two notions to the body of thought about conversion: the concept of the inflated Ego (capital "E" intended, to differentiate it from the Freudian "ego"); and the distinction between surrender and "compliance."

The Ego consists of a set of "immature traits carried over from infancy into adulthood, specifically, a feeling of omnipotence, inability to tolerate frustration, and excessive drive, exhibited in the need to do things precipitously" (Tiebout, 1954, p. 621). These unconscious attitudes constitute what James called the "habitual center" of the alcoholic's personal energy—that which must be surrendered, so that it can be replaced by a more mature and realistic unconscious attitude. Tiebout (1954) described alcoholics who have undergone this change as:

> people who are learning, for the first time in their lives, to live. They are neither dull nor wishy-washy. Quite the contrary, they are alive and interested in the realities about them. They see things in the large, are tolerant, open-minded, not close-mindedly bulling ahead. They are receptive to the wonders of the world about them, including the presence of a Deity who makes all this possible. They are the ones who are really living. (p. 616)

Tiebout (1949) was among the first to observe that alcoholics often *seem* to have surrendered and accepted the reality of their situations, while actually harboring strong unconscious reservations. He called this state of affairs *compliance* or (here) submission:

> One fact must be kept in mind, namely the need to distinguish between submission and surrender. In submission, an individual accepts reality consciously but not unconsciously. He accepts as a practical fact that he cannot at that moment conquer reality, but lurking in his unconscious is the feeling, "there'll come a day"—which implies no real acceptance and demonstrates conclusively that the struggle is still going on. (p. 9)

Compliance, then, is one of the chief obstacles to recovery from alcoholism. It allows the alcoholic—and those trying to help him or her—to believe that a surrender has occurred, while all along conscious control has been maintained, thus preventing the necessary unconscious events from taking place. Compliance is one of the most common and deceptive forms of resistance used by alcoholics in treatment programs.

OTHER THEORIES

Bateson's (1971) discussion of alcoholism centered on the alcoholic's *epistemology*—the "body of habitual assumptions or premises implicit in the relationship between man and environment" (p. 314). According to Bateson, a person's epistemology exists at "levels of the mind [which are] prelinguistic and . . . coded in *primary process*" (p. 327), that is, unconscious. Something in the alcoholic's epistemology is "wrong" and needs to be corrected: He or she is caught up in a symmetrical "schismogenesis," an escalating conflict between self and "other" in which the alcoholic struggles to conquer and control, first alcohol, then authority, other people, and eventually reality itself.

The solution is "a dramatic shift from this symmetrical habit . . . to an almost purely complementary view of his relationship to others and to the universe or God" (p. 326). Simply stated, the alcoholic must stop being *pitted against* reality and become *a part of it*. How this shift occurs "is complexly related to the experience of double bind" (p. 331). Bateson cites Dr. Silkworth's (Bill W.'s doctor) description of alcoholism—"*the obsession of the mind* that compels us to drink and *the allergy of the body* that condemns us to go mad or die"—as a double bind which forces the alcoholic "back and back to the point at which only an involuntary change in deep unconscious epistemology—a spiritual experience—will make the lethal description irrelevant" (p. 331).

Vernon Johnson (1980) emphasized the delusional systems which prevent alcoholics from becoming aware of their condition as it worsens:

> For many reasons, they are progressively unable to keep track of their own behavior and begin to lose contact with their emotions. Their defense systems continue to grow, so that they can survive in the face of their problems. The greater the pain, the higher and more rigid the defenses become; and this whole process is unconscious. (p. 27)

To combat the delusional system, Johnson recommended "interventions," planned confrontations in which families, friends, and associates present reality to the alcoholic "in a receivable form," which, when successful, overloads the unconsciously operating defense system and brings about its collapse. Subsequent treatment brings further presentations of reality, until the patient progresses from defiant denial, through halfhearted compliance, to acceptance and surrender. Once surrender has occurred, the state of affairs is dramatically different:

> The civil war is over, and the personality has "drawn together" again. Patients are open, self-accepting, warm, and willing to risk human relationships. (p. 91)

To maintain this attitude of surrender following treatment, Johnson prescribed lifelong participation in Alcoholics Anonymous.

CONVERSION AND ERICKSONIAN PSYCHOTHERAPY

For students of Erickson, much of the foregoing material will have seemed quite familiar, and for good reason: bypassing conscious limitations to facilitate change at an unconscious level is the essence of Ericksonian psychotherapy. As Erickson (1977) stated:

> The patient doesn't consciously know what the problems are, no matter how good a story he tells you, because that's a conscious story. What are the unconscious factors? You want to deal with the unconscious mind, bring about therapy at that level, and then translate it to the conscious mind. (p. 21)

In this context, one might say that a primary goal of Ericksonian therapy is to produce conversion experiences.

Previous workers have occasionally stumbled upon therapeutic approaches which seemed to facilitate conversion experiences: Silkworth's double bind, aspects of Jungian analysis, and Johnson's interventions. But none possessed skills or techniques even remotely approaching those of Erickson, who developed countless methods for minimizing conscious distraction and maximizing unconscious learning, e.g., the utilization technique (Erickson, 1967), confusion-restructuring, therapeutic binds, shock, paradox, metaphor (Erickson, Rossi & Rossi, 1976; Haley, 1973), and reframing (Watzlawick, Weakland, & Fisch, 1974).

The "fit" between Ericksonian psychotherapy and an AA-oriented approach to alcoholism treatment is remarkably good. Yet only a few workers have attempted such a combination (i.e., Lovern, 1980, 1981; Lovern & Zohn, 1982). This lack may be due to factors such as the limited popularity of alcoholism treatment among mental health professionals trained in Ericksonian techniques, and the accompanying lack of familiarity with the tenets of AA. Whatever the reasons, an increased use of Ericksonian approaches in alcoholism treatment is definitely indicated.

ERICKSONIAN PSYCHOTHERAPY AND AA— A SYNERGISTIC COMBINATION

Erickson typically accepted and then utilized both the patient's presenting behavior and response tendencies, and also elements of the context or environment which reinforced therapeutic learnings (Erickson, 1967). Insofar as AA reinforces unconscious therapeutic change among its members, it would be consistent with an Ericksonian approach to utilize, or join forces, with AA. To do so can create therapeutic synergy: not only can AA add to the power of Ericksonian therapy, but Ericksonian therapy can improve the effectiveness of AA.

How might an Ericksonian therapist join forces with AA? Basic training in alcoholism treatment and familiarization with the AA program are necessary prerequisites. This experience will provide the therapist with a clear understanding of the appropriate goals of treatment, familiarity with resistances typical of alcoholics, and the ability to "talk program," i.e., to present ideas in AA's language, ensuring that lessons learned in therapy will be transferred to and utilized in the patient's daily "working" of the AA program.

The first order of business in helping an alcoholic patient, after the acute withdrawal phase is over, is to facilitate the surrender of conscious self-will and promote the acceptance that one is powerless over alcohol. Techniques such as paradox, double bind, confusion-restructuring, and metaphor can all be useful here, particularly if the patient is simultaneously being exposed to AA concepts relevant to surrender and powerlessness.

An example of paradox might be to make a bet with a third person (either patient or co-therapist) that a certain patient will be unable to return sober to the clinic the next day. Many patients enjoy "showing up" the therapist by doing something the therapist was "certain" they could not do. This approach also utilizes the patient's defiance in a constructive way. A use of confusion-restructuring might consist of emphatically and convincingly describing to a patient the remarkable degree to which his or her behavior, drinking or sober, is controlled by processes of which he or she is completely unaware. The resulting confusion offers an opportunity to inject a bit of AA philosophy, which the patient will seize on in an attempt to reduce the uncomfortable confusion. After AA philosophy has been injected in this way a sufficient number of times, the patient's unconscious ecology must rearrange itself to accommodate the additions.

Another area where Ericksonian techniques and AA can team up productively is in the routine practice of therapeutic trance—or in AA terms: meditation and prayer, as suggested by Step Eleven (Anonymous, 1952):

> Step Eleven: "Sought through prayer and meditation to improve our conscious contact with God *as we understood Him*, praying only for knowledge of His will for us and the power to carry that out." (p. 8)

Therapeutic trance is defined as "a state of active learning on an unconscious level; that is, learning without the intervention of conscious purpose and design" (Erickson, Rossi, & Rossi, 1976, p. 147). In AA meditation, conscious processes are clearly subordinated to a Higher Power; the goal is to achieve a state of openness and receptivity, so that one might discover at a conscious level what plans, solutions, or directions have been arrived at unconsciously. To emphasize the similarity still further, one might try rereading the Step, substituting "our unconscious mind" for "God, *as we understood Him*" (AA would have no quarrel with this substitution, since members are encouraged to rely upon whatever Higher Power they accept, even an unconscious mind).

An Ericksonian therapist can teach patients how to experience therapeutic trance while labeling this activity as "teaching Step Eleven meditation." In doing so, the therapist opens up the possibility of combining the benefits of Ericksonian trance work with the benefits of the AA program, while at the same time capitalizing on AA members' desire to "work the Steps."

Additional methods of synergistically combining Ericksonian therapy with AA are likely to be discovered if more attention and effort are given to the task. Because of AA's tradition of emphasizing the need for unconscious change, the field of alcoholism treatment is a fertile one for the application of Ericksonian psychotherapeutic approaches.

CONCLUSION

The stage is set in the field of alcoholism treatment for widespread use of Ericksonian psychotherapeutic approaches. The philosophy of Alcoholics Anonymous—the orientation most frequently adopted by alcoholism treatment programs—views recovery from alcoholism as an unconscious process which can be obstructed by conscious, willful thought. Only when changes are made at an unconscious level, free from conscious interference, can recovery proceed. This view of recovery is consistent with Ericksonian approaches to therapeutic change.

Many possibilities exist for synergistically combining Ericksonian approaches with AA, such as employing Ericksonian techniques to facilitate the conversion experience or teaching therapeutic trance as Step Eleven meditation. Other approaches await exploration by creative Ericksonian therapists knowledgeable about alcoholism and AA.

REFERENCES

Anonymous. (1952). *Twelve steps and twelve traditions.* NY: Alcoholics Anonymous World Services.
Anonymous. (1957). *Alcoholics Anonymous comes of age.* NY: Alcoholics Anonymous World Services.
Anonymous. (1976). *Alcoholics Anonymous,* Third Edition. NY: Alcoholics Anonymous World Services.
Bateson, G. (1971). The cybernetics of "self": A theory of alcoholism. *Psychiatry, 34,* 1-18.
Erickson, M.H. (1967). Further techniques of hypnosis—Utilization techniques. In J. Haley (Ed.), *Advanced techniques of hypnosis and therapy.* New York: Grune & Stratton.
Erickson, M.H. (1977). Hypnotic approaches to therapy. *American Journal of Clinical Hypnosis, 20*(1), 20-35.
Erickson, M.H., Rossi, E.L., & Rossi, S.I. (1976). *Hypnotic realities.* New York: Irvington.
Haley, J. (1973). *Uncommon therapy.* New York: Norton.
James, W. (1958). *The varieties of religious experience.* New York: New American Library.
Johnson, V.E. (1980). *I'll quit tomorrow.* New York: Harper & Row.
Jung, C.G. (1968). *Analytical psychology: Its theory and practice.* New York: Vintage Books.
Lovern, J.D. (1980). Indirect hypnotic communication as a group therapy technique in alcoholism treatment. In H. Wain (Ed.), *Clinical hypnosis in medicine.* Chicago: Yearbook Medical Publishers.

Lovern, J.D. (1981). Starting at the bottom. *Alcoholism/The National Magazine*, Nov.-Dec., 28-30.

Lovern, J.D., & Zohn, J. (1982). Utilization and indirect suggestion in multiple-family group therapy with alcoholics. *Journal of Marital and Family Therapy, 8*, 325-333.

Tiebout, H.M. (1949). The act of surrender in the therapeutic process, with special reference to alcoholism. *Quarterly Journal of Studies on Alcohol, 10*, 48-58 (Reprinted by National Council on Alcoholism).

Tiebout, H.M. (1954). The Ego factors in surrender in alcoholism. *Quarterly Journal of Studies on Alcohol, 15*, 610-621.

W., Lois B. (1979). *Lois remembers*. New York: Al-Anon Family Group Headquarters.

Watzlawick, P., Weakland, J.H., & Fisch, R. (1974). *Change: Principles of problem formation and problem resolution*. New York: Norton.

PART VII

Cancer Treatment

Hypnotherapy techniques have often been applied to relieving the pain suffered by cancer patients. However, Ericksonian techniques can be used to help cancer patients deal with other aspects of their disease.

Sidney Rosen, M.D., is a psychiatrist in private practice in New York City. He is an assistant clinical professor of psychiatry at New York University Medical Center. Rosen has considerable background in psychoanalysis; he was appointed a training analyst at the American Institute of Psychoanalysis, and an adjunct psychoanalyst at the Karen Horney Clinic in New York City.

Rosen closely collaborated with Milton Erickson. He edited My Voice Will Go With You: The Teaching Tales of Milton Erickson, M.D. *(Norton, 1982). Rosen has served on the faculty of all of the yearly meetings sponsored by the Erickson Foundation, and he travels internationally to teach Ericksonian methods. He is founding president of the New York Society for Ericksonian Psychotherapy and Hypnosis.*

Ericksonian techniques, including age progression into the future, can alleviate side effects of chemotherapy. Additionally, patients can use hypnotic techniques to counteract preconceived ideas and negative suggestions from hospital personnel. A transcript demonstrates Rosen's dynamic approach.

Burkhard Peter, Dipl Psych, earned his diploma in psychology from the University of Munich. He has coauthored and coedited books in the German language on psychotherapy. As president of the Milton Erickson Gesellschaft für Klinische Hypnose, he organized the

385

*first German Congress for Hypnosis and Hypnotherapy of Milton H.
Erickson in October 1984 in Munich.*

*Wilhelm Gerl, Dipl Psych, has coauthored books with Burkhard
Peter and is vice-president of the Milton Erickson Gesellschaft für
Klinische Hypnose. Both Peter and Gerl are quite active in
conducting training programs on Ericksonian techniques in
Germany.*

*The traditional methods of using hypnosis for cancer patients
involves control of symptoms. Peter and Gerl have attempted to use
hypnosis to influence the actual disease process and enhance the
quality of the patient's life.*

Chapter 28

Hypnosis as an Adjunct to Chemotherapy in Cancer

Sidney Rosen

Patients who are undergoing chemotherapy for cancer sometimes feel that the side effects of the chemotherapy are so uncomfortable
that they would opt for a speedy death rather than endure the "extra
torture." Several investigators have reported that the side effects can be
ameliorated by the use of marijuana and behavioral desensitization
(Morrow & Morrell, 1982). In my experience and that of others, hypnotic
interventions are more helpful than these other approaches, especially
when they are directed toward the comfort and development of the
whole person (Redd, Rosenberger, & Hendler, 1982-3).

From my first contact with a patient with cancer I utilize approaches
such as projection into the future. In a trance state I guide patients to
see themselves at a mature age, perhaps in their eighties, looking back
upon this period of time, when they *had* suffered with cancer. They can
see not only that they learned to survive physically but that they went
through the chemotherapy treatment, comfortably and safely, and had
grown and learned from the entire experience. I usually include both
general suggestions, aimed at encouraging learning, comfort and healing, and specific ones, aimed at symptoms, such as nausea.

After an Early Learning Set induction, I may say:

> You can become a bodiless mind. And as a bodiless mind you
> can travel anywhere at all in time or in space. You can be three
> years old, or 10 years old. You can enjoy comfort at any age.

(Sometimes I will have the patients signal to me, with automatic movements, when they are comfortable.)

Then I may suggest:

> Today's date is not 1983. Today is not July 18, 1983. And you are not in New York City, in Dr. Rosen's office. This is 1993. And I don't know where you are. You could be at home. You could be on a vacation trip. You could be with friends, your children, your grandchildren. I don't know where you are, or what you are doing. But you are comfortable, aren't you? You do feel good, don't you?

CASE EXAMPLE

After I get a positive response to age progression I may go even further into the future. For example, with one hospitalized woman, age 43, who had both breasts removed, I said during my first contact with her:

> You are 80 years old—83 years old. And you can look back 40 years, seeing yourself at age 43. And you can realize that the period around age 43 was really a very important time in your life—a watershed, the time when you really began to understand the meaning of your life, the value of your life. A very important time for you. You can't say that you were actually lucky to have gotten cancer but, in a way, you feel that it was lucky for you.

I will then play with time:

> You are age 83, looking back at yourself, at age 43. And you see what happened after you saw Dr. Rosen. How did you go through that period? How did you go through the chemotherapy? Was the chemotherapy upsetting to you? Did it take one week, did it take two weeks after you saw Dr. Rosen, before the chemotherapy was accepted as a matter-of-fact treatment? As a helper? Or did it take only one session before you felt better? Did it take a month? Two weeks?

As I offer different times, I watch for responses and note them. Then I progress the patient, in the same way as I might bring her back from an early childhood regression:

> And that young woman of 43 grows older, hour by hour, day by day, week by week, month by month, year by year—and really enjoys her life, doesn't she? Life has become very meaningful. She appreciates the value of every moment. Of course, as Wordsworth

said, "Into every life some rain must fall, some days will be dark and dreary." There were sometimes when things were not so hot. There were times when you thought that you were not going to be able to make it, to get through another hour, another day. But you got through those times, didn't you (again looking back from age 83)?

Discussion

After the general approach, outlined above, I might have the patient hypnotically review the entire chemotherapy treatment, using imagery, when possible.

The progression into the future has three possible effects:

1) It implies that the person will survive and thereby adds to a sense of hope. Hope has been associated with greater survival rates and greater longevity (Newton, 1982-3).
2) It is an indirect way of requesting the unconscious mind to devise ways of dealing with the side effects of therapy and with the psychological and physiological impact of the cancer.
3) Patients are left with some sense of mastery and a feeling of process as they preview responses over the immediate future and through the next few months of therapy.

When we consider the reported results of the Simontons and Creighton (1978), and Hall (1982-3), in which it appears that the use of imagery or hypnotic and self-hypnotic approaches *may* prolong the life of cancer patients, it is possibly negligent *not* to make these approaches available to all cancer patients.

DEVELOPING TREATMENT APPROACHES

What specific suggestions do I give to a patient undergoing chemotherapy? I keep in mind Erickson's advice:

Maladies, whether psychogenic or organic, follow definite patterns of some sort . . . a disruption of this pattern could be a most therapeutic measure; it often matters little how small the disruption was, if introduced early enough. (Erickson, 1980, p. 254)

Details of the patient's response to chemotherapy to date can provide directions for treatment. For example, to a patient who reported the development of nausea about two hours after receiving intravenous chemotherapy, I suggested that, about two hours after the treatment, he could feel comfortable or he could sleep for two hours. If the situation was not one in which he could sleep, I would utilize time distortion, so that he could experience the feeling of having slept for several hours, even though the experience would take place during only a few minutes of clock time. He could rest his head on his office desk for two minutes, which could be experienced as several hours of sleep. On awakening from this "sleep," the patient could then have a feeling of hunger, with the understanding that hunger is the best antidote to nausea.

If patients have not had chemotherapy previously, their expectancy of sickness derives from stories they heard or read or from suggestions received from nurses or physicians. It is remarkable how specific treatment personnel can be in suggesting side effects. One patient was told, for example, "You will probably be O.K. for the first two treatments, but most people get very sick by the third treatment, from the cumulative effect of the medication."

It is often necessary to counteract these "helpful" suggestions. For example, I explain to patients the nature of indirect suggestions so that they can be alerted to them. Then, I make counter suggestions, such as, "You ought to get an increasing feeling of well-being and security as you realize that you have received an adequate dose of medication, perhaps after your third or fourth treatment."

Anticipatory nausea, a well-known phenomenon, is most obviously "purely psychological" in origin. An example is the patient who becomes violently nauseated on accidentally looking at a dressing gown worn in the hospital during chemotherapy. This type of nausea is easiest to treat. Simple desensitization, using visualizations, can be employed. For example, patients can visualize themselves in a comfortable situation, eating and enjoying a meal. Then, while maintaining the comfortable feeling, they can see and feel themselves looking at the robe. Later they can visualize or think of themselves as walking down the street towards the doctor's office for the therapy session, feeling comfortable and looking forward to the treatment.

Self-hypnosis can be taught to supplement therapeutic suggestions. Audiotapes, custom-made in the presence of the patient, can be helpful as a supplement, or can replace self-hypnosis in some patients. Because these tapes may be used before going to sleep at night, I often include sleep-promoting suggestions and suggestions for healing dreams.

Physiological responses to chemotherapy can be altered by the use of indirect or metaphorical suggestions. For example, I have decreased intestinal cramping and diarrhea by encouraging a patient to visualize a running stream which moved roughly at times and calmly at other times, with increasing periods of calm until it formed a large, tranquil pool.

CHANGING PATIENTS' ATTITUDES

The best way to change a fearful attitude towards chemotherapy is to intervene in ways that minimize discomfort. However, it is sometimes helpful to address attitudes directly, to correct historical misconceptions and to present the therapy in a positive light. Using patients' values and conceptions is a principal technique of the Ericksonian method.

For example, one patient was initially angry at the chemotherapy. She said, "I feel I'm just poisoning my body. The same way I did when I was seven years old and had X-ray treatment on my thymus." I reframed the situation and helped her see the chemotherapy as strengthening the defensive forces in her body, so that they could destroy the already poisoned, or potentially poisoned cancer processes.

Another patient who already saw chemotherapy as one of her "allies" conceived cancer as being "dirty." In working with her, chemotherapy and cleansing were repeatedly connected and associated.

For those patients who develop phobic responses to the chemotherapy, or to taking oral medication between intravenous treatments, therapy often can be quite simple. One successful method I have used is to have the patient practice visualizing swallowing the pills in a matter-of-fact manner.

Especially in cases which appear to be terminal I determine in which areas patients can find hope, whether it be through hope of a magical recovery, through ideas of an afterlife or reincarnation, or simply through the thought of living on through their children or their work. Looking forward to peace and the end of troubles may be relieving to some people.

APPROACHES TO HYPNOTIC INDUCTION

Induction techniques depend on what is available to the therapist and on the responsiveness of the patient. Healing suggestions often are incorporated into the induction. For example, with an arm levitation induction, I may casually mention, "It feels good, doesn't it, to be lighter? And, as your arm goes up, you can raise your sights; you can go beyond yourself as you look forward to periods of increasing enlightenment."

Case Example

One 63-year-old patient had undergone a radical mastectomy and was soon to begin chemotherapy. She was referred to me two years previously because of anxiety and fears that she *might* develop cancer. She associated her cancer with a type of dirtiness, contamination. In fact, she felt that the letter "c" generally referred to negatives—"cancer, calamity, contamination, crud, and, of course, chemotherapy." In the following induction it can be seen that posthypnotic suggestions, for healing in general, for comfort and specifically for minimal side effects from chemotherapy, are included from the beginning.

After a confusion-type induction, she was presented with time-distorting and disorienting suggestions:

> You know that St. Patrick's Day came last year and that it probably rained, as it always seems to do on St. Patrick's Day, this year, in 1981, just as it will in 1982 and as it did in 1979. You know that, a year or so ago, back in 1980, you were impelled to call Dr. Rosen, hoping that working with him would help you in dealing with some severe anxieties. When he didn't answer the telephone you decided that it wasn't the right time to do this. You don't know now, that two years from today you will actually be seeing Dr. Rosen, after some of your worst fears have materialized. You have a lot of conscious awareness of the importance of fantasy, the importance of listening to your own unconscious mind. When you do see Dr. Rosen, in March of 1982, you will want to be prepared to use whatever you have learned throughout your life so that you can redirect, not only your conscious thoughts, but your unconscious activity as well. You can do this by tapping that vast reservoir of unconscious learnings and extracting from it some of the most positive, the most helpful, the most creative experiences and moments. You can find yourself inspired, when the occasion arises, to lift yourself above yourself, or to take yourself outside of yourself, at times, or to go inside of yourself, in order to oversee or to direct those powerful healing forces which you know are present. You don't have to force those forces.
>
> You don't have to force yourself to concentrate. All you need to do is make gentle requests of your unconscious mind. "I would like to ask my unconscious mind to help me to go through this experience comfortably and effectively." Once you have made that request you can let yourself go into a deeper trance, knowing that

you have all the resources that you need. You can call on resources from inside and from outside—from your friends. You can allow them to nurture you, temporarily, putting aside your pride for a while, the feeling that you have to take care of everything, for yourself and for others. You can allow yourself to be sick, for a while, not needing to feel sick, but knowing that there is a cleaning up job to be done there, and that it will be done, as efficiently, as effectively and as comfortably as possible.

You know, deep down inside, do you not, that this will be done. It is not just a wish fulfillment, is it? You are going to be well very soon, are you not? I'm waiting for a signal. Yes! Like that! If you are wondering if that is just a wish fulfillment, that you are deliberately moving that thumb, try to stop it from going up, finding that the more you try to stop it the higher up it wants to go. That's right! Like that!

You can sense that force that is working inside you now. And that unconscious force that is working against you, too, can you not? That last force will become weaker and weaker as you become stronger.

You can have some understanding now of the question that was asked a long time ago. "What is the source of this unconscious part of you that is working against you now?" You can talk in words and tell me about it, if you like. (Patient: The source is fear. But it's not going to win—because fear is no good.)

Can you take that fear and wrap it up? Where is it located—in your left hand? Rather than try to fight against it, can you dispense with it, in some other way? Right now, when your hand becomes clenched so tightly, you can try to hold that fear in. The fingers and joints become locked tight. If you try to open that fist, the more you try to open it the tighter the fingers clench. That's right. Try to open it, finding that you can't. That's right. You can really feel the tightness, the tension. Locate all the tightness, all the tension from your body into that left hand; all of the despair. [A loud car horn is heard, persistently blowing outside the window.] And that damned irritating horn can make you feel more frustrated and angry, can't it—till you feel like smashing something—with that left fist. . . . And when you've had as much of it as you can stand for now . . . yes, let it build up further . . . there are times when we are in severe pain, that we naturally and instinctively hold on to something, just as you are holding on now . . . in that left fist . . . until the fist itself becomes painful . . . the hand be-

comes achy. . . . When you don't want to stand it for another
moment, just nod your head, once. . . . Now lean back and take
a deep breath, and let the fist relax and open, letting out the fear,
letting out the tension. Letting it out of your body. Letting it leave
your mind . . . like that . . . yes. . . .

You focus on your breathing for a moment or two, letting yourself
go into a more relaxed state, a deeper trance. Enter into your
cocoon . . . and you are not alone here. You become more and
more relaxed . . . and as you relax, more and more, you can listen
to your unconscious messages. . . . You've heard the negative
ones. You have seen them . . . in your dream . . . but you can
tune up the positive messages now, too . . . so that they become
not only messages from your conscious mind, not only the grim
determination of a very strong woman, to overcome this illness . . . it
will become a voice from a very very deep source, which just quietly
knows that you will become well . . . and safe . . . and able to
proceed with the living of your life again . . . very, very soon.

I don't know what images are going to come to you . . . to represent this very positive feeling . . . but I do know that you will
come up with some images that are meaningful to you . . . corrective
images, clean, clear, perhaps celestial . . . certainly comforting.
[Note the "good c's."] Can you see them, or hear them now? [She
shakes her head "no."] Would you like me to supply some? All
right. . . . You have a vast repertoire of music . . . much vaster
than mine. I do not want to limit you. You could think of "The
Ode to Joy". . . or a Schubert Mass . . . or even some Mozart. . . .
Just scan through your repertoire . . . until you hit on some small
piece of music that you can sense is a healing music for you. You
can hear that, in your mind, more and more vividly, more and
more clearly. You can see the orchestra. You can pick out various
parts of the orchestra. . . . So, you will remember these and they
will come back automatically. And they can be so vivid and so clear
that you will be not quite sure—is there really an orchestra, or is
it a record that I hear, or is it just in my own head? And it really
doesn't matter. All that matters is that you know that you're creative, your healing forces are liberated, more and more. . . .

You can go into a deeper trance and can take a look into your
future, if you like. You are with your family, your husband, and
everything is back to normal, isn't it?

Or, are you involved in newer projects, that interest you? I [your husband] is well, is he not? You had fears, back in 1982, that he might not be. And he is 74 years old now, isn't he? No? How old is he? (Patient: 72.) Yes, but now its 1984. He's 74. Can you see him being well, this year? And you are just a youngster—10 years younger.

And that chemotherapy is behind you. And that is a relief, isn't it? (Patient: Yes.) How did you go through it? Was it uncomfortable for you? Or were you able to utilize some of the things that you were working on with Dr. Rosen and others, to make it more comfortable? Did your hair fall out? That was not a serious problem, anyway, was it? You had the wig—a whole series of them, if you needed them. . . . And what about the nausea that people talk about? Did you have much nausea? Or were you able to just take a deep breath, whenever you felt it beginning, and let that feeling go out of you . . . blow it out . . . instead of having to throw it up . . . remembering that there was a desire at one time to want to throw something up, in despair, wasn't there? Were you able to let go of that despair, in some other way? . . . to focus on feeling relaxed and comfortable . . . and safe . . . during the treatment and after the treatment? (Patient nods "yes.")

This patient was seen for hypnotherapy and psychotherapy once or twice a week for about eight months. She completed her first series of chemotherapy treatments with no nausea or vomiting and a minimal amount of weakness. Periods of depression and anxiety were very brief, lasting for only hours. She maintained an active social and family life, philanthropic activities, and wrote and performed music.

After completion of this series she was given a series of radiotherapy treatments because of an unidentified mass in her upper thorax. She lost her voice, was hospitalized because of a pleural effusion, and died in hospital while undergoing a second series of chemotherapy sessions. I visited her in hospital, reinforced her ability to breathe relatively comfortably and to withdraw into a trance-sleep whenever she felt too tired to maintain contact with her family, during their frequent visits. She suffered more nausea than with her first series, but it was controlled with medication and self-hypnosis.

Following her death, a daughter told me that her mother had been calmer and more content with her life during her last year than ever before. This daughter attributed her mother's mental peace to her psychotherapy.

SUMMARY

There are several elements that form the basis of treating the side effects of chemotherapy in cancer patients:

1) Treatment of the whole patient, with emphasis on building hope. The hope may be invested in survival and resumption of life, or, in some terminal cases, may be attached to an expectation of prolongation of life, in relative comfort.
2) Management of unnecessary fear and pain are, of course, important. Fear, pain and nausea are interdependent.
3) Disruption of the pattern of symptoms, including pain and nausea. Sensory modalities can be modified.
4) Time sequences can be changed and time distortion may be utilized to alter patterns. A person can go through an entire response in a short time, perhaps minutes instead of hours.
5) All of the above can be connected with sleep or drowsiness, especially in patients who do not have to be active.
6) In lieu of sleepiness, a clear-minded meditative state may be induced, sometimes associated with "mystical" feelings or psychedelic experiences.
7) Sense of appetite can be enhanced. Suggestions of hunger can be followed by suggestions of sleep, especially before the patient has time to experience nausea or vomiting.

When everything else fails, the induction of a deep sleep can often be accomplished by means of hypnosis. This type of escape can be very helpful, not only from the torments of pain, fear and despair, but also from feelings of nausea and dizziness which may accompany the chemotherapy.

AFTERWORD

Working and living with cancer patients often evoke symptoms in treating personnel—mostly through the process of sympathetic identification. Physicians and nurses will develop pains and weakness, associated with hidden and sometimes not so hidden convictions that they have acquired cancer themselves. They also can become nauseated and feel febrile while dealing with the side effects of chemotherapy in their patients.

Psychotherapists or hypnotherapists who are working in these situations can develop similar responses. Obviously, we have tools—the ones I have outlined in this chapter—to deal with this kind of response. In fact, in alleviating our own nausea, our own pains, our own fears, we can develop a wider range of approaches to help our patients. We can explore different types of imagery, different types of relaxation suggestions, diversion suggestions and ways of evoking hopeful feelings in ourselves. By a combination of introspection, self-hypnosis and action we can reach a balanced perspective. Erickson once told me that he was able to maintain a type of separation from patients because, as he said, "I know my own voice." With the help of the techniques I have outlined we can find an optimal degree of joining and separation with our patients and can learn from and with them.

REFERENCES

Erickson, M.H. (1980). Migraine headache in a resistant patient. In E. L. Rossi (Ed.), *The collected papers of Milton H. Erickson, Vol. 4: Innovative hypnotherapy* (p. 254). New York: Irvington.

Hall, H.R. (1982-3). Hypnosis and the immune system: A review with implications for cancer and the psychology of healing. *American Journal of Clinical Hypnosis, 25*, 92-103.

Morrow, G.R., & Morrell, C. (December 9, 1982). Behavioral treatment for the anticipatory nausea and vomiting induced by cancer chemotherapy. *The New England Journal of Medicine*, 1476-1480.

Newton, B.W. (1982-3). The use of hypnosis in the treatment of cancer patients. *American Journal of Clinical Hypnosis, 25*(2-3), 112.

Redd, W.H., Rosenberger, P.H., & Hendler, C.S. (1982-3). Controlling chemotherapy side effects. *American Journal of Clinical Hypnosis, 25*, 161-171.

Simonton, D.C., Matthews-Simonton, S., & Creighton, J.L. (1978). *Getting well again*. Los Angeles: Tarcher-St. Martins.

Chapter 29

Clinical Hypnosis in Psychological Cancer Treatment

Burkhard Peter and Wilhelm Gerl

Clinical hypnosis traditionally has been used with cancer patients as a means of providing symptomatic relief, and Milton H. Erickson's own case reports provide examples of this treatment. In the case of Joe and the tomato plant, one of his most widely known cases, he suggested the use of a tomato plant possibly both as a metaphor for a growing tumor and to get the patient to address and accept the tumor for the purpose of pain control. We are aware of only two passages (Rosen, 1982, p. 54; Zeig, 1980, p. 189f) in which Erickson considers the possibility of moving beyond pain control and using the hypnotic method to influence the disease process itself. The work of Simonton et al. (1978) has brought this possibility into open discussion; they used a variety of psychological methods as possible means to reverse cancer growth. This chapter is a report of our experiences applying clinical hypnosis to cancer patients. Included in the report are the conditions and limitations which have emerged from our clinical experience and a discussion of our attempts to influence cancer growth with hypnotic methods.

As the following discussion will make clear, the authors differ in style, method, and interest. The report of our experience and theoretical reflection is consistent with our conviction that good work in the tradition of Milton H. Erickson requires a plurality of styles and methods; no

---

This paper was translated by Hunter Beaumont.

single "correct" style of hypnotherapy as yet has been identified and probably never will be. We wish to support experimentation within the limits of professional ethics in the quest for new knowledge.

CASE ONE

In 1980 one of us (B.P.) was asked to treat an intestinal cancer patient for insomnia. Because I was unable to visit him immediately in the hospital, I discussed with him on the telephone the possibilities and difficulties of counting a large flock of sheep. When I did visit him three days later, he reported to me the results of his counting attempts. He had devised a method of counting the flock by visualizing the sheep passing through a narrow gate one at a time. His failure to count the entire flock on each of the preceding nights due to having fallen asleep was a source of delight to him. Although the insomnia was apparently cured, his success with it led us to consider the possibility of using hypnotic technique to alleviate his considerable pain. He reported pain in the lower back, in the left side of the diaphragm, and in the lower abdomen, which had not responded significantly to medication. I agreed to work with him and the pain in the lower back responded quickly to suggestions of increasing muscle tonus in the area. The left-sided diaphragm pain did not respond in any way to my suggestions. I suggested to the patient that he could concentrate on his pain with the intention of discovering what it might mean. Approximately half an hour later he vomited a large quantity of fluid. The physician ordered the stomach pumped and additional large amounts of fluid were removed. The insertion of the tube successfully controlled the accumulation of fluid and the pain did not recur. The pain in the lower abdomen was near the tumor and appeared to be caused by the tumor itself. The patient learned to move his pain to his left arm and through the arm onto the floor, thereby achieving an adequate degree of pain control.

In spite of the fact that we had not practiced trance training as such, the patient had shown himself to be cooperative and had faithfully practiced all of the suggested exercises. He was now able to sleep comfortably and to control the pain so that it was no longer a major problem for him. He was nevertheless in a pitiful situation. The cancerous tissue in his abdomen was so substantial that it was necessary for him to be intravenously fed; the small amount of fluid he was allowed to take by mouth was drained by the stomach tube. The chemotherapy was having serious adverse side effects.

Prior to that time I had not worked with cancer patients. Still, I wanted to try something to help my patient. I began by talking about the function of the digestive system and the possibilities of various communication processes within the body itself and between the body and the unconscious. I explained these processes to him, partly using physiological information and partly by means of metaphor and analogy. I wove into the discussion indirect suggestions intended to strengthen his further cooperation and stimulate both his unconscious defenses against the cancer and his responsiveness to the chemotherapy. Simultaneously, again by means of embedded indirect suggestion, I hoped to encourage the growth of healthy tissue to replace that destroyed by the disease. The general condition of the patient improved visibly during this period. After four weeks he was able to eat and digest normally what he had eaten. He anticipated release from the hospital within the next week.

I also attempted to consider with him by means of stories and discussion the problems and possibilities of a continuing life after his release. This was difficult inasmuch as he had, to a large extent, already achieved his major life goals and did not have a deeply satisfying personal life. He had built a large business empire and had organized it so well that his continued participation was unnecessary. He filled his time with travel and attempts to write. Family ties were practically nonexistent. Other than occasional visits from one of his daughters, he did not have contact with his family; his only regular visitor and support person was his girlfriend.

On the day before his scheduled release from the hospital, he died suddenly from a lung embolism.

CASE TWO

The first practical experience of the co-author (W.G.) with a cancer patient was in 1979 and had a different character:

Together with my wife, I visited a 30-year-old relative in the hospital. He had been admitted for emergency surgery for cancer of the testes. His wife and son also were present during our visit. I surprised myself with a quite atypical reaction: I began to tell a story about a client of mine who rather suddenly had decided to leave her husband and family. As we left the hospital, my wife commented to me about the inappropriateness of this story. Several days later, this relative called me at my office and asked for an appointment. He reported that the story I had told him in the hospital had touched him personally and that he felt the need to talk with me about this and other things he had never discussed with anyone. The report of his personal situation and his seemingly insoluble problems seemed to be consistent with all my theoretical knowledge about cancer and cancer development. My theoretical knowledge turned out to be helpful in assisting me to communicate effectively with my patient and in giving him suggestions for reorganizing his life. During this session I used metaphor, indirect suggestion, quotes, and embedded commands in order to avoid resistance. This informal therapeutic format fit in well with the fact that our relationship was not only therapeutic, but also a friendship. It was fascinating for me to watch how successful he was in realizing the posthypnotic suggestions during the months following our session. His family was quite surprised at his decisions for reorganizing his life. He decided to move from the city in which he had lived to a beautiful house near the Alps. There, he and his wife opened a small hotel, and for newcomers they have done very well with it. He was able to improve his inner life and has been healthy since.

Moving from these first two experiences we will review our further experiences and thoughts regarding the role that an Ericksonian understanding of clinical hypnosis and psychotherapy can play with cancer patients.

Hypnotherapy for Pain Control and Other Side Effects of the Disease and Its Treatment

In contrast to patients whose complaint is pain of a psychosomatic origin, we have experienced good cooperation from our cancer patients. Patients in the advanced stages of cancer usually are highly motivated since the life-threatening quality of the disease reduces the attractiveness of secondary gains one might expect from being ill. These patients are receptive to suggestions to help reorganize their experience for purposes of reducing their discomfort. The unusually high suggestibility of these patients may be due to the fact that they have no other choice available for reducing their pain other than to accept the suggestions of the therapist. Specific hypnotic techniques for the control of pain have been described in the literature (Erickson & Rossi, 1979, p. 94ff; Hilgard & Hilgard, 1975).

We have found it difficult to facilitate the relief of pain caused by, or associated with, chemotherapy and radiation therapy. In these cases the patient often has doubts, open or hidden, as to the usefulness of treatments and is therefore unsure that the decision to undergo the treatment was a correct one. Occasionally, extreme reactions develop from this conflict.

CASE THREE

A melanoma patient developed a pronounced phobia to chemotherapy which generalized to all actual and imagined stimuli associated with the treatment. I (B.P.) predicted that a simple systematic desensitization would be of little use and attempted instead to facilitate a new interpretation (reframing) of the meaning of the anxiety-laden situation.

I began to work with her using embedded suggestions to communicate acceptance and to activate positive action. I told her that I could imagine that it must be *painful for an attractive and active, self-aware person* to suddenly be unable to *do the normal daily activities,* but rather to vomit continuously, to *look in the mirror and see correctly an image* of misery and wretchedness, to *have the normal nourishing activities of life* exist only as memories. Furthermore, she is *correct in understanding* that the chemotherapy does kill healthy as well as diseased cells. Her *impulse to protect herself* is *natural and correct.* To *maximize the positive effects and to minimize the negative side effects,* however, she should *do a good deal better* than she had been doing. The reactions of her body, for example, her extreme nausea, were to be seen as normal reactions. The chemicals act on all fast-growing cells and would be expected to kill other healthy fast-growing cells in addition to the cancer cells, cells, for instance, which line the stomach and intestine. She should *direct the intention* toward *aiming the effect of the chemicals more and more toward the cancer cells and away from the healthy cells.* She could also support the accidentally damaged healthy tissue in its effort to replace itself. She should *prepare the awareness* to *allow and accept the normal, although unpleasant body reactions and* to *adopt a position of increased friendliness to the body as a whole.*

The results of this treatment were successful insofar as she was able to resume the chemotherapy which required regular visits to the hospital, and she was able to cope better in the periods between treatments. The phobic reactions were reduced in spite of increased nausea after treatment which did not respond successfully to suggestions.

Special difficulties may emerge in cases where the surgical removal of tumors becomes necessary. In these cases it may appear as if the previous medical and psychological treatment had not been effective. A sense of failure and disappointment may tempt patients to blame themselves or the therapist with thoughts like, "If you had done a better job, this would not have been necessary." These reactions should be anticipated. It is helpful to give patients recognition for their efforts and to affirm that they have done the best that could be done at the time. "Therefore, it is now time to allow the surgeons to do their work." The patient's job is to use the time before the operation and the time of rest provided by the anesthesia to prepare the body for a speedy recovery.

Good communication between the therapist and the doctor is especially important during this phase because patients frequently ask if we think that this operation, or some other new treatment, might be useful. In this case, it is unjustified to contradict medical recommendations except in extreme cases since the full weight of the conflict then comes to rest upon the patient, adding to an already high level of stress. Instead of questioning the medical recommendations, we adopt a positive interpretation of the operation in the sense that it saves work. That is, it is highly plausible to assume that the operation, because it will remove large masses of tumorous tissue, makes the battle against any remaining cancer cells easier. The therapeutic goal is to organize the personality for renewed healing efforts after the surgery.

Our experience supports the previously reported observation that hypnotherapy can speed the healing process. However, that option of help is damaged when the patient gets the message of hopelessness. Indirect messages include things said by the doctors during the operation itself. Some highly suggestible persons appear to be able to "hear" what is said around them while they are under anesthesia. These messages may influence the postoperative healing process (Bowers, 1979).

Hypnotherapeutic preparation for surgery requires that all anxieties and skeptical thoughts of the patient should be accepted and, even if not directly expressed by the patient, should be addressed with the use of stories or metaphors. It is only when these so-called negative elements of a patient's experience are also accepted and viewed as being worthy that the patient feels accepted and is prepared to cooperate and to enter trance trustingly.

CASE FOUR

A histiocytosis patient had a large portion of cancerous lymph tissue removed. One year previously, the entire spleen had been removed. Following the surgery to remove the spleen, the patient had experienced multiple lung embolisms and barely survived. I (B.P.) said to him that his wife, his parents, and his whole family had fears that he would not survive and that I would *be surprised* if he did *have other thoughts sometimes.* It is the task of the conscious mind to consider all negative possibilities in order to *be better able to protect itself,* therefore, he should not try to keep himself from thinking negative thoughts. When he accepted his negative thoughts as a normal self-defense reaction, he would be able to *prepare calmly for the coming operation* and to *allow the unconscious mind to lay the groundwork for a speedy recovery.* I suggested to him, using examples, how he might use the anesthetic to remain sedated long after the surgery, thereby allowing the circulation to remain functionally reduced which in turn would have the effect of slowing the healing process and make it necessary for him to lay in the hospital bored to tears for an extended period of time; or, alternatively, he could choose to *return to full alertness immediately after the surgery* and to involve himself with the business of improving his condition and speeding his recovery. I waited with his wife to visit him as he came out of the recovery room. Remembering his condition after the prior surgery, she asked me to enter the room first and see how he was. As I entered the room, he smiled at me from his bed and appeared to be in good condition. He was released from the hospital ten days later.

Hypnotherapeutic Activation of the Coping and Immune Systems of the Physical Body and of the Unconscious Mind

The controversy on the effects of hypnosis was formulated by Sutcliffe (1960, 1961) with the categories, "Credulous" and "Skeptical." In essence, this controversy may be stated in terms of two questions: Are hypnotic phenomena only constructed fantasy and products of the imagination, as the Benjamin Franklin Commission thought of mesmerism in 1784? Or, do these phenomena bring about substantial changes?

In a recent article, I (Peter, 1983a) argued that both positions have relevance, depending on the application during long periods in the clinic, or for shorter periods in classical experiments. For present purposes, however, the question presents itself in a concrete form: Can hypnosis (or any other psychological method) affect the growth of cancer cells? At this time there is no definitive scientific answer. There are, of course, enormous experimental difficulties. From a purely experimental point of view, it would be ideal to have a control group of cancer patients who received no treatment, a group who received only medical treatment, a group who received only psychological treatment and a group receiving both medical and psychological treatment. This is hardly desirable in actual practice.

Research results from psychoneuroimmunology report individual cases and experiences which appear to support the possibility that patients can influence a life-threatening disease by using their own inner resources and that psychotherapy can assist the process (Ader, 1981; Hall, 1982/83).

We believe this area to be so serious, however, that we do not wish to arouse false hopes in the patient. Before more success under controlled conditions is reported and reviewed, extreme caution is advised. However, we are convinced that what we and other therapists are doing to help patients overcome their illness has value. It is our experience, and the experience of others working in this field, that as soon as patients begin to concern themselves with active healing work they do not experience the helplessness and hopelessness which is so common among terminal patients. Even when they die of the illness, death occurs after a period of meaningful living, often quite suddenly and unexpectedly. In many cases these patients possess their physical and mental faculties to a degree that they appear to themselves and to others to be living worthwhile lives up to the time of death. The trance experience seems to be especially effective in giving a sense of worthwhileness to this last period of life. The experiences which they have under trance are fascinating and satisfying. With the help of posthypnotic suggestion and amnesia it is possible to minimize the awareness of the unpleasant aspects and suffering of the disease, while focusing attention on the more positive life affirming aspects.

We usually do not discuss with patients nor attempt to convince them on a conscious level that they have the ability to influence body functions; we work primarily with stories and metaphors in which the possibility of influencing bodily functions plays an implicit role. We focus the first phase of the therapy on effects such as changes in muscle tone, breathing, pulse rate, and capillary tension. We use embedded commands to facilitate deepening the trance. Stories such as, "I once had a patient who . . .," are used for pacing patients' experiences and as an aid to define the therapeutic relationship and to prepare for induced therapeutic reactions. Further work begins to address patients' immune systems, opening "channels of communication" with the normal cells and with the cancer cells. At the beginning of the therapy patients are encouraged (through indirect suggestion and in later stages of the therapy through the addition of direct suggestion) to work with these systems so that gradually a transition from unconscious to conscious participation is effected. For this purpose we prefer to use descriptions of physiological channels or images of metamorphosis which are determined by the individual patient's needs and frame of reference. Patients select the specific contents of their fantasies and conceptual repertoire and then use these for independent work between sessions. We attempt to formulate the content according to the understanding, the language and the representational system of each patient.

In addition to the activation of the immune system, we have attempted to attend to the communication channels between the individual cells. We assume that in cancer this communication, for whatever reason, is disturbed. An appropriate psychotherapeutic task is to restore a correct and normal flow of communication.

A manifest advantage of clinical hypnosis here, as well as in other areas of psychological cancer treatment is that in trance, necessary processes can be worked with simply and satisfyingly. It is, however, premature to claim that the effectiveness of the work is increased by trance states.

Hypnotic Activation of the Will to Live

We are convinced that all possible psychological treatment of cancer including hypnotic attempts to activate the immune system are pointless unless the patient has the will to live and to fight for life. Recent studies (e.g., Grossarth-Maticek, 1979) indicate that it is possible to identify cancer patients and cancer candidates according to specific psychological characteristics. It may be possible to develop a construct of a certain personality type predisposed to cancer. This construct may have practical as well as heuristic value. In spite of the fact that we maintain a skeptical caution with constructs of this type, we cannot avoid the observation that most of the cancer patients we have worked with do appear to conform to a pattern. They display a marked tendency towards resignation, surrendering to the inevitability of the disease as if it were part of a predestined program which they are compelled helplessly to fulfill.

Hypnotic age regressions allow one to discover biographical experiences which may be considered typical for cancer patients. In the age regressions themselves we are careful to introduce only those suggestions which are appropriate for the patient, hoping to make a satisfying life possible. For examples of this kind, see the "February Man" case (Erickson & Rossi, 1979, p. 208; Peter, 1983b, p. 460). Projections into the future contain possibilities for reframing which are useful in supplying motivation for overcoming the present life threat.

With techniques applied in hypnotic trance, it must be remembered that the unconscious mind "knows" things which the conscious mind does not. We treat patients with utmost care, accepting resistances which emerge and inducing amnesia when it becomes clear in trance that they will not survive or do not want to survive, but consciously are convinced of a will to live. We accept that the fundamental decision to live or to die, to the degree that such a decision can be a determining factor in a multifactored disease process, will be made unconsciously by the patient. Because of this conviction, we reject certain "hard" treatment methods which are reported by other therapists (e.g., Simonton) especially the assumption that patients should either decide to fight unconditionally for their lives, or to prepare for death.

We have treated all our cancer patients in individual sessions, thereby avoiding the situation where an unmotivated patient or a conflicted patient could undermine the motivation of other patients. This model also allows us to accept patients exactly where they are, including their conflicts and idiosyncrasies. We can focus our attention on making the best of the situation without needing to worry about the effect of "negativity" on other patients. We are then free to take advantage of what we learned from Erickson, that even reactions which appear to be negative can be used therapeutically if the therapist is flexible enough to use these possibilities.

It is our opinion that a fixation on cure is an unnecessary and inhumane limitation of the treatment. The expectation or requirement for a cure can induce guilt in the patient quite easily and this certainly is an unnecessary burden. It may also be damaging to the therapeutic relationship and to further work. For example:

CASE FIVE

We (B.P. & W.G.) treated a 56-year-old patient with bronchial carcinoma. Only after a three-hour session did the patient agree to set aside his sarcasm and, in spite of his sense of hopelessness, make an attempt to care for his health and well-being. He accepted fully the idea that he would allow no metastasis. He developed a metaphor for himself which he called the "cell identification service." A sentence spontaneously occurred to him that he could apply in cases of questionable cell identification: "An ID card is not enough, fingerprints are required here!"

He also established six-month programs for himself in which he could transfer the future projections into his daily life. However, he obstinately rejected our efforts to activate the immune system and to support his making changes in his daily life which appeared to us to be necessary. Some of his arguments for this seemed clear and logical, others were questionable. At that time, we believed that we should attempt to steer the patient in what we thought would be a "correct" direction, using, of course, carefully chosen metaphors and direct questions which were appropriate for him.

This particular patient derived substantial secondary gain from his illness, and was able to control the occasional discomfort. He reacted to our attempts by rather unexpectedly breaking contact with first one therapist and then the other; he remained in contact with us only through a family member. Six months later, he resumed contact. During this period he had religiously done his program against the metastasis and had in fact begun the task of reordering his personal life. He continued to feel, as before, that any direct action against the tumor was pointless. He had not undertaken medical treatment for the tumor until recently, two and a half years after the discovery of the disease and the beginning of the psychological treatment. The tumor shows signs of a slow development, but there is no evidence of metastasis.

The fact that the therapeutic relationship remains stable to this day may be due to my (B.P.) willingness to give up the attempts to influence him to take any particular course of action against the tumor. Acceptance of his wish is communicated less through words than by the willingness to meet with him informally socially, e.g., at a nearby lake or with my family rather than in my office. In this informal context themes which previously had met with resistance were freely discussed and questions directly answered. A careful study of the videotape of the last two meetings before he broke off the therapy, does reveal errors in the therapeutic work. I had attempted to move the patient to make existential changes. In trance he clearly imagined the joylessness and desolateness of his existence as well as the beginning of a change. To speed the change effect, I tried to get the conscious side working by commenting that the session had been especially important and that he might think about how he could go about making the necessary changes in his life. In retrospect, this was a mistake. It would have been more useful to induce an amnesia and then in following sessions continue the work of restructuring or reframing the system. I didn't get that far. The patient apparently thought that he might make the changes, but because the timing was off, this served only to strengthen his sense of hopelessness and I was not successful in contacting again the fantasy images of beginning change which previously had emerged.

Hypnotherapy to Help Patients Deal with the Fact of Their Illness

For many of our patients, cancer is their first serious or life-threatening illness. The cancer often is viewed defensively as an immense insult to which they react with panic, despair, denial, or sarcasm. These reactions make it difficult to motivate conscious cooperation. If one accepts the idea that the cancer cells and the body defense system can be influenced more readily when patients are willing to identify with them and to accept them as their own, then it is important that patients develop awareness to the point where each says willingly, "I am my cancer" rather than "I have cancer!"

It is questionable if demanding this self-identification is justified and reasonable and if it is even therapeutically useful and meaningful. It is necessary that the conscious mind fight against the illness with every means at its disposal. Defenses must be respected and appreciated in order to be able to establish and maintain a therapeutic relationship. We acknowledge the patients' right to determine how many and which specific details they are consciously willing to accept and understand at any given point of time. We also accept their individual manner of doing this. Only after the defensive position is accepted can the patients' cooperation be freely given and his openness to utilize unconscious capabilities for change be assured.

CASE SIX

A 65-year-old patient with fibrosarcoma was expected to live only a few weeks. He was referred to me (B.P.) by his family physician because of his depressed mental state and poor physical condition. In the first session he wept almost continuously. I began to induce trance immediately by pacing his despair and hopelessness. I emphasized that I thought *it is indeed a shame to die such a miserable death after a long life of trying to function conscientiously and responsibly.* I then began to address his unconscious to help him use all of his resources in dealing with what was admittedly a heavy blow. During my discussion of his immune system, he developed the spontaneous image of a school of Piranhas attacking a white crocodile and tearing it to shreds. During the trance and in the waking state following, I suggested to him that he might just relax at home and try to activate his unconscious mind using this and similar images to work for a rich and worthwhile life.

The physician and the patient's wife reported that his mood improved dramatically following this session. In the following sessions he reported his plans for the coming year and for specific family-related events. In doing so he emphasized positive aspects, relating situations in which he had learned to overcome need, misery, and disaster. He mentioned, for example, the loss of his first wife to cancer ten years previously, how he coped with the difficulties of bringing up his children, and how he had survived the dangers of the war.

My task during his descriptions was only to appreciate his competence and to relate it gently to his present situation. He now appeared calm and tranquil in contrast to the weeping during the first session. His stories frequently gave rise to hearty laughter. He remained actively involved with his life, living each day to the fullest until his quick and painless death nine months after his first visit.

In such cases the question arises of whether patients diagnosed as terminal should know the full truth or not. We believe that this much-discussed question is problematic only when we, or others involved with patients, are not successful in determining what they want to know at a specific point in time, and what they prefer to hold at a distance. The danger that patients could decompensate as soon as the "hard facts" are known is especially great when time is short. They then die in depressed confusion without having had the time to come to terms with dying. As hypnotherapists we possess a rich palette of methods for indirect communication. Methods such as therapeutic metaphor, for example, allow us to offer patients indirect communication and then to watch reactions as a guide for further interventions. Such use of indirect techniques can aid the therapist in determining patients' limits without the need to speak directly about their personal situation.

CONCLUSION

A review of the literature shows that a growing number of researchers and clinicians are using hypnosis for cancer patients (e.g., *American Journal of Clinical Hypnosis,* 1982/83). Many controlled studies (e.g., Hilgard & LeBaron, 1982; Kellerman et al., 1983; Zeltzer et al., 1983) confirm our own experience: clinical hypnosis—when applied in a competent way—can effectively help cancer patients to deal with their illness and its symptoms, as well as with the side effects of the medical treatment. This means that clinical hypnosis can, at the least, contribute to a better life for cancer patients. Indeed, in a few special cases, hypnotic pain control seems to be the only possible way to help patients endure their lives.

What we do not yet know is whether hypnosis can help, or even help better than other psychotherapeutic treatment, to prolong the cancer patient's life significantly. Nor do we know if hypnosis can help to cure the disease. The work of Bernauer W. Newton (1982/83) and the positive outcomes with our patients are encouraging us to proceed with our clinical work as well as research.

REFERENCES

Ader, R. (Ed.). (1981). *Psychoneuroimmunology*. New York: Academic Press.

American Journal of Clinical Hypnosis. 25th Anniversary Commemorative Volume, 25(2/3), 1982/83.

Bowers, K. (1979). Hypnosis and dissociation. In D. Goleman & R. J. Davidson (Eds.), *Consciousness*. New York: Harper & Row.

Erickson, M. H., & Rossi, E. L. (1979). *Hypnotherapy*. New York: Irvington.

Grossarth-Maticek, R. (1979). Krankheit als biographie—Ein medizinsoziologisches modell der krebsentstehung und therapie. Köln: Kiepenheuer & Witsch.

Hall, H. R. (1982/83). Hypnosis and the immune system: A review with implications for cancer and the psychology of healing. *American Journal of Clinical Hypnosis*, 25(2/3), 92–103.

Hilgard, E. R., & Hilgard, J. R. (1975). *Hypnosis in the relief of pain*. Los Altos: W. Kaufmann.

Hilgard, J. R., & LeBaron, S. (1982). Relief of anxiety and pain in children and adolescents with cancer: Quantitative measures and clinical observations. *International Journal of Clinical and Experimental Hypnosis*, XXX(4), 417–422.

Kellerman, J., Zeltzer, L., Ellenberg, L., & Dash, J. (1983). Adolescents with cancer: Hypnosis for the reduction of the acute pain and anxiety associated with medical procedures. *Journal of Adolescent Health Care*, 4, 85-90.

Newton, B. W. (1982/83). The use of hypnosis in the treatment of cancer patients. *American Journal of Clinical Hypnosis*, 25(2/3), 104–113.

Peter. B. (1983a). Hypnotherapie. In R. J. Corsini (Ed.), *Handbuch der psychotherapie*. Weinheim: Beltz.

Peter, B. (1983b). Klinische hypnose. In C. Kraiker & B. Peter (Eds.), *Psychotherapieführer*. München: Beck.

Rosen, S. (1982). *My voice will go with you—The teaching tales of Milton H. Erickson*. New York: Norton.

Simonton, O. C., Matthews-Simonton, St., & Creighton, J. (1978). *Getting well again*. Toronto: Bantam Books.

Sutcliffe, J. P. (1960). "Credulous" and "skeptical" views of hypnotic phenomena. *International Journal of Clinical and Experimental Hypnosis*, 8, 73–101.

Sutcliffe, J. P. (1961). "Credulous" and "skeptical" views of hypnotic phenomena —Experiments on esthesia, hallucination, and delusion. *Journal of Abnormal and Social Psychology*, 62(2), 189–200.

Zeig, J. K. (1980). *A teaching seminar with Milton H. Erickson*. New York: Brunner/Mazel.

Zeltzer, L., Kellerman, J., Ellenberg, L., & Dash, J. (1983). Hypnosis for reduction of vomiting associated with chemotherapy and disease in adolescents with cancer. *Journal of Adolescent Health Care*, 4, 77–84.

PART VIII

Sexuality

In her volume, Disorders of Sexual Desire *(Brunner/Mazel, 1979), Helen Singer Kaplan described the condition of inhibited sexual desire. Hammond and Barbach describe their approach to the treatment of this problem.*

D. Corydon Hammond, Ph.D., earned his degree in counseling psychology from the University of Utah. As an assistant professor, he is codirector of the Sex and Marital Therapy Clinic and coordinator of training and research for the Alcohol and Drug Abuse Clinic of the University of Utah School of Medicine. Hammond is president of the Utah Society of Clinical Hypnosis and a clinical member of the American Association of Marital and Family Therapy. He has extensive publications in the fields of sexual dysfunction and alcoholism and coauthored Improving Therapeutic Communication: A Guide for Developing Techniques *(Jossey-Bass, 1977). Hammond presents a number of options for using hypnosis to assess and treat inhibited sexual desire, including induced dreams, metaphor, and age regression.*

Lonnie Barbach, Ph.D., earned her degree in social psychology at the Wright Institute in Berkeley, California. An assistant clinical professor of medical psychology at the University of California Medical School Human Sexuality Program in San Francisco, Barbach is active on the lecture circuit and has published articles in many popular magazines, including Family Circle, Mademoiselle, *and* Cosmopolitan. *Her books include:* For Yourself: The Fulfillment of Female Sexuality *(Doubleday, 1975),* Women Discover Orgasm: A Therapists' Guide to a New Treatment Approach

(Free Press, 1980), Shared Intimacies: Women's Sexual Experiences *(with Linda Levine) (Doubleday, Anchor Press, 1980)*, For Each Other: Sharing Sexual Intimacy *(Doubleday, Anchor Press, 1982)*.

Many problems involving lack of desire are interactional; they occur when there is a difference in level of sexual desire between partners. Lack of sexual desire has a number of causes. No matter what the cause, it soon becomes a habit and the habit pattern needs to be changed to promote satisfactory sexual expression.

Chapter 30

Treatment of Inhibited
Sexual Desire

D. Corydon Hammond

Inhibited sexual desire appears to be the most common sexual dysfunction and is probably seen in half or more of couples seeking sex therapy (Kaplan, 1979). However, Masters and Johnson (1970) did not originally identify inhibited sexual desire (ISD) as a diagnostic category of sexual dysfunction. It was not until 1977 that Kaplan distinguished inhibited sexual desire as another diagnosis.

Most patients with inhibited sexual desire experience little interest in sex; when they respond to sexual advances it is primarily out of a sense of duty rather than desire. It is not uncommon, however, for such patients to become aroused and perform adequately once they are sexually involved. Similar to other sexual dysfunctions, inhibited sexual desire may be primary (having always existed) or secondary, developing after previously experienced interest in sex. It may also be either global in nature or situational to the partner. When the inhibition of desire is so severe that the patient finds sex repulsive and wishes to avoid all sexual contact, the condition is referred to as sexual aversion. Multiple factors may inhibit sexual interest and a careful evaluation is required before initiating treatment. For example, sexual desire may be diminished by medications, illness, depression, fatigue, endocrine problems, stress, marital conflict, sexual ignorance, religious prohibitions and traumatic experiences.

There is limited research available on the treatment of ISD (Stuart & Hammond, 1980). However, more than forty years ago, Milton Erickson (Erickson & Kubie, 1941) provided the earliest known report of the successful treatment of a case. In three extended hypnotic sessions, he treated a woman who today would be diagnosed as having primary

415

sexual aversion. After proposing, the fiancé of the 23-year-old woman leaned over to kiss her. This caused her to vomit on him and afterwards develop a severe, intractable depression. Erickson brilliantly utilized the values she had internalized from her mother, gradually helping her realize that if her mother had lived longer she would have finished her sex education in a manner appropriate for a young adult. This is a classic case worthy of careful study. Others (August, 1959; Coulton, 1960; Levit, 1971; Oystragh, 1974) also have used hypnotic age regression to treat cases of inhibited sexual desire. Beigel (1969) worked with a woman with sexual aversion through hypnotically exploring and modifying negative attitudes and then using sex therapy techniques parallel to those later reported by Masters and Johnson (1970). More recently, Araoz (1980) reported the successful treatment of seven of ten cases of inhibited sexual desire using hypnotic techniques.

The purpose of this paper is to provide an overview of the variety of hypnotic strategies available for the treatment of inhibited sexual desire. The author utilizes various combinations of hypnotic techniques depending on the unique background factors and hypnotic talents of each patient.

HYPNOTIC ASSESSMENT & EXPLORATION

Inhibited sexual desire often seems somewhat mysterious in comparison with other dysfunctions. Following traditional evaluation, the therapist often has a sense that important information is still missing. The following methods of hypnotic exploration frequently provide invaluable additional information, particularly when "resistance" seems to be present.

Ideomotor Exploration

Methods of ideomotor signaling were popularized by Erickson (Erickson & Rossi, 1981) and Cheek (Cheek & LeCron, 1968). I often use these methods to identify the presence of unconscious dynamics or unresolved past experiences. Many patients who consciously indicated that they had never been involved in incest or negative childhood experiences have discovered early trauma during ideomotor exploration and subsequent age regression. Some patients with inhibited sexual desire are also found to have unresolved feelings of guilt and to be engaging in self-punishment without conscious awareness. Other patients may be unconsciously identifying with an inhibited parent. Cheek and LeCron (1968) discussed the concept of "imprints," which are statements made by authority figures, often in an atmosphere of strong emotion, that serve like prestige suggestions. It is not uncommon for inhibited sexual desire patients to have imprinted and internalized negative childhood messages about sex that may still be influential.

Age Regression

Age regression to the onset of a problem or to influential past events may be valuable in removing roadblocks to sexual desire. Some patients who reported feeling like their skin was "crawling" when touched by a partner have been regressed back to the first time they experienced such a sensation. In some cases, patients discovered an incest or molestation experience. In one instance, the patient found that during surgical anesthesia six years before, the physician had sexually fondled her breasts, leading to inhibited sexual desire and an aversion to breast stimulation (which she had previously enjoyed).

When traditional sex therapy assignments meet with resistance, age regression may be used to review task assignments that did not go well. The patient or couple may be hypnotized and regressed to the sexual assignment a few nights previous to obtain a detailed account of what occurred. This hypnotic review not only may include what was said and done, but may aid in clarifying feelings, sensations, and the internal dialogue accompanying the assignment. When a hypnotic review of an assignment is conducted, it usually removes any mystery about what went wrong.

HYPNOTIC TREATMENT STRATEGIES

After hypnotic and standardized assessment methods have identified some of the multiple factors causing inhibited desire, then an individualized treatment plan may be tailored to the couple. Treatment strategies may include traditional sex therapy assignments, marital therapy, communication training, and a variety of hypnotic methods that may be used individually or in combination with nonhypnotic techniques. In the remainder of the chapter, the author will overview some of the options for hypnotic intervention with inhibited sexual desire.

Age Regression

Age regression and hypnotic reframing may be helpful in resolving negative past experiences. However, age regression also may be focused on *positive* life experiences. Many patients with inhibited sexual desire have in the past enjoyed feelings of intimacy, desire and closeness to their partners. When romantic and sexual feelings have existed, age regression may aid in rekindling the attraction, love and passion that have withered. Age regression may revivify experiences both of sexual encounters and romantic courtship. Posthypnotic suggestions may then be given to aid in transferring the feelings of desire to situations when the patient is alone with the partner. Some patients also are able to utilize self-hypnosis in restimulating these feelings and desires.

Erotic Imagery

Sex therapists often encourage inhibited sexual desire patients to read erotic literature and to frequent romantic-erotic movies as a method for stimulating increased sexual interest. Sexual fantasies also have been encouraged as a method for distracting patients with performance anxiety from engaging in "spectatoring" (Kaplan, 1974).

Patients may be taught to induce erotic fantasies in a self-hypnotic state as a method to increase sexual desire, particularly prior to anticipated lovemaking or sexual assignments. In some cases I request that the patient construct one or two highly erotic fantasies. These fantasies are to be extremely detailed, including the sensory representational systems of sight, smell, taste, hearing and tactile sensations. When the patient brings the fantasies to the next interview, I may assist in further expanding the detail and vividness. Afterwards, the patient may be hypnotized and the fantasy material slowly presented. This process may be tape recorded as an aid for the patient to use in self-hypnosis. The patient also is strongly encouraged to practice self-hypnosis daily, independent of a recording, creating erotic imagery and fantasies to increase desire. One innovative patient created a pleasure mansion for herself to visit wherein she could open doors and find different and unexpected sexual environments and partners, including saunas, swimming pools, masseurs, outdoor settings, ballrooms, and parties. Each evening in self-hypnosis she would open doors until she encountered something interesting and provocative.

Induced Dreams

We all can reflect back to having a powerful dream that evoked strong feelings. Alfred Adler (1958) suggested that one of the functions of dreams was as a "factory of emotions," serving to generate feelings that move one toward action after awakening. One innovative use of hypnosis has been to give posthypnotic suggestions for erotic nocturnal dreams, including the suggestion that the feelings of increased sexual desire will remain and carry over into the day, after the patient has awakened. Giving posthypnotic suggestions for erotic dreams requires little time, but has been effective in some cases. This technique has the added advantage of allowing conservative and religious individuals to enjoy erotic imagery without feeling responsible for willfully creating the fantasies.

Ego-State Therapy

Patients with inhibited sexual desire are typically patients in conflict. They lack libido and yet part of them often desires to have sexual interest and please their mate. Ego-state therapy (Watkins & Watkins, 1978, 1981) is a hypnotic approach that is particularly useful with patients who experience conflict or a sense of compulsion. During a hypnotic state, the therapist may ask to speak with the inner part of the patient that is causing the lack of interest in sex. These ego states, much like miniature multiple personalities, typically give the therapist their name or title and provide a unique life history. Watkins has demonstrated that ego states, like Hilgard's (1977) hidden observer, may be elicited in normal subjects. The therapist seeks to develop a relationship with the unconscious part, to understand and positively reframe its goal and function within the person, and then to negotiate a cooperative relationship between the different inner parts of the patient. Watkins likened the method to doing internal diplomacy or family therapy with the "internal family of self." In many respects the method is similar to using gestalt therapy empty chair techniques.

Symbolic Hypnotic Techniques

Symbolic imagery techniques are often valuable in hypnotically modifying problematic feelings and attitudes in patients with inhibited sexual desire. Erickson (Haley, 1973) occasionally treated phobias or resistance through suggesting to hypnotized patients that they leave their fear or resistance in an envelope or an office chair. The patient with an excess of guilt or aversive feelings may visualize putting them into a basket, attaching a helium balloon, and then watching it float away to a distant mountain top (Walch, 1976). Araoz (1982) used metaphoric imagery by asking patients to visualize putting negative sexual attitudes or messages into a dump truck, then taking them to where they may be dynamited or burned.

Several other symbolic therapy methods have also been suggested (Stanton, 1977) that can be applied to some patients with inhibited sexual desire. A patient can visualize some kind of barrier (e.g., a brick wall) that is holding him back and imagine breaking through the barrier by smashing or blowing it up (Stanton, 1977). Parallel to Erickson's method, a patient can visualize placing negative attitudes or feelings into a compartment and locking them away where they will no longer be a bother or influence, such as in a safe or a remote castle (Stanton, 1977). The patient who is overfatigued can learn to withdraw in self-hypnosis to a serene or tranquil room, or to another peaceful (or erotic) scene (Stanton, 1977). In this restful place one can even feel one's batteries of sexual interest and energy being recharged in some symbolic manner.

Symbolic techniques are best when individualized to the patient's unique background and hypnotic talents. A golfer can imagine hitting a bucket of golf balls into a distant ravine or lake, with the balls symbolizing anger, guilt, or aversive feelings about something from the past. A patient responsive to visual and kinesthetic trance experiences can observe and feel himself writing negative parental messages about sex onto a paper and then putting it into the hot coals of a fire. While observing it burn, he can feel its warmth and an increasing sense of relaxation and relief.

The Silent Abreaction (Watkins, 1980) is a valuable symbolic technique for letting go of anger and hurt from negative past experiences. In this technique, the patient visualizes walking along a path (e.g., in the mountains) until coming to a large boulder that symbolizes hurt and anger. He is instructed to pick up a large stick and to beat on the boulder, yelling or screaming anything he wants (in his mind, "here in the mountains"). The patient is repetitively encouraged to continue until exhausted and to then give an ideomotor signal. In difficult cases, the patient may repeat the procedure as necessary in self-hypnosis. This technique facilitates abreactive release without the outward intensity that may embarrass a patient or disturb colleagues in nearby offices.

The Master Control Room technique (Araoz, 1982; Hammond, 1983a) is another symbolic method that has been used for increasing sexual desire, particularly after roadblocks to sexual interest have been removed. In a hypnotic state, the patient visualizes entering a master control room in the hypothalamus. Instructions are given that this is where all desires and feelings are controlled. Depending on the responsiveness of the patient to different sensory modalities, he or she be instructed to be aware of panels of colored lights, sense the temperature of the room, hear the hum of the computers, etc. The patient is instructed to find the panel regulating sexual desire, on which there is a lever or dial that may be set from 0-10. It is explained that zero represents the level of no desire and 10 the level of strong sexual desire. The patient can tell the therapist what number the dial is set on (it will often be one or two). Instructions are then given to gradually begin moving the dial upward. Simultaneously, suggestions are offered about how different feelings and sensations can be sensed. With each request to turn the dial up another number, suggestions are interspersed about the increasing desire, and hormones being released, pulsing and flowing through the body and particularly concentrating in certain places. Some patients are surprised to find sensual and aroused feelings during this experience.

When a patient does not sense different feelings, the therapist may proceed in a more fail-safe manner, e.g., "That just proves how subtle, almost imperceptible those changes are as they begin. And it's really not important, for you to fully sense these changes, in *this* environment. And I'm not sure just when, or where, you will begin to detect the difference. Your unconscious mind can bring about that awareness, of change, in a way that meets your needs. It may be that you suddenly and spontaneously become aware, that you feel urges, feelings, an impulse. Or perhaps there will be a gradual growing sense, of progressive changes, of a subtle, unhurried, natural evolution. And I don't know if you'll recognize those changes tomorrow, or Thursday, or next week. But in an interesting way, you'll realize that you *are* changing, in your own personal way."

Finally, the patient can decide what level the dial should remain set on, or the suggestion can be given that the patient's unconscious can regulate the level of sexual desire in accord with the appropriateness of the circumstances. In other cases, posthypnotic suggestions are given for sexual desire to occur in particular circumstances, such as whenever the patient snuggles with his or her partner in bed. Although this method seems simplistic, the spouses of several inhibited sexual desire patients have requested a dial change to lower reading after a couple of weeks of daily sexual activity!

Case example

Jane was a 22-year-old married woman who entered treatment with problems of serious depression, feelings of inadequacy, panic attacks, obesity, and strong sexual aversion. Following several sessions of general ego-strengthening and instruction in self-hypnosis, Jane's panic attacks stopped and her depression decreased. Jane's mother disliked sex and through age regressions we discovered many negative early messages that she received about sex and men. However, efforts to reframe or modify the influence of these early messages and her sexual aversion were unsuccessful. Jane still was dependent on her mother and controlled by mother's perceptions.

Jane was asked to picture imagery symbolizing the manner in which her mother had infused her with negativity about men. Almost immediately she described finding herself standing beside mother, trapped inside a spinning black circle of dirt and dust. Her husband, children and friends were outside the circle, looking black and dirty. Inside the circle she felt stifled and hardly able to breathe. When she looked at her mother, mother looked mean. The feelings of being stifled, unable to breathe, and the fear of her mother were accentuated to increase her motivation to escape. Nonetheless, Jane remained frightened.

I provided the encouragement that I would help her if she were willing to break out of the circle. Jane was familiar with the Star Wars movies. Therefore, I handed her a light saber that she could use to cut her way out of the circle to escape. She visualized herself cutting an opening in the spinning circle, we ran out, and the suggestion was given that the circle was closing again.

Once we were outside the circle, it was emphasized how good it felt to breathe the fresh air and how wonderful and bright everything looked now that we were no longer viewing things through the dirt and dust. Suggestions were given repetitively that she was now free to see things through her own eyes, to decide for herself what was right and wrong, and what was true for her. It was suggested that she no longer had to see things through her mother's perception from within the circle and that she was free of the stifling entrapment.

The patient could not be seen again for three weeks. Her first week was characterized by depression and frightening dreams filled with images of the spinning circle and her mother. However, the next two weeks were described as the happiest in her five years of marriage. A dramatic transformation began to occur. In the past, Jane had resisted buying new clothes, arguing that she was fat and ugly. She now purchased an attractive new wardrobe and began using appropriate makeup. She started fixing her hair and taking pride in her appearance. Following her mother's example, she had never ironed one article of her husband's clothes in five years. Now (although some may deny this was an improvement!), she began ironing and actually enjoyed doing it. Instead of wishing her husband would die in an automobile accident, she found herself sitting and looking adoringly at him, with a sense of great love. Instead of feeling occasionally depressed during the day, she felt happy, "light," and often on the verge of laughter. Whereas previously she had jealously forbidden her husband to play on a church softball team, she now encouraged him to play and was surprised how much she enjoyed making a picnic lunch and taking the children to watch. She experienced a pleasant sense of detachment from her mother, feeling warmly toward her, but free of her control.

The master control room technique was employed and the previous suggestions reinforced. Instead of hating to have sex twice a month, she now initiated sex twice daily and thoroughly enjoyed the experiences. She explained, "I used to never feel Steve touch me until this week." His touch was now described as "heavenly." After Steve began to plead for mercy, Jane was willing to use the imagery of the master control room to lower her sexual desire to a more moderate level. At six-month follow-up, the changes have maintained.

The Use of Metaphors

Erickson pioneered the concept of communicating on more than one level through indirect and interspersed suggestions and the use of metaphors. Metaphors create an atmosphere where patients feel less threatened and where suggestions can be interspersed in a way that bypasses defenses. After giving a suggestion, the therapist can quickly move on and distract the patient before resistance develops.

Zeig (1980) articulated the Ericksonian principle that, "In general, the amount of indirection necessary is directly proportional to the anticipated resistance" (p. 25). Metaphors can be valuable with inhibited sexual desire patients because, although appearing consciously cooperative, many of these patients are resistant to change. When considerable resistance is anticipated, I sometimes disguise metaphoric imagery and suggestions by further defining them as "deepening" techniques. They may be introduced with a phrase such as, "And now, to help you to go still deeper . . ." When the resistance is not strong, however, I follow another of Erickson's patterns—that of establishing an associative bridge between the metaphor and the patient's problem (E.L. Rossi, personal communication, 1983). I believe this to be valuable unless there is reason to believe that the patient's conscious mind will interfere with the suggestions. Examples of Erickson's use of such associative bridges may be found in Erickson and Rossi (1979, pp. 104-107).

Changes in food preference metaphor. The metaphor that follows is provided as a model of a metaphor designed for sexual aversion and inhibited sexual desire patients. Naturally, it is used selectively and individualized as much as possible.

> Most of us have some foods we like better than others. I can recall when I was a child I loved certain foods. I remember how much I just loved pancakes, and the smell of hot, fresh pancakes cooking in the morning. When I was hungry, they just seemed to melt in my mouth. And umm, after that warm, sticky feeling of the syrup, a glass of cold milk tasted so good. And I can recall the warm, comfortably full kind of feeling after eating them.
>
> "I don't know, when you were a child, what foods you liked. But *you* certainly remember, maybe not all of them, but some of them. I don't know for instance, if when you were a child, you liked eating pancakes, or pizza, or even strawberries. Maybe there was a particular food that you liked *very* much. (pause) I wonder how you are able to remember as a child, smelling the aroma, or seeing that food before you. Remember the taste of that food, the texture of it in your mouth as you relished it. Perhaps you remember the tingly juiciness of strawberries, and that feeling on your tongue. Or maybe you'd rather recall the crunchiness of fresh carrots out of the garden. For a moment, maybe you can just really enjoy the real memory of your favorite childhood foods again. (pause)
>
> Most of us as children, also had some foods that we disliked. I can recall as a child how I hated several kinds of foods. I didn't like peas, and at that time I hated clam chowder and enchiladas. I was turned off by all salads, and mushrooms, and yuk, the thought of eating a lobster or clam was repulsive. I'm sure you can remember some of the different foods that you disliked. (pause) There were so many things *then* that I didn't like, to eat. But you know, it's interesting, even surprising, how dramatically our tastes and preferences *can* change. Some of the foods that you avoided and disliked as a child can be enjoyed as an adult. And what I notice now is that the taste of an enchilada and the slipperiness of a clam seem different. And we learn that what was unappealing *can* become really pleasant and delicious.

And I guess that's because it's a part of nature, as we are continually growing and changing. Remember as children, we couldn't imagine how our parents could *enjoy* watching or listening to the news. It had no appeal to us then, but later, that changed. As a child, you can probably remember some television shows that you had no interest in. (pause) Many of us just couldn't understand how anyone could enjoy a movie that was romantic. A love story had no appeal to us then; we had no desire to see it. At the time, it seemed boring. But certain types of programs which once seemed uninteresting, *can* become enjoyable as we change. And it was the same with certain kinds of movies, and with certain kinds of music. (pause) We couldn't have imagined it at the time, but we changed in many ways that we could never predict. And most of the time, we aren't even quite sure exactly how or when those changes came about. But one thing that we can be sure of is that we will continue to change and to grow. Change is just a very natural part of life.

Developmental readiness metaphors are occasionally used with inhibited sexual desire patients. Anecdotes may be shared about late bloomers, variations in when individuals learn to walk and talk, etc. Toilet training requires a certain developmental readiness before it can be accomplished and learned. Similarly, a child cannot learn to read until development reaches a certain point at which the inner conditions are right. Relatedly, with female patients I sometimes use a metaphor I call the *Seasons of a Woman's Life*. The seasons of the year and their inevitable changes are discussed, including the changes associated with the blooming of spring and its new openness. The bridging association is that many women in like fashion do not come alive and evolve into their own sexually until their thirties or forties. Such metaphors can stimulate hope, seed ideas, and create a readiness or openness to change.

Trauma metaphors may be helpful for patients who have experienced trauma. For example, I describe the creation of a pearl, with the oyster transforming a harsh irritant into something different and beautiful, thereby providing stimulating creativity. Another way of reframing trauma or divorce is to tell a metaphor about vaccine and antibodies, likening this to being immunized by certain life experiences.

Physical metaphors and trance ratification. Demonstrating the ability of the unconscious mind to control the body can provide both a powerful metaphor and a dramatic experience that is convincing. I have used the experience of causing a patient to feel cold and then warm as a physical metaphor and simultaneous trance ratification experience. In treating a sexual aversion patient who experienced genital anesthesia, it was impressive to her to observe the capacity of her unconscious mind to create glove anesthesia and then witness a needle being painlessly inserted in the skin on the back of her hand. When she felt sensation return to her hand, it was suggested, "You now know the incredible power of your unconscious mind to influence your body and its feelings, and to produce change." During the following week, she perceived erotic genital sensation for the first time.

Other metaphors may be beneficial for patients more advanced in their treatment and close to the time when behavioral (sensate focus) exercises may be assigned (Kaplan, 1979). Depending on the interests of the patient, I may present (perhaps in the guise of a deepening technique) a discussion of enjoying a concert, caressing a pet, or swimming. As patients reexperience one of these types of activities, it is pointed out how pleasantly absorbed they have become in the experience and its sensations, shutting out other thoughts.

Relationship Enhancement Techniques

When relationship factors impair sexual interest, I use behavioral communication training exercises (Hammond, 1983b; Stuart & Hammond, 1980). In some cases, hypnosis can be a helpful adjunct to this training. When negative communication patterns have been identified, patients may visualize a model responding appropriately to various problematic situations, afterwards visualizing themselves responding similarly to the same situations. I subsequently request an unconscious (ideomotor) commitment for the new behavior to occur in similar situations. Failure to obtain the commitment alerts me to secondary gains requiring further exploration. After a commitment is obtained, posthypnotic suggestions can be given to further encourage transfer of learning and behavior change. Suggestions that were given in an awake state for enhancing communication also can be hypnotically reinforced. In this way, I use hypnosis in helping couples to avoid communication errors, to facilitate empathy, and to engage in constructive problem-solving and constructive management of anger.

Hypnosis also can be valuable in enhancing emotional intimacy and facilitating peak relationship experiences. Maslow (1964, 1972) originated the concept of the "peak experience." When one examines the description of these experiences, it is obvious that they are examples of spontaneous trance behavior. Maslow and subsequent researchers concluded that the prerequisite for a peak experience was an intense state of absorption and concentration on a present experience (e.g., dancing, mountain climbing, playing a musical instrument), or what Erickson called the "common everyday trance." I believe that part of the intensity of courtship results from informal trance experiences where both partners are deeply focused on one another, facilitating a feeling of union and intimacy. Dating couples often are literally entranced, feeling intensely close and experiencing a sense of time distortion when they are alone together. After marriage, however, many couples become preoccupied with other interests and with children. They spend time "around" each other, but not "with" one another, not unlike small children who engage in "parallel play activities." Gradually, feelings of closeness diminish.

When emotional distance is a factor in inhibited sexual desire, I teach the couple skills in being "fully present" with each other (Hammond, 1983a,b). In an exercise, they are asked to focus fully on what they are feeling, seeing, hearing, thinking and sensing with each other from moment to moment. As they focus fully on the present, they are asked to alternate speaking, beginning each sentence with the phrase, "Right now I'm aware of." Following several minutes of practice, they may move physically closer, hold hands and continue sharing their present awareness. With further practice, couples learn to narrow their focus of attention more fully to the interaction with their partner. Posthypnotic suggestions can also be given for facilitating greater present-centeredness. I often suggest that when they are alone together, they will become deeply absorbed in each other, and as they do so, the present will seem prolonged and expanded while the past and future will temporarily seem unimportant and distant. Couples also can be taught skills in mutual hypnosis. Through these methods, some of the intimacy and intensity of courtship may be rekindled.

CONCLUSION

As illustrated, inhibited sexual desire may be treated with a wide variety of hypnotic options. When individualized to the couple, hypnotic methods can enhance the effectiveness of traditional sex therapy.

REFERENCES

Adler, A. (1958). *What life should mean to you.* New York: Putnam.
Araoz, D.L. (1980). Clinical hypnosis in treating sexual abulia. *American Journal of Family Therapy, 8,* 48–47.
Araoz, D.L. (1982). *Hypnosis in sex therapy.* New York: Brunner/Mazel.

August, R.V. (1959). Libido altered with the aid of hypnosis: A case report. *American Journal of Clinical Hypnosis, 2,* 88.

Beigel, H.G. (1969). The use of hypnosis in female sexual anesthesia. *Journal of the Society of Psychosomatic Dentistry & Medicine, 19,* 4-14.

Cheek, D.B., & LeCron, L.M. (1968). *Clinical hypnotherapy.* New York: Grune & Stratton.

Coulton, D. (1960). Hypnotherapy in gynecological problems. *American Journal of Clinical Hypnosis, 3,* 92-100.

Erickson, M.H., & Kubie, L.S. (1941). The successful treatment of a case of acute hysterical depression by a return under hypnosis to a critical phase of childhood. *Psychoanalytic Quarterly, 10,* 583-609.

Erickson, M.H., & Rossi, E. (1979). *Hypnotherapy.* New York: Irvington.

Erickson, M.H., & Rossi, E.L. (1981). *Experiencing hypnosis.* New York: Irvington.

Haley, J. (1973). *Uncommon therapy.* New York: Norton.

Hammond, D.C. (1983a). Hypnosis in marital & sex therapy. In R. Stahmann & W. Hiebert (Eds.), *Counseling with marital & sexual problems* (3rd ed.). Lexington, MA: D.C. Heath.

Hammond, D.C. (1983b). *Enhancing couple communication.* Unpublished manuscript.

Hilgard, E.R. (1977). *Divided consciousness.* New York: Wiley.

Kaplan, H.S. (1974). *The new sex therapy.* New York: Brunner/Mazel.

Kaplan, H.S. (1979). *Disorders of sexual desire.* New York: Brunner/Mazel.

Levit, H.I. (1971). Marital crisis intervention: Hypnosis in impotence/frigidity cases. *American Journal of Clinical Hypnosis, 14,* 56-60.

Maslow, A.H. (1964). *Religions, values & peak-experiences.* New York: Viking.

Maslow, A.H. (1972). *Farthest reaches of human nature.* New York: Viking.

Masters, W., & Johnson, V. (1970). *Human sexual inadequacy.* Boston: Little, Brown & Co.

Oystragh, P. (1974). Hypnosis & frigidity. *Journal of the American Society of Psychosomatic Dentistry & Medicine, 21,* 10-18.

Stanton, H.E. (1977). Therapy, hypnosis and thought control. *Australian Journal of Clinical Hypnosis, 5,* 119-128.

Stuart, F., & Hammond, D.C. (1980). Sex therapy. In R.B. Stuart (Ed.), *Helping couples change* (pp. 301-366). New York: Guilford.

Walch, S.L. (1976). The red balloon technique in hypnotherapy. *International Journal of Clinical & Experimental Hypnosis, 24,* 10-12.

Watkins, H.H. (1980). The silent abreaction. *International Journal of Clinical & Experimental Hypnosis, 28,* 101-113.

Watkins, J.G., & Watkins, H.H. (1978). Theory & practice of ego-state therapy: A short-term therapeutic approach. In H. Grayson (Ed.), *Short-term approaches to psychotherapy* (pp. 176-220). New York: Human Sciences Press.

Watkins, J.G., & Watkins, H.H. (1981). Ego-state therapy. In R.J. Corsini (Ed.), *Handbook of innovative psychotherapies* (pp. 252-270). New York: Wiley.

Zeig, J.K. (1980). *A teaching seminar with Milton H. Erickson.* New York: Brunner/Mazel.

Chapter 31

Causes and Treatment of Lack of Sexual Desire

Lonnie Barbach

Before one can define the causes and treatment of lack of sexual desire, one must first define desire. Desire is the first stage in sexual arousal and response. Desire precedes arousal, physiological readiness, orgasm, and satisfaction. Often, people confuse desire and arousal. However, they are quite different. Desire is really a frequency variable. It determines how often one wants to make love, whereas arousal is a subjective response. It determines how turned on the person is.

A person can have a great desire for sex, yet not get aroused once stimulation begins. Sometimes this occurs when the lovemaking is too mechanical or when the person experiences considerable guilt over being sexually active. The reverse can also occur. Someone who has no difficulty getting aroused once the lovemaking begins may rarely feel desirous of sex. Sometimes this is seen among workaholics, to whom sex is regarded as a distraction from the task at hand, or among people who feel overwhelmed by the intimacy in a relationship and distance themselves sexually by lacking desire.

Since desire is a frequency variable, in order to determine a problem stemming from lack of desire, it is necessary first to arrive at what can be considered a normal level of desire. This becomes difficult if not impossible to do since every individual is unique. We differ in the clothes we wear, in the hobbies and vocations we choose; we differ in numerous predispositions, such as athletic, musical, or artistic abilities. As far as sex is concerned, hormonal balance, physical stamina, and the impor-

---

This paper is a synopsis of one section of *For Each Other: Sharing Sexual Intimacy*, by Lonnie Barbach. NY: Anchor/Doubleday, Inc. 1982.

tance of sex vary from person to person. All of these, plus the state of our physical health, affect the frequency with which we desire sex.

Most problems involving apparent lack of desire occur when the two members of a couple differ in their *levels* of sexual desire rather than because one partner has a lack of desire. This is a very important concept because discrepancies in desire are not treated in the same manner as cases of lack of desire.

When assessing lack of desire, it is necessary to determine the function sex plays in the lives of both members of the couple. In our culture, when it comes to sex, we generally consider *more* to be better. However, it is possible that the person with the higher sex drive is the one with the problem. For example, some people use sex as a distraction from boredom, for relaxation when frustrated or anxious, or as a pick-me-up when they are depressed, whereas others use sex solely as a way to express feelings of love and caring. When the members of a couple use sex for different purposes or when their basic sex drives vary considerably, a problem exists. However, the solution does not always lie in trying to increase the level of sexual desire of the person with the lesser interest. It may be necessary to teach the partner who satisfies various emotional needs through sex to derive satisfaction from nonsexual activities. Physical exercise, hobbies, and intimate discussions are some of the activities that could be instituted. In the same manner, the partner who is less interested in sex may need to learn that sex can be physically gratifying and can enhance the relationship when lovemaking is more frequent, even if he or she is not always entirely desirous at the outset.

As in every other area of intimate relating, the solution to discrepancies in desire involves compromise so that each person's needs are met part of the time. If a couple is planning a vacation together and one person wants to go to the mountains and the other wants to go to the beach, compromise is needed. In cases of discrepancies in desire, it may be necessary for the person who wants sex more often to be willing on some occasions to cuddle, take a walk, or have an intimate dinner together rather than make love. The less interested partner must be willing to engage in sex at times when he or she might not be as active or responsive as usual. It would be understood that the more interested partner would be expected to take the lead and invest most of the energy. When this is the case, it is important for the more interested person not to sulk or refuse the generous gesture of their mate just because he or she is less enthusiastic than would be preferred. Our partner's needs are important, and acts of generosity which are accepted graciously can enhance a relationship.

Further, it is possible for two people to engage sexually but to different degrees. Some couples have worked out a discrepancy in desire by having the more desirous person masturbate while being held and kissed by their partner. This allows both people to participate together, yet to different degrees, thereby meeting some of each person's needs.

Some couples are unable to institute the above solutions because of the secondary problem of stored anger and resentment that often result from discrepancies in sexual desire. When one partner wants sex more than the other, a number of additional problems inevitably occur. The person who wants sex more starts to feel unattractive, undesirable, unloved, and hence angry. The less desirous person begins to feel asexual, abnormal, guilty and resentful toward the partner who is making demands. Inevitably, the amount of physical touching, both sexual and nonsexual, decreases. The more interested partner does not want to get rejected and so avoids reaching out physically and emotionally. The less desirous partner does the same for fear of being accused of being a tease. The couple then drifts apart, partially due to lack of physical contact.

Often, the desire discrepancy grows larger over time. The more interested partner perceives the less interested one as *never* wanting sex and so demands sex whenever possible—the idea being that the more demands that are made, the more likely that at least some percentage will be accepted. The less interested partner sees each request as one more demand and begins to refuse almost automatically. After a while, neither partner pays attention to personal needs and begins to react to the anticipated response of the other. The power struggle that ensues is often more difficult to treat than the actual difference in levels of desire.

When this persist/resist battle occurs, it is often necessary to put a ban on sex. This changes the system of interaction so that the less interested partner has nothing to fight, and with this feeling of control, sexual interest generally rises of its own accord. However, in order to accomplish this goal, the more interested partner must somehow become convinced that he or she is more likely to get what is desired by becoming more patient and allowing the partner to initiate sex rather than pushing the partner further away by pursuit. This can often best be done by helping the more interested partner realize that since he or she is already making love only rarely, this ban on sex makes no practical difference in behavior—but it could change their process of interaction. It is at this point that Ericksonian and strategic techniques such as reframing, utilizing resistance, pacing, etc., can be of great value.

Sometimes a lack of desire, particularly on the woman's part, is not a lack of desire at all, but an inability to initiate sex. If her role scripting taught her that it was not ladylike to be overtly sexual but proper only to respond to the advances of her partner, she may have successfully cut off awareness of her sexual desire. If such a woman enjoys sex and experiences arousal while making love, the simplest approach is to help the partner understand that her lack of initiative in no way indicates a lack of interest and to encourage him to initiate sex as often as he likes. In addition, the woman can be given assignments to initiate sex even if she is not aware of feeling sexually turned on in order to indicate to her partner that he is indeed desirable to her.

In addition to discrepancies in levels of desire and discomfort in initiating sex, there are real cases of lack of desire. Determining a particular treatment approach for lack of sexual desire is complex because of the numerous potential causes for the problem and because often, the lack of desire is merely a symptom of some other problem in the relationship which needs to be resolved before sexual issues can be confronted. For example, a common cause of lack of desire is anger at one's partner. Being angry at a mate doesn't usually lead to feeling amorous toward them. Hence, before any attempt can be made to increase the couple's sexual contact, some headway must be made in handling the resentment.

Some medications can affect an individual's level of sexual interest even when it is not considered a normal side effect of that drug. Sexual desire is also affected by hormonal levels, particularly testosterone. If the adrenals are removed, there will be a loss of sexual desire. Consequently, taking a medical and drug history is essential when treating lack of desire.

Another medically related cause of lack of sexual desire can result from pain associated with sex. Pain is a negative reinforcer and sufficient experience of pain will curtail sexual desire. When pain is present, a medical examination is required to determine whether the pain is physiological or psychological. When it is physiological, the treatment may be simple. When it appears to be psychological, it is necessary to delve deeper to determine what is causing the partner to avoid sex.

There are three common causes of lack of sexual desire that are treated in a similar manner. Reduced desire resulting from pregnancy and childbirth, routine sex in a long-term relationship, and a major illness are all similar in that the reduced level of sexual activity forms a habit pattern that continues long after the precipitating factor is no longer present.

A lack of desire can be considered quite natural during the pregnancy and post-partum period, since both partners may be exhausted, anxious, and overwhelmed. However, if the sexual relationship is not reestablished within six months to a year, serious relationship problems can emerge. Many couples trace their sexual problems back to the post-partum period.

Sex often becomes routine and boring because it is relegated, by most couples, to a low priority. Both partners make appointments with colleagues for lunch, friends for dinner, PTA meetings, political meetings, etc. If time is left over for sex, it generally occurs late at night after bills are paid, phone calls made, and children put to bed. With little energy and not much enthusiasm, sexual satisfaction and frequency decline.

Any major illness will interfere with a couple's sexual relationship. However, in most situations where a major illness occurs, only a small percentage of couples who fully recover physically return to the same level of sexual frequency that existed prior to the illness.

For all of these three situations—pregnancy and post-partum, routine sex, and illness—a habit pattern of reduced sexual activity becomes a part of the relationship, and it is this habit pattern that must be broken before a satisfying sexual relationship can be reestablished. For couples who basically feel good about each other and who have not developed secondary relationship problems resulting from sexual inactivity, it is necessary to learn to refocus on sexuality. Methods of increasing sexual interest include making dates to be intimate together which may or may not develop into actual sexual contact, but at least will allow the time to foster it; reading erotica and attending erotic movies; buying lingerie; calling one another on the phone to express sexual interest; complimenting one another on their physical appearance; sharing or acting out sexual fantasies. All of these methods require the couple to think about sex during the day. Mentally focusing on sex naturally elicits a physical response. A gradual increase in quality sexual activity is self-reinforcing and leads to yet further increased desire.

When lack of sexual interest results from chronic stress or fatigue it is often necessary for the couple or partner involved to make significant changes in lifestyle or work if they want to increase their level of sexual activity. Work and other stresses can sap energy, leaving little to devote to sex with a partner. This seems obvious, but since most people consider sex a pleasure they often fail to recognize that it still requires physical energy and that an exhausting lifestyle interferes. In addition to reducing work obligations, it is particularly important for busy couples to set aside quiet time to be together. Many couples find that going away overnight regularly is a good way to establish some relaxed intimate time and to re-create the romance that may be lacking.

The most difficult cases of lack of desire are those that result from other problems in the relationship. Most commonly, the couple is in a struggle for power that is being enacted in the bedroom. Almost all couples go through a power struggle stage after the initial fantasy stage of the relationship wears off and each partner vies for control in certain areas of their joint venture. Use of force, whether verbal or physical—where one person, for example, yells loud and long, or just clearly states his or her position with authority—is one way of obtaining control. Withholding, however, is an equally powerful method of controlling the interaction. The partner who does *not* want to do something—go to the movies, go out to eat, want as strong a commitment to the relationship, or desire sex—is in a position of great power.

Not wanting sex is also a passive-aggressive way of expressing anger toward a partner. It indicates that the partner is undesirable or unattractive and, like other passive-aggressive tactics, is often used by a partner who feels no other power in the relationship. Consequently, while we see the symptom in the bedroom, the problem is not really sexual in nature. When lack of desire is the only sense of control people experience in the relationship, it is first essential to enable them to see the tremendous power they do have. Once a sense of control is established, it becomes possible to relinquish the power of withholding sexually by helping the person develop the tools necessary to get needs met in other ways.

In order to accomplish this when dealing with clients who experience themselves as victims and whose major form of interacting with the world is through withholding, it is essential not to be drawn into the power struggle. This makes treatment difficult because the mere act of helping a client regain sexual desire implies siding with the other partner who wants increased sexual activity. This may cause the client to resist the therapist in the same way they resist their partner. Paradox is useful in these cases. For example, it is more helpful to forbid sexual activity while helping clients become aware of the ways in which they are depriving themselves of enjoyment rather than trying to assist them in increasing frequency of sexual contact with their partner. Allowing clients to determine their own homework assignments and, in some cases stipulating less progress than they are capable of, can create a different kind of power struggle, one in which their attempts to thwart the therapist helps them attain their goals.

Relationship problems are absolutely indicated when a lack of sexual desire toward the partner is accompanied by sexual interest experienced toward others. In some cases, this behavior is an expression of anger and resentment felt toward the partner; in other cases, it may be the excuse that is necessary in order to act on an affair that has been brewing. And sometimes, a lack of desire is a manifestation of guilt feelings resulting from having had an extramarital affair, a way to gain the partner's attention so as to be able to confess and relieve some of the guilt. And in some instances a lack of sexual desire is a form of retaliation against the partner who has been the sexual transgressor.

Lack of desire also occurs among couples who appear to have no serious relationship problems. In some cases, a lack of sexual desire is a way to maintain emotional distance in a relationship where the two partners are in some ways overly dependent and enmeshed. People who fear intimacy, who lose their sense of themselves, or experience themselves as emotionally dependent yet fearful of being abandoned can, by creating distance in the most intimate aspect of their relationship, attempt to protect their vulnerability and ward off their fears. When this pattern is at play, we often see a rise in friction in the nonsexual aspects of the relationship as the sexual problems are resolved. These couples need to learn less devastating methods for creating emotional distance when necessary to prevent serious injury to the relationship.

Another problem that can occur with couples in good relationships is what Kaplan (1979) defines as a fear of success. In this case, a problem will be created in the sexual area to offset too much success in other areas. People who respond this way carry a magical belief that disaster descends when things are going too well. A lack of sexual desire therefore prevents some other unknown disaster from appearing. In these cases, it is necessary to help clients feel that they not only have control over their lives but are deserving of the rewards they are reaping. Only then can the lack of desire problem be reversed.

Clearly, the treatment for lack of sexual desire depends on the particular cause of the problem. A thorough medical, emotional, and relationship history is necessary in order to diagnose the problem accurately so that an appropriate treatment approach can be formulated.

REFERENCE

Kaplan, H. S. (1979). *Disorders of sexual desire*. New York: Brunner/Mazel.

PART IX

Pain Control

Milton Erickson was an expert on dealing with pain. Much of his expertise came from personal experimentation. Erickson used his methods on himself to control the chronic pain that he suffered from the residuals of poliomyelitis.

Bruce L.M. Tanenbaum, M.D., is a psychiatrist in Reno, Nevada. Tanenbaum earned his degree from the University of Maryland School of Medicine, and he is assistant clinical professor at the University of Nevada School of Medicine. He travels internationally to teach hypnotherapy.

Tanenbaum describes nine cases in which he used Ericksonian technique to guide the patient's association and behavior in such a way that the experience of pain was modified as the patient carried out the therapeutic directive. Formal induction is not necessary. In fact, naturalistic techniques may be preferable.

Deborah Ross, Ph.D., earned her degree in clinical psychology from the Fielding Institute in Santa Barbara. She also has an M.S.W. in community mental health from the University of California at Berkeley. Ross is based in Santa Cruz, California, but travels throughout the United States and Europe to present lectures on hypnosis, especially the medical applications of hypnosis.

Ross describes the diagnosis and treatment of functional pain. A case description and a second case transcript demonstrate Ross's mastery of Ericksonian multiple-level communication.

Sandra M. Sylvester, Ph.D., earned her degree in counseling from the University of Arizona. She is a psychologist in private practice in

Tucson, Arizona and is a faculty research associate in the Department of Anesthesiology at the University of Arizona School of Medicine. Sylvester is actively involved in teaching practitioners to use Ericksonian methods.

Hypnosis can be used as an alternative to preoperative medication. Stresses on the surgical patient are described. A transcript of a hypnotic tape that is given to patients prior to surgery is presented.

Chapter 32

Ericksonian Techniques in Emergency Situations: Pain Control

Bruce L.M. Tanenbaum

The *American Heritage Dictionary* defines an emergency situation as one "of a serious nature, developing suddenly and unexpectedly and demanding immediate action." The ability to communicate quickly and effectively, addressing the individual's needs, is essential in order to achieve an adequate response. The use of hypnosis often has not been considered because of the difficulty in using structured induction procedures which may be problematic or impossible to use in emergencies. However, Ericksonian techniques, communication directed towards the elicitation of hypnotic behavior, can be especially effective in evoking behavioral and physiological changes.

Erickson described hypnotic behavior as "a special but normal type of behavior, encountered when attention and the thinking processes are directed to the body of experiential learnings acquired from or achieved in the experiences of living" (Erickson, 1970, p. 72). It is "nothing more than a special state of conscious awareness in which certain chosen behavior of everyday life is manifested in a direct manner, usually with the aid of another person. But it is possible to be self-induced" (p. 72).

In this "special state of awareness the various forms of behavior of everyday life may be found—differing in relationships and degrees but always within normal limits. There can be achieved no transcendence of abilities, no implantation of new abilities, but only the potentiation of expression of abilities which may have gone unrecognized or not fully recognized" (p. 72).

It is important to keep in mind that the goals the patient wants so desperately to achieve are goals that may appear difficult, if not impossible, to the patient's conscious mind. "In the ordinary state of conscious awareness performance is too often limited by considerations which may actually be unrelated to the task at hand. Ideas, understandings, beliefs, wishes, hopes, and fears can all impinge easily upon performance in the state of ordinary conscious awareness-disrupting and distorting even those goals which may have been singly desired" (p. 72). By using Ericksonian techniques to depotentiate consciousness, "awareness is limited and tends to be restricted to exactly pertinent matters, other considerations being irrelevant" (p. 72).

Erickson uses "communication to evoke hypnotic behavior rather than hypersuggestibility per se" (Erickson & Rossi, 1976, p. 168). Hypnotic suggestion is actually the process of evoking, mobilizing and moving "a patient's associative processes and mental processes in ways that are outside his usual range of ego control . . . to *sometimes* achieve certain therapeutic goals" (p. 170). The first steps require a fixation of attention and depotentiation of consciousness. With continued effective communication a patient's attention can be directed inward, resulting in unconscious searching and unconscious processes, leading to a hypnotic response (Erickson & Rossi, 1976).

Hypnotic behavior can be evoked most successfully when the therapist adapts his communication to the patient's individual needs and the immediate situation. In an emergency situation, the ability to communicate quickly and effectively, addressing the patient's needs, is essential in order to achieve an adequate response. If the therapist utilizes the patient's own internal unconscious processes, abilities, and experiential learnings, the patient's goals often can be achieved via the elicitation of hypnotic behavior.

The use of hypnosis in emergency situations does not require formal induction or even the mention of the words "hypnosis" or "trance." In fact, Dr. Esther Bartlett describes patients experiencing a high degree of stress as "already in a state indistinguishable from hypnosis" (Bartlett, 1971, p. 276).

What is necessary is adequate, direct communication with the patient in a way that will be understood. This understanding will of necessity be a combination of conscious and unconscious understandings with the importance resting on the behavioral response achieved. In this manner the patient often can achieve seemingly remarkable results without the onus of attempting to respond to a structured hypnotic induction. In addition, the patient's lack of conscious understanding of the therapist's techniques can further help to facilitate responsive behavior. By interspersing suggestions (Erickson, 1967) in an indirect manner, the patient can make an adequate unconscious response without being limited by conscious biases. Erickson has stated (Erickson, Rossi, & Rossi, 1976) that anytime you give up your conscious biases you go into a trance (p. 180).

APPARENT NONINTERVENTION

Case One

While serving as on-duty physician at Western State Hospital in Stauntan, Virginia, I was called to see an employee who had caught her finger in a closing door. When I arrived the woman was sitting on the floor with her index finger wrapped in gauze, obviously in a state of distress. I asked her what had happened and if I could look at her finger. She had severed the nail about halfway down and about halfway through her finger, with the upper part almost like a flap.

Right away I realized that I could not repair her finger, that she needed to be sent to a nearby hospital for care by a qualified surgeon. I felt that the use of a formal hypnotic induction was not advisable, so I said to her, "I am going to call an ambulance to take you to the hospital where a surgeon will take care of your finger. In the meantime there is nothing you need to do but to remain sitting, keeping your finger tightly wrapped, and you can continue to relax more and more with each breath out." Then I went off to make the necessary arrangements.

Subsequent contact with this woman found her to be extremely grateful for this brief intervention and she noted marked pain relief. In fact, each time I encountered her she expressed repeated thanks. It seems this brief intervention, geared towards her needs in the immediate situation, had profound physiological and psychological significance.

PHYSIOLOGICAL CHANGES IN RESPONSE TO TRAUMA

Case Two

During a coed volleyball game a young woman was injured when hit near the eye by a teammate's elbow. She was led to the bleachers to lie down and I overheard someone say they were going across the street to get some ice. After the commotion subsided and the game resumed, I went over to talk to her.

I introduced myself as a doctor and proceeded, "You know you've been injured near your eye and any injury near the eye should be examined by a physician. Now someone's gone to get some ice and that can help *stop the swelling*. And later you can go to the emergency room to be examined so you can be sure that *everything is all right*. But right now there's really nothing you need to do so you could just imagine yourself lying comfortably in a pleasant place at the beach or in the mountains." I went on to elaborate in a general manner this pleasant scene using all sensory modalities. I continued talking in this manner with suggestions of comfort and healing, intermixing suggestions that she could carry out consciously (e.g., put ice on the injury, go to the emergency room, rest, etc.), and included suggestions that required an unconscious response (e.g., decrease swelling, increase comfort, healing, etc.).

At the completion of the game, she was calm and relaxed with no apparent discomfort. When I noticed her the following week she reported complete comfort and a quick recovery from her injury.

Case Three

A friend of mine was struck with a volleyball on her thumb while watching warm-ups before a game. I did not have much time, as I was preparing to play, so I made a brief intervention. I gently guided her hand up and said, "You can just let your hand *remain comfortably elevated* so the postural drainage can help your thumb *heal quickly*."

Throughout the game I could observe her sitting with her hand remaining cataleptically suspended. After the game she reported surprise that her hand had remained elevated and her injury was no longer bothering her.

EARLY LEARNING SET TECHNIQUE IN PAIN AND ANXIETY

Case Four

While on call for an acute psychiatric ward at the University of Virginia Hospital, I was asked to see a 29-year-old woman with menstrual cramps. I was told that because of problems with low blood pressure her doctor did not want her to receive medication.

After introducing myself and listening to her description of her problem, I said, "You've been having a problem with menstrual cramps and you know that your doctor really doesn't want to give you any medicine. And you want to do something so you can *feel better* and *go to sleep*. And sometimes talking can help you *feel better,* so why don't we talk, in fact, why don't I talk and you can *listen.* Now when you first went to school there was this task of learning to write the letters of the alphabet, and it really was a difficult task. How do you recognize the letter 'A' and how do you tell a 'Q' from an 'O'. . . ." And I continued to go through an early learning set induction similar to that in *Hypnotic Realities* (Erickson, Rossi, & Rossi, 1976). I concluded with suggestions to continue resting comfortably and to drift into a deep, restful sleep from which she could awaken refreshed and rested the following morning. The results obtained were completely satisfactory.

Case Five

After having finished working with the young woman in Case Four, I returned to my room to prepare to sleep. I received a phone call from a 20-year-old woman who was in an acutely agitated state. She reported that her Valium prescription was locked in her brother's car, trapped in a snowstorm, and that she had emptied all the drawers of her dresser in the middle of the floor.

I proceeded to tell her about the woman with menstrual cramps who could not take medication and how we had talked and it seemed to help her very much. I again suggested that "we talk, in fact, why don't I talk and you can listen," and I used almost the identical technique as with the previous woman. Along with pertinent suggestions I finished by suggesting that "when I hang up, you can *put the phone down, walk into your room* and you might find that you can *fall asleep as soon as your head hits the pillow."*

Several days later I received a letter that included the following: "Where can I find someone to talk to me like that? After I got off the phone I went to my room and seemed to fall asleep as soon as my head hit the pillow. I had the most beautiful dreams. The next day I cleaned up all the mess and straightened out my drawers. You can hit me with 1000mg of Thorazine or 50mg of Valium and I'm not that relaxed. You hypnotized me, didn't you?"

REMISSION OF A CHRONIC PAIN PROBLEM

Case Six

A ballet dancer twisted his ankle during rehearsal and limped off stage. As I was working backstage at the time, I followed him into the dressing room to see if I could help. He told me that he had a chronic ankle injury that hadn't given him any trouble for some time.

I asked if I could do "something to help your ankle *feel better*," and proceeded gently to guide his ankle upward, actually letting him unconsciously lift it. As I let go of it without his awareness, it remained suspended cataleptically and I continued to talk to him. "Now there is nothing you need to do but let your ankle remain elevated so it can begin to *feel better* and *heal quickly*. After you go home you can *put some ice on it* so it can continue to heal. Now you don't know how *it will heal*, but you can just *take some relaxing breaths* and *feel confident* that your subconscious mind can do whatever is necessary to allow your ankle to *feel better* and function adequately."

He then continued on to finish the rest of the rehearsal and performed in all the performances of that particular show. On casual inquiry two months later, he unexplainedly reported continued remission of this chronic problem.

AUTOHYPNOSIS

Case Seven

While playing volleyball, I was struck on the knuckle of my left thumb by the ball. Almost immediately the joint began to swell markedly. I suspended my arm with the thumb pointing upward and took a slow deep breath. I thought to myself that I needed to go into a trance to evaluate the extent of my injury. Almost instantly I noticed a feeling of dissociation in my arm and hand. I was able to move my thumb about and convince myself that there was no serious pathology. Comparison to my other thumb indicated I had probably broken a blood vessel running across the joint. Thinking in medical terms (consistent with my background and training), I suggested to myself that I was adequately attending to the injury and there was no need for continued acute response to the injury on a cellular level. Therefore, to decrease the swelling my body could stop sending white blood cells to the area and begin sending macrophages, those elements in the blood that clean up cellular debris.

I continued to play the last few minutes of the game, keeping my hand elevated with the suggestion that the postural drainage would continue to help the healing process.

Over the next two days, I continued this same process of elevation with the suggestion of healing. With only this treatment the swelling completely subsided and I had no further problems.

Case Eight

I sustained a painful injury to my left thumbnail during a basketball game. The nail was bent back about halfway down and began to bleed under the surface. I again suspended my hand to achieve dissociation and told myself that I would only feel pain if I needed to not use my left hand. With this suggestion I was able to continue playing for the next hour. Yet periodically I noted the return of pain, at which time I would suspend my hand until the pain was gone and then continue using my hand. In this manner, I was able to self-monitor the extent of my injury to determine the necessary action to take.

VISUAL IMAGERY TO CONTROL ACUTE PAIN

Case Nine

A nine-year-old boy, who I was seeing in ongoing therapy, came to his session complaining of knee pain. After a brief physical examination to check for pathology, I asked him if he would like me to show him something he could do to "help your knee *feel better*." He agreed, and I asked him to "close your eyes and I'd like you to see a boy about your age and about your size sitting in a chair like the one you're sitting in and as soon as you *see this* just easily nod your head." He successfully completed this task and I said to him, "and that boy's knee hurts him, just like your knee, doesn't it?" He again nodded his head and I asked him to see a box of switches on the back of that boy's head, switches that control pain and lead to different areas of his body. After this I asked him to find the switch leading to the painful knee and to turn it off. When he did this he was able to notice that the boy was no longer hurting. I then asked him to let that boy disappear and to see the box of switches on the back of his own head. He was then able to find the switch that controlled the pain sensation in his knee and turn it off. We were then able to return to our session and he had no further complaints of pain.

DISCUSSION

In the cases presented, normal abilities and potentials were not transcended, but demonstrated in ways outside usual conscious frames of awareness. Hypnotic behavior was achieved through the use of hypnotic techniques directed toward the individual's needs, rather than the application of rigid, structured hypnotic inductions.

Emergency situations require prompt, direct action. An adequate understanding and utilization of the principles of hypnosis and hypnotic techniques can help elicit desired behavioral and physiological changes.

REFERENCES

Bartlett, E. E. (1971). The use of hypnotic techniques without hypnosis *per se* for temporary stress. *The American Journal of Clinical Hypnosis, 2,* 273–278.

Erickson, M. H. (1967). In J. Haley (Ed.), *Advanced techniques of hypnosis and therapy.* New York: Grune & Stratton.

Erickson, M. H. (1970). Hypnosis: Its renascence as a treatment modality. *The American Journal of Clinical Hypnosis, 3,* 72.

Erickson, M. H., & Rossi, E. L. (1976). Two-level communication and the microdynamics of trance and suggestion. *The American Journal of Clinical Hypnosis, 3,* 168–170.

Erickson, M. H., Rossi, E. L., & Rossi, S. I. (1976). *Hypnotic realities: The induction of clinical hypnosis and the indirect forms of suggestion.* New York: Irvington.

Chapter 33

Symbolic Pain:
Metaphors of Dis-ease

Deborah Ross

DEFINITION AND INITIAL ASSESSMENT

All of us who work with pain have struggled with patients who appear to be genuinely suffering and genuinely in search of help but who, for some reason, do not respond well, if at all, to conventional treatment. Drug therapy, surgical intervention, psychotherapy, and conventional hypnotherapy appear unable to provide lasting relief. The patients continue to hurt and increasingly become hopeless and despondent. In these cases, the therapist should explore the symbolic function of such intractable pain. This chapter offers ways of recognizing symbolic pain patients early in treatment and provides hypnotic avenues for opening them up to change.

Symbolic pain can be defined as a chronic pain that may have originated from an organic trauma but whose continued existence serves some functional purpose of which the patient is consciously unaware. Symbolic pain often serves as an indicator of patients' ability to recognize and accept an important truth about themselves or their situation. To the extent that this truth is recognized, accepted, and assimilated, patients then make themselves available for treatment. Some of the clinical considerations that can aid the therapist in unraveling the functional aspect of the pain are as follows:

1) The therapist's ability to see the patient's systemic configuration is critical for getting an accurate diagnostic bearing.
2) Reading the unconscious body language of the patient is useful both in the diagnostic process and as a tracking device during therapy.

3) The use of age regression is perhaps the most fruitful hypnotic method for determining the strategic significance of the pain at its onset. Perhaps the pain *was* the best possible solution *then*; but *now* the mutual therapeutic task is to consider new strategic possibilities at both the conscious and unconscious levels.

Another indicator of functionality is the nature of the pain itself. For example, a patient reports a pain of unchanging intensity and tells you that the pain is consistently there every hour of the day and night and that it is unresponsive to warmth, cold, or change in position. It is terrible in the morning and just as bad at night. It is likely that this is a symbolic pain patient because that is not the nature of pain. Organic pain has fluctuations, times when it is more or less painful, and positions that are more or less comfortable. A patient who reports across-the-board pain whose only variation is that it is steadily growing worse is likely to have a pain that has a strong symbolic function.

I use the following three questions for eliciting information:

1) "Tell me about your experience of that sensation. Do you notice things, positions, temperatures, or times of day that allow you to be more comfortable? Tell me what you already know to make yourself more comfortable."

From the beginning of the first interview, it is important to establish a positive climate for change by phrasing suggestions positively, i.e., toward comfort and pleasure.

2) "What does that sensation keep you from doing that you would really like to do?"

This question can either supply some possibilities for trance metaphors or give more diagnostic information. The metaphors are both powerful and easily accepted because they originate from the patient.

This question may net an answer that points out either secondary gain or ambivalence, e.g., "I'd like to be going to graduate school, but how can I with this back pain?"; "I'd like to move out from my mom's, but with this pain I don't see how I could manage on my own"; or "Now that the kids are grown, I should start taking some courses at the community college, but with this pain. . . ." In these cases, the pain is clearly symbolic of ambivalence, and is often a way to delay passage to the next developmental level.

Developmental quagmires sometimes lead to reactivation of an old injury. These past and present stresses and their interconnection often may be uncovered through the use of age regression (see Case Two in the clinical examples). Simultaneously, age regression can help the patient explore how the unconscious mind is trying to provide protection by producing the symptom. The protective function of the symptom is suggested to the patient in a way conducive to maximizing rapport, therapeutic alliance, and agreement:

> I could help you learn to make that pain go away but I don't want to do that because that would be disrespectful to you. Now I know that the unconscious mind is caring and benevolent so, if that pain is there, it's there for a reason. We have to understand, you and I together, how that pain is protecting you so that we can find a better way for you to keep that protection, a comfortable way that allows you to live a full, rich life. Now do you agree with that?

The third question is best delivered with some sense of theater. I wait for the opportunity to fix the patient with a very intentful look, and then ask in a serious tone to invite confidences:

3) "And what else happened X years ago that you haven't told me *yet*?" Then I wait expectantly. This question often produces an immediate abreaction such as a release of tears and a confessional statement such as "my son-in-law suicided" or "my wife was having an affair."

INTRODUCTION TO CASE EXAMPLES

In the Neurology Department of UC Medical School/San Francisco, Howard Fields, M.D., Ph.D., and I have developed a team approach to treating ambulatory chronic pain patients. We interview the patient together. Dr. Fields does the neurological examination, and then I continue with the second half of the "examination," wherein I assess the efficacy of hypnosis for treating the patient's pain. I do not use the word "hypnosis," since this term may be met with a negative reaction, but rather present hypnosis as "some techniques our patients have found useful in increasing their level of comfort."

I generally teach a straightforward method of self-hypnosis based on eye catalepsy; hand-warming and progressive relaxation are used as deepeners. I like to suggest vasodilation in the hands because it allows me to establish early with the patient some important facets of control of sensation:

> Now . . . tell me, which hand is warmer? The left hand? Good,
> now I wonder how that left hand is going to teach the right hand
> to warm itself while you just enjoy the comfort and the pleasure
> of this very natural state of deep relaxation that your body is learn-
> ing all on its own.

I establish with the patient that one part of the body can teach another
part without any conscious mediation. This suggestion can be amplified
with pacing statements such as:

> Of course you're discouraged . . . you feel stuck and
> hopeless . . . but then again, you've only been using 10% of your
> brain capacity. I'm going to show you some techniques to add the
> wisdom of that other 90% that's been running your body all these
> years without any help from your conscious mind, without any
> need for you to think about it at all.

I often develop the theme that the body knows things it can teach the
mind:

> We might not understand, any of us, how an autoimmune system
> functions, how the body decides to turn it on or off, but our lack
> of understanding is irrelevant to the body's ability to do just
> that . . . and isn't it luck for us that the body has this knowing!

The basic metaphor is that the body, like the unconscious mind is a
powerful friend and ally that can share information with the mind. I
sometimes illustrate this idea with a personal story about my "safety-
belt," a feeling of constriction through the diaphragm that I get when
I am not being truthful with myself. For example, perhaps I agree to do
something for someone when I really want to refuse. When I figure out
what is "true" for me, the constriction goes away.

This is a particularly useful story with patients who use their symptom
when there is something they want to avoid and they have no other
way to say "no" except to produce an incapacitating pain.

Case Examples

Case one

Dr. Fields and I interviewed a woman in her mid-seventies who presented a three-year history of chronic pain in her right foot. Her de-

scription of the pain was typical of symbolic pain. Nothing helped alleviate it; it had no fluctuations and was steadily growing worse. She was a straight-backed farm lady who had a number of great-grandchildren and knitted and crocheted clothes for all of them. She had been an active woman, an extremely amiable lady who had enjoyed a busy, productive life. The type of lady that won blue ribbons at the county fair, she talked with great enthusiasm of her past involvement with family and community.

The pain in her right foot, a supposed neuroma, was incurred three years earlier when she was driving a truck and had to brake suddenly to avoid an accident. She broke a bone in her right foot and had a great deal of pain. She underwent surgery without any relief from the pain, which continued to grow in severity. Now she never left the house; she had become functionally agoraphobic.

She was asked what the foot prevented her from doing that she really wanted to do. Her answer was that she and her husband used to go salmon fishing every July. For the last 27 years, they chartered a boat and spent a week out at sea catching salmon which they smoked and gave as Christmas presents. This year she did not think the pain in her foot would let her go; her husband would be greatly disappointed. We conversed for a bit about the joys of deep-sea fishing. I used this conversation both to build rapport and to gather metaphors.

I took advantage of Dr. Fields' leaving the examination room to ask her the third question. "What else happened three years ago that you haven't told me *yet*? She burst into tears and told me her husband had been diagnosed as having bone cancer. We talked for a while and then I asked her permission to have her husband join us for the "examination." He was seated next to his wife. She began to talk about their 55 years of marriage. As she described what good years they had been, her hand kept coming down on her husband's thigh with a resounding slap. "Wasn't it, Henry? . . . (slap) . . . remember that time . . . wasn't it great . . . (slap) . . ." And I looked at that straight back and heard the unspoken words that that hand kept repeating, "Don't you dare die before me, I just couldn't bear it!"

Her body language gave me a strong hunch about how she developed that pain in her foot. As long as she had that pain and was housebound, he had to stay alive to take care of her. If she is well and functional, then maybe he will die. That is what was going on on the unconscious level. You could see her anger, her fear, and her frustration in that hand that kept slapping her husband's thigh.

I instructed the husband to watch his wife so I could do hypnosis by proxy. I instructed the wife to fix her gaze softly on a chart on the wall and I did the "rest of the neurological examination" which was an eye catalepsy induction. Then I talked to her about how wonderful it must be to go in that salmon-fishing boat, three, four, five miles out into the middle of nowhere . . . how one had all the time in the world in that peacefulness to ponder life . . . all the breaks in life, good ones and unfortunate ones, breaking bones, breaking with good companions, breaking through to a new understanding of an old situation . . . and then there's the lucky break . . . like the salmon that breaks the line and gets away . . . but sometimes he's really hooked good . . . there's nothing he can do to change that ending . . . but it's how he goes to the boat, the fight he makes right to the end . . . it's that good fighting spirit that makes salmon fishing such a great sport.

As the right foot had been the center of attention, I talked about my concern for that foot that was left. I was talking about her abandonment fears and her resources that she had thrown away. I remarked on how that left foot hadn't gotten any care for three years . . . it really had been neglected. I gave her some special exercises for that left foot so she could feel what a good, strong foot it was. I would give her some massage lotion for that left foot . . . after all, it really wasn't fair that that right foot got all the attention and that left foot was so left out. I commented on what good range of motion that left foot had and shared my conviction that that left foot could teach the other foot about that good range of motion. I excused myself and fetched Dr. Fields who did a short reexamination of the right foot and then moved on to the left foot," praising it and remarking on its responsiveness, what a good foot it was . . . with an excellent range of motion . . . so much good strength and possibilities that foot had.

I alerted the couple from trance. The wife looked at me thoughtfully and asked, "Is this what they call 'biofeedback'?" I replied, "You know 'bio' is the Greek for life, so I think you're right; you've been doing just that . . . you've been feeding so much life back to each other."

I wanted to give them another way to touch, so I instructed both of them in proper massage for the feet and remarked that the hands could benefit also. The husband said to me with a twinkle in his eye, "Doctor, we're going to be so busy holding hands that we won't have any time to go fishing. . . ." When the wife was asked to come back in six weeks for a reevaluation visit, she said, "I don't think that will be possible . . . we'll be out fishing then."

Did that couple understand what I was doing? Of course they did. Hypnosis does not have to be mysterious for it to work. Their good sense of humor and the strength of so many well-lived years together allowed them to accept my help in coming to a new mutual understanding that could remain implicit. This was a woman who was grieving her husband and unconsciously produced a pain to keep him around. She was very available for treatment.

Case two

Keith, a well-dressed, successful businessman in his mid-thirties, came at the request of his therapist to be a demonstration patient to illustrate the use of hypnosis with chronic pain. He had a radiating pain in his right arm incurred during a racquetball game three years earlier. He had undergone two cervical operations with no relief. He had tried an electric stimulator without success. His description of the pain was that it was continuous and getting worse. It kept him from sports which he missed; otherwise, he "just made the best of it" and continued to work hard at his business. He was a pleasant-appearing man, a "mister nice guy," with a set smile and a dearth of adjectives for describing his life. The arm "simply hurt"; life was "just fine" both three years ago and now. As I talked with him, I was struck by his controlled soft monotone, the essential blandness of his affect despite his supposed high pain level, his concrete, short responses to my queries, and the frequent references in his language to "stopping" and "cutting off."

I exhausted my whole repertoire of standard pain utilizations working with this young man. Nothing succeeded. He just sat there being agreeable and cooperative and reporting no change in sensation. Then I asked him to remove his jacket and I used some acupuncture release points. As soon as I touched him, his whole demeanor changed. His body visibly relaxed and he began to respond to whatever suggestion I gave him. He gave me carte blanche and the pain left. The audience and the patient were pleased. I was puzzled and unconvinced that any essential change had occurred. I had a strong hunch that the man's problem was not pain. The only thing that was clear to me was that he was touch-starved. However, he had reported that his marriage was "just fine." His manner was that of an alexithymic, that is, he had few words for physical feelings, even more marked difficulty in verbal expression of emotions, and little ability to use fantasy. Not to my great surprise, the pain returned within 12 hours.

Keith requested to see me again. I agreed with the proviso that I talk first with his former therapist. She gave me a different answer to "what else happened three years ago." Exactly coincident with the onset of the pain, his wife began to have an affair with her boss. Keith claimed not to have known about the affair until later. Therefore, he could see no possible connection with the pain in his right arm. The wife finally told him nine months after onset of the pain and then left him for another ten months. He did not remember grieving. Almost immediately, he got involved with another woman. Without any warning, the wife asked to come back and to give the marriage another go. Keith left the other woman with whom he had a supposed deep involvement immediately, and in his own words, never gave her another thought. He just "cut off" the other relationship.

When Keith came to see me the second time, the questions on my mind were: 1) What had he done with all the hurt and grieving from his wife's affair and their subsequent separation? 2) How had he cut off his relationship with the other woman without any hesitation? and 3) What interconnection was there between his present physical pain, emotional barrenness, alexithymic affect, and previous life events?

Keith reported that he had tried to use self-hypnosis five to six times daily without any success. He asked if he conned himself that first time with me, maybe the pain never left and he just fooled himself into not feeling it. I asked him to show me how he had been using what I'd taught him and as he put his hand into a catalepsy, I changed my voice and suggested that he just go into the lightest of trances, so he could listen to me more comfortably. He cooperated and I continued:

Dr. Ross: You know, Keith, I can help a burn patient to feel comfortable through using hypnosis; does that mean that the burn's not there? Is he conning himself into that comfort . . . and does it matter? After all there are so many sources for pain, and psychological and physical and emotional pain can get all mixed up. . . . It's real confusing. A psychological pain is as real as a physical pain. An emotional pain that's not attended to festers the same way a physical pain can. Now, Keith, as I talk with you, that deeper part of your brain can begin to review who and what a long time ago taught you that it wasn't OK to have any emotional pain . . . that life was just real cut and dry. Now I don't know if they taught you with words or you learned by just watching what they did or didn't do because you know how kids learn. They learn as much as from what's not said and done just as much as from what is said and done. And I can remember when I was six my dog got run over. No one grieved that dog but me. I couldn't stop crying and the response from my folks was, that's ridiculous, it's only a dog, we'll buy you another one. And that to me was even more painful, how little they understood my relationship with that dog, how important it was to me. I had a grandmother who died about the same time and that was of much less significance to me. My family got upset with me for that too. I wasn't mourning the right critter. And Keith, you can just continue to review what you learned about what's OK to feel, what's not OK to feel, and what you feel and what you cut off. . . .

Keith: I can't remember my early childhood . . . my parents talking or acting like that.

Dr. Ross: That's right, you'll just have to go even deeper into trance and see what comes that you don't know you know. If you knew, you wouldn't have to see me. Your conscious mind doesn't know but the other part of your brain is like a super file cabinet . . . and as you continue to go into the trance . . . deeper with every breath . . . some part of your deeper brain . . . not your ordinary thinking brain, but that other part . . . can select just the right file and you can begin to know what you know and don't know you know . . . it was . . . so . . . long . . . ago . . . without thinking about it at all. All you need to do is let go of trying to remember, just go into your breathing while I talk with you and let the memories come all by themselves and surprise you. It might not even make sense, Keith . . . like watching someone else's story on a TV show, watching some other little kid. You know, Keith, in many families, male children have it tough. They're told be a man . . . keep a stiff upper lip . . . don't cry, only sissies cry, and don't whine and don't complain . . . and don't and don't and don't. And they're told that sometimes in words and sometimes just by a look. Why I had an aunt who had a look that could freeze every hair on the back of your neck . . . and when she would look in your direction with that look . . . you just stopped. You might not even know what you were doing wrong but you knew something you were doing was wrong. Funny the way pain works; figuring out what's happening can be so confusing. Now I had a patient once whom you would have liked. She was a real friendly lady, a real hard-working lady all her life. You could see how industrious and hard-working she had been by looking at her hands and face. She wasn't a complainer, a real straight-backed nice lady. She had a pain in her foot from a broken bone. She had to have surgery, in fact she had two surgeries and the doctors tried everything they knew to give her relief from that pain which got more and more constant over the next three years. Now something else was happening for this lady and she wasn't really aware of it. She wasn't aware of it at all with her conscious mind. But that deeper part of your mind picks up so much more and understands so much more of what's happening than the conscious mind does, and often times it protects by not allowing the conscious mind *at that time* to know what's going on. Now what was going on for this lady although she didn't know it was that her husband had come down with a very rapid cancer just about the time she had the accident that broke the bone, or maybe just a little bit before. And she didn't know that and yet she *knew* it. Now her unconscious mind, again without any co-operation from her conscious mind, developed a strategy. The strategy was that if she hurt enough and became crippled enough which was real hard on her because she was such an active lady . . . then her husband would have to hang around and take care of her and she couldn't stand the thought of his dying and leaving her alone. None of this was conscious. And as soon as she began to understand how really important that pain was, how much that pain was serving her interest in keeping her husband there, then she could begin to allow the same part of her brain that had so cleverly produced the pain to find another way . . . now go all the way down, Keith, and begin to understand for yourself how important that pain is . . . and I really want to tell your unconscious mind that I respect how it's taking care of you, that I respect its need to keep that pain until you understand on all levels of your mind and body how that pain is protecting you. You know how to withstand physical pain and now you can begin to understand just for yourself the other pain that the physical pain protects you from . . . the one you don't understand yet . . . just what you might have to deal with if that pain went away and there were nothing to distract you from that other pain. You learned that so long ago; it became so natural to cut it off and feel it somewhere else. It's OK to come home because you're hurt from a football game or falling on a tennis court . . . that's acceptable . . . but there's some other pain that's not so acceptable . . . until you realize how legitimate it is to have the pain that comes from outrage . . . that other pain.

Keith: Everything's whirling . . . I can't grasp anything. . . .

Dr. Ross: That's OK . . . just let it whirl. Now what images come and go?

Keith: Maybe my parents overprotected me because I was sick and in the hospital for a year.

Dr. Ross: How old are you and what's wrong?

Keith: I'm six. I guess I had polio. I remember the little Indian boy in the bed next to me. He's burned all over and he cried and screamed all night and then he died.

Dr. Ross: Did you cry?

Keith: Yes.

Dr. Ross: How afraid were you that you were going to die?

Keith: I don't remember.

Dr. Ross: Can you see that child now?

Keith: Yes. (starts to cry)

Dr. Ross: Let the feelings come now because that's terribly scary to be six and not know whether you're going to be alive or dead. Old people die, but not little boys. Breathe with your whole chest, and talk with that boy . . . now.

Keith: I tried. I couldn't. I tried to help him but there was nothing I could do. He just cried and screamed. And died.

Dr. Ross: And what did you tell yourself?

Keith: I don't remember . . . (eye movements indicative of visualization are evident)

Dr. Ross: What are you seeing now?

Keith: I'm at school. It's recess. I'm in the wheelchair . . . I can't walk . . . I can't play . . . and the other kids are laughing and making fun of me because I can't walk (weeping increases) . . . and I want them to be my friends . . . (attempts a smile)

Dr. Ross: So you smile?

Keith: I laugh with them.

Dr. Ross: What do you do with all the pain and anger?

Keith: Hide it, I guess. I just sit there and smile, try to keep talking . . . I want to be their friend.

Dr. Ross: So telescope back now and look at that kid . . . he's come through so much terror and he hasn't let himself feel that either. That was just too scary and he was only six. Does he know he's going to walk?

Keith: They told me I wouldn't walk until high school but by sixth grade I was walking without a brace. I went to therapy every day.

Dr. Ross: So you learned how to work hard. But what did you do with all those feelings? You cut them off and you stashed them somewhere. And that's what's getting in your way. Not only then but now. Maybe they're in your head, maybe your knee, maybe your eyes, maybe your groin, maybe your toe, maybe in that jaw . . . and maybe it isn't finding them but just releasing them from all those places. Now you survived and you learned to walk and you did more than that because

no one could ever tell you had polio. And the only part that you need
to complete is to let the feelings catch up . . . to let them release. And
that's the most courage of all. That takes the most strength of
all . . . to allow those feelings. Now that you know you survived you
don't really have to hold them in anymore.

Keith: I don't know how to do that though. When I was in high school,
when I hurt, nobody believed it. They told me it was all in my
head . . . the teacher, the doctor. Even now it's the same. Maybe
they're right. Maybe I just wanted pity; maybe that's what I'm doing
now.

Dr. Ross: Who from?

Keith: My wife.

Dr. Ross: What do you want to hear from your wife?

Keith: That she understands.

Dr. Ross: How much you hurt?

Keith: Yes.

Dr. Ross: And as long as you go on hurting, that means . . . ?

Keith: That she doesn't understand.

Dr. Ross: Aren't you punishing the wrong person? And haven't you
suffered long enough?

Keith: I guess so . . . I just always thought that something was wrong
with me.

Dr. Ross: And now?

Keith: I don't know.

Dr. Ross: That's a good first step. Go into that "I don't know" and see
what some of the other possibilities are all about.

Keith: I don't think I need acceptance from people anymore like I used
to . . . just from my wife.

Dr. Ross: What interests me is what did you do with all that rage?

Keith: I just tried to channel it the best way I could. Just like a teacher
in grade school who called me gregarious. I resented that.

Dr. Ross: Tell that teacher now.

Keith: I did tell him.

Dr. Ross: Tell him again because your voice still sounds so friendly.

Keith: I don't like to be called gregarious or aggressive. (still no affect)
I didn't know how to get people to like me so I just put on a mask.

Dr. Ross: And what would happen if you decided that it was OK to
disagree, OK to be angry, OK to hurt?

Keith: I wouldn't have any friends. I'd be alone.

Dr. Ross: But physical pain's OK?

Keith: No . . . I don't want to have any pain; I don't know how to get rid of it.

Dr. Ross: Which one? There's so many of them.

Keith: (smile) You're trying to confuse me. Everything's just spinning.

Dr. Ross: Let it spin and understand that you have a whole warehouse full of pain because you've been accumulating it so long. You just didn't know what to do with it. (Keith begins to sob) And let your eyes do what they're doing . . . they're very smart . . . and as your jaw relaxes see if you can release some of that confusion. Your thinking brain doesn't know what to do. Your body might if you just allow it to begin to grieve, to feel . . . the six-year-old, the ten-year-old, the twelve-year-old, the fourteen-year-old, the thirty-two-year old . . . that's right . . . and let the other pain begin to leave. Breathe and support and trust your body . . . up to now you've never allowed yourself to do that. That's the challenge now. Do you have the courage to allow the pain that really was to begin to leave through your eyes, the pain that you've been storing at least since you were six? And if I let the pain come out, will I be all alone? The Indian boy cried and look what happened to him. You know what happens when you swallow it down, you're a real expert at that. The real courage, the new strength is coming from your eyes beginning to release that old pain which was so much more horrible than anything your body can produce.

Keith: I don't know what to do . . . it just doesn't seem fair . . . I don't know what to do. . . .

Dr. Ross: Breathe . . . and see that Indian boy and let yourself feel that helplessness . . . and your body will help you. (loud voice) PLEASE DON'T DIE . . . PLEASE DON'T CRY! (patient begins to sob deeply) . . . PLEASE . . . it frightens me too much. DON'T LEAVE.

Keith: (crying hard) It's just not fair.

Dr. Ross: That's right . . . it's just not fair and it frightens me so much. Don't swallow it down . . . you're too good at that. The real challenge is to let it out. So much unfairness and scare . . . then and now. I'm tired of hurting this much. I don't want to be alone.

Keith: (fighting for control) I'm not frightened. I just want my wife to understand. I want to have a happy marriage. There's just nothing I can do . . . (begins to sob again)

Dr. Ross: Just like with the Indian boy. Let the tears come now, the tears you didn't cry then. No reason to cry . . . the pain either leaves here (touching his eyes) or lives here (touching his arm). To the degree that you allow yourself to understand that grieving is a real natural human process and let those tears come . . . (patient again is struggling for control) Do you feel that tension?

Keith: Yes.

Dr. Ross: And the pain?

Keith: It's worse.

Dr. Ross: To the degree that you swallow it down, do you understand what happens to your body? You got real good at your masquerade. You got super-training.

Keith: I can't let go . . . no reason to. . . .

Dr. Ross: Can you let it out irrationally? Feelings aren't rational. Feelings just are. It wasn't rational to cry more for a cocker spaniel than a grandmother . . . it doesn't make any sense. But the dog meant more to me. I don't want you to release it *all* today. That would be too much; after all, you've had some thirty years of learning and you've got a certain pride invested in that ability to be an excellent masquerade artist.

Keith: (smiles) That's true. I learned to talk with people, look at them, see what they want.

Dr. Ross: Good! Look at Keith and see what he wants.

Keith: I just want to be happier. To play sports. To work less and have more time with my family. I just don't understand how this pain comes in.

Dr. Ross: This is the one you're used to . . . you're a pro, aren't you? You can write a book on it.

Keith: (smiling) You're getting me mad.

Dr. Ross: Do you always smile at people who are trying to get you mad? That's the training too. So what happens to the rage?

Keith: I don't get mad that often.

Dr. Ross: Do you ever get mad?

Keith: Not very often. (smiles) No reason to be irrational. . . .

Dr. Ross: No reason to be irrational! A six-year-old dies in the bed next to you . . . no reason to cry, no reason to be irrational. Dead is dead. Your family is breaking up, you don't know whether your wife is coming back, you don't know what you're doing with another woman, you don't know what the heck is right or wrong . . . no reason to cry or feel . . . that's irrational. How are you handling all that anger and hurt and fear?

Keith: Guess I'm not very well.

Dr. Ross: You sure aren't. I know you like challenges. That's the challenge now. And you'll know how well you're doing because as you deal with the other pains, this pain will start to go away. (Keith's hands begin to tense and move.) Let your hands keep going . . . let them think for you. What do they really want to do?

Keith: I don't know.

Dr. Ross: Yeah? Try letting them loose. See what happens when you make a fist.

Keith: There's no reason to get mad.

Dr. Ross: Can you get mad without a reason?

Keith: Not very often.

Dr. Ross: You're going to have to learn. Let your hand move up and down on that nice upholstered chair and use a word, any word. No's a good one.

Keith: I don't have any reason to do that.

Dr. Ross: That's right . . . I want you to do that without a reason. OK? Use more of your arm and now the word, "NO!" C'mon, Keith, a two-year-old would have more energy than that.

Keith: There's no reason to be doing this. I'm not angry at anything.

Dr. Ross: That's right. Angelic Keith. Happy with the world. Everything's just wonderful. Perfect wife, perfect job, perfect marriage, perfect city . . . tell me how wonderful the world is, Keith. Let's see what your hands have to say about it.

Keith: I do enjoy the world, I do enjoy my job.

Dr. Ross: I don't believe you. Can you hit any weaker?

Keith: Sure.

Dr. Ross: Let's see how completely powerless you can be. If you cut your breathing, you can make yourself even weaker. That's pretty good. Now turn the volume up the other way. Harder . . . HARDER! Hard as you can . . . release your jaw. Breathe. Now some words.

Keith: I just feel silly doing this.

Dr. Ross: Stupid!

Keith: Right.

Dr. Ross: DUMB!

Keith: You're trying to get me mad. (voice consistently bland)

Dr. Ross: Dumb bitch trying to get me mad. But I won't. I'll keep my mask. I'm real good at it and I've got some 30-odd years of practice and I'm an expert.

Keith: There's nothing mad inside . . . nothing at all. Just my arm hurts.

Dr. Ross: Right. Only your arm hurts. That's the whole idea. And that's why you'll keep the pain. So only your arm hurts. . . . Now, you can pick your time to get angry . . . it doesn't have to be here. Now, just take a minute to allow all we've worked on to assimilate. And the process will continue and you'll pick the right time and place to do what you have to do.

Keith: I don't want to blame others.

Dr. Ross: You don't have to blame anyone. But you do have to do the grieving and the feeling and the releasing of all the many things you've stored up to now. That's the work.

Keith: Won't that be trying to make people feel sorry for me?

Dr. Ross: No. You're doing that now.

Keith: I don't understand.

Dr. Ross: Well, you're such a nice guy, such a controlled guy. Who would ever leave somebody who's such a nice guy, such a good father, such an excellent provider, so pleasant, such a nice smile . . . and he's struggled so hard all his life with nary a complaint. And you don't understand how that's a manipulation?

Keith: You say I'm manipulating my wife . . . putting guilt feelings on her?

Dr. Ross: That's the only thing you've learned up to now. You've got a lot of new learning ahead of you. But to have the learning, you're going to have to learn to let yourself feel fully. You're crippling yourself in many many ways. You're using one-tenth of what you've got. It's like having a whole piano and you pick four notes. And that's all you let yourself play because the others aren't rational.

Keith: So, how do I learn?

Dr. Ross: You started today. There were some moments when you let some release happen, when you actually allowed yourself to be irrational. You're going to have to experiment and learn about the other side.

Keith: Will you help me? I don't think I can do it alone.

Dr. Ross: I agree that you need some help and you've been alone long enough. You know the job and you started today.

Keith: Thank you.

I quote this second session with Keith in its entirety because I believe that the combination of symbolic pain and alexithymia is one of the most difficult challenges for the psychotherapist. Keith didn't need to learn about pain control or producing anesthesias; he was a master at that. He needed to learn how to accept his feelings, past and present, and how to share them verbally and physically first with himself and then with his wife.

I saw the couple conjointly for two months. In the first conjoint session, Keith was able to express his hurt and loneliness to his wife. A full release of tears followed and much to Keith's surprise, his wife spontaneously embraced him and cried with him. I left them alone in my office for an hour and returned to find a couple that had finally started to share the feelings of pain and isolation each had felt in the marriage. They were ready to do some new learning together. The pain in Keith's arm left after that session and has not returned.

MAINTAINING WELLNESS

Many chronic pain patients, whether organic or symbolic, will respond to hypnotherapeutic treatment in four to six weeks. However, it is important to have continuing contact with these patients even if all symptoms have abated. I strongly recommend having them drop by the office or clinic just to let you know "how *well* they're doing." This is an important point with most pain patients.

In a sense, one could say that they have to be paced like well-compensated schizophrenics. It is not that they are crazy. It is just that it takes a lot of energy to control pain and restructure life, to assume new interests and responsibilities, a lot of energy and discipline and practice. So often, once a patient is well, there is no reinforcement from the physician, psychotherapist, or family. Patients may have spent many years of their lives with the hospital staff and doctors being the most important people in their lives. All of a sudden, no one is interested in them. No one has time for them because they are "well" and health professionals are not trained to think in terms of wellness. Those of you who treat schizophrenics know that once that patient is well-functioning, your job is not over. Once you have been that patient's therapist, you're the therapist for life. You may only hear from the patient once or twice a year. The contact may be no more than a shared cup of coffee, a phone call, or a Christmas card, but that's the kind of anchoring that reinforces and helps to continue good healthy functioning. The same is true for chronic pain patients. Therefore, I recommend to those who treat pain to schedule regular visits, even if they are only twice a year, to pace the wellness. Invite the successful patient back to tell you how well he or she continues to do. Let the patient know that you would not be a bit surprised to see even more good changes happening in other areas of life now that energy is so much freer and now that he or she knows what a powerful and caring friend and ally there is in that deeper part of the mind.

Chapter 34

Fear in the Management of Pain: Preliminary Report of a Research Project

Sandra M. Sylvester

In 1965, Milton H. Erickson delivered an important paper at the International Congress for Hypnosis and Psychosomatic Medicine, held in Paris and organized by Jean Lassner, M.D. Here, he spoke of the naturalistic ways by which unrecognized psychological, physiological, and neurological learnings and associations make pain control possible. For example, a suffering mother forgets her pain when she sees her infant seriously threatened, or a severely wounded soldier does not discover his injury until after he has helped a wounded buddy to safety. "These unconscious learnings, repeatedly reinforced by additional life experiences, constitute the source of the potentials that can be employed through hypnosis to control pain intentionally without resorting to drugs" (1967).

Few subjects have generated as much interest and controversy in the area of medical hypnosis as the subject of pain (Goodman, 1983). However, little attention has been given to the role of fear in pain management.

For the hospitalized patient, fear of surgery, fear of a medical procedure, and fear of the unknown promote a condition of increased awareness so that each new sensation is evaluated by the patient as a possible cause of concern, and henceforth of more fear and anxiety (Fraulini, 1983).

This chapter addresses the role of fear in pain management of the surgical patient and the nature of stress for the surgical patient, and previews a model using hypnosis as an alternative to preoperative medication for the surgical patient. This model is being used at the Anesthesia Department of the University of Arizona Hospital.

THE ROLE OF FEAR IN PAIN MANAGEMENT OF THE SURGICAL PATIENT

Fear has both a positive and a negative function. So often practitioners work hard to alleviate fear in patients, when perhaps the most helpful way to begin is to listen to the fear and learn what it has to say. Fear is a barometer of vulnerability, an indicator of a patient's position on the continuum of locus of control, and an open door to communication.

When a patient manifests fear, he or she is in a hyperalert phase and certain physiological correlates are present. These include increased heart rate, more rapid and shallow respiration, higher blood pressure (Sylvester, 1974), and also production of endorphins and other endogenous morphines (Amir, Brown, & Amit, 1980; Jacob, 1982; Milloy, 1982). While their precise role remains elusive, these changes are important in their ability both to regulate pain and to filter stimuli. It is believed that endogenous morphines may be released at times when pain impulses are triggered excessively, and in this way they provide natural pain control (Hole, 1981).

Fearful patients also may appear to be agitated. Usually these patients are given preoperative medications to help manage their distress. These medications, rather than working preoperatively, catch up with the patient in the recovery room where their effect is additive to the effect of the general anesthetic. Thus, during the immediate postoperative period, when the surgical patient faces the risk of aspiration, cardiac arrest, and circulatory or respiratory depression, he or she must also recover from the depressive side effects of the preoperative drugs. Hypnosis, on the other hand, has no side effects.

THE NATURE OF STRESS FOR THE SURGICAL PATIENT

Fear and anxiety are caused by stress. However, the *intensity* of the fear and the concomitant disruption of the patient depends on the nature of the stress, the duration, the individual's attitude toward the stressor and his or her ability to deal with it (Parker, 1983).

Nature of the Stress

In this case, the stressors are surgery and anesthesia. Knowing about the surgery and the surgical procedure, even if the individual cannot control it, usually reduces the severity of fear. During the pre-op visit, the night before surgery, both the anesthesiologist and the surgeon visit patients, review the nature of the surgery, the procedure which will be used (including what time patients will be taken to the preparation room, how long they will be there, when they will be taken to surgery, how long it will take, how long they will be in the recovery room, etc.) and answer any questions which patients may have.

Attitude Toward the Stressor

How the patient perceives or interprets sensations surrounding the surgery and the recovery period greatly influences the degree of comfort. During times of pain or discomfort, the patient is in a state of arousal, constantly orienting to new sensations. If these sensations are unexpected, uncomfortable, or perceived in a negative way, the patient will keep them central in awareness, constantly monitoring them, and report the experience as pain. If, on the other hand, the patient is prepared for the changes experienced, there is less need to be so vigilant.

Duration of the Stress

Controlling the duration of a stressful event also reduces its severity. Since patients cannot control the surgical procedure consciously because they are rendered "unconscious" and often paralyzed, we have developed a procedure by which patients can develop some autonomic control prior to the surgery. With autonomic control they are able to maintain a relaxed, low arousal state as measured by skin conductance, blood pressure, and heart rate. To this end, the night before surgery patients are taught relaxation coupled with suggestions of cooperating with the body's healing processes. They are also given a tape player and cassette recording of this procedure and given total control over its use.

Ability to Cope

To this end specific skills are taught. The night before surgery, patients are given a tape entitled "Preparation for Surgery." This tape is a hypnotic induction procedure coupled with specific direct and indirect suggestions for relaxation and healing. Patients are taught to go into trance while skin conductance is being monitored by an electrodermograph. If a patient has difficulty, as indicated on the electrodermograph, further induction work is initiated. If the patient proceeds successfully, he or she is given the tape and tape recorder to be used as desired.

Patient preparation, addressing each of the preceding factors, enables the individual to decrease the severity of anxiety and fear.

MODEL USING HYPNOSIS AS AN ALTERNATIVE TO PREOPERATIVE MEDICATION FOR THE SURGICAL PATIENT

Presently, in the Anesthesia Department at the University of Arizona Hospital, we are pursuing a series of research questions related to drug dosage, pre-, inter-, and post-op. The first study in this series addresses the question, "Can clinical hypnosis be used instead of preoperative medication?" We would like to show that postoperatively, patients who use hypnosis in lieu of pre-op medication recover from the anesthesia more quickly and more easily than patients who have pre-meds or patients who have no treatment.

The variables we are looking at preoperatively, interoperatively, and postoperatively are: vital signs (blood pressure, heart rate, temperature, respirations); color, consciousness, circulation, movement, G.I. indicators, drugs requested, length of stay in recovery room, length of post-op hospital stay, and various verbal reports.

The patient population consists of 45 adults who are having either abdominal or orthopedic surgery. The Hypnosis Group has no pre-op medication, receives 30 minutes of hypnosis training via cassette tape while being monitored on an electrodermograph, and has unlimited use of the tapes until discharge from the recovery room. As was mentioned above, the tapes contain a conversational hypnotic induction interspersed with suggestions of healing. A partial transcript of this tape appears below.

The Medication Group receives pre-op medication and follows normal hospital protocol. The Control Group receives no pre-op medication and follows normal hospital procedure. All patients receive a comparable dose of the same volatile anesthetics.

Since this study is still in progress, statistical data are not yet available; however, there is one anecdote I would like to share. The morning after being introduced to hypnosis, a 65-year-old mastectomy patient met me in the holding area before her surgery. She said that she had really enjoyed the tape. During the night she was unable to sleep because she said she "felt a cold coming on." Her nose was running, her eyes tearing, and she had an uncontrollable cough. She decided that she was probably nervous about the next day's surgery. Then she recalled how good she felt when she listened to the tape earlier that evening. So she got her tape recorder and began to listen to the tape. All of a sudden, her nose and eyes stopped running and she stopped coughing. She fell asleep only to be awakened at 3 A.M. by a nurse who said she woke her because she hadn't moved all night. The patient fell asleep a second time and again slept until awakened by the nurse, this time to go to surgery.

TRANSCRIPT: "PREPARATION FOR SURGERY" (SYLVESTER, 1983)

Hello, this is Dr. Sandra Sylvester and I am here to help you prepare for your surgery. What I am going to do at this time is to speak to you a little about surgery and the healing process and also give you some instructions that will help you become more comfortable and more relaxed as you prepare for your surgery.

Now, would you please lie in a position which is very comfortable for you. Take time to arrange your body, position your pillows, so that you feel poised and balanced and very comfortable and at ease. Take a few moments to do this. Adjust your head so that you are comfortable . . . your back . . . your arms . . . your feet . . . and legs. As we continue, if you would like to change your position to become even more comfortable, please feel free to do so.

The process of coming into the hospital for surgery is a very common and routine procedure for all of us here at the hospital. But for you it may be a once in a lifetime experience. And so, if I may, I would like to talk with you about what we have learned about the healing process so that you can prepare yourself in the best possible way for your surgery.

And so to begin: As you are lying in this comfortable position, look up at the ceiling and find a spot which is easy for you to see. Just any spot on the ceiling will do. Please continue to look at that spot while I continue to speak with you. Already as you are looking at that spot you may begin to perceive some very subtle changes in your vision. For example, you may notice that that spot becomes very easy to see. And you may also notice that the periphery of your vision surrounding that spot may begin to get hazy, so that as you keep that spot in focus, the rest of your vision moves out of focus. You may also notice that your eyes begin to tire and fatigue . . . and sometimes your eyes will indicate that by tearing. So you may notice your eyes watering a bit. You may notice that as your eyes blink, you sense a feeling of comfort come over your body in that brief moment when your eyes are closed. And as your eyes continue to tire, and they continue to blink, you will find more and more comfort and pleasure as your eyes are closing. And soon you will notice that it is more comfortable for you to just allow your eyes to close. When you notice that it is more comfortable for you to allow your eyes to close, let them close, so that you can notice the changes which occur when you have turned off your sense of vision.

One thing you may notice almost immediately is how easy it is to hear the words that I speak directly to you. It is also easy to hear and continue to hear all of the sounds around you. And yet, those sounds which are not important to you at this moment can fade into the background, and even though they are still there, they need not disturb you in any way. You can hear pages in the hallway and know that you do not need to listen to them. You may hear talking or sounds from your neighbor, the television set, snatches of conversations. While these go on, notice how pleasant it is to know that you need not bother to respond to anything unless it is directed specifically at you.

You may also notice how easy it is to begin to tune in to the rhythm of your breathing, noticing that when you are still, your body takes a rhythm of breathing which is most beneficial for you at this moment. As you inhale and exhale, your chest goes up and down in a comfortable, easy rhythm. An interesting thing about your breathing is that you breathe day and night every moment of your life without having to think about it. Your autonomic nervous system directs and controls your breathing in a comfortable way; in a way that is so much better than you could ever do consciously; in a way that occurs without any effort on your part. Your body, in a sense, breathes by itself. As you continue to breathe, you may notice that each time you exhale, you can relax more and more. Each time you exhale you can feel as if you are sinking deeply into the support of the mattress. Each time you exhale you can feel as if you are letting go of more and more muscle tension. So that each time you breathe out, it is as if you are letting go of tightness and you feel your muscles becoming soft and loose. You may experience this as a comfortable feeling of heaviness, so that each time you exhale, you feel your body becoming soft and loose and heavy. If you notice that there is any part of your body which is still tense, which is holding on to tension, imagine as you exhale, that you breathe out through that body part which was holding tension and let your breath melt the tension so that, as you breathe out, those muscles too become soft and loose and comfortable. Take a few moments to make a tour of your body, taking time to notice if there is any tension anywhere within your body. If you notice any tension in your body, take a few moments of extra care, letting yourself breathe out through that part of your body and melt the tension away.

You may also notice that your heartbeat assumes a regular, even, rhythmical pattern, which is most beneficial for you at this time. You know again that your unconscious mind directs the beating of your heart day and night, every moment of your life whether you consciously think about it or not. It is the circulation of oxygenated enriched blood throughout your body which aids very much in the healing process. And so for these few moments, just feel the rhythm of your heartbeat. You may notice somewhere within your body a pulsing, regular, even rhythm. Sometimes your heartbeat may be so subtle that perhaps the only way to feel it is on a cellular level, for every single living cell in your body feels the regular influx of nutrients with every beat of your heart. This process also cleanses away all waste products in each and every cell in your body. And, as mentioned earlier, this process goes on automatically whether you think about it or not.

Your blood pressure lowers to a level which is best for you right now. Because you are lying down in a position of relaxation and comfort and you feel a certain sense of stillness, your blood pressure can lower. If you were to get up and move around, your blood pressure would rise so that you could carry on that activity. So the important thing about your blood pressure is that it be flexible, rising when you need it to rise and lowering when you are not doing anything which places a demand on your body.

You may also notice that as I continue to speak with you, thoughts continue to drift through your mind, as if your thoughts are like drops of water in a river. And you know, sometimes those drops of water move very quickly in the form of white water rapids, bubbling over rocks, moving very quickly downstream. Yet, in the very same river, if you walk downstream far enough, you will come to a spot in the river where the water is so deep that it is almost impossible to detect any movement at all. In fact, perhaps you cannot see the water move until you wait and watch a leaf detach itself from a branch of a tree, begin to drift downward toward the surface of the water, touch the surface of the water, pause for just a moment and then begin its journey downstream.

Feel the rhythm of your thoughts without bothering to pick out any one thought to think about. Just feel the gentle drifting rhythm of your thoughts as they drift through your mind like drops of water.

Know that at this moment there is nothing special for you to do, there are no demands being placed upon you, no expectations. There is no one to please, no one to satisfy. The only thing for you to do right now is to feel and experience the rhythms going on within your body—feeling a sense of comfortable stillness, feeling a sense of quiet deep within you, allowing your unconscious mind to work freely and easily in this process of healing.

One of the ways that your body heals itself is by circulating rich oxygenated blood to every single living cell in your body, filling that cell with nourishment and carrying away waste products and poisons, and filtering them outside of your body. This process is a process that you can participate in and facilitate. One of the ways that you can facilitate this process is to keep in mind that your body is constantly healing itself, sloughing off dead cells, nourishing that area, and growing new cells all of the time. As part of your healing process you will experience many different kinds of physical sensations. You may feel the sensation of stretching and shrinking as tissues join together and mend themselves. You may experience sensations of warmth as the healing process continues, or sensations of pressure as swelling begins to subside. It is important to know that, as your body heals itself, changes do occur and those changes may be perceived by you. You can cooperate with the work of your body by remaining calm, as you are now, continuing to breathe in a rhythmical easy rhythm, letting your breath enrich your blood supply, which in turn will carry nutrients to your cells, allowing your blood pressure to go to a level which is most beneficial to you now. If you are feeling any sense of discomfort, breathe in and out through that area so that your warm breath can soothe those muscles and allow them to feel soft and warm and relaxed. So let yourself rest and let your body take its time to heal.

Now, leaving you with these thoughts, allow yourself to continue to breathe, relaxing more and more with each breath, fully enjoying that feeling of deep comfort and peace. Allow the drifting of your thoughts to match the easy rhythm of your breathing as you inhale and exhale. Then, give to your unconscious the task of directing your healing process with the same efficiency that it directs your respiration, digestion, and circulation—knowing that your unconscious can direct your healing process, whether or not you consciously think about it.

In a few moments, you will begin to rouse yourself and reorient yourself to this room. You can begin to do so when, and only when, you are ready to do so, taking all the time you need; allowing yourself to retain that feeling of comfort and a sense of well-being. As you do begin to move around a bit, you may feel sensations returning to your hands and feet. Be curious as you open your eyes, and notice how bright the colors can appear. You can feel refreshed as if you have just awakened from a long and restful sleep.

I invite you to play this tape as often as you wish so that you can use it to help put yourself in the best possible mind-set for your surgery and for the healing process, which for the next few days and weeks will be your full-time job. Thank you.

REFERENCES

Amir, S., Brown, Z.W., & Amit, Z. (1980). The role of endorphins in stress: Evidence and speculations. *Neuroscience Biobehavior Review, 4,* 77-86.

Erickson, M.H. (1967). An introduction to the study and application of hypnosis for pain control. In J. Lassner (Ed.), *Hypnosis in psychosomatic medicine.* New York: Springer-Verlag.

Fraulini, K.E. (1983). Coping mechanisms and recovery from surgery. *AORN Journal, 37*(6), 1198-1208.

Goodman, C.E. (1983, March). Pathophysiology of pain. *Archives of Internal Medicine, 143,* 527-530.

Hole, J.W. (1981). *Human anatomy and physiology.* Dubuque, IA: Wm. C. Brown.

Jacob, J. (1982). Endogenous morphines and pain control. *Panminerva Medica, 24*(2), 155–159.

Milloy, D. (1982, Dec.). Enkephalins and endorphins: The endogenous opiates. *Journal of the American Association of Nurse Anesthetists, 50*(6), 569-73.

Parker, J.C. (1983, Jan.). Psychological factors that influence self-reported pain. *Journal of Clinical Psychology, 39*(1), 22-25.

Sylvester, S.M. (1974). *Physiological correlates of emotion.* Unpublished paper.

Sylvester, S.M. (Speaker). (1983). *Preparation for surgery* [Audio-Cassette]. Sandra Sylvester, 2500 E. River Rd., Tucson, AZ 85718.

PART X

Case Studies

This section consists of single case studies in which Ericksonian techniques are applied to a variety of problems. Each practitioner has adapted Ericksonian methods to his or her own style.

Ronald A. Havens, Ph.D., is an associate professor of psychology at Sangamon State University who earned his degree in clinical psychology from West Virginia University. He has authored and/or coauthored more than 20 publications, mostly in the areas of hypnosis and the training of psychologists. He edited a volume entitled The Wisdom of Milton H. Erickson which is in press with Irvington Publishers.

When one of the scheduled speakers cancelled, a place became available for Ronald Havens to present a second paper. Havens describes the dynamics and treatment of a case of "negative hypnosis." (Daniel Araoz, Ed.D., has used this term to describe the untoward effects of detrimental suggestions presented when a patient is in a focused state of attention.) Havens uses hypnotic technique to effectively break through a repression that caused a school phobia.

F. William Hanley, M.D., died prior to publication of this book. In fact, illness prevented him from attending the Congress, and his paper was read by one of his colleagues from British Columbia.

Hanley received his M.D. from the University of Toronto and served as a clinical associate professor in the Department of Psychiatry at the University of British Columbia. He was president of the BC Division of the Canadian Society of Clinical Hypnosis and was a member of the Board of Directors of the Canadian Psychiatric Association. Hanley was a Life Fellow of the American Psychiatric

Association and a Fellow of the American Society of Clinical Hypnosis. As an extraordinary teacher and practitioner, he was known as "Mr. Hypnosis" in western Canada.

Hanley described the microdynamics of a single session of hypnotherapy for a patient suffering from depression. A follow-up indicates the effectiveness of the therapy.

Dawn M. White, Ph.D., earned her degree in clinical psychology from the United States International University. She also has a Master's degree in psychiatric social work. Employed in Whiteriver, Arizona, Dr. White works with Native Americans. She studied extensively with Milton Erickson from 1976 until his death and was one of the more frequent visitors at Erickson's teaching seminars.

Dr. White surveys Erickson's writings on weight reduction. She describes the dynamics of her approach in successfully treating a woman who suffered obesity.

Eric Greenleaf, Ph.D., earned his degree in clinical psychology from New York University. He conducts a practice of psychotherapy and hypnosis in Berkeley, California. Greenleaf has a number of publications on active imagination and hypnosis. He was recipient of the 1970 Milton Erickson Award for Scientific Excellence in Writing in Hypnosis from the American Journal of Clinical Hypnosis.

Greenleaf describes the use of his active imagination technique in successfully treating a case involving sexual disinhibition. His sensitive approach shows through in the transcripts that he presents of his work.

Alan F. Leveton, M.D., is a psychiatrist who earned his degree at the University of California in San Francisco. He is an associate clinical professor at the Pediatric Mental Health Unit of the University of California Medical Center in San Francisco. Leveton is founding director of the Family Therapy Center in San Francisco. An accomplished teacher and practitioner of family therapy, he has been a supervisor of family therapists for almost twenty years.

Leveton's remarkable sensitivity as a clinician is shown in his treatment of a woman dying of cancer. He uses concepts from the philosopher Bachelard, the pediatric psychoanalyst Winnicott, and Milton Erickson to demonstrate the depth and power of reverie.

Chapter 35

The Unintentional Creation of a School Phobia Using Hypnotic Dynamics of Interaction

Ronald A. Havens

Although hypnosis typically is presented as a potentially powerful treatment tool, it also has been recognized that hypnosis has the potential to produce unintended, undesirable and unpleasant effects. Erickson (1964b) described several instances wherein the use of inappropriate suggestions by untrained lay hypnotists resulted in destructive outcomes for their patients. One woman, who wished to quit smoking, was told emphatically during trance that "the thought, mention or sight of a cigarette would induce convulsive vomiting." Not surprisingly, the end result was several days of unrelieved convulsive vomiting and the need to consult a professional hypnotherapist to undo the effects of the ill-conceived suggestion.

The literature and folklore surrounding hypnosis contain similar examples of the dangers involved in saying the wrong thing at the wrong time to a deeply hypnotized person. There is little doubt that most professional hypnotherapists are sensitive to these issues.

On the other hand, hypnotic events are not limited to situations involving trained or untrained hypnotists engaged in formal induction and suggestion procedures with a willing subject. Indeed, Erickson himself frequently noted that his most innovative and effective hypnotic procedures (such as those which use boredom, surprise, shock or confusion) were derived from his observations of the unintended hypnoidal consequences of certain patterns of interpersonal interaction in everyday life (cf. Erickson, 1964c). In other words, Erickson's approach to hypnosis was based largely upon a recognition that hypnotic events are a normal, if sometimes unintended, part of life. Erickson noted that he could create these events naturalistically through careful duplication of the circumstances which his observations had taught him were responsible for such events.

For example, Erickson traced the origin of his "confusion technique" to a chance encounter with a stranger in 1923 (Erickson, 1964a). Having accidently bumped into a man, Erickson glanced at his watch, told the gentleman the wrong time and walked on. When he turned and looked he saw the victim of his unusual behavior standing looking at him in an obviously puzzled, virtually catatonic state. Erickson realized that he had literally stumbled across an effective induction procedure.

There is no reason to believe that unintentional hypnotic events of everyday life are invariably positive or neutral in effect. If hypnosis under controlled or formal circumstances has the inherent possibility of detrimental consequences, then hypnotic events in informal, uncontrolled situations also could produce unwanted or unintended outcomes.

LeCron (1964) briefly describes several cases wherein the presenting problem evidently had been precipitated by hypnosis-like incidents in everyday life. A case of uncontrollable promiscuity, for example, was eventually traced to a mother's forceful admonition, "Don't you ever say no again! Don't ever say that word 'no' again!" Forceful repetition of this command while the girl was beaten with a stick apparently implanted it as a subconscious directive to be followed under all circumstances, even when being propositioned by a stranger.

CASE DESCRIPTION

A 24-year-old single female student who suffered from intense anxiety in a classroom setting was referred to me. This young woman had moved to the United States several years previously and recently decided to continue her education at the university level. Unfortunately, the anxiety she experienced whenever she attended a class was so extreme and uncontrollable that she considered leaving school if it continued.

The patient was mildly anxious during our initial interview. However, she was quite cooperative and seemed to be highly motivated to overcome her problem. She was unable to specify exactly when her school anxiety had begun, though she indicated that she thought it was present in a milder form as far back as high school. She stated that what terrified her the most was the possibility of being called on to answer a question or to read out loud. Whenever this had happened in the past she was totally unable to say anything and was forced to sit there utterly humiliated by her own silence. She was so embarrassed by these incidents that she lived in terror of their recurrence. Each time she entered a classroom this terror reappeared.

She could offer no explanation for her inability to speak when called on. She indicated that she had no trouble speaking in other social situations and noted that, aside from this difficulty, her performance as a student was excellent. She performed well on written exams and had no trouble writing term papers.

Because she remained somewhat anxious and continued to profess an inability to be able to recall the etiology of her problem in any detail, it was decided to utilize a hypnotic trance to help her relax and, perhaps, to facilitate her recollection of historical information pertinent to the problem.

She proved to be highly responsive, and entered a mild trance almost immediately. Her light trance state was utilized to direct her thoughts and attention toward memories associated with school. In reviewing memories of junior high school, she reported that she had no problems during that time; in fact, she enjoyed school enormously. As she turned her attention toward high school, however, she became increasingly anxious and began remembering various ploys she had used to avoid attending class.

Having roughly localized the onset of her difficulties, she then was told that her unconscious mind could provide her with a detailed memory of the events in high school that led to her fears, and that she could remember these events calmly and with an understanding of their significance.

Almost instantaneously she began describing the event that precipitated her problems. Rather than attempt to summarize the description myself, I present an edited version of a description she wrote after the session.

> School was fun until that one day in September. It was the third hour and I think nobody was ready for serious studies after a long summer vacation. We were all telling each other about our vacations and our plans for the upcoming weekend. I turned around to talk to my classmates in back of me and we were giggling and laughing when all of a sudden my teacher started to shout at me. He was very angry. He shouted my name and told me to turn around and be quiet. I did not expect that reaction and his loud

angry voice just hit me. He really scared me, his voice hit me like thunder. I think I could have handled that, but then he commanded me right away to read a business letter aloud to the class. My mind could not understand two commands at once like "Shut up—read that letter!" Suddenly I could not talk, I could not read and my heart was beating like crazy. I was in shock and felt terrible. I was not able to say one word and I wanted to hide because I felt so ashamed. Here I was, a high school student, and I could not read a simple paragraph. Everybody in class stared at me and could not understand what was going on. Somebody else had to read. After class my teacher did not make any comments to me and just left me in that confused state.

Afterwards, the whole thing haunted me. I hated school because subconsciously I was afraid it could happen again. I was petrified to read and was even afraid to talk in class. Every time I had to do it I had that painful feeling. I couldn't relax and feel comfortable anymore. School was connected with tension, fear and frustration.

After I was out of school for a while, I didn't think about that scary feeling because I had it only in classroom situations. I almost forgot about it. I just can't see why one moment in my life should change everything. But when my teacher shouted at me and told me to be quiet and at the same moment told me to read, my mind could not understand what was going on. I could not get one word out and the teacher and the entire class just stared at me. It was like a shock treatment for me, and I never got rid of it. I have to start to get rid of that moment in my life, forget the shock and the terrible feeling.

Whenever I read about school phobias and hear about kids who just hate school, I wonder what happened to them. Teachers have a great impact on students and sometimes don't realize what confusion they cause. I finished high school without talking to anybody about my problem. After years I talked about it and it was an incredible relief. There was somebody who understood and was willing to listen. I wish I could have done it earlier, maybe with the teacher who caused all of these unpleasant situations. I am sure my teachers could tell how I felt in class, but nobody ever asked the important question, "Why?" I think I always knew why I acted that way, but I was scared and embarrassed to communicate. But now I can work to get rid of it and go back to normal behavior in classroom situations. I can't say I like to go to class yet or that

I am eager to be called on. It happened and nobody can make it unhappen, but the difference is now I can talk about it.

DISCUSSION

In many respects this case involves a typical example of the creation of a phobic response. There are, however, several intriguing features which are worth noting.

First of all, it should be recognized that the hypnotic state apparently was not responsible directly for the retrieval of the memory of the precipitating event. As indicated in the report written by the patient and by discussions with her afterwards, she evidently knew all along what incident had started her anxiety attacks. The hypnotic state merely provided a calm climate wherein she was able to verbalize what she already consciously knew but previously had been too afraid or embarrassed to discuss.

This particular use of hypnosis to facilitate patient cooperation was described by Erickson on numerous occasions. One of his more straightforward discussions of this issue contains the following statement: "Usually, however, hypnotic questioning serves to elicit the information more readily than can be done in the waking state, but the entire process of overcoming the resistance and reluctance depends on the development of a good patient-physician relationship rather than upon hypnotic measures, and the hypnosis is essentially, in such situations, no more than a means by which the patient can give the information in a relatively comfortable fashion" (Erickson, 1939, pp. 401-402). This certainly seems to be an accurate description of the role played by hypnosis in this case.

Moreover, the traumatic experience which precipitated this young woman's anxiety in classroom situations was not simply the circumstance of being yelled at by her teacher. Rather, the truly devastating reaction occurred when she found herself totally unable to speak. She realized that she had been told to read and that the class was waiting expectantly for her to do so. However, she was unable to do so no matter how hard she tried. The teacher responded to her muteness by calling on another student, thereby leaving the patient terrified, confused and embarrassed by her condition. As she described it later, "It felt like I was under a spell or something and I had no way to explain it to myself or anyone else."

Although it would be easy to explain her inability to read merely by attributing it to the fear created by her teacher's yelling, the patient's own description of the event suggests a more subtle and powerful process at work. Her analysis indicates that the teacher first captured and focused her attention by yelling her name, then told her in no uncertain terms to be quiet, then challenged her compliant quietness with an instruction to read. Her subsequent inability to talk in that setting, or in other classroom settings for that matter, suggests that she may have been placed in a trance by the surprise and shock of hearing her name yelled by the teacher and that consequently his directive to shut up then seemed to have the impact of a hypnotic suggestion. When asked to read, she apparently was unable to do so because she was still responding to his "hypnotically" implanted suggestion.

Except for its rapidity, this induction-suggestion-challenge process is identical in structure and outcome to the strategies commonly used during tests of hypnotizability. An induction is followed by a suggestion which the subject is then challenged to overcome. Inability to consciously overcome the suggested effect, such as paralysis of an arm, is scored as a positive hypnotic response.

Erickson (1964c) discussed the use of shock or surprise as an induction process. He noted that a shocking or surprising statement can create a momentary trance which then can be utilized quickly to generate a hypnotic response. The case presented here would seem to be a prime example of this process compressed into a few brief seconds. Apparently, whenever the microdynamics of an interaction consist of the elements necessary to capture attention and then convey a suggested response to the captivated subject, compliance is almost automatic or unconscious. The effectiveness of this strategy may explain its frequent utilization in everyday life by parents, teachers, etc. In most situations where it is used, the recipient responds appropriately and that is the end of the matter. In the situation described above, however, the teacher followed this intervention with a directive that challenged the young woman to violate his previous instruction. Her inability to do so puzzled, embarrassed and frightened her to such an extent that she began taking steps to avoid a recurrence of the experience at all costs. She started skipping school and refused to participate verbally when she did attend. Eventually her anxiety generalized and, as she wrote later, "Since that time, I have known what people mean by a school phobia."

Eventually this woman's speaking difficulties were resolved completely. The events which led to this resolution offer an intriguing insight into the shifts in perspective that were needed to break the "spell" she felt she was under.

After she described the incident which had precipitated her condition and before she emerged from trance, she was asked to allow her unconscious to present her with an awareness of what she could do to overcome her problem. She reported in a puzzled manner that she had the feeling that she should write her teacher a letter explaining what had happened so that he could avoid doing the same to someone else. She was encouraged to do so and did. However, this act by itself had minimal effect upon her anxiety.

Several weeks later, however, she received a reply from the teacher. Instead of being understanding, concerned or even apologetic, as she had anticipated he would be, he refused to accept any responsibility for the incident and indicated that it was entirely her fault. Such a rude and rejecting reply coming from a person she previously had admired and respected stimulated considerable anger and she completely revised her opinion of him. It also removed any concerns about speaking in classroom settings. Within the next week she gave an oral presentation in one class and was active in asking and answering questions in her others.

It is interesting to speculate upon the wisdom of her "unconscious" prescription for a cure. In hindsight, it seems perfectly predictable that anyone who would ignore the obviously detrimental effects of the precipitating incident probably would respond as the teacher did. On the other hand, it may be that any response would have sufficed. An understanding or sympathetic reaction might have allowed her to let go of his directive whereas a total lack of response might have had the same effect as his rudeness. In any event, the way he did respond generated a total reevaluation of him and a complete remission of the problem.

CONCLUSION

There is little doubt that hypnotic dynamics are present in many everyday interactions. A majority of these events probably are benign and simply go unnoticed by everyone concerned. It may be important to recognize, however, that these events involve the same processes employed by skilled hypnotists and, as such, have the same if not greater potential for misuse or unpleasant outcomes. Accordingly, psychotherapists should be aware of the possibility that a patient's apparently unconscious or seemingly irresistible neurotic patterns of behavior may have been initiated by such unintentional hypnotic processes. In such cases, hypnosis may be of use both in identifying the precipitating incident and in removing the offending hypnotic suggestion. In other words, it may be as useful to learn how to dehypnotize patients as it is to learn how to hypnotize them.

REFERENCES

Erickson, M.H. (1939). An experimental investigation of the possible anti-social use of hypnosis. *Psychiatry, 2*, 391-414.

Erickson, M.H. (1964a). The confusion technique in hypnosis. *American Journal of Clinical Hypnosis, 6*, 193-207.

Erickson, M.H. (1964b). Editorial. *American Journal of Clinical Hypnosis, 78*, 1-3.

Erickson, M.H. (1964c). The "surprise" and "my-friend-John" techniques of hypnosis: Minimal cues and natural field experimentation. *American Journal of Clinical Hypnosis, 6*, 293-307.

LeCron, L.M. (1964). *Self-hypnotism: The techniques and its use in daily living.* Englewood Cliffs, NJ: Prentice-Hall.

Chapter 36

A Case of Brief Psychotherapy

F. William Hanley

Psychotherapy is a cooperative enterprise between patient and therapist in which the therapist facilitates change in the patient to meet the patient's therapeutic needs. The therapist's understanding of the psychotherapeutic process determines how effectively and rapidly patients can use their unique resources, assets, learnings, and experiences to alter perceptions and understandings which will result in more effective and satisfying living.

The past cannot be changed; its experience is useful. The future is constantly becoming the present, and it is now that the patient can choose how to change as a result of altered perceptions and understandings. This process occurs mostly at an unconscious level. The conscious mind may know of the change during the therapeutic experience or it may not know of the change until it discovers it later. The therapist respects the patient's uniqueness to make changes in perception and behavior in one's own time, one's own way and in places of one's own choosing. The therapist aids those changes by understanding unconscious needs as they are presented and by responding appropriately.

Some patients accomplish therapeutic change in a few sessions or even less, some require more than a few sessions, and some achieve it in one meeting. Sheri is a patient who used a single session to achieve satisfying therapeutic change. In describing the process I will tell you important things I know about psychotherapy.

Sheri had been in the inpatient unit for some weeks when I was asked

Dr. Hanley died on July 16, 1984, following a brief illness. The videotape of the therapeutic encounter described in this chapter is on file at the University of British Columbia.

to see her. I was told that there had been only limited response to treatment, which consisted of antidepressant medication and group and individual psychotherapy.

As Sheri entered the room it was noted immediately that she had an expression of sadness and resignation. She sat down with head and shoulders slightly drooping; she moved little and spoke in a low monotone.

I gestured toward the empty chair and noted that the patient responded to the nonverbal suggestion by sitting down with her hands in her lap. I let my arm rest on the arms of my chair and allowed my feet to remain flat on the floor.

T: As you know, I'm Dr. Hanley and I want to be sure I have your name
   correctly.
P: Sheri M——.
T: Sheri M—— and how do you spell Sheri?
P: S, H, E, R, I.
T: And what do you prefer to be called?
P: Sheri.

(In this brief interchange I indirectly asked Sheri to give *her* name and told her I wanted correct information about her. A person's name stands for the total self with its unique experiences. I received that capsule statement with my ears and eyes, noting the patient's self-attitude in tone of voice, hesitations, etc. I received it with respect and returned it with respect. I showed with the simple question "What do you prefer to be called?" that I gave the patient the choice of distance. The patient was assured in the first, intense and indelibly recorded moments of the relationship that this will be a cooperative, respectful relationship. Moreover, attention has been focused and in that sense trance induction has begun.)

T: And how old *are* you, Sheri?
P: 34.

(The patient provided more personal information which was received with great interest and respect—the patient did not hear how *old* are you. Now the therapeutic relationship has begun.)

T: And you're a patient in this hospital.
P: Right.

(A yes response.)

T: Can you give me some idea of the reason for your being in this hospital *now*.

(This invites another yes response—to the word "can." The intervention both elicits the patient's response to an indirect suggestion and refers to the present: tell me *now*, you are here now. It permits the patient to bring the whole problem, including feelings, into the interview situation by asking for only part of it.)

P: When I came in it was because I was self-destructive and that's what they're treating me for—depression, and to channel the problems elsewhere instead of into myself; that's what we're working on.

(The therapist's task now is to understand the patient's problem; to meet the patient at her level; to bring the problem into the consulting room; to facilitate an appropriately intense emotional involvement; and to maximize the effectiveness of whatever therapeutic intervention is made. I was also listening and watching for clues to formulate a therapeutic intervention. When one really pays attention, patients will explain how to treat them.)

T: I see . . . depressed?
P: Yes. (without affect).
T: Tell me what it's like for *you* to be depressed.
P: It's horrible—it's no sleeping and worrying all the time and being really unhappy . . . I just can't stay asleep very long because whatever I'm dreaming or thinking keeps waking me up.
T: What dreams do you *remember*?

(I asked for dreams rather than thoughts in order to obtain information from the patient's unconscious and to focus attention inward, thereby directing the developing trance. "Remember" is emphasized. It is a powerful tool. I wanted to learn more about the patient's early life and to prepare her for age regression if that should be useful.)

P: At home, my teeth keep falling out and it bothers me when they do. I have it all the time in different circumstances. If I touch my teeth with my tongue they just fall out . . . I dream it all the time . . . I hate it, I hate my teeth to fall out. It upsets me.

(As affect begins to intensify, I show increasing interest.)

T: What time do you wake in the morning?
P: 5:30.
T: When does the depression begin?
P: Probably, at that time . . . I can't get rid of it.

(The patient is asking for help and is stating a goal. I made notes of her phrase.)

T: Could you tell me what it was like before you came in.

(I was suggesting she go back to a time when it was worse and tell me about it.)

P: It would get worse by evening, because when I was working all day it helps . . . days off were horrible.
T: You're working?
P: Yeh, I *was*.
T: What was your work?
P: Hairdresser . . . now I'm going to work for someone else in the city . . . I enjoy it. (without affect.)

(I then chose to postpone intensification of the affect in order to get more information; I was interested in learning about when and in what context she feels well.)

T: What do you like about it?
P: I like making people look better when they leave. I usually like listening to them . . . they put me into their confidence.

(The patient is telling me how to treat her. When she used the word confidence, I nodded my head. I then inquired about the severity of the depression and suicidal thoughts. The patient said that she took overdoses of tranquilizers and aspirins on about 10 occasions in the previous 10 years, usually followed by emergency admission to hospital.)

P: They sent me home every morning until the last time . . . when I'd wake up they'd send me home . . . there were happy times in between—I just don't remember them.

T: It began when you were about 24. What was going on in your life at that time?

(A request for information about the context in which the depression began.)

P: Venturing out on my own from a marriage and having kids and having to look after them. Sometimes I tell people I've been depressed for 30 years but they don't believe me. I guess they don't think it's possible.

T: It's possible for four-year-olds to be depressed. What was going on in your life at the age of four?

P: It started when I was three. My mother got married when I was three to a man that she didn't tell she had a daughter until they were married, so I went into their marriage "in the way."

T: In the way?

P: Yeh, in the way, I guess, of their happiness. I think she should have told him. I mean, I was disliked before he even met me. He was resentful that she hadn't told him.

T: And you were the only child at the time?

P: Yeh—I still am. I left when I was seven. My mother left first and she left me there for it seemed like a long time before she sent for me but she . . . I thought she made me stay there too long. She sent for me when I was seven.

T: What was your mother like?

P: I think she was resentful that she had me. When I was about 14 or so she asked me to call her by her first name so people wouldn't think I was her daughter. It upset me . . . anyway, it's taken me a long time to get here. I'm glad I'm here.

(I have learned that the patient felt abandoned, disliked and resented by her mother. However, affect has not intensified. I noted that the patient did not ask for help with this, but handled it herself by moving into the present and expressing a good feeling. I also noted that she left out a large segment of her life—a "long time." I found out that her mother left the marriage and moved in with another man when she was 14. He was "just a bum" and kicked Sheri out when she was 17.)

P: He was mad. It was Christmas day. When they came home he got really mad at me . . . they were drinking . . . he just told me to get out.

(She went to stay with a friend. She married at 18, had two children, and broke up at 24.)

T: And what is the age and sex of each child?

(Sex is also a powerful word. Through its use, the patient's unconscious can hear that it has permission to speak about sexual problems if they exist.)

P: A daughter 15, a son 12. I have custody of them.
T: What happened in that marriage?
P: I thought it would last forever because I wanted something solid and he knew that and took advantage of it. I finally got tired of it—I packed his bags. I've had relationships since then but none of them have worked.
T: What was your main learning from that marriage?
P: That he didn't have to be my mother—I just went from one mother to another.
T: Any close friends?
P: No.
T: You move around a lot.
P: Yeh—from one town to another. I was trying to get away from me. I haven't talked to anyone about that. When I was in the other hospital before this, the doctor told me to get an apartment and a job and I could get out of the hospital. I didn't want to live by myself.

(The patient then told of declaring bankruptcy and being without her children, who had been placed before the hospital admission. After 10 days of living alone in her apartment without work, she came into the hospital. I have now learned enough about the patient's life experiences, her needs, the context in which depression occurs, her present situation, her strengths and the context in which pleasurable feelings occur. I know her goal is to get rid of the depression. Therapeutic intervention can begin. Therefore I chose a word to intensify her affect.)

T: Living can be pretty *lonely* at times.
P: I've lost everything. (She touches her teeth and cries.) I'm just going in a circle.
T: You have that tremendous task of starting all over again, just like at the beginning.

P: All over. I used to be so proud when I got everything for myself and didn't have to ask for anything. Everything's all gone now.

T: Many people have lost everything and started over and done better because they have learned so much. One of the best ways to be successful . . . is to fail.

P: It was hard. (referring to her business)

T: You have ten years of experience and learning in your work. (pause) You must know it thoroughly. (pause)

(The totality of the depression has been brought into the now. The touching of the teeth told me a deep level of the depression had been reached. "I'm just going in a circle" indicated her feelings of helplessness. I suggested total change: starting *all over*, like at the *beginning*. When was that? Perhaps age 3?

I then reframed her problem: One of the best ways to be successful . . . is to fail. Depressed people ruminate on the past and their present helplessness and see no future. The reframing alters the perception of the past to make it an asset. The patient hears "be successful" and the paralogical unconscious mind can accept that failure is success. I tried to activate the unconscious memories of her 10 years of experience and learning to reinforce the reframing. To make sense of this the patient needed time and I paused to allow her to go into as deep a trance as she needed.)

P: Yes. By coincidence I worked in T——for a fellow and he's giving me a job now. He gave me my first job and now he's giving it to me again—it's really strange. It's great—the circle's come right around. (She rotates her hand in a circle, smiles for the first time in the interview and puts her hand supportively to her mouth.)

(Surprise is associated with altered perception. The circle of helplessness has changed to something to smile about. Nonverbally she told me she can keep her teeth from falling out.

A turning point has been reached. The therapeutic task is to facilitate and consolidate the patient's development, using the potential she had been neglecting by focusing on her past. Notice how she does this.)

T: It's surprising how things happen like that.

(What things?)

P: Yeh—he's given me a definite day but this time it's harder—the kids aren't here (pause)—but I imagine I'll do it. They (the staff and patients) keep telling me I have a lot of strength. I'll just have to find it in me.

T: You imagine you'll do it.

(A suggestion for age progression—to rehearse the future.)

P: Yeh. I think I can get out and work and build up something. I've got to learn I can do it just for me. That's what I have to do.

T: Would you mind taking a few minutes to do a little of that imagining. Would you mind closing your eyes and *imagine* your next job (patient closes her eyes) and you're working—and the people—and the things you're doing. Enjoy that imagining and *really* enjoy that imagining. (When one is with people one doesn't feel abandoned and good feelings replace feelings of being disliked and resented; when one is doing work that one enjoys one is building something.) Give yourself a comfortable, pleasant mental image. You may recall many times when you are working and enjoying your work, many times when you are doing things you like to do and feeling confident doing what you like to do and having a feeling of confidence in yourself and in doing the things you really know you can do.

You may remember some time when you felt secure and comfortable. Be aware of the tremendous importance of a feeling of security. Be willing to discover the strengths and abilities within yourself. Your unconscious mind knows you really have strengths and abilities. Be very interested to find those strengths and that confidence growing within yourself. You can be pleased to find yourself becoming stronger, more confident, more secure, more comfortable and you can leave the unhappiness way back in the past and look forward to the good things that are going to happen and the good things you are going to do. I wouldn't be surprised if you begin to find yourself sleeping better and begin to find yourself having different dreams. Certain changes are taking place and those changes can go on, and you can look forward to accomplishing the things that are important and satisfying to you, and you can look forward to being the person who is satisfying to you and more and more comfortable with yourself and with others, and more and more effective in anything and everything you do, and keep that picture of your next job in your unconscious mind available at all times for your well-being, and let yourself have that feeling of well-being. (long pause)

All right. Any time you wish you can open your eyes . . . *now.* (long pause during which the patient opened her eyes and sat dreamily)

(Termination of therapy ought to be part of the therapeutic task and consistent with the patient's therapeutic needs. The therapy then has unity and integrity. In the end is the beginning and in the beginning therapists ready themselves for the end. This patient was abandoned by her mother, kicked out by her stepfather, and had comparable experiences when discharged from the previous hospitals. She needs to feel in control of any separation. The corrective emotional experience of the therapy session is completed by the simple communication:)

T: Are you ready to go back to the ward now?
P: (dreamily) Mm-hmm. Thank you. Good-bye.

One Week Later

(The patient entered briskly, with changed demeanor and voice; she was smiling. Notice in her remarks the suggestions she had accepted and the corresponding modifications she made. I was surprised to discover other changes she had made—therapists ought to be willing to be surprised.)

P: I'm sleeping better. Not as hungry, too—I was eating excessively. Using my voice a lot more. It feels good.
T: When was the best time in your life?
P: I was very happy when my daughter was born. This might be my best year.

(The patient resisted the therapist's attempt to look at the past!)

T: The best time of one's life is always *now.* You can't change the past.
P: You can plan the future. I feel a lot better, a lot more positive—just go out there and work and do it and take care of myself.
T: You got rid of that depression?
P: I think it's gone. I don't know where it went. All of a sudden, about a week—just a cloud sort of lifted.
T: And how do you account for that?
P: I don't know . . . maybe talking . . . getting it out instead of keeping it in . . . I'm glad I'm here, really glad. (with affect)

T: What do you remember of our session?

P: The best part was at the end when you had me relax and told me positive things. I guess I so much wanted to hear them that that's what I remember best—not the negative things. When I left I was ready to tackle something. I left not thinking about memories but thinking ahead. I just feel a lot better, really happy.

T: I suppose you'll be leaving.

P: I suppose so—I'm looking forward to it.

COMMENT

Patients are commonly in an altered state of consciousness on entering a therapist's office, or soon after. This may be augmented by the nature of the communication used for history taking and acquiring understanding of a patient's therapeutic needs, and in turn enables the most rapid expression and understanding of those needs. At the appropriate time, specific therapeutic intervention is made to meet the individual needs, allowing the patient to alter maladaptive patterns or to replace them with more adaptive patterns derived from their experience. The therapist facilitiates such change and reinforces it. In short, the patient enters the therapeutic situation with focused attention; and the therapist, using his or her knowledge of and skill in hypnosis, consciously deepens and utilizes the trance (informally or formally), while learning about and understanding the patient, to facilitate and consolidate change. In this way the therapeutic process develops at an optimal rate and is called brief therapy. Many maneuvers used without recognition of the existence and potential of the altered state of consciousness, especially those based on theoretical preconceptions, may impede, prolong, or prevent therapeutic change. The result may be designated long-term therapy and ascribed to the patient's resistance or inability to change.

The altered state in which Sheri entered the therapeutic situation, with its ideational preoccupations and affective content, is known as depression. It is sometimes asked if hypnosis can be effective in depression. In this case, it is a question of discovering how. An immediate therapeutic relationship is established through the use of the patient's name, which both focuses on and begins to access inner realities. Then the pattern of the problem is elucidated—how it has occurred and is being maintained, and also the contexts that produce a feeling of well-being. This is done in such a way as to maintain the altered state (the nonverbal aspects, such as inflections, emphases, and gestures can be appreciated on the videotape but are not recorded in this chapter). The patient is met at her level throughout. The next step is to intensify the affect, further deepening the trance. This allows increased communication with the unconscious and the use of a paradoxical suggestion or reframing (the more failure, the more success), which again increases the trance. The process and timing are monitored by the "yes" responses (verbal and head nodding) and the patient's altered verbalization and affect. The patient's use of the word "imagine" offers the therapist the choice of using imagery to deepen and utilize the trance further and to introduce numerous general, appropriate, positive suggestions for which the patient is ready and which she can apply in her unique case. She is unhooked from her preoccupation with depression-generating ideas and memories, and hooked to positive, constructive, optimistic thoughts and images. Hence the therapeutic task—to get rid of the depression and allow separation from the hospital—is completed.

The follow-up visit tests and further consolidates the change. Outpatient therapy, if indicated, would be based on changes made in this session.

Chapter 37

Ericksonian Hypnotherapeutic Approaches: The Treatment of Obesity Using Indirect Suggestion

Dawn M. White

OVERVIEW OF ERICKSON'S WRITINGS ON WEIGHT REDUCTION

Of nearly 150 articles written by Milton H. Erickson, only one deals exclusively with the treatment of obesity (Erickson, 1960). It describes the successful treatment of three cases of obesity.

In the first case, a woman who would agree to only one session reduced from 240 to 125 within a nine month period. During the session Erickson taught her subjectively to distort her experience of time. She learned to eat each meal in a state of time expansion. As she finished a meal it would be as if she had been eating for "hours on end with complete satisfaction" (Erickson, 1960, p. 112). She was to have her husband, a physician, prescribe a proper diet and supervise her weight loss. This approach utilized her stated enjoyment of eating: "I enjoy eating, I could spend all the time in the world just eating."

In the second case, the patient was required to add nearly 20 pounds to her existing weight of 180 pounds, before reaching her goal of 125 pounds. Erickson successfully interrupted a recurring pattern of losing and then gaining weight by insisting that this patient gain weight before she could lose. Previously she ate frantically as soon as she reached her goal, thereby gaining back all the weight lost.

The third case described treatment of a woman of 270 pounds who

494

wished to weigh 130 or 140 pounds. For 13 years she sought medical help and used many diets. These efforts were unsuccessful because she "always overate." A medium trance could be induced, but she would repeatedly arouse herself by laughing. Therefore, Erickson directed her to develop and maintain a light trance. Further, she was directed to listen to and understand what she was told without arousing from the trance.

He told her that she now weighed 270 pounds and that she was to cooperate with him by overeating as she always did. During the next week she was to overeat, "doing so carefully and willingly, and to overeat enough to support 260 pounds" (Erickson, 1960, p. 115). One week later she weighed 260 pounds and reported that for the first time in her life she had enjoyed overeating. She was told to overeat enough to support 255 pounds the next week and 250 pounds the week after. With this procedure she lost 80 pounds in six months. She was still in treatment when the article was written and looking forward to over-eating enough to weigh 130 or 140 pounds.

The therapeutic goal in each of the above cases was weight reduction; previously, each patient failed to achieve this goal. Erickson explained:

> By employing hypnosis a communication of special ideas and understandings ordinarily not possible of presentation was achieved in relation to personality needs and subjective attitudes toward weight reduction. Each was enabled to undertake the problem of weight loss in accordance with long established patterns of behavior but utilized in a new fashion. Thus one patient's pleasure in eating was intensified at the expense of quantity; a change of sequence of behavioral reactions led to success for the second, and a certain willfullness of desire to defeat the self was employed by the third to frustrate the self doubly and thus to achieve the desired goal. (Erickson, 1960, p. 116)

In 1970 Erickson reported another case of obesity. As in the cases reported above, the extent to which Erickson went to suit his therapy to the needs of the patients, resulted in a number of unusual treatment methods.

At the onset of treatment Ann weighed nearly 260 pounds. Both of her parents were alcoholic and treated her with brutality. Erickson felt that in order to gain rapport he had to speak to her truthfully and unemotionally. Therefore, trance was induced in an insulting and unorthodox manner. She was asked various questions which established the nature of her relationships with significant people and their attitudes towards her. Then she was told to spend as much time as she could in the library for the next two weeks and asked to return for another session. She was to take out anthropological books with pictures of women from other cultures, and to search through them to discover which strange looking women were successful in the marriage market. She returned two weeks later and described some of the most unpleasant pictures.

During the next two weeks she was directed to stand on a street corner of the busiest section of the city and notice the peculiar shapes and faces of married men and women. She reported seeing women wearing wedding rings who were almost as homely as she was, and hideously fat couples walking together. Erickson advised the patient that she was beginning to learn something and gave her further assignments on cosmetology, customs and dress, including visits to women's apparel stores. She was to wear the polka dot dress that she appeared to live in, and ask the clerks earnestly for advice on what she should wear. She reported that many of the clerks kindly explained how unbecoming polka dots were for her figure.

The next two weeks were spent obsessively thinking about why she had become so fat. Since this did not bring forth any conclusions, she was asked to

> . . . discover if there was any reason why she had to weigh what she did . . . to be curious about what she might look like if she weighed only 150 pounds and were dressed appropriately . . . to awaken in the middle of the night with that question in mind only to fall asleep again restfully. (Erickson, 1970, p. 84)

In the next few sessions she was asked to review all of her assignments and see whether they applied to her.

After six months the patient decided that there was no need to weigh so much and dress so unbecomingly. With great urgency she asked Erickson for permission to change things according to all that she had learned. A year later she weighed 150 pounds, her taste in clothes had vastly improved, and she had enrolled in a university. By graduation she was maintaining her weight at 140 pounds. Her smile had improved through dental work, she had a job as a fashion artist and was engaged to be married. When Erickson last heard from her, she had been married 15 years and had three children.

In remembering her therapy, she told Erickson:

> When you said those awful things about me, you were so truthful, I knew that I could trust you. But if you hadn't put me in trance I wouldn't have done any of the things you made me do. (Erickson, 1970, p. 85)

In this case, the patient did not begin to lose weight until six months after the first session. During this period, she was absorbed in learnings that heightened her motivation and provided her with what she needed for overall improvement.

The assignments helped her learn how to achieve maximum attractiveness, and kindled her motivation to lose weight. She also was asked to survey the reasons why she had to weigh as much as she did. A variation of this procedure was used in my own case study.

THE CASE OF C.T.

I met this patient at a social gathering where she expressed an interest in hypnosis to lose weight. When she called for an appointment, I expressed optimism to create a positive expectancy.

The treatment sessions typically lasted an hour. The first ten minutes or so were spent in going over events since the last session. Trances lasted about a half hour on the average. The remaining time was spent in discussion of whatever the patient wanted to bring up regarding the trance experience, or any other subject.

There were 16 treatment sessions over a 15-month period. For the entire period, sessions were arranged according to her inclination and my own availability (this casualness is also reflected in the way Erickson worked . . . he said on occasion that therapy was best done in intermittent fashion). For the first three months, sessions averaged two a month. At the end of this period I naively suggested that further treatment was unnecessary but that I would be available if the patient wished. Four months passed before she reinitiated treatment.

In the first session information was gathered about the patient's frame of reference, and misconceptions about hypnosis were cleared up. She was informed about Milton Erickson's psychotherapeutic methods and about my own training with him.

As was customary in Erickson's practice, the patient was asked to write down the following information: date; name; address; telephone number; age and birth date; education; occupation; siblings and birth order; marital status; number, sex and age of children, if any; and whether she grew up in an urban or rural setting.

In addition I asked her to record:

1) Her starting weight (232 pounds) and her desired weight (150 pounds);
2) A drawing of how she thought she looked and another of how she would like to look after she lost weight;
3) Her goals in therapy.

A history of her weight problem was taken, eating patterns discussed and her commitment to lose weight confirmed.

The patient made the following statement regarding her goals: "I hope to be able to alter my behavior so that I can eat and enjoy food like a normal person . . . to rid myself of the excess weight I have accumulated and to wipe out permanently my obsessive eating habits."

She reported that she was "inspired" for a few days after our phone conversation and then "backslid." She said she had been reluctant to call until she was really sure she wanted to try to lose weight as she had tried just about everything else and felt there would be no turning back once she started.

An accomplished potter, the patient often overate while doing detailed glaze work on her pottery. She did this work at home on her kitchen table. She said that the work was often tedious and tiring and she had a habit of stopping for a snack (cheese, cookies, etc.) about every 20 minutes. Besides, the patient could not bear to throw food away or to leave it on her plate.

She presented an intriguing fantasy system that she used to help relieve guilt about overeating. It involved two little characters named "Nosher" and "Fresser" who were always urging her to eat. They even had ropes and pulleys all rigged up inside of her so that her arm and hand would move to the food and put it in her mouth. It was as if her legs and arms and mouth were carrying her around and feeding her.

The initial trance work addressed the two fantasy characters:

> And it is nice to know that we can give up imaginary playmates as we grow older. Having served their purpose for a time in our lives, we can bid them goodbye, however regretfully, as we realize that they get in the way of more grown-up wishes. So you can take time to bid goodbye to fantasy characters that are no longer useful given your new resolutions and wishes. There are so many ways

to usher them out of your life and I wonder which imaginative method you will choose.

Following this session, and to the patient's relief, Nosher and Fresser "packed their bags and left."

Next the problem of eating while doing her glaze work was addressed by indirect suggestion:

> I wonder what new and interesting things will occur to you as you take a break from glazing. I wonder what your garden looks like outside, and I wonder if there are any books that might be enjoyable to read, and I wonder if you enjoy the taste of carrots and celery. How surprising it is to suddenly find the most tedious tasks absorbing so that all sense of time is forgotten.
>
> I talked about the pleasures of leisurely meals, the savoring of food with great concentration and satisfaction "Your unconscious mind knows just what sorts of food you need for a healthy state and how much of these foods are really needed to keep you in good health." I talked about how interesting it would be to try self-hypnosis and its use was recommended. She was advised to find a quiet private place, to sit comfortably in a favorite chair; to fix her eyes on an interesting object while she counted slowly from one to twenty, attending to that developing sense of relaxation and serenity. The suggestion was given that while she might consciously have an idea of about how long she wanted to stay in trance, her unconscious mind would determine the depth of trance and it really knew a lot more about these matters than she did.

The patient came to the second session smiling broadly. She was energetic and she showed an aliveness that had not been there previously. She reported many significant changes.

"Following the session, I went home feeling that nothing had happened and wondering if anything had. Then I had a light lunch and started working at my glazing. I didn't think of food again until 5 P.M." (The session had been at 11 A.M.) She also mentioned some habit changes that she couldn't explain. For example, she no longer wanted butter on her vegetables, and she no longer drank a glass of wine with her husband when he got home from work. She decided she really did not enjoy that glass of wine, but she could enjoy talking with her husband while he drank his glass of wine.

The patient did self-hypnosis three times a day. She would sit in a

comfortable chair and stare at a bulb until her eyes closed with a sensation that she was unable to open them. She would then dwell on
themes such as "The body needs very little food to maintain itself in a
healthy condition."

Trance work proceeded with suggestions about the small amount of
food needed to stay in good health, how interesting it is to discover that
certain foods are better than others, that small tasty portions are sometimes more satisfying than large portions, natural balance and homeostasis, the joys of savoring food, enjoying meals in leisurely and elegant
fashion, changes and discoveries, and the surprise of discovering what
she might give up today or change tomorrow, the next day, next week
and next month.

Trance was deepened and she was dissociated as follows:

> As you go as deeply into trance as you wish, it may be surprising
> to you how deeply detached you can become—like a wise friend
> looking at you in a wise and friendly manner. And from this de-
> tached vantage point you might want to review all past efforts at
> reducing, seeing all the details and all the angles and discovering
> why these efforts failed. And you can also review the experiences
> of this past week and think about the changes. And I wonder what
> it is that is different about this weight reducing experience. And
> you can take as long as you need, and when you are through you
> can awaken gradually at your own pace with the realization that
> you have accomplished a great deal. You can retain feelings of calm
> and relaxation yet be wide awake and alert, remembering only
> what it is useful for you to remember at this point.

Smiling and stretching the patient reoriented from trance and said,
"That was so nice, I'm so relaxed." She mentioned feeling deprived and
punished during previous attempts to lose weight but now it was ef-
fortless; it seemed to come naturally from within her.

Despite having attended cocktail parties and luncheons, the patient
reported a 20-pound weight loss in the first month.

In the third session, trance was induced, the paradox of gaining
through losing was presented, and age regression was employed:

> You might want to go back to a very pleasant time when you were
> five years old. A time when you were feeling really loved and
> secure. And it is so nice to feel loved, to take in all those good
> feelings." (By now the patient was smiling and appeared to be

enjoying the experience.) I reinforced good feelings of security and being loved as she enjoyed her regression. When asked where she was she said that she was sitting on her father's knee and he was making faces to make her laugh.

It was next suggested that she might want to go back to another pleasant time at age ten, when she could experience love and security once again. It would be most interesting and "it was nice to feel loved and secure." She regressed to a time when she was with her grandmother.

She was then regressed to age 15 and a pleasant experience in which she felt loved and secure. When asked where she was she said she was with "Toby." She was asked to remain deeply in trance and "think of many things."

The patient was reoriented from trance and asked about her experiences. She went into light trance as she recalled them.

In the first regression she realized how much her father had given her: that he had comforted her during difficult times and made her laugh. I commented that it must have felt good to get all that unconditional love, and she nodded with moist eyes, obviously moved by the memory.

In the regression at age ten, she was at a cowboy movie with her grandmother who did not understand English very well. They would go to the movies as a Saturday afternoon treat and she would translate dialogue for her grandmother.

In back of her grandmother's store was a dining room and kitchen. The patient enjoyed watching her grandmother who was immensely pleased when her granddaughter enjoyed her cooking. Grandmother even gave her meat and milk at the same meal (a practice disapproved of by other family members). In this the grandmother aligned herself with the patient; food was love, a reward, and a way of pleasing grandmother.

During the regression to age 15, the patient was with her first boyfriend, Toby. They attended an opera, "Don Giovanni," and skipped home singing arias.

Treatment continued with the following suggestions:

> You can go right back to feelings of comfort and as you become more comfortable you can go deeper and deeper into trance. It's nice to know that you can become more and more detached, so detached that you feel almost like a wise intelligence floating in

space. And from this wise and distant vantage point you can begin
to realize many things about yourself. You might even like to look
at two very different aspects of yourself. On the one hand, you
can see a very confident, secure self. You might want to go back
to a time when you were feeling very loved, secure, confident,
strong; and really savor those feelings because very soon you can
become aware of a very different self. (Long pause). A self that
was feeling insecure, unloved, unsure and afraid. And as you
observe, that strong, confident self can comfort the self that needs
comforting, give her all the comforting she needs.

Tears came to her eyes and I remarked that it must feel good to cry
tears of release. I wondered how the earth felt after the spring rain—it
surely felt great comfort from the blessings of rain. Rain was important
and soothing; as far as food was concerned, it was possible that very
little of it was needed for good health.

Upon awakening from trance the patient said that she saw herself at
a party and that she cried tears of relief as she felt a sort of global,
abstract comfort coming from within herself.

At the fourth session the patient reported she stopped eating ice
cream, formerly a favorite food. This session included suggestions about
the aesthetics of delicately arranged plates with color and texture and
dainty portions.

During the sixth session, the patient spontaneously regressed to an
incident that involved a dress belonging to her sister. She had zipped
herself into a beautiful dress that was so tight she could hardly breathe.
The seam ripped and she felt badly about it.

During the next three months she lost only three pounds and she felt
she reached a plateau. She knew her old habits had not come back full
force; although she was under stress she did not go back to ice cream
and cookies but ate fruit instead.

It was a mistake to suggest that further treatment might be unnecessary following the patient's loss of 25 pounds. Her pattern was to gain
weight after losing 15 to 30 pounds. She may have felt particularly
anxious and vulnerable around the time my suggestion was made. She
said, "I didn't want to bother you because I knew you were busy. But
I feel if I can come in once a month or so until I get down to where I
want to be, I know that I'll be perfectly fine because there doesn't seem
to be any problem maintaining myself."

The following metaphor was constructed to treat a delicate matter of family relationships without raising resistances through more direct methods:

> You can imagine three healthy plants growing up together in a small space of rich earth. As these plants grow toward the sun, they will have to make accommodations for each other in order to grow. As one lifts up a branch the other will need to move over so that that branch may have room to grow. And so as close as they are, they can never be totally intertwined because if they were intertwined they would constrict each other's growth. And each one will learn to allow the other to grow freely and to accommodate and adapt so that free growth may take place in all three. And all three plants can then reach out to the sun with their branches in all directions without constricting the other two, the other one. And so it is in any grove of trees; be there two trees, or four or six, they all learn to grow with the sun and nature, their own nature. You can imagine how comfortable and how wonderful it is to grow in an open and free manner and yet maintain the closeness that comes from shared goals and shared roots, and even the inter-twined roots still enable the branches to move outward freely without constriction and restriction. All things can learn to bring their apparent opposition into harmonious balance. When seeds are planted, they can begin to send their shoots up out of the earth eagerly claiming their place in the sun.

When awakened the patient commented, "Your analogy of the plants hits home because of what I am going through in this period of letting go of my last child. I was anxious about him all this week because he is a pilot. That plane crash (there was a recent crash in California) . . . of course I identified it with him. I always have anxieties. I am overcoming this. It is also an excuse for comforting myself with food."

During the ninth session two months later, anxieties about becoming a grandmother were addressed, and the importance of enjoying fully all the joys of new experiences was emphasized.

At the tenth session, four months later, the patient summarized:

> I've lost 40 pounds but there it has remained. Why, I'm not sure. With hypnosis, for the first time, I felt that I was helping myself and that I myself was in control. Those horrible cravings vanished. I'd just go about my business and then I'd just eat normally and

be satisfied. And I don't mean stuffed like I used to be. When I do
self-hypnosis everything is fine. That hasn't diminished at all. It'll
last a day or two and if I don't do it, I resume my former behavior
to a certain degree. I haven't been able to eat ice cream. I've developed an aversion to chicken skin which used to be my favorite.
Now, whether I've hypnotized myself or not I can't tolerate it. I
don't eat butter or margarine and I don't like the idea of fried foods.
Since Thanksgiving we've had guests on and off and I haven't been
hypnotizing myself because I haven't had the privacy or the desire.
But, I don't feel horrible about myself and I can go out and face
the public. I don't have to turn my head away when I pass plate
glass windows that might reflect my image suddenly. I don't have
that problem any more and I can go out in the evening, get dressed
and feel that I look nice.

At the eleventh session, trance was induced and age regression was
accomplished.

I'd like you to go back and you may be surprised where it will take
you. Go back to a time that has a direct bearing on some of the
blocks you are experiencing. Go back there and reexperience it and
free yourself. It might be just a feeling or maybe you'll hear something or see something and it'll be nice to know that whatever it
is, you can understand it in a very different light and it can free
you still further.

The patient gasped as if in pain and sobbed briefly. Upon awakening
she said her own reactions surprised her greatly. She regressed to a time
when her mother was making her clean her plate, admonishing her
about "starving Armenians" and reminding her that her older sister had
been close to starvation in Russia. Although shaken by these feelings,
she also experienced a sense of relief.
Later she remarked:

On one level I was thinking how ridiculous, the cliche to end all
cliches . . . the starving Armenians . . . but on the other hand I
was really feeling it and was helpless and profoundly upset. Now
today, and a little bit the last time also, I had this feeling about my
sister. I know that since childhood I've worshipped my sister and
I know she adores me. We have a close and wonderful relationship,
but on the other hand all my life I've tried to be like her and there's

absolutely no way. She's a high achiever, went to the most pres-
tigious schools and got a Ph.D. Her children went to Harvard and
Radcliffe. She is everything my mother dreamed of having. A child
in America accomplished all these things and I've never been able
to match this. And besides everything she was thin. She was born
in Russia and when she was two there was a famine. She was one
of those starving children . . . one of the factors that prompted my
parents to emigrate.

The next two sessions dealt mainly with anxieties about her imminent
European vacation and her fear of flying. Allusions were made to the
easy flight of birds, air currents, the elements of water, fire, earth and
air and how man had learned to utilize these elements. Indirect suggestions were given about travel and adventure, excitement and comfort.
It was suggested that the anxieties would gradually turn into excited
anticipation. An excerpt from *Biplane* (Bach, 1972, pp. 45-48) was read
as a reframing. Systematic desensitization was accomplished by going
through the steps from home to airport to Europe and back. She was
also regressed to a trip to Mexico City that she had enjoyed in the past.
    As an artist, color had special meaning for this patient. Therefore, a
monologue about color was created in accord with Erickson's (1966)
interspersal technique:

> There are so many variations of green. There's deep forest green
> and *lighter* green and mixtures of green and blue and turquoise
> and the very *lightest* greenish yellow getting *lighter* and *lighter*. The
> warm yellow of the sun, getting *lighter* and *lighter*, till it's the palest
> of yellow and getting even *lighter* until it is almost white.

And so all the colors of the spectrum were mentioned always emphasizing the *lightness* of the colors.
    The patient weighed 181 pounds upon returning from her month-long
vacation in France. She gained four pounds, this being the first weight
gain reported during the treatment period. She said the custom was to
eat two five-course meals and a light breakfast with no snacks in between. She walked a great deal.
    The patient was anxious during this last session. She was coughing
and clearing her throat and experiencing difficulty going into trance. A
special induction was used to help calm her restlessness. It concerned
watching a butterfly flit from flower to flower. She was asked to watch
the jerky and sudden movements and to observe the restlessness, and

then, to watch as the butterfly flitted less and lighted on flowers for longer periods until it finally became still and quiet, blending into the background. As the coughing ceased and the patient became motionless and calm I talked about how it is sometimes interesting to gain a few pounds in order to find out how quickly they could be lost. It was only human to gain a few pounds now and then and it was good to reaffirm one's ability to lose weight. Former suggestions were repeated regarding the pleasure of walking and being discriminating about food.

Her weight was back to 178 pounds when recorded 12 days later. This was in August 1979. There was no further treatment due to the fact that I moved.

During a follow-up phone call in September 1983, the patient reported that she had started gaining weight about one year after treatment ended. She had abandoned self-hypnosis and gained all the way back to her original weight. In August 1982 she began going to a clinic that supervised a nutritious liquid diet and went to weekly maintenance groups that continued to meet even after goal weight had been reached. Within five months she reached 140 pounds and had maintained that weight since January 1983. Now when she loses her resolve, she uses self-hypnosis effectively to get back on track.

The patient attributed her relapse to the fact that therapy was discontinued before she reached her desired weight (she was only halfway there), and to the fact that she had not had a support group. She had been under stress and developed high blood pressure and other health problems. She did, however, retain her habit of daily walks. She now walks about three miles a day. I agree with the patient's assessment but also feel strongly that cessation of the self-hypnotic sessions was particularly harmful. This was my first attempt at using hypnosis for weight reduction and was carried out as a research study with tape recording of sessions on a no-fee basis. My present knowledge and experience indicate that monthly therapy sessions should have continued indefinitely until she maintained a stable weight for a reasonable time once goal weight was reached.

REFERENCES

Bach, R. (1972). *Biplane*. New York: Avon Books.

Erickson, M. H. (1960). The utilization of patient behavior in the hypnotherapy of obesity: Three case reports. *American Journal of Clinical Hypnosis, 3,* 112-116.

Erickson, M. H. (1966). The interspersal hypnotic technique for symptom correction and pain control. *American Journal of Clinical Hypnosis, 8,* 198-209.

Erickson, M. H. (1970). Hypnosis: Its renascence as a treatment modality. *American Journal of Clinical Hypnosis, 13,* 71-79.

Chapter 38

Conjoint Hypnotherapy with an Imagined Co-therapist

Eric Greenleaf

I remember later, in another part of the dream, I am in an upstairs room of my grandmother's house. My husband and I are going to live there and I am complaining about the lack of mirrors. He suggests bringing one from our bedroom but I don't want to do that. I want a new one.

Then I begin to notice many small doors along the bottom part of the wall, and I remember that one is a secret passageway to an attic area, and that I used to know the way there as a child. At the same time I have the feeling that I have visited these attic rooms in my dreamlife as an adult.

Yet I am afraid to open any of the doors. It has been many many years since anyone has opened them and looked in and I think there are probably terrible, awful things behind them now which I wouldn't want to see.

Recently, I was consulted by a happily married woman, Melody, who, although orgasmic with her husband and experiencing a wide range of sexual activity and emotion, suffered a feeling of sexual restraint. Her inhibition, though shameful and secret to her, was manifest in a fearful reluctance to undergo routine gynecological examination. She also experienced nausea and dizziness when attempting to use tampons. In addition, and more unsettling still to Melody, herself a psychotherapist, she had contracted a series of "crushes" on a succession of therapists she consulted, the first one some three months following her marriage, the others over the course of the next 15 years. Melody's therapy with me began in September, 1981 and continued

507

through the resolution of her inhibition in April, 1983. We met for an hour each week and dealt in turn with themes in her life which seemed to offer a way to the relief of her distress. Each path in dreams, relationship, strategic intervention, hypnotherapy or conversation seemed to reach some resolution, only to turn into another unsolved puzzle. Meanwhile, Melody's "crush" on her therapist grew and flourished. As Melody said, "I need to keep doing this until I exhaust myself and let go of it."

So, Melody was encouraged repeatedly to express all her sexual feelings by words and in letters, and to thoroughly enjoy these feelings as the natural expression of her strong, womanly emotions. As she said, "It happens a little bit with the writing, but the experience of relief is much stronger after I actually have put these letters and dreams in your box."

Now, the experience of having an attractive, intelligent woman of honest conviction declare sexual passion week after week is a heady one, no matter how trivialized in the therapeutic literature, no matter how expectable. My box was piled high with letters. I thought I could use some help here (about July of 1982) and so suggested that Melody solicit a woman's view of her intense emotions. To save the expense involved, she was to consult, in her active imaginings, with a woman therapist of her choosing. She chose the distinguished and innovative family therapist, Mara Selvini Palazzoli. Then, at home, she held the first of four long conversations with Mara.

In the first talk, Mara gives Melody a blue and red cloth blanket. She tells her that this blanket "belonged to your grandmother many years ago. She gave it up, put it away, far away, so that it was lost even in memory, when her first love died. . . . This was the mantle of her womanhood. . . . Under its warm protection, she would surrender fully to him—but more importantly, she would yield to the mysteries of her own nature. "Mara tells her, too, that Melody's husband will be enriched as she is by her "secret treasure."

The second conversation has Melody ask Mara for understanding of "this dream about the small girl-child and the male torso with the large penis." Placing Melody and the three-year-old girl on the magic blue blanket, Mara transports them to the hill which is the dream's most frightening place. She says, "No harm will come to either of you. I will help you discover what to do." Melody and the child are naked. "Suddenly I am aware that a shadow has fallen over us. Mara calls to me, 'Melody, open your eyes and look now.' "

It is a tall, dark, handsome stranger. Mara coaxes Melody to speak with him, sit with him, touch him, make love with him. Mara takes the child away with her to the tree. Melody and the man are caressing. "Suddenly I feel afraid. At that moment, Mara's singing comes to me with the breeze—she's comforting the child, and I, too, feel soothed." Melody and the stranger make love until both are satisfied. The child returns and Mara tells Melody, "Your body holds all the meaning which you need."

So, Mara brought together the themes of the frightened little girl, the alluring stranger, and a grown woman's sexual knowledge. And she placed these in the context of the patient's history—her imitation of a grandparent's inhibited love. For their third conversation, I encouraged Melody to speak with Mara about her strong, sexual feelings towards me.

Mara leads Melody to describe her sexual imaginings and emotions. Then, Mara suggests she imagine being in the office with me. Melody asks that Mara accompany her in this fantasy and warns her, "If you get me into hot water, I'm leaving!" She is encouraged to express her natural feelings in words—they turn out to be ones of warmth and affection—and is told, "It's the holding back that creates difficulty. Long ago you learned to suppress these natural and very right feelings."

The fourth conversation with Mara concerned ways Melody might schedule her time and care for herself in the world, at work, among her friends. Of the conversations with Mara, Melody said:

> They seem to be supporting this important shift from my regarding you as the one to be revered and idolized to simply one who is my equal. I'm not speaking here of the content of the conversations; rather, the structure itself. In addition, Mara's femaleness . . . in some way is allowing me to re-own my own wisdom and power, rather than projecting them onto some male figure (you, most recently). I feel happy. Yes! I feel happy! I think I am finally falling in love with myself.

As before, the resolution of issues of emotion was not accompanied by sexual disinhibition, although it did produce real changes in Melody's sense of herself, changes noted with approval by her friends and husband. Even into the next year, Melody insisted on bringing forth the remaining aspects of her family drama for experiencing, talking about, dreaming with and understanding:

> I dreamed that as I was looking into the deepest part of the water, which was at the beginning, a man who was alternately my husband and my father came up behind me as I was looking.

Also, feelings about grandmother and great-grandmother surfaced again, as well as feelings about her father's rages and sadness. In February of 1983, Melody tearfully "confessed" that she had yet to overcome her sexual inhibition, and in March, she asked to discontinue therapy, then changed her mind and continued until her successful completion of the sexual experiences she had set for herself as the task of therapy. Her ability to endure gynecological examination comfortably occurred early in 1982, the disinhibition of her sexual fear in April, 1983, and the ability to insert a tampon without nausea and dizziness was hers by September of 1983.

Before she could accomplish these tasks, it was important that she understand the emotional origins of her distress in her family life. This is, in part, because there were undiscovered issues, such as "Can I let go of 26 years of feeling ugly?" which had to be brought into the therapy before the goals which were the ostensible cause of treatment could be accomplished.

These sexual goals and investigations had to be accomplished, as Erickson always insisted, "In your own way; in your own good time; in the right way; at the right time." So, the acknowledgment of sexual passion as a natural emotion, the expression of sexual activity toward the right partner, respect for the emotions brought forward in psychotherapy and between therapist and patient, and trust in one's own wisdom, power and love—in one's right to one's own life and liveliness—all these themes of emotion must coexist and be expressed. As Melody put it: "The charm would be to feel what I feel neither more nor less than what is actually so in the moment, and to find a way to stay in contact with you at the same time."

To illustrate the work further, and to give the reader its flavor, I include a transcript of the session of October 12, 1982, in which Melody and I met in person and employed the aid of Mara as an imagined co-therapist. Here, "G" is Eric Greenleaf and "P" is Melody Palmer:

G: I thought we might have a joint session today.
P: A what?
G: A joint session.
P: With?
G: Mara.
P: I thought about that the other day. (laughs) And?
G: I had the idea that she and I could show you something about this dilemma that you're in. Alright. Just suppose you just sit back and close your eyes. (pause) Now, I don't know when you started going

to "Blue Movies," but if you started going to Blue Movies a long time ago, you probably remember that the male characters in those movies often wore masks. If you didn't start going that long ago, take my word for it.

P: (laughs)

G: Now, in the letters you wrote to me you told me some interesting things. And, one of the interesting things you told me was that it's different to have sexual feelings in a daydream than it is to have a variety of feelings right here, talking with me, and that the contrast is intriguing to you—wasn't bedeviling you. So, I thought, Mara and I would sit with you, and let you see a Blue Movie of your daydream, and then, at some point, when you are satisfied with the erotic content of this daydream, the male character in it will peel off his mask, and then you could see, and then he will peel off his mask again, and then you could see, and then he could peel off his mask again—as many masks as he has. And so, Mara will turn on the film. You can watch to your heart's content. Just have to watch the screen—you'll see it. She'll sit to one side of you and I'll sit to the other, and you can just watch, and when you finish watching the movie, open your eyes and tell me what you saw.

P: And this male is supposed to have a mask?

G: Well, you know, he'll probably look like your therapist, to begin with.

P: (laughs)

G: At least, that's the mask he's always had in the past.

P: How true. (laughs) Oh, God.

G: Now, while you watch the movie, I'm not going to watch you. I'm going to get coffee. Do you want coffee? Do you want tea? Do you want milk?

P: You're supposed to say, "Coffee, tea or me?" (laughs) Alright. Tea, with one sugar. Thank you.

G: OK.

(Ten minutes pass, during which time P sits by herself, while G leaves to get coffee and tea. Then, he returns.)

P: You came in just at the good part.

G: Well, there it is. You kinda get caught trying to mess the old lady up. Should I go out for a little bit longer?

P: Uhn-uh. Now, what about this "mask" business?

G: Just keep watching and see the guy take the mask off. (pause) Then, it's very possible he'll take several masks off, one after another.

P: But am I supposed to know who he is?

G: No. No, not really. Not necessarily at all. He might look like a complete stranger. If you have any questions, ask Mara what she knows about this odd event, that this complete stranger has such strong sexual attraction for you.

P: So strange.

G: What is?

P: Well, I have this little, vague image of this older man. I imagined more masks—it's the same.

G: Just an old man—is the stranger. Ask Mara . . .

P: She doesn't know.

G: She doesn't know who he is (sounds surprised)? Does she know why he's such a stranger?

P: (pause) I'm sort of surprised though that even . . . like when I saw this older man that's a stranger I didn't feel horrified.

G: I wonder if you'd ask Mara if she's felt in her life strong, powerful sexual attraction for strangers, or if she knows that in other women?

P: Uh-huh.

G: Just listen as she tells you about it.

P: She has a very positive view on this subject. (laughs)

G: What does she say?

P: She says that it's an experience many people have and it's not something to be afraid of or ashamed of, but something you should be glad for.

G: Why "be glad"?

P: Just a different way of . . . sometimes it's easy to have your head up in a cloud perhaps, and these feelings can be reminders of something more rooted.

G: Something more lifelike. Is her stranger an older stranger?

P: She doesn't have only one. Well, she's older. (laughs) She has older and younger ones. Likes variety. (laughs)

G: Yes, she does. (pause) And you can just open your eyes.

P: Well?

G: Well, how did you enjoy it?

Following this experience, Melody asks, "What do you say I do when I do that? When I get into my thing, what am I doing? When I get into these fantasies it's like I give over conscious function to you. You being the teacher or being in charge. And then, that lets me imagine myself to get more and more intensely into sexual feelings. But actually, I'm doing the whole thing. I'm just using you in a sort of convenient way."

I reply, "Ah! That's me—a sexual convenience!" Melody laughs, "But here, that's appropriate." And I answer, "I think that's exactly so."

Following this exchange, Melody was treated to a long, complicated lecture on the various psychoanalytic and Jungian analytic interpretations of the "stranger" in sexuality and of the utility of denial as a gradual way of allowing information to consciousness. The concept of the archetypes of the collective unconscious was invoked to encourage a rearrangement of emotions and actions better suited to Melody's individual needs and sensibilities than the arrangement bequeathed her by her family.

Then, in the last minutes of the hour, I spoke about relationship:

P: So . . . (laughs)

G: So, what makes people special is the experience of doing something unique together. And that's what it is to be special to somebody. . . . You know about "The Little Prince"? You know what the fox says to the Little Prince? When he's leaving?

P: Refresh my memory.

G: He says, "There are millions of little boys in the world, and millions of foxes. But, what is it that makes you special to me? You're special to me because you've 'tamed' me," says the fox to the boy. "So, wherever I go I will see the color of your hair in the waving wheat and the color of your eyes in the blue sky." He rhapsodizes for a while. That's it. He had a special experience with another critter. He didn't think he was the most blond boy in the world or the most red fox in the world, but it was special because of the relationship, not for any comparative reason, since the world is full of foxes and boys and many of them are just fine.

P: While you were telling that story, I said to myself, "Listen, Eric is saying something about *this* relationship." And then, I felt pleased, and then I felt myself go in a sort of haze, and don't take it in.

G: Do. Take it in. And see how pleasurable it is.

P: I don't trust the pleasure.

G: Feel some more. It is pleasant, is it not? No matter what you think about it, taking it in is very pleasant. So, you're welcome to think what you like, but you do have the experience of the pleasure taking in that special feeling. And what you discover is something about your special quality of feeling. You're not a boy, I'm not a fox. I'm not a little boy, you're not a fox; some French guy wrote the story. But you want to know what it means to be special to someone. That's what it means.

It is important, when doing psychotherapy, to respect the emotions brought forth and the reality of the relationships formed during the work. Everyone has recognized, though, that these relationships and emotions are imbedded in a complex context, now thought of in terms of structures, or families; or conceived of as complexes or introjects. Even Freud said that "psychoanalysis is in essence a cure through love" (1983).

When interacting with others, we are all aware of the "voice of conscience" and some of us, too, of "voices" or "visions," the haunting presence of our dealings with others, or of the aspects of our "unconscious minds," carried by persons in dreams, or in waking life. Wise counsel from friends, family, and therapists, also provides us with authority for our conduct. We may remember the voice of a friend, or, indeed, of Milton Erickson, during periods of doubt, or struggle.

So, it is easy to see the usefulness of the imagined co-therapist in psychotherapy. But I believe it to be a hallmark of effective therapy that patients come more and more to depend on their own wisdom and emotions in living life, and to feel equal with all other humans they may meet along their way. As Melody said to me this past August:

> You will perhaps enjoy hearing what my friend said to me this morning as we were standing on the porch at work: "Melody, you have been looking so sexy lately. Are you going through a little sexual revolution or something?" I said, "Yes!!"

REFERENCE

Freud, S. (1983). A letter to Jung. In B. Bettelheim, (Ed.), *Freud and man's soul*. New York: Knopf.

Chapter 39

Between: A Study Showing the Relationships Between Erickson, Winnicott, and Bachelard

Alan F. Leveton

The philosopher who gives himself enough solitude to enter the region of shadows bathes in an atmosphere without obstacles where no being says no. He lives by his reverie in a world homogeneous with his being, with his demi-being. The man of reverie is always in space which has volume. Truly inhabiting the whole volume of his space the man of reverie is from anywhere in his world in an inside which has no outside. It is not without reason that people commonly say that the dreamer is plunged into his reverie. The world no longer poses any opposition to him. The I no longer opposes itself to the world. In reverie there is no more non-I. In reverie the no, no longer has any function; everything is welcome. A philosopher enamoured of the history of philosophy could say that the space in which the dreamer is plunged is a "plastic mediator" between man and the universe. It seems that in the intermediary world where reverie and reality mingle, the plasticity of man and his world is realized without one ever needing to know where the principle of this double malleability lies. (Bachelard, 1969, p. 167)

I have found it useful to organize my thinking about Erickson's work with the help of studies made by two authors, D. W. Winnicott (Appendix A) and Gaston Bachelard (Appendix B). Winnicott, an English pediatric psychoanalyst, studied the state of reverie in which children play with their first possessions. He called these possessions "transitional objects." Examples are the favored blanket, the teddy bear, the thumb that children apparently believe is part of themselves and not quite part of themselves. Children act as if there is a special place in the space around that possession and themselves and this Winnicott called the "transitional space." I believe that trance work as Erickson taught it recreates many of the conditions of transitional space and objects.

Bachelard, a French philosopher and historian of science, was also interested in the special qualities that characterize a state of reverie. He was interested in how certain poetic images evoke reveries of childhood wonderment and awe. Erickson drew on many early poetic images to evoke deeper trance and childhood reverie—images of fire, trees, child-hood rooms—to start his patients and students on the track of change that existed in the latent or forgotten possibilities of their childhoods.

I am going to designate the term "between" as a concept that unifies the thoughts of these three men. "Between" names that realm of action between therapist and patient, parent and child, sleep and wakefulness, now and then, here and there, and inside and outside.

I will demonstrate how I used the idea of between in the way I worked with a woman dying of cancer.

THE REALM OF BETWEEN

> . . . there is the third part of the life of a human being, a part we cannot ignore, an intermediate area of experiencing, to which inner reality and external life both contribute. It is an area which is not challenged, because no claim is made on its behalf except that it shall exist as a resting place for the individual engaged in the perpetual human task of keeping inner and outer reality sep-arate yet interrelated. (Winnicott, 1951, p. 230)

Watch a child at play. Perhaps it is this way; the child collects little things from places in the room. Perhaps he or she will go to a corner of the room. The little objects can be encompassed by a glance of the eyes, the reach of both hands. The objects are not necessarily toys. Their value is not that of the manufacturer but in the interest invested by the child. A box, a stick, a piece of ribbon, a leaf, anything will do. The child can be so concentrated on play that he or she will not wonder where these objects came from. We need not limit the physical space in which play occurs. Right now it is there, in that corner. It may suit the child to come here, to this one, or to the center of the room, or out to the garden. Wherever he is at play, *that* is the center of play. And it is fixed only as long as his interest marks it.

We are there, watching. He seems totally absorbed in his play. Still, he knows we are there. We are watching. Indeed, our being there is part of his play. We are connected with his play through our awareness of him. How does he know? He glances up to locate us. He may come to us for a moment, to touch home base and, reassured, return to his play. If tension, frustration, or anxiety intrude, we will sense it and help him—that has happened so many times already. We have done enough of the right things so that he trusts us and that trust is palpable in the zone of play that encompasses the child, the things he is playing with, our watching him, his knowing we are watching him, our pleasure in being with him at play. There is trust between us, a charmed space between us. There is respect for play between us. There is caring between us.

Watch Erickson telling a story. He is awake so another may sleep in reverie. His words are there as a reliable container for the affect and imagery of the listener. Is he leading or following? Are the subject's eyes almost closing so that Erickson can say they may *now* close? The subject is convinced that Erickson suggested eye closure. Erickson is convinced the eyes were beginning to close and he timed his intervention accordingly. Now a story unfolds. Who suggests its contents? The subject is convinced the story is told just for him. Erickson is convinced the patient has given him the cues necessary to produce that story.

And *where* is the story in relation to the subject? To Erickson? Notice the holding quality of Erickson's voice. Street noises, other people, even the telephone will not be experienced as intruding into the charmed circle. The story that emerges from Erickson's store of memories is embroidered by the listener with reveries and reminiscences from a personal history rich in details unknown to Erickson. Each is associating, elaborating. The stories evoke the presence of figures from the past. Many stories, many landscapes, many companions take shape between hypnotist and subject—belonging to each, belonging to both.

A TRANSITIONAL OBJECT

I have introduced the terms "transitional object" and "transitional phenomena" for designation of the intermediate area of experience between the thumb and the teddy bear, between the oral eroticism and true object relationship, between primary creative

activity and projection of what has already been introjected, between primary unwareness of indebtedness and the acknowledgment of indebtedness.

By this definition an infant's babbling or the way an older child
goes over a repertory of songs and tunes while preparing for sleep
come within the intermediate area of transitional phenomena along
with the use made of objects that are not part of the infant's body,
yet are not fully recognized as belonging to external reality.

The transitional object and the transitional phenomena start each
human being off with what will always be important for them, i.e.,
a neutral area of experience which will not be challenged. Of the
transitional object it can be said that it is a matter of agreement
between us and the baby that we will never ask the question "did
you conceive of this or was it presented to you from without?" The
important point is that no decision on this point is expected. The
question is not to be formulated. (Winnicott, 1951, p. 230)

We were hiking on a rather dry, sparsely forested region of a Greek
island. Sasha, our eldest son, who was then eight years old, suddenly
told us: "I used to think I could make a bottle of milk in the night by
sticking out my hand." We were astonished that he remembered and
I knew what he remembered. When he was between a year and 18
months old we always replaced the empty bottle with which he fell
asleep with a full one so that he could have milk should he awaken in
the night. The eight-year-old was puzzled about something the infant
could not know. The infant Sasha in the magic of the transitional space
believed his action alone had created a second full bottle of milk in the
middle of the night simply by reaching out his hand—mysteriously in
the very place his hand reached when the need for it arose. Did he find
that bottle? Did he create that bottle? It pleased him very much to have
it there.

Another example. This one is about Julian, our younger son. We had
trouble deciphering his first complex word "savorite." He used it often
when we put him to bed. Finally we discovered that it applied to special
objects he wanted to have with him when he awakened. One "savorite"
was a pair of jeans whose rear pocket was studded in the shape of a
whirling star. Without our knowing why these pants were important to
him, there was no doubt he wanted them. They were his "savorite
cowboys." What to do when they no longer fit? Eva, his mother, thought
of a diplomatic solution. Without comment, she patched the pockets

onto the next-sized jeans. He was content. No explanations were asked for, given, or needed.

STARTING TO PLAY

> Psychotherapy takes place in the overlap of two areas of playing, that of the patient and that of the therapist. Psychotherapy has to do with two people playing together. The corollary of this is that where playing is not possible, then the work done by the therapist is directed towards bringing the patient from a state of not being able to play into a state of being able to play. (Winnicott, 1971b, p. 38)

Now I am going to tell you a story. A woman I knew very well was suffering greatly from pain caused by metastasis of breast cancer. Alexis knew, and her friends knew, that I had been studying pain relief through hypnosis and that I wanted to work with her and thought I could be of help. I also knew she was an extroverted woman, intensely involved with her personal relationships, her family, and her work. She was generous and self-sacrificing, not much given to introspection and reflection. There were earlier occasions in her life when psychotherapy might have been useful to her and I knew she had not pursued that course.

Often when you seek to bring someone into a state of being able to play, you must do a certain amount of calculation and preparation. The work you intend to do is focused, condensed, and intense. When the person is frightened, distrustful, and skeptical, the work can be directed initially toward creating a safe place, a safe realm for play. The therapist can begin by simply starting to play. The action itself does not demand a specific response and demonstrates safe play. Think of Erickson's funny stories about the Marx brothers, Carl Whitaker's crawling around on the floor, the irresistible urge grownups feel when they clown in order to engage the attention of a child. Playing indicates a realm of safety and is engaging, possibly surprising and exciting, protected from danger or anxiety.

I knew I would need a plan to entice Alexis into making a first appointment. It happened this way. It was her birthday. Many people were sending her presents, expressing the great love they had for this remarkable woman. They sent her flowers, inspirational poetry. I expected the presents would speak to that part of Alexis that was most known publicly—her generosity and extroversion. I went in the opposite direction. I made a storybook of drawings, based on the protagonist "Mad Dog," whose adventures I depicted in vivid graphic form (see pp. 522 and 523 for a selection from this storybook). Mad Dog was as unlike the public persona of Alexis as I could make her. Mad Dog was scruffy, antisocial, eccentric. Mad Dog snarled at mere facts, took revenge on menacing trees by peeing, blew her top. Said in the midst of a party for which she was hostess, "To hell with socializing." She was outrageous. That drawing showed Mad Dog upside down and taking a nap. Mad Dog sent her heart flying over the rainbow and over the rough edges of the world to explore what might lie beyond.

I heard by way of the grapevine that Mad Dog captured Alexis's attention. She was keeping the book by her bed, opening its pages to different pictures according to her mood. Some time went by. Her condition worsened. Heavy doses of medication were not helping her sleep through the night. At last she called for an appointment.

We began with a review of her physical symptoms: terrible pain and insomnia, unrelieved by medication. She was hyperalert, irritable, frightened, clearly in pain. We talked of Mad Dog. She smiled at Mad Dog's imperious unreasonableness. I asked her to notice if she could remember the pictures I had drawn. She shut her eyes. I lingered on the pictures of Mad Dog's great satisfaction at being able to take a nap even when there was that great pressure to be the hostess, to give a social response when someone else was present. I described that picture in detail. And she went into trance.

OPPORTUNITIES IN THE TRANSITIONAL SPACE

It is good to remember always that playing is itself a therapy. To arrange for children to be able to play is itself a psychotherapy that has immediate and universal application. It is helpful to think of the preoccupation that characterizes the playing of a young child. The content does not matter. What matters is the near withdrawal state akin to the concentration of older children and adults. The playing child inhabits an area that cannot easily be left nor can it easily admit intrusions. (Winnicott, 1971b, pp. 50–51)

Now Alexis was in trance and already more comfortable. I had set her to concentrate on Mad Dog's ability to take care of herself, to lose her temper, to withdraw, to nap. I would keep watch so Alexis could sleep. I told her so. She had to confront so many real-life facts that were frightening: her cancer had metastasized, her ribs had spontaneous fractures, her hip had fractured and corrective surgery had failed. She needed time off for comfort, for rest, for play. I already knew how to conduct two-hour sessions with her using pain-altering suggestions in which she showed no signs of discomfort. She could listen to tapes I prepared for her at night if she wakened in pain and these allowed her to sleep. What could I do in addition?

I knew she generally neglected her inner life and herself.

In the very first session she described her imagination as "relentlessly blank." She valued primarily her ability to engage in intense relationships in her work and with her family. She had little contact with her private self and very little recall of her childhood. She said, "I flattened my life out, I 'bland' my personal feelings away. When I'm by myself, I'm bored. The pain is worse. My childhood is totally blank." I wanted to offer her something that might change that emptiness. I thought of her inner state as being so vague that she might fill it with the experience of pain. I wanted to change that, but how?

VALUING THE IMAGE

With the theme of drawers, chests, locks, and wardrobes we shall resume contact with the unfathomable store of daydreams of intimacy. Wardrobes with their shelves, desks with their drawers, and chests with their false bottoms are veritable organs of the secret psychological life. Indeed, without these objects and a few others in equally high favor, our intimate life would lack a model of intimacy. Does there exist a single dreamer of words who does not respond to the word wardrobe? Every poet of furniture, even if he is to be a poet in a garret and therefore has no furniture, knows that the inner space of an old wardrobe is deep. A wardrobe's inner space is also intimate space, space that is not open to just anybody. (Bachelard, 1964, p. 78)

This is how I see the confluence of ideas of Erickson, Winnicott, and Bachelard and their use in thinking through my plans for Alexis's treatment. Erickson taught the power of trance work. He demonstrated that patients can listen in trance and still roam freely and elaborate their own stories. Rather than demand memory, the therapist offers the opportunity to remember. Bachelard, in his exploration of the material world of poetic evocation, gave his readers just those categories of things and places which are of the greatest value to the self in reverie, particularly

FROM A CHARACTER INVENTED
By Richard Stine

MAD DOG SNARLS AT MERE FACTS....

MAD DOG BLOWS TOP........

MAD DOGS HEART FLYING
ON THE RAINBOW BRIDGE
OVER THE ROUGH EDGES
OF THE WORLD...........

the child part. His chapter headings alone are pointers to topics of relevance for a utilizer of trances: The House, The Significance of the Hut, The House and Universe, Drawers, Chests, Miniatures, Shelves and Nests. Winnicott defines how a guardian of play can put forth objects and words for objects in a space that belongs to two people—a therapist, a patient; a parent, a child; and, I hoped, Alexis and myself.

In the next trance, remembering Bachelard's notions about wardrobes, I used a story told by a colleague. It was a simple image. A woman remembered spending many hours as a little girl arranging and rearranging the contents of a special dresser drawer. A girl at play alone in her room, taking out her dresses, her skirts, her ribbons, her barrettes, her stockings, her underwear—arranging and rearranging them in her drawer. She particularly enjoyed arranging and rearranging her ribbons. They were red, blue, pink, purple, white. She never knew how much actual time this took, nor did she ever seem finished. She never tired of arranging and rearranging.

I told that story slowly, lingering on its details. That story could also be one for all children, all drawers, all reveries, all houses, and all childhoods spent in quiet rooms.

Alexis became less restless. She appeared to be less bothered by her pain. She began to smile in that way people smile and move when they are in trance—which is to say, slightly and slowly. Now I taught Alexis how she could speak in trance without awakening. She spoke in the dreamlike sparse, economical manner that is the mark of speech during trance. I asked her where she was.

She told me she was in her bedroom. She knew she was a little girl. She clearly saw the sunlight streaming in through the window. She was sitting half in shade and half in light. She could hear the chirping of her canary in its cage in her room. At her left hand was her favorite doll given to her by her grandmother. Directly in front of her was her most prized childhood possession—a little copy in miniature of an old-fashioned steamer trunk. She described the beauty of its brass hinges, the complexity of its lock, the miniature hangers that hung on one side and the little drawers covered with and lined by a satin fabric that occupied the other. While I was telling her a story of one little girl arranging her drawer, Alexis had been remembering that she loved to pack her doll's clothing into the miniature steamer trunk, all in preparation for her dolly's magic trips to foreign countries. Sometimes she put all the clothing in one drawer and the shoes and socks in another. Sometimes she would take winter clothing, sometimes her doll's summer frocks. The packing of the trunk was *very* important. On the outside of the steamer trunk were replicas of stickers from famous hotels the world over. She could also decide *where* her doll was going. Was she going to the mountains? Was she going to the seashore? Was she going to take a train ride across Europe?

There was intense satisfaction in the preparation and packing for her doll's voyages. When I asked her if there were other people around her, she said yes. Her mother was downstairs, her father had not yet come home from work, and the house was peaceful and quiet so no one would interrupt her and the time could pass in a sweet, unhurried way.

THE VALUE OF HAVING A BETWEEN

We comfort ourselves by reliving memories of protection, something closed must retain our memories while leaving them their original values as images. Memories of the outside world will never have the same tonality as those of home and by recalling these memories we add to our store of dreams; we are never real historians but always near poets. And our emotion is perhaps nothing but an expression of a poetry that was lost. This being the case, if I were asked to name the chief benefit of the house, I would say, "The house shelters daydreaming, the house protects the dreamer, the house allows one to dream in peace. (Bachelard, 1964, p. 6)

Poetry extends well beyond psychoanalysis on every side, from a dream it always makes a daydream and a poetic daydream cannot content itself with the rudiments of a story. It cannot be tied to a knotty complex. The poet lives a daydream that is awake, but above all his daydream remains in the world facing worldly things. It gathers the universe together, around and in an object. We see it open chests or condense cosmic wealth in a slender casket. All of that is so much greater than a key in its lock. The casket contains the things that are unforgettable, unforgettable for us but also unforgettable for those to whom we are going to give our treasures. Here the past, the present, and a future are condensed. Thus, the casket is memory of what is immemorial. (Bachelard, 1964, p. 84)

It is joy to be hidden, but disaster not to be found. (Winnicott, 1971a, p. 197)

Alexis began a series of adventures related to her steamer trunk. She, who had been stopped by a "relentlessly blank" wall against memory, began to utilize the details of the single memory by following the suggestion that each aspect of the trunk, each sticker, each detail of her room was itself a story relevant to her. She remembered details first of the floor around her, the effect of light and shadow with the sunshine streaming through the windows. She remembered particularly "Cheepsie." Her father had bought that canary. It was yellow and white, and sang in its cage even when the cage was covered. There was a mirror in that cage. She began wondering if behind the mirror was another room. She even had a fragrant box for the downy feathers shed by her bird and for other treasures as well.

Here are some stories.

Mt. Vesuvius

She saw a hotel sticker with a smoking volcano. She wanted to find the source of the lava. People could be fooled by the appearance of a volcano. To some it looked like a peaceful mountain, but the volcano knew that the pressure was building up. Fire and steam issued from the rocks. Some foolish people ignored the warnings. The earth trembled. The boulders were dislodged and careened down the mountainside. Still, there were some people who failed to respect the wrath of a mountain and pretended everything was peaceful. Then came the explosion. The mountain blew its top. It had to. It could not be bothered about foolish people. The power of its molten lava swept aside all obstacles.

As she visualized this in her trance, her face went from frowning to smiling. This came at a time when she felt besieged by the well-meaning advice of her friends. She felt at the mercy of well-wishers, some of whom went so far as to tell her that her cancer was under her control and therefore self-induced. After the trance, without reference to Mt. Vesuvius, she talked openly about her extreme discomfort in the presence of these well-wishers. She said she felt like letting off steam but that people would be shocked if she blew her top.

The Western Desert

Cactus. A great expanse of sand. Suddenly she saw a girl on horseback, hair streaming in the wind. She thought it was herself on vacation, a vacation she took at age 12. Powerful and riding alone in control of her horse. She remembered that feeling. Now she was not just pretending to be a cowgirl, she *was* a cowgirl riding without effort or pain across the mesas of the Great West.

After this, she began a systematic review of all her childhood vacations. She did much of the work on her own. She had tapes of our sessions and tapes I had prepared for her. She could use them and go at her own pace. There were many nighttime hours, many anxious moments to be filled with her work. She learned that the steamer trunk could be the starting point. "Where shall I go with my doll? What shall I bring along?"

Her greatest surprise was in the wealth of detail she could remember. She had thought of herself as blank, yet there was a space for everything: her whole childhood, a whole series of remembered and imagined worlds. There were trees, cacti, rocks. She did not know then why she remembered rocks, but she would discover the reason later.

The Room Behind the Canary's Mirror

I suggested she examine Cheepsie's cage. She loved Cheepsie's singing. He was an active, real companion. He was fascinated with his mirror image. I suggested she look very closely at the mirror. I remembered *Alice Through The Looking Glass* and Cocteau's *Orpheus*. I mentioned casually that sometimes mirrors are doors. After a long silent trance she said she had been in the room behind the mirror. It was a way out of the cage. Cheepsie had talked to her in her childhood language (English was a second language to her). They talked and laughed. The bird showed her how to fly, even over dangerous obstacles. She felt delighted in being weightless. She remembered the fragrant cigar box filled with Cheepsie's feathers. She felt light as a feather.

This was the greatest flight of imagination she shared with me. It came at a time when she was increasingly confined to her bed and experiencing spontaneous fractures. I thought I was getting an echo of Mad Dog teaching her heart to fly over the rainbow. Friendly human qualities could be discerned in a talking bird. She could go anywhere she wanted.

BETWEEN NOW AND ALMOST FOREVER

In reverie, image values become psychological facts.

When reverie goes so far one is astonished by his own past. Astonished to have been that child. There are moments in childhood when every child is the astonishing being, the being who realizes the astonishment of being. We thus discover within ourselves an immobile childhood, a childhood without becoming. Liberated from the gear wheels of the calendar.

Poets convince us that all our childhood reveries are worth starting over again. . . . It would be then for us a matter of awakening within us through a reading of the poets and sometimes thanks to nothing more than a poet's image, a state of new childhood which goes farther than memories of our childhood, as if the poet was making us continue, complete a childhood which was not well-accomplished. And yet which was ours of which we have doubtless dreamed on many occasions. (Bachelard, 1969, pp. 106, 116)

Of all the images and stories that emerged, two stood out as important markers.

The Portrait

She had been thinking of the steamer trunk again. It was so beautiful. A photographer had come to the house to take her picture. Her mother had dressed her up in velvet with a nice bow. The photographer wanted to have her pose, hands folded, in an ornate chair in her bedroom. This was a real memory and she recalled wanting the trunk included in the picture with her dolly sitting on top. The photographer refused and her mother took his side. She had made a mild protest but had not prevailed. During a trance, she reported rage. She wanted her treasured trunk and doll in that picture.

I told her that years later she would meet Mad Dog who would teach her the value of being angry and noncompliant. And that, unknown to her, Mad Dog and her canary Cheepsie were already great friends and Cheepsie would know what to do. And he did. He flew down and made an enormous ruckus, and would only stop when Alexis got her way. In imagination, the photo session was redone. Slowly and in great detail she arranged things the way she had always wanted them to be. In the completed picture she sat with her trunk and her dolly, with a look of triumphant satisfaction.

The Talking Rocks

She had been fascinated by the landscape of the American West. In her cowgirl reverie she had noticed cacti, sagebrush, and boulders. This resonated with a memory of mine. Our family had been hiking on the top of a mesa on the Hopi Indian Reservation. We had seen a day-long Kachina dance at Shongopavi. Our boys caught the deep religious concentration of the dancers. Now it was dusk. The colors and textures of the desert were sharply etched. Half-embedded in the sandy top of the mesa were smooth rocks, still warm, really flesh warm from the day.

One of the boys said, "I wonder what stones dream about?" For the next while they decided that stones do dream, that they could talk to one another. It is clear you would have to listen very carefully to hear them. And it might just sound like very slow, low human language. I told Alexis that I wondered too about the life of those desert stones, so warm and present, to be there for the hands of a child's curiosity and wonder.

In her trance she slowly nodded yes. She could hear the rocks. It was a little like putting a seashell to your ear but you could hear the earth in movement, not the sea. The time the rocks knew about was deep time, far greater than the time experienced by a single human being. Seasons were like minutes to the rocks and minutes might last for seasons. The desert may seem empty but rocks mark it, the way the emptiness of the Zen sand garden is marked by the arrangement of rocks that may be large or small, but are immense in the way they anchor that bit of earth. Rocks can wait almost forever, she said. And they love it when children remember to say hello.

EPILOGUE

Alexis died of her illness in a coma 10 months after I sent her Mad Dog. She had many pain-free months. She had lived longer than some of her physicians expected and on her good days could leave home for brief periods. She had time to make arrangements for her children and to be with her friends. The series of cards she sent me kept me posted on her achievements in pain relief and memory. They began with her first card showing a mass scene of an incredibly crowded beach and ended with a tranquil photo of a quiet meadow surrounded by a cool forest, lofty mountains, grasses and flowers.

SUMMARY

Erickson showed that there were ways to awaken and protect reverie. Particularly in his later storytelling years, he valued the state of light trance or reverie because of his recognition that patients would be free to do their own work. In organizing and thinking about Erickson's work it is useful to use Winnicott's notion of the transitional space and transitional objects as a kind of general map of that general region existing in the between where trance seems to reside. Bachelard would probably not be surprised to discover that a miniature steamer trunk would be so important to a woman, since he thought so long and well about those items of value to the imagination. And a study of Bachelard will help orient a clinician to that wonderous realm.

The work that took place between Alexis and me was in that realm between us; her room is vivid to me, my desert rocks blend with hers. Neither had to explain precisely how those things came to be there, they simply were.

REFERENCES

Bachelard, G. (1964). *Poetics of space.* New York: Orion Press.

Bachelard, G. (1969). *Poetics of reverie.* Boston: Beacon Press.

Winnicott, D. W. (1951). Transitional objects and transitional phenomena. In *Collected papers: Through pediatrics to psychoanalysis,* London: Tavistock Press.

Winnicott, D. W. (1971a). Dreaming, fantasying and living. In *Playing and reality.* New York: Basic Books.

Winnicott, D. W. (1971b). Playing: A theoretical statement. In *Playing and reality.* New York: Basic Books.

APPENDIX A

Biographical Note

D. W. Winnicott (1896-1971) began with an interest in being a general practitioner in a country area. After reading Freud he decided to explore psychoanalysis. During his 40 years on the staff of Paddington Green Children's Hospital he developed many methods based upon the simplest of play situations, offering a child a tongue depressor, a squiggly line, a piece of string, in order to study the child's development. His writing is that of a careful clinician, without jargon, colorful. Many concepts are relevant to Ericksonian work in addition to those of the transitional objects and transitional space. He wrote of the "good enough mother," making an attempt to free parents from the tyranny of perfection and the "holding" that a good enough parent provides for the security of a young child. Both of these ideas are relevant to the safe conduct of hypnotherapy. Like Erickson he was not at all sentimental about childhood; full measure is paid to aggression, destruction, and hatred as necessary aspects of childhood, playing, and therapeutic interaction.

He was a great daydreamer. He prefaced his article *The Location of Cultural Experience* with the following:

On the seashore of endless worlds, children play.—Tagore

Winnicott commented, "The quotation from Tagore has always intrigued me. In my adolescence I had no idea what it could mean, but it found a place in me, and its imprint has not faded."

His major papers are most easily found in the following collected volumes:

1. Winnicott, D. W. (1965). *The maturational process and the facilitating environment.* New York: International Universities Press.
2. Winnicott, D. W. (1975). *Through pediatrics to psychoanalysis.* New York: Basic Books.

APPENDIX B

Biographical Note

Gaston Bachelard (1884–1962) was born in the small Champagne town of Bar-Sur-Aube. He was a postman in his youth, studying chemistry and physics. At the age of thirty-five he became a college professor of natural sciences. He became interested in ideas that influenced scientific theories. He predicted changes in philosophy that would follow the development of quantum physics. He described how philosophical ideas influenced scientific theories of fire. In the great works that followed, he posed the question: "Why are some poetic images so powerful, so productive of reverie?" He saw himself as a phenomenologist. He began to use some theories of Jung. I can only read him slowly; his language is so evocative. I pause, I daydream. When he writes of nests, I am sitting in a nest I found in the leafy arm of my favorite tree.

Note: His works are being reissued. New translations are going to be printed. The Second International Congress on Ericksonian Approaches to Hypnosis and Psychotherapy (1983) coincided with the First American Congress on Bachelard which was held at the Dallas Institute of Humanities and Culture.

Bibliographies of Translations in English

1. Bachelard, G. (1964). *The poetics of space.* New York: Orion Press.
2. Bachelard, G. (1964). *The psychoanalysis of fire.* Boston: Beacon Press.
3. Bachelard, G. (1969). *The poetics of reverie.* Boston: Beacon Press.
4. Bachelard, G. (1982). The Charon complex: The Ophelia complex. *Spring Quarterly* , pp. 171–193. Dallas: Spring Publications.
5. Gaudin, C. (Ed.). (1970). *On poetic imagination and reverie.* New York: Bobbs-Merrill.